INDEX OF

NOTICES APPEARING IN 23

EARLY CINCINNATI NEWSPAPERS

1793 – 1853

INDEX OF

NOTICES APPEARING IN 23

EARLY CINCINNATI NEWSPAPERS

1793 – 1853

Indexed by

Jeffrey G. Herbert

HAMILTON COUNTY CHAPTER OF
THE OHIO GENEALOGICAL SOCIETY

Cincinnati, Ohio
2015

Published by the
Hamilton County Chapter, OGS
P.O. Box 15865
Cincinnati, OH 45215-0865
513-956-7078
http://hcgsohio.org

Printed in the United States of America.
ISBN-13: 978-0692378038
LCCN 2015901640

Table of Contents

Introduction

This index is intended to give the researcher another means of discovering information about their early Hamilton County, Ohio ancestors who lived in the greater Cincinnati area between 1793 and 1853. Many families, while not settling here permanently lived in the area for a time, and had spouses and children who were married or died here while they were passing through this region. Traces of these early pioneer families are hard to find through cemetery or court records during the time when the area was part of the Northwest Territory, and later during the first half of the nineteenth century. This index is intended to serve as another tool in the family history researcher's toolbox.

The scope of this index covers death, marriage, and other miscellaneous notices that were published during this time period. The twenty-three early Cincinnati newspapers that were published and covered by this index are:

Centinel of the North-Western Territory	Nov. 1793 – June 1796
Cincinnati American	Feb. 1830 – Apr. 1832
Cincinnati Chronicle and Literary Gazette	Dec. 1826 – Sept 1842
Cincinnati Daily Sunbeam	Nov. 1848 – Feb. 1849
Cincinnati Daily Whig & Commercial Intelligencer	Mar. 1834 – Dec. 1839
Cincinnati Dispatch and Democratic Union	July 1850 – Nov. 1850
Cincinnati Emporium	Mar. 1824 – Feb. 1825
Cincinnati Evening Mercury	Feb. 1849 – July 1849
Cincinnati Daily Microscope	Jan. 1842 – Aug. 1842
Cincinnati Daily Nonpareil	May 1850 – Jan. 1853
Cincinnati Gazette	July 1815 – Aug. 1815
Cincinnati Independent Press & Freedom Advocate	July 1822 – Dec. 1826
Cincinnati Journal and Western Luminary	Jan. 1831 – Dec. 1837
Cist's Daily Advertiser	Mar. 1847 – Apr. 1848
Coon-Skinner	Sept 1842 – Oct. 1842
Freeman's Journal	July 1796 – Oct. 1799
Literary Cadet and Cheap City Advertiser	Jan. 1820 – Apr. 1820
National Republican	Jan. 1823 – Aug. 1842
Spirit of the West	July 1814 – Apr. 1815
Western Episcopal Observer	Sept 1841 – Nov. 1841
Western Spy	May 1799 – Dec. 1822
Western Tiller	Aug. 1826 – Aug. 1828
The Whig	Apr. 1809 – May 1810

And the page number codes used for the notices in this index under the 'Page' column are:

A1 – A4	Cincinnati American
B1 – B4	Cincinnati Daily Sunbeam
C1 – C4	Centinel of the North-Western Territory
D1 – D4	Literary Cadet and Cheap City Advertiser
E1 – E4	Cincinnati Emporium
F1 – F4	Freeman's Journal
G1 – G4	Cincinnati Gazette
H1 – H4	The Whig
J1 – J4	Cincinnati Independent Press and Freedom Advocate
K1 – K4	Cist's Daily Advertiser
L1 – L4	Cincinnati Evening Mercury
M1 – M4	Cincinnati Daily Microscope
N1 – N4	National Republican
P1 – P4	Cincinnati Daily Nonpareil
Q1 – Q4	Western Tiller
R1 – R4	Cincinnati Chronicle
S1 – S5	Western Spy
T1 – T4	Cincinnati Daily Whig and Commercial Intelligencer
V1 – V4	Western Episcopal Observer
W1 – W4	Spirit of the West
X1 – X4	Cincinnati Journal and Western Luminary
Y1 – Y4	Cincinnati Daily Dispatch and Democratic Union
Z1 – Z4	The Coon-Skinner

The letter portion of the code refers to the name of the newspaper, and the numeric portion of the code refers to the page number where the information can be found on the indicated date of the specified newspaper. In some cases, items may have been published in multiple newspapers at the time, so each item is listed with a reference to the specified newspaper, publication date and page number for the researcher to view. Many multiple notices contain the same information, although some may have a better preserved copy, and in other cases, different notices contains different pieces of information and it is beneficial for the researcher to review all notices in order to maximize any information on a given ancestor.

Existing copies from the Cincinnati History Library and Archives (CHLA) and the Public Library of Cincinnati and Hamilton County (PLCH) have been used in order to create the most complete and comprehensive index. The gaps in the combined collection with respect to the complete runs dates that are listed above are as follows:

The Western Spy	Feb. 1804 – May 1804
	Aug. 1808 – Aug. 1810
Cincinnati Chronicle	April 1835 – Dec. 1836
	Oct. 1838 – Sept. 1839

National Republican   June 1838 – Sept. 1838
                                                 Jan. 1839 – Sept. 1840
Cincinnati Daily Microscope   Feb. 1842 – June 1842
Cincinnati Daily Non-Pareil   Dec. 1851 – June 1852
Cincinnati Independent Press and Freedom Advocate
                                                 Dec. 1823 – May 1826

Some of these early newspapers merged, changed owners and names over the years. Some of the alternate names for each newspaper are listed below.

The Western Spy
        The Western Spy, and Hamilton Gazette   May 1799 – Aug. 1805
        The Western Spy, and Miami Gazette   Sept 1805 – Apr. 1809
        The Western Spy   Sept 1810 – Dec. 1818
        Western Spy, and Cincinnati General Advertiser Jan. 1819 – Apr. 1820
        Western Spy and Literary Cadet   Apr. 1820 – Dec. 1822

Cincinnati Chronicle
        Saturday Evening Chronicle   Dec. 1826 – Aug. 1827
        Saturday Evening Chronicle of General Literature Aug. 1827 – Dec. 1828
        Cincinnati Chronicle and Literary Gazette   Jan. 1829 – Apr. 1835
        Cincinnati Mirror and Chronicle   Apr. 1835 – Oct. 1835
        Cincinnati Chronicle and Literary Gazette   Nov. 1835 – Sept 1842

National Republican
        National Republican and Ohio Political Register   Mar. 1824 -- 1833
        National Republican and Cincinnati Daily
        Mercantile Advertiser   Mar. 1831 – July 1833
        Daily Cincinnati Republican & Commercial Register Jan. 1835 – Dec.1838
        Daily Cincinnati Republican   1835 – Aug. 1842

Cincinnati Daily Whig and Commercial Intelligencer
        Cincinnati Democratic Intelligencer and Commercial Advertiser

This index contains over 8,800 deaths, over 3,200 marriages, and over 3,100 miscellaneous notices which were reported and published before 1853 in Hamilton County and surrounding counties. It should be noted that the names in this index are not only from the Cincinnati and Hamilton County area, but for much of the former Northwest Territory during the early years, and as far north as Dayton, as far east as Columbus and Chillicothe, south to Lexington, Kentucky, and west as far as Indianapolis and Richmond, Indiana for the period in the mid-19th century.

The information in this index was compiled using the most complete set of collections from both the Public Library of Cincinnati and Hamilton County (PLCH) and the Cincinnati History Library and Archives in the Cincinnati Museum Center (CHLA), and using both the microfilm collection as well as the original hardbound paper copies when the microfilm copies were not available. This provides the most comprehensive and complete index using all the available existing sources. Researchers should request the microfilm copies first in order to avoid wear on the hardbound paper copies.

The *Centinel of the North-Western Territory* was the first newspaper published in the Northwest Territory, and the first published in Ohio. It was established on November 9, 1793 by William Maxwell in Cincinnati, just five years after the founding of the town of Cincinnati, and nine years before Ohio became a state. It was discontinued in June 1796 when Maxwell sold the newspaper to Edmund Freeman. The new owner changed the name of the newspaper to *Freeman's Journal*, and it remained published in Cincinnati until 1800, when Freeman moved to Chillicothe. The relocation happened as Ohio prepared to be admitted as a state in 1802, and the new capital was located there. This paper later merged with the Chillicothe Gazette, and later became the Scioto Gazette. Even though this paper was published in Cincinnati through March 1800, the latest surviving edition dates to October 1, 1799.

The next newspaper to be published in Cincinnati was the *Western Spy*, which was established on May 28, 1799 by Joseph Carpenter. This newspaper was published under various names and with various partners during its brief history, and briefly suspended publication in 1800 and in June 1801 due to a paper shortage in the city. The last surviving copy is from December 1822. The paper also ceased publication for a brief period from 1809 through 1810 when the newspaper *The Whig* took its place. Copies of this newspaper are available at PLCH on microfilm for the few issues that remain. *The Whig* was succeeded by the *Cincinnati Advertiser*, which in turn only existed for two years, from 1810 through 1811. *The Whig* was a weekly publication of which only 14 issues survive, and are found on microfilm at PLCH and filed under the collection "Miscellaneous Ohio Newspapers 1809 - 1818".

The *Literary Cadet and Cheap City Advertiser* was published by Joseph Buchanan and began in November 1819 under the title *The Literary Cadet,* however only after a month, the title was changed to *Literary Cadet, and Cheap City Advertiser* and the size of the publication was increased. The paper existed for only a brief period of time, and in April 1820 was likewise consolidated with the *Western Spy*.

The *Cincinnati Gazette* was published under many variations of its name, but for this index, the issues included are when it existed briefly as a stand-alone newspaper published by Thomas Palmer, and then it merged with the Liberty Hall in December 1815. The copies of this brief period are bound together with the Liberty Hall newspaper in the collection at CHLA from its establishment in July 1815 until it merged with the Liberty Hall in Dec. 1815.

The *Cincinnati Chronicle* published its first issue on December 30, 1826 and continued under various names through 1849.

The *Cincinnati Daily Non-Pareil* published its first issue in May 1850 and continued under various names through January 1853 from its offices on the corner of 5th and Main Streets. Its motto was "Association against monopoly – the profits of labor belong to the laborer", and it listed itself as the "Official Paper of the City" in 1851.

The *Cincinnati Emporium* published its first issue on March 2, 1824 and continued through February 3, 1825. This short lived newspaper was printed by Samuel J. Browne, and had the motto of "Where liberty dwells, there is my country."

The *Cincinnati Evening Mercury* was also a short-lived paper. Existing copies span only from February 2, 1849 to July 14, 1849, and are located at the Cincinnati History Library and Archives (CHLA). The motto of the newspaper on the top of the front page was "The Advocate of Truth, Industry, Internal Improvements, Commerce, and our Country".

The Coon-Skinner was also had a very brief lifespan. It was started in advance of the election of the fall of 1842, and was a pro-Democratic newspaper that was focused on removing the Whigs from office and defeating Whig candidates running for office. The newspaper was reminiscent of Davie Crockett and his attire in a coon-skin cap, thus the name of the newspaper was the image of a simple politician fighting bureaucracy. Existing issues of this newspaper are only for the months of September and October of 1842.

The *Spirit of the West* was also only published for a brief time period by Melancton S. Pettit, and bound copies of this paper are stored with the Liberty Hall newspaper at PLCH. The paper began in July 1814 and suspended publication in April 1815.

For additional information on these early newspapers and additional repositories that may house additional copies of these early Cincinnati newspapers please consult the following references.

Brigham, Clarence S., *History and Bibliography of American Newspapers 1690 – 1820 Volume 2*, American Antiquarian Society, Worcester, Massachusetts, 1947

Gutgesell, Stephen, *Guide to Ohio Newspapers 1793 – 1973*, Ohio Historical Society, Columbus, Ohio, 1974

Section 1 – Death, Estate and Probate Notices and Obituaries

This section contains over 8,800 deaths, which were reported and published before 1853 in Hamilton County and surrounding counties. It should be noted that the names in this index are not only from the Cincinnati and Hamilton County area, but are as far north as Dayton and Wilmington, as far east as Chillicothe, south to Lexington and Shelbyville, Kentucky, and west as far as Indianapolis and Richmond, Indiana.

If the birthplace of the person is listed in the death notice, an " * " is placed before the page number in the index to alert the researcher to additional vital information.

During the early periods of this index, it was not very common to take out a death notice or obituary, but in some cases there were administrator and executor notices or estate sales listed when someone who owned property died, and their estate was being sold off. These notices were published so that creditors and debtors of the deceased could file a claim against the estate. These notices were recorded in this index, and instead of the age of the person, the word "**estate**" is listed in that column so that the researcher will know to look in the original papers for an estate notice or sale vs. a death notice. While a death notice will most likely give the date of death and age, the administrator or estate notice will give the name of the deceased, where they owned property (i.e. the township), and the name of the administrator or executor. In many cases this will be the name of the surviving spouse or the name of one of the sons. This can be an important clue before 1850 when only the head of the household was listed in the census data.

If the word "executor" (man) or "executrix" (woman) was listed, then it means that the deceased left a will and this person was named as the executor of the will to dispose of the property in the estate. This was usually the surviving spouse or a son, or son-in-law of the deceased person, or some other close relative that was trusted. The researcher should check Hamilton County wills to see if a will is still available and would most likely contain additional family information.

If the word "administrator" (man) or "administratrix" (woman) was listed, this person was formally appointed at a quarterly session of the Common Pleas Court (before 1852) or Probate Court (after 1852). The surviving court records should be searched for additional information. The appointment of an administrat(or/rix) could mean that the deceased died intestate or without a will, or the requested execut(or/rix) declined to serve, or in the court's opinion was not capable of serving. This could just be that the person didn't feel capable because of age or infirmity or they now lived out of Hamilton County, or because of the size of the estate, could not post an adequate bond. If the widow declined, perhaps she felt uncomfortable dealing with the management and/or sale of property left to her. In some cases, multiple administrators were named, like brother and son, or two brothers for example. If the administratrix was a woman, she was most likely the widow of the deceased. If her last name is different that the deceased, there are a number of examples in the Probate Court account records were she had remarried while the estate was still being settled. These may provide many additional clues to follow up on.

In a similar manner, sometimes the Probate Court published a list of recent cases brought before the court. These have also been included in the index and listed as "**probate**" in the age column. The actual date of death would not be listed in the notice, but it would provide the latest possible date when a death would have occurred, and that they owned property or owed debts in Hamilton County that needed to go before the Probate Court for disposition. In the earlier years, the Probate Court met in quarterly sessions and typically handled 25 to 30 cases a quarter. This may lead the researcher to other court documents for additional information since there was a case filed in Probate Court on that date. These notices will typically be listed on the page of the newspaper as "PROBATE NOTICE" or "Probate Court".

There may be a great deal of variation in the information recorded in these early notices. In some cases there is only the name of the deceased, the date of death, their age, and when and where the funeral will take place. In other cases, the surviving spouse might be listed, especially in the case where the wife died, and occasionally more information about their life and where they were born or when they migrated to the area. For almost all the cases, where the person was a small child, the names of the parents are listed in the notice.

During the cholera outbreak of 1832, 1833, and 1849, there were many deaths in the city on a daily basis. During the height of these epidemics, this issue consumed the city, and was the topic of many articles in the newspaper each day. During these times of epidemic, a list of deaths on a daily basis was gathered and published for three of these major outbreaks and has been included in this index.

Section 2 – Marriage Notices

This section contains over 3,200 marriages, which were reported and published before 1853 in Hamilton County and surrounding counties. It should be noted that the marriage notices listed are not only from the Cincinnati and Hamilton County area, but are from surrounding counties and even from the neighboring states of Kentucky and Indiana.

For a marriage notice, the situation was similar. In most of the cases, the date and place of the marriage was listed along with the name of the minister or justice of the peace that performed the marriage. In many cases, the name of the father of the bride or both of her parents was listed. The notice date in the index is the date of the publication in the newspaper, not the date of the marriage.

Section 3 – Miscellaneous Notices

This section contains over 3,100 notices of divorce cases, bankruptcy lists, guardianships, Army desertions, run away apprentices, lost and found farm animals, and other valuable notices that were reported and published before 1853 in Hamilton County by the various courts as notice to the public. These notices include guardianships, where a minor child inherited property, and an adult guardian was appointed by the court to administer and protect this property until the child reached adulthood. Another important set of notices published was debt relief notices. This was the equivalent of our modern bankruptcy laws, where the individual could not pay his expenses and filed for protection under the insolvent debtor laws in existence at the time. This would provide notice to the individuals that he owned money to, and they could plead their case before the judge to recover some of their investments. In the case of the early 1830s when a financial panic occurred, these lists were quite extensive.

Along with many other useful notices that appear in these early issues of Cincinnati newspapers, there were notices of divorce or abandonment by one spouse or another, and later in the 1850s the Common Pleas Court notices that appear in the newspaper started listing hearings for divorce. When a divorce hearing was requested, there needed to be a notice given in the local newspapers to the public, and in many cases these listed both names and a short reason for the divorce petition. In the earliest newspapers, these notices were more common when one spouse abandoned the other one or just disappeared (e.g. went west but was never heard from again and did not return). These notices were to protect the other person from being responsible for the debts incurred by the other spouse, and for permission for the spouse left behind to legally remarry. In other cases where the domestic environment was intolerable due to mistreatment or habitual drunkenness, a wife might simply flee the marriage, since there was little legal alternative available at the time. An example of an early notice appearing the newspaper where the wife left is as follows.

> "I do hereby notify the public that my wife *<Wife's name>* has voluntarily left my bed and board, and that debts contracted by her will not be paid by me." *<Husband's name>*

This can be especially useful information since before 1850 only the head of household was listed in the census. These kinds of early notices would give the name of the wife, and that a marriage had existed before the date of the notice.

Table 1 on the following page contains the individual newspapers codes used in this index, the most common name of the newspaper, the years covered by this index for this given newspaper, and the call numbers needed to retrieve a given newspaper at CHLA and PLCH. For the issued housed at the Public Library of Cincinnati and Hamilton County (PLCH), please ask for a given issue at the Newspapers and Magazines Desk and they will retrieve the copy for you.

Code	Name of Newspaper	CHLA	PLCH	Years Covered
A	Cincinnati American	071.771 fC5am	Newspaper Desk	1830 - 1832
B	Cincinnati Daily Sunbeam	071.771 fC5sb		1848 - 1849
C	Centinel of the North-Western Territory	071.771 fC5ce RB	Newspaper Desk	1793 - 1796
D	Literary Cadet and Cheap City Advertiser	071.771 fC5Li RB	Newspaper Desk	1820
E	Cincinnati Emporium	071.771 fC5em	Newspaper Desk	1824 - 1825
F	Freeman's Journal	071.771 ffC5F		1796 - 1799
G	Cincinnati Gazette	071.771 fC5L		1815
H	The Whig		Newspaper Desk	1809 - 1810
J	Cincinnati Independent Press and Freedom Advocate	071.771 ffC5if RB		1822 - 1826
K	Cist's Daily Advertiser	071.771 fC5Cid		1847 - 1848
L	Cincinnati Evening Mercury	071.771 fC5m		1849
M	Cincinnati Daily Microscope	071.771 fC5mi		1842
N	National Republican	071.771 fC5R	Newspaper Desk	1823 - 1842
P	Cincinnati Daily Nonpareil	071.771 fC5Np		1850 - 1853
Q	Western Tiller	071.771 ffC5Wt RB		1826 - 1828
R	Cincinnati Chronicle and Literary Gazette	071.771 fC5Chz	Newspaper Desk	1826 - 1842
S	Western Spy	071.771 fC5We	Newspaper Desk	1799 - 1822
T	Cincinnati Daily Whig and Commercial Intelligencer	071.771 fC5Wh		1834 - 1839
V	Western Episcopal Observer	071.771 fC5W		1841
W	Spirit of the West	071.771 fC5L	Newspaper Desk	1814 - 1815
X	Cincinnati Journal and Western Luminary	071.771 fC5J		1831 - 1837
Y	Cincinnati Dispatch and Democratic Union	071.771 fC5DiS		1850
Z	The Coon-Skinner	Unbound	Newspaper Desk	1842

Table 1

Name	Notice Date	Death Date	Age		Page	Maiden Name
----, Charles	28, June 1849	June	30		L2	
----, SC, Anna (Sr)	17, July 1851	16, July	23	*	P2	
----, Susanna	24, June 1828	June	4m		N3	
Abbot, Nathaniel	17, Apr. 1819		estate		S3	
Abbott, W.	26, July 1834	July	1- 2m		R3	
Abbott, William	22, July 1834	July	1- 2m		T2	
Abraham, Kate	25, Sept 1852	23, Sept	2- 9m		P2	
Abrams, Jacob Strader	6, Dec. 1841	4, Dec.	25m-14d		N2	
Abrams, Louisa H.	30, July 1842	25, July			R3	
Ackerman, Richard (Capt)	21, Aug. 1852				P2	
Ackley, Alphonzo	7, June 1849	June	36		L2	
Adam, (son of Jesse M.)	6, Oct. 1827	Oct.	5m		R3	
Adam, Charles	25, July 1850	July	2		Y2	
Adams, (child of A.)	29, Oct. 1830	Oct.	stillborn		N3	
Adams, Adelaide	10, Nov. 1827	4, Nov.	24	*	R3	
Adams, David	9, Feb. 1807		estate		S3	
Adams, Edwin (Dr)	6, Nov. 1827	4, Nov.	24	*	N2	
Adams, Francis M.	10, Apr. 1829	Apr.	1- 7m		N3	
Adams, Hannah	7, Jan. 1832	16, Dec.			R3	
Adams, Harriet	24, Oct. 1850	Oct.	1d		Y2	
Adams, Jane	5, Apr. 1849	Apr.	85		L2	
Adams, Jane S.	24, Aug. 1847	13, Aug.	33		K2	
Adams, John	5, Nov. 1830	Nov.	36		N3	
Adams, John (President)	22, July 1826	4, July			J3	
Adams, John S.	18, Aug. 1835	16, Aug.			T2	
Adams, John V.	4, Nov. 1830	2, Nov.	37		A3	
Adams, John W.	30, Nov. 1830		estate		N3	
Adams, Joseph	18, Dec. 1840	16, Dec.	3		N2	
Adams, N.F. (Capt)	26, May 1815	21, May			S3	
Adams, Nathaniel F.	18, Aug. 1815		estate		S3	
Adams, Thomas J.	26, Feb. 1842	3, Feb.	infant		R3	
Adams, William	5, Sept 1828	Sept	2m-26d		N3	
Addams, A.A.	21, Mar. 1851				P2	
Adkinson, Annie Silvester	1, Sept 1852	29, Aug.	28		P2	
Aelerney, Ruth	19, Aug. 1831	Aug.	40		A3	
Agnew, Jane	20, Aug. 1830	Aug.	41		N3	
Aguial, Annette	3, Mar. 1827	28, Feb.			R3	
Ahearn, Dennis	13, July 1849	July	35		L2	
Airey, Joseph	24, Mar. 1838	9, Mar.	49		R3	
Alcoke, James B.	22, June 1849	21, June	39		L2	
Aldick, Henry	31, July 1850	July	1		Y3	
Aldred, George	10, Jan. 1837		estate		N3	
Aldrich, Gustavus	5, June 1841	2, June	41	*	R3	
Aldrich, Gustavus	4, June 1841	2, June	41	*	N2	
Aldrich, Henry Clay	24, Sept 1842	17, Sept	15		R3	
Aldrige, Richard	8, Aug. 1850	Aug.	9m		Y2	
Aldy, Isaac	12, Apr. 1849	Apr.			L2	
Alexander, Horace	3, Feb. 1835		estate		N2	
Alexander, Horace	7, Sept 1836		probate		N2	
Alexander, Joseph	23, July 1850	July	1- 5m		Y2	
Alexander, Margaret	27, Oct. 1847	25, Oct.	5		K2	
Alexander, Mary A.	6, Sept 1833	Sept	23		X3	
Alexander, W.F.	22, Oct. 1830	Oct.	31		N3	
Alkson, Jane	2, Aug. 1834	July	1- 6m		R3	

Name	Notice Date	Death Date	Age	Page	Maiden Name
Alkson, Jane	29, July 1834	July	1- 6m		T2
Allcorn, James (Capt)	31, May 1847	29, May	74		K2
Allen, Andrew	6, Aug. 1830	Aug.	1		N3
Allen, Charlotte	6, Nov. 1839	4, Nov.			T2
Allen, Eliza	4, Oct. 1839	1, Oct.	33	*	T2
Allen, Emily Rhoda	4, Sept 1841	25, Aug.	6- 8m		V3
Allen, George	10, Sept 1830	Sept	51		N3
Allen, George	2, Aug. 1834	July	2m		R3
Allen, George	29, July 1834	July	2m		T2
Allen, Harriette	25, June 1830	June	2- 6m		N3
Allen, Hugh	9, Nov. 1841	6, Nov.			N2
Allen, Joseph	5, Jan. 1811	31, Dec.	73		S3
Allen, Joseph	3, June 1811		estate		S3
Allen, Joseph	18, Jan. 1812		estate		S3
Allen, Joseph	28, Aug. 1827		probate		N3
Allen, Lewis	13, Nov. 1841	4, Nov.	19		R3
Allen, Martha	30, Dec. 1830	28, Dec.			A3
Allen, Martha	31, Dec. 1830	28, Dec.			N2
Allen, Paul	1, Sept 1826	19, Aug.			N3
Allen, Samuel	14, Dec. 1835		probate		N2
Allen, Samuel R.	14, Dec. 1835		probate		N2
Allen, Samuel W.	19, Feb. 1820		estate		S3
Allen, Samuel W.	14, Dec. 1824		probate		N3
Allen, Samuel W.	16, Dec. 1824		probate		E3
Allen, Samuel W.	19, Feb. 1820	12, Feb.		*	S2
Allen, Samuel W.	17, Feb. 1820	14, Feb.		*	D3
Allen, William	20, Sept 1833	Sept	42		X3
Allin,	30, Dec. 1828	Dec.	10		N3
Alling, Lymen	22, Mar. 1837		estate		N3
Alling, Sarah Ann	14, July 1849	8, July	30- 7m		L2	Sibley
Allison, James	8, Oct. 1814		estate		S3
Allison, Richard	20, Sept 1816		estate		S3
Allison, Richard	23, Mar. 1830		probate		N3
Allison, Richard (Dr)	22, Mar. 1816	22, Mar.			S3
Allsop, Henry	1, Aug. 1840	July	11		R3
Alms, Charles Frederick	19, July 1852	16, July	6-11m		P2
Alter, (child of William)	8, July 1828	July	stillborn		N3
Alter, Frederick	13, Nov. 1819		estate		S3
Alter, Frederick	14, Dec. 1824		probate		N3
Alter, Frederick	19, Aug. 1828		probate		N3
Alter, Frederick	16, Dec. 1824		probate		E3
Alter, William	1, Dec. 1841		estate		N3
Althoreseren, Mary	28, June 1849	June	40		L2
Altman, Dirk	18, May 1838		probate		N2
Amberg, John	7, June 1849	June	70		L2
Ames, (child of Henry)	18, June 1830	June	stillborn		N3
Ames, Benjamin	15, Oct. 1835	28, Sept	58		T2
Ames, Cyrus	16, Oct. 1847	2, Oct.	74		K2
Ames, Dobarro	13, Aug. 1830	Aug.	42		N3
Ames, Margaret	9, Dec. 1828	Dec.	21		N3
Amidon, Abner	31, Oct. 1804	24, Oct.			S4
Ammon, Sarah	28, Sept 1852	24, Sept	71		P2
Amon, Charles H.	9, 10, May 1850	8, May			P2
Anderson, (child of J.)	6, Aug. 1830	Aug.	2		N3

Name	Notice Date	Death Date	Age	Page	Maiden Name
Anderson, Charles G.	22, Mar. 1849	21, Mar.	12	L2	
Anderson, Charles Winton	5, Feb. 1849	5, Feb.	3- 6m- 5d	Y2	
Anderson, Daniel	16, May 1828		estate	N3	
Anderson, Enoch	6, Dec. 1852	2, Dec.	79	P2	
Anderson, George	10, Oct. 1823		estate	N3	
Anderson, George S.	10, Aug. 1852	6, Aug.	11	P2	
Anderson, James	27, June 1849	26, June	30	L2	
Anderson, John	6, Feb. 1829	Feb.	19	N2	
Anderson, Julia	1, Sept 1827	Aug.	20m	R3	
Anderson, Maria J.	11, Oct. 1852	29, Sept	19	P2	Gano
Anderson, Martha Anne	18, Mar. 1831	14, Feb.		* X3	
Anderson, Mary	14, Nov. 1840	9, Nov.	46	R3	
Anderson, Mary	3, Sept 1830	Aug.	1-10m	N2	
Anderson, Mary Barstow	28, Oct. 1837	28, Oct.	1- -25d	T2	
Anderson, Mary D.R.	23, July 1830	July	3m	N3	
Anderson, Matilda	17, May 1849	May	40	L2	
Anderson, Matilda S.	30, July 1830	July	3m	N3	
Anderson, R.C. (Col)	24, Oct. 1826	16, Oct.	76	N3	
Anderson, Rebecca	16, June 1821	12, June		S3	
Anderson, Richard	8, Sept 1826			N3	
Anderson, Richard	15, Sept 1826	24, July		Q3	
Anderson, Robert	11, July 1828	19, June	39	* N3	
Anderson, Robert	12, July 1828			R3	
Anderson, Sally	27, Oct. 1832	18, Oct.		R3	
Andress, Gabriel	27, Aug. 1852	Aug.	30	P2	
Andrews, (child of Dudley)	12, Aug. 1828	Aug.	3w	N3	
Andrews, (child of John)	14, Oct. 1828	Oct.	18m	N3	
Andrews, Bela	25, July 1818	22, July		* S3	
Andrews, Charles Willdott	1, July 1852	29, June	8m	P2	
Andrews, Dudley	14, Dec. 1835		probate	N2	
Andrews, Harry	5, Oct. 1852	2, Oct.		P2	
Andrews, Isaac	7, June 1849	June	45	L2	
Andrews, J.	1, June 1849	May	45	L2	
Andrews, Mary Elizabeth	4, May 1849	3, May	1- 4m- 9d	L2	
Andrews, Samuel	7, Sept 1852	5, Sept		P2	
Annable, Dorus H.	3, Mar. 1827	17, Feb.		* R3	
Annes, Horace	17, Sept 1830	Sept	17	N3	
Annis, Andrew	30, July 1830	July	1	N3	
Anthony, Christopher	3, Nov. 1815	28, Oct.	71	S3	
Anthony, Christopher	19, Jan. 1816		estate	S3	
Anthony, Mary	23, June 1838	16, June	89	R3	
Applegate, Abner	3, Dec. 1824		estate	N3	
Applegate, Abner	9, Dec. 1828		probate	N3	
Applegate, George	16, Feb. 1830		estate	N3	
Applegate, Henry S.	31, Dec. 1852	30, Dec.	33- 4m-23d	P2	
Applegate, John	1, June 1835		probate	N2	
Appleton, William	21, Oct. 1830	19, Oct.	22	A3	
Appleton, William	22, Oct. 1830	Oct.	22	N3	
Appleton, William W.	20, Nov. 1838	17, Nov.	32	* N2	
Appleton, William W.	17, Nov. 1838	17, Nov.		T2	
Arbegust, George	20, Mar. 1838		probate	N3	
Arbigust, George	22, Dec. 1829		probate	N3	
Arbigust, George	21, Dec. 1830		probate	N3	
Arcamble, Elizabeth	6, Apr. 1837	4, Apr.	75	T2	

Name	Notice Date	Death Date	Age		Page	Maiden Name
Archibald, Elizabeth	23, Jan. 1837		estate		N3	
Ardener, Andrew	7, June 1849	June	3		L2	
Armer, John M.	24, Dec. 1830	Dec.	1- 9m		N3	
Armistead, Theodorick	19, Dec. 1812	20, Nov.			S3	
Armstrong, Anna Eleanor	11, Feb. 1831	13, Jan.			X3	
Armstrong, James	26, Feb. 1841	24, Feb.	57		N2	
Armstrong, James	20, July 1811		estate		S4	
Armstrong, Jane	7, July 1838	2, July			R3	
Armstrong, John	9, Aug. 1816		estate		S3	
Armstrong, John (Col)	1, Mar. 1816	4, Feb.			S3	
Armstrong, Mary	12, May 1836	17, Apr.	67		X3	
Armstrong, Nathaniel	18, July 1840	4, July	91		R3	
Armstrong, Reuben	23, Apr. 1849	Apr.	20		L2	
Armstrong, Robert	31, July 1850	July	96		Y3	
Armstrong, Samuel	9, Feb. 1807		estate		S3	
Armstrong, Thomas (Rev)	28, Sept 1835	27, Aug.			T2	
Armstrong, Thomas (Rev)	25, Sept 1835	27, Aug.		*	X2	
Arnold, F.	5, Sept 1828	Sept	23		N3	
Arnold, Magdalena	16, Sept 1851	14, Sept			P2	
Arnold, William	17, Jan. 1835		estate		N2	
Arnold, William	27, Mar. 1835		estate		N2	
Arnold, William	17, June 1837		probate		N2	
Arons, David C.	20, Sept 1852	17, Sept	29		P2	
Artchey, Benjamin	23, Aug. 1852	18, Aug.	39		P2	
Arthur, (child of William)	27, Feb. 1829	Feb.	4m- 9d		N3	
Arthur, William	19, Sept 1835	16, Sept	38	*	T2	
Arthur, William (Rev)	24, Feb. 1827	19, Feb.	59		R3	
Arwood, Thomas R.	24, May 1849	May	45		L2	
Asbury, Francis	3, May 1816	31, Mar.	73		S3	
Aschraft, Emeline	29, July 1834	July	34		T2	
Asgill, Charles (Sir)	10, Oct. 1823		70		N1	
Ashburn, Ann	10, Nov. 1815	3, Nov.	76		S3	
Ashcraft, Emeline	2, Aug. 1834	July	34		R3	
Ashcroft, George	19, Sept 1828	Sept	19		N3	
Ashley, (son of Stephen)	11, Nov. 1838	Nov.	9m		N3	
Ashley, John	17, May 1849	May	40		L2	
Ashton, Cecilia	9, July 1835	2, July	51		N2	
Askeen, Joseph M.	7, Aug. 1852	26, July			P2	
Askew, Elenor V.	12, Sept 1840	4, Sept	1		R3	
Asseleneau, Edward Numa	18, Dec. 1841	18, Dec.	6- -23d		R3	
Atchison, George	22, Aug. 1828	Aug.	4- 1m- 5d		N3	
Atchison, William	24, Oct. 1828	Oct.	2m-15d		N2	
Atherton, Aaron	27, May 1825				N3	
Atherton, Wesley	8, Dec. 1836	30, Sept	26		X3	
Atkins, Ann	26, Nov. 1830	Nov.	70		N3	
Atkins, Thomas	1, Aug. 1850	July	2		Y2	
Atkinson, (child of Jane)	26, Apr. 1849	Apr.	child		L2	
Atkinson, Andrew	26, Apr. 1849	Apr.	38		L2	
Atkinson, Henry (Gen)	22, June 1842	14, June			N2	
Atkinson, Isaac	8, Aug. 1829	27, June	64	*	R3	
Atkinson, James	3, May 1849	May	3		L2	
Atkinson, James	14, June 1849	June	45		L2	
Atkinson, Jane	17, May 1849	May	21		L2	
Atkinson, Mary	24, May 1849	May	34		L2	

Name	Notice Date	Death Date	Age		Page	Maiden Name
Atkinson, Thomas	26, Apr. 1849	Apr.	4		L2	
Atkinson, Thomas E.	14, June 1849	June	5		L2	
Atla, (Mr)	29, Jan. 1842	23, Jan.			R3	
Atlee, Henry Yorke	30, May 1837	7, May	2m		T2	
AtLee, Richard J.	29, Dec. 1841				N2	
Atret, Joseph	15, Sept 1827	Sept	64		R3	
Attee, William	11, Oct. 1841	9, Oct.		*	N2	
Atwater, Alfred	23, June 1849	20, June	6m		L2	
Atwater, Anna Clarissa	3, Nov. 1847	31, Oct.	5m- 6d		K2	
Atwick, Gustavus	3, June 1841	2, June	41	*	N2	
Augusta, Caroline	14, Oct. 1828	Oct.	4w		N3	
Augustus, Henry	23, June 1835	22, June	8m		T2	
Aumberger, (child of Eliz.)	4, Sept 1852	2, Sept	infant		P2	
Austin, Benjamin	25, May 1820	4, May	68		S3	
Austin, Warren B.	17, Sept 1835		probate		T2	
Auten, Ralph	2, May 1836		estate		N2	
Avery, (child of John C.)	13, Aug. 1830	Aug.	stillborn		N3	
Avery, Charles	30, Dec. 1806	25, Dec.	57		S2	
Avery, Charles	9, Feb. 1807		estate		S3	
Avery, Howard B.	3, July 1849	29, June	13m		L2	
Avery, Jemima	10, Apr. 1829	4, Apr.	68		N3	
Avery, John	27, Feb. 1829	Feb.			N3	
Avery, Mary Ann	15, Sept 1836	19, Aug.			T2	
Avery, Mary Ann	14, Sept 1836	19, Aug.			N2	Brown
Avery, Nancy	19, Sept 1828	Sept	39		N3	
Awes, Henry	23, July 1850	July	1- 3m		Y2	
Aydelott, Daniel Brainard	19, 26, Dec. 1840	12, Dec.	15		R3	
Aydelotte, Caroline	18, July 1840	15, July			R3	
Aydelotte, Caroline	15, Aug. 1840	15, July			R3	
Aydelotte, David Brainerd	18, Dec. 1840	12, Dec.	15		N2	
Ayer, (child of Rufus)	3, Dec. 1830	Nov.	stillborn		N3	
Ayer, John	17, June 1823		estate		N3	
Ayer, John	18, July 1823		estate		N3	
Ayer, John	19, Aug. 1828		probate		N3	
Ayr, John	28, Sept 1822		estate		S3	
Ayre, John	9, Sept 1825		probate		N3	
Ayres, Mark	21, Dec. 1830		probate		N3	
Ayres, Martha	12, Aug. 1831	Aug.	45		A3	
Ayres, Martha Jane	1, Aug. 1840	22, July	infant		R3	
Ayres, Samuel	22, Feb. 1840		estate		R3	
Babcock, Elisha	28, Apr. 1821	7, Apr.	37		S3	
Babcock, Gideon	8, Nov. 1816	1, Nov.			S3	
Babinger, Abraham	8, Oct. 1830	Oct.	15		N3	
Backover, Benedict	27, Aug. 1852	Aug.	40		P2	
Bacon, Catharine Eberle	2, Oct. 1841	28, Sept	28		R3	
Bacon, Catharine Eberle	5, Oct. 1841	28, Sept	28		N2	
Bacon, Nathan	6, June 1818		estate		S3	
Badgely, Ellen S.	28, July 1832	24, July		*	R3	
Badgley, Rachel	27, Mar. 1805		estate		S3	
Badollet, Relief	14, Jan. 1831	8, Jan.			X3	
Bads, Emma	29, Oct. 1830	Oct.	55		N3	
Bagley, Catharine A.	16, Feb. 1839	15, Feb.			T2	
Bagley, Frank Clifford	3, June 1847	2, June	6m		K2	
Bagott, Margaret	10, Dec. 1830	Dec.	8m		N3	

Name	Notice Date	Death Date	Age		Page	Maiden Name
Bailes, John	25, Aug. 1852	23, Aug.			P2	
Bailey, Andrew	25, Nov. 1823		estate		N2	
Bailey, Charles S.	8, Aug. 1837	7, Aug.			N2	
Bailey, Charles S.	17, Aug. 1837	7, Aug.			X3	
Bailey, Daniel	11, Dec. 1827		probate		N3	
Bailey, Eleanor	19, May 1832	12, May	76	*	R3	
Bailhache, Sarah A.D.	13, May 1836	5, May	6		T2	
Bailhache, Sarah A.D.	19, May 1836	5, May	6		X3	
Bailiff, Daniel	29, Apr. 1831		estate		A3	
Baily, (child of John)	28, June 1849	June	1		L2	
Baily, Ann	28, June 1849	June	34		L2	
Baily, James K.	19, Aug. 1828		probate		N3	
Baird, John B.	17, Mar. 1837		estate		T2	
Baker, (child of Adam)	25, June 1830	June	stillborn		N3	
Baker, (child of Charles)	12, Aug. 1828	Aug.	infant		N3	
Baker, (child of Mrs)	17, Feb. 1829	Feb.	2m		N3	
Baker, Albert	27, July 1850	July	8		Y3	
Baker, Benjamin F.	5, July 1849	3, July	21		L3	
Baker, Elizabeth	5, Nov. 1830	Nov.	20		N3	
Baker, Francis	19, Nov. 1824	8, Nov.	40		N2	
Baker, George	19, July 1834	July	8m		R3	
Baker, Henry	7, June 1849	June	67		L2	
Baker, Hilary	14, Nov. 1840	29, Oct.	51		R3	
Baker, Isaac	6, Nov. 1838		probate		N2	
Baker, James H.	28, Nov. 1828	Nov.	41		N3	
Baker, Mary	9, July 1830	July	74		N3	
Baker, Mary	22, May 1841	May	6m		R3	
Baker, Nathan	23, Oct. 1841	18, Oct.			R3	
Baker, Nathan	22, Oct. 1841	18, Oct.			N2	
Baker, Philip H.	19, Aug. 1828	Aug.	21d		N3	
Baker, Stephen V.	12, Aug. 1828	Aug.	1-10m		N3	
Baker, Timothy	24, Aug. 1852	21, Aug.	54		P2	
Bakewell, Howard	5, Apr. 1849	Mar.	23		L2	
Balanges, (child of Peter)	16, Dec. 1828	Dec.	stillborn		N3	
Baldera, Mary	12, Apr. 1849	Apr.	3		L2	
Balding, James	25, Aug. 1829		probate		N3	
Balding, John	9, Dec. 1828		probate		N3	
Baldwin, (Dr)	23, Oct. 1819	31, Aug.			S3	
Baldwin, (Judge)	6, Nov. 1837	4, Nov.			T2	
Baldwin, Arden W.	22, Apr. 1847	20, Apr.	34		K2	
Baldwin, Christopher C.	5, Sept 1835	21, Aug.			T2	
Baldwin, Christopher C.	4, Sept 1835	21, Aug.		*	X3	
Baldwin, E.	10, Jan. 1837		estate		N3	
Baldwin, Elisha W. (Rev)	7, Nov. 1840				R3	
Baldwin, Elizabeth Elliot	15, Sept 1841	13, Sept	7m		N2	
Baldwin, Elizabeth Elliott	18, Sept 1841	13, Sept	6m-20d		R3	
Baldwin, Mary Elizabeth	25, Sept 1852	23, Sept	12		P2	
Bales, Mary P.	26, July 1850	July	2		Y2	
Ball, (child of Amos)	5, Nov. 1830	Nov.	stillborn		N3	
Ball, (child of William)	13, July 1849	July	stillborn		L2	
Ball, (child)	29, Mar. 1834	Mar.	infant		R3	
Ball, Alice Daveraux	16, Aug. 1852	14, Aug.	9m		P2	
Ball, Mary	30, Apr. 1824	26, Apr.	25		N3	
Ball, Mary Elizabeth	10, Apr. 1829	Apr.	6w		N3	

Name	Notice Date	Death Date	Age	Page	Maiden Name
Ball, Samuel Candler	19, July 1836	17, July	1- 5m- 7d	T2	
Ballance, Charles Howard	25, June 1849	21, June	5- 6m-10d	L2	
Ballard, David	28, Dec. 1820			S3	
Ballard, Sarah Ella	29, July 1851	27, July	infant	P2	
Ballard, William	20, Mar. 1829	Mar.	20	N3	
Ballinger, Temple	5, Apr. 1830	23, Mar.		A3	
Baltzell, Charles	9, Nov. 1832	5, Nov.	*	X3	
Bangs, Louisa	4, June 1849	2, June	39	L2	
Banks, Catharine	17, Sept 1830	Sept	40	N3	
Banks, Linn	24, Jan. 1842	21, Jan.		N2	
Banks, Symmes Harrison	12, Aug. 1847	8, Aug.	20m	K2	
Banks, Thomas	29, Dec. 1837		estate	N3	
Banks, Thomas	19, Dec. 1826		probate	N3	
Barbee, Mary	24, July 1850	July	1- 3m	Y2	
Barber, Charles P.	4, June 1830	June	37	N3	
Barber, William	9, June 1837	June	22	* T2	
Barbour, Edward	10, Dec. 1830	Dec.	39	N3	
Bard, James	27, Aug. 1830	Aug.	70	N3	
Bard, John	21, Dec. 1830		probate	N3	
Bard, Joseph H.	12, May 1851	9, May	27	P2	
Bard, Mary E.	14, May 1830	May	3	N3	
Barham, John	14, Oct. 1825		73	N2	
Barkalo, Lydia	22, Sept 1852	18, Sept	14- - 9d	P2	
Barker, John	2, July 1830	June	33	N2	
Barker, Mary Jane	26, Feb. 1831	23, Feb.		R3	
Barker, Thomas (Dr)	9, June 1815	7, June		S3	
Barker, Thomas C. (Dr)	11, Aug. 1815		estate	S3	
Barkley, Elizabeth C.	31, Dec. 1852	24, Dec.		P2	Best
Barnard, (child of Charles)	19, Nov. 1830	Nov.	20d	N3	
Barnes, James	29, May 1841	May	26	R3	
Barnes, Josephine	21, Jan. 1841	19, Jan.		N2	
Barnes, Mary Frances	27, Aug. 1842	7, Aug.	19m	R3	
Barnes, Nathan	4, Mar. 1797		estate	F3	
Barnes, William (Dr)	13, May 1837	23, Apr.		R3	
Barnes, William (Dr)	10, May 1837	23, Apr.		T2	
Barnes, William D.	12, Aug. 1836	11, Aug.	18- 5m	T2	
Barnes, William D.	12, Aug. 1836	11, Aug.	18- 5m	N2	
Barnet, Elizabeth	13, Aug. 1808	11, Aug.		S3	
Barnet, James R.	1, July 1828	June	2	N3	
Barnet, John	15, Jan. 1806		estate	S3	
Barnet, Lucinda	1, July 1828	June	27	N3	
Barns, Catharine	17, Oct. 1851	16, Oct.	73	P2	
Barns, Nathan	25, Mar. 1797		estate	F3	
Barnschmit, William	18, Sept 1852	17, Sept		P2	
Barnum, Horace L. (Capt)	21, Aug. 1837	20, Aug.		N2	
Barnum, Horace L. (Capt)	31, Aug. 1837	20, Aug.		X3	
Baron, Samuel	1, Dec. 1810	28, Nov.		S3	
Barr, Enos	21, June 1849	June	48	L2	
Barr, Mary	17, July 1819			S3	
Barr, Thomas T.	14, Dec. 1824		47	N3	
Barr, Thomas T.	3, Dec. 1824	27, Nov.		N3	
Barr, William	21, Mar. 1837	16, Mar.	60	T2	
Barr, William	17, May 1816	14, May	74	S3	
Barr, William	6, Nov. 1838		probate	N2	

Name	Notice Date	Death Date	Age	Page	Maiden Name
Barret, John	9, Oct. 1819		estate	S3	
Barret, Theodore	27, Nov. 1830		estate	R3	
Barret, Theodore B.	30, June 1827	25, June		R3	
Barrett, Dudley	20, Apr. 1824	5, Mar.	14	N3	
Barrett, Dudley	22, Apr. 1824	5, Mar.	14	E3	
Bartholomew, Daniel	14, June 1849	13, June		* L2	
Bartle, John	14, Dec. 1839	10, Dec.	94	* R3	
Bartlett, (child of Andrew)	9, Dec. 1828	Dec.	7m	N3	
Bartlett, Caroline V.	19, July 1834	July	7m	R3	
Bartlett, Maria Raymond	16, July 1842	9, July	6	R3	
Bartlett, Roswell	3, Apr. 1805		estate	S3	
Bartlett, Roswell	30, Mar. 1807		estate	S3	
Bartlett, Stephen	23, May 1840		86	R3	
Bartlett, William Henry	23, July 1842	17, July	3	R3	
Bartley, Joseph	17, May 1849	May	27	L2	
Barton, Benjamin Smith (Dr)	5, Jan. 1816	19, Dec.	49	S3	
Barton, David	15, Nov. 1837	19, Oct.		T2	
Barton, James	29, Oct. 1830	Oct.	32	N3	
Barwise, Catharine	22, July 1834	July	18	T2	
Barwise, Catherine	26, July 1834	July	18	R3	
Barwise, Thomas	25, Nov. 1824		estate	E3	
Basey, Bassel	6, Oct. 1827	Oct.	19	R3	
Bass, Moses T.	6, Apr. 1837	3, Apr.	26	* T2	
Bassett, Benjamin	9, Jan. 1830	2, Jan.	78	* R3	
Bateman, Aaron	17, Sept 1835		probate	T2	
Bates, David	31, Oct. 1840	19, Oct.		R3	
Bates, Frederick	26, Aug. 1825	2, Aug.		N3	
Bates, George H.	2, Aug. 1850	1, Aug.	35	P2	
Bates, George H.	3, Aug. 1850	1, Aug.	35	Y2	
Bates, Nancy E.	12, Sept 1828	Sept	6w- 3d	N3	
Bauch, Mary E.	28, May 1835	12, May		T2	
Bauer, George C.	12, Apr. 1849	Apr.	50	L2	
Baughman, John	19, Dec. 1828		estate	N3	
Baum, Jacob	9, Nov. 1841	6, Nov.	34	N2	
Baum, Kershner	21, Sept 1838	10, Sept		T2	
Baum, Martin	1, June 1835		probate	N2	
Baum, Martin	14, Dec. 1835		probate	N2	
Baum, Martin	7, Sept 1836		probate	N2	
Baum, Martin	17, Dec. 1831	14, Dec.		R3	
Bavis, Andrew	11, Dec. 1827		probate	N3	
Baxter, Andrew	13, Jan. 1826		estate	N3	
Baxter, Andrew	9, Dec. 1828		probate	N3	
Baxter, Andrew (Capt)	23, Dec. 1825	1, Dec.	35	N3	
Baxter, Greenbury	31, Dec. 1830	Dec.		N3	
Bayard, James A.	19, Aug. 1815	7, Aug.		S1	
Bayley, James K.	11, Apr. 1818		estate	S3	
Bayley, James K.	14, Nov. 1818		estate	S3	
Bayley, James K.	27, Dec. 1816	26, Dec.		S3	
Bayly, James K.	17, Jan. 1817		estate	S3	
Baymiller, Anna T.	5, Dec. 1817	3, Dec.		S3	
Baymiller, Jacob	24, June 1825		estate	N3	
Baymiller, Jacob	22, Dec. 1829		probate	N3	
Baymiller, Samuel Davies	11, Sept 1819	2, Sept		S3	
Beach, Aaron	6, July 1822		96	* S2	

Name	Notice Date	Death Date	Age		Page	Maiden Name
Beach, Benjamin C.	18, Aug. 1836	21, July	26		X3	
Beach, Solomon (Dr)	17, Aug. 1850	12, Aug.	67	*	Y2	
Beal, Nathaniel G.	20, Oct. 1827	Oct.	18		R3	
Beall, Clara Frances	23, July 1852	22, July	infant		P2	
Beall, Mary	28, Mar. 1812	21, Mar.			S3	
Bealle, George	16, Apr. 1835	11, Apr.			T3	
Beals, Celena Augusta	10, Dec. 1852	27, Nov.	17- 6m-20d		P2	
Beaman, Elizabeth G.	31, Oct. 1834	27, Sept	32	*	X3	
Beamon, David	20, Nov. 1835		estate		T3	
Bean, Alexander	12, Nov. 1830	Nov.	30		N3	
Bean, Thomas	7, May 1830	May	3		N3	
Beard, John	20, Jan. 1829		estate		N3	
Beard, Sarah E.	26, Dec. 1840	Dec.	4m		R3	
Beard, William	15, Jan. 1806		estate		S3	
Beard, William	13, Nov. 1805	6, Nov.			S3	
Bears, Mary	16, Oct. 1852	14, Oct.	52		P2	
Beata, Arthur	2, Aug. 1834	July	34		R3	
Beatty, (dau. of Samuel T.)	14, Oct. 1828	Oct.	stillborn		N3	
Beatty, Arthur	17, June 1837		probate		N2	
Beatty, H.T.	21, Oct. 1823	27, Sept	30	*	N3	
Beaty, Arthur	29, July 1834	July	34		T2	
Beaty, Nancy	19, Aug. 1828	Aug.	23		N3	
Beauvels, Samuel	22, Oct. 1830	Oct.	44		N3	
Beck, (Miss)	14, Mar. 1823				N3	
Beck, Margaret	29, Oct. 1830	Oct.	39		N3	
Beck, Margaret	28, Oct. 1830	23, Oct.	40	*	A3	
Beckett, Elizabeth	23, Oct. 1852	19, Oct.			P2	
Beckman, Lewis	26, Sept 1850	Sept			Y2	
Beckwith, (child)	19, July 1834	July	child		R3	
Beckwith, Nicholas (Capt)	9, Nov. 1837	29, Oct.			T2	
Bedoun, (child of J.E.)	23, Sept 1831	Sept	1		A3	
Beecher, Harriet	8, July 1835	6, July			T2	
Beecher, Harriet	10, July 1835	7, July			X3	
Beecher, Jacob (Rev)	29, July 1831	15, July	30	*	X3	
Beeker, Charles	13, Nov. 1852	12, Nov.	4- 1m-21d		P2	
Beeler, Daniel	22, Dec. 1829		probate		N3	
Beeler, Daniel	7, Sept 1830		probate		N3	
Beeman, David	6, Nov. 1838		probate		N2	
Beer, Jacob	1, Oct. 1830	Sept	23		N3	
beeson, Amos	12, Oct. 1837	18, Sept			T2	
Beggs, (Mrs)	1, Aug. 1828	July			N3	
Beker, Bernard	11, June 1842	June			R3	
Belcher, George	6, July 1849	July	27		L2	
Bell, Charles M.	25, July 1850	July	6m		Y2	
Bell, Charles Murdoch	25, July 1850	24, July	6m-12d		Y2	
Bell, Charles Murdock	24, July 1850	24, July	7m-10d		P2	
Bell, Jane	16, Feb. 1836	29, Jan.			T3	
Bell, Peter	11, May 1830	9, May	60		N2	
Bell, Peter	18, June 1830		estate		N3	
Bell, Peter	13, May 1830	9, May			A3	
Bell, Reuben	6, July 1849	July	48		L2	
Bell, Samuel	3, Mar. 1826		estate		N3	
Bell, Samuel	9, Dec. 1828		probate		N3	
Bell, Samuel	10, Mar. 1829		probate		N3	

Name	Notice Date	Death Date	Age	Page	Maiden Name
Bell, Washington	30, July 1850	July	14m	Y3	
Belman, Clarissa	12, Oct. 1852	8, Oct.	26	P2	
Bemiss, Elijah	9, Jan. 1823		estate	J2	
Benby, Mary	12, Jan. 1829	Jan.	30	N2	
Benedict, Mary S.	14, Sept 1837	5, Sept		X3	
Benefiel, Israel	17, Sept 1835		probate	T2	
Benford, Paton	23, Dec. 1828	Dec.		N3	
Benham, Isabella	1, Nov. 1828	29, Oct.		R3	
Benham, Isabella G.	11, Nov. 1838	Nov.	32	N3	
Benham, Joseph S.	18, July 1840	17, July	43	R3	
Benham, Nancy	3, July 1849	2, July	63	L2	
Benjamin, Benjamin	22, Oct. 1830	Oct.	37	N3	
Benjamin, Levi	29, May 1829		100	N3	
Bennet, (child of Sarah)	11, June 1842	June	2w	R3	
Bennet, Ann	27, Aug. 1808	16, Aug.	60	S3	
Bennet, Caleb P.	26, May 1836		78	X3	
Bennet, Patrick	10, May 1849	May	40	L2	
Bennet, William	31, May 1816		estate	S1	
Bennett, A.D.	21, June 1849	June	23	L2	
Bennett, Elizabeth	7, May 1842	3, May	23	R3	
Bennett, Elizabeth	13, Nov. 1838	4, Nov.	*	T2	Weare
Benson, (child of Daniel)	22, Oct. 1830	Oct.	stillborn	N3	
Benson, (child of Peter)	30, Dec. 1828	Dec.	stillborn	N3	
Benson, Charles Lea	24, Aug. 1836	21, Aug.	8	T2	
Benson, Jane	6, Mar. 1829	Mar.	58	N2	
Benson, Mary Elizabeth	9, June 1847	5, June	20m	K2	
Benson, Mary Jane	8, Oct. 1838	23, Sept	20m	T2	
Benson, Peter H.	26, July 1834	July	7- -4d	R3	
Benson, Peter Howell	14, 22, July 1834	11, July	7- -4d	T2	
Benson, Sarah Ann	27, Oct. 1832	19, Oct.		R3	
Benson, William	17, Feb. 1829	Feb.	46	N3	
Benson, William	27, Mar. 1835		estate	N2	
Benson, William	19, Nov. 1835		estate	N2	
Bentley, William (Rev)	22, Jan. 1820	25, Dec.		S3	
Benton, F. Stanley	16, Nov. 1835	14, Nov.		T2	
Benton, F. Stanly	24, Dec. 1835		estate	X3	
Benton, F.S.	7, Mar. 1836		estate	T3	
Beresford, William H.	17, Nov. 1851	14, Nov.		P2	
Bergen, Daniel	3, May 1849	May	37	L2	
Bergen, Judith	26, Apr. 1849	Apr.	28	L2	
Bergen, Margaret	14, June 1849	June	3	L2	
Bergen, Mary	21, June 1849	June	9w	L2	
Berisford, Richard	5, Sept 1828	Sept		N3	
Berkley, Alexander	31, Mar. 1826	Oct.	114	N3	
Bermagem, Thomas	27, July 1803	8, July		S3	
Bermagem, William	27, July 1803	8, July		S3	
Berman, Leurent	2, Aug. 1834	July	1	R3	
Berman, Leurent	29, July 1834	July	1	T2	
Bernegobre, Mary B.	23, July 1850	July	3	Y2	
Berry, Emily	4, Feb. 1831	Jan.		X3	
Berry, James	20, Mar. 1847	17, Mar.	88	K2	
Berry, Joseph	2, Oct. 1827		estate	N3	
Berry, William	24, Jan. 1810		estate	H4	
Berry, William G.	24, Apr. 1838		estate	T3	

Name	Notice Date	Death Date	Age	Page	Maiden Name
Bessam, R.C. (Mrs)	22, July 1841	21, July	43	N2	
Best, Emma	23, Apr. 1842	19, Apr.		R3	
Best, John	24, July 1850	July	9w	Y2	
Best, Samuel	7, July 1821	3, July	10	S3	
Best, Thomas	22, May 1813	13, May		* S3	
Better, Agness	28, June 1849	June	36	L2	
Betterton, Oliver K.	8, Aug. 1842	31, July	20- 3m-19d	N2	
Betts, Eliza Ann	4, Oct. 1833	12, Sept		X3	
Betts, Elizabeth	3, Dec. 1852	29, Nov.	70	P2	
Betts, John	18, July 1828	July	18m	N3	
Betts, Samuel	27, Feb. 1830		estate	R3	
Betts, William	26, May 1815	25, May		S3	
Betty, (child of Sarah E.)	4, June 1830	June	1	N3	
Betz, John	12, Aug. 1801		murdered	S3	
Bevis, Anna	29, Oct. 1835		estate	N4	
Bevis, Anna	11, Sept 1837		probate	N2	
Bevor, William	21, Sept 1838		probate	N3	
Biddle, Thomas	3, May 1825		probate	N3	
Biddle, William S.	17, June 1835			T2	
Bidgley, Rachel	20, Mar. 1805		estate	S3	
Bidwell, Penelope	13, Sept 1852	10, Sept		P2	
Bigalow, Aaron	18, Oct. 1816		estate	S3	
Bigalow, Daniel	18, Oct. 1816		estate	S3	
Bigalow, Jonathan	18, Oct. 1816		estate	S3	
Bigelo, (child of Horace)	18, June 1830	June	5d	N3	
Bigelow, John	6, Sept 1833	Sept	58	X3	
Bigelow, John	17, Sept 1835		probate	T2	
Bigelow, Russel (Rev)	17, July 1835	1, July		X3	
Bigelow, Russell	15, July 1835	1, July	43	T2	
Biggar, George D.	7, June 1847	29, May	33	K2	
Biggin, Ann	7, June 1849	June	27	L2	
Biggs, Dorington	10, Jan. 1837		estate	N3	
Biggs, Zacheus	13, Oct. 1826		estate	N3	
Biggs, Zacheus	7, Sept 1830		probate	N3	
Biggs, Zacheus	23, Dec. 1831			X3	
Biggs, Zacheus (Major)	8, Sept 1826	4, Sept		N3	
Bigham, Benjamin	20, Oct. 1827	Oct.	25	R3	
Billings, Wright S.	2, Aug. 1834	July	1	R3	
Billings, Wright S.	29, July 1834	July	1	T2	
Billins, (twins of E.)	7, May 1830	May	stillborn	N3	
Bills, (Mr)	27, Mar. 1813	26, Mar.		S3	
Bills, James	17, Apr. 1813		estate	S3	
Bingham, Amos	30, Jan. 1841	Jan.	43	R3	
Bingham, Rebecca	10, July 1841	July	42	R3	
Bingham, Sabra	26, Dec. 1840	Dec.	1- 7m	R3	
Birch, (Mrs)	19, July 1834	July	35	R3	
Birch, Fanny Childs	16, Apr. 1842	7, Apr.	5	R3	
Birch, George DeWitt	25, Dec. 1841	18, Dec.	20m	R3	
Birch, Richard	24, Oct. 1817		estate	S2	
Bird, Amos	10, Apr. 1829	Apr.		N3	
Bird, Norman	27, Mar. 1837	23, Mar.	52	T2	
Bird, Norman	25, Mar. 1837	23, Mar.	52	N2	
Bird, Norman	1, Apr. 1837		estate	N2	
Birdsell, John	25, July 1829	24, July		R3	

Name	Notice Date	Death Date	Age		Page	Maiden Name
Birdseye, Lucinda P.	12, July 1828			*	R3	
Birkbeck, Morris	14, June 1825				N3	
Birkel, Michael	21, June 1849	June	19		L2	
Birmingham, Daniel	26, July 1850	July	36		Y2	
Birne, Henry	21, June 1849	June	39		L2	
Bishop, Catharine W.	12, July 1828				R3	
Bishop, Hezekiah	25, Apr. 1810		estate		H4	
Bishop, James M.	17, July 1841	20, June			R3	
Bishop, Mary Rosina	28, May 1842	21, May	11m-12d		R3	
Bishop, Mary Rosina	24, May 1842	21, May	11m-12d		N2	
Bishop, Thomas	7, Sept 1824		probate		N3	
Bishop, Thomas	9, Sept 1824		probate		E3	
Bishop, Truman	27, Jan. 1829	Jan.	48		N2	
Bishop, Truman (Rev)	12, 16, Jan. 1829	11, Jan.	48		N2	
Bislen, Elijah	19, Aug. 1831	Aug.	37		A3	
Bissell, Edward Meade	7, Mar. 1840	29, Feb.	16m		R3	
Bissell, George Meade	12, Feb. 1842	11, Feb.	infant		R3	
Blachly, Elizabeth	23, Feb. 1833	1, Feb.	32		R3	
Blachly, Elizabeth	8, Mar. 1833	11, Feb.	32		X3	
Blachly, Oliver B.	26, Jan. 1837		estate		T2	
Blachly, Oliver B.	14, Sept 1836	12, Sept			N2	
Black, Anne	29, Oct. 1836		estate		N2	
Black, Harriet	16, Oct. 1841	10, Oct.	27		R3	Jones
Black, Harriet	14, Oct. 1841	10, Oct.	27	*	N2	Jones
Black, Henry	9, Dec. 1841	28, Nov.			N2	
Black, Matthias	9, Sept 1828		estate		N3	
Black, Matthias	22, Dec. 1829		probate		N3	
Black, Matthias	7, Sept 1830		probate		N3	
Blackburn, Bryson	20, Aug. 1814		estate		S3	
Blackburn, Edward S.	2, Aug. 1850	25, July	65		P2	
Blackburn, George (Rev)	20, Oct. 1837	4, Oct.			T2	
Blackburn, Joseph	11, Aug. 1852	6, Aug.	20-10m- 1d		P2	
Blackburn, Samuel Emmons (Rev)	10, Oct. 1835	23, Aug.			T2	
Blackleach, Charity A.	20, July 1820	8, July	18	*	S3	
Blackmore, Elizabeth	2, July 1852	22, June			P2	
Blades, Benjamin	4, June 1836		probate		N2	
Blair, James	27, Jan. 1837	7, Jan.	75	*	N2	
Blair, Letitia	6, July 1849	July	16		L2	
Blair, William	19, Aug. 1828	Aug.	2w		N3	
Blake, Francis A.	9, Apr. 1824	5, Apr.		*	N3	
Blake, John	1, Aug. 1828	July	2- 4m		N3	
Blanch, Matthew	21, Nov. 1840	Nov.	22		R3	
Blanding, Abraham (Col)	12, Oct. 1839			*	R3	
Blatchly, (child)	10, Apr. 1829	Apr.	stillborn		N3	
Blatzee, John	24, May 1849	May	40		L2	
Blazdell, Polly	29, May 1819				S3	
Blew, John	22, Aug. 1850	Aug.	3m		Y2	
Blinn, Mary	30, Oct. 1841	19, Oct.	101		R3	
Bliss, (child)	29, Mar. 1834	Mar.	stillborn		R3	
Bliss, Elizabeth Jelf	10, Nov. 1832	4, Nov.	55- -12d		R3	
Bliss, Margaretta	5, Nov. 1824	17, Oct.	19		N1	
Bliss, Margaretta	4, Nov. 1824	17, Oct.			E3	
Bliss, Mary M.	11, Apr. 1828	10, Apr.			N3	
Bliss, Mary M.	11, Apr. 1828	10, Apr.			Q3	

Name	Notice Date	Death Date	Age		Page	Maiden Name
Blodget, Darius (Mrs)	9, Nov. 1832	7, Nov.		*	X3	
Blood, Hosea (Dr)	25, Oct. 1816	12, Sept			S2	
Bloom, (child of Ellen)	22, Mar. 1849	Mar.	1d		L2	
Bloom, Ephraim	20, Jan. 1829	17, Dec.	100- -4d	*	N3	
Bloomfield, Joseph (Gen)	21, Oct. 1823	3, Oct.			N3	
Blossom, (child of Nancy)	13, Aug. 1830	Aug.	7m		N3	
Bloxton, Mary	12, July 1828				R3	
Blue, (Mrs)	30, Dec. 1828	Dec.			N3	
Blue, David	18, Aug. 1821	7, Aug.			S3	
Blue, Jackson	19, Sept 1828	Sept	8- 6m		N3	
Blythe, Mary S.	2, July 1830	June	1		N2	
Boal, James	11, Sept 1837		probate		N2	
Boal, Thomas	31, Dec. 1814	25, Dec.			S3	
Boardman, Charles	26, July 1834	July	33		R3	
Boardman, Charles	22, July 1834	July	33		T2	
Boardman, Charles T.	16, July 1834	13, July	33	*	T2	
Boardman, Elizabeth	10, Dec. 1840	9, Dec.	64	*	N2	
Boardman, Mary Ellen	6, Aug. 1841	4, Aug.	2- 8m		N2	
Bockdalage, Jane	21, Oct. 1828	Oct.	10m		N2	
Bode, Elizabeth	24, July 1850	July	24		Y2	
Bodley, Ann Griffith	17, Nov. 1852	15, Nov.	5- 6m-22d		P2	
Bodmann, Adelaide A.	13, Dec. 1847	10, Dec.			K2	
Bogardus, Abraham	1, Sept 1821	30, Aug.		*	S3	
Bogen, Jacob	14, May 1830	May	53		N3	
Boggs, Andrew J.	20, Mar. 1847	18, Mar.	30		K2	
Boggs, Elizabeth	25, July 1828	24, July			Q3	
Bogie, John	1, June 1835		probate		N2	
Bohannan, Margaret Ann	31, Dec. 1841	24, Dec.	19		N2	
Bohlman, Margaret E.	28, June 1849	June	79		L2	
Bohmert, Henry	27, July 1852	July			P2	
Boiles, (Mrs)	4, Nov. 1824	28, Oct.	75		E3	
Bolander, John	26, Mar. 1842		estate		R3	
Bollmann, Errich (Dr)	22, June 1822	9, Dec.			S4	
Bolser, Henry	4, Mar. 1828		probate		N3	
Bolser, Reason	20, Mar. 1838		probate		N3	
Boltzell, Peter	1, June 1835		probate		N2	
Bonnel, Emmeretta	9, July 1830	July	10m		N3	
Bonnel, Lewis	28, Oct. 1831		estate		A3	
Bonnell, Moses E.	17, Aug. 1842	16, Aug.			N2	
Bonnell, Samuel	18, Sept 1819	7, Sept	27		S3	
Bonnell, Stephen	21, Nov. 1829	31, Oct.	21	*	R3	
Bonner, Hugh	2, Apr. 1842	31, Mar.	3- 4m		N2	
Bonner, Hugh (Dr)	3, Mar. 1837	27, Feb.	37		T2	
Bonsall, Ann	15, July 1830	1, July	58		A3	
Bonsall, Isaac	8, Oct. 1831	3, Oct.	66	*	R3	
Bonsall, Isaac	14, Oct. 1831	3, Oct.	66	*	X3	
Bonsell, Sidney	12, Nov. 1830	Nov.	5		N3	
Bonte, Mary Amelia	26, June 1849	24, June	2- -16d		L2	
Boon, Jane	1, Aug. 1828	July	11		N3	
Boon, William	6, Oct. 1826		probate		N3	
Boone, Daniel	19, Oct. 1820	26, Sept	90		S3	
Boone, George	30, Nov. 1820		83		S3	
Boone, John R.	23, Apr. 1842				R3	
Bootee, Eliza	13, July 1849	July	40		L2	

Name	Notice Date	Death Date	Age	Page	Maiden Name
Booth, Benjamin	7, Sept 1824		probate		N3
Booth, Benjamin	3, May 1825		probate		N3
Booth, Benjamin	9, Sept 1824		probate		E3
Booth, Eliza	10, Nov. 1836	5, Nov.	18		T2
Booth, Joseph	2, Oct. 1841	30, Aug.		*	R3
Boothe, Edward (Capt)	31, Oct. 1840	20, Oct.			R3
Borden, Francis Carr	16, July 1830	July	1		N3
Borden, Francis Carr	15, July 1830	8, July	12m		A3
Borden, Louisa	6, Jan. 1848	4, Jan.	12		K2
Borden, Samuel	14, Dec. 1835		probate		N2
Borden, Samuel	7, Sept 1836		probate		N2
Borden, Samuel (Gen)	25, Oct. 1834	22, Oct.	53		T2
Bordon, William F.	21, Oct. 1852	18, Oct.	31		P2
Bosley, M.	4, Sept 1852	2, Sept			P2
Boss, Thomas	12, Sept 1828	Sept	19m		N3
Bosse, Henry	22, Aug. 1850	Aug.	27		Y2
Bosson, John S. (Dr)	11, Apr. 1818	5, Apr.	25	*	S3
Bosson, Joseph	27, Oct. 1838	23, Oct.		*	T2
Bosson, Mary H.	31, July 1819	26, July			S3
Boswell, Ann	10, Mar. 1829		probate		N3
Boswell, John	7, Sept 1830		probate		N3
Boswell, Mary	6, July 1849	July	40		L2
Boswell, Rachel	6, Sept 1839	4, Sept			T2
Boswell, W.E. (Gen)	21, June 1828				R3
Bottomly, Mary A.	13, July 1849	July	37		L2
Boudinot, Elias	17, Nov. 1821	24, Oct.	82		S3
Bouge, Aaron J. (Rev)	1, Aug. 1826		74		N2
Boughman, Isabella	19, Aug. 1831	Aug.	20m		A3
Boulware, James	1, Aug. 1828	July			N3
Bourne, Jason	2, July 1849	29, June	14m		L2
Bowdle, Catharine	1, July 1837	26, June		*	R3
Bowdle, Daniel (Mrs)	27, June 1837	26, June			T2
Bowen, Anderson	30, Dec. 1847				K2
Bowen, Benjamin	30, Dec. 1847				K2
Bowen, James	20, Mar. 1830		estate		R3
Bowen, James	11, Sept 1837		probate		N2
Bower, James	27, Mar. 1830		estate		R3
Bower, John George	12, Sept 1850	Sept			Y2
Bowles, William	2, July 1835		estate		T2
Bowlin, Jesse B.	29, June 1850	28, June	66		P2
Bowman, Daniel	20, Aug. 1830	Aug.	18m		N3
Bowman, John	7, Mar. 1828		estate		Q3
Bowman, Jonas	5, May 1829		estate		N3
Bowman, Richard	11, Sept 1829		estate		N3
Bowman, Richard	21, Dec. 1830		probate		N3
Bowmar, Robert	28, June 1828		88		R3
Bowne, William H.	29, Dec. 1815	24, Nov.	12		S3
Bowring, John	28, June 1849	June	48		L2
Boyd, (child of Henry)	21, May 1830	May	child		N3
Boyd, Jane	4, June 1830	June			N3
Boyd, John	21, Oct. 1837	19, Sept	23		R3
Boyd, John	18, Oct. 1837	19, Sept	23	*	T2
Boyd, John	7, Sept 1836		probate		N2
Boyd, John (Rev)	27, Oct. 1832	23, Oct.		*	R3

Name	Notice Date	Death Date	Age		Page	Maiden Name
Boyd, Joseph	28, Aug. 1827		probate		N3	
Boyd, Mary	21, Aug. 1852	19, Aug.	65	*	P2	
Boyer, G.A.	26, June 1849	24, June	29		L2	
Boynton, Mary	8, Aug. 1823	21, July	62	*	N3	
Bozher, Phillipine	31, July 1841	July	33		R3	
Bracaw, John	20, Aug. 1799	18, Aug.			S3	
Brackenridge, Joseph	8, Sept 1826	28, Aug.			N3	
Bradbury, G.W. (Col)	2, Nov. 1847	1, Nov.	31		K2	
Bradey, James	16, Mar. 1803		estate		S4	
Bradford, C.B. (Mrs)	8, Apr. 1820	13, Mar.	28		S3	
Bradford, James	4, Nov. 1828	Oct.	3- 5m		N3	
Bradford, John	22, Apr. 1830	2, Mar.			A3	
Bradford, Sarah Hickling	14, July 1832	1, July			R3	
Brading, Jeremiah (Dr)	18, May 1838		probate		N2	
Bradley, Abraham	14, May 1838	14, May			T2	
Bradley, Charles	27, Sept 1838	Sept			T2	
Bradley, Samuel	15, Nov. 1834		estate		R3	
Bradly, William	25, May 1849	23, May	35		L3	
Bradstreet, Lidia	14, July 1852	13, July	71		P2	
Brady, James	10, Nov. 1802		estate		S3	
Braham, C.	12, Sept 1828	Sept	75- 2m		N3	
Brail, Jane	18, July 1828	July	16m		N3	
Brainerd, Carlos	31, Aug. 1837	28, Aug.	22		X3	
Brainerd, Sarah	24, June 1835	20, June	28	*	T2	Langstroth
Brainerd, Thomas (Mrs)	26, June 1835	20, June			X2	
Braislin, Ann	16, June 1835	14, June			T2	
Braken, Jesse (Major)	19, June 1805	31, May			S3	
Bramble, Elow	6, Oct. 1826		probate		N3	
Bramlege, Anna Gertrude	14, July 1852	12, July	64		P2	
Brammer, S.	1, June 1849	May	25		L2	
Branch, James	16, Nov. 1839	30, Oct.	27		T2	
Brand, William	16, Mar. 1827		estate		N3	
Brand, William	9, Dec. 1828		probate		N3	
Brandon, Maria E.B.	18, Dec. 1838	17, Dec.			T2	Dorman
Brandriff, Timothy	15, Sept 1827	Sept	43		R3	
Brandruff, Elizabeth	12, Aug. 1828	Aug.	20		N3	
Brandruff, Timothy	10, Mar. 1829		probate		N3	
Brandt, Francisco	27, Aug. 1852	Aug.	4w		P2	
Brannon, Andrew	31, Oct. 1817	30, Oct.			S3	
Brannon, Elenor	4, Mar. 1828		probate		N3	
Brant, Nathaniel Todd	10, Sept 1830	Sept	13m		N3	
Brat, Lucinda	28, June 1849	June	35		L2	
Bratton, James	21, Dec. 1830		probate		N3	
Bray, Francis	19, July 1852	16, July	42		P2	
Breading, (child)	24, Sept 1830	Sept	stillborn		N3	
Brecaw, Michael	15, July 1825		estate		N2	
Breckenridge, Alice	12, Oct. 1820				S3	
Breckenridge, Cabell	31, Aug. 1837	10, Aug.			X3	
Breckenridge, John	21, Feb. 1810		estate		H4	
Breckenridge, John (Rev)	11, Aug. 1841	14, July	44		N2	
Breckenridge, Joseph Cabell	9, Sept 1823	1, Sept			N3	
Breckinridge, John	23, Dec. 1806	14, Dec.			S3	
Breeding, Mason P.	13, Feb. 1830		estate		R3	
Breeding, Mason P.	21, Dec. 1830		probate		N3	

Name	Notice Date	Death Date	Age		Page	Maiden Name
Brekeng, Elizabeth	30, July 1850	July	3		Y3	
Brennan, Sarah	5, July 1828				R3	
Brent, Robert	25, Sept 1819	4, Sept			S3	
Breslan, Bridget	17, May 1849	May	2		L2	
Breslan, Mary	17, May 1849	May	11		L2	
Breslan, Timothy	17, May 1849	May	37		L2	
Breslau, Rosa	7, June 1849	June	28		L2	
Brewen, Jabez	7, Jan. 1815		estate		S3	
Brewer, Aaron	12, Aug. 1828	Aug.	50		N3	
Brewster, Bowen	23, Apr. 1835	3, Jan.		*	N2	
Brewster, George	2, Nov. 1847	28, Oct.	18	*	K2	
Brewster, Lot E.	23, June 1849				L2	
Briant, Charles	7, Dec. 1837		probate		N3	
Brick, John	16, May 1828		estate		N3	
Brick, Thomas	25, Aug. 1829		probate		N3	
Brick, Thomas	23, Mar. 1830		probate		N3	
Bridge, Edward	14, Oct. 1825		86		N2	
Brigham, John	20, Oct. 1827	Oct.	35		R3	
Brigham, Marcus M.	4, July 1840	1, July			R3	
Brigham, Matilda	22, Oct. 1830	Oct.	2- 6m		N3	
Brimstone, Maria E.	2, Aug. 1834	July			R3	
Brimstone, Maria E.	29, July 1834	July			T2	
Brinker, Henry	13, July 1849	July	30		L2	
Britt, Peter	20, Apr. 1820				D3	
Britt, William	8, Aug. 1818	5, Aug.	infant		S3	
Broadmeadow, Simeon	24, May 1849	May	65		L2	
Broadwell, Jacob	11, Nov. 1835	10, Nov.			T2	
Broadwell, Jacob	11, Nov. 1835	10, Nov.			N2	
Broadwell, Jacob (Admrs. of)	21, Sept 1838		probate		N3	
Broadwell, Jerome	18, Dec. 1840	13, Dec.	3- 4m-15d		N2	
Broadwell, Mahlon L.	4, June 1836		probate		N2	
Broadwell, Maria	21, Nov. 1840	15, Nov.	15		R3	
Broadwell, Nathaniel	9, Jan. 1805		estate		S2	
Broadwell, Samuel	26, Dec. 1826		estate		N3	
Broadwell, Samuel	10, Nov. 1826	Nov.			Q3	
Broady, Philip	13, Mar. 1829	Mar.	52		N3	
Brockenbrough, William	27, Dec. 1838	10, Dec.	61		T2	
Brockman, James	9, Sept 1831	Sept	31		A3	
Brockmiller, Augustus	23, Sept 1831	Sept	32		A3	
Brockoff, John	7, June 1849	June	56		L2	
Brogan, Michael	5, Apr. 1849	Apr.	57		L2	
Brokaw, John	10, Sept 1799		estate		S3	
Bronson, Charles H.	31, July 1850	July	34		Y3	
Bronson, Charles H.	30, July 1850	29, July	34- 9m		P2	
Bronson, Charles H.	30, July 1850	29, July			Y2	
Bronson, Sarah M.	17, Nov. 1851	15, Nov.	28		P2	
Brooke, Harriet	27, June 1828	20, June	23		N2	
Brooke, Harriet	1, July 1828	June	23		N3	
Brooke, Louisa	16, Oct. 1841		18m		R3	
Brooke, Louisa	16, Oct. 1841	9, Oct.	18m		V3	
Brooke, Richard	27, Oct. 1838	24, Oct.	10		T2	
Brooke, Robert	2, Apr. 1800	27, Feb.			S3	
Brookes, Maria Lovelace	28, Nov. 1840	24, Nov.	infant		R3	
Brooks, David	8, Sept 1826	3, Sept	23		N3	

Name	Notice Date	Death Date	Age		Page	Maiden Name
Brooks, Edwin	16, May 1826	12, May	7		N3	
Brooks, George C. (Dr)	7, Jan. 1832	31, Dec.	23		R3	
Brooks, John	10, Dec. 1824	4, Dec.	26		N3	
Brooks, John	22, Mar. 1825	Mar.	73		N3	
Brooks, John	14, Dec. 1824		probate		N3	
Brooks, John	6, Oct. 1826		probate		N3	
Brooks, John	16, Dec. 1824		probate		E3	
Brooks, John	25, Sept 1819	23, Sept		*	S3	
Brooks, Ransom	2, July 1831	5, June	19		R3	
Brooks, Sarah	29, Oct. 1830	Oct.	29		N3	
Brotherton, Mary	9, Oct. 1841	25, Sept	55		R3	
Brotherton, Robert (Col)	8, Nov. 1837	4, Nov.			T2	
Brough, William P.	4, Nov. 1841	27, Oct.	23		N2	
Brown, (child of John)	23, July 1830	July	4d		N3	
Brown, (child)	30, July 1830	July	8m		N3	
Brown, (man)	3, Nov. 1852	2, Nov.			P2	
Brown, Aaron	10, Dec. 1814		estate		S3	
Brown, Ann	4, Mar. 1828		probate		N3	
Brown, Ann	4, Nov. 1830	26, Oct.			A3	
Brown, Benjamin	1, Dec. 1838	26, Nov.	34		T2	
Brown, Carlitle	12, Apr. 1794		estate		C3	
Brown, David	29, May 1829	30, Apr.	31		N3	
Brown, E.	3, May 1825		probate		N3	
Brown, Elias T.	2, Aug. 1834	July	21d		R3	
Brown, Elias T.	29, July 1834	July	21d		T2	
Brown, Elijah	5, Dec. 1823		estate		N2	
Brown, Eliza	3, Sept 1800	24, Aug.			S3	
Brown, Eliza	28, June 1828				R3	
Brown, Eliza Coffin	19, May 1838	18, May		*	T2	
Brown, Elizabeth H.	31, July 1850	July	12m		Y3	
Brown, Ephraim	17, June 1837		probate		N2	
Brown, Ephraim (Capt)	4, July 1835	23, June			N3	
Brown, Frances	19, Jan. 1838	17, Jan.			N2	
Brown, George Washington	1, Oct. 1831	23, Sept	20		R3	
Brown, Henry Shenstone	14, Aug. 1835	13, Aug.	11m		N2	
Brown, Ida Leonora	3, July 1852	21, June	8m-23d		P2	
Brown, Jackson	15, Oct. 1830	Oct.	7m		N3	
Brown, James	21, Oct. 1828	Oct.	29		N2	
Brown, James	1, Nov. 1830	24, Oct.			A3	
Brown, James	6, Sept 1839	4, Sept			T2	
Brown, Jane W.	4, Nov. 1852	29, Oct.	23	*	P2	Williams
Brown, Jenks	29, Oct. 1830	Oct.	35		N3	
Brown, Jenks	19, Aug. 1828	Aug.	11m		N3	
Brown, Jenks	19, Nov. 1830		estate		N3	
Brown, Jenks	14, Dec. 1835		probate		N2	
Brown, Jenks	30, Oct. 1830	24, Oct.		*	R3	
Brown, Jesse G.	27, Apr. 1841		estate		N2	
Brown, John	1, July 1828	June	38		N3	
Brown, John	7, Dec. 1811		estate		S3	
Brown, John	23, Apr. 1814		estate		S3	
Brown, John	28, Jan. 1825		estate		N3	
Brown, John	21, May 1830		estate		N3	
Brown, John	30, Aug. 1837		estate		N3	
Brown, John	17, July 1838	14, July			T2	

Name	Notice Date	Death Date	Age	Page	Maiden Name
Brown, John (Capt)	3, Dec. 1824		74	N3	
Brown, John (Capt)	2, Dec. 1824		74	E2	
Brown, Jonathan	29, May 1829	2, May	31	N3	
Brown, Jonathan	7, July 1836		83	X3	
Brown, Louisa	8, July 1828	July	18m	N3	
Brown, Mary	17, Oct. 1840	Oct.	45	R3	
Brown, Mary	12, Aug. 1831	Aug.	8m	A3	
Brown, Nathaniel	26, July 1830	27, June	25	A3	
Brown, Nathaniel	30, July 1830	July	26	N3	
Brown, Nicholas	27, Sept 1852	24, Sept		P2	
Brown, Rachael	6, July 1849	July	40	L2	
Brown, Robert C.	30, July 1830	July	1- 8m	N3	
Brown, Rosetta	1, Sept 1827	Aug.	6	R3	
Brown, Sarah	17, July 1852	14, July	57	P2	
Brown, Sophia	15, Oct. 1830	Oct.	56	N3	
Brown, Thomas	6, Feb. 1829	Feb.	69	N2	
Brown, Thomas	6, Mar. 1813		estate	S3	
Brown, Thomas	30, Oct. 1805	23, Oct.		S3	
Brown, Vincent	18, May 1838		probate	N2	
Brown, William	21, Nov. 1804		estate	S3	
Brown, William	16, Dec. 1825		probate	N3	
Brown, William	28, Sept 1820	23, Sept		* S3	
Brown, William (Col)	31, Oct. 1804	23, Oct.		S4	
Brown, William J.	13, Dec. 1836		estate	N2	
Brown, William J.	10, Jan. 1837		estate	N3	
Brown, William James	6, Nov. 1838		probate	N2	
Brown, Wilson N.	7, Aug. 1841			R3	
Brown, Wilson N. (Mrs)	5, Aug. 1841	3, Aug.		N2	
Browne, Eliza	30, Dec. 1828	Dec.	1- 6m	N3	
Browne, Eliza Emma	18, May 1838	17, May	8	T2	
Browne, Eliza Emma	18, May 1838	17, May	8	N2	
Browne, Frances	20, Jan. 1838	17, Jan.		R3	
Browne, Frances	18, Jan. 1838	17, Jan.		T2	
Browne, John	27, Jan. 1825		estate	E3	
Browne, John W.	2, Sept 1824		estate	E3	
Browne, John W. (Rev)	9, Jan. 1813		58	* S3	
Browning, Elizabeth	20, Apr. 1847	19, Apr.	75	* K2	
Browning, Martha Ann	13, Oct. 1847	11, Oct.	23	K2	Holmes
Brownson, Asa	11, Sept 1805	9, Sept		S3	
Brownson, John	1, Sept 1826		estate	N3	
Brownson, Norman S.	23, Dec. 1824		estate	E3	
Brownson, Norman S.	7, Oct. 1823	3, Oct.		* N3	
Bruce, (child of B.)	24, July 1850	July	18m	Y2	
Bruce, Andrew	23, July 1838	21, July	60	* T2	
Bruce, Catharine W.	9, Dec. 1852	8, Dec.	28	P2	
Bruce, Charles	23, Apr. 1849	Apr.	35	L2	
Bruce, Charles	4, Oct. 1816		estate	S3	
Bruce, Charles	14, Feb. 1817		estate	S3	
Bruce, David	20, Jan. 1838		estate	N2	
Bruen, Mary	17, Dec. 1852	9, Dec.	67	P2	
Brugelman, John B.	30, July 1850	July	24	Y3	
Bruix, (Admiral)	19, June 1805	17, Feb.		S3	
Brumwell, Washington	13, Aug. 1830	Aug.	20d	N3	
Brunswick, Louisa	26, July 1850	July	7m	Y2	

Name	Notice Date	Death Date	Age	Page	Maiden Name
Bryan, Julia	24, May 1849	May	18	L2	
Bryan, William J.	19, May 1847	5, May		K2	
Bryant, Alex.	19, Aug. 1831	Aug.	15	A3	
Bryant, James	20, Mar. 1829	Mar.		N3	
Bryden, Elizabeth	13, Sept 1838	Sept	9	T2	
Bryon, (child of J.)	7, May 1830	May	stillborn	N3	
Bryson, James W. (Capt)	19, Dec. 1818	16, Dec.	87	S3	
Bucan, Charles	5, Nov. 1830	Nov.	40	N3	
Buchanan, Eva Louisa	4, June 1850	2, June	13m-26d	P2	
Buchanan, James	4, June 1841	3, June	4- 6m	N2	
Buchanan, James	5, June 1841	3, June		R3	
Buchanan, Mary	2, Sept 1828	Aug.	13m	N3	
Buchanan, Robert	12, Aug. 1831	Aug.	1- 1m	A3	
Buchanan, Sarah	3, July 1841	26, June	8- 8m	R3	
Buchanan, Sarah	28, June 1841	26, June	8- 8m	N2	
Buchanan, Susan	19, Oct. 1822	11, Oct.	31	S3	Teater
Buck, Thomas	6, July 1849	July	2	L2	
Buckler,	8, July 1828	July	5	N3	
Buckley, (child of Joseph)	1, Aug. 1828	July	infant	N3	
Buckley, Joseph	25, May 1836		estate	N2	
Buckley, Joseph	20, Mar. 1838		probate	N3	
Buckley, Thomas (Capt)	7, Nov. 1838	6, Nov.	46	T2	
Buckman, Eliza	13, Mar. 1829	Mar.	18	N3	
Buckrell, William	21, Aug. 1852	19, Aug.		P2	
Budd, Alice G.	26, July 1834	July		R3	
Budd, Alice G.	22, July 1834	July		T2	
Budd, George (Capt)	4, Oct. 1837	3, Oct.		T2	
Buell, Ephraim	24, Mar. 1821		estate	S3	
Buell, Ephraim	4, Mar. 1828		estate	N3	
Buell, Leonard	15, Oct. 1835	30, Sept	31	T2	
Buell, Salmon	25, Aug. 1829		probate	N3	
Buell, Salmon	23, Mar. 1830		probate	N3	
Buffum, Jane	7, 14, Nov. 1818	6, Nov.	31	S3	
Buffum, John	8, June 1820		estate	S3	
Buffum, John	11, Dec. 1827		probate	N3	
Buffum, John	25, May 1820	21, May		* S3	
Bull, Eleanor	15, Mar. 1833	10, Mar.		X3	
Bullard, Anna Maria	10, May 1833	28, Apr.	9m-19d	X3	
Bullard, Artemas Everett	12, May 1836	12, Apr.	5- 9m	X3	
Bullard, Jacob	30, July 1830	July	32	N3	
Bullock, Elizabeth	3, Dec. 1830	Nov.	30	N3	
Bullock, Millard Fillmore	30, Dec. 1852	21, Dec.	3- 7m-20d	P2	
Bullock, Rice	23, July 1800		estate	S3	
Bullock, William	17, May 1828	1, Mar.	29	R3	
Bullock, William	23, May 1828	1, Mar.	29	Q2	
Bumgardner, John	6, July 1849	July	38	L2	
Bumgardner, Mary	6, July 1849	July	40	L2	
Bunker, Paul	31, July 1827		26	N3	
Bunnell, Daniel	27, Oct. 1798	25, Oct.		F3	
Burber, Cinthia	4, Apr. 1818	25, Mar.	3	S3	
Burge, Jonathan	16, Feb. 1822		estate	S3	
Burgell, Isaac	18, July 1828	July	15	N3	
Burgess, George	16, Mar. 1827		estate	N3	
Burgoyne, John	11, Sept 1829	30, July	63	N2	

Name	Notice Date	Death Date	Age		Page	Maiden Name
Burgoyne, John	19, Mar. 1830		estate		N3	
Burgoyne, Mary Ann	16, Nov. 1847	15, Nov.	14m		K2	
Burhans, John William	28, Mar. 1851	27, Mar.	6m- 9d		P2	
Burk, Andrew	6, July 1849	July	36		L2	
Burk, Edward	6, July 1849	July	6		L2	
Burk, Elisha	11, Dec. 1827		probate		N3	
Burkart, George	14, June 1849	June	40		L2	
Burke, Robert	6, Oct. 1836	11, Sept	36		X3	
Burland, W.H. (Dr)	6, July 1849	5, July	40	*	L2	
Burley, Charles	16, July 1830		estate		N3	
Burley, Frances	4, June 1849	2, June	88	*	L2	
Burnes, Catharine	4, Mar. 1828		probate		N3	
Burnes, Dixon	19, Sept 1850	Sept	26		Y2	
Burnet, George W.	22, Oct. 1800		estate		S1	
Burnet, George W.	13, May 1801		estate		S3	
Burnet, George W.	23, July 1800	14, July			S3	
Burnet, James	3, May 1838				N2	
Burnet, Margaret	23, Jan. 1836	26, Dec.		*	T3	Curry
Burnet, William	19, Mar. 1836	16, Mar.	10m		T2	
Burnet, William (Dr)	1, Oct. 1799	9, Sept			S3	
Burnet, William, Jr.	22, Apr. 1801		estate		S3	
Burnett, Joseph Augustus	1, July 1852	30, June	14m		P2	
Burnham, Lewis	11, Aug. 1850	24, July	34	*	Y2	
Burnham, William A.	7, Sept 1836		probate		N2	
Burns, A.	3, May 1838			*	N2	
Burns, James	16, Feb. 1827		estate		Q3	
Burns, James	1, June 1835		probate		N2	
Burns, Margaret	23, July 1850	July	30		Y2	
Burrowes, Ambrose Dudley	2, July 1849	1, July	13m		L2	
Burrows, Nehemiah Tunis	1, Apr. 1818	21, Mar.			S3	
Burson, Edward (Dr)	27, Aug. 1852	24, Aug.	73		P2	
Burt, Andrew	14, Feb. 1817	11, Feb.			S3	
Burt, Mary A.	31, May 1838	27, May			T2	
Burt, Sallie G.	30, Oct. 1847	29, Oct.	4- 8m-23d		K2	
Buschman, Henry	10, May 1849	May	45		L2	
Bush, Alexander	24, July 1850	July	5		Y2	
Bush, Edward Smith	17, July 1841	25, June			R3	
Bush, John E.	4, June 1836		probate		N2	
Bush, Presley	11, May 1850		estate		P1	
Bush, Zebulon	24, Sept 1830	Sept	1- 5m		N3	
Bushnell, A.L. (Dr)	23, July 1852	22, July			P2	
Bushnell, Austa	19, Dec. 1828	30, July	20		N3	
Bushnell, B. (Mrs)	19, Dec. 1828	18, July	71		N3	
Bushnell, Fanny	19, Dec. 1828	1, Sept	36		N3	
Bushnell, Jane	19, Dec. 1828	26, July	27		N3	
Bushnell, Lester	19, Dec. 1828	5, Aug.	38		N3	
Bushnell, Nancy	19, Dec. 1828	31, Mar.	30		N3	
Bushnell, Sarah P.	6, Mar. 1851	5, Mar.			P2	
Bushnell, William	19, Dec. 1828	25, July	25		N3	
Bushnell, Willson	19, Dec. 1828	30, Aug.	51		N3	
Buskey, Enos	29, May 1841	May	50		R3	
Bussell, Charles	17, Oct. 1850	Oct.	44		Y2	
Butcher, Edward	26, July 1850	July	22		Y2	
Butcher, John	14, June 1849	June	35		L2	

Name	Notice Date	Death Date	Age	Page	Maiden Name
Butland, Lydia	27, June 1842	18, June	78	N2	
Butler, (Mrs)	25, July 1850	July	30	Y2	
Butler, Adeline	9, Sept 1831	7, Sept		A3	
Butler, Adeline	10, Sept 1831	7, Sept		* R3	
Butler, Adeline	9, Sept 1831	7, Sept		X3	
Butler, Amy	7, May 1830	May	1m	N3	
Butler, Frederick Tomlin	31, Oct. 1840	31, Oct.	2	R3	
Butler, Henry	24, May 1849	May	20	L2	
Butler, Jacob	16, Dec. 1828	Dec.	36	N3	
Butler, Julia Bayard	15, Oct. 1852	13, Oct.	4- 8m	P2	
Butler, Lawrence (Major)	25, May 1811	3, May		S3	
Butler, Letta	25, July 1850	July	75	Y2	
Butler, Mahitable	18, Aug. 1821	6, Aug.		S3	
Butler, Nancy	4, Aug. 1815	3, Aug.		S3	
Butler, O.P.	26, Sept 1840	23, Sept	49	R3	
Butler, Pamela	7, Apr. 1836	15, Mar.	49	X3	
Butler, William (Capt)	22, Sept 1827	Sept	71	R3	
Butterbaugh, George	5, Nov. 1814		estate	S3	
Butts, Samuel	16, Jan. 1836	13, Jan.	43	* T3	
Buxton, Abram Sandford	17, Sept 1835	15, Sept	30	* T2	
Byers, Anna	3, Feb. 1829	Jan.	13m	N3	
Byers, Israel	12, Sept 1826		estate	N3	
Byers, James	9, Aug. 1852	6, Aug.		P2	
Byers, Matilda	19, Oct. 1832	4, Oct.		X3	
Byrd, C.W.	6, Sept 1828	Aug.		R3	
Byrd, C.W.	2, Sept 1828			N3	
Byrnes, Nicholas	12, Apr. 1849	Apr.	27	L2	
Byrns, Mary	23, July 1850	July	6	Y2	
Bywaters, H.R.	2, Oct. 1852	29, Sept	68	P2	
Bywaters, Robert	1, Oct. 1830	Sept	8m	N3	
Byxbee, Ebenezer	2, Aug. 1834	July	40	R3	
Byxbee, Ebenezer	29, July 1834	July	40	T2	
Cable, George	13, July 1849	July	3	L2	
Cadey,	31, Dec. 1830	Dec.	17	N3	
Cadwallader, Inez	6, Sept 1852	30, Aug.		P2	
Cady, Ann Eliza	11, Mar. 1848	11, Mar.		K2	Clingman
Cady, Henry H.	22, Nov. 1841	17, Nov.	47	N2	
Cady, John C.	9, July 1849	7, July	51	L2	
Caffery, Thomas	1, Oct. 1830	Sept	1- 8m	N3	
Cafield, Nathan	4, June 1814		estate	S3	
Cahill, Margaret	31, Aug. 1852	28, Aug.	8m-12d	P2	
Caldbrook, William	21, June 1849	June	38	L2	
Caldwell, Anne	28, June 1849	27, June	49	L2	
Caldwell, Ford	30, July 1830	July	35	N3	
Caldwell, James S.	6, Aug. 1830	Aug.	25	N3	
Caldwell, John	24, Oct. 1828	Oct.	45	N2	
Caldwell, John	26, Oct. 1835	9, Oct.		T2	
Caldwell, Margaret D.H.	17, Jan. 1837	16, Jan.		N2	
Caldwell, Margaretta D.	28, Jan. 1837	16, Jan.	20	* R3	
Caldwell, Samuel	1, Aug. 1840	12, July		R3	
Callahan, Hugh	22, Apr. 1801		estate	S3	
Cally, Mary	28, July 1850	July	28	Y3	
Calvin, James	4, June 1836		probate	N2	
Cambell, John	21, Sept 1807		estate	S3	

Name	Notice Date	Death Date	Age		Page	Maiden Name
Cambell, Precilla Jane	12, Nov. 1830	Nov.	1m		N3	
Cameron, Samuel	12, Aug. 1831	Aug.	2		A3	
Cameron, William	27, Aug. 1852	25, Aug.	5- 5m		P2	
Camp, Job D.	18, Mar. 1820		estate		S1	
Campbell, Alexander W.	1, Aug. 1840	July	34		R3	
Campbell, Archibald	3, Dec. 1796	13, Sept			F3	
Campbell, Charles	14, June 1849	13, June	infant		L2	
Campbell, George W.	23, Feb. 1848	17, Feb.	80		K2	
Campbell, Hiram	27, July 1850	July	31		Y3	
Campbell, Hugh P.	30, Nov. 1820	11, Nov.			S3	
Campbell, John B.	27, Dec. 1852	24, Dec.	infant		P2	
Campbell, Julian	9, Sept 1831	Sept	1-10m-14d		A3	
Campbell, Laty	29, Sept 1851	28, Sept	18m		P2	
Campbell, M. (Capt)	6, Sept 1794	20, Aug.			C3	
Campbell, Margaret	24, July 1850	July	28		Y2	
Campbell, Matilda	15, Oct. 1830	Oct.	6d		N3	
Campbell, Thomas	21, Sept 1847	17, Sept			K2	
Campbell, Virginia Dickinson	2, Oct. 1841	14, Sept	1-11m		R3	
Campbell, Virginia Dickinson	27, Sept 1841	14, Sept	1-11m		N2	
Campbell, William	16, July 1830	July	27		N3	
Campbell, William (Dr)	23, Mar. 1830		29- 6m- 7d	*	N2	
Campton, Rachel A.	15, Aug. 1850	Aug.	8		Y2	
Can, Lydia	26, Sept 1828	Sept	52		N3	
Canan, William P.	29, Aug. 1840	24, Aug.			R3	
Canbey, Thomas	1, June 1835		probate		N2	
Cane, Jane	21, Oct. 1828	Oct.	36		N2	
Canfield, Edward	27, Feb. 1829	Feb.	13d		N3	
Canfield, George	14, Oct. 1828	Oct.	18		N3	
Canfield, George	12, June 1841	June	56		N2	
Canfield, Ida Maria	17, Nov. 1852	14, Nov.	5w		P2	
Cannahan, Anna O.	26, Sept 1828	Sept	35		N3	
Cannon, Amos	17, Sept 1835		probate		T2	
Cannon, Michael	26, Sept 1850	Sept	26		Y2	
Carey, (Rev)	2, Jan. 1835	9, June	73		X3	
Carey, Olive	21, Sept 1852	19, Sept	14m		P2	
Carigan, Samuel	22, Oct. 1830	Oct.	8m		N3	
Carl, John	14, Dec. 1835		probate		N2	
Carlin, Emily	3, Oct. 1840	16, Sept	19		R3	
Carlisle, George L.	21, Apr. 1832	19, Apr.	3		R3	
Carlisle, George L.	27, Apr. 1832	19, Apr.	3		X3	
Carlisle, James	24, Sept 1830	Sept	28		N3	
Carlos, Sarah Ann	29, June 1833	17, June			R3	Wood
Carlton, Jonathan	14, Sept 1822	7, Sept			S3	
Carman, Charles	20, Mar. 1841	Mar.	37		N2	
Carnahan, Patrick	6, July 1849	July			L2	
Carnell, Tobias	30, Dec. 1828	Dec.	48		N3	
Carnes, John	13, July 1849	July	30		L2	
Carney, Thomas	5, Apr. 1849	Apr.	27		L2	
Carnot, (Count)	28, Nov. 1823		70		N1	
Carpenter, Abraham	14, Dec. 1836	11, Dec.			T2	
Carpenter, Ezekiel	21, Apr. 1832				R3	
Carpenter, Ezekiel	27, Apr. 1832	18, Apr.		*	X3	
Carpenter, J.	30, Apr. 1814		estate		S3	
Carpenter, J.	7, July 1815		estate		S3	

Name	Notice Date	Death Date	Age		Page	Maiden Name
Carpenter, James	4, Apr. 1795		estate		C3	
Carpenter, Joseph	17, Sept 1835		probate		T2	
Carpenter, Joseph	7, Sept 1830		probate		N3	
Carpenter, Joseph (Capt)	2, Apr. 1814	10, Mar.	36	*	S3	
Carr, Dabney Overton	21, Dec. 1830	17, Sept	24		N3	
Carr, F.	2, Aug. 1836		estate		N2	
Carr, Francis	15, May 1838		estate		N3	
Carr, Francis	1, June 1835		probate		N2	
Carr, Francis	6, Nov. 1838		probate		N2	
Carr, Francis (Col)	27, July 1833	July			R3	
Carr, John	30, Dec. 1852	29, Dec.			P2	
Carr, John A.	23, May 1837				T2	
Carr, Sarah	17, Nov. 1821	14, Nov.			S3	
Carrack, C.	27, July 1833	July			R3	
Carrel, (child of Rachel)	4, June 1830	June	2m		N3	
Carrel, Rachel	8, Apr. 1847	3, Apr.	22		K2	
Carrick, Cunningham	17, June 1837		probate		N2	
Carrigan, W. (Mrs)	13, May 1824	11, May			E3	
Carrington, Lester	14, Dec. 1835		probate		N2	
Carrol, Almira	24, June 1828	June	1		N3	
Carroll, Dennis	24, Sept 1852	23, Sept			P2	
Carroll, Patrick	29, Mar. 1849	Mar.	63		L2	
Carroll, Thomas	27, Sept 1838	Sept	30		T2	
Carson, Enoch	25, Apr. 1817	14, Apr.	53		S3	
Carson, John	13, Apr. 1809		estate		H3	
Carson, John Q.A.	14, Apr. 1851	13, Apr.			P2	
Carson, Ruth Ann	26, Aug. 1847	24, Aug.			K2	
Carson, Samuel P. (Col)	28, Nov. 1838	23, Nov.	50		T2	
Carson, William	9, June 1815		estate		S3	
Carson, William	8, Feb. 1840				R3	
Carter, (child of John)	19, Aug. 1831	Aug.	15m		A3	
Carter, Ada A.M.	16, July 1842	11, July	18- 6m		R3	
Carter, Ada A.M.	13, July 1842	11, July	18- 6m		N2	
Carter, Charlotte	19, Aug. 1831	Aug.	1		A3	
Carter, James	30, July 1850	July	2		Y3	
Carter, Jewell D.	6, Nov. 1838		probate		N2	
Carter, Mary	23, Sept 1831	Sept	37		A3	
Carter, Nathaniel H.	5, Mar. 1830	2, Jan.			N2	
Carter, Sarah	12, Aug. 1831	Aug.	1		A3	
Carter, Thomas	22, Apr. 1823		estate		N3	
Carter, Warren	4, May 1849	3, May			L2	
Cartwright, Rachel	17, Sept 1830	Sept	1- 2m		N3	
Carver, Augusta Cornelia	10, Nov. 1852	7, Nov.	18d		P2	
Carver, G.W.	11, July 1828		estate		N3	
Carver, George W.	24, June 1828	June	26		N3	
Carver, George W.	23, Mar. 1830		probate		N3	
Carver, George W.	21, Dec. 1830		probate		N3	
Cary, J. Addison (Rev)	10, Aug. 1852	7, Aug.	39		P2	
Cary, Leah	24, Dec. 1830	Dec.	67		N3	
Cary, Maria Louisa	28, Sept 1847	26, Sept			K2	
Cary, Samuel	27, Mar. 1805		estate		S3	
Case, Henry J.	23, July 1850	July	10m		Y2	
Casey, H.B.	3, May 1838				N2	
Casey, James	14, June 1849	June	25		L2	

Name	Notice Date	Death Date	Age	Page	Maiden Name
Cash, James M.	13, July 1852	11, July		P2	
Casin, James H.	23, July 1850	July	43	Y2	
Casseday, Eliza	25, June 1849	20, June		L2	
Casserty, Barney	6, July 1849	July	20	L2	
Cassiday, John	29, Jan. 1814		estate	S3	
Cassiday, John	18, Dec. 1813	15, Dec.		S3	
Cassiday, Patrick	30, Apr. 1814		estate	S3	
Cassily, Sarah	5, July 1828	1, July	infant	R3	
Cassin, Margaret	8, July 1830	14, June		A3	
Caster, John	4, July 1812		estate	S3	
Castillo, Joseph	16, Jan. 1841	Jan.	54	R3	
Castillo, Joseph	16, Jan. 1841	Jan.	54	N2	
Castle, Roswell	19, Apr. 1833		estate	X3	
Castman, Clement	5, Sept 1828	Sept	3	N3	
Catlin, Ruth E.	14, Oct. 1828	Oct.	28	N3	
Cato, Carle	6, July 1849	July	32	L2	
Catterlin, Joseph (Capt)	23, Nov. 1822	10, Nov.	81	* S3	
Caughliss, Michael	29, Mar. 1849	Mar.	40	L2	
Caulfield, Thomas	22, Apr. 1815	22, Apr.	45	* W3	
Caullet, Benjamin	7, Nov. 1834		estate	T2	
Cavender, Allen McLean	24, June 1828	June	10m	N3	
Caverly, Peter J.	29, May 1835	24, May		* T2	
Caverly, Peter T.	26, May 1835	24, May		* T3	
Cerdell, William B.	23, Sept 1831	Sept	43	A3	
Ceward, (child of John)	10, Dec. 1830	Dec.	1	N3	
Cezanne, Henry D.	21, Aug. 1827	18, July		N3	
Chalfant, Henry Clay Motier	27, Aug. 1841	26, Aug.		N2	
Chalkley, Jacob	28, June 1849	June	18	L2	
Chamberlain, John	24, Oct. 1828	Oct.	19	N2	
Chamberlain, William	1, June 1835		probate	N2	
Chamberlin, Elijah	2, Nov. 1837	10, Oct.	67	X3	
Chamberlin, George	23, Apr. 1814		estate	S3	
Chamberlin, Milton Lawrence	17, Sept 1850	15, Sept	22	Y2	
Chamberlin, Richard	19, Mar. 1830		estate	N3	
Chamberlin, William	28, Nov. 1835		estate	N3	
Chamberlin, William	7, Jan. 1836		estate	N2	
Chambers, Catherine	27, July 1850	July	4	Y3	
Chambers, Clara Francis	2, Nov. 1847	31, Oct.	6m	K2	
Chambers, John	3, Apr. 1829		estate	N3	
Chambers, John R.	31, Dec. 1830	Dec.	1	N3	
Chambers, Ruth	3, Sept 1800	28, Aug.		S3	
Chapin, Manley	30, June 1849	29, June	36	L2	
Chapman, J.	3, May 1838			N2	
Chapman, John	14, Aug. 1802		estate	S3	
Chapman, William Daniel	22, Oct. 1841	14, Oct.	14m-16d	N2	
Chappel, John George	1, Sept 1852	30, Aug.	7m-17d	P2	
Charter, James	18, Jan. 1836		estate	N2	
Charters, Ann	26, Feb. 1820	25, Feb.		* S3	
Charters, Georgiana	12, July 1830	10, July		* A3	
Charters, Georgianna	16, July 1830	July	23	N3	
Charters, James	11, Sept 1837		probate	N2	
Charters, William	25, Mar. 1801		estate	S3	
Chase, (Rev)	26, Mar. 1824	3, Mar.		N3	
Chase, Abram L.	4, June 1836		probate	N2	

Name	Notice Date	Death Date	Age		Page	Maiden Name
Chase, Alexander P.	27, Mar. 1847	23, Mar.	49		K2	
Chase, Catharine Jane	8, Feb. 1840	6, Feb.	4- 3m		R3	
Chase, Dudley	19, Aug. 1852	31, July	30		P2	
Chase, Isaac	4, June 1836		probate		N2	
Chase, Josephine	9, Aug. 1850	27, July	1- -22d		P2	
Chase, Josephine Ludlow	7, Aug. 1850	27, July			Y2	
Chase, S.P. (Mrs)	3, Dec. 1835	1, Dec.			X3	Garniss
Chase, Sarah S.	12, May 1836			*	X3	Bailey
Chatfield, Leonard	4, Jan. 1838				T2	
Cheasman, Keziah	6, Aug. 1830	Aug.	16		N3	
Cheeney, John (Deacon)	29, Dec. 1821	16, Sept	73		S3	
Cheesbrough, Julia E.	19, Aug. 1828	Aug.	10		N3	
Cheesman, Richard W.	20, Mar. 1838		probate		N3	
Cheney, Ernest H.	8, Nov. 1852		1- 8m-20d		P2	
Chenoworth, Frank G. (Capt)	22, Dec. 1847	19, Dec.			K2	
Chester, Franklin	21, June 1849	June	59		L2	
Chester, Mary Elizabeth	17, Aug. 1841	15, Aug.	1		N2	
Chester, Mary Elizabeth	21, Aug. 1841	15, Aug.	14m-25d		R3	
Chevers, Jacob	2, Sept 1828	Aug.	2- 7m		N3	
Cheves, Mary Elizabeth	13, May 1836	6, May	47		T2	
Chew, Aaron	19, June 1835	16, June			T3	
Chew, Maria Theodora	1, Aug. 1837	31, July			T2	
Chew, Samuel Lloyd (Col)	24, June 1795	28, Apr.		*	C3	
Child, A.L. (Dr)	30, Jan. 1849	28, Jan.			B2	
Child, David	3, July 1841		40	*	R3	
Child, David	28, June 1841		40	*	N2	
Child, James	23, July 1850	July	2		Y2	
Child, Richard Eberle	4, July 1840	27, June	22m		R3	
Childs,	3, Apr. 1829	Mar.	infant		N2	
Childs, Amos	10, May 1849	May	26		L2	
Chipman, Horace D.	13, Jan. 1851	12, Jan.	infant		P2	
Chipman, Horace G.	18, Feb. 1851	16, Feb.	25		P2	
Chona, George C.	3, May 1833		estate		X3	
Chonn, Jonathan	3, Apr. 1829	Mar.	18		N2	
Chopson, Elizabeth	25, Apr. 1840	15, Apr.	34		R3	
Chrisman, Elizabeth	4, June 1836		probate		N2	
Christian, Martha	3, Sept 1830	Aug.	2- 6m		N2	
Christie, Jannett	8, Feb. 1839	7, Feb.	41		T2	
Christie, William B. (Rev)	2, Apr. 1842				R3	
Christy, (child of Elizabeth)	27, June 1840	June	2w		R3	
Christy, James	12, Aug. 1828	Aug.	1- 7m		N3	
Chull, Philip	15, Jan. 1814	16, Nov.	115	*	S3	
Church, Robert	11, Nov. 1838	Nov.	35		N3	
Churchill, Abigail	1, Sept 1826	27, Aug.	77	*	N2	
Churchill, Almistead	25, July 1795	22, July			C3	
Churchill, Armistead	1, Aug. 1795		estate		C3	
Churchill, Jesse (Major)	22, Jan. 1820				S3	
Churchill, Simeon	23, Dec. 1828	Dec.	43		N3	
Chute, James (Rev)	16, Jan. 1836	28, Dec.			T3	
Chute, James Thurston	11, Sept 1819	1, Sept	infant		S3	
Cilly, Jonathan	17, Apr. 1813		estate		S3	
Cinckner, Harvey	22, Sept 1827	Sept	18m		R3	
Ciser, Casper	7, June 1849	June	22		L2	
Cisson, Caroline A.	26, Sept 1828	Sept	21		N3	

Name	Notice Date	Death Date	Age	Page	Maiden Name
Cist, (daughter of Charles)	24, Nov. 1840		17	N2	
Cist, Jane Martha	28, Nov. 1840	22, Nov.	17	R3	
Cist, Mary	29, May 1837	26, May	3	N2	
Cist, William	27, May 1837	26, May	3	N2	
Claiborne, Elizabeth	7, Nov. 1804	26, Oct.		S3	
Claiborne, William Charles C.	19, Dec. 1817	23, Nov.		S3	
Clark, (child of James)	6, Mar. 1829	Mar.	9m	N2	
Clark, (child of William)	4, June 1830	June	1	N3	
Clark, Alice P.	1, Sept 1847	30, Aug.		K2	
Clark, Andrew	10, May 1849	May	30	L2	
Clark, Ann	28, May 1838	27, May	41	T2	
Clark, Ann	28, May 1838	27, Mar.	41	N2	
Clark, Eliza	20, Sept 1825	19, Sept	26	N3	
Clark, Elizabeth S.	23, Nov. 1835	22, Nov.	2- 5m	T2	
Clark, Elizabeth S.	23, Nov. 1835	22, Nov.	2- 5m	N2	
Clark, George	23, Jan. 1838	14, Jan.		T2	
Clark, Hanna	25, Nov. 1852	23, Nov.	65	P2	
Clark, James (Mrs)	25, Aug. 1836	22, Aug.		T2	
Clark, Jeremiah	13, Sept 1833		estate	X3	
Clark, Mary Eddy	14, July 1836	17, June	14d	X3	
Clark, Nathan (Major)	9, Apr. 1836	18, Mar.		T2	
Clark, Peter	20, Aug. 1830	Aug.	2m	N3	
Clark, Samuel	8, July 1823		estate	N3	
Clark, Sarah	13, May 1835	9, May		T3	Ewing
Clark, Thomas	22, Nov. 1830	6, Nov.	37	A3	
Clark, Thomas	31, Dec. 1830		estate	N3	
Clark, Thomas	23, Nov. 1830	6, Nov.		N3	
Clark, Thompson	5, Dec. 1823		estate	N2	
Clark, Thompson	9, Dec. 1828		probate	N3	
Clark, Virginia	30, Aug. 1852	26, Aug.	4- 2m	P2	
Clark, William (Gen)	22, Sept 1838	1, Sept	68	R3	
Clarke, Aaron	31, July 1819	25, July		S3	
Clarke, Adam (Rev)	19, Oct. 1832	14, Oct.	69	X3	
Clarke, Charles	7, May 1830	May	2- 5m	N3	
Clarke, Henry R.	5, Sept 1834	2, Aug.	*	X3	
Clarke, John	12, Mar. 1800		estate	S3	
Clarke, John	10, Apr. 1819		estate	S3	
Clarke, John L.	10, Aug. 1836	9, Aug.	*	T2	
Clarke, Samuel	25, May 1841			N2	
Clarkson, Charles S.	30, Dec. 1837	26, Dec.	2-10m	R3	
Clarkson, Thomas B. (Rev)	14, July 1836	12, July		X3	
Clarkson, William	3, Feb. 1832	29, Jan.	72	X3	
Clary, James	23, Apr. 1849	Apr.	30	L2	
Clason, Frank	23, Aug. 1852	19, Aug.	18m	P2	
Claxton, James	7, May 1824		estate	N3	
Claxton, James	7, Sept 1824		probate	N3	
Claxton, James	11, Dec. 1827		probate	N3	
Claxton, James	9, Sept 1824		probate	E3	
Clay, Matthew	23, June 1815	27, May		S3	
Clay, William	29, Mar. 1849		1- 4m	L2	
Claypool, Joseph	16, Feb. 1835		estate	N2	
Claypoole, Abraham G.	19, Sept 1829	25, Aug.	*	R3	
Clayton, James H.M.	15, June 1836	7, June	26 *	T2	
Clayton, Jane	26, July 1834	July	10m	R3	

Name	Notice Date	Death Date	Age	Page	Maiden Name
Clayton, Jane	22, July 1834	July	10m	T2	
Clayton, Mary Ann	12, June 1849	8, June	22	L2	
Cleary, Thomas	9, Aug. 1841	Aug.	35	N2	
Cleaveland, Francis A.	18, July 1822	17, July		J3	
Clement, Sarah	22, Aug. 1828	Aug.	41	N3	
Clement, Stephen James	10, Nov. 1852	8, Nov.	2- 1m	P2	
Clement, William Morrow	20, June 1849	19, June	5	L2	
Clements, Daniel	8, Oct. 1852	Oct.	64	P2	
Clements, Ephraim	28, Apr. 1827	26, Apr.	42	R3	
Cleneay, John	10, Nov. 1852	8, Nov.	39- 9m	P2	
Cleveland, F.A.	27, July 1822			S3	
Cleveland, Levi	16, Apr. 1814		estate	S1	
Climer, William F.	20, Aug. 1852	7, Aug.	14m	P2	
Clinch, Elizabeth Bayard	11, Sept 1838	21, Aug.	38	T2	Houston
Cline, Joseph	1, Aug. 1828	July	3	N3	
Cline, Mary Helen	21, July 1852	19, July	22	P2	
Cline, Oliver	30, July 1850	July	10m	Y3	
Clingman, Enoch	24, July 1850	July	32	Y2	
Clingman, Sarah	27, Oct. 1838	26, Oct.	52	T2	
Clinton, DeWitt	26, Feb. 1828	11, Feb.		N2	
Clinton, George	2, May 1812	24, Apr.		S3	
Cloon, Philip B.	26, Sept 1828	Sept	14m	N3	
Clopper, Edward D.	8, Aug. 1840	15, July	11	R3	
Clough, Mary	3, Jan. 1853	31, Dec.	71	P2	
Clouser, John	20, Sept 1852	17, Sept	27	P2	
Clyme, Philip	8, Aug. 1840		96	R3	
Cobb, Catharine	19, July 1834	July	7m	R3	
Cobb, James	18, May 1838		probate	N2	
Cobb, James	27, July 1833	July		R3	
Cobb, Mary A.	17, Sept 1852	15, Sept	2- 9m-28d	P2	
Cobb, Mary E.	26, July 1834	July	1- 1m	R3	
Cobb, Mary E.	22, July 1834	July	1- 1m	T2	
Cobourn, Joseph A.	31, May 1847	31, May		K2	
Coburn, Francis T.	16, May 1840		30	R3	
Cochlin, (Mrs)	14, June 1849	June	40	L2	
Cochlin, Daniel	14, June 1849	June	45	L2	
Cochlin, T. (Mrs)	13, Aug. 1852	11, Aug.	29	P2	
Cochnower, Charles F.	20, July 1852	18, July	infant	P2	
Cochran, John	17, May 1837		estate	N3	
Cochran, John	21, Sept 1838		probate	N3	
Cochran, Richard	12, Oct. 1836		estate	N2	
Cochran, Richard	21, Sept 1838		probate	N3	
Cochran, William	7, Dec. 1827		estate	N3	
Cochran, William	19, Feb. 1830		estate	N3	
Cochran, William	21, Dec. 1830		probate	N3	
Cocke, Samuel B.	17, June 1835	31, May		T2	
Cockram, William (Rev)	30, Aug. 1833		77	X3	
Coddington, Stephen	15, Dec. 1836		estate	N2	
Coe, Harvey L.	29, Nov. 1833	18, Nov.		* X3	
Coffin, H.B.	23, July 1841		36	N2	
Coffin, Henry B.	24, July 1841	18, July	36	R3	
Coggshall, James	19, Sept 1850	16, Sept	21	Y2	
Coghill, Angeletta	6, July 1849	July	16	L2	
Cogswell, (child of O.)	8, July 1828	July	stillborn	N3	

Name	Notice Date	Death Date	Age		Page	Maiden Name
Cogswell, Asa H.	21, Dec. 1830		probate		N3	
Cogswell, Osmond	3, Apr. 1841		estate		R3	
Cogswell, Osmond	2, Apr. 1842		estate		R3	
Cogswell, Osmond	13, Mar. 1841	9, Mar.			R3	
Cogswell, Osmond	11, Mar. 1841	9, Mar.			N2	
Cohoon, Robert D.	17, June 1841	15, June	8m		N2	
Colby, A.C. (Mrs)	20, Jan. 1838	19, Jan.	38		T2	
Colby, A.C. (Mrs)	20, Jan. 1838	19, Jan.	38		N2	
Colby, Z.	7, Mar. 1826	26, Feb.			N3	
Colden, Maria	20, May 1837	10, May			T2	Provoost
Cole, Helen A.	9, Aug. 1850	7, Aug.	24		Y2	
Cole, Isaac	27, June 1840	June	46		R3	
Coleman, Adbel (Rev)	9, Dec. 1824		42	*	E2	
Coleman, Alfred	2, Sept 1847	14, Aug.		*	K2	
Coleman, E.W. (Dr)	28, Dec. 1838	18, Dec.			T2	
Coleman, James	12, Apr. 1849	Apr.	53		L2	
Coleman, James	26, June 1823		estate		J3	
Coleman, James	3, May 1825		probate		N3	
Coleman, P.	19, July 1834	July			R3	
Coleman, Rebecca	5, Nov. 1830	Nov.	28		N3	
Coleman, Theodore	10, Dec. 1830	Dec.	1m		N3	
Colerick, Charles (Capt)	10, Feb. 1838	7, Feb.		*	N2	
Coles, Henry	26, Feb. 1841	Feb.	20		N2	
Coles, Sarah	8, Aug. 1842	7, Aug.	69- 4m- 7d		N2	
Coley, Joseph	23, Apr. 1849	Apr.	21		L2	
Collard, (child of Samuel W.)	10, Dec. 1830	Dec.	1- 6m		N3	
Collier, Hazel	29, Sept 1826		estate		N3	
Collier, Hazel	25, Aug. 1829		probate		N3	
Collier, Lydia Frances	24, July 1852	22, July			P2	
Collier, William B.	30, Nov. 1852	24, Nov.			P2	
Collins, Agnes A.	10, Dec. 1835		13		X3	
Collins, Elizabeth	10, Sept 1830	Sept	54		N3	
Collins, J.J.	11, Sept 1847				K2	
Collins, James	21, June 1849	June	29		L2	
Collins, John A.	22, June 1850	10, June	26	*	P2	
Collins, John J.	9, Sept 1847	7, Sept			K2	
Collins, Mary Ann	3, Nov. 1836	1, Nov.	33		T2	Armstrong
Collins, Sarah	12, Aug. 1815	19, July	76		G3	
Collins, William	10, Dec. 1835		17		X3	
Collogs, Abraham	26, July 1834	July	2		R3	
Collogs, Abraham	22, July 1834	July	2		T2	
Colohon, Ann	26, July 1850	July	3		Y2	
Colson, Ichabod	10, Sept 1830	Sept	55		N3	
Colton, Francis Fellowes	28, May 1842	24, May	10m		N2	
Colton, Francis Fellowes	4, June 1842	24, May	child		R3	
Colton, Rachel	21, Aug. 1834	16, Aug.		*	T2	
Colvin, (child of F.)	25, June 1830	June	stillborn		N3	
Colvin, James	2, Oct. 1830		estate		R3	
Colvin, James	25, June 1831		estate		R3	
Colvin, James	17, Sept 1835		probate		T2	
Colvin, James	1, June 1835		probate		N2	
Colvin, James	14, Dec. 1835		probate		N2	
Colvin, John	24, Oct. 1828	Oct.	1m		N2	
Colwell, Cyrus	12, Aug. 1826	9, Aug.	20	*	J3	

Name	Notice Date	Death Date	Age		Page	Maiden Name
Colwell, Thomas	3, Dec. 1830	Nov.	55		N3	
Comfort, Patrick	14, June 1849	June	25		L2	
Comley, Elizabeth F.	18, Aug. 1827	14, Aug.	40	*	R3	
Comley, Reney	29, May 1819	26, May			S3	
Comley, Sarah	29, May 1819	23, May			S3	
Comly, Mary	17, Feb. 1838	12, Feb.			T2	
Compton, Henry	14, Dec. 1835		probate		N2	
Compton, Jacob R.	3, Nov. 1821		estate		S3	
Compton, John	19, Dec. 1812		estate		S3	
Comstock, Joab	2, Sept 1825		estate		N3	
Concklin, Mary	22, Sept 1852	20, Sept	73		P2	
Conckling, Phebe Ann	2, Apr. 1842	29, Mar.			R3	
Conclin, Caleb	2, Sept 1825	31, Aug.	25		N3	
Conclin, Caleb	4, Oct. 1825		estate		N3	
Conclin, Hannah	4, Nov. 1825	27, Oct.			N2	
Cone, Rufus	21, Feb. 1810	28, Jan.			H3	
Cones, Margaret C.	16, Apr. 1849	14, Apr.	24		L2	
Conger, John	11, Sept 1837		probate		N2	
Conklin,	10, Oct. 1840	Oct.	stillborn		R3	
Conklin, (twins of Caleb)	21, May 1830	May	stillborn		N3	
Conklin, David	21, Dec. 1830		probate		N3	
Conklin, Freelove	6, May 1841	4, May			N2	
Conklin, Halstead	14, Dec. 1824		probate		N3	
Conklin, Halstead	9, Dec. 1828		probate		N3	
Conklin, Halstead	16, Dec. 1824		probate		E3	
Conklin, Isaac	22, Dec. 1829		probate		N3	
Conklin, Joseph	11, Dec. 1827		probate		N3	
Conklin, Joseph L.	27, Aug. 1830	Aug.	3- 6m		N3	
Conklin, Stephen	18, Aug. 1826		estate		N3	
Conkling, David	20, Mar. 1841	15, Mar.	48		N2	
Conkling, David	20, Mar. 1841	19, Mar.			R3	
Conkling, Josiah	11, Sept 1819		estate		S3	
Conn, Charles	23, Apr. 1808		estate		S3	
Conn, Charles	11, Jan. 1808	5, Jan.			S3	
Conn, James	27, Dec. 1825		53		N2	
Conn, James M.	13, Sept 1825	12, Sept			N3	
Conn, Joseph	27, May 1806	22, May	61		S3	
Conn, Joseph	1, Aug. 1818		estate		S2	
Conn, Joseph	3, May 1825		probate		N3	
Conn, Joseph	9, Dec. 1828		probate		N3	
Conn, Joseph	7, Sept 1836		probate		N2	
Conn, Joseph	18, Aug. 1815	12, Aug.			S3	
Conn, Joseph	19, Aug. 1815	12, Aug.			G3	
Conn, Joseph (heirs)	14, Dec. 1824		probate		N3	
Conn, Joseph (heirs)	16, Dec. 1824		probate		E3	
Conn, Sarah	21, Jan. 1832	14, Jan.	100		R3	
Conn, Sarah	27, Jan. 1832	14, Jan.			X3	
Connell, William	10, Sept 1830	Sept	54		N3	
Conner, Daniel	27, Feb. 1805	23, Feb.			S3	
Conner, Jacob	21, June 1849	June	40		L2	
Conner, Margaret	30, July 1850	July	24		Y3	
Conover, Harriet Key	29, June 1833	24, June	infant		R3	
Conover, Henry Shreve	1, Feb. 1836	30, Jan.	9m-15d		T3	
Conover, Joseph	22, Dec. 1826		estate		N3	

Name	Notice Date	Death Date	Age	Page		Maiden Name
Conover, Julia Ann	25, Mar. 1836	24, Mar.	24- 3m		T2	Sellman
Conover, Julia Ann E.	26, Mar. 1836	24, Mar.	24- 3m		N2	Sellman
Conover, Margaret	20, June 1836	10, June	61	*	T2	
Conover, Margaret	23, June 1836	10, June	61	*	N2	
Conover, William A. (Capt)	22, Nov. 1838				T2	
Conrad, Jacob	22, Dec. 1829		probate		N3	
Conrod, Daniel	18, May 1807	11, May			S3	
Conroy, Peter	27, Aug. 1852	Aug.	32		P2	
Constable, George	11, Jan. 1837		estate		N2	
Contee, Eliza	9, Jan. 1837	18, Dec.	18		T2	
Conway, Margaret	8, Oct. 1852	Oct.	3		P2	
Conway, Oney	27, Aug. 1852	Aug.	7		P2	
Cook, (child of Samuel V.)	3, Dec. 1830	Nov.	stillborn		N3	
Cook, Charles	27, Aug. 1830	Aug.	14		N3	
Cook, Daniel P.	26, Oct. 1827	16, Oct.			N3	
Cook, Jesse S.	30, May 1828		estate		Q3	
Cook, Lucy	1, Oct. 1830	Sept	1- 5m		N3	
Cook, Martha Jane	27, Nov. 1852	24, Nov.	23- 2m- 1d		P2	
Cook, Mary	1, Nov. 1852	30, Oct.	46- 1m- 5d		P2	
Cook, Mary F.	1, June 1835		probate		N2	
Cook, Milton G.	1, June 1835		probate		N2	
Cook, Sarah G.	1, June 1835		probate		N2	
Cook, Shubael P.	11, Oct. 1816	9, Oct.	27		S3	
Cook, Theodore M. (Dr)	8, June 1849	22, May			L2	
Coolidge, Eliza	17, May 1842	14, May			N2	
Coolidge, Elizabeth B.	17, July 1835	14, July	18	*	T2	
Coolidge, Henry James	6, July 1842	30, June	infant		N2	
Cooly, Ebenezer	21, Feb. 1810		estate		H2	
Coombe, William	16, Sept 1823		81		N3	
Coombs, Alfred	8, Oct. 1838	5, Oct.	15m		T2	
Coombs, Annis D.	10, July 1841	2, July			R3	
Coombs, Annis D.	3, July 1841	2, July			N2	
Coombs, John	27, July 1827	26, July			Q3	
Coombs, John (Capt)	28, July 1827	26, July			R3	
Coombs, Samuel A.	4, June 1836		probate		N2	
Coombs, Samuel Armor	27, Oct. 1834		25		T2	
Cooms, John	29, Aug. 1836		estate		N2	
Coon, Aaron	31, July 1850	July	52		Y3	
Coon, Mary Ann	18, July 1828	July	11m		N3	
Coons, Frederick	16, Feb. 1816		estate		S3	
Cooper, (child of Joseph)	24, Sept 1830	Sept	stillborn		N3	
Cooper, Betsy	13, July 1849	July	40		L2	
Cooper, Elizabeth	28, May 1830	May	6m		N3	
Cooper, Francis E.	3, June 1847	1, June	33		K2	
Cooper, Isaac	6, Oct. 1826		probate		N3	
Cooper, Isaac	11, Dec. 1827		probate		N3	
Cooper, Isaac	23, Mar. 1830		probate		N3	
Cooper, James	1, Feb. 1849	29, Jan.		*	B2	
Cooper, John W.	31, May 1847	29, May			K2	
Cooper, Loyd	29, Jan. 1842	23, Dec.	42		R3	
Cooper, M. Le	19, Aug. 1831	Aug.	13m		A3	
Cooper, Margaret	13, Aug. 1830	Aug.	67		N3	
Cooper, Peter	28, June 1849	June	35		L2	
Cooper, William	27, Jan. 1835		estate		N2	

Name	Notice Date	Death Date	Age		Page	Maiden Name
Cooper, William	14, Dec. 1835		probate		N2	
Cooper, William	31, July 1847	30, July		*	K2	
Cope, Emma	7, May 1830	May	4m		N3	
Cope, Mary	6, Jan. 1826	7, Dec.			N3	
Copeland, Jonathan	2, Oct. 1813		estate		S3	
Coppin, John	6, Aug. 1830	Aug.	77		N3	
Corbin, Mary Ann	24, May 1842	27, May	28	*	N2	
Corbley, George Washington	2, July 1849	3, June			L2	
Corbley, John	18, Sept 1819		estate		S3	
Corbly, Paul	1, June 1835		probate		N2	
Corcoran, J.	30, July 1850	July	19m		Y3	
Corey, Oliver Smith	12, June 1835	8, June	13m		X3	
Corey, Zebia	2, June 1836	1, June	34		T2	
Corey, Zebia Smith	16, Aug. 1836	13, Aug.	5m-15d		T2	
Corey, Zebia Smith	18, Aug. 1836	13, Aug.	5m-15d		X3	
Corliss, Angelia	18, Nov. 1852	17, Nov.	8- 5m		P2	
Corn, George	5, May 1826		estate		N3	
Cornell, J.P.	21, Dec. 1847				K2	
Cornick, David	4, June 1836		probate		N2	
Cornman, (child of George)	12, Sept 1828	Sept	2m		N3	
Cornwright, Thomas	22, Aug. 1828	Aug.	56		N3	
Corry, Alice	23, Oct. 1847	22, Oct.			K2	
Corry, Elenor	16, Sept 1852	15, Sept	72		P2	
Corry, William	20, Dec. 1833	16, Dec.			X3	
Corson, Susan	17, Sept 1814	15, Sept			S3	
Corwine, Aaron H.	15, July 1830	4, July	28	*	A3	
Corwine, Joab H.	13, Mar. 1848	12, Mar.	20- 9m		K2	
Corwine, Laura Jane	11, Nov. 1852	9, Nov.	3- 4m		P2	
Cosgrove, Margaret	1, July 1852	28, June	35		P2	
Costler, Elizabeth	12, Mar. 1849	10, Mar.	38		L2	
Cotter, Mary	24, July 1850	July	3- 3m		Y2	
Cottle, (man)	6, July 1849	July			L2	
Cottom, Elizabeth	2, Aug. 1834	July	9m-14d		R3	
Cotton, Elizabeth	29, July 1834	July	9m-14d		T2	
Cotton, Hiram B.	31, Oct. 1850	Oct.	23		Y2	
Cottorne, Mary Ann	28, Nov. 1828	Nov.	2-10m		N3	
Couch, Jessup N.	14, July 1821	7, July	42	*	S3	
Coufman, Henry	2, Aug. 1834	July	1		R3	
Coufman, Henry	29, July 1834	July	1		T2	
Coughlin, Rebecca	30, July 1850	July	73		Y3	
Coughlin, William	3, Oct. 1838	29, Sept	70	*	N2	
Coughlin, William	22, Oct. 1838		estate		N2	
Coulte, J.D. (Capt)	6, Oct. 1829	22, Sept			N3	
Coulter, Susan	20, Mar. 1849	19, Mar.	29		L2	
Councellor, Jerome	7, June 1849	June	5m		L2	
Counter, (Mrs)	22, Aug. 1828	Aug.	100		N3	
Courtly, John	1, June 1835		probate		N2	
Covalt, Bethuel	7, Sept 1837		estate		N3	
Covalt, Isaac	22, Mar. 1837		estate		N2	
Covalt, Isaac	19, Oct. 1837		estate		N3	
Covalt, Isaac	4, June 1836		probate		N2	
Covert, Joseph	13, Dec. 1833		estate		X3	
Coverts, Joseph	14, Dec. 1835		probate		N2	
Cowan, (Mrs)	30, Nov. 1835				T2	Sinclar

Name	Notice Date	Death Date	Age	Page	Maiden Name
Cowan, John	7, Nov. 1804		estate	S3	
Cowan, Margaret	25, Apr. 1840		79	R3	
Cowden, Joseph Fox	26, Dec. 1818	23, Dec.	infant	S3	
Cowdin, Charlotte May	27, May 1823	20, May	24	N3	
Cowdrey, Cornelia Maria	6, Apr. 1837	4, Apr.		* T2	
Cowen, (Mrs)	3, Dec. 1835	Nov.		X3	Sinclair
Cowles, Samuel	21, Dec. 1837	22, Nov.	62	X3	
Cowly, Patrick	8, Oct. 1852	Oct.		P2	
Cox, Asa	9, Aug. 1816		estate	S3	
Cox, Benjamin	7, Feb. 1795	2, Feb.		C3	
Cox, Edward	2, Aug. 1834	July	2- 3m	R3	
Cox, Edward	29, July 1834	July	2- 3m	T2	
Cox, Eliza A.H.	19, Aug. 1828	Aug.	11	N3	
Cox, Eliza Ann	22, Aug. 1828	Aug.	11	N3	
Cox, Garret	4, Jan. 1821		estate	S3	
Cox, Garret	3, May 1825		probate	N3	
Cox, Garrett	9, Feb. 1822		estate	S3	
Cox, John	20, Feb. 1813	13, Feb.		* S3	
Cox, Matthew T.	2, Aug. 1834	July	27	R3	
Cox, Matthew T.	29, July 1834	July	27	T2	
Cox, Sarah E.	26, Nov. 1830	Nov.	21	N3	
Cox, William P.	8, Oct. 1830	Oct.	25	N3	
Coxe, Susan B.	4, Oct. 1837	1, Oct.		T2	
Cozyes, Mary	24, Oct. 1850	Oct.	2	Y2	
Crabb, Alexander	28, July 1852	27, July	10m	P2	
Craffort, Henry	15, Aug. 1828		estate	N3	
Craig, (Lt)	5, July 1794	30, June		C3	
Craig, Martha	19, Aug. 1828	Aug.		N3	
Crain, Abigail	21, Sept 1838		probate	N3	
Crain, Daniel	21, June 1849	June	22	L2	
Crain, Isaac	10, Apr. 1802		estate	S3	
Crainbert, John	3, May 1849	May	42	L2	
Cranaer, John	17, Sept 1835		probate	T2	
Crane, Abigail	10, Jan. 1837		estate	N3	
Crane, Ann	23, June 1849	22, June		L2	
Crane, Ebenezer	30, June 1838	22, June	41	* R3	
Crane, Elias	17, May 1816		estate	S3	
Crane, Elihu	9, Jan. 1824		estate	N3	
Crane, Elihu	11, Dec. 1827		probate	N3	
Crane, Elizabeth B.	6, Oct. 1827	Oct.	4	R3	
Crane, Elizabeth Burt	6, Oct. 1827	3, Oct.	5	R3	
Crane, Henry Francis	26, Aug. 1852	22, Aug.	infant	P2	
Crane, Ichabod	24, Jan. 1818		estate	S3	
Crane, Ichabod	12, June 1819		estate	S3	
Crane, Ichabod	1, Sept 1821		estate	S3	
Crane, Mary E.	28, May 1830	May	5m	N3	
Crane, Noah	4, Sept 1810	21, Aug.	28	S3	
Crane, Phebe	6, Mar. 1829		estate	N3	
Crane, Samuel	17, Sept 1835		probate	T2	
Crane, William E.	16, June 1837	14, June	23	T2	
Cranmore, Rachel	30, Mar. 1811	27, Mar.		S3	
Crary, Pamela	27, Aug. 1808	21, Aug.		* S3	
Crawford, Alexander	20, Jan. 1821	7, Jan.		* S3	
Crawford, John	13, Feb. 1819		estate	S3	

Name	Notice Date	Death Date	Age		Page	Maiden Name
Crawford, John A.	5, Nov. 1830	Nov.	1d		N3	
Crawford, Sampson	28, Aug. 1829		estate		N3	
Crawley, James M.	19, Nov. 1830	Nov.	3m		N3	
Crawley, Michael	2, Oct. 1852	30, Sept		*	P2	
Creach, Rebecca Ann	6, Mar. 1829	Mar.			N2	
Creaven, Michael	3, May 1849	May	28		L2	
Cregar, Hannah	6, Sept 1833	Sept	27		X3	
Cregar, Peter	2, Sept 1825		estate		N3	
Cregar, Peter	19, Aug. 1828		probate		N3	
Creighton, William	30, Apr. 1842	18, Apr.	72	*	N2	
Crippen, Jacob	19, Sept 1828	Sept	14		N3	
Crisman, Elias	19, Mar. 1830		estate		N3	
Crisman, Osman	23, Dec. 1828	Dec.	10m		N3	
Crispin, Jonathan	15, Sept 1815		estate		S3	
Crispin, Jonathan	11, Dec. 1827		probate		N3	
Crist, Joseph	4, Mar. 1828		estate		N3	
Crittenden, Eugenia A.	26, May 1837	20, May	18		T2	
Crittenden, Martin	26, Sept 1840	5, Sept			R3	
Crocketts, (child of William)	10, Dec. 1830	Dec.	11m		N3	
Crogker, James H.	21, July 1842	20, July	36	*	N2	
Crome, Henry Francis	24, Aug. 1852	22, Aug.	infant		P2	
Cromwell, John William	26, May 1837	25, May	6		T2	
Cronan, Catharine	28, June 1849	June	6		L2	
Cronan, Catharine	6, July 1849	July	3w		L2	
Crone, John	17, Oct. 1818		estate		S3	
Crookshank, Elizabeth	17, Mar. 1826	12, Mar.		*	N3	
Crookshank, Nathaniel (Dr)	15, Apr. 1847	1, Apr.	76		K2	
Crosby, Barnabas	9, July 1830	July	1		N3	
Crosby, Enoch	14, July 1835	25, June	88		N2	
Crosby, Simeon	16, Feb. 1835		estate		N2	
Crosley, Ross	19, Dec. 1817		estate		S3	
Cross, John J.	4, Oct. 1852	29, Sept	76		P2	
Cross, Joseph	21, May 1830	May	4- 8m		N3	
Cross, Sarah Agness	18, Apr. 1837	10, Apr.	2- 5m-11d		T2	
Cross, Thomas	19, Sept 1817	9, Sept	48		S3	
Cross, William	16, Dec. 1823		estate		N3	
Crossman, W.A.	17, Mar. 1838	14, Mar.			R3	
Crosson, Margaret	7, June 1825	31, May			N3	
Crosson, Maria	20, Sept 1825	16, Sept			N3	
Croul, John	3, May 1849	May			L2	
Crouse, Charles F.	7, Mar. 1849		18		L2	
Crouse, David	18, Apr. 1837				T2	
Crowell, Peter	9, July 1830	July	3		N3	
Crowing, Mary	6, July 1849	July	6w		L2	
Crowley, Jeremiah	23, Dec. 1828	Dec.	51		N3	
Crowly, Jeremiah	27, Dec. 1828	Dec.	51		R3	
Crozier, Kennedy	6, Oct. 1826		probate		N3	
Crumblick, Christopher	19, Mar. 1830		estate		N3	
Culberson, John	27, Nov. 1805		estate		S3	
Culbertson, (Mrs)	26, July 1834	July	25		R3	
Culbertson, (Mrs)	22, July 1834	July	25		T2	
Culbertson, Henry Duncan	30, Apr. 1842		5m-20d		R3	
Culbertson, Henry Duncan	26, Apr. 1842		5m-20d		N2	
Culbertson, Margaret Hamilton	16, 17, July 1834	13, July		*	T2	

Name	Notice Date	Death Date	Age		Page	Maiden Name
Culbertson, Samuel W.	20, June 1840	15, June	60		R3	
Culbreth, Robert Emmet	21, Sept 1837	8, Sept	26		T2	
Culen, Edward	11, Dec. 1827		probate		N3	
Cullum, George	25, Aug. 1829		probate		N3	
Culter, Caroline	19, June 1835	8, June	35		T3	
Cumming, Mary	6, Aug. 1814		estate		S3	
Cumming, Robert	8, Sept 1826	2, Sept	67		Q3	
Cummings, Jeremiah	6, July 1849	July	23		L2	
Cummings, John	1, June 1835		probate		N2	
Cummins, Alexander	28, Oct. 1823		estate		N2	
Cummins, Alexander	7, Sept 1830		probate		N3	
Cummins, Alexander (Rev)	30, Sept 1823	27, Sept	37		N3	
Cummins, Eliaxer	11, June 1814		estate		S3	
Cummins, John	2, June 1826		estate		N3	
Cummins, John	11, Dec. 1827		probate		N3	
Cummins, John	21, Dec. 1830		probate		N3	
Cummins, John N.	20, Jan. 1825		estate		E3	
Cummins, Peter	21, Dec. 1835		estate		N3	
Cummins, Peter	4, Apr. 1837		probate		N2	
Cune, Roswell	25, Apr. 1835	18, Mar.	44		T3	
Cunningham, Ann S.	10, Sept 1830	Sept	31	*	N3	
Cunningham, Francis	7, June 1849	June	35		L2	
Cunningham, Janet	7, Dec. 1837		probate		N3	
Cunningham, Jenet	17, June 1837		probate		N2	
Cunningham, John	11, Apr. 1826	9, Apr.	27		N3	
Cunningham, John	6, July 1830		estate		N1	
Cunningham, Joshua	31, Oct. 1850	28, Oct.			Y2	
Cunningham, Thomas	18, June 1830	June	47		N3	
Curless, (Mrs)	3, Dec. 1835				T2	
Curlis, John	3, Apr. 1813	31, Mar.	20		S3	
Currie, James	4, Aug. 1832	28, July		*	R3	
Curry, Betsy	15, Aug. 1840	Aug.	69		R3	
Curry, Mary A.	24, July 1850	July	6		Y2	
Curry, Mary A.P.	6, Mar. 1849	5, Mar.	13- 1m		L2	
Curry, Robert	11, Feb. 1835		estate		N2	
Curry, William	23, July 1838	21, July	8- 6m		T2	
Curtis, (Mrs)	16, Dec. 1828	Dec.			N3	
Curtis, Benjamin R.	25, July 1850	24, July	infant		Y2	
Curtis, Jane C.	23, Nov. 1852	21, Nov.	14- 6m		P2	
Cushing, Ellen	17, May 1849	May	27		L2	
Cushing, William V.H.	31, Mar. 1838	27, Mar.	35		T2	
Cushion, Philip	22, Aug. 1850	Aug.	37		Y2	
Cushman, Ralph (Rev)	2, Sept 1831	27, Aug.			X3	
Cusick, A.	25, July 1850	July	18m		Y2	
Cuskey, William	2, Jan. 1841	Dec.	25		R3	
Cutter, Andrew	15, Sept 1826	13, Sept	36	*	N3	
Cutter, John	5, Dec. 1795		estate		C3	
Cutter, Joseph	5, Dec. 1795		estate		C3	
Cutter, Seth	4, Sept 1805		estate		S3	
Cutter, Seth	7, Sept 1824		probate		N3	
Cutter, Seth	9, Sept 1824		probate		E3	
Cutter, William W.	9, Dec. 1828		probate		N3	
Dackey, George	9, Sept 1825	4, Sept	38		N3	
Dackey, George	13, Sept 1825		estate		N3	

Name	Notice Date	Death Date	Age		Page	Maiden Name
Dackey, George	21, Dec. 1830		probate		N3	
Dagneaux, Mary	1, June 1835		probate		N2	
Dagnell, Martha	28, June 1849	June	58		L2	
Daily, (child of Mary)	22, Aug. 1850	Aug.	stillborn		Y2	
Daily, Lydia Ann	2, Dec. 1834	29, Nov.	16		T2	
Daily, Patrick	21, June 1849	June	30		L2	
Dair, Mary Alice	19, June 1841	17, June	child		R3	
Dair, Mary Alice	19, June 1841	17, June	child		N2	
Dakin, Phoebe	5, Sept 1817	20, Aug.		*	S2	
Dalany, Betsey	26, July 1834	July	50		R3	
Dalany, Betsey	22, July 1834	July	50		T2	
Dallas, Alexander James	31, Jan. 1817	16, Jan.			S3	
Dalton, Joseph	7, May 1830	May	3m		N3	
Dalton, Josiah	2, Aug. 1834	July	28		R3	
Dalton, Josiah	29, July 1834	July	28		T2	
Dalton, Richard	14, June 1849	June	24		L2	
Damrell, William (Capt)	14, Apr. 1826		36		N3	
Dana, Francis	25, May 1811				S3	
Dana, James G.	2, Dec. 1840	26, Nov.			N2	
Dana, William Greene	12, Aug. 1835	7, Aug.	8m		T2	
Danaugh, John	19, Sept 1840		estate		R3	
Danby, Thomas	14, Sept 1820		estate		S3	
Danby, Thomas	25, May 1820	20, May			S3	
Dangerfield, Martha	1, Aug. 1828	July	1		N3	
Daniels, Isaac	17, Sept 1830		estate		N3	
Dantt, H. (Mrs)	8, Oct. 1852	Oct.	29		P2	
Dark, Sarah	28, Aug. 1834	19, Aug.		*	T2	
Darragh, John	24, May 1828	21, May	56		R3	
D'Arusmont, Frances Wright	16, Dec. 1852	13, Dec.	57		P2	
Dashiell, George	1, Apr. 1825	21, Mar.	14m		N3	
Daugherty, Alex.	8, Aug. 1850	Aug.	37		Y2	
Daulton, Naomi	10, Mar. 1829		probate		N3	
Daulton, Naomi	21, Dec. 1830		probate		N3	
Davenport, Charles	28, July 1850	July	2		Y3	
Davenport, Charles	28, July 1850	27, July	2- 4m-29d		Y2	
Davenport, Elijah	24, Sept 1830	Sept	5m		N3	
Davenport, Moses	8, July 1828	July	1		N3	
Davenport, Ruth	27, Aug. 1830	Aug.	28		N3	
Davenport, Thomas D.	9, July 1851	5, July			P2	
Davidson, Carlos	13, July 1833	2, July	22- 5m		R3	
Davidson, Carlos	12, July 1833	2, July	22- 5m		X3	
Davidson, James D.	16, Dec. 1825		probate		N3	
Davidson, Nancy	23, June 1836	3, June	29	*	X3	Goodwin
Davidson, Peter	27, June 1850	26, June			P2	
Davidson, William	6, Feb. 1836	11, Jan.	30		T3	
Davidson, William	11, Feb. 1836				X3	
Davies, Daniel	28, June 1849	June	35		L2	
Davies, Francis	18, May 1833	16, May			R3	
Davies, John	22, Aug. 1829	18, Aug.	85		R3	
Davies, Mary G.	5, Mar. 1814	2, Mar.			S3	
Davies, W.	9, Feb. 1833	1, Jan.	75	*	R3	
Davies, William	23, July 1830	July	11		N3	
Daviess, Nancy	4, Nov. 1847	22, Oct.			K2	
Davis,	1, Aug. 1828	July	1- 7m		N3	

Name	Notice Date	Death Date	Age		Page	Maiden Name
Davis,	1, Mar. 1849				L3	
Davis, (boy)	7, Aug. 1805	29, July	8		S3	
Davis, (boy)	7, Aug. 1805	29, July	14		S3	
Davis, (Mrs)	17, Feb. 1829	Feb.	41		N3	
Davis, Benjamin	1, Oct. 1799		estate		F2	
Davis, Daniel	10, May 1849	May	22		L2	
Davis, David	5, May 1835	24, Apr.	70	*	N2	
Davis, George M.	22, Sept 1827	4, Sept	29		R3	
Davis, Hannah	14, Aug. 1830	13, Aug.			R3	
Davis, John	10, Nov. 1832	19, Oct.	14		R3	
Davis, John	3, May 1837	30, Apr.	22		N2	
Davis, John	12, Mar. 1842	7, Mar.	68	*	R3	
Davis, John	9, Mar. 1842	7, Mar.	68		N2	
Davis, John	26, May 1815		estate		S3	
Davis, Joseph	10, May 1849	May	23		L2	
Davis, Joseph	20, Aug. 1830	Aug.	70		N3	
Davis, Mary J.	12, Oct. 1852	10, Oct.	22		P2	
Davis, Rebecca F.	9, July 1842	30, June			R3	Trimble
Davis, Samuel	9, May 1812		estate		S3	
Davis, Sarah	20, Aug. 1830	Aug.	49		N3	
Davis, Sarah	16, Dec. 1825		probate		N3	
Davis, Sarah	11, Dec. 1827		probate		N3	
Davis, Thomas	14, June 1849	June	25		L2	
Davis, Thomas	23, Oct. 1805		estate		S3	
Davis, Thomas	9, June 1821	12, Apr.			S3	
Davis, William	6, May 1837	30, Apr.	22		R3	
Davis, Zadock	7, Sept 1836		probate		N2	
Davison, Elizabeth	14, July 1849		70		L2	
Davison, Peter	26, June 1850	25, June			P2	
Daviss, Benjamin	8, Oct. 1800				S3	
Daviss, Benjamin	25, Mar. 1801				S3	
Davorid, (child of David)	18, June 1830	June	10d		N3	
Davy, Eliza	3, Nov. 1838	2, Nov.	22		T2	
Davy, Mary	7, Jan. 1832	2, Jan.			R3	
Dawson, (Mrs)	4, Nov. 1828	Oct.			N3	
Dawson, George Washington	18, Sept 1835	13, Sept			T2	
Day, (heirs of Daniel)	1, June 1835		probate		N2	
Day, C.	28, Nov. 1828	Nov.			N3	
Day, Daniel	17, June 1823		estate		N3	
Day, Elias Harvey	30, Dec. 1850	29, Dec.	22		P2	
Day, Hannah	4, Mar. 1841	21, Feb.	56		N2	
Day, Jehiel	17, Sept 1835		probate		T2	
Day, Samuel	14, May 1830	May	30		N3	
Day, Samuel	1, June 1835		probate		N2	
Day, William	14, Dec. 1835		probate		N2	
Day, William	17, June 1837		probate		N2	
Dayer, Frederick	19, Feb. 1841	Feb.	25		N2	
Dayton, Aaron	2, July 1830	June	55		N2	
Dayton, Jonathan	21, Dec. 1824		estate		N3	
Dayton, Jonathan	23, Dec. 1824		estate		E2	
Dayton, Jonathan	10, Mar. 1829		probate		N3	
Dean, Eleanor	3, Sept 1830	Aug.	22		N2	
Dean, John	8, Sept 1827	Sept	6		R3	
Dean, Lewis Judson	17, July 1852	15, July	10m		P2	

Name	Notice Date	Death Date	Age	Page	Maiden Name
Dean, Samuel	2, May 1840	28, Apr.	85		R3
Death, John C.	31, Oct. 1850	14, Oct.			Y2
Deats, Adam	14, Dec. 1835		probate		N2
DeBarr, Clara Julia	27, Apr. 1849	23, Apr.	19-9m-17d		L2	Levassor
Debolt, George	12, Mar. 1835		estate		N3
Debolt, George	4, June 1836		probate		N2
DeCamp, James	12, Sept 1850	Sept	41		Y2
Decater, W.D.	15, Oct. 1830	Oct.	50		N3
Deen, C.	3, Feb. 1829	Jan.	1-8m		N3
Deen, William C.	8, Sept 1827	Sept	3		R3
Deeters, Abraham	30, July 1830	July	44		N3
Deffenbaugh, Francis H.	2, Sept 1850	31, Aug.	17m		P2
Deffenbaugh, George	29, Nov. 1851	27, Nov.			P2
DeForest, Henry	14, Mar. 1840	12, Mar.	2		R3
Defrees, Joseph	29, Aug. 1826	13, Aug.	72	*	N3
Degler, Leopold	13, July 1849	July	26		L2
DeGolyer, Joseph	13, Dec. 1847	27, Nov.	85		K2
DeGray, Amanda	8, Oct. 1852	Oct.	21		P2
DeGroff, Oliver G.	3, July 1849	1, July	50		L2
Dehon, Theodore (Rev)	12, Sept 1817	6, Aug.	41		S3
Dekins, Walter	31, Oct. 1834		estate		X3
Dekins, Water M.	29, Mar. 1834	Mar.			R3
Delafield, Charles	16, May 1840	15, May	2		R3
Delancy, Susan	19, July 1834	July	1		R3
Delano, Amasa	21, Feb. 1826	15, Feb.	15		N2
Delano, Amasa (Dr)	3, Sept 1830	26, Aug.	56		N2
Delany, Dennis	13, Sept 1852	10, Sept			P2
Delaplaine, Joshua	9, Mar. 1807	26, Jan.	68		S3
DeLean, Emanuel G.	26, Apr. 1849	Apr.	21		L2
DeLizardi, Francisco	4, May 1842				N2
Dellinger, Frederick	19, Nov. 1830	Nov.	26		N3
Delorac, Michael	14, Sept 1822	31, Aug.			S3
Demas, Samuel M.	2, Aug. 1834	July	1m		R3
Demas, Samuel M.	29, July 1834	July	1m		T2
Dembling, Sophia	31, July 1850	July	30		Y3
Dement, (Mrs)	27, Dec. 1828	Dec.	44		R3
Dement, (Mrs)	23, Dec. 1828	Dec.	44		N3
Deming, (child of W.H.)	23, Sept 1831	Sept	stillborn		A3
Deming, Cynthia Robbins	28, Jan. 1832	24, Jan.	6		R3
Deming, James Allyn	9, June 1832	3, June	2-9m		R3
Deming, Walter H.	20, Oct. 1837	6, Oct.			T2
Dempsey, Bridget	19, Sept 1850	Sept	64		Y2
Dempsey, Elizabeth	2, Sept 1828		estate		N3
Dempsey, John	15, Sept 1827	15, Aug.			R3
Dempsey, John	11, Sept 1827	15, Aug.			N2
Dempsey, Joseph	5, Nov. 1830	Nov.	44		N3
Denham, Sarah	1, Sept 1827	Aug.	36		R3
Denholm, Archibald (Major)	12, Aug. 1815	16, July			G3
Denis, Julien L.	27, Oct. 1832	19, Oct.	58	*	R3
Denman, Nathaniel	21, May 1836		estate		N2
Denman, Nathaniel	21, Jan. 1837		estate		N3
Dennison, William W.	22, Apr. 1847	19, Apr.	35		K2
Denny, Eliza Jane	1, Nov. 1833	18, Oct.	18		X3
Denny, George	30, Sept 1823	20, Sept			N3

Name	Notice Date	Death Date	Age	Page	Maiden Name
Denny, Hannah E.	23, Mar. 1833	15, Mar.		R3	Birdsall
Denny, Henry Baldwin	28, Apr. 1841	20, Apr.		N2	
Denny, Sarah	30, Sept 1823	20, Sept		N3	
DeNoailles, (Duke)	28, Jan. 1825	6, Nov.	85	N3	
Dentler, William G.	17, Dec. 1852	16, Dec.	29	P2	
Depriest, (child of L.)	4, June 1830	June	child	N3	
Derbigny, Peter	3, Nov. 1829	7, Oct.		N2	
Derby, Charles	25, Oct. 1852	23, Oct.	4m	P2	
Desalis, J.F.	16, Dec. 1825		probate	N3	
Desalis, J.F.	4, Mar. 1828		probate	N3	
DeSalis, Julius Ferdinand	21, Sept 1822		estate	S3	
Deutsch, George	17, May 1849	May	46	L2	
Deval, Stephen	28, June 1828		*	R3	
Devaul, Richard	28, Mar. 1795		estate	C3	
Devaul, Richard	1, Aug. 1795		estate	C3	
Deveny, Frances	20, Aug. 1830	Aug.	1	N3	
Devinney, J.M. (Capt)	9, Aug. 1841	14, July		N2	
Devor, John	8, Aug. 1828	24, July	70	N3	
Devou, (infant of Samuel)	31, Dec. 1830	Dec.	infant	N3	
Dewees, William P. (Dr)	25, May 1841		75	N2	
Dewett, Mary	23, Sept 1831	Sept	9m	A3	
Dexter, Julia	25, Aug. 1836	23, Aug.	4- 3m	T2	
Dexter, Julia	24, Aug. 1836	23, Aug.	4- 3m	N2	
Dexter, Norman	19, July 1834	16, July	50 *	R3	
Dexter, Normand	18, July 1834	16, July	49 *	X3	
Dexter, Samuel	24, May 1816	17, May	*	S3	
DeYoung, John	15, Mar. 1842	11, Mar.	19	N2	
DeYoung, M.J.	1, Sept 1847	31, Aug.	*	K2	
Dial, Oliver P.	12, Sept 1828	Sept	19m	N3	
Dickeson, Samuel	19, Sept 1850	Sept	73	Y2	
Dickey, John McClelland	27, Oct. 1810	23, Oct.		S3	
Dickey, Joseph	28, July 1847	27, July	40	K2	
Dickey, Margaret	24, Nov. 1832	27, Oct.		R3	
Dickey, Patrick	5, Jan. 1816	20, Dec.		S3	
Dickey, Samuel	20, Feb. 1813		estate	S3	
Dickinson, Samuel	19, Aug. 1837	16, Aug.	31	R3	
Dickman, Henry	17, May 1849	May	20	L2	
Dickson, Michael	14, Oct. 1825		95	N2	
Dignan, Luke	6, Apr. 1847	5, Apr.	50	K2	
Dill, Eliza	28, Jan. 1825	16, Jan.	62	N3	St.Clair
Dill, Elizabeth	12, June 1841	June	7	N2	
Dill, Isaac	12, June 1841	June	48	N2	
Dill, James	5, Aug. 1841		estate	N3	
Dill, Lydia	3, Sept 1830	Aug.	3	N2	
Dill, Martha Ann	18, July 1840	July	3	R3	
Dill, Richard	13, Sept 1825		estate	N3	
Dillon, (Mr)	9, Nov. 1852	21, Sept	55	P2	
Dillon, Alfred Gerard	6, July 1850	29, June	15m	P2	
Dillon, F.C.	3, May 1838			N2	
Dillon, J.	3, May 1838			N2	
Dillon, James	1, June 1849	May	30	L2	
Dillon, Samuel	28, June 1849	June	50	L2	
Dinsmore, Silas G.	29, June 1849	28, June	40	L2	
Diserens, Henry	26, Sept 1850	26, Sept	3- 3m-17d	P2	

Name	Notice Date	Death Date	Age	Page	Maiden Name
Diserens, John Louis	23, May 1849	22, May	1- 7m-12d	L2	
Disney, Ann	15, Apr. 1828	13, Apr.	23	N3	
Disney, Ann	26, Apr. 1828	14, Apr.		R3	
Disney, Mary	4, Jan. 1825	31, Dec.	40	N3	
Distin, Edward H.	27, Mar. 1847	25, Mar.	20	K2	
Dix, Clarendon	10, Apr. 1813		estate	S1	
Dixon, Benjamin	30, Dec. 1828	Dec.	3m	N3	
Dockwilder, Peter	13, July 1849	July	40	L2	
Doddridge, Joseph (Rev)	24, Nov. 1826	8, Nov.	58	N3	
Dodson, Alexander W.	29, Sept 1832	13, Sept	17- 1m-11d	R3	
Dodson, John	20, May 1825	16, May	73	N2	
Dodson, John	27, May 1825		estate	N2	
Dodson, John R.	23, Nov. 1847	21, Nov.	39	K2	
Dodwell, John C.	14, Sept 1852	12, Sept	40	P2	
Doherty, William A. (Dr)	25, June 1849	22, June		L2	
Dolan, Rebecca	21, June 1849	June	10m	L2	
Dolan, Thomas	21, June 1849	June	3	L2	
Doll, Henry	28, June 1849	June	24	L2	
Doll, William	17, Oct. 1850	Oct.	34	Y2	
Dolson, E.	24, Oct. 1828	Oct.	4m	N2	
Dolson, Jacob	3, Sept 1852			P2	
Donahoo, James (Mrs)	20, Jan. 1821	17, Jan.		S3	
Donahue, Thomas	7, June 1849	June	21	L2	
Donaldson, John W.	24, June 1831	21, June	28	A3	
Donberger, Frederick	1, June 1849	May		L2	
Donelly, Alexander Lewis	23, Oct. 1852	20, Oct.	7m-20d	P2	
Donelson, Andrew (Mrs)	10, Jan. 1837	19, Dec.		N2	
Donelson, Emily	27, Jan. 1837	19, Dec.	29	N2	
Donley, Hugh	13, Mar. 1841	Mar.	52	R3	
Donnahue, Catharine	21, June 1849	June	43	L2	
Donnigan, Michael	17, Oct. 1850	Oct.	32	Y2	
Donohugh, John	6, July 1849	July	35	L2	
Donough, Joseph	12, Aug. 1831	Aug.	9	A3	
Donovan, Mary E.	12, Sept 1828	Sept	2-10m	N3	
Donovan, Tim.	24, July 1850	July	65	Y2	
Dooley, Mary	28, Dec. 1852	24, Dec.	31	P2	
Doolittle, Curtis Miller	16, June 1849	1, June	50	* L2	
Doolittle, Leonora Ann	14, June 1850	12, June	9m- 6d	P2	
Doren, John (Mrs)	17, May 1849	May		L2	
Dorham, Nancy	12, Aug. 1831	Aug.	70	A3	
Dorkins, Thomas	11, Nov. 1838	Nov.	30	N3	
Dorman, Jesse Byrd	13, July 1852	11, July	69	P2	
Dorman, Sarah	18, July 1828	July	73	N3	
Dornin, Bernard	28, Feb. 1837	24, Feb.	76	* N2	
Dornin, Bernard	28, Feb. 1837	24, Feb.		* T2	
Dornwoody, John	31, Dec. 1830	Dec.	42	N3	
Dorr, William	27, July 1850	July	6m	Y3	
Dorsey, (child of Hannah)	25, Nov. 1828	Nov.	stillborn	N3	
Dorsey, Edward	5, May 1836	23, Apr.		X2	
Dorsey, J.L.	14, Dec. 1835		probate	N2	
Dorsey, John L. (Dr)	3, Aug. 1833	29, July	26	* R3	
Dorsey, Sarah Johnson	13, Sept 1834	25, Aug.	45	R3	Johnson
Dorton, Andrew	31, Dec. 1830	Dec.	32	N3	
Dosey, Hamilton Horatio	23, Dec. 1840	19, Dec.	3- 4m	N2	

Name	Notice Date	Death Date	Age		Page	Maiden Name
Doty, Caroline	23, July 1830	July	4		N3	
Doty, Eliza	20, July 1842	19, July	40	*	N2	
Doty, Samuel	14, Dec. 1835		probate		N2	
Dougan, William	4, Apr. 1837		probate		N2	
Dougherty, Charles	26, July 1852	23, July			P2	
Dougherty, John	24, Oct. 1840	Oct.	25		R3	
Dougherty, Thomas	12, Apr. 1849	Apr.	20		L2	
Doughty, Mary Isabella	27, July 1852	25, July	2- 9m		P2	
Douglass, John D.	14, May 1847	10, May			K2	
Douglass, Joseph	3, May 1838			*	N2	
Douglass, Luke (Dr)	21, Sept 1820	4, Sept		*	S3	
Douglass, Mary	8, July 1828	July	1		N3	
Douglass, Samuel (Lt)	5, Nov. 1852	3, Nov.	41		P2	
Douglass, William H.	10, Nov. 1827	6, Nov.	16		R3	
Douthitt, Solomon	24, Mar. 1836		60		X3	
Dover, James	9, June 1815	8, June		*	S3	
Doverner, Peter	17, May 1849	May	28		L2	
Dowler, Thomas	24, June 1835	29, May	53		T2	
Downer, John	2, Nov. 1835	28, Oct.	60	*	T2	
Downes, Elisha	3, Feb. 1829	Jan.	18		N3	
Downes, Henry	9, Aug. 1841	Aug.	20		N2	
Downes, W.P.	15, July 1823		estate		N3	
Downes, William P.	5, Oct. 1822		estate		S3	
Downes, William P.	17, June 1823		estate		N3	
Downes, William P.	3, Aug. 1822	30, July		*	S3	
Downs, William P.	1, Aug. 1822	30, July			J3	
Dowtey, Reuben	26, Feb. 1814		estate		S3	
Dowty, Reuben	25, July 1817		estate		S4	
Doxon, James N.	12, Aug. 1852	10, Aug.	30		P2	
Doyle, Calvin F.	24, Feb. 1829	Feb.	7m-18d		N3	
Doyle, Michael	28, June 1849	June	43		L2	
Doyle, Thomas (Major)	20, Feb. 1805	17, Feb.	45		S3	
Doyle, Thomas (Major)	13, Mar. 1805		estate		S3	
Doyle, William	14, Dec. 1835		probate		N2	
Drake Uriah	17, Aug. 1811	27, July	21		S2	
Drake, Alexander	13, Feb. 1830	10, Feb.			R3	
Drake, Andrew C.	31, Dec. 1830	Dec.	1m		N3	
Drake, Benjamin	22, May 1841		estate		R3	
Drake, Benjamin	10, Apr. 1841			*	R3	
Drake, Benjamin	15, Apr. 1841			*	N2	
Drake, Daniel	20, Aug. 1830	Aug.	29		N3	
Drake, Daniel (Dr)	6, Nov. 1852	5, Nov.			P2	
Drake, Edward L.	11, Jan. 1840	11, Dec.		*	R3	
Drake, Elizabeth	12, Nov. 1831	8, Nov.	71		R3	
Drake, Harriet	4, Nov. 1825	30, Sept	38	*	N2	
Drake, Harriet	4, Oct. 1825	30, Sept			N3	
Drake, Harriet Elizabeth	30, July 1841	23, July	9m-12d		N3	
Drake, Isaac	20, Oct. 1832	13, Oct.	76	*	R3	
Drake, John Mansfield	9, Feb. 1816	3, Feb.			S3	
Drake, John T.	9, Mar. 1830	12, Feb.	35		N3	
Drake, Joseph Charles	12, 13, July 1849	11, July	13		L2	
Drake, Martha Ella Taylor	24, Jan. 1842		30		N2	
Drake, Mary	15, Aug. 1817	8, Aug.			S3	
Drake, William	9, Nov. 1822		estate		S3	

Name	Notice Date	Death Date	Age	Page	Maiden Name
Drake, William	9, Dec. 1828		probate	N3	
Dramont, Alanson	8, Sept 1827	Sept	21	R3	
Draper, James	14, Nov. 1840	28, Oct.	27	R3	
Draught, (child of James)	8, Oct. 1852	Oct.	18m	P2	
Drennan, Alexander	27, Mar. 1835		estate	N2	
Drenning, Alexander	4, June 1836		probate	N2	
Drenning, Mary	10, Dec. 1830	Dec.	49	N3	
Drese, William	13, July 1849	July	27	L2	
Dresser, Leather	29, May 1802		estate	S3	
Drew, Robert	20, Jan. 1825		estate	E3	
Drew, Stephen E.	16, Sept 1852	14, Sept	40	P2	
Dromgoole, George C.	5, May 1847	29, Apr.		K2	
Drummond, Mary	31, July 1850	July	55	Y3	
Drury, Mary E.	21, July 1838	15, July	27	R3	
Drury, Mary E.	18, July 1838	15, July	27	T2	
Dryden, Samuel	27, Jan. 1827	13, Jan.	18	R2	
Dryer, Georgette	24, July 1841	July	2m	R3	
Dudley, Elizabeth	27, Dec. 1828	Dec.	2	R3	
Dudley, Elizabeth	23, Dec. 1828	Dec.	2	N3	
Dudley, Elizabeth	7, Nov. 1840	13, Oct.		R3	
Dudley, Margaret	2, Sept 1828	Aug.	26	N3	
Dudley, Sarah J.	2, Aug. 1834	July	1- 9m	R3	
Dudley, Sarah J.	29, July 1834	July	1- 9m	T2	
Dudley, William Scott	20, Mar. 1829	Mar.	4	N3	
Duer, Robert	24, Sept 1847	21, Sept	21	K2	
Duffee, James	15, May 1841	May	32	R3	
Duffie, Benjamin	10, July 1841	July	50	R3	
Duffield, Catharine	2, Oct. 1841	2, Oct.	6	R3	
Duffield, Catharine	25, Sept 1841	24, Sept	6	N2	
Duffield, Edward	23, July 1834			T2	
Duffield, Margaret	26, Dec. 1840	20, Dec.	26	R3	
Duffield, Margaret	22, Dec. 1840	20, Dec.	26	N2	
Duffield, Margaret	19, June 1841	11, June		R3	
Duffield, Margaret	12, June 1841	11, June		N2	
Dugan, Alexander	2, Jan. 1829	Dec.	19 *	N3	
Dugan, William	4, June 1836		probate	N2	
Dugan, William	20, Mar. 1838		probate	N3	
Duhrman, Henry	21, June 1849	June	28	L2	
Duke, Basil (Dr)	7, June 1828	June		R3	
Duke, James Currie	8, Mar. 1836	1, Mar.	7m	T3	
Dukes, Isaac	16, July 1838		estate	T2	
Dulic, Barbara	1, July 1828	June	50	N3	
Dull, John	1, May 1837		estate	T2	
Dumass, (child of Alfred)	14, May 1830	May	2m	N3	
Dumass, (child of B.)	12, Aug. 1831	Aug.	2d	A3	
Dumass, Albert	9, July 1830	July	4m	N3	
Dumont, Peter	15, Sept 1821	31, Aug.	77	S3	
Dumoss, Benjamin	7, Oct. 1828	Oct.	infant	N3	
Dunaway, Thomas	7, Mar. 1837	27, Feb.		T2	
Dunbar, Catharine	9, July 1830	July	66	N3	
Dunbar, Seth	4, Sept 1829		estate	N3	
Dunbar, Seth	21, Dec. 1830		probate	N3	
Dunbar, Seth	18, May 1838		probate	N2	
Duncan, Jesse S.	23, Jan. 1835	18, Jan.	25	X3	

Name	Notice Date	Death Date	Age	Page	Maiden Name
Duncan, John	17, May 1849	May	57	L2	
Duncan, John	2, Apr. 1842		estate	R3	
Duncan, Mary	24, July 1841	18, July	7- 3m	R3	
Duncan, Thomas	4, Dec. 1827	16, Nov.		N3	
Dunham, (Miss)	3, May 1838			N2	
Dunham, Isaac	11, Mar. 1831		estate	X3	
Dunham, Joseph	9, Dec. 1828	Dec.	65	N3	
Dunham, Phoebe	10, Dec. 1835			X3	
Dunker, Caroline Bernardine	25, Aug. 1852	21, Aug.	1- 7m- 8d	P2	
Dunkinson, Ann B.	18, Sept 1837	1, Sept		* T2	Williams
Dunlap, (child)	30, July 1830	July	5m	N3	
Dunlap, Mary Ann	6, Feb. 1829	Feb.	34	N2	
Dunlap, Rebecca	1, Aug. 1828	July	8	N3	
Dunlap, Richard C.	9, July 1841		45	* N2	
Dunlap, Robert	7, Sept 1836		probate	N2	
Dunlap, Robert	27, Oct. 1832	19, Oct.		R3	
Dunlap, Robert (Rev)	26, Mar. 1847	21, Mar.		K2	
Dunlap, Robert F.	9, Apr. 1831	27, Mar.	25	R3	
Dunlap, Robert Jameel	28, May 1842	24, May	2- 3w	R3	
Dunlap, Robert James	26, May 1842	24, May	2- -21d	N2	
Dunlap, William	26, July 1834	July	60	R3	
Dunlap, William	22, July 1834	July	60	T2	
Dunlap, William	7, Sept 1836		probate	N2	
Dunlavy, Francis	11, Nov. 1839	4, Nov.	78	T2	
Dunlop, Edward	26, Jan. 1803		estate	S3	
Dunn, Abner Martin	25, July 1795	18, July		C3	
Dunn, E.	3, May 1838			N2	
Dunn, Eleanor	18, July 1828	July	16	N3	
Dunn, James	28, June 1849	June	20	L2	
Dunn, James	30, May 1818		estate	S2	
Dunn, John	22, Aug. 1834	13, Aug.		* T2	
Dunning, Duncan Dunbar	3, Jan. 1853	30, Dec.	27	P2	
Dunseth, Andrew	28, Sept 1824		estate	N3	
Dunseth, Crawford	17, July 1841	14, July		R3	
Dunseth, David	23, Mar. 1830		probate	N3	
Dunseth, David	5, Sept 1818	21, Aug.		S3	
Dunseth, George	28, Sept 1824		estate	N3	
Dunseth, Patty	25, Dec. 1829		estate	N3	
Dunseth, Patty	7, Sept 1830		probate	N3	
Dunseth, Stephen	3, May 1847	2, May	29	K2	
DupontdeNemours, Peter S.	19, Sept 1817	6, Aug.	78	S3	
Durant, Nancy	24, Dec. 1830	Dec.	2- 7m	N3	
Durfee, Charles H.	24, July 1850	23, July	18	* P2	
Dury, Henry	20, Oct. 1832		estate	R3	
Dury, Henry	27, Apr. 1832	28, Mar.		* X3	
Dusbach, Catharine	17, Nov. 1852	14, Nov.	15	P2	
Duskey, Eli	7, Mar. 1828		estate	N3	
Duskey, Eli	23, Mar. 1830		probate	N3	
Dusky, Eli	29, Jan. 1828	23, Jan.	67	N2	
Dutton, A.S.	14, Dec. 1835		probate	N2	
Duval, James S.	12, July 1828		infant	R3	
Duval, Stephen	24, June 1828	June	41	N3	
Duvall, James S.	24, Aug. 1833	Aug.		R3	
Duvall, Lamech	18, Sept 1830		estate	R3	

Name	Notice Date	Death Date	Age	Page	Maiden Name
Duwell, (child of John)	2, Aug. 1834	July	1-10m	R3	
Duwell, (child of John)	29, July 1834	July	1-10m	T2	
Dwight, (Rev)	7, Feb. 1817	11, Jan.		S3	
Dwyer, James	29, Mar. 1849	Mar.	40	L2	
Dwyer, Richard	26, Apr. 1828		estate	R4	
Dwyer, Richard	15, Jan. 1830		estate	N3	
Dyer, Sarah	26, July 1834	July	9m	R3	
Dyer, Sarah	22, July 1834	July	9m	T2	
Dywer, Richard	23, Feb. 1828		estate	R3	
Eads, William H.	3, Dec. 1835		55	T2	
Eagan, Catharine	2, Aug. 1834	July		R3	
Eagan, Richard	31, Oct. 1850	Oct.	26	Y2	
Eagun, Catherine	29, July 1834	July		T2	
Earhart, George	13, Oct. 1826		estate	N3	
Earhart, George	25, Aug. 1829		probate	N3	
Earhart, George	4, June 1836		probate	N2	
Early, Eleazar	11, July 1840			* R3	
East, Hueston	5, Sept 1828	Sept	9	N3	
Eastman, Clement	4, Nov. 1828	Oct.	3	N3	
Eastman, Daniel	25, Apr. 1840		55	R3	
Easton, Ann	28, July 1850	July	30	Y3	
Easton, Charlotte	9, Nov. 1839	2, Nov.	30	R3	
Easton, Emily Farrin	9, Oct. 1841	1, Oct.	18m	R3	
Easton, Samuel	26, June 1835	11, June		T2	
Eastres, Oliver	14, June 1849	June	1	L2	
Eaton, (daughter of William)	8, Aug. 1818	6, Aug.	infant	S3	
Eaton, Jeremiah A.	24, Oct. 1850	Oct.	45	Y2	
Eaton, John	1, Nov. 1852	29, Oct.	50	P2	
Eaton, Pamela	4, July 1826		estate	N3	
Eaton, Richard Keys	24, Jan. 1839	23, Jan.	24	T2	
Eberle, John	8, Mar. 1839	8, Mar.	28	T2	
Eberle, John (Dr)	5, Feb. 1838	4, Jan.		T2	
Eberle, John (Dr)	6, Feb. 1838	5, Feb.		N2	
Eberly, Ellen	30, Dec. 1852	28, Dec.		P2	Decker
Eccles, James Robert	22, July 1851	21, July	2- 7m	P2	
Echler, H.	11, Oct. 1852	10, Oct.		P2	
Eckford, Charles E.	31, July 1850	July	35	Y3	
Ecklan,	30, July 1850	July	2	Y3	
Eckstein, Jane	20, July 1833	7, July		* R3	
Eddy, Isaac	10, Apr. 1849	9, Apr.		L3	
Eddy, Mary	7, Apr. 1836	20, Mar.	2- 9m	X3	
Edgeworth, Robert	1, June 1835		probate	N2	
Edmiston, John (Dr)	4, June 1824		45	N2	
Edmonds, John D. (Capt)	6, Feb. 1841	5, Feb.	35	R3	
Edsall, Richard, Jr.	26, Dec. 1818	29, Nov.		S3	
Edstrom, Andrew	3, Aug. 1836	30, July	40	* N2	
Edwards, (child of Willey)	12, Aug. 1831	Aug.	1- 5m	A3	
Edwards, Alexander	29, Mar. 1849	Mar.		L2	
Edwards, Hester	29, Sept 1852	26, Sept	19	P2	
Edwards, Isaac	11, May 1827		estate	Q3	
Edwards, Isaac	7, Sept 1830		probate	N3	
Edwards, John S. (Col)	20, Feb. 1813	29, Jan.	35	S3	
Edwards, Jonathan	9, Sept 1801			S3	
Edwards, Lucy	21, Jan. 1841	Jan.	40	N2	

Name	Notice Date	Death Date	Age	Page	Maiden Name
Edwards, Lucy	23, Jan. 1841	Jan.	49	R3	
Edwards, Mary Ann	12, Aug. 1828	Aug.	1- 7m	N3	
Edwards, Robert (Capt)	13, Apr. 1820		estate	D3	
Edwards, Sylvester D.	3, June 1837			T2	
Eells, James H. (Rev)	29, Dec. 1836	10, Dec.		X3	
Eells, Samuel	19, Mar. 1842	13, Mar.		R3	
Eells, Samuel	15, Mar. 1842	16, Mar.		N2	
Eggbert, Andrew	15, Aug. 1850	Aug.	3	Y2	
Eggbert, Anna	15, Aug. 1850	Aug.	5	Y2	
Eggbert, Edward	8, Aug. 1850	Aug.	7	Y2	
Eggbert, Herbert	8, Aug. 1850	Aug.	4	Y2	
Egleston, Joseph (Major)	16, Mar. 1811	13, Feb.	57	S3	
Eichelberger, Ferdinand	19, July 1834	July	1- 6m	R3	
Eichelberger, Margaret	5, Apr. 1816	27, Mar.	109	* S3	
Eichler, John	13, July 1849	July	36	L2	
Eickhoff, Charles L.	8, Oct. 1841	Oct.	38	N2	
Elby, David	17, Nov. 1810	12, Nov.		S3	
Elder, Ann T.	25, June 1830	June	1	N3	
Elder, Mary P.	30, July 1842	25, July	27	R3	
Elder, Mary P.	26, July 1842	25, July	27	N2	
Eldgenoss, Ditha	13, July 1849	July	6m	L2	
Elistone,	8, Oct. 1841	22, Sept	38	* N2	
Ellery, William	19, Feb. 1820	29, Jan.	93	S2	
Ellery, William	11, Mar. 1820	15, Feb.	93	S3	
Elliot, Robert	11, Oct. 1794	6, Oct.		C3	
Elliott, Elizabeth Gertrude	27, Mar. 1849	19, Mar.	4- 6m	L2	
Elliott, Hattie	20, Nov. 1852			P2	Jones
Elliott, Stephen	19, Apr. 1830	28, Mar.	58	A3	
Ellis, David	4, June 1836		probate	N2	
Ellis, Francis	30, Aug. 1833	19, July		X3	
Ellis, George W.	10, July 1841	4, July	child	R3	
Ellis, George W.	7, July 1841	5, July	child	N2	
Ellis, John	30, Aug. 1833	20, July		X3	
Ellis, Otis	24, Feb. 1821		estate	S3	
Ellis, Thomas	23, Mar. 1830		probate	N3	
Ellit, John	19, Aug. 1831	Aug.	16m	A3	
Elmes, Francina A.	22, July 1834	July	1- 6m	T2	
Elmes, Francis A.	26, July 1834	July	1- 6m	R3	
Elmes, Fransina Adelaide	15, July 1834	13, July	1- 6m-13d	T2	
Elwell, Jane	4, June 1830	June	21	N3	
Elwell, Thomas	28, Oct. 1823		estate	N2	
Ely, Jonathan	9, June 1847	8, June	50	K2	
Emans, John	18, Feb. 1835		estate	N2	
Embree, Elihu	20, Jan. 1821			S3	
Embree, Jesse	9, Sept 1823	14, Aug.		N3	
Embrick, Philip	23, Sept 1852	17, Sept	65	P2	
Emerson, Jonathan	10, June 1824		estate	E3	
Emery, Charles	21, Sept 1838		probate	N3	
Emison, Thomas	7, Dec. 1838		estate	T2	
Emmons, John	11, Dec. 1827		probate	N3	
Emmons, John	19, Aug. 1828		probate	N3	
Emons, John	9, Dec. 1828		probate	N3	
Empson, Thomas Jefferson	2, June 1847	1, June		K2	
Enalt, Benjamin	8, Oct. 1841	29, Sept	83	N2	

Name	Notice Date	Death Date	Age		Page	Maiden Name
Endus, George	3, May 1838				N2	
Endus, Johannes	3, May 1838				N2	
Engart, (child of J.S.)	19, Aug. 1831	Aug.	5m		A3	
England, Samuel T.	24, Apr. 1835	8, Apr.	22-10m		T3	
English, James	15, Dec. 1837	8, Dec.	23	*	T2	
English, Phebe	24, Feb. 1829	Feb.	3		N3	
English, Susan	15, Jan. 1828	2, Jan.			N3	
Ennes, Sarah	12, Aug. 1828	Aug.	1m		N3	
Enness, Susan	16, Aug. 1831				A3	
Enness, Susan	6, June 1826	4, June			N3	
Ennis, J.W.	21, Sept 1837	17, Sept			T2	
Ennson, John Henry	16, July 1851	13, July	7		P2	
Enright, Frances Josephine	26, Aug. 1852	22, Aug.	3		P2	
Entwisle, Mary	21, Nov. 1840	Nov.	49		R3	
Enyart, Anna	26, July 1852	21, July	82		P2	
Enyart, Samuel	30, Jan. 1835		estate		N2	
Enyart, Samuel	14, Dec. 1835		probate		N2	
Enyart, William	27, Aug. 1830	Aug.	45		N3	
Epley, Joseph	11, Sept 1837		probate		N2	
Eply, William	14, Dec. 1835		probate		N2	
Eppes, John W.	7, Oct. 1823				N3	
Erbert, Margaret	13, July 1849	July	75		L2	
Erexon, James	14, May 1830	May	21		N3	
Ernest, Catharine	28, June 1828				R3	
Ernst, Dorothy Maria	30, Oct. 1841	25, Oct.	71		R3	
Ernst, Dorothy Maria	27, Oct. 1841	25, Oct.	71		N2	
Ernst, Elizabeth	11, Jan. 1840	11, Jan.	44		R3	
Ernst, Emily Jane	18, Nov. 1847	16, Nov.	23		K2	
Ernst, Francis M.	28, July 1838	27, July	11		R3	
Ernst, Francis M.	27, July 1838	26, July	11		T2	
Ernst, Lydia A.	17, July 1841	13, June			R3	Bush
Erwin, (child of James)	5, Nov. 1830	Nov.			N3	
Erwin, Ann	16, Dec. 1835	10, Dec.			T3	Clay
Escavaille, Joseph	21, June 1828				R3	
Eshelby, James Alexander	26, Dec. 1840	23, Dec.	5- 3m		R3	
Eshelby, James Alexander	24, Dec. 1840	23, Dec.	5- 3m		N2	
Eshelby, Margaret Jane	22, July 1850	22, July	1- 9m-14d		P2	
Eshelby, Sarah Emily	29, June 1847	26, June	8m- 4d		K2	
Este, George Washington	11, June 1836	10, June	infant		T2	
Este, John	20, Aug. 1842	17, Aug.	2		R3	
Este, Lucy	11, Apr. 1826	7, Apr.			N3	Harrison
Estell, Levi	24, Sept 1830	Sept	53		N3	
Esther, Sarah A.	24, May 1849	May	10		L2	
Estill, Levi	8, Oct. 1830	Oct.	28		N3	
Estle, Levi	3, Jan. 1831		estate		A3	
Etheridge, T.	1, Nov. 1816	29, Oct.			S3	
Eubank, James T.	13, Apr. 1824		estate		N4	
Eubank, John J.	3, Sept 1852	1, Sept	29- 6m		P2	
Eugene, William	26, Sept 1840	Sept	1- 6m		R3	
Eustis, William	22, Feb. 1825		75		N3	
Eute, John Adolphus	30, July 1852	24, July	10		P2	
Evans, (man)	21, Oct. 1852	19, Oct.			P2	
Evans, Abraham	28, Dec. 1838		estate		N2	
Evans, Catharine	24, May 1849	May	47		L2	

Name	Notice Date	Death Date	Age		Page	Maiden Name
Evans, Griffin	15, May 1849	14, May	24		L2	
Evans, Harvey D.	19, July 1825	12, July	28		N3	
Evans, James M.	13, Jan. 1838	3, Jan.		*	T2	
Evans, John (Col)	12, Jan. 1842	10, Jan.	76	*	N2	
Evans, Joseph	23, July 1850	July	4- 3m		Y2	
Evans, Oliver	8, May 1819				S3	
Evans, Owen	7, July 1827	2, July			R3	
Evans, Sarah Elizabeth	7, Aug. 1852	3, Aug.	1		P2	
Evans, Watson	6, 7, Oct. 1852	5, Oct.	17m		P2	
Eve, (Mrs)	31, July 1805	27, July			S3	
Evens, Eliza Jane	21, July 1827	20, July	infant		R3	
Everett, Amanda M.	24, Oct. 1840	15, Oct.	23		R3	Broadwell
Everett, William	30, Nov. 1841	29, Nov.	28		N2	
Everingham, Enoch	16, Dec. 1825		probate		N3	
Everson, Almira	29, Mar. 1834	Mar.	6		R3	
Everson, Charles	29, Mar. 1834	Mar.	3		R3	
Everson, Jacob	23, Jan. 1837		estate		N2	
Everson, Juletta	29, Mar. 1834	Mar.	10m		R3	
Evert, Frederick	13, July 1849	July	28		L2	
Ewing, Alexander H.	30, Aug. 1847	28, Aug.	45	*	K2	
Ewing, Charles Albert	17, July 1852	13, July	10m- 9d		P2	
Ewing, Charlotte	14, Aug. 1838	11, Aug.	56		T2	
Ewing, Elizabeth	27, Aug. 1800	23, Aug.	31		S3	
Ewing, Robert	23, Oct. 1819		22		S3	
Ewing, Samuel	4, Mar. 1825		49		N2	
Ewing, Samuel	8, Aug. 1804		estate		S4	
Facemine, Joseph T.	19, Aug. 1828	Aug.	2-11m		N3	
Fahy, Martin	6, July 1849	July	14m		L2	
Fairbank, Daniel	11, Aug. 1835	9, Aug.	29		T2	
Fairbank, Daniel W.	14, Aug. 1835	10, Aug.	29	*	X2	
Fairbank, Daniel W.	2, Oct. 1835		estate		X3	
Fairbank, Ebenezer	6, Dec. 1816		estate		S3	
Fairchild, (child of Walter)	24, June 1828	June	infant		N3	
Fairchild, (Dr)	15, Aug. 1840				R3	
Falls, James	28, June 1849	June	12		L2	
Falls, James	6, July 1849	July	12		L2	
Falmer, Valentine	13, July 1849	July	46		L2	
Fanshaw, Ann	28, Sept 1852	26, Sept	65	*	P2	
Farel, (child of Samuel)	25, June 1830	June	stillborn		N3	
Farichild, Alpheus	3, Feb. 1826	27, Jan.	77	*	N3	
Faris, Ida Elizabeth	31, Aug. 1852	20, Aug.	10m-16d		P2	
Faris, Mary Paulina	7, June 1849	5, June			L2	
Farley, John	13, Apr. 1824		estate		N3	
Farlin, James	27, Oct. 1802		estate		S3	
Farly, John	16, Dec. 1825		probate		N3	
Farmer, James	19, Sept 1850	Sept	63		Y2	
Farmer, James	18, May 1838		probate		N2	
Farmer, Jemima	9, July 1830	July	46		N3	
Farmer, John	15, Sept 1838	10, Sept	50	*	R3	
Farmer, William	24, Nov. 1832	18, Nov.	38	*	R3	
Farmer, William	1, Dec. 1832		estate		R3	
Farnham, Margaret P.	20, Apr. 1847	18, Apr.	23		K2	Aydelotte
Farrar, (child of A.S.)	24, June 1828	June	stillborn		N3	
Farrar, Henry	19, Aug. 1831	Aug.	32		A3	

Name	Notice Date	Death Date	Age		Page	Maiden Name
Farrar, John	3, Oct. 1817	28, Sept	20		S3	
Farrar, John	9, July 1814		estate		S3	
Farrar, John (Major)	5, Mar. 1814	1, Mar.			S3	
Farrell, John	1, Aug. 1850	July	32		Y2	
Farrell, John	22, Aug. 1850	Aug.	50		Y2	
Farrell, Mary	1, Feb. 1849	30, Jan.	5		B2	
Farris, H.S.	22, July 1834	July	8		T2	
Farwell, Augustus	22, Aug. 1850	Aug.	45		Y2	
Faulcon, Sally	2, Dec. 1840	14, Nov.	66		N2	
Faux, Abraham	3, May 1849	May	37		L2	
Fawcett, Henrietta Shotwell	2, July 1847	30, June	infant		K2	
Fayarty, Edward	15, Aug. 1850	Aug.	19		Y2	
Febiger, C.C.	3, Feb. 1829	Jan.	42		N3	
Febiger, C.C.	24, Jan. 1829	22, Jan.			R3	
Febiger, C.C.	23, Jan. 1829				N3	
Febiger, Caroline	16, Oct. 1852	15, Oct.	23		P2	
Feeld, Elizabeth O.	10, Dec. 1830	Dec.	4- 4m		N3	
Felter, David	1, Dec. 1829		estate		N3	
Felter, Jacob	25, Oct. 1841	18, Oct.			N2	
Femmirman, Margaret	9, July 1830	July	1		N3	
Fenington, John	11, Sept 1841	4, Sept	65	*	R3	
Fenner, Arthur	20, Nov. 1805				S3	
Fenton, Alfred T.	12, Oct. 1835		estate		N2	
Fenton, Alfred T.	1, Aug. 1836		estate		N3	
Fenton, Alfred T.	6, Nov. 1838		probate		N2	
Fenton, Joseph Brush	28, Feb. 1848	25, Feb.			K2	
Fenton, Roswell	6, Oct. 1810		estate		S3	
Fenton, Roswell	24, Dec. 1830		estate		N3	
Fenton, Roswell	14, Dec. 1835		probate		N2	
Ferances, Daniel	13, July 1849	July	40		L2	
Ferguson, Abijah F.	3, Mar. 1836	28, Feb.	35		X3	
Ferguson, Abijah Franklin	1, Mar. 1836	28, Feb.			T3	
Ferguson, Abijah Franklin	1, Mar. 1836	28, Feb.			N2	
Ferguson, Addison M.	9, Aug. 1833	4, Aug.	38		X3	
Ferguson, Arthur	26, Sept 1828	Sept	69		N3	
Ferguson, Arthur	23, Jan. 1837		estate		N3	
Ferguson, Edward	17, Oct. 1835		estate		N2	
Ferguson, Edward	20, Mar. 1838		probate		N3	
Ferguson, James	23, Jan. 1837		estate		N3	
Ferguson, John	21, Sept 1830		estate		N3	
Ferguson, John	17, Sept 1835		probate		T2	
Ferguson, Salome	1, May 1835	6, May	30	*	X3	Snow
Ferguson, Susan M.	8, Oct. 1821	1, Oct.			S3	
Ferguson, William	1, Aug. 1812	28, July		*	S3	
Fernading, John	13, July 1849	July	22		L2	
Fernsher, Paul	6, Mar. 1829		estate		N3	
Ferrell, Felix	6, July 1849	July	50		L2	
Ferrell, Thomas	21, June 1849	June	20		L2	
Ferret, Philip H.	11, Apr. 1826	6, Apr.		*	N3	
Ferrill, Elizabeth	18, July 1828	July	2		N3	
Ferrill, John	24, Aug. 1836		estate		T2	
Ferris, Andrew (Capt)	16, June 1849	15, June	70		L2	
Ferris, H.S.	26, July 1834	July	8		R3	
Ferris, Harriet	10, Sept 1842	5, Sept	26		R3	Foreman

Name	Notice Date	Death Date	Age	Page	Maiden Name
Ferris, Henry	25, Nov. 1828	Nov.	1	N3	
Ferris, Henry	14, Dec. 1824		probate	N3	
Ferris, Henry	3, May 1825		probate	N3	
Ferris, Henry	16, Dec. 1824		probate	E3	
Ferris, Joseph	17, Sept 1835		probate	T2	
Ferris, Joseph	1, June 1835		probate	N2	
Ferris, Nancy	24, Sept 1850	23, Sept		Y2	
Fessenden, Thomas Green	20, Nov. 1837	18, Nov.		T2	
Fiegler, Charlotte	26, July 1834	July	26	R3	
Fiegler, Charlotte	22, July 1834	July	26	T2	
Field, Elizabeth	2, June 1827	27, May	54	R3	
Field, John	10, Apr. 1829	Apr.	40	N3	
Field, Seth	11, Sept 1805		estate	S3	
Field, William H.	16, Aug. 1841	10, Aug.	1- 1m	N2	
Fiestag, Martin	24, May 1849	May	54	L2	
Fifield, Mary Abbey	8, Aug. 1840	30, July	7	R3	
Fifield, Nancy O.	26, Feb. 1848	25, Feb.	45	K2	
Filson, John L.	20, Mar. 1838		probate	N3	
Finan, Andrew	31, Oct. 1850	Oct.	1w	Y2	
Finch, William	1, May 1849	18, Apr.		L2	
Findlay, (Mrs)	6, Aug. 1824	26, July	60	N2	
Findlay, (Mrs)	5, Aug. 1824	26, July	60	E3	
Findlay, Elizabeth	20, 22, July 1847	18, July	34	K2	Patterson
Findlay, James	12, Apr. 1836		estate	N2	
Findlay, James (Gen)	30, Dec. 1835	28, Dec.		N2	
Findlay, John (Col)	13, Nov. 1838	5, Nov.	73	T2	
Findley, Robert	7, June 1849	June	32	L2	
Findley, William	28, Apr. 1821			S3	
Findly, James	30, Dec. 1835	28, Dec.		T3	
Fine, Abraham	9, Dec. 1828		probate	N3	
Finkbine, Mary M.	6, Nov. 1852	4, Nov.		P2	
Finley, J.	9, Sept 1831	Sept	50	A3	
Finley, Rachel	9, June 1827	23, May		R3	
Finley, Robert	18, Aug. 1852	13, Aug.	49	P2	
Finley, Thomas	20, Sept 1852	17, Sept	72 *	P2	
Finney, E.W.	9, Dec. 1828		probate	N3	
Finney, Ebenezer W.	21, Jan. 1823		estate	N3	
Finney, James P.	17, Sept 1835		probate	T2	
Finney, James P.	1, June 1835		probate	N2	
Fishback, John	22, Aug. 1850	Aug.	26	Y2	
Fisher, Abigail	25, Oct. 1825	24, Sept		N3	
Fisher, Anderson C.	19, Nov. 1852	17, Nov.	3- 7m-17d	P2	
Fisher, Andrew	1, June 1849	May	42	L2	
Fisher, Arthur	28, July 1850	July	23	Y3	
Fisher, Helen	11, Apr. 1828	9, Apr.	*	Q3	
Fisher, James	26, June 1802		estate	S3	
Fisher, James	14, July 1821		estate	S3	
Fisher, John	23, Dec. 1841		estate	N3	
Fisher, John	11, Dec. 1841	3, Nov.		R3	
Fisher, Joseph	7, June 1849	June	26	L2	
Fisher, N.	17, Feb. 1829	Feb.	34	N3	
Fisher, Perry	9, July 1830	July	4- 6m	N3	
Fisher, Samuel	21, Dec. 1830		probate	N3	
Fisher, Thomas	3, May 1838			N2	

Name	Notice Date	Death Date	Age		Page	Maiden Name
Fishover, Sepheld	8, Oct. 1852	Oct.	65		P2	
Fishover, Sepheld	6, Sept 1852	4, Sept			P2	
Fisk, Amos	9, Aug. 1825	11, Aug.	40		N3	
Fisk, Amos	19, Dec. 1826		probate		N3	
Fitch, Daniel	21, June 1849	June	59		L2	
Fitch, Jeremiah	25, July 1840	10, July			R3	
Fitch, Phoebe	8, Feb. 1837	6, Feb.	41	*	N2	
Fitten, Thomas	18, May 1833		estate		R3	
Fitton, Francis	16, Dec. 1828	Dec.	55		N3	
Fitzpatric, Michael	7, June 1849	June	58		L2	
Fitzpatrick, Andrew	1, June 1835		probate		N2	
Flagg, Benjamin	19, Nov. 1830	Nov.	13		N3	
Flagg, Catharine	2, Sept 1828	Aug.	21		N3	
Flanagan, William	23, June 1835	12, June			T2	
Flanagan, William	1, July 1835	12, June			T2	
Flannagan, John	22, Mar. 1849	Mar.	40		L2	
Flannegan, Matthew	24, May 1849	May	28		L2	
Fleak, Peter	6, Oct. 1826		probate		N3	
Fleak, Peter	25, Aug. 1829		probate		N3	
Fleetwood, Mary Columbia	18, Aug. 1852		26		P2	
Fleming, Dorcas B.	8, Dec. 1852	7, Dec.			P2	
Fleming, Robert	25, Aug. 1829		probate		N3	
Fleming, Tarlton (Capt)	21, June 1794	17, June			C3	
Fleming, Thomas (Capt)	9, Dec. 1837	6, Dec.	88	*	R3	
Flemming, J.	3, May 1838				N2	
Flemming, Robert	15, Nov. 1816		estate		S3	
Fletcher, Albert M.	19, Sept 1840	18, Sept	23		R3	
Fletcher, John	22, Feb. 1794		estate		C3	
Fletcher, Rosanna F.	2, June 1849	1, June	infant		L2	
Fling, Thomas	26, Nov. 1830	Nov.	68		N3	
Flinn, Ann	28, June 1849	June	10w		L2	
Flinn, Elizabeth	29, Sept 1829		estate		N3	
Flinn, John	7, June 1849	June	31		L2	
Flinn, Stephen	22, Jan. 1830		estate		N3	
Flinn, Stephen	4, June 1836		probate		N2	
Flinn, William	13, Apr. 1836		estate		N2	
Flinn, William	9, Jan. 1838		estate		N3	
Flinn, William	4, June 1836		probate		N2	
Flint, Isaac O.	2, Nov. 1827		estate		N3	
Flint, Osgood	4, July 1826		estate		N3	
Flint, Pamela	4, July 1826		estate		N3	
Flint, Timothy	5, Sept 1840	18, Aug.	60	*	R3	
Flint, Timothy (Mrs)	5, Sept 1840	18, July			R3	
Flintham, Susan	4, Nov. 1830	2, Nov.	52		A3	
Flintham, Susan	5, Nov. 1830	Nov.	52		N3	
Flintham, Susan	6, Nov. 1830	1, Nov.			R3	
Flomerfelt, Peter	16, Dec. 1825		probate		N3	
Flood, Betsy	13, July 1849	July	40		L2	
Flood, William	16, May 1823	21, Apr.			N3	
Flora, Mary A.	7, Sept 1837	6, Sept	25		T2	
Flourney, John J.	23, June 1835	22, June			T2	
Flowers, Catharine	5, Sept 1828	Sept	35		N3	
Flowers, Catharine B.	7, Sept 1830		probate		N3	
Flowers, Elizabeth	7, June 1849	June	50		L2	

Name	Notice Date	Death Date	Age	Page	Maiden Name
Flowers, Lucy Ann	1, July 1828	June	1- 6m	N3	
Flowers, Michael	30, Nov. 1827		estate	N3	
Flowers, Michael	23, Mar. 1830		estate	N3	
Flowers, Michael	9, Dec. 1828		probate	N3	
Flowers, Michael	25, Aug. 1829		probate	N3	
Flowers, Michael	21, Dec. 1830		probate	N3	
Flowers, Michael	7, Aug. 1827	28, July		N3	
Flyn, Michael	24, Feb. 1851			P2	
Flynn, Catharine	24, May 1849	May	20	L2	
Foley, Timothy	24, Oct. 1850	Oct.	30	Y2	
Folger, Charles C.	29, May 1841	28, May	17	N2	
Folger, David	1, June 1835		probate	N2	
Folger, Eleonora Elizabeth	30, Apr. 1842	25, Apr.	28	R3	
Folger, Elizabeth	9, Jan. 1838		estate	N3	
Folger, Emma	13, Mar. 1829	Mar.		N3	
Folger, Hebsabeth	1, June 1835		probate	N2	
Folger, Hepsey	21, Feb. 1823	16, Feb.	68	* N3	
Folger, Mary	11, Mar. 1823	8, Mar.		* N3	
Folger, Sarah	25, Aug. 1827	Aug.	3	R3	
Follick, Isaac	25, Aug. 1836		estate	N2	
Follie, Isaac	20, Mar. 1838		probate	N3	
Foot, Daniel	16, Jan. 1824		estate	N3	
Foot, Ziba	2, Mar. 1807		estate	S3	
Foote, Dan	14, Dec. 1824		probate	N3	
Foote, Dan	9, Dec. 1828		probate	N3	
Foote, Dan	16, Dec. 1824		probate	E3	
Foote, George A.	8, Nov. 1834	3, Nov.		R3	
Foote, Sarah T.	9, June 1827	6, June		R3	
Forbes, William	6, Oct. 1826		probate	N3	
Forbus, Edward L.	12, July 1849	11, July	20	L2	
Ford, Bridget	30, July 1850	July	36	Y3	
Ford, Emily	18, July 1828	July	8m	N3	
Ford, John	25, July 1850	July	1	Y2	
Ford, Nathan	4, Oct. 1825	1, Oct.	20	N3	
Forde, Catharine B.	3, Sept 1830	Aug.	15	N2	
Forden, Christopher	15, Feb. 1836		estate	N2	
Forden, Christopher	6, Nov. 1838		probate	N2	
Fore, Emeline	14, 15, May 1849	13, May	32	L2	
Foreman, Mary	24, Mar. 1838		estate	N2	
Forgey, Edgar Sinton	13, July 1852	10, July	4- 4m	P2	
Forpes, Mary E.	26, July 1834	July	1	R3	
Forpes, Mary E.	22, July 1834	July	1	T2	
Forquer, George	22, Sept 1838	12, Sept	40	R3	
Forquer, George	18, Sept 1838	12, Sept		T2	
Forrer, James A.	1, Oct. 1830	Sept	4m	N3	
Forrer, John	28, Apr. 1827	26, Apr.		R3	
Forrer, John	20, Apr. 1827	12, Apr.		N3	
Forrester, R.	4, July 1828		estate	N3	
Forrester, Robert	4, June 1824		estate	N3	
Forrester, Robert	13, May 1828		estate	N3	
Forrester, Robert	9, Dec. 1828		probate	N3	
Forrester, Robert	21, Dec. 1830		probate	N3	
Forsha, Caroline	20, Aug. 1830	Aug.	15m	N3	
Forshay, John B.	15, Oct. 1830	Oct.	1- 4m	N3	

Name	Notice Date	Death Date	Age		Page	Maiden Name
Fortune, Charles Alfred	11, Nov. 1837		7m- 2d		R3	
Fosdick, Charles Updike	8, Jan. 1835	6, Jan.	20		N2	
Fosdick, Henry N.	11, Sept 1841	6, Sept	32		R3	
Fosdick, Henry N.	7, Sept 1841	6, Sept	33		N2	
Fosdick, Phebe	7, Nov. 1826	3, Nov.			N3	
Fosdick, Richard (Capt)	21, 23, Aug. 1837	20, Aug.	72	*	T2	
Fosdick, Richard (Capt)	21, Aug. 1837	20, Aug.			N2	
Fosdick, Thomas R.	21, Aug. 1829	1, Aug.			N2	
Foster, Anna Maria	24, Nov. 1847	23, Nov.	25		K2	Huntington
Foster, Catharine Stanhope	7, Nov. 1826	5, Nov.	infant		N3	
Foster, Elizabeth	25, July 1850	20, July			P2	
Foster, Hepziba	20, Nov. 1805	19, Nov.			S3	
Foster, J.T.	19, Aug. 1831	Aug.	1-11m		A3	
Foster, John P.	12, Aug. 1828	Aug.	38		N3	
Foster, Joseph C.	13, July 1849	12, July	48		L2	
Foster, Julius H.	24, Sept 1830	Sept	2		N3	
Foster, William S. (col)	25, Jan. 1840	26, Nov.	50		R3	
Fotler, Crete	3, May 1838			*	N2	
Fotler, Filben	3, May 1838			*	N2	
Fotler, Jacob	3, May 1838			*	N2	
Fotler, Joseph	3, May 1838			*	N2	
Fotrell, Jacob	21, Sept 1838		probate		N3	
Fotterage, Harriet	24, Oct. 1828	Oct.	3		N2	
Foulds, Elizabeth	7, Apr. 1838	17, Feb.	33	*	R3	Lowry
Foulds, William H.	17, Sept 1838	2, Sept		*	T2	
Foulke, (Mr)	11, July 1822	3, July			J3	
Foulke, Cassandra M.	20, Sept 1825	18, Sept			N3	
Foulke, Lewis	7, Nov. 1834	22, Oct.	71		T2	
Fowble, Margaret	12, Oct. 1811	11, Oct.			S3	
Fowler, (child of Joseph)	12, Nov. 1830	Nov.	2w		N3	
Fowler, John	23, July 1850	July	7		Y2	
Fowler, Libby	19, Sept 1840	Sept	37		R3	
Fowler, Margaret	25, July 1850	July	15		Y2	
Fowler, Reft.	23, Sept 1831	Sept	37		A3	
Fox, (Mr)	2, Aug. 1834	July			R3	
Fox, (Mr)	29, July 1834	July			T2	
Fox, Richard	1, July 1828	June	8m		N3	
Francisco, (Mrs)	6, Oct. 1827	1, Oct.			R3	
Francisco, A.	12, Sept 1828	Sept	18m		N3	
Francisco, Henry	30, Nov. 1820	25, Oct.	134		S3	
Francisco, Mary C.	2, Aug. 1834	July	21		R3	
Francisco, Mary C.	29, July 1834	July	21		T2	
Francomb, Elizabeth	28, May 1830	May	10m		N3	
Frane, James	11, Aug. 1850	30, Apr.			Y2	
Frank, Augustus	30, July 1850	July	33		Y3	
Frank, Ida Catharina Eliza	19, Aug. 1852	16, Aug.	16m-17d		P2	
Frankenstein, J.A.	4, June 1842	29, May	53		R3	
Frankenstein, J.A.	31, May 1842	29, May	53		N2	
Franklin, Alexander	1, Oct. 1830	Sept	1		N3	
Franklin, Benjamin	15, Oct. 1830	Oct.	3		N3	
Franklin, Benjamin	6, July 1849	July	3		L2	
Franklin, John	4, Mar. 1828		probate		N3	
Franromb, Francis	18, June 1830	June	2- 9m		N3	
Fraser, Agnes	17, May 1833	10, May			X3	

Name	Notice Date	Death Date	Age	Page	Maiden Name
Fratabas, Maurice	20, Mar. 1838		probate	N3	
Frazer, J.	9, Sept 1831	Sept	1	A3	
Frazer, John T.	16, Jan. 1829	Jan.	1- 4m	N2	
Frazer, Robert	3, Oct. 1836	2, Oct.		T2	
Frazer, Robert Tyler	3, Oct. 1836	2, Oct.	5m-11d	T2	
Frazer, Robert Tyler	4, Oct. 1836	2, Oct.	5m-11d	N2	
Frazer, Susan A.	30, May 1840	27, May	22	R3	
Frazier, (child)	27, Feb. 1829	Feb.	stillborn	N3	
Frazier, John	9, Dec. 1828		probate	N3	
Frazier, John B.	6, Mar. 1819	1, Jan.		* S3	
Frazier, John S.B.	31, Jan. 1823		estate	N3	
Frazier, Solomon (Capt)	31, Mar. 1826	2, Mar.	72	N3	
Freake, Sophia	26, July 1850	July	9m	Y2	
Frederick, John	24, Oct. 1850	Oct.	37	Y2	
Freeland, John	19, Sept 1828	Sept	56	N3	
Freeman, Edmund	5, Nov. 1800	25, Oct.		S3	
Freeman, Elijah	23, Nov. 1832	15, Oct.	20	* X3	
Freeman, J.G.	3, May 1838			N2	
Freeman, Martha	7, June 1849	June	4	L2	
French, Laura H.	19, May 1847	18, May	7m-26d	K2	
French, Mary	1, Sept 1852	28, Aug.	75	P2	
French, Mary Jane	11, Nov. 1838	Nov.	11w	N3	
French, Z.P.	7, Dec. 1837		probate	N3	
Friermutte, Joseph	27, Aug. 1852	Aug.	31	P2	
Frigh, (child of Joseph)	27, Aug. 1830	Aug.	stillborn	N3	
Frilingsdorf, William	21, Oct. 1826		estate	J3	
Frintz, Charles M.	28, June 1850	27, June	2- -9d	P2	
Fritman, Dorotha	6, July 1849	July	40	L2	
Fritsch, Victoria	31, July 1841	July	54	R3	
Frohmingk, Anthony	6, July 1849	July	20	L2	
Fromeier, Henry	19, Sept 1850	Sept	26	Y2	
Fromentin, Elegius	9, Nov. 1822	6, Nov.		S3	
Fromentin, Elizabeth	9, Nov. 1822	5, Nov.		S3	
Froome, Mary Elizabeth	29, June 1849	27, June	1- 9m	L2	
Frost, Isaac	11, Dec. 1827		probate	N3	
Frost, Isaac	4, Mar. 1828		probate	N3	
Frost, John	21, Dec. 1830		probate	N3	
Frost, Nathaniel (Major)	5, Oct. 1835		88	T2	
Frost, Thomas	11, Dec. 1827		probate	N3	
Frost, Thomas	4, Mar. 1828		probate	N3	
Frothingham, Nathaniel	4, Mar. 1825		79	N2	
Frute, George	8, Feb. 1812		estate	S3	
Fry, Ann Penrose	15, Nov. 1837	9, Nov.		T2	
Fry, John	10, July 1830		estate	R3	
Fry, Zaver	25, July 1840	July	26	R3	
Fuchs, (Mr)	29, July 1834	July		T2	
Fudira, George	5, Sept 1828	Sept	19- 7m	N3	
Fuller, George	23, Apr. 1841	Apr.	36	N2	
Fuller, Henry	28, Apr. 1847	25, Apr.	51	K2	
Fuller, John	7, May 1847	6, May	70	K2	
Funk, (child of Henry B)	21, Oct. 1828	Oct.	1d	N2	
Funk, Eliza Ely Selden	24, Feb. 1838	15, Feb.		T2	
Furman, J.F.	3, May 1838			N2	
Fyffe, Martha	29, July 1852	26, July	6m-10d	P2	

Name	Notice Date	Death Date	Age		Page	Maiden Name
Fyne, Jane	27, Dec. 1847	25, Dec.			K2	
Gaddis, Thomas	18, Mar. 1831	7, Feb.	60		X3	
Gage, William Albert	7, Apr. 1836	Oct.	18m		X3	
Gaines, (Mrs)	12, Dec. 1836	29, Nov.			T3	
Gaines, Elizabeth Virginia	8, June 1841	22, May	8m-11d		N2	
Gains, Nancy	6, Sept 1833	Sept	20		X3	
Gale, John (Dr)	27, Aug. 1830	27, July	35		N2	
Gales, Joseph	2, Sept 1841	24, Aug.	80	*	N2	
Galey, Margaret	20, Aug. 1830	Aug.	90		N3	
Gallagher, Abigail	30, Sept 1835	25, Sept	63	*	T2	
Gallagher, Abigail	30, Sept 1835	25, Sept	63	*	N2	
Gallagher, Margaret	25, June 1849	22, June			L2	
Gallitzin, Demetrius (Rev)	30, May 1840	6, May	70	*	R3	
Galloway, James	14, Aug. 1838	7, Aug.	89		T2	
Gallup, Elizabeth Stone	9, Aug. 1834	29, July	19- 9m	*	R3	
Gamage, Julia	17, Sept 1830	Sept	14		N3	
Gamage, Samuel	29, Apr. 1824	24, Apr.	42	*	E3	
Gamage, Samuel	4, Mar. 1828		probate		N3	
Gamage, Samuel	19, Aug. 1828		probate		N3	
Gamble, William	17, June 1837		probate		N2	
Gammel, Thomas	22, Dec. 1829		probate		N3	
Gammell, Thomas	16, May 1828		estate		N3	
Gannett, Deborah	25, May 1827	29, Apr.	67		N3	
Gannon, Eleanor	26, Sept 1828	Sept	72		N3	
Gano, A.G. (Mrs)	13, May 1837	9, May			R3	
Gano, A.G. (Mrs)	10, May 1837	9, May			T2	
Gano, Charles B.	13, Mar. 1848	12, Mar.	9m-21d		K2	
Gano, Isaac E. (Dr)	2, Nov. 1811	8, Oct.	42		S3	
Gano, John (Rev)	29, Aug. 1804	23, Aug.	79	*	S2	
Gano, John S. (Gen)	5, 19, Jan. 1822	3, Jan.			S3	
Gano, Rebecca L.	27, May 1836	25, May	2		T2	
Gano, Richard M. (Gen)	3, Nov. 1815	22, Oct.	41		S3	
Gano, Stephen (Lt)	12, Sept 1812	8, Sept			S3	
Gano, Stephen (Rev)	6, Sept 1828	18, Aug.			R3	
Gano, Theodore	9, Sept 1831	Sept	11m		A3	
Gano, Theodore S.	27, Aug. 1830	Aug.	35		N3	
Gaphart, Peter	6, Nov. 1805		estate		S3	
Garard, John	3, Oct. 1823		estate		N3	
Garber, A.W.	28, June 1834	24, June			R3	
Gard, Gersham	16, Dec. 1825		probate		N3	
Gard, Gershum	19, Jan. 1807	28, Dec.	70		S3	
Gard, Seth	11, Dec. 1827		probate		N3	
Gard, Seth	10, Mar. 1829		probate		N3	
Gardiner, Benjamin	4, Feb. 1825	24, Jan.		*	N2	
Gardner, (dau. of Rachel)	8, July 1828	July	14m		N3	
Gardner, (heirs)	14, Dec. 1835		probate		N2	
Gardner, (man)	13, Nov. 1852	12, Nov.			P2	
Gardner, Enoch	12, Feb. 1828		92	*	N3	
Gardner, George	25, June 1830	June	18- -21d		N3	
Gardner, James	11, June 1838	4, June	65	*	T2	
Gardner, James	31, Oct. 1804		estate		S4	
Gardner, Josiah	1, June 1835		probate		N2	
Gardner, Sarah	30, Sept 1831	29, Sept			X3	
Garfforth, John	28, June 1849	June	50		L2	

Name	Notice Date	Death Date	Age	Page	Maiden Name
Garnett, Elijah	19, Sept 1835	16, Sept	52	T2	
Garran, Michael	12, Apr. 1849	Apr.	35	L2	
Garrard, Abner	15, May 1819	21, Apr.		S3	
Garrard, J.	15, Feb. 1836		estate	T3	
Garrard, J.D.	5, Mar. 1836		estate	T3	
Garrard, J.D.	6, Apr. 1836		estate	N2	
Garrard, Jeptha D.	28, Jan. 1836	27, Jan.		T3	
Garrard, Nancy	10, Dec. 1835	17, Nov.	62	X3	
Garrard, Nancy	16, Dec. 1835	17, Nov.		T3	
Garrard, William	7, Dec. 1837		probate	N3	
Garretson, Sarah	15, June 1836	10, June		T2	
Garrigus, David	1, Nov. 1816		estate	S2	
Garrison, Elizabeth	23, July 1830	July	10m	N3	
Garrison, Margaret A.	10, July 1849	9, July		L2	Handy
Garrison, Susan M.	20, Dec. 1852	17, Dec.		P2	
Gaskil, George	24, Oct. 1828	Oct.	9m	N2	
Gasley, Jane	20, Aug. 1830	Aug.	20	N3	
Gassam, Hannah	15, Aug. 1850	Aug.	4	Y2	
Gassaway, H.	2, Jan. 1829	Dec.	1d	N3	
Gassaway, Henry	3, Aug. 1835	12, July		T2	
Gassaway, Nicholas G.R.	31, Oct. 1829	21, Oct.		R2	
Gaston, J.B.P.	31, Aug. 1820	28, Aug.	55	S3	
Gaston, Joseph H.	9, Dec. 1828		probate	N3	
Gaston, Joseph H.	21, Dec. 1830		probate	N3	
Gates, Abner	17, June 1837		probate	N2	
Gates, Elizabeth	26, Dec. 1840	Dec.	20	R3	
Gatewood, Sarah	27, Feb. 1829	Feb.	70	N3	
Gause, John D.	22, Aug. 1834			X3	
Gay, James	9, Oct. 1841	21, Sept	96	* N2	
Gazlay, James (Mrs)	26, Dec. 1817	17, Dec.		S3	
Gazley, James	4, Nov. 1828	Oct.	2- 2m	N3	
Gazzam, (child of C.W.)	13, Aug. 1830	Aug.	2d	N3	
Gazzam, Harriet B.	5, Sept 1838	27, Aug.		T2	
Geary, (child)	25, July 1850	July	9m	Y2	
Gee, Thomas	20, July 1850	20, July		P2	
Gehalt, Benjamin (Dr)	19, July 1834	July	44	R3	
Gehrum, Philip J.	13, July 1849	July	83	L2	
Geizer, Samuel	7, June 1849	June	87	L2	
George, (Capt)	5, July 1837	3, June	70	T2	
Gerard, William	1, May 1837		estate	N2	
German, Caleb	28, Apr. 1821		estate	S3	
German, Caleb	6, Oct. 1826		probate	N3	
German, Caleb	19, Dec. 1826		probate	N3	
Geskel, Patrick	8, Aug. 1850	Aug.	7m	Y2	
Gest, William	12, June 1819	6, June		S3	
Gib, Eliza	28, May 1830	May	6m	N3	
Gibbs, John W.	22, July 1851	21, July		P2	
Gibbs, Justus	27, July 1836	22, July	71	T3	
Gibson, Alfred Alexander	3, June 1824	18, May	8m	E3	
Gibson, Crawford	6, Jan. 1831	3, Jan.		* A3	
Gibson, Elizabeth	27, Jan. 1832	13, Jan.		X3	
Gibson, Emaline	3, June 1824	29, May	3- 3m	E3	
Gibson, James	3, Apr. 1829	Mar.	70	N2	
Gibson, James	7, Apr. 1829	28, Mar.	72	N3	

Name	Notice Date	Death Date	Age		Page	Maiden Name
Gibson, James	2, Oct. 1829		estate		N3	
Gibson, John (Gen)	1, June 1822		82	*	S4	
Gibson, Lydia	3, June 1824	1, June	67	*	E3	
Gibson, Martha	10, June 1841	29, May			N2	
Gibson, Mary	21, July 1852	16, July	31		P2	
Gibson, Thomas	5, Sept 1818				S3	
Gibson, William	21, Sept 1838		probate		N3	
Gibson, Woolman (Capt)	10, Oct. 1835	21, Sept		*	T2	
Gibson, Woolman (Capt)	10, Oct. 1835	21, Sept		*	N2	
Gideon, Elizabeth Ann Shaw	23, July 1852	14, July	2- 1m-17d		P2	
Gilbert, Ashley M. (Rev)	2, Nov. 1837	9, Sept		*	X3	
Gilbert, Chauncy G.	13, Sept 1847	12, Sept	32	*	K2	
Gilbert, Sarah	13, Dec. 1847	9, Dec.	64		K2	
Gilbreath, (child of Hugh)	15, Sept 1827	Sept	11m		R3	
Gilbreath, (heirs)	4, June 1836		probate		N2	
Gilbreath, Hugh	17, Sept 1835		probate		T2	
Gilbreath, Hugh	1, June 1835		probate		N2	
Gildersleve, Nelly	2, Feb. 1803	30, Jan.			S3	
Gilderslieve, Isaac	28, Aug. 1805		estate		S3	
Giles, Ezekiel (Major)	28, Apr. 1827		85		R3	
Giles, Ezekiel (Major)	20, Apr. 1827		85		N3	
Giles, George B.	16, Apr. 1830		estate		N3	
Giles, William B.	21, Dec. 1830	4, Dec.	69		N3	
Giles, William B.	20, Dec. 1830	4, Dec.			A3	
Giles, William Lewis	28, Sept 1852	25, Sept	2- -3d		P2	
Gill, Mary	21, June 1849	June	3m		L2	
Gill, Michael	28, Aug. 1852	26, Aug.			P2	
Gillaspey, James H.	19, July 1809	14, July			H3	
Gillaspie, Robert	14, Oct. 1825	8, Sept	40		N2	
Gilleland, David	22, Dec. 1829		probate		N3	
Gilliland, Israel	9, Oct. 1841	4, Oct.	28		R3	
Gilliland, Israel	8, Oct. 1841	4, Oct.	28		N2	
Gilliland, James	30, Apr. 1814		estate		S1	
Gillman, Joseph	3, June 1806	14, May	68		S3	
Gilman, Andrew	3, May 1838				N2	
Gilman, Emeline	9, July 1830	July	19m		N3	
Gilman, Hannah	21, Sept 1837	24, Aug.	69		X3	
Gilman, Joseph	19, Aug. 1823	17, Aug.	31	*	N3	
Gilmore, Gurdon R.	14, Dec. 1835		probate		N2	
Gilmore, Gurdon R.	27, Oct. 1832	21, Oct.			R3	
Gilmore, Jane	18, Jan. 1836				N2	
Gilmore, John	18, May 1838		probate		N2	
Gilmore, John	18, Jan. 1836				N2	
Gilpin, Gideon	14, Oct. 1825	20, Aug.	88		N2	
Gilson, Jacob	26, July 1850	July	30		Y2	
Gimble, Henry	20, Oct. 1826		estate		Q3	
Gimble, Margaret	27, June 1812	22, June			S3	
Gin, (child of Austin)	14, May 1830	May	1d		N3	
Girard, Stephen	7, Jan. 1832	26, Dec.			R3	
Girard, Stephen	6, Jan. 1832				X3	
Given, Sarah	7, Sept 1836		probate		N2	
Glaize, John	16, Jan. 1841	Jan.	51		N2	
Glaize, John	16, Jan. 1841	Jan.	54		R3	
Glancey, William A.	6, Sept 1852				P2	

Name	Notice Date	Death Date	Age	Page	Maiden Name
Glancy, William A.	1, Sept 1852	27, Aug.		P2	
Glasco, George M.	16, July 1830	July	1- 6m	N3	
Glasco, Susan J.	9, Sept 1831	Sept	7	A3	
Glascoe, Henry Reese	2, 9, July 1842	25, June	6	R3	
Glascoe, James Dill	9, July 1842	4, July	7	R3	
Glascoe, James Dill	6, July 1842	4, July	7	N2	
Glascoe, Josephine	6, July 1842	3, July	2- 3m	N2	
Glasgow, Samuel R.	3, Sept 1830	Aug.	20	N2	
Glass, James	24, Dec. 1830	Dec.	30	N3	
Glass, James	21, Dec. 1830	18, Dec.	40	N3	
Glendening, Adam	6, Feb. 1829	Feb.		N2	
Glenn, Ann B.	3, Feb. 1829	Jan.	34	N3	
Glenn, Elizabeth	23, Oct. 1819	20, Oct.		S3	Drake
Glenn, Hannah	26, Sept 1840	16, Sept	58	* R3	
Glenn, Hugh	1, June 1833			R3	
Glenn, Jonathan	21, June 1849	June	2	L2	
Glenn, Mary Jane	22, Aug. 1828	Aug.	8m	N3	
Glenn, Wilson	6, June 1835	3, June		T2	
Glover, (child)	26, July 1834	July	stillborn	R3	
Glover, (child)	22, July 1834	July	stillborn	T2	
Glover, Elias	2, July 1814		estate	S3	
Glover, Elias	12, Oct. 1811	5, Oct.		S3	
Glover, William Flintham	17, Aug. 1842	7, Aug.		N2	
Gobel, William K.	22, Oct. 1830	Oct.	25	N3	
Goddard, Stephen	8, Oct. 1841			N2	
Godden, Eliza	28, Oct. 1852	26, Oct.	16m-26d	P2	
Godfrey, Calvin	18, Apr. 1840			R3	
Godman, John D. (Dr)	1, May 1830	17, Apr.	32	* R3	
Goforth, A.	23, Oct. 1813		estate	S3	
Goforth, Aaron	16, Nov. 1811	10, Nov.	36	S3	
Goforth, Aaron	30, July 1814		estate	S3	
Goforth, Aaron	10, Oct. 1823		estate	N3	
Goforth, Aaron	14, Dec. 1824		probate	N3	
Goforth, Aaron	16, Dec. 1824		probate	E3	
Goforth, William (Dr)	13, June 1817		51	* S2	
Goforth, William (Dr)	16, May 1817	13, May		S3	
Goforth, William (Mrs)	26, May 1827			R3	
Golden, Barnabas	26, Oct. 1835		estate	N4	
Golden, Barnabas	6, Feb. 1836		estate	N4	
Golden, Barnabus	20, Mar. 1838		probate	N3	
Goldsmith, Abraham	1, Dec. 1810			S3	
Goldtrap, John	17, Sept 1830		estate	N3	
Goliver, Ruth	19, Aug. 1831	Aug.	45	A3	
Gooch, John A. (Capt)	3, Apr. 1807	7, Mar.		S3	
Goodall, John William	27, Nov. 1852	25, Nov.	3- 3m	P2	
Goodall, Martha Ann	27, Nov. 1852	20, Nov.	6- 9m	P2	
Goodall, Mary Frances	27, Nov. 1852	20, Nov.	18m	P2	
Gooddel, Lucy C.	2, Dec. 1831	16, Oct.		* X3	Childs
Goode, Sarah Crane	22, Oct. 1852	20, Oct.	30	P2	
Goodell, John	3, Jan. 1826		estate	N3	
Goodell, John	27, Jan. 1826		estate	N3	
Goodenow, John M.	20, July 1838	20, July	56	T2	
Goodenow, John M.	21, July 1838	20, July		R3	
Goodheart, A.	7, July 1852	4, July	20	P2	

Name	Notice Date	Death Date	Age		Page	Maiden Name
Goodhouse, Susanna P.	26, July 1834	July	5- -31d		R3	
Goodhouse, Susanna P.	22, July 1834	July	5- -31d		T2	
Goodin, Daniel R.	29, Dec. 1852	7, Dec.			P2	
Goodin, Philip	18, June 1830	June	25		N3	
Goodles, Adam	3, Sept 1830	Aug.	60		N2	
Goodman, Edwin Adams	4, Feb. 1848	31, Jan.	5m		K2	
Goodrich, Edward	26, Sept 1828	Sept	2w		N3	
Goodrich, Jeremiah	9, May 1812		estate		S3	
Goodwin, (child of Griffith)	24, Feb. 1829	Feb.	stillborn		N3	
Goodwin, Catharine	19, Aug. 1831	Aug.	6m		A3	
Goodwin, Edward	8, July 1828	July	5		N3	
Goodwin, Edward	13, July 1849	July	35		L2	
Goodwin, Edward	2, Sept 1835		estate		N2	
Goodwin, Nathan	6, Feb. 1841	Feb.	17		R3	
Goodwin, Oliver	17, Mar. 1838	11, Mar.	78	*	R3	
Goodwin, Oliver (Dr)	12, Mar. 1838	11, Mar.	78		T3	
Goodwin, William R.	23, Sept 1824		estate		E3	
Goodwin, William R.	13, Jan. 1825		estate		E3	
Goodwin, William R.	11, Dec. 1827		probate		N3	
Goodwin, William R.	4, Mar. 1828		probate		N3	
Goodwin, William R.	19, Aug. 1828		probate		N3	
Gorden, Daniel	3, Sept 1830	Aug.	10m		N2	
Gordon, George	30, Aug. 1837		estate		N3	
Gordon, H.G.	14, June 1836		estate		N2	
Gordon, H.G.	11, Sept 1837		probate		N2	
Gordon, Horatio G.	21, Sept 1838		probate		N3	
Gordon, Jane	19, Nov. 1831	2, Nov.	24		R3	
Gordon, Lewis W.	9, Mar. 1841	6, Mar.	62		N2	
Gordon, Mary	21, May 1849	20, May			L2	
Gordon, Sally W.	13, Mar. 1819	6, Mar.			S2	
Gordon, William	16, July 1830	July	10m		N3	
Gorham, Parsons	31, May 1837	31, May	60		T2	
Gorman, (child of James)	31, May 1841	27, May	3m		N2	
Gorman, Alice	1, Sept 1852	31, Aug.			P2	
Gorman, George	3, Feb. 1842	1, Feb.			N2	
Gorman, James (Mrs)	2, Sept 1852	29, Aug.			P2	
Goshorn, (child of Nicholas)	9, Dec. 1828	Dec.	1d		N3	
Goshorn, David	16, Oct. 1841		estate		R3	
Goshorn, Margaret	9, Dec. 1828	Dec.	21		N3	
Goshorn, Theodore	3, Feb. 1829	Jan.	22m		N3	
Goslee, George	2, June 1837		estate		T2	
Gosman, Ann	27, Oct. 1832	22, Oct.	59		R3	
Gossin, (son of B.F.)	2, Aug. 1850	1, Aug.	4- 6m		P2	
Gossin, Catharine	9, Oct. 1847	8, Oct.			K2	Bowman
Gossin, Harriet	21, July 1850	20, July	49		Y2	
Gossin, Malvira	2, Sept 1836	31, Aug.	8		N2	
Gossin, Margaretta Ann	27, Nov. 1852	11, Nov.	20		P2	
Gotschalk, Augustus	6, July 1849	July	23		L2	
Gott, Henry Conrad	11, Aug. 1850	8, Aug.	18m-12d		Y2	
Gottermutte, Philip	17, Oct. 1840	Oct.	28		R3	
Goudy, Richard (guardian of)	7, Dec. 1837		probate		N3	
Goudy, Thomas	21, May 1814		estate		S3	
Gould, James	26, May 1838	11, May	68		R3	
Gould, Lauretta Theresa	21, July 1852	20, July	1w- 5d		P2	

Name	Notice Date	Death Date	Age		Page	Maiden Name
Gould, Nathan	7, Sept 1824		probate		N3	
Gould, Nathan	14, Dec. 1824		probate		N3	
Gould, Nathan	9, Sept 1824		probate		E3	
Gould, Nathan	16, Dec. 1824		probate		E3	
Gould, Uzal W.	30, Oct. 1823		estate		J3	
Gourdin, Louis J.	27, Oct. 1832	25, Oct.		*	R3	
Gourgas, Jacob	17, Nov. 1821	16, Nov.			S3	
Gove, Ann Eliza	23, Jan. 1838	20, Jan.	6		T2	
Gove, Lucinda Maria	23, Jan. 1838	16, Jan.	4		T2	
Gowan, John	7, Oct. 1851	4, Oct.			P2	
Gowdy, Theo.	24, July 1850	July	45		Y2	
Gowen, Andrew	7, May 1830	May	7m		N3	
Grabe, Louis	22, Aug. 1850	Aug.	30		Y2	
Grace, Edward Fenwick	24, July 1829	21, July			N3	
Grace, Eliza	26, Sept 1840	27, Aug.	16		R3	
Grace, Michael	24, Oct. 1840	Oct.	28		R3	
Grade, James M.	17, May 1849	May	50		L2	
Grady, Matthew	24, May 1849	May	28		L2	
Graham, Aaron	6, Feb. 1829	Feb.	72		N2	
Graham, Abner	15, Aug. 1829		estate		R3	
Graham, Archibald	10, Feb. 1832	31, Jan.			X3	
Graham, Elizabeth	25, July 1817	21, July			S3	
Graham, Ellen D.	8, Aug. 1834				X3	Strickland
Graham, George	23, Aug. 1830				A3	
Graham, John	4, Nov. 1837	18, Oct.	42		R3	
Graham, Julia	18, Mar. 1831	17, Mar.			A3	Yeatman
Graham, Thomas	31, Mar. 1838				N2	
Graham, W.L. (Capt)	24, Oct. 1835	6, Oct.			T2	
Graham, William	12, Jan. 1829	Jan.	33		N2	
Graham, William	8, July 1828	July	2m		N3	
Graham, William L.	3, Nov. 1835		estate		N3	
Graland, James	15, Nov. 1852	10, Nov.			P2	
Grandin, Martha Ann	27, Oct. 1821	22, Oct.	infant		S3	
Grandin, Mary Frances	13, June 1818	12, June	infant		S3	
Granger, Artimetia	19, Dec. 1829	27, Nov.			R3	
Grant, (child of John)	24, June 1828	June	3m		N3	
Grant, Alfred R.	10, Feb. 1851	9, Feb.			P2	
Grant, Benjamin	14, Dec. 1835		probate		N2	
Grant, Henry	21, Dec. 1830		probate		N3	
Grant, John H.	29, Aug. 1818	27, Aug.		*	S3	
Grant, Sidney S.	9, July 1830	July	8m		N3	
Grany, Mary	10, May 1849	May	3		L2	
Gratiot, Henry	19, May 1836	27, Apr.			X3	
Graves, John C. (Capt)	2, May 1840		83		R3	
Gray, James	17, Feb. 1829	Feb.	50		N3	
Gray, James	27, Jan. 1832	13, Jan.			X3	
Gray, Samuel	1, June 1835		probate		N2	
Gray, Samuel	4, June 1836		probate		N2	
Gray, William	22, Nov. 1825	4, Nov.	75		N3	
Gray, William	18, Mar. 1837	4, Mar.			T2	
Grealy, Mary	14, June 1849	June	19		L2	
Greely, M.T.	22, Aug. 1828	Aug.	16m		N3	
Green, Anderson	9, Aug. 1841	Aug.	29		N2	
Green, Charles	15, Aug. 1818	7, Aug.		*	S3	

Name	Notice Date	Death Date	Age		Page	Maiden Name
Green, David	21, Nov. 1840	14, Nov.			R3	
Green, Fenelon	31, Aug. 1833		estate		R3	
Green, Hope	8, Sept 1827	Sept	66		R3	
Green, John (Mrs)	4, Nov. 1825	31, Oct.			N2	
Green, Michael	21, Oct. 1828	Oct.	22		N2	
Green, Michael	23, Mar. 1830		probate		N3	
Green, Michael	20, Mar. 1838		probate		N3	
Green, Nancy	21, Nov. 1840	11, Nov.	23		R3	
Green, Nancy	20, Aug. 1830	Aug.	50		N3	
Green, William	2, May 1823		estate		N3	
Green, William	22, Aug. 1823		estate		N3	
Green, William	4, Mar. 1823	28, Feb.		*	N3	
Greenan, Patrick	21, Nov. 1840	Nov.	28		R3	
Greenawalt, George	1, Oct. 1841	15, Sept	35	*	N2	
Greene, Elizabeth	7, Jan. 1832	1, Jan.			R3	
Greene, Elizabeth	6, Jan. 1832	1, Jan.			X3	
Greene, Emily Ann	19, Nov. 1841	16, Nov.	4- 3m		N2	
Greene, T.C. (Dr)	7, Nov. 1840	19, Oct.	29		R3	
Greener, John	17, Sept 1835		probate		T2	
Greener, John	7, Sept 1830		probate		N3	
Greener, John	21, Dec. 1830		probate		N3	
Greener, John	1, June 1835		probate		N2	
Greener, John	3, Aug. 1822	27, July			S3	
Greenham, Daniel	15, Jan. 1814	12, Jan.			S3	
Greenham, Richard	13, June 1840	June	49		R3	
Greenleaf, Edmond H.	20, Aug. 1830	Aug.	2- 8m		N3	
Greenleaf, Mariam	25, Dec. 1841	25, Dec.			R3	
Greenwell, Barnabas	25, Aug. 1829		probate		N3	
Greenwood, Howard W. (Mrs)	7, Sept 1835	31, Aug.	23		T2	Hill
Greenwood, Howard W. (Mrs)	8, Sept 1835	31, Aug.	23	*	N2	Hill
Greenwood, Margaret Howard	9, Apr. 1842	5, Apr.	7		R3	
Greer, Dixon	10, Sept 1808		estate		S2	
Greer, Dixon	18, Oct. 1816		estate		S3	
Greer, James	18, June 1814		estate		S3	
Greer, John	18, Oct. 1816		estate		S3	
Gregg, Amos	11, Sept 1837		probate		N2	
Gregg, Israel (Capt)	26, June 1847	20, June	72		K2	
Gregg, Jarvis (Rev)	14, July 1836				X3	
Gregg, Thomas R.	22, Sept 1827	Sept	65		R3	
Gregor, (child of David)	25, June 1830	June	9m		N3	
Gregor, Frederick L.	12, Aug. 1831	Aug.	8m		A3	
Gregory, Benjamin	22, Mar. 1842	14, Mar.	68		N2	
Gregory, Caroline H.	26, Oct. 1852	24, Oct.			P2	
Gregory, Ellen Antoinette	25, July 1840	15, July			R3	
Grenning, John	7, June 1828	June			R3	
Grery, Charles	20, Aug. 1847	17, Aug.	1- 3m		K2	
Gresemeere, George	14, Apr. 1837		estate		N2	
Grib, Henry B.	25, June 1849	23, June			L2	
Gridley, E.G.	14, Mar. 1828		estate		N3	
Gridley, E.G.	7, Sept 1830		probate		N3	
Griffin, Bridget	7, June 1849	June	20		L2	
Griffin, George Hancock (Capt)	29, Oct. 1839	7, Oct.			T2	
Griffin, Rosetta	7, June 1849	June	9		L2	
Griffith, Benjamin	23, Jan. 1841	Jan.	25		R3	

Name	Notice Date	Death Date	Age	Page	Maiden Name
Griffith, Benjamin	21, Jan. 1841	Jan.	25	N2	
Griffith, Benjamin	15, Jan. 1835		estate	N2	
Griffith, Benjamin	11, Mar. 1831		estate	X3	
Griffith, Benjamin	21, Sept 1838		probate	N3	
Griffith, Elizabeth	19, Nov. 1834			T2	
Griffith, Josephine	19, June 1850	18, June	25	* P2	
Griffith, Maria	14, June 1849	June	30	L2	
Griffith, Mary A.	2, Aug. 1834	July	1- 2m	R3	
Griffith, Mary A.	29, July 1834	July	1- 2m	T2	
Griffith, Thomas	2, Sept 1825			N3	
Griffith, Walter	30, Nov. 1822		estate	S3	
Griffith, William	11, Sept 1837		probate	N2	
Grigar, Margaret	28, June 1849	June	2w	L2	
Grigg, Samuel	2, Jan. 1829	Dec.	27	N3	
Griggs, Ebenezer	20, Feb. 1823		estate	J3	
Griggs, Ebenezer	6, July 1822	4, July		S3	
Griggs, Ebenezer	7, Nov. 1822			J3	
Griggs, Jane	28, June 1849	June	24	L2	
Grill, Catherine	12, Aug. 1831	Aug.	2m	A3	
Grimans, John	23, July 1830	July	35	N3	
Grimes, James	17, Sept 1835		probate	T2	
Grimes, James	4, June 1836		probate	N2	
Grimes, James	28, June 1828			R3	
Grimes, John (Col)	26, May 1836	13, May		X3	
Grimke, Thomas S.	16, Oct. 1834	11, Oct.	48	* T2	
Grismore, George	18, Mar. 1835		estate	N2	
Grismore, George	4, Apr. 1837		probate	N2	
Grismore, George	17, June 1837		probate	N2	
Grismore, George	6, Nov. 1838		probate	N2	
Grisson, (child)	3, May 1849	May	child	L2	
Grisson, Henrietta	3, May 1849	May	28	L2	
Gristall, Margaret	6, July 1849	July		L2	
Griswold, James F.	9, Nov. 1811	16, Oct.	22	S2	
Griswold, Stanley	13, Oct. 1815	21, Aug.		S3	
Griswould, Roger	21, Nov. 1812	Oct.	51	S3	
Groesbeck, Mary A.	10, Dec. 1852	7, Dec.	14- 2m	P2	
Groff, Sarah	17, Sept 1835		probate	T2	
Groshon, Belinda	2, Feb. 1822	31, Jan.		S3	
Gross, George Frederick	26, May 1834	25, May	2	T2	
Gross, Jacob	6, Mar. 1841	Feb.		R3	
Gross, Nicholas	2, Aug. 1834	July	54	R3	
Gross, Nicholas	29, July 1834	July	54	T2	
Grout, Jonathan	5, Apr. 1825	12, Mar.	60	N3	
Grove, William Barry	2, May 1818	30, Mar.		S3	
Grover, Fancis	21, Oct. 1828	Oct.	39	N2	
Groves, Margaret	12, Nov. 1847	5, Nov.		K2	
Gruba, Sabina	28, June 1849	June	53	L2	
Grumbine, Laura Louisa	23, Nov. 1852	22, Nov.	6- 2m	P2	
Grundy, John R.	14, July 1836	6, July	33	X3	
Guest, Henry	3, Aug. 1820	9, July	61	S3	
Guest, Henry C.	18, Nov. 1828	3, Nov.	34	* N3	
Guest, Lydia	12, Oct. 1822	9, Oct.	50	S3	
Guest, Moses (Capt)	25, 28, Mar. 1828	22, Mar.	73	* N3	
Guesuard, Marie	11, Sept 1837		probate	N2	

Name	Notice Date	Death Date	Age	Page	Maiden Name
Guider, Abraham	24, May 1849	May	20	L2	
Guion, Benjamin Coombs	26, June 1849	24, June	31	L2	
Gulick, Henry	11, Nov. 1828		estate	N3	
Gulick, John	19, May 1838	14, May	72	* T2	
Gulick, William G.	7, July 1832	2, July	46	R3	
Gunning, Robert	28, Aug. 1827		probate	N3	
Gunning, Robert	25, Aug. 1829		probate	N3	
Gunning, Robert	21, Dec. 1830		probate	N3	
Guthrie, Edward	23, July 1850	July	2	Y2	
Guthrie, Hannah	25, July 1817	23, July		S3	
Guy, Susan A.L.	16, Sept 1852	14, Sept	48	P2	
Gwer, Charlotte	23, July 1850	July	40	Y2	
Gwinn, David	29, Mar. 1834	Mar.	32	R3	
Gwynne, John W.	19, July 1834	July	5m	R3	
Gwynne, Mary Flagg	29, Aug. 1842	16, Aug.	18m- 8d	N2	
Gwynne, Thomas	8, July 1825	5, July		N3	
Hackenger, George	17, Sept 1835		probate	T2	
Hacket, Catharine	21, June 1849	June	3	L2	
Hackney, Isaac M.	7, Nov. 1840	20, Oct.	2- 3m	R3	
Haddlesey, Elizabeth	23, June 1849	22, June	22	L2	
Hafer, Henry	25, Mar. 1825	22, Mar.	40	N2	
Hafer, Henry	6, Apr. 1826		estate	N3	
Hafer, Henry	28, Aug. 1827		probate	N3	
Hafer, Henry	9, Dec. 1828		probate	N3	
Hafer, Henry	25, Aug. 1829		probate	N3	
Hafer, Henry	22, Dec. 1829		probate	N3	
Hafer, Henry	21, Dec. 1830		probate	N3	
Hafer, Mary Ann	26, June 1835	22, June	18	X2	
Haffner, John L.	9, Dec. 1828		probate	N3	
Hafner, John L.	27, July 1827		estate	N2	
Hagal, George	13, July 1849	July	43	L2	
Hagarty, Bridget	1, Aug. 1850	July	15m	Y2	
Hageman, Adrian L.	14, Dec. 1839		estate	R3	
Hageman, Christian	4, Apr. 1837		probate	N2	
Hageman, Laura D.	26, June 1841	24, June		R3	Bishop
Hagerdy, Julia Ann	18, July 1828	July	19m	N3	
Hagerman, Adrian	6, Oct. 1826		probate	N3	
Hagerman, Laura D.	26, June 1841	24, June		N2	Truman
Haggeford, Charlotte Bowers	21, Aug. 1834		11m	T2	
Haggeford, John	21, Aug. 1834		43	* T2	
Haggerty, J.H.	19, Dec. 1840	18, Dec.	45	N2	
Hagherty, Bryan	3, July 1852	2, July		P2	
Hailey, Patrick	27, Sept 1852	24, Sept		P2	
Hailman, Mary	24, Sept 1830	Sept	60	N3	
Hailman, Simon	8, Sept 1838	6, Sept	72	T2	
Haines, A.	20, Oct. 1826		estate	Q3	
Haines, Amos	27, Oct. 1821		estate	S3	
Haines, Amos	19, Aug. 1828		probate	N3	
Haines, Charles G.	19, July 1825	3, July		N3	
Haines, Robert	16, Dec. 1825		probate	N3	
Hains, Daniel S.	24, Dec. 1814		estate	S3	
Hains, Robert	2, Jan. 1805		estate	S2	
Halderman, Elizabeth	17, Sept 1852	16, Sept	4- 7m	P2	
Halderman, Peyton S.	2, Aug. 1834	July	20	R3	

Name	Notice Date	Death Date	Age		Page	Maiden Name
Halderman, Peyton S.	29, July 1834	July	20		T2	
Hales, Mary	29, June 1833	23, June			R3	
Hall, (child of James)	8, Oct. 1852	Oct.	13m		P2	
Hall, Anna L.	17, Aug. 1852	15, Aug.	53		P2	
Hall, Dominick A.	20, Jan. 1821	19, Dec.			S3	
Hall, Elijah	16, July 1830	29, June	88		N3	
Hall, Eliza W.	2, Apr. 1847	1, Apr.	32		K2	
Hall, Elizabeth	7, June 1849	June	1w		L2	
Hall, Elizabeth	4, May 1811	28, Apr.			S3	
Hall, Hugh	17, May 1816		estate		S3	
Hall, Hugh	10, Oct. 1817		estate		S2	
Hall, James	13, July 1849	July	33		L2	
Hall, James (Mrs)	1, Sept 1832			*	R3	Posey
Hall, Jane	8, Oct. 1852	Oct.	39		P2	
Hall, Jane	3, Aug. 1822	29, July			S3	
Hall, John A.	18, Nov. 1830	3, Nov.	24		A3	
Hall, Mary E.	1, Aug. 1828	July	1- 8m		N3	
Hall, Samuel	15, Nov. 1828				R3	
Hall, Samuel G.	10, Mar. 1829		probate		N3	
Hall, Samuel M.	11, Nov. 1828	10, Nov.			N3	
Hall, Stephen	30, Dec. 1828	Dec.	37		N3	
Hall, Stephen	31, Jan. 1829		estate		R3	
Hall, Stephen	19, Dec. 1828	18, Dec.			N3	
Hall, Thomas	6, Feb. 1841	1, Feb.	60	*	N2	
Hallain, Deborah	18, June 1830	June	9m		N3	
Hallam, Charles J.	26, July 1834	July	11m		R3	
Hallam, Charles J.	22, July 1834	July	11m		T2	
Hallam, Sarah	23, July 1824	16, July	42		N2	
Hallam, Sarah	22, July 1824	16, July		*	E3	
Hallenbrant, John	21, June 1849	June	67		L2	
Halley, Allen	12, Jan. 1807	4, Jan.	18		S3	
Halley, Josiah	29, Nov. 1816		estate		S3	
Halley, Josiah (Major)	8, Nov. 1816	29, Oct.			S3	
Halley, Margaret	24, Mar. 1847	23, Mar.	77		K2	
Halley, Maria	31, July 1819	28, July			S3	
Halley, Samuel	18, Sept 1813		estate		S1	
Halley, Samuel	5, Dec. 1818		estate		S1	
Halley, Samuel (Capt)	23, May 1812	14, May	47		S3	
Halliday, Horace C.	10, July 1849	6, July	6w- 5d		L2	
Halloway, Joseph	8, Jan. 1814		estate		S3	
Halsall, Mary	23, July 1850	July	2		Y2	
Ham, Hiram	7, Oct. 1828	Oct.	18		N3	
Hamel, John	11, Dec. 1827		probate		N3	
Hamet, James	12, Nov. 1830	11, Nov.			N3	
Hamet, John (Capt)	4, Apr. 1840	3, Apr.	63	*	R3	
Hamilton, Alexander (Gen)	5, Sept 1804				S4	
Hamilton, Catherine Ann	18, July 1828	July	19		N3	
Hamilton, Charles	24, May 1849	May	55		L2	
Hamilton, E.	20, Mar. 1847	15, Mar.	53		K2	
Hamilton, Emma Ann	10, Dec. 1830	Dec.	21d		N3	
Hamilton, Hiram	1, Oct. 1830	Sept	23		N3	
Hamilton, James	10, May 1849	May	20		L2	
Hamilton, John	11, Jan. 1808		estate		S1	
Hamilton, John T. (Rev)	9, Sept 1831	10, Aug.	39		X3	

Name	Notice Date	Death Date	Age		Page	Maiden Name
Hamilton, Martha Ludlow	31, Aug. 1852	29, Aug.			P2	
Hamilton, Martha Ludlow	1, Sept 1852	29, Aug.			P2	
Hamilton, Matilda	3, July 1852	1, July			P2	
Hamilton, Samuel	15, Aug. 1850	Aug.	40		Y2	
Hammel, John	8, Oct. 1824		estate		N3	
Hammil, (child)	27, Feb. 1849	26, Feb.			L3	
Hammond, Charles	11, Apr. 1840	3, Apr.	60	*	R3	
Hammond, George	3, May 1849	May			L2	
Hammond, Henry	7, Nov. 1829		20		R1	
Hammond, Henry	3, Nov. 1829	23, Oct.	20		N2	
Hammond, John	21, June 1849	June	75		L2	
Hammond, Michael	3, May 1849	May	40		L2	
Hammond, Sally C.	1, Aug. 1826	31, July			N2	
Hammond, Thomas	30, July 1831	24, June			R3	
Hammond, Timothy	26, July 1834	22, July	47	*	R3	
Hammond, Timothy	17, Sept 1835		probate		T2	
Hampton, Wade (Gen)	14, Mar. 1835	4, Mar.	81		N2	
Hamrick, James	19, Nov. 1830	Nov.	30		N3	
Hanagan, Jeffrey	3, May 1849	May	18		L2	
Hanahan, Cornelius	6, July 1849	July	35		L2	
Hanan, John	7, Feb. 1839	7, Feb.	30	*	T2	
Hancock, Edith	24, May 1849	May	44		L2	
Hand, James	8, July 1828	July	infant		N3	
Handley, Joanna	14, Feb. 1818	5, Feb.			S3	
Handley, N.P.	19, Sept 1818		estate		S3	
Handley, N.P.	19, Dec. 1817	18, Dec.			S3	
Handy, James	24, Oct. 1828	Oct.	38-11m		N2	
Hanes, Robert	15, Aug. 1804		estate		S3	
Hanna, Philomena	28, May 1835	20, May			T2	
Hannaford, Harriet	26, July 1850	July	55		Y2	
Hannah, (child of James)	2, Sept 1828	Aug.	10m		N3	
Hannegan, George A.	14, June 1837	20, May	25		T2	
Hans, Henry M.P.	16, Jan. 1841	Jan.	32		R3	
Hans, Henry M.P.	16, Jan. 1841	Jan.	32		N2	
Hanson, (Miss)	22, July 1834	July	19- 4m		T2	
Hanson, Alexander C.	15, May 1819		33		S3	
Hanson, Thomas	21, Nov. 1840	Nov.	48		R3	
Harbach, Justina	6, June 1840	June	69		R3	
Harbaugh, John	21, Jan. 1825		estate		N3	
Harbeson, Jane Morris	23, Feb. 1839	21, Feb.	3		T2	
Hardesty, Richard	20, Apr. 1847	28, Mar.	91- 6m		K2	
Hardin, Juliet	20, Oct. 1836	20, Sept	55	*	X3	
Hardin, Martin D. (Gen)	21, Oct. 1823	8, Oct.	43		N3	
Harding, Jonathan	3, Apr. 1830	1, Apr.	63	*	R3	
Harding, Josiah	14, Dec. 1835		probate		N2	
Harding, Mary P.C.	23, July 1850	July	39		Y2	
Harding, Simeon	18, June 1830	June	3m		N3	
Hardy, Elizabeth	16, July 1850	15, July	53		P2	
Hardy, William	30, July 1850	July	15m		Y3	
Hargan, Mary Virginia	3, Sept 1852	1, Sept	10m		P2	
Hargin, Mary	26, July 1834	July	31		R3	
Hargin, Mary	22, July 1834	July	31		T2	
Hargraves, Maxwell	20, Mar. 1838		probate		N3	
Hargy, Priscilla	2, Sept 1828	Aug.	1- 2m		N3	

Name	Notice Date	Death Date	Age		Page	Maiden Name
Harker, Eliza G.	12, Aug. 1828	Aug.	1- 6m		N3	
Harker, Jarvis Moss	23, Nov. 1852			*	P2	
Harkins, Alfred	23, Jan. 1837		estate		N2	
Harkins, Alfred	21, Sept 1838		probate		N3	
Harkness, Amanda	18, June 1830	June	1- 7m		N3	
Harlan, Carter B.	20, June 1840	9, June			R3	
Harman, Daniel	12, Nov. 1830	Nov.	48		N3	
Harman, Joseph	26, July 1834	July	2m		R3	
Harman, Joseph	22, July 1834	July	2m		T2	
Harness, Michael	8, June 1827		estate		Q2	
Harness, Michael	7, Sept 1836		probate		N2	
Harney, John M. (Dr)	8, Feb. 1825		25		N2	
Harper, Edward C.	26, Feb. 1842	26, Feb.	42	*	R3	
Harper, Francis J.	28, Mar. 1837	18, Mar.	38		T2	
Harper, James	3, Jan. 1848				K2	
Harper, Mary	19, Dec. 1826		probate		N3	
Harper, Rachel	23, May 1835	16, May	38		T2	Reeve
Harper, Rachel	29, May 1835	16, May	38		T2	
Harper, Robert Goodloe (Gen)	25, Jan. 1825	14, Jan.	60		N3	
Harper, Robert Goodloe (Gen)	27, Jan. 1825	13, Jan.			E3	
Harper, Samuel H.	1, Aug. 1837	18, July			T2	
Harran, Michael	24, May 1849	May	32		L2	
Harrington, Ira P.	10, Oct. 1835	12, Sept			T2	
Harrington, William	4, Mar. 1828		probate		N3	
Harris, Cora	14, July 1852	13, July	1- 6m-20d		P2	
Harris, Elizabeth	11, Mar. 1831				X3	
Harris, Francis Coldstream	31, Mar. 1849	26, Mar.	15- 7m		L2	
Harris, George W.	15, Sept 1827	Sept	3m		R3	
Harris, Jane	24, July 1850	July	46		Y2	
Harris, John	3, May 1849	May			L2	
Harris, Joseph	9, Sept 1825		probate		N3	
Harris, Joseph	16, Dec. 1825		probate		N3	
Harris, Joseph	4, June 1836		probate		N2	
Harris, Noah	25, May 1822		estate		S3	
Harris, Phebe	24, Feb. 1836	23, Feb.			N2	
Harris, Phoebe	25, Feb. 1836	23, Feb.			T3	
Harris, Robert	10, Aug. 1827		estate		N3	
Harris, Robert	29, Feb. 1828		estate		N3	
Harris, Robert	23, Sept 1828		estate		N3	
Harris, Robert	25, Aug. 1829		probate		N3	
Harris, Thaddeus M. (Rev)	15, Apr. 1842				N2	
Harris, Thomas (Rev)	27, Oct. 1832	19, Oct.		*	R3	
Harris, William	14, Dec. 1835		probate		N2	
Harrison, (child of David)	8, July 1828	July	infant		N3	
Harrison, Albert G.	12, Oct. 1839				R3	
Harrison, Benjamin	5, Jan. 1842		estate		N3	
Harrison, Benjamin (Dr)	20, June 1840	16, June	34		R3	
Harrison, Carter Basset	16, Aug. 1839	13, Aug.	27		T2	
Harrison, Clarissa B.	17, Feb. 1837	1, Feb.			T2	Pike
Harrison, Clarissa B.	20, Mar. 1837	1, Feb.			T2	Pike
Harrison, Edmund J.	3, Dec. 1824	27, Nov.	24		N3	
Harrison, Ephraim	24, Aug. 1852	23, Aug.	23		P2	
Harrison, George M.	2, Sept 1828	Aug.	1- 4m		N3	
Harrison, Henry L.	20, Aug. 1850	13, Aug.	3		Y2	

Name	Notice Date	Death Date	Age	Page	Maiden Name
Harrison, J. Symmes	5, Jan. 1842		estate	N3	
Harrison, J.C. Symmes	6, Nov. 1830	30, Oct.		R3	
Harrison, James L.	26, Sept 1828	Sept	23	N3	
Harrison, James L.	20, Sept 1828	18, Sept		R3	
Harrison, Job	22, Mar. 1837		estate	N2	
Harrison, Job	6, Nov. 1838		probate	N2	
Harrison, John C. Symmes	2, Nov. 1830	30, Oct.	32	N2	
Harrison, John Cleves Symmes	1, Nov. 1830	30, Oct.	32	A3	
Harrison, Joseph H.	23, July 1830	July	1- 7m	N3	
Harrison, Laura	9, Oct. 1840	8, Oct.	infant	N2	
Harrison, Louisa	10, Oct. 1840	8, Oct.	infant	R3	
Harrison, Mary Ann	3, Sept 1830	Aug.	1	N2	
Harrison, Mary J.	19, May 1847	18, May	34	K2	
Harrison, William H.	10, Feb. 1838	6, Feb.	36	N2	
Harrison, William H. (Gen)	5, Jan. 1842		estate	N3	
Harrison, William H., Jr.	5, Jan. 1842		estate	N3	
Harrison, William Henry	9, Apr. 1849	18, Mar.	21	L2	
Harrison, William Henry	10, Apr. 1841	4, Apr.		R3	
Harrison, William Henry (Gen)	9, Apr. 1841	4, Apr.		N2	
Hart, Abram	29, May 1819		estate	S3	
Hart, Abram	28, Jan. 1835		estate	N2	
Hart, Henry	16, Jan. 1829	Jan.	68	N2	
Hart, Jacob	28, Oct. 1835		estate	N4	
Hart, Jacob	17, June 1837		probate	N2	
Hart, John	23, Mar. 1830		probate	N3	
Hart, John S.	26, July 1838	20, July		T2	
Hart, Joseph	13, July 1849	July	33	L2	
Hart, Thomas	26, July 1834	July	42	R3	
Hart, Thomas	22, July 1834	July	42	T2	
Hartbun, Charles Christopher	9, Nov. 1852	6, Nov.	18m	P2	
Hartick, F.	11, July 1842		estate	N2	
Hartsgrave, Theodore	29, Mar. 1834	Mar.	3m	R3	
Hartshorn, (Capt)	5, July 1794	30, June		C3	
Hartshorn, Solomon	19, Aug. 1828	Aug.	25	N3	
Hartshorne, William	10, Nov. 1836	8, Nov.	61	T2	
Hartshorne, William	10, Nov. 1836	8, Nov.	61	N2	
Hartshorne, William Burrows	28, May 1842	28, May	8m- 8d	R3	
Hartshorne, William Burrows	24, May 1842	23, May	8m- 8d	N2	
Hartwell, Abbott Lawrence	2, Apr. 1847	1, Apr.	1	K2	
Hartwell, Eliza W.	4, May 1847	3, May	34	K2	
Hartwell, Francis Baymiller	22, Sept 1847	21, Sept	7m- 5d	K2	
Hartwell, Peter P.	12, July 1841	10, July		N2	
Harvey, Asa	10, Oct. 1804		estate	S3	
Harvey, Esther	27, Oct. 1826		estate	Q3	
Harvey, Mary	18, Aug. 1835	13, Aug.		T2	
Harvy, Andrew	6, Nov. 1838		probate	N2	
Harwood, George D.	30, May 1837	20, May	6- 9m	T2	
Harwood, William C.C.	3, Dec. 1852	1, Dec.	53	P2	
Haskins, Eliza	20, Sept 1833	Sept	33	X3	
Haskins, Mary J.	12, Aug. 1831	Aug.	3m	A3	
Haslam, Christopher Wells	27, Sept 1852	25, Sept	17	P2	
Hassenger, Henry	1, June 1849	May	34	L2	
Hastings, Cornelia	24, Feb. 1842	23, Feb.	16	N2	
Hastings, Henry V. Johns	28, Nov. 1840	16, Nov.	2- 6m	R3	

Name	Notice Date	Death Date	Age		Page	Maiden Name
Haston, William Allen	22, Sept 1852	20, Sept	5w- 4d		P2	
Hatch, Abner	2, Oct. 1819	26, Sept	66	*	S3	
Hatch, Jane	20, Mar. 1819	15, Mar.			S2	
Hatch, Jerusha A.	10, Apr. 1849	9, Apr.			L2	
Hatchett, Elizabeth	24, May 1849	May	25		L2	
Hatfield, Eliza	17, Sept 1830	Sept	25		N3	
Hatfield, Willis	26, Jan. 1848	21, Dec.			K2	
Hathaway, Henry	2, Nov. 1852	31, Oct.	83		P2	
Haughton, Ann	7, Sept 1822	3, Sept	72	*	S3	
Haughton, J. (Rev)	6, Mar. 1841	1, Mar.			R3	
Haughton, J. (Rev)	3, Mar. 1841	1, Mar.			N2	
Haughton, John	20, Mar. 1841		estate		R3	
Haughton, Richard	26, Apr. 1841	24, Apr.	45		N2	
Havens, Mary	21, Sept 1827	7, Sept			N3	
Hawes, Elliott Hastings	6, Oct. 1847	4, Oct.	infant		K2	
Hawkins, Andrew J.	2, Mar. 1849	16, Feb.			L2	
Hawkins, Carvel	19, Dec. 1826		probate		N3	
Hawkins, Eliza Jane	18, June 1830	June	3- 9m		N3	
Hawkins, Hannah M.	28, May 1830	May	1- 3m		N3	
Hawkins, Joseph	19, Dec. 1826		probate		N3	
Hawkins, Joseph	1, June 1835		probate		N2	
Hawkins, Josiah	6, Sept 1836		estate		T2	
Hawkins, Josiah	22, Dec. 1829		probate		N3	
Hawkins, Mary M.	8, July 1828	July	15m		N3	
Hawkins, Richard	16, Dec. 1825		probate		N3	
Hawkins, Robert	24, Dec. 1830	Dec.	50		N3	
Hawkins, William	8, Feb. 1839	7, Feb.	32		T2	
Hawley, Daniel Webster	29, May 1837	27, May	infant		N2	
Hay, George	7, Oct. 1830				A3	
Hay, Jacob	9, Feb. 1822		estate		S3	
Hay, William	16, Mar. 1807		estate		S1	
Hayden, Alfred	1, July 1831	29, June	34		A3	
Hayden, Benjamin	4, June 1830	3, June	35	*	N2	
Hayden, Benjamin	7, June 1830	3, June		*	A3	
Hayden, Benjamin	5, June 1830	3, June		*	R3	
Hayden, Benjamin	6, June 1828				Q3	
Hayden, Daniel	29, Oct. 1835		estate		N2	
Hayden, Daniel	7, Jan. 1836		estate		N2	
Hayden, Daniel	13, Mar. 1837		estate		N3	
Hayden, Daniel	11, Sept 1837		probate		N2	
Hayden, Joshua	14, Sept 1820	6, Sept	28	*	S3	
Hayden, Meriam Sumner	1, May 1829	29, Apr.		*	N2	
Hayden, Miriam	18, May 1833	12, May	71	*	R3	
Hayden, William	3, Mar. 1829		estate		N3	
Hayden, William	21, Dec. 1830		probate		N3	
Hayden, William	21, Sept 1838		probate		N3	
Hayes, James	26, Feb. 1835		estate		N2	
Hayes, John	6, June 1835		estate		N1	
Hayes, Joseph	29, Nov. 1816		estate		S3	
Hayes, R.P. (Dr)	10, Apr. 1837	8, Apr.	50		T2	
Hayes, R.P. (Dr)	11, Apr. 1837	8, Apr.	50		N2	
Hayne, Robert T. (Col)	12, Oct. 1839		49		R3	
Haynes, Henry	8, Dec. 1827	3, Dec.			R3	
Hays, David	22, Oct. 1851	20, Oct.			P2	

Name	Notice Date	Death Date	Age		Page	Maiden Name
Hays, Franklin	17, Sept 1830	Sept	3		N3	
Hays, John	20, Jan. 1825	18, Jan.			E3	
Hays, Oliver	26, Mar. 1830		estate		N3	
Hays, William	26, Apr. 1849	Apr.	36		L2	
Hayt, Charles James	9, Nov. 1833	31, Oct.	8		R3	
Hayward, Ann	21, Nov. 1840	8, Oct.	27		R3	McLean
Hayward, Caleb	12, Apr. 1836		estate		N2	
Hayward, Eliza	27, May 1834	19, May	46		T2	
Hazen, Bounetta	2, Aug. 1834	July	64- 6m		R3	
Hazen, Bounetta	29, July 1834	July	64- 6m		T2	
Hazen, Murat	1, July 1828	June	1		N3	
Hazen, Nathan L.	19, Feb. 1842	18, Feb.			N2	
Hazler, Henry	2, Aug. 1834	July	2		R3	
Hazler, Henry	29, July 1834	July	2		T2	
Hazleton, Horace	2, July 1830	June	37		N2	
Hazzard, Thomas K.	16, Dec. 1825		probate		N3	
Healy, James	1, June 1849	May	40		L2	
Hearn, Elizabeth	1, June 1835		probate		N2	
Hearsey, Mary Caroline	19, Apr. 1830	9, Mar.	24	*	A3	
Heath, David	9, Dec. 1828		probate		N3	
Heaton, George	16, Aug. 1841	13, Aug.	child		N2	
Heckewelder, John	21, Feb. 1823	31, Jan.	79		N3	
Hedge, Barnabas	25, July 1840		76		R3	
Hedger, Thomas	30, May 1836	29, May		*	T2	
Hedger, Thomas	31, May 1836	29, May		*	N2	
Hedges, (child of William)	4, June 1830	June	child		N3	
Hedges, Elias	18, Dec. 1813		estate		S3	
Heffener, Mary	30, July 1830	July	43		N3	
Heffner, Frederick	19, Dec. 1828		estate		N3	
Heffner, Frederick	1, June 1835		probate		N2	
Hegerty, William	25, June 1850	24, June			P2	
Heidelback, Simon	27, June 1849	26, June	31		L2	
Heighway, John	30, Dec. 1828	Dec.	42		N3	
Heil, Daniel	8, Aug. 1850	Aug.	1		Y2	
Heilman, John	8, Oct. 1841	Oct.	33		N2	
Heinger, George	19, July 1834	July			R3	
Helker, Ann	23, July 1850	July	2- 6m		Y2	
Heller, S.W.	22, Aug. 1828	Aug.	2m-15d		N3	
Hellstern, Eliza	13, July 1849	July	23		L2	
Helmick, Elizabeth	21, Dec. 1830		probate		N3	
Hempstead, Edward	5, Sept 1817	8, Aug.	38		S2	
Henderson, Aaron B.W.	17, Aug. 1820	14, Aug.	6		S3	
Henderson, Frederick	23, Feb. 1835	19, Jan.	43		N2	
Henderson, James	31, Oct. 1840	Oct.	6		R3	
Henderson, James	12, Feb. 1842		estate		R3	
Henderson, James	4, Apr. 1837	3, Apr.			T2	
Henderson, Mary A.	21, June 1849	June	19		L2	
Henderson, Mary W.	2, June 1849	24, May	69	*	L2	
Henderson, Mary W.	26, May 1849	23, May			L2	
Henderson, Nancy	21, June 1849	June	1w		L2	
Henderson, Thomas	27, Jan. 1832		estate		A3	
Hendreckson, William	14, June 1849	June	25		L2	
Henecy, Michael	8, Oct. 1841	Oct.	41		N2	
Hengehold, Philomena	25, July 1850	July	3		Y2	

Name	Notice Date	Death Date	Age	Page	Maiden Name
Henlock, William	5, May 1821		estate	S3	
Hennessey, Margaret	28, June 1849	June	37	L2	
Hennessy, Mary	14, Oct. 1852	11, Oct.	child	P2	
Henrie, (son of E.)	8, July 1828	July	6m	N3	
Henry, Isaac	14, July 1852	11, July	27	P2	
Henry, Mary Duke	14, Apr. 1832	13, Apr.	infant	R3	
Henry, Robert P.	8, 12, Sept 1826	24, Sept		N3	
Henry, Virginia Reese	4, 5, Oct. 1852	2, Oct.	14	P2	
Henson, James	1, Aug. 1850	July	1	Y2	
Henson, Melinday	24, Oct. 1828	Oct.	9	N2	
Henzelbrook, George	23, July 1850	July	9m	Y2	
Heom, Perry	19, July 1834	July	32	R3	
Hepburn, James S. (Dr)	8, June 1833	2, May	34	R3	
Hereman, John	26, June 1805		estate	S3	
Herman, (child of William)	1, Oct. 1830	Sept	stillborn	N3	
Herrick, Ephraim	2, Dec. 1825		100	N3	
Herron, Anna Maria	24, Dec. 1852	22, Dec.	2- 1m	P2	
Herron, Otho M. (Dr)	15, Mar. 1837		estate	N2	
Herzog, Catharine	3, Nov. 1852	1, Nov.	29	P2	
Hess, Abraham	23, July 1850	July	1	Y2	
Hess, Michael	2, Mar. 1827		estate	N3	
Heuber, Caroline	2, Aug. 1834	July	9m	R3	
Heuber, Caroline	29, July 1834	July	9m	T2	
Heuchan, Robert	18, Oct. 1852	16, Oct.	60	* P2	
Heuer, William A.	21, Sept 1838		probate	N3	
Heunmel, Joseph	2, Aug. 1834	July	7	R3	
Heunmel, Joseph	29, July 1834	July	7	T2	
Heuston, William	18, Dec. 1813	16, Dec.		S3	
Hewes, Roxanna	24, Dec. 1814	18, Dec.	21	S3	
Hewes, Roxanna	20, Dec. 1814	13, Dec.	21	W3	
Hewitt, Daniel T.	27, Aug. 1824	24, Aug.		* N2	
Hewitt, Daniel T.	26, Aug. 1824	24, Aug.		* E3	
Hey, Aaron	22, Aug. 1829		estate	R3	
Heyden, Christopher	9, Dec. 1828		probate	N3	
Hickermon, James (Mrs)	18, Oct. 1814	11, Oct.		W4	
Hickman, John	14, Sept 1850	13, Sept	39	P2	
Hickman, Joseph	10, Oct. 1836		estate	N3	
Hickman, Joseph	18, May 1838		probate	N2	
Hicks, (Mr)	16, Aug. 1852	13, Aug.	24	P2	
Hicks, Benjamin	15, Aug. 1850	Aug.	18	Y2	
Hicks, Charles	10, May 1828	9, May	27	* R3	
Hicks, Frances Mary	28, Apr. 1841	26, Apr.	32	N2	
Hicks, Jemima	7, Apr. 1829	17, Mar.	79	* N3	
Hicks, Robert	12, Sept 1840	10, Sept	91	R3	
Hicks, Robert	19, Sept 1840	10, Sept	91	R3	
Hieatt, G.W.	2, Dec. 1825		estate	N3	
Hieatt, George Whitfield	14, Dec. 1847	11, Dec.	6	K2	
Higbee, Benjamin	25, Sept 1835	20, Sept		T2	
Higbee, Charles	13, Mar. 1841	14, Feb.	73	R3	
Higbee, Charles	3, Mar. 1841	14, Feb.	73	N2	
Higby, wife of D.)	3, May 1838			N2	
Higgins, A.J. (Dr)	31, Aug. 1822	3, Aug.		S1	
Higgins, Archibald J.	30, Nov. 1822		estate	S3	
Higgins, Nathaniel	1, June 1835		probate	N2	

Name	Notice Date	Death Date	Age		Page	Maiden Name
Higgins, Ophelia	14, Oct. 1828	Oct.	1		N3	
Higgins, Sarah Ann	30, June 1836	27, June			N2	
Higgins, Thomas	14, Sept 1827		estate		N3	
Higgins, Thomas	22, Dec. 1829		probate		N3	
Higgins, Thomas	7, Sept 1830		probate		N3	
Hight, Samuel	18, June 1830	June	1- 3m		N3	
Highwarden, Amos	8, July 1828	July	50		N3	
Hilditch, Hannah	25, Aug. 1815	22, Aug.	47		S3	
Hilditch, Hannah	15, Sept 1815		estate		S3	
Hilditch, Hannah	6, July 1820		estate		S3	
Hilditch, Hannah	25, Apr. 1823		estate		N3	
Hilditch, Hannah	26, Aug. 1815	22, Aug.	47		G3	
Hilditch, Samuel	13, Oct. 1810	6, Oct.	52		S3	
Hilditch, Samuel	22, Dec. 1810		estate		S3	
Hilditch, Samuel	6, July 1820		estate		S3	
Hilditch, Thomas	6, July 1820		estate		S3	
Hill, Alice	15, Aug. 1837	15, Aug.	24	*	T2	Rhoades
Hill, Benjamin	12, June 1837		estate		N2	
Hill, Benjamin	21, Sept 1838		probate		N3	
Hill, Caroline	3, Sept 1830	Aug.	1- 3m		N2	
Hill, D. Greenwood	19, June 1841	17, June	5m		R3	
Hill, D. Greenwood	19, June 1841	17, June	5m		N2	
Hill, David	20, Aug. 1852	19, Aug.			P2	
Hill, Doerceas E.	2, July 1830	June	1		N2	
Hill, H.W. (Prof)	15, May 1849	13, May			L2	
Hill, Jacob	22, Dec. 1829		probate		N3	
Hill, James	6, Nov. 1834				T2	
Hill, John	27, Jan. 1821		estate		S3	
Hill, Letitia M.	30, July 1842	26, July	23		R3	
Hill, Letitia M.	28, July 1842	26, July	23		N2	
Hill, Samuel H.	14, Apr. 1826		estate		N3	
Hill, Samuel H.	11, Dec. 1827		probate		N3	
Hill, Samuel H.	9, Dec. 1828		probate		N3	
Hill, W.B.	17, July 1838	16, July	49	*	T2	
Hill, William C.	3, May 1841	21, Apr.			N2	
Hillhouse, Benjamin	30, Dec. 1828	Dec.			N3	
Hillman, Zebulon	16, Dec. 1825		probate		N3	
Hillman, Zebulon	12, Nov. 1817	6, Nov.		*	S3	
Hills, Eliza	1, June 1835		probate		N2	
Hime, Charles	12, Aug. 1831	Aug.	10d		A3	
Hinde, Thomas (Dr)	7, Oct. 1828	28, Sept	92		N3	
Hindman, Jacob (Col)	6, Mar. 1827	17, Feb.	38		N3	
Hinds, James	17, Oct. 1835		estate		N2	
Hine, Ward Chapin	23, Dec. 1850	21, Dec.	2- 1m-16d		P2	
Hines, Thomas (Rev)	1, May 1805				S2	
Hinkle, (child of Rampson)	3, Sept 1830	Aug.	stillborn		N2	
Hinkle, Elizabeth	24, June 1847	24, June	66		K2	
Hinkle, Frances	27, June 1849		37		L2	
Hinkle, George	26, Nov. 1830	Nov.	35		N3	
Hinsdlae, Mary J.	2, Dec. 1836	1, Dec.	15	*	N2	
Hinton, Elijah	7, Oct. 1828	Oct.	2		N3	
Hinton, Eliza	8, July 1828	July			N3	
Hinton, L.T. (Rev)	11, Sept 1847	28, Aug.	48		K2	
Hinton, Thomas	10, Apr. 1829	Apr.	5		N3	

Name	Notice Date	Death Date	Age	Page	Maiden Name
Hoag, James	10, Aug. 1852	8, Aug.	75		P2	
Hoaton, Samuel	8, July 1828	July	1		N3	
Hobart, Anne Newell	20, Mar. 1847	18, Mar.		*	K2	
Hobbs, William	15, Sept 1827	Sept	24		R3	
Hobson, George	18, May 1838		probate		N2	
Hobson, William	14, Sept 1852	12, Sept	1- 2m		P2	
Hodges, (Rev)	12, Sept 1840	29, Aug.			R3	
Hodgson, Sophia	1, Sept 1821	30, Aug.			S3	
Hodson, John B.	12, Jan. 1842	10, Jan.			N2	
Hoel, Phoebe	12, Jan. 1829		estate		N3	
Hofer, Frederick	9, Sept 1852	6, Sept	24		P2	
Hoffman, Adam	6, July 1849	July	49		L2	
Hoffman, Hariett	23, July 1850	July	27		Y2	
Hoffman, Isaac	24, Aug. 1824		estate		N3	
Hoffman, Isaac	25, Aug. 1829		probate		N3	
Hoffman, John	4, May 1824		estate		N3	
Hoffman, John	16, Dec. 1825		probate		N3	
Hoffman, Margaret	15, Aug. 1840	Aug.	1		R3	
Hoffman, William C.	13, Mar. 1841	Mar.	28		R3	
Hoffmier, Peter	6, July 1849	July	40		L2	
Hoffner, Catharine A.	12, Nov. 1830	Nov.	19		N3	
Hoffner, Nancy	28, Nov. 1818	14, Nov.	85		S3	
Hogan, Patrick	12, Apr. 1849	Apr.	40		L2	
Hogdook, Margaret	13, Aug. 1830	Aug.	80		N3	
Hoich, Rosina	23, July 1850	July	19m		Y2	
Holaway, Benjamin	9, Sept 1831	Sept	37		A3	
Holcomb, (child of C.B.)	22, Aug. 1828	Aug.	11d		N3	
Holcomb, Alice Penthea	7, Oct. 1847	4, Oct.	infant		K2	
Holcomb, James W.	27, Feb. 1829	Feb.	34		N3	
Holcomb, Mary Ann	7, 10, Nov. 1834	29, Oct.	22	*	T2	Murray
Holcomb, Milton Everest	24, Apr. 1835	12, Apr.	4m		T3	
Holcombe, Theadore Emley	23, Mar. 1833	19, Mar.	12m		R3	
Holden, Amos P.	4, Oct. 1852	2, Oct.	46		P2	
Hole, Margaret	19, Apr. 1849	18, Apr.	53- 6m		L2	
Hollabird, Amos B.	21, Sept 1852	18, Sept	65		P2	
Holland, George	22, Oct. 1796	18, Oct.			F3	
Holland, George (Mrs)	22, Oct. 1796	18, Oct.			F3	Kennedy
Holland, Samuel	7, Mar. 1826		estate		N3	
Holley, (Mr)	25, Aug. 1827	Aug.			R3	
Holliday, John	30, May 1840	20, May	32		R3	
Hollinshead, Mercy M.	25, June 1830	June	8m		N3	
Hollmann, Henry	28, June 1849	June	30		L2	
Hollowell, Delmot L.	9, Nov. 1847	8, Nov.			K2	
Hollowell, Orlando	6, Mar. 1851	5, Mar.	34		P2	
Holman, Joseph George	19, Sept 1817	24, Aug.	53		S3	
Holman, Sarah	17, Sept 1852	16, Sept			P2	
Holmes, And. L.	9, Sept 1831	Sept	26		A3	
Holmes, Elnathan	22, Aug. 1828	Aug.	4m		N3	
Holmes, James	8, July 1828	July	infant		N3	
Holmes, James M.	18, Mar. 1806	17, Mar.		*	S3	
Holmes, William	16, July 1842	12, July		*	R3	
Holmes, William	13, July 1842	12, July		*	N2	
Holmes, William	12, July 1842	12, July		*	M2	
Holroyd, E.B.	12, July 1849	10, July	30		L2	

Name	Notice Date	Death Date	Age		Page	Maiden Name
Holt, Francis	29, Aug. 1828		estate		N3	
Holt, William	24, Sept 1830	Sept	25		N3	
Hontz, Bolser	17, Sept 1835		probate		T2	
Hook, (child of Orson)	19, Sept 1828	Sept	1d		N3	
Hook, Charles B.	28, July 1850	July	1m		Y3	
Hook, Elijah	17, Sept 1830	Sept	27		N3	
Hoops, Catharine	19, Nov. 1830	Nov.	53		N3	
Hoops, John	7, Dec. 1820	1, Dec.	18		S3	
Hoover, Edward S.	5, Dec. 1840	Dec.	5m		R3	
Hoover, Matthias	11, July 1837				T2	
Hopes, (child of Adam)	24, Feb. 1829	Feb.	3m		N3	
Hopkins, Augustus	5, Mar. 1842	25, Feb.			R3	
Hopkins, Augustus	26, Feb. 1842	25, Feb.			N2	
Hopkins, Benjamin	19, Oct. 1837		estate		N3	
Hopkins, Benjamin W.	30, Nov. 1835		estate		T2	
Hopkins, John	3, May 1849	May	21		L2	
Hopkins, Mary	7, Dec. 1838	5, Dec.	61		T2	
Hoppel, John	9, Nov. 1852		74		P2	
Hopper, Eliza	19, July 1834	July	29		R3	
Hopper, Samuel	10, May 1849	May	28		L2	
Hopple, Andrew	21, Sept 1820		' estate		S3	
Hoppock, John	19, Dec. 1828		estate		N3	
Hoppock, John	12, Jan. 1829		estate		N3	
Hoppock, John & Nancy	9, Dec. 1828		probate		N3	
Hopson, Ann	19, July 1834	July	28		R3	
Horn, John	5, May 1835	19, Apr.	19	*	T3	
Horne, John S.	31, July 1841	24, July	61		R3	
Horner, Samuel D.	5, Sept 1818	24, Aug.			S3	
Horner, William	8, Sept 1827	Sept	70		R3	
Horton, Caroline Mowrey	2, Apr. 1842	27, Mar.	2		R3	
Horton, Jonathan K.	22, Feb. 1848	22, Feb.	71	*	K2	
Horton, Peter L.	31, July 1852	30, July	66		P2	
Hosack, Hamilton	30, Sept 1837	13, Sept		*	T2	
Hosea, Robert	13, Mar. 1848	12, Mar.	61		K2	
Hossler, Henry Clay	9, Nov. 1841	2, Nov.	3- 6m		N2	
Host, Joseph	6, July 1849	July	28		L2	
Hotchkiss, Augusta	12, June 1849	11, June		*	L2	
Hotchkiss, Phoebe G.	6, Oct. 1847	2, Oct.			K2	
Hothe, Nancy	24, June 1828	June	1		N3	
Hough, Catharine	29, Feb. 1828	10, Feb.	55		N2	
Hough, Frances	18, Nov. 1830	12, Nov.	56		A3	
Hough, Frances	16, Nov. 1830	12, Nov.	56		N2	
Hough, Frances	19, Nov. 1830	Nov.	56		N3	
Hough, John	19, Aug. 1831	Aug.	2		A3	
Houglan, Ellen	16, Mar. 1837	15, Mar.	34		X3	
House, John	19, July 1834	July	9m		R3	
Houser, Christian N.M.	30, May 1840		35		R3	
Housman, Mary C.	24, July 1850	July	38		Y2	
Houston, Mary Ann	27, Sept 1838	26, Sept			T2	
Houten, Benjamin	22, Oct. 1830	Oct.	55		N3	
Houvall, Peter	26, Nov. 1830	Nov.	39		N3	
Howard, (Gen)	15, Oct. 1814	18, Sept			S3	
Howard, Charles (Mrs)	26, June 1850	25, June			P2	
Howard, Frederick	29, Nov. 1825		78		N3	

Name	Notice Date	Death Date	Age	Page	Maiden Name
Howard, Jane	30, July 1830	July	15m	N3	
Howard, John	21, June 1849	June	67	L2	
Howard, John E. (Col)	27, Oct. 1827	12, Oct.		R3	
Howard, John Eager (Col)	26, Oct. 1827			N3	
Howard, Lucy	8, Dec. 1827	4, Dec.	17	R3	
Howard, Mary	27, Dec. 1828	Dec.	22	R3	
Howard, Mary	23, Dec. 1828	Dec.	22	N3	
Howard, Rolla	1, Aug. 1828	July	1-10m	N3	
Howard, Sarah	28, May 1830	May	49	N3	
Howe, Elizabeth	13, June 1840	11, June		R3	
Howe, John	10, Oct. 1829		estate	R3	
Howe, Persis	1, Mar. 1833	31, Dec.	22	X3	
Howell, Eliza Longworth	7, June 1833	May	2- 6m	X3	
Howell, Harton	24, Aug. 1833	Aug.		R3	
Howell, J.	12, Aug. 1831	Aug.	1- 3m	A3	
Howell, Jacob H.	4, Nov. 1830	24, Oct.	29	A3	
Howell, Jacob H.	6, Nov. 1830	24, Oct.	29	R3	
Howell, Lewis	7, Nov. 1834	1, Nov.		X3	
Howell, Silas (Major)	11, Apr. 1812	10, Apr.		S2	
Howell, Thomas P.	22, Oct. 1830	Oct.	1- 6m	N3	
Howes, Thomas	6, June 1840	June	22	R3	
Hubbard, John	15, June 1827		estate	Q4	
Hubbard, John	9, Dec. 1828		probate	N3	
Hubbard, Joshua	15, May 1849	13, May	67	L2	
Hubbel, Jacob	19, Aug. 1825		estate	N3	
Hubbell, Gabriel	2, May 1828	28, Apr.	40	N3	
Hubbell, Jacob	22, July 1825	18, July	47	N3	
Hubbell, Jacob	26, June 1830		estate	R3	
Hubbell, Thomas	22, Jan. 1842	17, Jan.	95	R3	
Huber, Eary	14, June 1849	June	27	L2	
Huddart, Amelia	25, Mar. 1847	24, Mar.	3m	K2	
Hudson, (dau. of Guy)	19, Aug. 1828	Aug.	3m	N3	
Hudson, G.	20, Aug. 1836		estate	N2	
Hudson, James	13, July 1849	July	40	L2	
Hudson, John	24, July 1847	23, July	80	K2	
Hudson, John (Mrs)	2, June 1827			R3	
Hueston, (man)	6, Mar. 1802	21, Feb.		* S3	
Hueston, Samuel	20, Mar. 1838		probate	N3	
Huffman, (son of William)	26, Sept 1828	Sept	9m	N3	
Huffman, Robert	7, Dec. 1837		probate	N3	
Huggeford, Charlotte Bowers	23, Aug. 1834	Aug.	11m	R3	
Huggeford, John	23, Aug. 1834	Aug.	43	* R3	
Huggerford, C.O.	11, Sept 1837		probate	N2	
Hughes, James (Rev)	19, May 1821	2, May		S3	
Hughes, John	4, June 1836		probate	N2	
Hughes, Joseph S. (Rev)	7, Oct. 1823	24, Sept	54	N3	
Hughes, Patrick	25, Apr. 1837	11, Apr.		N2	
Hughes, Thomas	19, Aug. 1828		probate	N3	
Hulbert, Adolphus H.	19, Aug. 1850	18, July	_m- 9d	P2	
Hulbert, Amelia	10, July 1850	9, July	34	P2	
Hulbert, Stephen	6, June 1818		estate	S3	
Hull, Jane	30, July 1830	July	3	N3	
Hull, Julius	10, July 1852	8, July		P2	
Hull, Lucy Amelia	13, July 1852	11, July	29-11m-22d	P2	

Name	Notice Date	Death Date	Age	Page	Maiden Name
Hull, William (Gen)	16, Dec. 1825			N3	
Huller, V.H.	22, Aug. 1828	Aug.	1- 2m-16d	N3	
Hulm, Barnard	24, May 1849	May	35	L2	
Hulse, (child of George)	17, Sept 1830	Sept	stillborn	N3	
Hultzscar, John	6, July 1849	July	58	L2	
Humel, Mary	23, Sept 1831	Sept	1-10m	A3	
Humes, Margaret	1, Jan. 1806	28, Dec.		S3	
Humphrey, Jacob (Col)	31, Mar. 1826	21, Jan.	74- 3m	N3	
Humphreys, Jane	13, July 1849	July	9m	L2	
Humphreys, Robert	16, July 1852	15, July	8	P2	
Hunewell, Jonathan	15, Apr. 1842		83	N2	
Hunn, (Mrs)	9, June 1827	10, Mar.	81	R3	
Hunt, Abijah	27, July 1811	21, July	38	S3	
Hunt, Andrew	7, Sept 1830		probate	N3	
Hunt, Andrew Jackson	12, Oct. 1835	19, Sept		* T2	
Hunt, B.P.	26, Dec. 1840	6, Dec.	27	R3	
Hunt, B.P.	22, Dec. 1840	6, Dec.	27	N2	
Hunt, Eliza Louisa	5, 12, Nov. 1814	31, Oct.	15	S3	
Hunt, Flavel	5, Nov. 1841	1, Nov.		N2	
Hunt, George N.	11, Mar. 1825	6, Mar.	23	N2	
Hunt, Henry L.	8, Oct. 1838	5, Oct.		* T2	
Hunt, James	13, July 1849	July	32	L2	
Hunt, James A.	21, June 1849	June	33	L2	
Hunt, Jeremiah	27, Oct. 1821	25, Oct.	55	S3	
Hunt, Jesse	26, Aug. 1835	24, Aug.	75	T2	
Hunt, Jesse	27, 28, Aug. 1835	24, Aug.	75	* N2	
Hunt, Joshua	29, June 1833	24, June	76	R3	
Hunt, Louisa	1, Nov. 1814	31, Oct.	17	W3	
Hunt, Nehemiah	4, Nov. 1824	21, Oct.	50	E3	
Hunt, Philip Grandin	8, Aug. 1818	3, Aug.	infant	S3	
Hunt, R.E.A.	8, Dec. 1827	29, Nov.	19	R3	
Hunt, Rhoda	3, Feb. 1829	Jan.	24	N3	
Hunt, Rhody	30, July 1830	July	22	N3	
Hunt, Samuel	26, July 1834	July	25	R3	
Hunt, Samuel	22, July 1834	July	25	T2	
Hunt, Samuel	15, Oct. 1830	Oct.	3- 9m	N3	
Hunt, Samuel F.	21, Mar. 1838		estate	N2	
Hunt, William	13, Oct. 1815	10, Oct.	96	S3	
Hunt, William Gibbs	24, Aug. 1833	Aug.		R3	
Hunt, William Hazel	12, July 1841	3, July		N2	
Hunt, William L.	20, Mar. 1841		estate	R3	
Hunter, George	28, July 1852	26, July	45	P2	
Hunter, Jonathan	28, Mar. 1818		estate	S2	
Hunter, Larry	26, Sept 1828	Sept	24	N3	
Hunter, Lydia	28, June 1849	June	10	L2	
Hunter, Serena	18, Sept 1850	17, Sept	4	Y2	
Hunter, Thomas	18, June 1842		estate	R3	
Hunter, William	14, Dec. 1835		probate	N2	
Huntington, E.	14, Oct. 1852	1, Oct.	53	P2	
Huntington, Margaretta	30, Mar. 1849	29, Mar.	2- -24d	L2	
Huntop, John	2, Aug. 1834	July	4	R3	
Huntop, John	29, July 1834	July	4	T2	
Hurdus, Adam	16, July 1831	14, July		R3	
Hurdus, Hannah	29, Oct. 1836	27, Oct.	74	T2	

Name	Notice Date	Death Date	Age	Page	Maiden Name
Hurdus, Hannah	28, Oct. 1836	27, Oct.	74	N2	
Hurdus, James	15, May 1850	14, May	62	P2	
Hurley, Mary	14, June 1849	June	51	L2	
Hurrold, Caroline	23, Sept 1831	Sept	1- 5m	A3	
Huston, James	26, Feb. 1814	24, Feb.	100	S3	
Huston, James H.	12, Aug. 1828	Aug.	45	N3	
Huston, John	16, July 1830	July	46	N3	
Hutchens, George D.	2, June 1847	1, June	11- 7m	K2	
Hutcheson, John	24, Dec. 1830	Dec.	27	N3	
Hutchins, Samuel	14, Oct. 1828	Oct.	1	N3	
Hutchins, Sarah B.	10, Nov. 1832	27, Oct.	24	R3	
Hutchinson, Ann	1, Apr. 1801	4, Jan.	101	S3	
Hutchinson, Edward	9, Feb. 1839	8, Feb.	44	T2	
Hutchinson, Jonathan	18, June 1830	June	52	N3	
Hutchinson, Mary	11, Jan. 1828	4, Jan.	20	N2	
Hutchinson, Robert	17, June 1837		probate	N2	
Hutchinson, Thomas	25, Aug. 1829		probate	N3	
Hutchinson, Thomas	1, June 1835		probate	N2	
Hutchinson, William	2, Sept 1825		estate	N3	
Hutchinson, William	25, Aug. 1829		probate	N3	
Hutchinson, William (heirs of)	7, Sept 1836		probate	N2	
Hutchison, James	22, Aug. 1850	Aug.	4	Y2	
Hutchison, L.	26, Sept 1828	Sept	5	N3	
Hutchison, Thomas	8, Oct. 1821		estate	S3	
Hyatt, James	22, Aug. 1850	Aug.	6	Y2	
Hyatt, John	8, Aug. 1850	Aug.	25	Y2	
Hyde, William	24, May 1849	May	23	L2	
Igray, William	12, Sept 1828	Sept	1- 4m	N3	
Iliff, Margaret	20, July 1852	18, July	63	P2	
Ilis, (child of Robert)	16, Jan. 1829	Jan.	4m-15d	N2	
Illiff, Francis	16, Jan. 1829	Jan.	1m	N2	
Ingalsbe, Sarah	23, June 1849	22, June		L2	
Ingalsbe, Sarah Augusta	20, Jan. 1848	19, Jan.	2- 3m	K2	
Ingersoll, Jared	23, Nov. 1822	31, Oct.		S3	
Ingleking, Henry	20, Mar. 1838		probate	N3	
Innes, Emeline	27, Oct. 1841	14, Oct.	28	* N2	Dunham
Innis, Francis	25, Feb. 1801		estate	S4	
Innis, Francis	5, June 1819		estate	S3	
Iratabos, Maurice	4, Apr. 1837		probate	N2	
Ireland, Aaron	27, Mar. 1813	19, Mar.		S3	
Irish, John H.	28, June 1849	June	53	L2	
Irons, Ruth	21, May 1842	5, Apr.	55	R3	
Irvin, Samuel	27, July 1850	July	42	Y3	
Irvine, Callender (Gen)	23, Oct. 1841	16, Oct.	67	R3	
Irvine, John	12, June 1841	June	12	N2	
Irwin, Archibald	9, Sept 1852	8, Sept	46	P2	
Irwin, Archibald	6, Sept 1852	4, Sept	56	P2	
Irwin, Green W.	17, May 1849	May	24	L2	
Irwin, Jane	13, June 1817	12, June		S3	
Irwin, John	2, Aug. 1834	July	53	R3	
Irwin, John	29, July 1834	July	53	T2	
Irwin, John (Capt)	15, Aug. 1840	29, July		R3	
Irwin, John V.	21, Jan. 1839	19, Jan.	32	T2	
Irwin, Mary	20, Sept 1825	17, Sept		N3	

Name	Notice Date	Death Date	Age		Page	Maiden Name
Irwin, Mary Jane	14, Dec. 1847	13, Dec.			K2	
Irwin, Rebecca	12, Aug. 1831	Aug.	35		A3	
Irwin, William	18, Nov. 1824		estate		E3	
Irwin, William	21, Dec. 1830		probate		N3	
Irwin, William	22, July 1824	16, July			E3	
Isaacks, Jacob C.	13, Oct. 1835				T2	
Isdell, Thomas	14, Apr. 1826	12, Apr.	26		N3	
Isham, William	2, Aug. 1833	25, July	3- 8m		X3	
Isherwood, Thomas C.	29, June 1842		estate		N2	
Izard, Ralph	27, Aug. 1831	25, Aug.	27		R3	
Jackson, (child of James)	22, Oct. 1852	21, Oct.	5		P2	
Jackson, (child of Robert)	12, Jan. 1829	Jan.	stillborn		N2	
Jackson, David	10, Feb. 1841		estate		N3	
Jackson, David	16, Jan. 1841	12, Jan.			N2	
Jackson, George	27, Aug. 1852	Aug.	2		P2	
Jackson, George A.	5, Oct. 1838	4, Oct.	31	*	T2	
Jackson, George A.	5, Oct. 1838	4, Oct.		*	N2	
Jackson, James	22, Oct. 1852	21, Oct.			P2	
Jackson, John	25, Aug. 1827	Aug.	26		R3	
Jackson, John	15, July 1825	10, July	87	*	N2	
Jackson, Rachael	6, Jan. 1829	22, Dec.	62		N3	
Jackson, Rachael	30, Dec. 1828	22, Nov.			N2	
Jackson, Sarah	18, June 1838	17, June	53	*	T2	Pierce
Jackson, William	11, Mar. 1806		estate		S3	
Jacobs, Freelove H.	17, Apr. 1849	15, Apr.	32		L2	
Jacobs, Harriet Lilie	7, Oct. 1847	6, Oct.	13m		K2	
Jacobs, John	6, June 1812		estate		S3	
Jacobs, Mary Ellen	21, July 1852	20, July	1- 9m		P2	
Jacobs, N.	17, May 1849	May			L2	
James, David	27, May 1824		estate		E3	
James, David	9, Sept 1825		probate		N3	
James, David	4, Mar. 1828		probate		N3	
James, David	3, May 1838				N2	
James, Eliza	25, Sept 1852	21, Sept	45- 8m		P2	
James, George W.	16, Dec. 1828	Dec.	22		N3	
James, Isaac	23, Dec. 1828	Dec.	6m		N3	
James, Jane	2, Sept 1828	Aug.	1- 8m		N3	
James, Jane	22, Aug. 1828	Aug.	20m		N3	
James, John A.	19, Aug. 1828	Aug.	1-11m		N3	
James, John Keating	14, June 1841	11, June	2-10m		N2	
James, Lucy Audubon	7, Oct. 1847	5, Oct.	19m-10d		K2	
James, Margaret K.	14, Aug. 1839	12, Aug.			T2	
James, Mary	19, Aug. 1828	Aug.	1- 5m		N3	
James, Mary Ann	28, July 1815	19, July			S3	
James, Mary Ann	22, July 1815	18, July			G3	
James, Nathan	14, Dec. 1835		probate		N2	
James, Philip	13, July 1849	July	1- 9m		L2	
James, Reuben Langdon	28, Dec. 1852	25, Dec.	2- 4m		P2	
James, Sarah	9, Mar. 1807		estate		S3	
Jameson, John G.	6, Oct. 1837	27, Sept	43		T2	
Jamison, Edward	11, Sept 1837		probate		N2	
Janson, Anthony	26, Apr. 1849	Apr.	45		L2	
January, Fanney P.	26, Nov. 1835	4, Nov.	34		X3	Irvin
Jaques, Abiel	18, Oct. 1852	7, Oct.	73		P2	

Name	Notice Date	Death Date	Age	Page	Maiden Name
Jaquess, Martha	26, Oct. 1847	24, Oct.	48		K2
Jaquish, Amos	18, Mar. 1837		estate		N2
Jardine, Thomas	5, Feb. 1842	27, Jan.	74		R3
Jarvis, (child of Henry)	27, Jan. 1829	Jan.	1d		N2
Jasper, Conrod	7, Dec. 1837		estate		N3
Jay, Sarah	19, June 1802	28, May	45		S3
Jefferson, George	8, July 1828	July	4		N3
Jefferson, Thomas (President)	18, July 1826	4, July			N2
Jefferson, Thomas (President)	15, July 1826	4, July			J3
Jengrat, Mary Serafini	1, Jan. 1831	12, Dec.	39		R3
Jenings, Obediah (Rev)	27, Jan. 1832	14, Jan.			X3
Jenkins, Benjamin	24, Oct. 1818		estate		S3
Jenkins, Benjamin	16, Dec. 1825		probate		N3
Jenkins, Benjamin	6, Oct. 1826		probate		N3
Jenkins, Josiah	11, Dec. 1827		probate		N3
Jenkins, Josiah	4, Mar. 1828		probate		N3
Jenkins, Prince	29, Sept 1815		estate		S3
Jenks, Emma	28, Nov. 1840	21, Nov.	19	*	R3
Jennings, George	24, July 1850	July	3- 5m		Y2
Jennings, John	15, Mar. 1828	11, Mar.	68	*	R3
Jennings, Martin	8, Dec. 1852	4, Dec.	31	*	P2
Jennison, (son of James)	16, Aug. 1852	12, Aug.	infant		P2
Jenz, Jacob	26, Sept 1850	Sept	41		Y2
Jeppenis, (child of C.)	23, Sept 1831	Sept	2		A3
Jeremiah, Warren	19, July 1834	July	7m		R3
Jessop, Aaron	7, Oct. 1835	1, Oct.		*	T2
Jessup, John	19, Dec. 1826		probate		N3
Jessup, Samuel	1, Aug. 1817	25, July			S3
Jewel, Thomas	15, May 1805		estate		S3
Jewell, John	27, Feb. 1829	Feb.			N3
Jewels, Henry	2, Jan. 1829	Dec.			N3
Jewett, Ebenezer (Lt)	23, Feb. 1827	11, Dec.	82		N3
Jewett, Mary	24, Mar. 1838	15, Mar.	23		R3	Ferris
Jinkins, Henry	18, June 1830	June	9m		N3
Jocelin, Mary E.	23, Apr. 1849	Apr.	16d		L2
John, Lemuel	18, Aug. 1852	16, Aug.	61- 8m		P2
John, Levi	19, Dec. 1826		probate		N3
John, Nancy	16, Oct. 1835	3, Oct.			X3
Johns, Abijah	9, Dec. 1828		probate		N3
Johns, Abijah	25, Aug. 1829		probate		N3
Johnson, Alexander	6, Feb. 1823		estate		J3
Johnson, Annie	25, Aug. 1852	23, Aug.	5m		P2
Johnson, Archibald	2, Oct. 1819	16, Sept	26		S3
Johnson, Archibald (Rev)	21, Aug. 1819	16, Aug.			S3
Johnson, Benjamin (Col)	29, Mar. 1834	Mar.	23		R3
Johnson, Benjamin S.	18, July 1828	July	16m		N3
Johnson, Charles	20, Oct. 1829		estate		N3
Johnson, Charles	23, Mar. 1830		probate		N3
Johnson, Christopher	5, Sept 1835	2, Sept		*	T2
Johnson, David	13, June 1840		63		R3
Johnson, David	6, July 1822		estate		S3
Johnson, David	20, Mar. 1838		probate		N3
Johnson, David I.	18, Jan. 1842	15, Jan.	47	*	N2
Johnson, Edward I.	2, Aug. 1836		estate		T2

Name	Notice Date	Death Date	Age		Page	Maiden Name
Johnson, Edward I.	1, Aug. 1836		estate		N2	
Johnson, Francis (Col)	20, May 1842	16, May	65		N2	
Johnson, George	16, Dec. 1828	Dec.	32		N3	
Johnson, George Alexander	17, Apr. 1849	15, Apr.			L2	
Johnson, James (Col)	8, Sept 1826				Q3	
Johnson, James Dunlop	7, Sept 1835	30, Aug.		*	T2	
Johnson, Jane	11, Nov. 1851	10, Nov.	69		P2	
Johnson, John	13, July 1849	July	6		L2	
Johnson, John	16, Apr. 1814		estate		S3	
Johnson, Joseph J.	29, Sept 1852	25, Sept	47		P2	
Johnson, L.M.	21, May 1830	May	4m		N3	
Johnson, Lizzie Frances	30, July 1852	28, July	1-11m		P2	
Johnson, Nicholas	13, July 1822		estate		S3	
Johnson, Rhoady	19, Jan. 1837	13, Jan.	57		T2	
Johnson, Rhoda	14, Jan. 1837	13, Jan.	57		R3	
Johnson, Richard M.	8, Aug. 1837	7, Aug.	10m		N2	
Johnson, Thomas	19, Aug. 1836	7, Aug.	17		N2	
Johnson, Thomas	24, Jan. 1823		estate		N3	
Johnson, Thomas	3, May 1825		probate		N3	
Johnson, Walter	6, Oct. 1826		probate		N3	
Johnson, William M.	17, July 1841	10, July	29	*	N2	
Johnson, William Samuel	4, Dec. 1819	14, Nov.	93		S3	
Johnston, (heirs of Nicholas)	1, June 1835		probate		N2	
Johnston, Alexander	16, Dec. 1825		probate		N3	
Johnston, Alexander	30, Apr. 1842	27, Apr.			R3	
Johnston, Ann J.	12, July 1850	10, July			P2	
Johnston, Charles	2, Aug. 1834	July	2- 5m		R3	
Johnston, Charles	29, July 1834	July	2- 5m		T2	
Johnston, Charles	19, Dec. 1828		estate		N3	
Johnston, Charles	7, Sept 1830		probate		N3	
Johnston, Daniel	19, Dec. 1828		estate		N3	
Johnston, Daniel	23, Mar. 1830		probate		N3	
Johnston, Daniel	7, Sept 1830		probate		N3	
Johnston, Edward	21, Dec. 1830		probate		N3	
Johnston, Elizabeth	12, Aug. 1828	Aug.	23		N3	
Johnston, George M.	12, Sept 1804	23, July			S2	
Johnston, James	30, Jan. 1836	29, Jan.	infant		N2	
Johnston, John (Major)	28, Nov. 1826	21, Oct.	80	*	N3	
Johnston, Joseph	29, June 1833	23, June	38		R3	
Johnston, Margaret D.	22, 23, June 1849	21, June	22		L2	
Johnston, Matilda Elisabeth	6, Aug. 1850	5, Aug.	16m		Y2	
Johnston, Nicholas	19, Dec. 1826		probate		N3	
Johnston, Nicholas	11, Dec. 1827		probate		N3	
Johnston, Parmeli	27, Aug. 1852	Aug.	38		P2	
Johnston, Phebe	25, July 1826	6, June	114	*	N1	
Johnston, Robert	8, Jan. 1828		estate		N3	
Johnston, Samuel (Rev)	25, May 1833	22, May			R3	
Johnston, Walter	19, Dec. 1826		probate		N3	
Johnston, William	19, Aug. 1836	13, Aug.	75		T2	
Johnston, William	16, July 1830	July	5m		N3	
Johnston, William	2, May 1817		estate		S3	
Joiner, Rebecca Ann	1, Aug. 1828	July	7m		N3	
Jolley, Edward	26, 29, July 1836	25, July	39		N2	
Jolley, Edward	26, July 1836	25, July			T2	

Name	Notice Date	Death Date	Age	Page	Maiden Name
Jolley, Henry	9, Aug. 1842	29, July	84- 7m	M3	
Jolley, John	30, Nov. 1841	29, Nov.	73	N2	
Jolley, William D.	17, Oct. 1829	24, Sept	28	R3	
Jolly, Ann	3, Apr. 1829	Mar.	32	N2	
Jonas, Gershom S.	10, Aug. 1827	23, July	6m	N3	
Jonas, Gershon	11, Aug. 1827	23, July	infant	R3	
Jones, (child of Betsy)	19, July 1834	July	child	R3	
Jones, (child of Harrietta)	27, Aug. 1830	Aug.	stillborn	N3	
Jones, (child of Jane)	25, July 1840	July	1d	R3	
Jones, (child of Jesse)	9, Sept 1831	Sept	2m	A3	
Jones, (heirs of Mary)	4, June 1836		probate	N2	
Jones, Aaron	14, July 1836		81	X3	
Jones, Anne Lucinda	29, May 1835	15, May	45	T2	Lee
Jones, Daniel	13, Dec. 1825	11, Dec.		N3	
Jones, Esther	7, May 1830	May	46	N3	
Jones, Frederick	22, Aug. 1850	Aug.	3w	Y2	
Jones, George A.	28, July 1850	July	9m	Y3	
Jones, George W.	7, Dec. 1820	1, Dec.	25	* S3	
Jones, George W.	3, May 1825		probate	N3	
Jones, George W.	25, Aug. 1829		probate	N3	
Jones, George W.	10, Aug. 1836	9, Aug.		T2	
Jones, George W.	11, Aug. 1836	10, Aug.		N2	
Jones, Helen	22, June 1841	29, May	4m	N2	
Jones, Henry	30, Oct. 1838	27, Oct.		N2	
Jones, James	31, July 1850	July	3w	Y3	
Jones, James	7, Sept 1820		estate	S3	
Jones, James	10, June 1828		estate	N3	
Jones, James	3, May 1825		probate	N3	
Jones, James	16, Dec. 1825		probate	N3	
Jones, James	19, Aug. 1828		probate	N3	
Jones, Jane	31, Mar. 1836	26, Mar.	69	* X3	
Jones, Job	3, May 1838			N2	
Jones, John	17, Jan. 1817		estate	S3	
Jones, John	16, Dec. 1825		probate	N3	
Jones, John	19, Dec. 1826		probate	N3	
Jones, John	9, Dec. 1828		probate	N3	
Jones, John	22, Dec. 1829		probate	N3	
Jones, John	3, May 1838			* N2	
Jones, John (Col)	7, Sept 1824		probate	N3	
Jones, John (Col)	9, Sept 1824		probate	E3	
Jones, John (Col)	31, Mar. 1821	24, Mar.		S3	
Jones, John L.	14, Dec. 1835		probate	N2	
Jones, John L.	7, Sept 1836		probate	N2	
Jones, John T.	1, June 1835		probate	N2	
Jones, Lorenzo	21, Oct. 1837	6, Oct.		R3	
Jones, Lorenzo	20, Oct. 1837	6, Oct.		T2	
Jones, Margaret	26, Jan. 1803	21, Jan.		S3	
Jones, Margaret	10, Feb. 1832	2, Feb.		X3	
Jones, Margaretta Evelina	11, Feb. 1832			R3	
Jones, Maria	27, Feb. 1829	Feb.	80	N3	
Jones, Maria	21, Dec. 1830		probate	N3	
Jones, Mary	2, Mar. 1835		estate	N2	
Jones, Mary	7, Sept 1836		probate	N2	
Jones, Moses	7, Sept 1824		probate	N3	

Name	Notice Date	Death Date	Age	Page	Maiden Name
Jones, Moses	9, Sept 1824		probate	E3	
Jones, Nimrod (Dr)	14, Sept 1835	31, Aug.	24	T2	
Jones, Philip	2, Dec. 1831		estate	A3	
Jones, Philip	14, Dec. 1835		probate	N2	
Jones, Rachel	31, July 1850	July	23	Y3	
Jones, Rachel J.	2, Aug. 1834	July	10	R3	
Jones, Rachel J.	29, July 1834	July	10	T2	
Jones, Rachel Johnston	22, July 1834		10	T2	
Jones, Reuben	5, Nov. 1830	Nov.	25	N3	
Jones, Richard	28, June 1849	June	37	L2	
Jones, Salmon	4, June 1830	June		N3	
Jones, Salmon	5, June 1849	4, June		L2	
Jones, Samuel	28, Nov. 1817			S2	
Jones, Samuel	17, Oct. 1822	15, Oct.		J2	
Jones, Sarah Fracker	29, 30, Dec. 1852	28, Dec.	7-11m-26d	P2	
Jones, Thomas A.	19, Aug. 1831	Aug.	25	A3	
Jones, Thomas Allibone	13, Aug. 1831	10, Aug.	24	R3	
Jones, Thomas C.	21, Sept 1838		probate	N3	
Jones, William	18, July 1828	July	6m	N3	
Jones, William	28, July 1827	27, July		R3	
Jones, William Henry	3, June 1824	19, May	infant	E3	
Jonte, Catharine E.	3, Dec. 1830	Nov.	19	N3	
Jordan, William	14, June 1849	June	50	L2	
Jordan, William Hugh	8, Aug. 1840		83	R4	
Joseph, Charles	6, July 1849	July	38	L2	
Joseph, Samuel	4, Mar. 1828		probate	N3	
Joseph, Samuel	28, Feb. 1826	23, Feb.	*	N2	
Jouitt, (Mr)	18, Aug. 1827	Aug.		R3	
Jourdan, James	21, Apr. 1836		estate	N2	
Joyce, Elizabeth	18, Dec. 1813	10, Dec.	56	S3	
Joyce, James	18, Dec. 1813	3, Dec.	28	S3	
Joyce, James	22, Jan. 1814		estate	S3	
Joyce, Thomas	7, Sept 1836		probate	N2	
Judd, Nelson	27, Feb. 1829	Feb.	38	N3	
Judd, William C.	7, Sept 1830		probate	N3	
Judkins, Susan	20, Jan. 1838	18, Jan.		R3	
Junker, George	10, May 1849	May	26	L2	
Justice, Anna Rebecca	21, July 1852	19, July	11m-10d	P2	
Justice, Jesse	26, July 1850	25, July	55	Y2	
Kaeltering, Ann	14, June 1849	June	25	L2	
Kaerber, George	7, June 1849	June	77	L2	
Kain, Rebecca	9, Dec. 1828	Dec.	1	N3	
Kain, Thomas	12, Mar. 1814		estate	S3	
Kairman, Anthony	7, June 1849	June	70	L2	
Kalley, William	1, Sept 1827	Aug.	6	R3	
Kane, Elias K.	22, Dec. 1835	11, Dec.		N2	
Kane, Francis	31, July 1850	July	35	Y3	
Kaney, Madaline	23, July 1850	July	7	Y2	
Karr, John	6, Oct. 1826		estate	N3	
Karr, William	15, Sept 1821	9, Sept	40	S3	
Kats, Jacob	21, June 1849	June		L2	
Kaufman, Michael	19, July 1834	July	3	R3	
Kean, Rhoda	19, Nov. 1799	16, Sept		S3	Cadwell
Keck, Ann	29, June 1833	23, June		R3	

Name	Notice Date	Death Date	Age	Page	Maiden Name
Kecke, Godfrey	19, July 1834	July	30	R3	
Keel, Benjamin	16, Mar. 1830		estate	N3	
Keeler, Philander	31, Dec. 1831	24, Dec.	27	R3	
Keeler, Philander	14, Apr. 1832		estate	R3	
Keenan, James	8, May 1829	4, Apr.	80	N3	
Keenan, Thomas	18, Sept 1851	16, Sept		P2	
Keene, Arthur F.	9, Nov. 1837			T2	
Kegan, Patrick	8, Oct. 1841	Oct.	43	N2	
Kehoe, Samuel	22, Dec. 1829		probate	N3	
Kehoe, Samuel	6, July 1822	2, July		S3	
Keiler, Dennis	14, Jan. 1831	10, Dec.	24	X3	
Kelley, Clifton W.	25, Nov. 1851	22, Nov.	2	P2	
Kelley, George	8, Oct. 1852	Oct.	29	P2	
Kellog, Horace E.	2, Aug. 1834	July	8m	R3	
Kellog, Horace E.	29, July 1834	July	8m	T2	
Kellogg, Almira Kilborn	4, Jan. 1821	15, Dec.	33	S3	
Kellogg, Caleb Bingham	29, July 1831	17, July	25	* X3	
Kellogg, Elizabeth B.	10, Mar. 1842	13, Feb.	11m	N2	
Kellogg, Lizzie	5, July 1852	2, July		P2	
Kellogg, Virginia	24, July 1850	23, July	8	Y2	
Kellogg, Virginia	24, July 1850	July	8	Y2	
Kellogg, Warren Converse	4, Jan. 1821	7, Dec.	infant	S3	
Kelly, Bridget	22, Aug. 1850	Aug.	7	Y2	
Kelly, Bridget	11, Sept 1847	7, Sept		* K2	
Kelly, Charlotte	1, Oct. 1830	Sept	9	N3	
Kelly, Christopher	6, July 1849	July	9	L2	
Kelly, Hannah A.	23, Apr. 1849	Apr.	4	L2	
Kelly, James	4, June 1836		probate	N2	
Kelly, Jane	1, July 1828	June	69	N3	
Kelly, Jane	8, July 1828	July	6m	N3	
Kelly, Joseph	16, Sept 1852	15, Sept	38	P2	
Kelly, Michael	27, Aug. 1852	Aug.	8m	P2	
Kelly, Nathaniel	29, Mar. 1849	Mar.	25	L2	
Kelly, Oliver	6, Oct. 1827	Oct.	70	R3	
Kelly, Oliver	9, Dec. 1828		probate	N3	
Kelly, Patrick	31, Oct. 1850	Oct.	50	Y2	
Kelly, Peter	1, June 1849	May		L2	
Kelly, Thomas O.	1, Sept 1852	31, Aug.		P2	
Kelly, William	14, Dec. 1835		probate	N2	
Kelsey, George W.	1, July 1828	June	6	N3	
Kelsey, Henry C.	9, Aug. 1825	7, Aug.	5	N3	
Kelso, Sarah	20, July 1820	17, July	18	S3	
Kemp, James (Rev)	10, Nov. 1827	28, Oct.		R3	
Kemp, James (Rev)	9, Nov. 1827	28, Oct.		N2	
Kemper, Caleb	17, Sept 1835		probate	T2	
Kemper, James	9, June 1835		estate	N2	
Kemper, James (Rev)	22, Aug. 1834	20, Aug.	81	* X3	
Kemper, Reuben (Col)	23, Feb. 1827	29, Jan.		N3	
Kendal, James	6, Jan. 1837		estate	N2	
Kenedy, Patrick	14, June 1849	June	25	L2	
Keniston, Lowell	13, Feb. 1841	Feb.	35	R3	
Kennady, James	23, Mar. 1830		probate	N3	
Kenneally, (Capt)	26, Jan. 1848	21, Dec.		K2	
Kennedy, (child of James)	18, July 1828	July	stillborn	N3	

Name	Notice Date	Death Date	Age	Page	Maiden Name
Kennedy, A.	8, Aug. 1850	Aug.	50	Y2	
Kennedy, Ann	30, July 1850	July	25	Y3	
Kennedy, Hannah	18, July 1828	July	36	N3	
Kennedy, James	21, Dec. 1830	probate		N3	
Kennedy, James A.	15, Aug. 1828	2, July	23	N3	
Kennedy, Julia Ann	4, Apr. 1818	31, Mar.		S3	
Kennedy, Nancy	14, Aug. 1802	7, Aug.	27	S3	
Kennedy, Samuel	16, Feb. 1835	estate		T2	
Kennedy, Thomas	18, Aug. 1821	10, Aug.	80	S3	
Kennedy, Thomas	8, Dec. 1821	estate		S3	
Kenneedy, John	17, Nov. 1802	estate		S3	
Kenner, George R.	26, Oct. 1852	25, Sept		P2	
Kenney, Robert (Capt)	1, June 1807	30, May		S3	
Kennidy, Archibald	23, July 1850	July	26	Y2	
Kennister, James	6, Nov. 1838	probate		N2	
Kenny, Michael	13, July 1849	July	23	L2	
Kent, Charles Woodward	24, Nov. 1847	16, Nov.	18m-16d	K2	
Kent, Elizabeth	18, July 1850	17, July	55	P2	
Kent, Jacob	27, June 1840	3, June	87	R3	
Kent, Louisa Elgel	6, July 1849	July	7m	L2	
Kent, Luke	14, May 1842	6, May	71	R3	
Kent, Nicholas	1, June 1835	probate		N2	
Kent, William	25, Apr. 1840		75	R3	
Kenton, Simeon (Gen)	19, May 1836	29, Apr.	82	X3	
Kenyon, William	6, Oct. 1826	probate		N3	
Keown, John	25, July 1851	estate		P2	
Kepper, Hiram L.	26, July 1834	July	1	R3	
Kepper, Hiram L.	22, July 1834	July	1	T2	
Keral, (child of Jesse)	10, Dec. 1830	Dec.	1m	N3	
Kereding, Anna	14, June 1849	June	1	L2	
Kerner, William C.	28, May 1842	27, May		N2	
Kerns, Samuel	17, June 1837	probate		N2	
Kerr, John	5, Aug. 1823	20, July		N3	
Kerr, Thomas	21, Aug. 1852	19, Aug.	63	P2	
Kesler, Joseph	1, June 1835	probate		N2	
Kesse, Ann	6, July 1849	July	40	L2	
Kettenhorn, Rebecca	30, Sept 1852	28, Sept	34	P2	
Keys, Elizabeth Ann	18, June 1830	June	9m	N3	
Keys, James	11, Aug. 1826	estate		N3	
Keys, Margaret	6, Aug. 1817	2, Aug.	5	S3	
Keys, Richard	1, May 1830	28, Apr.	74	R3	
Keys, Richard	7, May 1830	May	74	N3	
Keys, William B.	20, Apr. 1836	14, Apr.	26	T2	
Keysor, John	14, June 1849	June	66	L2	
Keyt, David R.	6, Oct. 1815	estate		S3	
Keyt, David R.	31, Jan. 1817	estate		S3	
Kibby, Emma Louisa	1, Sept 1827	Aug.	15m	R3	
Kidd, John	6, Feb. 1819	1, Feb.	72	S3	
Kidd, John	27, Feb. 1819	estate		S1	
Kidd, John	7, Sept 1824	probate		N3	
Kidd, John	9, Sept 1824	probate		E3	
Kidd, Samuel (Mrs)	18, Apr. 1817	15, Apr.		S3	
Kidder, Henry Augustus	18, Mar. 1820	Jan.	16	* S3	
Kieser, Francis	1, June 1849	May	69	L2	

Name	Notice Date	Death Date	Age	Page	Maiden Name
Kiger, Francis	6, July 1849	July	42		L2	
Kilburn, Joseph	23, May 1823		estate	N3	
Kile, (child of B.)	19, Aug. 1831	Aug.	13m	A3	
Kiles, (child of Hannah)	1, Aug. 1828	July		N3	
Kiles, Jane	20, Feb. 1841	Feb.	14	R3	
Kiles, Jane	19, Feb. 1841	Feb.	14	N2	
Kiles, Julia	8, Aug. 1850	Aug.	2	Y2	
Kilgour, David	11, Oct. 1830	9, Oct.	63	A3	
Kilgour, Henry	11, Aug. 1837	10, Aug.		T2	
Kilgour, Sarah	1, Sept 1821	14, Aug.	52	S3	
Killbuck, Peter	15, Oct. 1800	8, Oct.		S3	
Killgore, Charles	5, Oct. 1807	2, Oct.		S3	
Kilmartin, John	26, July 1850	July	45	Y2	
Kiloh, Maria Anna	15, Oct. 1847	11, Oct.	*	K2	
Kilroy, James	24, May 1849	May	20	L2	
Kimball, Charles	21, Jan. 1842	20, Jan.	29	N2	
Kimball, Jesse	4, May 1835	2, May	44	T3	
Kimball, Mary Elizabeth	1, Jan. 1836	30, Dec.		T3	
Kimball, P.F. (Capt)	16, Oct. 1847	2, Oct.		K2	
Kimball, William	18, Mar. 1824		estate	E3	
Kimball, William	31, Aug. 1822	24, Aug.	*	S3	
Kimble, Martha R.	24, July 1850	July	1-10m	Y2	
Kimble, William	22, Aug. 1828	Aug.	2m	N3	
Kinch, Thomas W.	23, July 1850	July	34	Y2	
Kinemost, (child of Alexander)	2, July 1830	June	stillborn	N2	
King, Charles W.	24, June 1828	June	5m	N3	
King, Cyrus (Gen)	23, May 1817		44	S3	
King, E. (Mrs)	5, July 1828			R3	
King, Edward (Gen)	8, 9, Feb. 1836	6, Feb.	40	T3	
King, Edward (Gen)	9, Feb. 1836	6, Feb.	*	N2	
King, Elizabeth	13, 20, Mar. 1841	26, Feb.	24	R3	
King, Fanny W.	25, Nov. 1828	Nov.	1	N3	
King, John	24, Sept 1830	Sept	6m	N3	
King, John	11, Mar. 1806		estate	S3	
King, John (Mrs)	18, Aug. 1836	29, July	50	X3	
King, John E. (Gen)	28, June 1828		70	R3	
King, Joseph	9, July 1852	8, July	41	P2	
King, Julia	22, Aug. 1850	Aug.	36	Y2	
King, Rufus	15, May 1827	29, Apr.	73	N2	
King, Rufus	12, May 1827	25, Apr.		R3	
King, Thomas D.	29, Aug. 1829		estate	R3	
Kinkaid, (Mr)	6, Dec. 1852	2, Dec.		P2	
Kinkaid, Maria	4, Dec. 1852	2, Dec.	21- -7d	P2	
Kinlock, Francis	31, Mar. 1826		70	N3	
Kinmont, Alexander	22, Sept 1838	16, Sept		R3	
Kinmont, Alexander	17, Sept 1838	16, Sept		T2	
Kinnard, G.L.	30, Nov. 1836	27, Nov.		N2	
Kinnard, George L.	1, Dec. 1836	26, Nov.	35	X3	
Kinney, Altha L.	3, July 1852	2, July		P2	
Kinshallow, Jacob	30, July 1830	July	17d	N3	
Kirby, Fanny	29, June 1841	26, June	child	N2	
Kirby, Fanny	3, July 1841	26, June		R3	
Kirby, John H.	19, Oct. 1852	2, Sept		P2	
Kirby, Mary Jane	15, Dec. 1852	13, Dec.	8- 1m-23d	P2	

Name	Notice Date	Death Date	Age		Page	Maiden Name
Kirby, Richard	1, June 1835		probate		N2	
Kirk, William	12, Aug. 1828	Aug.	11		N3	
Kirkendal, Stephen	29, Mar. 1834	Mar.	50		R3	
Kirkland, John Thornton (Rev)	9, May 1840				R3	
Kissinger, (child of Samuel)	8, July 1828	July	7m		N3	
Kitchell, Benajah	19, Dec. 1826		probate		N3	
Kitchell, Benajah	11, Dec. 1827		probate		N3	
Kitchell, Benajah	4, Mar. 1828		probate		N3	
Kitchell, Calvin	20, Sept 1816		estate		S1	
Kitchell, Calvin	7, Feb. 1817		estate		S2	
Kitchen, Henry	28, July 1850	July	11m		Y3	
Kittera, John Wilkes	15, July 1801	6, June			S3	
Kitty, Thomas	11, Sept 1852	9, Sept			P2	
Klamroth, Anthony	21, June 1849	June	65		L2	
Klausing, William	2, July 1851		estate		P3	
Klien, George	14, June 1849	June	18		L2	
Kloppenberg, Otto Frederick	26, July 1852	20, July	11m- 1d		P2	
Knapke, Joseph	24, Sept 1852	23, Sept			P2	
Knicely, Jacob	11, Dec. 1827		probate		N3	
Knight, Abby H.	25, Oct. 1850	25, Oct.			P2	Jones
Knight, Francis Gates Adamson	4, May 1847	3, May	33		K2	
Knight, Henry	10, Apr. 1841	6, Apr.	32	*	R3	
Knight, Henry	9, Apr. 1841	6, Apr.	32	*	N2	
Knight, Henry	12, Mar. 1842		estate		R3	
Knight, Horace G.	16, July 1852	7, July			P2	
Knight, James	30, Sept 1825	31, Aug.	24		N2	
Knight, James	30, Oct. 1852	29, Oct.	1- 3m		P2	
Knight, Jonathan	19, Dec. 1826		probate		N3	
Knight, Mary E.	10, Dec. 1830	Dec.	1m		N3	
Knight, Thomas	10, May 1849	May	35		L2	
Knight, William Henry	20, Mar. 1841	18, Mar.	22m		N2	
Knoblaugh, John	11, June 1842	June	43		R3	
Knopp, (child of Joseph)	8, Oct. 1852	Oct.	11		P2	
Knox, Catharine	25, Aug. 1827	Aug.	50		R3	
Knox, Vicesimus (Rev)	17, Nov. 1821		68		S3	
Koeffer, John	5, Apr. 1849	Apr.	27		L2	
Koehler, Gottlib	28, June 1849	June	44		L2	
Koeller, Christian	3, May 1849	May	46		L2	
Kohn, Charles	25, July 1850	July	18m		Y2	
Konning, John H.	9, Sept 1831	Sept	6m		A3	
Kown, Charlotte	19, Aug. 1828	Aug.	11m		N3	
Kramer, (children of George)	3, May 1838				N2	
Kramer, Christina	6, Sept 1852	4, Sept			P2	
Kramer, George	3, May 1838				N2	
Kramer, George (Mrs)	3, May 1838				N2	
Kriesler, Joseph	4, Sept 1852	3, Sept			P2	
Krone, C.F.	17, Sept 1835		probate		T2	
Krout, Hannah	22, Aug. 1835	16, Aug.	24		T2	
Kugler, Christian	22, Aug. 1836	18, Aug.	24		T2	
Kugler, Christian	22, Aug. 1836	19, Aug.	24		N2	
Kugler, Matilda Caroline	31, Oct. 1840	24, Oct.	32- 9m		R3	Brower
Kuhlman, Theodore	21, June 1849	June	28		L2	
Kuhn, Joseph	28, June 1849	June	23		L2	
Kunzman, Anthony	19, Dec. 1840	Dec.	51		R3	

Name	Notice Date	Death Date	Age		Page	Maiden Name
Kunzman, Anthony	18, Dec. 1840	Dec.	51		N2	
Kyle, Jane	12, Sept 1840	17, Aug.	47	*	R3	
Kyle, Margaret	16, Apr. 1835	11, Apr.	76		T3	
Kyler, George	14, Aug. 1819		estate		S3	
Kyler, George	13, Mar. 1819	11, Mar.			S2	
Labrot, Marie Estelle Fleurie	8, Sept 1847	4, Sept	13m-15d		K2	
Lachlan, John	27, Nov. 1819			*	S3	
Lackey, (child of Patrick)	3, Apr. 1829	Mar.	stillborn		N2	
Lackey, George	22, Dec. 1829		probate		N3	
Lackey, John	11, Dec. 1827		probate		N3	
Lackey, Mary	3, May 1825		probate		N3	
Lacount, (man)	27, Nov. 1852	26, Nov.			P2	
Lacy, Elizabeth	30, July 1850	July	65		Y3	
Lafayette, (General)	26, June 1834	20, May	77		T2	
Laferty, James	7, June 1849	June	6		L2	
Lafferty, (child)	29, Mar. 1834	Mar.	stillborn		R3	
Lafferty, Lydia	21, June 1849	June	36		L2	
Lafferty, Robert	14, May 1830		estate		N3	
Laggerty, William	24, Sept 1830	Sept	30		N3	
Lain, Emma	20, Aug. 1830	Aug.	2		N3	
Laing, John	21, Mar. 1838		estate		N2	
Lakey, Cynthia	10, Sept 1842	30, Aug.			R3	
Lallemand, Henry (Gen)	3, Oct. 1823	15, Sept			N3	
Lallemand, Henry (Gen)	10, Oct. 1823	15, Sept			N1	
Laman, John H.	13, Sept 1852	11, Sept			P2	
Lamb, Abial	16, Dec. 1823		estate		N3	
Lamb, James	13, July 1849	July	55		L2	
Lamb, Susan G.	12, Aug. 1836	8, Aug.			T2	
Lambert, Daniel	7, Sept 1824		probate		N3	
Lambert, Daniel	9, Sept 1824		probate		E3	
Lambert, Mary	21, Dec. 1830		probate		N3	
Lamburn, Samuel	6, Oct. 1815		estate		S3	
Laming, (heirs)	14, Dec. 1835		probate		N2	
Lamme, Robert	12, Dec. 1801		estate		S3	
Lamme, Robert	17, July 1802		estate		S3	
Lamon, Charles	6, July 1849	July	50		L2	
Lamont, James	5, Dec. 1840	29, Nov.	29	*	R3	
Lamont, James	26, Sept 1840	18, Sept	2- 6m		R3	
Lamont, James	30, Nov. 1840	29, Nov.			N2	
Lamphear, Lucinda	23, Mar. 1841	20, Mar.	57		N2	
Lancaster, Elizabeth	28, Dec. 1820				S3	
Lancaster, J.R.H. (Lt)	24, July 1841	5, July			R3	
Land, Mary Ann	26, Apr. 1842	25, Apr.			N2	
Landers, Charles	15, Aug. 1850	Aug.	3		Y2	
Lane, Benjamin	2, July 1830	June	45		N2	
Lane, George	3, Jan. 1853	30, Dec.	16m		P2	
Langarl, William	5, Oct. 1822		estate		S3	
Langarl, William	16, Apr. 1824		estate		N3	
Langarl, William	16, Dec. 1825		probate		N3	
Langarl, William	3, Aug. 1822	25, July			S3	
Langdon, Esther	1, Sept 1827	26, Aug.	72	*	R3	
Langdon, James Burke	28, Apr. 1832	24, Apr.	17m		R3	
Langdon, John	23, Sept 1831	Sept	47		A3	
Langdon, John	8, Aug. 1818	3, Aug.			S3	

Name	Notice Date	Death Date	Age		Page	Maiden Name
Langdon, Nancy	16, Mar. 1824	7, Mar.	38		N3	
Langdon, Oliver	31, Jan. 1829		estate		R3	
Langdon, Oliver (Rev)	27, Sept 1828	21, Sept	59	*	R3	
Langdon, Solomon	7, Mar. 1817		estate		S3	
Langdon, Solomon	19, Sept 1817		estate		S3	
Langdon, Solomon (Rev)	11, Oct. 1816	8, Oct.			S3	
Langstaff, Euphema	30, Nov. 1852	27, Nov.	?- -10d		P2	
Langtry, Sarah	6, Aug. 1830	Aug.	10m		N3	
Lanman, James	16, Aug. 1841	7, Aug.	71		N2	
Lapham, Darius	21, July 1850	20, July	42		Y2	
Lardner, Mary Ann	22, Nov. 1839	8, Nov.	18		T2	Keys
Large, Lucinda	3, May 1849	May	20m		L2	
Lark, George	21, May 1830	May	32		N3	
Lark, Sebastian	13, July 1849	July	39		L2	
Larkin, John	15, Aug. 1850	Aug.	15m		Y2	
Larkin, William	7, June 1849	June			L2	
Larned, Attaresta	28, June 1834	27, June		*	T2	
Larvin, Alfred	23, July 1850	July	35		Y2	
Latschaw, Andreas	29, Mar. 1849	Mar.	40		L2	
Latta, Robert (Col)	11, Oct. 1837	23, Sept	40		T2	
Latte, Henry	15, May 1841	May	24		R3	
Latton, Elizabeth	4, Nov. 1828	Oct.	2- 6m		N3	
Laurison, Andrew	6, July 1849	July	7		L2	
Laurison, Ann	6, July 1849	July	35		L2	
Lavurna, Mary	30, July 1850	July	8		Y3	
Law, Thomas	9, July 1830	July	17m		N3	
Law, William	28, June 1849	June	33		L2	
Lawler, Ann	30, Mar. 1835	25, Mar.	74	*	T2	
Lawler, Ann	17, June 1837		probate		N2	
Lawler, Matthew	16, July 1831	14, July	77	*	R3	
Lawner, Bartlett	28, June 1849	June	25		L2	
Lawrence,	30, Dec. 1828	Dec.	2		N3	
Lawrence, (child of Dean)	24, Dec. 1830	Dec.	1d		N3	
Lawrence, Alanson J.M.	7, Nov. 1840	14, Oct.	21		R3	
Lawrence, Caroline	16, Jan. 1829	Jan.	5		N2	
Lawrence, Edmund	15, Aug. 1850	Aug.	3		Y2	
Lawrence, Elias D.	28, June 1828				R3	
Lawrence, Jonathan	2, Mar. 1833		estate		R3	
Lawrence, Lorenzo (Dr)	24, Dec. 1836	21, Dec.	44		R3	
Lawrence, Lorenzo (Dr)	24, Dec. 1836	21, Dec.	44		T2	
Lawrence, Lorenzo (Dr)	29, Dec. 1836	21, Dec.	44	*	X3	
Lawrence, Robert	26, Oct. 1835		estate		N2	
Lawrence, Robert	4, Apr. 1837		probate		N2	
Lawrence, Sophia Williamson	14, Dec. 1833	11, Dec.	5- 7m		R3	
Lawrence, Thomas (Sir)	5, Mar. 1830		50		N2	
Lawrence, William C.	2, Aug. 1834	July	3m-15d		R3	
Lawrence, William C.	29, July 1834	July	3m-15d		T2	
Lawson, (child of J.)	8, Sept 1827	Sept	1m		R3	
Lawson, (child of Thomas)	25, Nov. 1828	Nov.	stillborn		N3	
Lawson, Emma	25, June 1830	June	1- 2m		N3	
Lawson, Harriet	7, June 1828	June			R3	
Lawson, Jesse	1, June 1835		probate		N2	
Lawson, Thomas	22, Dec. 1852	21, Dec.	35		P2	
Lawson, Thomas	8, June 1841	4, June	53		N2	

Name	Notice Date	Death Date	Age		Page	Maiden Name
Lawson, William H.	23, July 1850	July	1- 5m		Y2	
Lawson, Wilson	8, Aug. 1850	Aug.	32		Y2	
Layer, Frederick	20, Feb. 1841	Feb.	25		R3	
Laygham, Elias (Col)	29, Apr. 1830	3, Apr.	73		A3	
Lazarus, Eleazar	23, July 1850	July	5		Y2	
Lea, (Mrs)	29, Mar. 1834	Mar.	42		R3	
Lea, Elizabeth	16, Mar. 1833	13, Mar.		*	R3	
Lea, James	4, Oct. 1825	30, Sept	66	*	N3	
Lea, James M.	8, May 1830		estate		R3	
Leach, Charles E.	20, Jan. 1848	18, Jan.	3- 6m		K2	
Leach, L.D.	22, June 1849	20, June	32		L2	
Leahy, James	25, July 1850	July	40		Y2	
Leake, Samuel	8, Apr. 1820	8, Apr.	63	*	S3	
Leatherman, Michael	13, June 1835		estate		N2	
Leathers, Jane	17, May 1841	11, May	59		N2	
Leathers, Thomas P.	29, Apr. 1828		estate		N3	
Lebosley, Elizabeth	23, July 1830	July	18		N3	
Leckey, Andrew	9, Aug. 1816		estate		S3	
Lecky, Alex.	16, Dec. 1825		probate		N3	
Lecky, Andrew	16, Dec. 1825		probate		N3	
Ledbetter, Daniel B.	28, July 1850	July	13		Y3	
Ledyard, Herman L.	23, Nov. 1839	23, Nov.	26		R3	
Lee, (child of William)	30, July 1830	July	10d		N3	
Lee, Adam	6, July 1836		estate		N2	
Lee, Adam	4, Apr. 1837		probate		N2	
Lee, Adelia	12, Sept 1828	Sept	10d		N3	
Lee, Amos	16, Aug. 1851	14, Aug.			P2	
Lee, Ann E.	27, July 1850	July	11		Y3	
Lee, Arthur	9, Aug. 1841	3, Aug.		*	N2	
Lee, Arthur	21, Aug. 1841	17, Aug.			V3	
Lee, Betsey C.	3, Nov. 1837	2, Nov.	35		T2	
Lee, Charles	28, July 1815	1, July	58		S3	
Lee, Clinton W.	16, Oct. 1851	15, Oct.	26		P2	
Lee, Gideon	4, Sept 1841			*	R3	
Lee, Henry (Gen)	25, Apr. 1818	25, Mar.	61	*	S3	
Lee, Jane	20, Oct. 1827	Oct.	7m		R3	
Lee, John	7, June 1849	June	38		L2	
Lee, John G.	21, Sept 1827	12, Sept	24		N3	
Lee, Margaret	7, Sept 1830		probate		N3	
Lee, Mary	8, Dec. 1827	4, Dec.	33		R3	
Lee, Robert	25, Sept 1838	24, Sept	21		N2	
Lee, Robert	22, Sept 1838	22, Sept		*	T2	
Lee, Samuel	3, May 1825		probate		N3	
Lee, Samuel	19, Dec. 1826		probate		N3	
Lee, Samuel M.	11, Sept 1841	2, Sept	33		N2	
Lee, Thomas	1, Dec. 1835		estate		N2	
Leech, William	3, Feb. 1829	Jan.	80		N3	
Leethem, Aaron	19, July 1834	July	14d		R3	
Lefferson, Garret	15, July 1828		estate		N3	
Leffler, Joseph	13, July 1849	July	41		L2	
Lefler, David	26, Nov. 1830	Nov.	26		N3	
Lehmanowsky, Mary Salome	12, Jan. 1837	18, Dec.	42		X3	
Leibert, Joseph B.	29, July 1806	25, July			S3	
Leien, Frank	14, June 1849	June	33		L2	

Name	Notice Date	Death Date	Age		Page	Maiden Name
Leigh, Benjamin Watkins	8, Dec. 1837	1, Dec.			T3	
Leiper, Thomas	26, July 1825	8, July	80		N3	
Leland, Julia	23, Dec. 1840	27, Nov.	23	*	N2	
Lembar, Joseph	15, Aug. 1850	Aug.	43		Y2	
Lemming, Samuel	11, Nov. 1835		estate		N2	
Lemon, Andrew	6, Oct. 1826		probate		N3	
Lemon, Joshua	18, Feb. 1841	17, Feb.			N2	
Lemond, Benjamin F.	6, Aug. 1830	Aug.	16		N3	
Lenhart, Sarah	1, Dec. 1848				B2	
Lentner, Sarah Ann	22, Aug. 1828	Aug.	24		N3	
Lentz, Catharine	10, July 1841	July	3m		R3	
Leny, Thomas M.	28, June 1849	June	42		L2	
Leonard, Charles	17, June 1850	14, June			P2	
Leonard, Charlotte	19, Aug. 1831	Aug.	8m		A3	
Leonard, George	24, June 1850	22, June	12		P2	
Leonard, Patrick	17, Aug. 1822	11, Aug.	84		S3	
LePage, Edwin	22, Aug. 1826	21, Aug.	28		N3	
LePage, Hannah	8, Oct. 1830	Oct.	40		N3	
Leque, Edward	8, Aug. 1835		estate		N2	
Letherby, Amos R.	16, Aug. 1852	9, Aug.	20		P2	
Lewis, (child of Enson)	2, July 1830	June	stillborn		N2	
Lewis, (child of James)	1, Aug. 1828	July	infant		N3	
Lewis, (Mr)	31, July 1852	28, July	66		P2	
Lewis, Benjamin Henry	12, Aug. 1852	10, Aug.	1- 7m- 4d		P2	
Lewis, Elizabeth G.	13, Sept 1847	12, Sept	19		K2	
Lewis, Ellen	24, July 1850	July	18		Y2	
Lewis, Francis C.	7, June 1828	June			R3	
Lewis, John	3, Aug. 1822	26, July		*	S3	
Lewis, Martha	31, Oct. 1840	26, Oct.	50	*	R3	
Lewis, Mary	17, Aug. 1837	17, July	38	*	X3	Cornelius
Lewis, Nancy E.	27, Sept 1841	26, Sept			N2	
Lewis, Rachel Miller	26, Sept 1840	22, Sept	3		R3	
Lewis, Sylvia	12, Sept 1828	Sept	20		N3	
Lewis, Theodore	12, Jan. 1829	Jan.	52		N2	
Lewis, Watson	21, Dec. 1839		estate		R3	
Lewis, Watson	19, Sept 1840		estate		R3	
Lewis, William	18, July 1828	July	60		N3	
Lewis, William	25, Sept 1819	16, Aug.	69		S3	
Lewis, William (Gen)	5, Apr. 1825	17, Jan.	58	*	N3	
Lewis, William H.S.	15, Dec. 1852	13, Dec.	22m		P2	
Lewis, Zachariah	21, Nov. 1840	14, Nov.	68		R3	
L'Hommedieu, Charles	21, Aug. 1813		estate		S3	
L'Hommedieu, Charles (Capt)	17, Apr. 1813	10, Apr.		*	S3	
L'Hommedieu, Charles Hammond	5, Sept 1840	3, Sept	10m-13d		R3	
L'Hommedieu, Samuel	8, Sept 1838	3, Sept	37		R3	
L'Hommedieu, Samuel	5, Sept 1838	3, Sept	37		T2	
Libea, Josephine M.	24, July 1841	20, July	13m		R3	
Libeau, Josephine M.	23, July 1841	20, July	13m		N2	
Lieman, Gotleeb	3, Oct. 1840	Sept	21		R3	
Lifthouse, William	6, Aug. 1830	Aug.	62		N3	
Liggett, Elizabeth	27, Oct. 1852	22, Oct.	27		P2	
Light, Mary	13, July 1849	July	14d		L2	
Lightfoot, S.	19, Aug. 1831	Aug.	7m		A3	
Lighton, William P.	13, Mar. 1829	Mar.			N3	

Name	Notice Date	Death Date	Age		Page	Maiden Name
Lilly, Eleanor	19, Nov. 1830	Nov.	19		N3	
Lilly, Silas	25, Oct. 1831	Sept	65		A3	
Limthecome, J.	28, Mar. 1795		estate		C3	
Lincoln, Henry (Rev)	26, Aug. 1847	18, Aug.	64		K2	
Lindenger, John	6, July 1849	July	26		L2	
Lindinger, Magdalena	6, July 1849	July	28		L2	
Lindley, Emma	7, Aug. 1852	4, Aug.	5		P2	
Lindley, Martha	27, Oct. 1821	4, Oct.	18		S3	
Lindley, Martha	3, Nov. 1821	4, Oct.	18		S3	
Lindley, Martha	27, Oct. 1821	28, Sept	51		S3	
Lindley, Martha	3, Nov. 1821	28, Sept	51		S3	
Lindley, Mary	27, Aug. 1852	Aug.	1		P2	
Lindley, Thaddeus	21, Dec. 1830		probate		N3	
Lindley, Thadeus	22, Sept 1821	11, Sept	34		S3	
Lindley, William	7, Aug. 1852	2, Aug.	19m		P2	
Lindo, A.A.	10, July 1849	8, July	73	*	L2	
Lindsay, Elizabeth	13, May 1847	12, May	44		K2	
Lindsay, William (Col)	21, Sept 1838	21, Sept			T2	
Lindsay, William C.	5, Sept 1823	2, Sept		*	N3	
Lindsey, Beulah	5, June 1835		80		T2	
Lindsey, Eliza	26, Sept 1840	12, Sept			R3	
Lindsey, Mary Elizabeth	30, July 1852	27, July	10m-22d		P2	
Linn, John	20, Jan. 1821	5, Jan.	57		S3	
Linskey, James	10, Nov. 1852	9, Nov.			P2	
Linton, William	13, Mar. 1848	12, Mar.	67		K2	
Lippencott, David A.	24, Jan. 1837	23, Jan.	40		T2	
Lippencott, David A.	27, Jan. 1837		estate		T2	
Lippincott, David A.	6, Nov. 1838		probate		N2	
Lister, Richard	21, June 1849	June			L2	
Little, Francis B.	11, Nov. 1834	25, Oct.	63	*	T2	
Little, James M.	24, Apr. 1838		estate		N2	
Little, Jane	26, Sept 1840	22, Sept		*	R3	
Little, Lucy	7, Nov. 1834		30	*	X3	
Little, Rachel	18, June 1830	June	1- 6m		N3	
Little, William	19, Sept 1828	Sept	19	*	N3	
Littleken, Catharine Christina	14, Aug. 1852	13, Aug.	2- 7m-10d		P2	
Littleton, Elizabeth Maria	16, Nov. 1852	4, Nov.	64		P2	
Liverpool, (child of Esick)	19, July 1834	July	1d		R3	
Livezey, Elizabeth B.	8, Sept 1852	5, Sept			P2	
Living, David	17, Sept 1835		probate		T2	
Livingston, Brockholst	1, Apr. 1823	18, Mar.	66		N2	
Livingston, Edward	9, June 1836	6, June	72		X3	
Livingston, John H. (Rev)	11, Feb. 1825	20, Jan.	79		N3	
Livingston, Robert R.	3, Apr. 1813		70		S1	
Lloyd, (Mr)	28, July 1821	27, July			S3	
Lloyd, John	27, Aug. 1800	20, Aug.	31		S3	
Loar, G.	18, May 1838		probate		N2	
Loar, George	7, Dec. 1837		probate		N3	
Locke, James	13, Feb. 1841	Feb.	22		R3	
Lockman, (child of William)	21, Oct. 1828	Oct.	child		N2	
Lockman, Hugh W.	6, Aug. 1830	Aug.			N3	
Lodge, James	22, Dec. 1835	19, Dec.		*	N2	
Lodge, Jozabad	23, July 1830	July	62		N3	
Lodge, Jozabad	6, Aug. 1830		estate		N3	

Name	Notice Date	Death Date	Age		Page	Maiden Name
Lodge, Seline	10, Oct. 1818	6, Oct.			S3	
Lodock, Thomas	12, Aug. 1828	Aug.	48		N3	
Lodwick, William	17, Sept 1835		probate		T2	
Lodwick, William	14, Dec. 1835		probate		N2	
Lodwick, William	18, June 1831	12, June			R3	
Lofsinger, Albert	17, May 1849	May	20		L2	
Lofthouse, Larry	13, July 1849	July	45		L2	
Logan, Samuel C.	14, Apr. 1836	12, Apr.			X3	
Lognwatts, John	5, Sept 1828	Sept	32		N3	
Lohse, F.	8, Oct. 1852	Oct.	80		P2	
Londerloch, John	15, Sept 1827	Sept	66		R3	
Long, Agnes	21, Sept 1838		probate		N3	
Long, Andrew	2, Dec. 1828		estate		N3	
Long, Andrew	21, Dec. 1830		probate		N3	
Long, Herman	26, Oct. 1824	24, Oct.	58		N3	
Long, Herman	7, Dec. 1824		estate		N3	
Long, Herman	27, Jan. 1825		estate		E3	
Long, Herman	9, Dec. 1828		probate		N3	
Long, James	10, July 1841	July	69		R3	
Long, John D.	22, Sept 1827	Sept	2- 8m		R3	
Long, Joseph	20, Aug. 1830	Aug.	30		N3	
Long, Michael	23, Mar. 1830		probate		N3	
Longenecker, Charles H.	27, Nov. 1852	26, Nov.	3- 2m-10d		P2	
Longshore, John	21, Sept 1838		probate		N3	
Longshore, Mary R.	23, July 1850	July	13		Y2	
Longshore, William	4, Apr. 1842		25		N2	
Look, Silas C.	16, July 1830	July	3- 9m		N3	
Looker, Ada	12, May 1836	11, May	15m		N2	
Looker, Allison C.	3, Aug. 1824	27, July	33	*	N2	
Looker, Allison C.	5, Aug. 1824	3, Aug.	33	*	E3	
Looker, Allison G.	10, July 1852	9, July	30		P2	
Looker, Frances J.	27, July 1850	July	21		Y3	
Looker, James Harvey	10, Mar. 1827	3, Mar.	19		R3	
Looker, James Hervey	6, Mar. 1827	3, Mar.	19		N3	
Looker, John M.	19, Dec. 1812	17, Dec.			S3	
Looker, Lydia	24, Nov. 1827	19, Nov.			R3	
Looker, Lydia	23, Nov. 1827	19, Nov.			N3	
Looker, R.A.	4, June 1836		probate		N2	
Looker, Silas C.	12, Oct. 1830		estate		N3	
Looker, Silas C.	7, Nov. 1835		estate		N2	
Looker, Silas C.	5, Apr. 1830	1, Apr.			A3	
Looker, Silas C.	2, Apr. 1830	1, Apr.			N2	
Loomis, Elisha	6, Oct. 1836	28, Sept			X3	
Loomis, William Dorwin	23, Nov. 1837	21, Nov.	6m- 2d		T2	
Lord, Frederick French	15, Feb. 1848	13, Feb.	4-10m		K2	
Lord, Mary	26, Sept 1828	Sept	26		N3	
Lorens, Caleb	21, Oct. 1828	Oct.	72		N2	
Loring, David	5, Feb. 1849	22, Jan.	64	*	L2	
Loring, David	5, Feb. 1849	22, Jan.	64	*	Y2	
Lough, Joseph	28, Sept 1820	3, Aug.	40	*	S3	
Loughburough, Sarah	13, Aug. 1852	11, Aug.	83		P2	
Loundsberry, (child of Joseph)	19, Aug. 1828	Aug.	3w		N3	
Louns, William L.	25, June 1830	June	14d		N3	
Lourrig, Henry	8, Aug. 1850	Aug.	55		Y2	

Name	Notice Date	Death Date	Age		Page	Maiden Name
Love, Margaret	12, Aug. 1852	1, Aug.	20- 7m		P2	
Love, Sally Ann	27, Jan. 1824		estate		N3	
Love, Sally Ann	3, May 1825		probate		N3	
Lovejoy, E.P. (Rev)	16, Nov. 1837				X2	
Lovejoy, Elizabeth	14, May 1830	May	37		N3	
Lovejoy, Lewis	24, Feb. 1829	Feb.	11m		N3	
Lovejoy, Samuel	26, July 1834	July	41		R3	
Lovejoy, Samuel	22, July 1834	July	41		T2	
Lovejoy, Samuel	24, July 1834		estate		T2	
Lovejoy, Samuel	1, Sept 1834		estate		T3	
Lovejoy, Samuel (heirs of)	18, May 1838		probate		N2	
Lovejoy, William G.	4, Nov. 1847	6, Oct.	26		K2	
Lovelace, Sarah Maria Mellor	8, Feb. 1840	7, Feb.	18		R3	
Lovelace, Seneca	25, Apr. 1828	22, Apr.			Q3	
Lovelace, Seneca James	25, Apr. 1840	24, Apr.	infant		R3	
Lovell, Joseph (Dr)	28, Oct. 1836	27, Oct.			T2	
Lovell, William	22, Aug. 1850	Aug.	26		Y2	
Lowe, Cornelius	2, Sept 1828		estate		N3	
Lowes, James	29, Dec. 1810	15, Dec.			S3	
Lowman, Levi	27, Feb. 1829	Feb.	22		N3	
Lowrey, Margaret	26, Jan. 1803	21, Jan.			S3	
Lowrey, Thomas	18, Feb. 1806		estate		S3	
Lowry, Rebecca	6, Nov. 1841	21, Sept	43		N2	
Loyes, Chester	14, June 1849	June	42		L2	
Lucas, William	25, Sept 1805	24, Aug.			S3	
Ludlow, Israel	8, Nov. 1809		estate		H3	
Ludlow, Israel (Col)	25, Jan. 1804	20, Jan.	38		S3	
Ludlow, James C.	17, Sept 1841		estate		N2	
Ludlow, James C.	21, Aug. 1841	15, Aug.			R3	
Ludlow, James C.	16, Aug. 1841	15, Aug.			N2	
Ludlow, John	11, Apr. 1823	26, Mar.	71		N3	
Ludlow, John	27, Oct. 1826		estate		N2	
Ludlow, John	16, Sept 1851	14, Sept			P2	
Ludlum, Henry	13, Feb. 1819		estate		S1	
Ludlum, Henry	7, Sept 1824		probate		N3	
Ludlum, Henry	4, Mar. 1828		probate		N3	
Ludlum, Henry	9, Sept 1824		probate		E3	
Ludlum, James A.B.	1, Aug. 1828	July	11m		N3	
Ludlum, James M. (Dr)	26, Aug. 1852	23, Aug.	60		P2	
Luke, William	19, May 1834	16, May	49	*	T2	
Lumsden, Mary Jane	12, Sept 1840	8, Sept	6m-21d		R3	
Lungren, William P.	1, Nov. 1837	23, Oct.		*	T2	
Lupton, Anna Buck	28, Apr. 1849	27, Apr.	11m		L2	
Lupton, Harriet	17, July 1837	16, July	7m-16d		T2	
Lupton, Harriet B.	8, Dec. 1836	2, Dec.	19		X3	Lawrence
Lupton, Harriet O.	5, Dec. 1836	2, Dec.	20		T2	Lawrence
Lupton, Mary F.	19, May 1849	3, May	32		L2	Leslie
Luth, Mary Emma	28, June 1849	June	4- 3m		L2	
Lutz, Samuel H.	25, July 1829	19, July		*	R3	
Luzenburg, Mary L.	20, June 1849	19, June	20		L2	
Lyle, Agnes	24, July 1850	July	50		Y2	
Lynch, Miles	30, July 1850	July	13m		Y3	
Lynch, William	25, June 1836	June	17		N2	
Lyncoya,	8, July 1828	1, July	16		N3	

Name	Notice Date	Death Date	Age		Page	Maiden Name
Lynes, Mary	30, Dec. 1825	29, Dec.	76		N3	
Lynes, William (Rev)	9, Dec. 1841	6, Dec.	83		N2	
Lynk, Andrew	4, June 1836		probate		N2	
Lynk, Elmira	13, Sept 1838	Sept	9		T2	
Lyon, Eliza	12, Sept 1840	7, Sept			R3	
Lyon, Harriet Elizabeth	9, Dec. 1828	Dec.	1- 7m		N3	
Lyon, James	21, Sept 1841	10, Sept	87		N2	
Lyon, John	6, July 1849	July	2		L2	
Lyon, Mary	2, Jan. 1835	22, Dec.	72		X3	
Lyon, Peter	10, Aug. 1824		80		N2	
Lyons, Ella	17, Nov. 1852	14, Nov.	1		P2	
Lyst, John	3, Dec. 1824		estate		N3	
Lyst, John	16, Dec. 1825		probate		N3	
Lytle, Andrew J.	18, June 1842	2, June	26	*	R3	
Lytle, Andrew J.	15, June 1842	2, June	26	*	N2	
Lytle, Eliza N.	19, May 1821	15, May			S3	
Lytle, Elizabeth	1, Jan. 1842	1, Jan.			R3	
Lytle, Elizabeth	30, 31, Dec. 1841	29, Dec.			N2	
Lytle, Elizabeth H.	15, Jan. 1842	29, Dec.			N2	
Lytle, John S.	24, May 1841		estate		N2	
Lytle, Lucien	28, July 1815				S3	
Lytle, Lucien	29, July 1815	26, July			G3	
Lytle, Robert T. (Gen)	18, Jan. 1840	21, Dec.		*	R3	
Lytle, Sarah S.	8, June 1833	3, June	25		R3	Biddle
Lytle, William (Gen)	19, Mar. 1831	18, Mar.	61		R3	
Lytle, William (Gen)	9, Apr. 1831	18, Mar.	61	*	R1	
Lytle, William H.	6, June 1826	4, June			N3	
MacAlester, Eliza Ann	9, 11, Sept 1835	31, Aug.			T2	Lytle
MacFarland, Robert	30, Nov. 1827	23, Oct.			N2	
MacGregor, James	27, July 1827	27, May	100	*	N2	
MacIntyre, Duncan	9, June 1838	7, June	35	*	N2	
Mack, Thomas	24, July 1850	July	2		Y2	
Macker, John	20, Jan. 1825		estate		E3	
Mackey, Alexander	16, Mar. 1811	9, Mar.			S3	
Mackey, George	29, May 1813	16, May			S3	
Macomb, Alexander (Gen)	1, July 1841	25, June	60	*	N2	
Macomb, Mary Tiffin	28, Mar. 1837	Mar.			T2	Worthington
Macraken, James C.	22, Oct. 1852	5, Sept	32		P2	
MacRee, Marion	2, Nov. 1847	1, Nov.	16m		K2	
Madarie, William	21, Sept 1838		probate		N3	
Madden, J.	3, May 1838				N2	
Maddigan, Edward	19, Dec. 1840	Dec.	20		R3	
Maddigan, Edward	18, Dec. 1840	Dec.	20		N2	
Maddock, John	26, Sept 1828	Sept	76		N3	
Madeira, J.	28, Nov. 1835		estate		N2	
Madeira, Jacob	19, Jan. 1830		estate		N3	
Madeira, Jacob	1, June 1835		probate		N2	
Madeira, Jacob	1, Jan. 1830	30, Dec.			N2	
Maderea, William	1, Nov. 1836		estate		N2	
Madiera, George Dashiell	6, Oct. 1827	3, Oct.	infant		R3	
Madison, George (Gov)	25, Oct. 1816	14, Oct.			S2	
Madison, James (President)	8, July 1836	28, June	85- 3m-12d		T2	
Madison, Margaret	5, Dec. 1838	5, Dec.			T2	
Maffit, John N.	7, June 1850	15, May			P2	

Name	Notice Date	Death Date	Age	Page	Maiden Name
Magill, Catharine	10, July 1849	8, July	60	L2	
Magilly, Owen	8, Oct. 1852	Oct.	25	P2	
Magman, (child of Patsy)	2, July 1830	June	2d	N2	
Magowan, Ursica O.	19, Aug. 1828	Aug.	14	N3	
Mahaffy, Mary Ann	12, July 1828		infant	R3	
Mahana, Timothy	26, Apr. 1849	Apr.	23	L2	
Mahany, Thomas	29, July 1834	July	57	T2	
Mahary, Thomas	2, Aug. 1834	July	57	R3	
Mahony, John	26, Apr. 1849	Apr.	36	L2	
Malone, Mercy	27, Aug. 1830	Aug.	29	N3	
Malony, Daniel	13, Sept 1852	9, Sept	38	P2	
Malsbury, Samuel	10, Jan. 1837		estate	N2	
Manly, Abraham	19, Aug. 1828	Aug.	4m	N3	
Manly, Bridget	25, July 1850	July	2	Y2	
Manly, Catherine	28, July 1850	July	10	Y3	
Mann, Hebe Carter	20, Mar. 1838	16, Mar.	*	N2	
Mann, Leah P.	25, Jan. 1842	24, Jan.	27	N2	
Mann, Phebe Carter	24, Mar. 1838	19, Mar.		R3	
Mann, Phoebe Carter	17, Mar. 1838	16, Mar.		T2	
Mann, W.	28, Oct. 1835		estate	N3	
Mann, William	14, Dec. 1835		probate	N2	
Manning, Harriet	15, Nov. 1838	8, Nov.	29	T2	
Manning, Patrick	28, June 1849	June	36	L2	
Mansfield, Jared (Col)	5, Mar. 1830	3, Feb.	71	* N2	
Mansfield, John F. (Capt)	2, Jan. 1813		estate	S3	
Mansfield, John Fenno (Capt)	19, Sept 1812	14, Sept	25	S2	
Mansfield, Mary	14, Mar. 1837	13, Mar.		T2	
Mansfield, Mary W.	16, Mar. 1837	10, Mar.	36	X3	
Mansfield, Mary W.	11, Mar. 1837	10, Mar.		R3	
Mansfield, William V.	24, June 1837	18, June	infant	R3	
Manson, (Miss)	26, July 1834	July	19- 4m	R3	
Manuire, Catharine	2, Aug. 1834	July		R3	
Manuire, Catherine	29, July 1834	July		T2	
Maphet, John	16, Oct. 1819		estate	S3	
Maples, Thomas	25, Sept 1805	29, Aug.		S3	
Mappen, Joseph	22, Dec. 1829		probate	N3	
Mappett, John	9, May 1817		estate	S4	
March, Joseph H.	27, Mar. 1835		estate	X3	
Marchant, Nathan	1, June 1835		probate	N2	
Markland, Thomas	20, Mar. 1838		probate	N3	
Marks, Eliza R.	4, Sept 1841		40	* V3	
Marks, William	8, July 1852	6, July		P2	
Markwood, Sarah Ann	18, July 1828	July	17m	N3	
Marnan, Catharine	26, July 1850	July	13	Y2	
Marony, Mary	13, Mar. 1837	11, May	12	R3	
Marony, Mary	10, May 1837	9, May	12	T2	
Maroony, Margaret	6, July 1849	July	6	L2	
Marrion, Louisa	13, July 1849	July	25	L2	
Marrion, Mary	13, July 1849	July	1	L2	
Marse, Martha N.	24, July 1850	July	28	Y2	
Marsh, Charles	15, Aug. 1850	Aug.	35	Y2	
Marsh, Charles	13, Nov. 1819		estate	S3	
Marsh, Charles	7, Nov. 1818	31, Oct.		* S3	
Marsh, Daniel, Sen.	18, Mar. 1820		estate	S1	

Name	Notice Date	Death Date	Age	Page	Maiden Name
Marsh, Darius	8, Oct. 1799		estate	S3	
Marsh, Harriet S.	2, July 1849	1, July	38	L2	
Marsh, Harry Blatchford	29, Aug. 1850	27, Aug.	6- 7m	P2	
Marsh, Isaiah	19, Nov. 1814		estate	S3	
Marsh, Jacob	18, Mar. 1820		estate	S1	
Marsh, Richard	5, Nov. 1814		estate	S3	
Marsh, Sarah J.	23, July 1850	July	1	Y2	
Marsh, Thomas	15, Dec. 1832		estate	R3	
Marsh, Thomas	19, Jan. 1833		estate	R3	
Marsh, William	19, July 1834	July	2m	R3	
Marsh, Zebulon M.P.	27, Mar. 1841	20, Feb.	25	R3	
Marshal, John	21, Aug. 1805	19, July		S3	
Marshal, William	6, June 1818		estate	S3	
Marshall, David	1, June 1835		probate	N2	
Marshall, Elihu F.	19, Sept 1840	29, Aug.		R3	
Marshall, Eliza	13, Nov. 1838	12, Nov.	24	T2	
Marshall, George	29, Aug. 1823		estate	N3	
Marshall, Jimmy	1, Sept 1837	6, Apr.	140	N2	
Marshall, John	18, July 1828	July	13m	N3	
Marshall, John	13, July 1835	7, July		T2	
Marshall, Leah	20, Apr. 1824	16, Apr.		N3	
Marshall, Margaret	24, Nov. 1827	18, Nov.		R3	
Marshall, Margaret	23, Nov. 1827	18, Nov.		N3	
Marshall, Mary	14, Dec. 1839	9, Dec.	81	R3	
Marshall, Rebecca	14, Oct. 1828	Oct.	2	N3	
Marshall, William	9, Nov. 1841	23, Oct.	35	N2	
Marshall, William	29, Apr. 1828		estate	N3	
Marshall, William	16, June 1829		estate	N3	
Marshall, William P.	8, May 1849	6, May	80- 5m	* L2	
Marshell, William	27, June 1826		estate	N3	
Marten, George	17, July 1841	July	29	R3	
Martin, (child of Hugh)	22, Aug. 1828	Aug.	9d	N3	
Martin, Alexander	18, July 1828	July	16m	N3	
Martin, Alvira	1, May 1835	14, Apr.		T3	
Martin, Amelia L.	19, June 1813	14, June	23	S3	
Martin, Arthur	13, Mar. 1848	11, Mar.	57	K2	
Martin, Benjamin	11, Aug. 1850	24, July	19	Y2	
Martin, C.A.	9, Sept 1831	Sept	1- 5m-11d	A3	
Martin, Edward M.	11, Aug. 1850	23, July	29	* Y2	
Martin, Elizabeth	24, Jan. 1837	22, Jan.	30	T2	
Martin, Francis	26, Mar. 1808		estate	S3	
Martin, Francis	4, July 1828		estate	N3	
Martin, Francis D.	17, Sept 1835		probate	T2	
Martin, George W.	17, Sept 1835		probate	T2	
Martin, Henriett	24, Aug. 1850	20, Aug.	infant	P2	
Martin, Hugh	14, Jan. 1832	11, Jan.	58	R3	
Martin, Hugh	27, Jan. 1832	11, Jan.	58	X3	
Martin, Isaac	26, Jan. 1803		estate	S3	
Martin, Jacob O.	17, Sept 1835		probate	T2	
Martin, Jacob O.	21, Sept 1838		probate	N3	
Martin, James Thomas	24, Mar. 1832	24, Feb.	24	R3	
Martin, John	14, June 1849	June	30	L2	
Martin, John	22, Nov. 1852	18, Nov.	74	P2	
Martin, John	11, July 1836		estate	N2	

Name	Notice Date	Death Date	Age		Page	Maiden Name
Martin, John	18, May 1838		probate		N2	
Martin, John Edwin	22, 23, Sept 1852	20, Sept	14-10m		P2	
Martin, Joseph	9, June 1847	8, June	70		K2	
Martin, Joseph	27, Mar. 1835		estate		N2	
Martin, Lucinda	30, Oct. 1852	28, Oct.		*	P2	
Martin, Luther	8, Aug. 1826	9, July	82	*	N3	
Martin, Lydia D.	7, June 1825	3, June			N3	
Martin, Margaret	21, Oct. 1828	Oct.	36		N2	
Martin, Mary Ann	27, Sept 1838	Sept	3		T2	
Martin, Mary Blair	18, Sept 1852	15, Sept	93		P2	
Martin, Oliver	12, May 1829	8, Apr.	68		N3	
Martin, Oliver	1, May 1830		estate		R3	
Martin, Richard	25, Apr. 1817		estate		S3	
Martin, Robert	27, July 1850	July	50		Y3	
Martin, Samuel	27, June 1835	22, June	3		T2	
Martin, Samuel J.	23, Sept 1831	Sept	10m		A3	
Martin, Samuel M.	25, Nov. 1825	24, Nov.			N3	
Martin, Thomas (Major)	23, Jan. 1819	18, Jan.	68		S3	
Marvin, Elizabeth	2, Jan. 1829	Dec.	2m		N3	
Mash, (son of Aaron)	16, Jan. 1802	13, Jan.	15		S3	
Mash, Aaron	16, Jan. 1802	13, Jan.			S3	
Mashulatubbee, Mingo	12, Oct. 1838	30, Sept	60		N2	
Mason, Ana S.	23, Mar. 1824	22, Mar.	21		N3	
Mason, Anna S.	25, Mar. 1824	22, Mar.	21		E3	Fosdick
Mason, Benjamin	20, Oct. 1847		76		K2	
Mason, Catharine	6, Feb. 1829	Feb.	42		N2	
Mason, Clementina	10, Aug. 1852	30, July			P2	
Mason, James M.	21, Dec. 1839		estate		R3	
Mason, James M.	27, Feb. 1838		estate		T2	
Mason, James M. (Dr)	1, July 1837	26, June			R3	
Mason, James M. (Dr)	26, June 1837	26, June			T2	
Mason, Joseph	21, Apr. 1821	16, Apr.	58		S3	
Mason, Sarah B.	4, 5, Nov. 1852	3, Nov.	93-10m		P2	
Mason, William	30, July 1850	July	15		Y3	
Mass, Isaac	3, Sept 1852	2, Sept			P2	
Matchett, C.M. (Mrs)	9, Nov. 1841	8, Nov.	44	*	N2	
Mathews, Clara Curtis	7, June 1849	3, June	1		L2	
Mathews, Joseph	9, Sept 1825		probate		N3	
Matile, Daniel Francis	25, May 1820		estate		S3	
Matlack, Timothy	12, Oct. 1839	30, Sept			T2	
Matson, Enoch	10, Sept 1808		estate		S4	
Mattewson, J.	2, Dec. 1825		83		N3	
Matthews, Caorline Sheppard	28, July 1852	23, July	infant		P2	
Matthews, Edmond L.	22, Oct. 1830	Oct.	25		N3	
Matthews, Edwin	6, Oct. 1827	Sept	49		R3	
Matthews, Edwin	6, Oct. 1827	29, Sept			R3	
Matthews, Edwin Stanley	30, Dec. 1852	28, Dec.	child		P2	
Matthews, Epaphra	20, Dec. 1814	20, Aug.			W4	
Matthews, Harriet J.	21, Nov. 1822	19, Nov.			J3	
Matthews, Jackson	8, July 1828	July	50		N3	
Matthews, Mary	8, Oct. 1852	Oct.	9m		P2	
Matthews, Nehemiah	1, Sept 1827	Aug.	26		R3	
Matthews, Sarah	10, May 1847	8, May	49		K2	
Matthews, Sarah Ann	14, June 1849	June	26		L2	

Name	Notice Date	Death Date	Age	Page	Maiden Name
Matthews, Sarah Ann	16, June 1849	12, June	28	L2	
Matthews, Thomas J.	11, Nov. 1852	10, Nov.	65	P2	
Mauer, Robert Halstead	7, Aug. 1841	4, Aug.	child	R3	
Maulsbury, Samuel	18, May 1838		probate	N2	
Maver, Robert Walsted	5, Aug. 1841	14, July		N2	
Maw, Jacob	18, May 1838		probate	N2	
Maxfield, John	24, Apr. 1837		estate	N2	
Maxwell, Eliza H.	5, Feb. 1842	24, Jan.	35	R3	
May, Andrew	19, Apr. 1837		estate	N2	
Mayall, (child of James)	6, Aug. 1830	Aug.	stillborn	N3	
Mayhew, Charles Henry	28, May 1851	27, May	6- 9m	P2	
Mayhew, Eber	10, June 1841	6, June		N2	
Mayhew, John	19, Nov. 1830	Nov.	23	N3	
Mayhew, Nathaniel	11, Sept 1837		probate	N2	
Mayhew, Rhoda	22, Apr. 1825	Apr.	21	N2	
Mayo, Daniel	5, Jan. 1839	25, Dec.		T2	
Mayo, Frances M.	6, Dec. 1838	Nov.		T3	St.Clair
Mays, Dabney	3, Dec. 1830	Nov.	17	N3	
Mays, Thomas	10, Dec. 1830	Dec.	12	N3	
Mays, Thomas	10, Sept 1830	Sept	42	N3	
Maythe, Walter	17, Feb. 1849	16, Feb.		L3	
McAber, David	24, July 1850	July		Y2	
McAboy, James (Rev)	22, Nov. 1833			* X3	
McAdams, John	14, Aug. 1819		estate	S3	
McAlister, Ann	23, July 1850	July	8	Y2	
McAlister, I.T.	6, Mar. 1829		estate	N3	
McAnally, James	7, Nov. 1840	Nov.	63	R3	
McArthur, Nancy	8, Nov. 1836	23, Oct.	58	T2	
McCahill, Richard	19, Apr. 1847	16, Apr.	32	K2	
McCain, John	22, Jan. 1814		estate	S3	
McCalla, Martha C.	16, July 1830	July	2	N3	
McCallion, Mary Bertha (Sr)	1, Oct. 1841	12, Sept	24	* N2	
McCallister, Isaac T.	1, June 1835		probate	N2	
McCandless, Alexander	12, Sept 1834	13, Aug.		T2	
McCartney, Margaret	10, Dec. 1830	Dec.	66	N3	
McCarty, Dennis	9, Aug. 1847	9, Aug.	79	K2	
McCarty, John	13, July 1849	July	40	L2	
McCarty, Thomas	12, Sept 1850	Sept	20	Y2	
McCarty, William	30, Aug. 1852	28, Aug.		P2	
McCashen, John	2, Mar. 1811		estate	S3	
McCaulley, John C.	20, Oct. 1835	29, Sept		T2	
McCauly, John C.	17, Oct. 1835	29, Sept		N2	
McChesney, William R.	17, Sept 1847	16, Sept	30	K2	
McClain, Alex	31, Mar. 1826		84	N3	
McClaine, Alexander (Mrs)	19, May 1815	16, May		S3	
McClanahan, Maria J.	23, June 1836	24, May	30	X3	Nourse
McClane, Allen	17, July 1802		estate	S3	
McClean, Elizabeth	9, July 1852	7, July	40	P2	
McClean, Jane	4, June 1830	June	1- 6m	N3	
McClean, John	24, Aug. 1824		estate	N3	
McCleland, Sam.	29, Mar. 1834	Mar.	30	R3	
McClelland, James	26, July 1834	July	26	R3	
McClintock, John	11, Nov. 1838	Nov.	35	N3	
McCloskey, Henry	3, Sept 1808		estate	S3	

Name	Notice Date	Death Date	Age		Page	Maiden Name
McCluer, John	10, July 1819		estate		S3	
McClure, James	7, Sept 1807	26, Aug.			S3	
McClure, James	5, July 1828				R3	
McClure, Margaret Catharine	20, Dec. 1847	19, Dec.	15		K2	
McClusky, James (Major)	7, Feb. 1829				R1	
McCollock, (child)	28, Nov. 1828	Nov.	stillborn		N3	
McCollum, Thomas	3, Mar. 1835		estate		N2	
McCollum, Thomas	19, Feb. 1838		estate		N2	
McComas, Daniel	7, July 1835	3, July	32	*	T2	
McCombs, Margaret	15, Oct. 1830	Oct.	41		N3	
McConnaughey, Cynthia Ann	28, Sept 1852	27, Sept	18		P2	
McConnell, Lucinda Carolina	19, Aug. 1852	17, Aug.	infant		P2	
McConnell, Robert	28, Jan. 1832	26, Jan.	24		R3	
McConnell, Robert	11, Aug. 1841	3, Aug.	65		N2	
McCook, James John	3, June 1842	30, Mar.	18		N2	
McCord, Asenath Brown	19, Apr. 1847	17, Apr.	30		K2	
McCord, Elizabeth	2, June 1827	29, May			R3	
McCord, Mary	24, May 1849	May	20		L2	
McCord, Rachel	28, May 1830	May	26		N3	
McCormick, Mary	21, Aug. 1852	19, Aug.	52		P2	
McCormick, Samuel	22, Feb. 1836	21, Feb.	34		T3	
McCormick, Thomas	17, Nov. 1826		estate		N3	
McCormick, William W.	30, June 1849	28, June			L2	
McCorril, D.	12, Aug. 1831	Aug.	35		A3	
McCoy, Henry B.	20, June 1834		estate		T2	
McCoy, Henry B.	14, Dec. 1835		probate		N2	
McCoy, Mary	14, Dec. 1837	6, Dec.			X3	
McCoy, Robert	20, Aug. 1830	Aug.	40		N3	
McCoy, Robert	24, Dec. 1830		estate		N3	
McCoy, William	6, July 1849	July	44		L2	
McCray, Samuel	6, June 1817		estate		S3	
McCulloch, Robert	12, July 1828	7, July	44		R3	
McCulloch, Sampson	25, May 1822		estate		S3	
McCullough, H.U.	23, July 1850	July	23		Y2	
McCullough, James	31, Aug. 1822	28, Aug.			S1	
McCullough, John	25, Aug. 1829		probate		N3	
McCullough, Mary	9, Apr. 1849	8, Apr.	87		L2	
McCullough, Mary	23, July 1850	July	19m		Y2	
McCullough, Robert	21, Dec. 1830		probate		N3	
McCullough, Sampson	6, Oct. 1826		probate		N3	
McCullough, Sampson	19, Dec. 1826		probate		N3	
McCullum, Thomas	7, Sept 1836		probate		N2	
McCune, Cornelius	12, Apr. 1849	Apr.	18		L2	
McCune, Michael	24, Nov. 1851	16, Nov.			P2	
McCurdy, Daniel	2, Apr. 1800		estate		S3	
McCurdy, Robert	3, Dec. 1830	Nov.	78		N3	
McDarcey, Mary	24, July 1850	July	20		Y2	
McDonald,	21, Apr. 1838	Apr.			R3	
McDonald, Angus	31, Mar. 1826	1, Mar.	106		N3	
McDonald, Anthony	17, Oct. 1850	Oct.	60		Y2	
McDonald, Archibald	30, Apr. 1808	29, Apr.			S3	
McDonald, Barnard	17, June 1837		probate		N2	
McDonald, Bridget	26, Apr. 1849	Apr.	35		L2	
McDonald, Bridget	1, July 1852	30, June			P2	

Name	Notice Date	Death Date	Age		Page	Maiden Name
McDonald, Henry	26, July 1850	July	28		Y2	
McDonald, John	26, Apr. 1849	Apr.	40		L2	
McDonald, Samuel	24, June 1851	21, June			P2	
McDonald, Spencer	3, Dec. 1830	Nov.	10m		N3	
McDonald, William Alexander	3, June 1847	1, June	21		K2	
McDonold, John	15, Aug. 1850	Aug.	18m		Y2	
McDonough, (child of Pat.)	13, July 1849	July	2w		L2	
McDonough, Ann	20, Nov. 1852	18, Nov.	4m		P2	
McDonough, Patrick	24, July 1841	July	35		R3	
McDonough, Rosanna	1, Aug. 1850	July	35		Y2	
McDougal, Hamilton	2, May 1826	22, Apr.	5- 4m		N2	
McDowell, Benjamin Drake	25, June 1847		estate		K3	
McDowell, Lucy E.	5, Mar. 1831	4, Mar.	21m		R3	
McDuell, John A.	9, Jan. 1837	30, Dec.			T2	
McDuffie, Mary Rebecca	7, Oct. 1830	14, Sept		*	A3	Singleton
McElheny, Daniel	13, Sept 1838	Sept	38		T2	
McElroy, William	21, June 1849	June	14m		L2	
McEvoy, Owen	27, July 1850	July	40		Y3	
McFall, Elizabeth	22, Dec. 1847	20, Dec.	60		K2	
McFall, Elizabeth	11, Aug. 1850	10, Aug.	9m		Y2	
McFall, Margaret	2, Feb. 1849	2, Feb.	49		L2	
McFall, Mary Ann	25, July 1850	July	18		Y2	
McFarland, (son of Capt)	15, Oct. 1814	13, Oct.			S3	
McFarland, Catharine	19, July 1809	13, July			H3	
McFarland, James B.	3, May 1838			*	N2	
McFarland, John (Col)	25, Aug. 1827				R3	
McFarland, John (or Joel)	3, May 1838				N2	
McFarland, Stephen (Col)	17, Nov. 1832	15, Nov.	61	*	R3	
McFarland, Thomas	18, Oct. 1814	13, Oct.	10		W4	
McFeely, Richard G.	20, Feb. 1837		estate		N2	
McFerrin, Andrew	14, July 1821		estate		S3	
McGechin, William	11, July 1849	8, July	19m- 9d		L2	
McGee, Daniel	9, Sept 1852	6, Sept			P2	
McGee, Henry F.	21, Nov. 1840	14, Nov.	28		R3	
McGee, John	27, Aug. 1852	Aug.	36		P2	
McGibben, J.	17, Feb. 1829	Feb.	25		N3	
McGill, (Mr)	9, Nov. 1852	23, Sept			P2	
McGill, Christopher	8, Feb. 1808		estate		S3	
McGill, Robert	1, June 1835		probate		N2	
McGilliard, John	26, Apr. 1837		estate		N2	
McGilliard, Susan	4, Oct. 1825	23, Sept	59		N3	
McGioney, James	27, July 1850	July	45		Y3	
McGlosson, (child of John)	30, Dec. 1828	Dec.	stillborn		N3	
McGoon, Josiah	18, Dec. 1813	15, Dec.			S3	
McGregor, Anna E.	26, July 1834	July	3		R3	
McGregor, Anna E.	22, July 1834	July	3		T2	
McGregor, Helen	16, Nov. 1847	14, Nov.	35		K2	
McGrew, Aurelia	20, July 1820	7, July	27		S3	Haywood
McGrew, Elvira L.	13, Apr. 1824	9, Apr.	28		N2	
McGrew, Sarah	12, Dec. 1836	10, Dec.	29		T3	
McGrew, Sarah	12, Dec. 1836	10, Dec.	29		N3	
McGuff, Bridget	10, May 1849	May	18		L2	
McGuff, Bridget	3, May 1849	May	60		L2	
McGuffey, Daniel Drake	22, May 1841	14, May	infant		R3	

Name	Notice Date	Death Date	Age		Page	Maiden Name
McGuffey, Daniel Drake	17, May 1841	14, May	infant		N2	
McGuier, Emily	13, Aug. 1830	Aug.	5m		N3	
McGuire, Isaac	22, Dec. 1835	21, Dec.			T3	
McGuire, James	26, Apr. 1849	Apr.	32		L2	
McHaddle, Francis	26, Sept 1828	Sept	50		N3	
McHenry, Sarah	27, June 1849	26, June			L2	
McHough, Michael	19, Nov. 1851	16, Nov.			P2	
McHugh, Sarah	6, July 1849	July	20		L2	
McIlroy, Enos	21, Dec. 1830		probate		N3	
McIlvaine, Emily Harriet	26, May 1836	1, May	7- 7m		X3	
McIntire, David	13, July 1849	July			L2	
McIntire, John	12, Aug. 1815	29, July	56		G3	
McIntire, William T.	21, Jan. 1825		estate		N3	
McIntire, William T.	16, Dec. 1825		probate		N3	
McIntire, William T.	4, Mar. 1828		probate		N3	
McIntyre, Duncan	8, June 1838	7, June	35	*	T2	
McKawe, Mary A.	24, July 1850	July	3		Y2	
McKean, Neil	8, Oct. 1841	Oct.	28		N2	
McKee, (child of Charles B.)	29, Oct. 1830	Oct.	stillborn		N3	
McKee, James	15, July 1852	13, July	45		P2	
McKee, Rebecca	17, Oct. 1835		estate		N2	
McKee, W.G.	19, Sept 1828	Sept	3- 6m		N3	
McKibben, Joseph	20, Mar. 1835	2, Mar.	57		X3	
McKinley, James	24, July 1850	July	11		Y2	
McKinley, James	23, May 1840		42		R3	
McKinley, William	1, Oct. 1830	Sept	29		N3	
McKinney, (child of John)	19, Sept 1828	Sept	1- 8m		N3	
McKinney, Mary Ann	9, Oct. 1852	22, Sept	24- 5m-27d	*	P2	
McKinney, Thomas	10, July 1813	23, June			S3	
McKinny, William	1, Aug. 1829	22, July			R3	
McKinon, Simeon	2, Jan. 1818	1, Jan.		*	S3	
McKnight, Dan.	20, Aug. 1830	Aug.	19m		N3	
McKnight, David	19, May 1821	13, May			S3	
McKnight, James	25, May 1811	17, May			S3	
McLain, Thomas	31, July 1841	July	25		R3	
McLane, Daniel (Capt)	14, Aug. 1805	30, June			S3	
McLane, Lucinda	1, July 1828	June	4m		N3	
McLasty, John	13, July 1849	July	13m		L2	
McLaughlin,	12, Aug. 1828	Aug.	14m		N3	
McLaughlin, Dolly	24, May 1849	May	2		L2	
McLaughlin, Ellen	24, May 1849	May	8		L2	
McLaughlin, John	31, Jan. 1818		estate		S3	
McLean, Allen	12, Dec. 1801		estate		S3	
McLean, Anna	28, Dec. 1852	24, Dec.	5- 6m- 7d		P2	
McLean, Arabella Margaret	5, Aug. 1835	4, Aug.	2		T2	
McLean, Ellen	22, Sept 1852	12, Sept	41		P2	
McLean, Fergus	25, Feb. 1837	Feb.	91		T2	
McLean, Hugh	28, Aug. 1841		estate		R3	
McLean, J.	1, Nov. 1830	14, Oct.			A3	
McLean, John	2, Nov. 1830	24, Oct.			N2	
McLean, John (Mrs)	9, Dec. 1841				N2	
McLean, Margaret	7, Sept 1836		probate		N2	
McLean, William	23, Feb. 1839	14, Feb.	7m		T2	
McLean, William M.	5, Dec. 1829	3, Dec.	9		R2	

Name	Notice Date	Death Date	Age	Page	Maiden Name
McLean, William Monroe	4, Dec. 1829	3, Dec.	8- 9m	N3	
McLeary, E.H.(Rev)	10, Dec. 1835	29, Sept	26	X3	
McLene, Jeremiah	28, Mar. 1837	26, Mar.	70	T2	
McLung, Cloyd	9, June 1836	18, May		X3	
McLure, Felix G.	16, Nov. 1847	16, Nov.	24	K2	
McMachen, (Major)	5, July 1794	30, June		C3	
McMahon, Elizabeth	20, Apr. 1847	19, Apr.		K2	
McManama, James	14, Mar. 1840		estate	R3	
McManie, Benjamin	24, Feb. 1821		estate	S3	
McMeans, Benjamin	22, Dec. 1829		probate	N3	
McMickle, John	29, Aug. 1840	Aug.	25	R3	
McMillan, William	19, Sept 1804		estate	S3	
McMillan, William	17, Apr. 1805		estate	S3	
McMillen, William Arthur	18, Nov. 1847	16, Nov.	19m	K2	
McMinn, Joseph	17, Dec. 1824	17, Nov.		N3	
McMullen,	17, Nov. 1852	16, Nov.	child	P2	
McMullen, James	21, Dec. 1852	19, Dec.	37	P2	
McMullen, Samuel (Mrs)	15, Sept 1810	5, Sept	56	S3	
McMurchy, William	20, Mar. 1838		probate	N3	
McMurchy, William	6, Nov. 1838		probate	N2	
McMurphy, Catharine	22, May 1847	20, May	6- 8m	K2	
McMurray, Joseph	14, Dec. 1835		probate	N2	
McNabb, John	8, June 1807		estate	S3	
McNally, Catharine	3, May 1849	May	25	L2	
McNamaraugh, John	26, July 1850	July	27	Y2	
McNaughton, Isaac	25, Apr. 1840		estate	R3	
McNeely, Elizabeth	11, Dec. 1829		estate	N3	
McNeely, Elizabeth	22, Jan. 1830		estate	N3	
McNeely, Lorenzo	26, Dec. 1840	18, Dec.	3	R3	
McNeely, Lorenzo	23, Dec. 1840	18, Dec.	3	N2	
McNeill, John W.	28, Aug. 1841	19, Aug.		R3	
McNeill, Robert (Dr)	23, Dec. 1835	22, Dec.		T3	
McNicelson, Anthony	13, July 1852	11, July		P2	
McNight, Mary	21, Jan. 1801		estate	S3	
McPhee, Charles D.	1, Aug. 1850	July	19m	Y2	
McPherrin, William	16, Aug. 1833	3, Aug.	50	X3	
McPherson, Alexander	2, Dec. 1831	18, Nov.	80	X3	
McPherson, R.H. (Col)	4, Apr. 1817			S3	
McPherson, Samuel	4, June 1830	June	30	N3	
McPike, James	20, May 1825	15, May	78	N2	
McQuillen, Cynthia Holland	15, Sept 1836	14, Aug.	37	T2	Prince
McReynolds, John D.	19, Jan. 1822	16, Jan.		S3	
McRoberts, Virginia	9, Aug. 1841	25, July	child	N2	
McSorley, James	5, Sept 1828	Sept	78	N3	
McUlaph, Lydia	2, Aug. 1834	July	36	R3	
McUlaph, Lydia	29, July 1834	July	36	T2	
McWilliam, Patrick	12, Apr. 1849	10, Apr.		L3	
McWilliams, Patrick	23, Apr. 1849	Apr.	22	L2	
Mead, Henry	12, Apr. 1849	Apr.	45	L2	
Mead, Marcy	8, July 1828	July	37	N3	
Mead, Richard W.	12, July 1828			R3	
Mead, Sally Ann	28, Nov. 1828	Nov.	7- 6m	N3	
Meade, Richard K. (Col)	10, Apr. 1805	9, Apr.		S3	
Meader, Flora Jane	9, Oct. 1841	3, Oct.	19m-18d	R3	

Name	Notice Date	Death Date	Age		Page	Maiden Name
Meader, Flora Jane	5, Oct. 1841	3, Oct.	20m		N2	
Meakings, Mary Elizabeth	10, July 1852	4, July	10		P2	
Mearldy, Mary	26, July 1834	July	8		R3	
Mearldy, Mary	22, July 1834	July	8		T2	
Mearldy, Sarah A.	2, Aug. 1834	July	11m		R3	
Mearldy, Sarah A.	29, July 1834	July	11m		T2	
Mears, Esther	24, Nov. 1827	19, Nov.	69		R3	
Mears, Esther	23, Nov. 1827	19, Nov.	69		N3	
Meason, Isaac	26, Feb. 1842	21, Feb.			R3	
Medary, George	5, May 1847				K2	
Medary, Jacob	25, Mar. 1847				K2	
Medary, Lucious P.	28, July 1851	26, July	2- 2m		P2	
Medary, William	7, Apr. 1849	6, Apr.	54		L2	
Meddock, Moses	16, Dec. 1825		estate		N3	
Meddock, Moses	11, Dec. 1827		probate		N3	
Meddock, Moses	19, Aug. 1828		probate		N3	
Meddock, Moses	9, Dec. 1828		probate		N3	
Medkiad, W.R.	26, July 1834	July	26		R3	
Medkiad, William R.	22, July 1834	July	26		T2	
Meeker, Caroline	20, May 1841	19, May	11	*	N2	
Meeker, Harvey	1, June 1833	30, May			R3	
Meeker, John	26, Oct. 1835		estate		N4	
Meeker, John	30, Jan. 1836		estate		N3	
Meeker, John	4, June 1836		probate		N2	
Meeker, John	17, June 1837		probate		N2	
Meeker, Randolph	22, Dec. 1829		probate		N3	
Meeks, Edward	6, May 1825		estate		N3	
Meeks, William J.D.	8, Sept 1827	Sept	18		R3	
Meigs, Josiah	21, Sept 1822	20, Sept	70	*	S3	
Meigs, Return J. (Col)	4, Mar. 1823	28, Feb.			N1	
Meigs, Return Jonathan	22, Apr. 1825	29, Mar.			N2	
Meigs, Return Jonathan (Col)	25, Mar. 1823	28, Jan.		*	N1	
Melendy, Mary Elizabeth	16, Sept 1831	12, Sept	1- 8m		X3	
Melendy, Thomas	26, July 1834	July	10m		R3	
Melendy, Thomas	22, July 1834	July	10m		T2	
Mellen, Isabel	6, June 1849	19, May	6m		L2	
Menclon, Dorthy	20, Mar. 1838		probate		N3	
Mendenhall, George	6, July 1850	6, July	17m		P2	
Menken, Eliza	17, Nov. 1832	13, Nov.	32		R3	
Menkin, Alexander	9, Oct. 1834	7, Oct.	75	*	T2	
Mennessier, Francis	16, Apr. 1814		estate		S3	
Mennessier, Francis	17, Dec. 1814		estate		S3	
Mennessier, Francis	15, Jan. 1814	9, Jan.			S3	
Mentle, Mary A.	15, Aug. 1850	Aug.	13m		Y2	
Menzies, Christian	14, July 1832		112	*	R3	
Mercer, John	30, Mar. 1807		estate		S3	
Mercer, John	25, July 1818		estate		S2	
Mercer, John (Capt)	18, Nov. 1806	15, Nov.			S3	
Mercer, Susan	26, Sept 1828	Sept	75		N3	
Merideth, Alfred Bosler	10, Sept 1852	7, Sept	4- -12d		P2	
Meriwether, David (Gen)	23, Nov. 1822	13, Nov.	68		S3	
Merklein Y Onis, Frederica	6, June 1817	22, May			S3	
Merrefield, Joseph	30, Sept 1825	22, Sept	55	*	N2	
Merrefield, Sarah	21, Oct. 1825	13, Oct.		*	N2	

Name	Notice Date	Death Date	Age		Page	Maiden Name
Merrell, Horace C.	3, Nov. 1838	31, Oct.	22	*	T2	
Merrell, Levisa	16, Nov. 1838	14, Nov.	20		T2	Stockbridge
Merrell, Warren Kellogg	16, Oct. 1852	13, Oct.	2m-26d		P2	
Merrick, J.F.	12, Dec. 1836	24, Nov.	22		N3	
Merrick, Roswel	5, May 1821		estate		S3	
Merrie, James B.	6, May 1830	5, May	21		A3	
Merrie, Robert	19, Aug. 1837	17, Aug.			R3	
Merrie, Robert	18, Aug. 1837	17, Aug.		*	T2	
Merril, John	24, Oct. 1828	Oct.	4d		N2	
Merril, Moodey	24, Oct. 1828	Oct.	10d		N2	
Merrill, Mary Anne	2, June 1836	21, May			X3	Hughes
Merrill, Sophia E.H.	1, Aug. 1850	July	31		Y2	
Merritt, Elizabeth	1, June 1835		probate		N2	
Merritt, Elizabeth	7, Sept 1836		probate		N2	
Merritt, Elizabeth	20, Mar. 1838		probate		N3	
Merritt, Elizabeth (heirs of)	20, Mar. 1838		probate		N3	
Merritt, Margaret Adelia	28, Nov. 1835	24, Nov.	20		T2	Dunseth
Merriweather, Nicholas	28, Sept 1852		estate		P2	
Merriweather, Thomas H.	18, Aug. 1835	11, Aug.			T2	
Merry, James B.	14, May 1830	May	21		N3	
Merry, John	11, Sept 1837		probate		N2	
Mershonway, E.	5, Sept 1828	Sept	3m- 4d		N3	
Mervey, Jane Ann	21, May 1830	May	5m		N3	
Meskill, Dennis	1, Aug. 1850	July	1		Y2	
Mess, Christopher	7, June 1849	June	38		L2	
Metcalf, Agnes	18, Dec. 1840	17, Dec.	infant		N2	
Metcalf, Thomas	21, Oct. 1828	Oct.			N2	
Metcalf, William Henry	11, Sept 1847	7, Sept	13m		K2	
Mets, H.	23, Dec. 1828	Dec.	32		N3	
Meyer, Christian	3, May 1851	22, Apr.	64	*	P2	
Meyer, Frederick	8, Oct. 1841	Oct.	21		N2	
Meyers, Mary	13, Oct. 1852	10, Oct.			P2	Clark
Miall, Nathaniel	28, June 1849	June	47		L2	
Michael, Joseph	24, July 1850	July	2		Y2	
Micke, Mary	1, Aug. 1850	July	14m		Y2	
Middlesworth, Elizabeth	3, Apr. 1829	Mar.	5m		N2	
Middlesworth, John	2, July 1830	June	66		N2	
Middleton, Mary	21, Oct. 1828	Oct.	18m		N2	
Middleton, William T.	18, May 1838		probate		N2	
Mifflin, Thomas	12, Feb. 1800	20, Jan.	57		S3	
Milder, A.G.	25, Sept 1852	24, Sept			P2	
Miles, Benjamin	4, June 1836		probate		N2	
Miles, John	28, June 1828				R3	
Miles, Robert H.	1, June 1835		probate		N2	
Miles, Sarah	9, Jan. 1838		estate		N3	
Milfield, Henry	24, July 1850	July	27		Y2	
Milford, James	23, July 1834	20, July		*	T2	
Milford, Sarah Ann	5, Jan. 1833	1, Jan.		*	R3	
Millan, Samuel	13, May 1835	25, Apr.			T3	
Miller, (child of William)	23, Apr. 1849	Apr.	7d		L2	
Miller, Anderson	15, July 1835	7, July			T2	
Miller, Charles Ludlow	19, Jan. 1822	16, Jan.	6		S3	
Miller, Charles W.	27, Mar. 1847	18, Mar.	37		K2	
Miller, Christopher	13, Sept 1838	Sept	48		T2	

Name	Notice Date	Death Date	Age	Page	Maiden Name
Miller, Elizabeth	2, Jan. 1824	31, Dec.		N3	
Miller, Francis	20, Aug. 1852	18, Aug.	61- 4m	P2	
Miller, Henry	10, May 1849	May	52	L2	
Miller, Henry	5, May 1835			T2	
Miller, Henry	5, May 1835			N2	
Miller, Humphrey	19, May 1829		estate	N3	
Miller, John	21, Dec. 1827		estate	N3	
Miller, John	4, Apr. 1837		probate	N2	
Miller, John B.	17, Sept 1830	Sept	1- 8m	N3	
Miller, John R.	6, Nov. 1838		probate	N2	
Miller, Joseph	28, June 1850	27, June		P2	
Miller, Lewis	9, July 1850	8, July		P2	
Miller, Magdalene	11, Dec. 1841	30, Nov.	20	* R3	
Miller, Margaret	2, Sept 1835		estate	N2	
Miller, Mary	25, Nov. 1828	Nov.	27	N3	
Miller, Mary A.	2, Aug. 1834	July		R3	
Miller, Mary A.	29, July 1834	July		T2	
Miller, Mary Ann	11, Sept 1819	3, Sept		S3	
Miller, Nicholas	6, June 1840	June	29	R3	
Miller, Rebecca	3, Sept 1830	Aug.	1- 5m	N2	
Miller, Rebecca C.	12, Nov. 1830	Nov.	12	N3	
Miller, William	10, May 1849	May	20	L2	
Miller, William	22, Aug. 1828	Aug.	28	N3	
Miller, William	23, July 1796		estate	F3	
Miller, William	30, Dec. 1847			K2	
Milles, John (Major)	27, Aug. 1796		estate	F3	
Millikan, Jesse	2, Sept 1835	19, Aug.	51	T2	
Millman, Henry F. (Rev)	16, May 1840	8, May	35	R3	
Millon, Sarah	12, Aug. 1831	Aug.		A3	
Mills, (Mrs)	14, Aug. 1805		118	S3	
Mills, Abner	13, Aug. 1836		estate	N2	
Mills, Abner	7, Dec. 1837		probate	N3	
Mills, Benjamin	23, Dec. 1831	6, Dec.		X3	
Mills, Isaac	4, Apr. 1837		probate	N2	
Mills, Isaac	3, July 1849	1, July		L2	
Mills, John	13, June 1817		estate	S3	
Mills, John (Major)	9, July 1796	8, July		F3	
Mills, John R.	9, Mar. 1811		estate	S3	
Mills, Martha Gazlay	22, Jan. 1842	12, Jan.	3- 3m	R3	
Mills, Mary	30, Sept 1837	29, Sept	62	T2	
Mills, Peter	8, Nov. 1847	2, Nov.		K2	
Mills, Robert	20, Sept 1833	Sept	37	X3	
Mills, Sallie A.	13, June 1849	12, June	32	L2	
Mills, Samuel	19, Aug. 1828	Aug.	34	N3	
Mills, William	14, Oct. 1828	Oct.	17	N3	
Mills, William	14, May 1835	13, May	65	N2	
Mills, William	11, Oct. 1828	6, Oct.	17- 8m	R3	
Millspaugh, William	4, June 1836		probate	N2	
Milot, Patrick	17, June 1837		probate	N2	
Minegar, William	26, Nov. 1824	4, Oct.	30	N2	
Miner, Asher	3, Apr. 1841	13, Mar.	65	* R2	
Miner, Elizabeth	21, Sept 1837	25, Aug.		X3	
Miner, Emma	9, July 1849	8, July	12m	L2	
Miner, Jacob	14, Aug. 1819		estate	S3	

Name	Notice Date	Death Date	Age		Page	Maiden Name
Minett, Juliet	14, Aug. 1852	11, Aug.	3		P2	
Minor, John Mercer	4, Feb. 1831	11, Jan.			X3	
Minshall, Margaret	24, Mar. 1838		estate		N2	
Minshall, Mary	6, Oct. 1827	Oct.	33		R3	
Mint, Samuel	16, Jan. 1829	Jan.			N2	
Mitchel, (child of Patrick)	19, July 1834	July	4		R3	
Mitchel, (child of Richard)	17, Sept 1830	Sept	stillborn		N3	
Mitchell, B.	3, May 1838				N2	
Mitchell, Emma Louisa	27, Sept 1852	25, Sept	child		P2	
Mitchell, John	11, Dec. 1827		probate		N3	
Mitchell, Matilda	9, Dec. 1828	Dec.	25		N3	
Mitchell, Sarah	6, Oct. 1827	Oct.	2- 8m		R3	
Mitchell, Simeon	19, Mar. 1836		estate		N2	
Mitchell, Simeon	11, Sept 1837		probate		N2	
Mitchell, Simeon	20, Mar. 1838		probate		N3	
Mitchell, Thomas	17, June 1837		probate		N2	
Mitchell, Thomas	27, July 1833	July			R3	
Mitchell, William	22, Sept 1826		estate		Q3	
Mitchell, William H. (Rev)	19, May 1836	8, Apr.	36		X3	
Mittendorf, Henry Andolph	25, Nov. 1852	24, Nov.			P2	
Mitts, Margaret	26, Nov. 1830	Nov.	62		N3	
Mix, Marvin P.	19, Feb. 1839	18, Feb.	52		T2	
Mixer, Charles T.	16, July 1835	29, June	30	*	T2	
Mixer, Jessica Megowan	13, Apr. 1836	10, Apr.	5		T2	
Mixer, Nathaniel	18, Aug. 1852	12, Aug.	5		P2	
Mixer, William H.	19, July 1834	July	25		R3	
Moerlan, Elizabeth	19, July 1834	July	60		R3	
Moes, Ann	2, Jan. 1829	Dec.	1m		N3	
Mogevin, Michael	28, July 1850	July	10m		Y3	
Moghen, Patrick	22, Mar. 1849	Mar.	33		L2	
Mohaber, Alonzo	24, Feb. 1829	Feb.	27		N3	
Moier, Henry	5, Dec. 1804		estate		S5	
Molleston, Henry	4, Dec. 1819				S3	
Monegan, Jane	6, July 1849	July	40		L2	
Monfort, Peter H.	1, May 1829		estate		N3	
Monfort, Peter H.	7, Sept 1830		probate		N3	
Mongelfier,	1, Dec. 1810	9, July	77		S3	
Monsarrat, Ann	24, Feb. 1838	18, Feb.			T2	
Montfort, (child of W.P.)	30, Dec. 1828	Dec.	stillborn		N3	
Montgomery, Caroline	1, Aug. 1828	July	4m		N3	
Moody, (man)	25, Sept 1851	22, Sept			P2	
Moody, Moses B.	7, Jan. 1836		estate		N3	
Moody, William	10, Dec. 1830	Dec.	10m		N3	
Moon, Daniel C.	28, July 1852	21, July	35		P2	
Mooney, (Mrs)	20, May 1835	20, May			T2	
Mooney, John	20, May 1835	20, May	9		T2	
Mooney, Mary	20, May 1835	20, May	7		T2	
Mooney, Richard	20, May 1835	20, May	12m		T2	
Mooney, Sampson	10, Apr. 1813	1, Apr.			S3	
Mooney, William Joseph	7, Sept 1852	5, Sept	1- 2m		P2	
Moore, (child)	3, Sept 1830	Aug.	9m		N2	
Moore, (daughter of Hugh)	30, Mar. 1807	28, Mar.	infant		S3	
Moore, Adeline	4, Sept 1810	25, Aug.			S3	
Moore, Barbara	4, Feb. 1841	28, Jan.	61	*	N2	Schroeder

Name	Notice Date	Death Date	Age		Page	Maiden Name
Moore, Bustard	16, Jan. 1824		estate		N3	
Moore, Bustard	10, Mar. 1829		probate		N3	
Moore, Charles	15, July 1825		estate		N2	
Moore, Eleanor	14, Oct. 1806	4, Oct.	80		S3	
Moore, Henry	7, Feb. 1795		estate		C3	
Moore, Hetty Anne	12, Jan. 1829	Jan.	6w		N2	
Moore, Isaac	10, May 1849	May	38		L2	
Moore, Isaac	9, July 1835		estate		T2	
Moore, Isaac	25, July 1836		estate		N2	
Moore, Isaac	17, June 1837		probate		N2	
Moore, Isaac	11, Sept 1837		probate		N2	
Moore, Isaac	18, May 1838		probate		N2	
Moore, James	13, Aug. 1830		estate		N3	
Moore, James	18, May 1838		probate		N2	
Moore, John	10, Sept 1830	Sept	9- 7m		N3	
Moore, John	20, Nov. 1851	19, Nov.			P2	
Moore, John	20, July 1852	18, July			P2	
Moore, John R.	23, June 1851	20, June	36		P2	
Moore, Jonathan	18, 19, June 1849	16, June	64	*	L2	
Moore, Lucy	13, June 1812	26, May			S3	
Moore, Margaret	14, June 1849	June	5		L2	
Moore, Mary A.	19, July 1834	July	20		R3	
Moore, Mary E.	26, July 1834	July	21d		R3	
Moore, Mary E.	22, July 1834	July	21d		T2	
Moore, Mary J.	1, Aug. 1840	July	2w		R3	
Moore, Michael A.	11, June 1842	June	24		R3	
Moore, Patrick	8, Nov. 1809		estate		H3	
Moore, Patrick	24, Aug. 1852	7, Aug.		*	P2	
Moore, Samuel P.	16, June 1832		estate		R3	
Moore, Thomas	28, May 1800		estate		S3	
Moore, William	1, Oct. 1830	Sept	29		N3	
Moore, William	7, Dec. 1830		estate		N3	
Moorehead, Maria M.	15, May 1849	2, May	6- 2m		L2	
Moorehead, Samuel	17, June 1837		probate		N2	
Moorehead, William	30, May 1850	29, May			P2	
Moores, John	7, Dec. 1837		probate		N3	
Moorhead, Henrietta	6, Nov. 1841	31, Oct.	32		R3	
Moorhead, Samuel	20, Mar. 1838		probate		N3	
Moorhouse, William	9, Dec. 1828	Dec.	1w		N3	
Moorman, Maria Doretta	23, May 1849	22, May	24		L2	
Moran, Eliza	17, Oct. 1850	Oct.	18		Y2	
Moran, Jason	2, Aug. 1834	July	45		R3	
Moran, Jason	29, July 1834	July	45		T2	
More, Isabella	23, Jan. 1837		estate		N3	
Morehead, Theodore Espy	23, July 1841	1, July	infant		N2	
Moreland, John R. (Rev)	9, Nov. 1832	16, Oct.	48	*	X3	
Moreland, William	25, Sept 1852				P2	
Moren, Edward	10, May 1849	May	26		L2	
Morgan, Collins	23, Apr. 1849	Apr.	22		L2	
Morgan, Daniel	31, July 1802	6, July			S3	
Morgan, Enoch	11, Mar. 1815		estate		S1	
Morgan, Harriet	11, July 1849	10, July		*	L2	Stone
Morgan, Jacob	30, Apr. 1836	26, Apr.	77		T2	
Morgan, James	28, Nov. 1828	Nov.	22		N3	

Name	Notice Date	Death Date	Age	Page	Maiden Name
Morgan, John	28, July 1835		estate	T3	
Morgan, John	5, Sept 1836		estate	T4	
Morgan, John	18, May 1838		probate	N2	
Morgan, John	20, May 1850	18, May		P2	
Morgan, Mary	28, July 1850	July	19	Y3	
Morgan, Mordecai (Dr)	16, Aug. 1841	22, Aug.	51	N2	
Morison, Virginia	9, Sept 1831	Sept	9m	A3	
Morloody, Elizabeth	2, Aug. 1834	July	28	R3	
Morloody, Elizabeth	29, July 1834	July	28	T2	
Morrell, (Mrs)	8, Aug. 1804		44	S4	
Morrell, Anna Eliza	16, Sept 1852	14, Sept	10	P2	
Morrell, Francis (Rev)	15, Sept 1838	9, Sept	90- 7m	R3	
Morrey, Larrey	3, Apr. 1841	Mar.	44	R3	
Morris, (child of Benjamin)	28, Nov. 1828	Nov.	stillborn	N3	
Morris, Abigail	21, May 1842	17, May		R3	
Morris, Cavileer	10, Apr. 1813		estate	S3	
Morris, David	28, Aug. 1829	14, Aug.		N3	
Morris, Emily	26, July 1850	July	11m	Y2	
Morris, Frank	13, July 1849	July	37	L2	
Morris, George	5, Mar. 1842	20, Jan.	98	* R3	
Morris, James C.	24, Oct. 1828		estate	N2	
Morris, James C.	18, May 1838		probate	N2	
Morris, James C.	6, Nov. 1838		probate	N2	
Morris, James C.	27, June 1828	25, June		Q3	
Morris, James C. (Capt)	28, June 1828	25, June		R3	
Morris, Jane	18, May 1838		probate	N2	
Morris, Jane	28, July 1832	23, July		R3	
Morris, Rachel	11, Aug. 1852	9, Aug.	42	P2	
Morris, Sarah	25, Aug. 1832	22, Aug.	7	R3	
Morrison (child)	1, Oct. 1830	Sept	1-10m	N3	
Morrison, Isaac	16, Dec. 1825		probate	N3	
Morrison, Moses	4, June 1836		probate	N2	
Morrison, William C.	11, Sept 1837		probate	N2	
Morrison, William C.	7, Dec. 1837		probate	N3	
Morrow, James	20, Feb. 1796		estate	C3	
Morrow, John	17, Sept 1830	Sept	32	N3	
Morrow, Robert A.	17, Aug. 1830	1, Aug.		N2	
Morrow, Samuel	6, Oct. 1827	Oct.	40	R3	
Morrow, Thomas V.	17, July 1850	16, July	48	P2	
Morse, Benjamin	6, Oct. 1852	4, Oct.	64	P2	
Morse, Dolly Dresser	13, Aug. 1841	11, Aug.	40	* N2	
Morse, Eleazer	2, Dec. 1823	1, Dec.	22	N2	
Morse, Isaac	26, May 1821		estate	S3	
Morse, John C.	31, Jan. 1831	28, Jan.	24	A3	
Morse, John C.	4, Feb. 1831	3, Feb.	24	X3	
Morse, Joseph	11, Dec. 1819		estate	S3	
Morsell, James C.	4, May 1835		estate	N2	
Morsell, James C.	5, Jan. 1833	30, Dec.		R3	
Morten, Henry	1, Nov. 1852	29, Oct.		P2	
Mortimer, John	2, Sept 1831			* A3	
Morton, Henry	21, Sept 1838		probate	N3	
Morton, Mary	9, Jan. 1837	7, Jan.	21	T2	
Morton, Rebecca	1, June 1849	30, May		L2	
Morton, Sarah Ann	23, Nov. 1832	1, Nov.	20	X3	Fairbank

Name	Notice Date	Death Date	Age		Page	Maiden Name
Mosby, Benjamin (Capt)	22, July 1815		38		G3	
Mosby, Littleberry	16, July 1842	14, July	33		R3	
Moss, James	27, June 1840	June	37		R3	
Mothershead, Ruth	2, May 1840	15, Apr.	77		R3	
Mount, William	19, Sept 1850	Sept	34		Y2	
Mount, William	8, Dec. 1826		estate		N3	
Mount, William	4, Mar. 1828		probate		N3	
Mowen, John	19, Aug. 1831	Aug.	30		A3	
Mowry, Barbara	29, Oct. 1830	Oct.	4		N3	
Mowton, James	9, July 1850	9, July	3m-25d		P2	
Mowton, Joan	30, July 1850	28, July	4m-14d		Y2	
Moyer, Henry	11, Sept 1805		estate		S3	
Muchmore, Samuel	7, Dec. 1837		probate		N3	
Muckins, Henry	3, Dec. 1830	Nov.	36		N3	
Muckridge, Johanna	30, July 1850	July	5		Y3	
Mudge, Hannah	7, Oct. 1831	26, Sept	53	*	X3	
Mudge, Hannah C.	30, Sept 1831	26, Sept	55		X3	
Muhl, Sarah	27, Sept 1852	23, Sept	18m		P2	
Muhlenberg, Frederick August	1, July 1801	4, June			S3	
Mulford, Amanda Clifford	25, May 1837	17, May	14m-14d		X3	
Mulholland, Daniel	12, Apr. 1849	Apr.	32		L2	
Munday, Benjamin	28, June 1849	June	50		L2	
Mundong, (child)	27, Aug. 1830	Aug.	stillborn		N3	
Munsell, Levi	12, Apr. 1849	1, Mar.	87		L3	
Munson, Roderick W.	2, Nov. 1830		estate		N3	
Murdock, Lizzie H.	8, Sept 1852	6, Sept			P2	
Murphey, Edward	28, June 1849	June	33		L2	
Murphy, Edward	23, July 1850	July	14m		Y2	
Murphy, John	1, June 1849	May	28		L2	
Murphy, John	14, June 1849	June	1- 6m		L2	
Murphy, John	26, Mar. 1842	17, Mar.			R3	
Murphy, Michael	23, Apr. 1849	Apr.	21		L2	
Murphy, Neal	26, Oct. 1837	22, Sept	29		T2	
Murphy, Neal	23, Jan. 1838		estate		N3	
Murphy, Peter	7, Jan. 1827		estate		R4	
Murphy, Peter	19, Aug. 1828		probate		N3	
Murphy, William	8, Aug. 1850	Aug.	25		Y2	
Murphy, William	17, Feb. 1829	Feb.	30		N3	
Murphy, William	14, June 1849	June	39		L2	
Murphy, William	21, June 1828				R3	
Murray, Reuben J.	22, Apr. 1847	20, Apr.	37		K2	
Murry, Samuel P.	2, July 1830	June	44		N2	
Muscroft, Christiana	7, Aug. 1841	3, Aug.			R3	
Muscroft, George	23, Apr. 1842	17, Apr.	58	*	R3	
Muscroft, Hannah	24, Oct. 1829	18, Oct.			R3	
Musgrove, Elizabeth	6, Aug. 1830	Aug.	10m		N3	
Mussey, (child)	1, Oct. 1830	Sept	child		N3	
Myer, Philapenia	23, July 1850	July	5w		Y2	
Myers, Adam	6, Nov. 1838		probate		N2	
Myers, John	25, Aug. 1829		estate		N3	
Myers, John	16, July 1830		estate		N3	
Myers, John	17, Apr. 1835		estate		X3	
Myers, Joseph	11, Sept 1837		probate		N2	
Myers, Marcus	17, Oct. 1840	Oct.	6		R3	

Name	Notice Date	Death Date	Age	Page	Maiden Name
Myers, Mary	20, Aug. 1842	17, Aug.	45	R3	
Myers, Ruth	4, June 1836		probate	N2	
Myers, Samuel	22, Dec. 1829		probate	N3	
Myneke, (child of C.T.)	9, July 1830	July	stillborn	N3	
Myres, Mary	2, Aug. 1834	July	8- 3m	R3	
Myres, Mary	29, July 1834	July	8- 3m	T2	
Mysenburg, Richard	12, Sept 1850	Sept	37	Y2	
Nancarrow, John	20, Feb. 1805	14, Feb.	63	S3	
Nancarrow, John	13, Mar. 1805		estate	S3	
Napoleon, Sarah	12, Apr. 1849	Apr.		L2	
Napton, Nancy	24, Apr. 1835	Mar.		T3	
Narry, Patrick	29, Mar. 1849	Mar.	34	L2	
Nash, Josephine Bowers	26, Jan. 1833	19, Jan.	3	R3	
Nash, Mary	14, Sept 1835	27, Aug.	67	T2	
Nash, Solon	1, Aug. 1840	17, July		* R3	
Nash, Theodocia	31, Dec. 1830	Dec.	42	N3	
Nashee, George	25, May 1827		40	N3	
Nashee, George	26, May 1827			R3	
Nashee, Sarah	22, July 1815			G3	
Nathan, Moses	25, Mar. 1828		estate	N3	
Nead, Patrick	27, Jan. 1838	24, Jan.		N2	
Neal, William	21, May 1808		estate	S2	
Nealand, Thomas	6, July 1849	July	50	L2	
Neave, Alexander	22, Jan. 1820	15, Jan.	22- 5m-24d	S3	
Neave, Charles	28, Dec. 1841	25, Dec.	infant	N3	
Neave, Jeremiah	7, May 1824		59	* N3	
Neave, Jeremiah	28, Dec. 1824		estate	N3	
Neave, Jeremiah	3, Mar. 1826		estate	N3	
Neave, Mary S.	13, Mar. 1841	12, Mar.	8- 6m	R3	
Neave, Michael S.	23, Mar. 1830		probate	N3	
Neave, Susannah	7, Apr. 1832	3, Apr.	3	R3	
Neave, Thomas J.	9, Dec. 1828	Dec.	1- 8m	N3	
Neely, Benjamin	21, June 1849	June	22	L2	
Neely, George	21, Oct. 1828	Oct.	15m	N2	
Neely, Thomas	27, Sept 1852	20, Sept	23	P2	
Neely, Thomas	6, Oct. 1829		estate	N3	
Neely, Thomas	6, Oct. 1829	16, Sept		N3	
Neff, Elizabeth Clifford W.	30, Jan. 1841	24, Jan.	infant	R3	
Neff, Elizabeth Clifford Wayne	26, Jan. 1841	25, Jan.	infant	N2	
Neff, George	31, Oct. 1840	9, Oct.	82	* R3	
Neff, George	14, Oct. 1828	Oct.	infant	N3	
Neff, George W.	11, Aug. 1850	9, Aug.		Y2	
Neff, John Randolph	28, Sept 1839	27, Sept		T2	
Neff, Juliana Wayne	9, Feb. 1837	8, Feb.	4- 4m- 7d	T2	
Neff, Juliana Wayne	9, Feb. 1837	8, Feb.	4- 4m- 7d	N2	
Neil, Robert	15, Oct. 1830	Oct.	7m	N3	
Neill, Lewis	16, Feb. 1841		estate	N2	
Neill, Lewis	26, Mar. 1841		estate	N2	
Neise, A. (Dr)	6, July 1849	July		L2	
Neitlord, Patrick	6, July 1849	July	53	* L2	
Nelson, David A.	18, Oct. 1828	1, Oct.		* R3	
Nelson, Elizabeth	28, Apr. 1849	25, Apr.	66	L2	
Nelson, Jane	17, May 1849	May	50	L2	
Nelson, John	18, May 1838		probate	N2	

Name	Notice Date	Death Date	Age		Page	Maiden Name
Nelson, L.F.	13, Aug. 1830	Aug.	29- 5m		N3	
Nelson, Mary L.	8, Sept 1836	9, Aug.	41	*	X3	Trimble
Nelson, Philipe	2, Aug. 1834	July	60		R3	
Nelson, Philipe	29, July 1834	July	60		T2	
Nemor, Herman	14, Dec. 1835		probate		N2	
Nesbit, James A.	13, Aug. 1830	Aug.	6		N3	
Nesler, Frederick	22, Aug. 1828	Aug.	56		N3	
Nette, Elizabeth	22, Mar. 1849	Mar.	11		L2	
Neveille, E. Lawson	30, Nov. 1847	26, Nov.	18m		K2	
Neville, George Byron	25, Aug. 1832	22, Aug.	4		R3	
Neville, John	31, Oct. 1840	Oct.	29		R3	
Neville, Morgan	1, May 1838	30, Apr.	15		N2	
Neville, Morgan	1, Jan. 1842		estate		N2	
Nevins, William	28, Sept 1835	15, Sept	38		T2	
Nevins, William (Rev)	25, Sept 1835	15, Sept			X2	
Newberry, Joshua	12, Aug. 1831	Aug.	17		A3	
Newbrough,	12, Jan. 1829		estate		N3	
Newbrough, John	23, Dec. 1828		estate		N3	
Newcom, Mathew	13, Nov. 1805	27, Oct.	26		S3	
Newell, Abigail	19, Mar. 1839	17, Mar.	50		T2	
Newell, Benjamin	29, June 1827		estate		N3	
Newell, Benjamin	9, Dec. 1828		probate		N3	
Newell, Benjamin	28, Apr. 1827	25, Apr.			R3	
Newell, George W.	19, Sept 1828	Sept	9		N3	
Newell, Harriet	29, July 1815		infant		G3	
Newell, Margaret	29, Sept 1829	26, Sept	infant		N3	
Newell, Samuel	11, Nov. 1836		estate		N2	
Newell, Samuel	18, May 1838		probate		N2	
Newell, Thomas	20, Mar. 1847	19, Mar.	55		K2	
Newell, William H.	8, July 1852	5, July	33		P2	
Newkirk, Mary	3, May 1825		probate		N3	
Newsteckel, Eliza	21, June 1849	June	30		L2	
Newton, Abby B.	11, May 1830	7, May	32		N2	Wood
Newton, Eliza	24, Oct. 1828	Oct.	32		N2	
Newton, Eliza	24, Oct. 1828	18, Oct.		*	N2	
Newton, Joseph	3, Sept 1830	Aug.	34		N2	
Niblett, Margaret	30, July 1850	July	20		Y3	
Nichol, Arthur	24, May 1849	May	7m		L2	
Nichol, Margaret	24, May 1849	May	20		L2	
Nicholas, George	6, Aug. 1799	25, July			S3	
Nicholds, Francis	20, Apr. 1811		estate		S3	
Nichols, Charles	17, Oct. 1850	Oct.	30		Y2	
Nichols, John	2, Aug. 1834	July	45		R3	
Nichols, John	29, July 1834	July	45		T2	
Nichols, Perry	4, Mar. 1828		probate		N3	
Nichols, Samuel	19, Dec. 1812				S3	
Nicholson, John G.	6, July 1849	July	43		L2	
Nicholson, William Rozelle	13, July 1849	12, July	11m		L2	
Nickerson, Uriah	5, Apr. 1825		estate		N3	
Nickols, Arthur Hugh	26, Sept 1840	25, Sept	7m-21d		R3	
Nicoll, Edward	7, Sept 1820	2, Sept	30	*	S3	
Nider, Catherine E.	26, Sept 1828	Sept			N3	
Niel, John	15, Oct. 1831	9, Oct.	19	*	R3	
Niles, Hezekiah	22, June 1824	3, June	43		N3	

Name	Notice Date	Death Date	Age		Page	Maiden Name
Niswanger, Jacob	13, May 1835	5, May			T3	
Nixon, (child of John)	12, Aug. 1831	Aug.	2d		A3	
Nixon, Ellen B.	2, Oct. 1841	28, Sept		*	V3	
Nixon, William	9, July 1830	July	10m		N3	
Nixon, Wilson (Capt)	5, Feb. 1831	1, Feb.	77	*	R3	
Nixon, Wilson (Capt)	4, Feb. 1831	1, Feb.	77	*	X3	
Noble, James	11, Mar. 1831	28, Feb.	48		X3	
Noble, James (Gen)	11, Mar. 1831	26, Feb.			A3	
Noble, John (Lt)	28, Mar. 1817	26, Feb.			S3	
Noble, Lewis R.	21, 24, Dec. 1830	16, Dec.	24		N3	
Noble, Lewis R.	20, Dec. 1830	17, Dec.			A3	
Noble, Mary	26, July 1834	July	38		R3	
Noble, Mary	22, July 1834	July	38		T2	
Noble, Samuel	28, Apr. 1835	20, Apr.	17- 5m		T3	
Noble, Teham (Major)	22, Apr. 1825		82		N2	
Noble, William	22, Dec. 1829		estate		N3	
Noble, William	21, Dec. 1830		estate		N3	
Noble, William	25, May 1827	23, May			Q3	
Noble, William (Capt)	25, May 1827	23, May	47		N3	
Noble, William (Capt)	26, May 1827	23, May			R3	
Noe, Abraham	9, July 1830	July	62		N3	
Noe, Washington	18, July 1828	July	19m		N3	
Nolan, Harriet	18, June 1830	June	10m		N3	
Noland, Bridget	24, May 1849	May	21		L2	
Noodman, Barnard	12, Sept 1850	Sept	23		Y2	
Noonan, Timothy	26, Feb. 1841	Feb.	34		N2	
Norman,	2, Aug. 1834	July	50		R3	
Norman,	29, July 1834	July	50		T2	
Norris, Charles	29, July 1837		estate		R3	
Norris, George	19, Feb. 1841	Feb.	21	*	N2	
Norris, George	20, Feb. 1841	Feb.	22		R3	
Norris, Gersham	14, Dec. 1835		probate		N2	
Norris, John Dorsey	15, Jan. 1839	12, Jan.	2- -7d		T2	
Norris, P. Nelson (Dr)	6, Oct. 1836	22, Sept			T2	
Norris, Phebe	19, Nov. 1830	Nov.	16		N3	
Norris, Uriah	1, June 1849	May	37		L2	
Norris, William E.	30, Mar. 1849	27, Mar.	25- 3m		L2	
North, Caleb (Col)	21, Nov. 1840	7, Nov.	88		R3	
North, Elijah	3, May 1838				N2	
Northrop, Henry A.	5, Oct. 1839	3, Oct.	20		R3	
Northrup, Charles	27, Oct. 1852	26, Oct.		*	P2	
Norton, Francis Louisa	7, Sept 1837	20, Aug.	19m		X3	
Norton, Harriet	24, Oct. 1817	23, Oct.	22	*	S3	
Norton, Shoral	4, Apr. 1818	29, Mar.	52	*	S3	
Norvell, Hendrick	30, Mar. 1837	18, Mar.	28		T2	
Norwood, John	2, Dec. 1825		98		N3	
Nott, Abraham	8, July 1830	6, July	67		A3	
Nourse, (child of Charles)	30, July 1850	July	1d		Y3	
Nourse, Charles F.	12, May 1836	26, Apr.			X3	
Nourse, Elizabeth M.J.	6, Apr. 1847	4, Apr.	4		K2	
Nourse, George	29, Oct. 1835	23, Oct.	31	*	X3	
Nowland, Mary	20, Oct. 1827	Oct.	42		R3	
Noyes, Charles C.	10, Sept 1852	8, Sept	38		P2	
Nugent, William	13, July 1849	July	42		L2	

Name	Notice Date	Death Date	Age		Page	Maiden Name
Nutt, Adam	7, Dec. 1837		probate		N3	
Nutt, Adam (heirs of)	7, Dec. 1837		probate		N3	
Nutt, Edward J.	13, July 1849	July	35		L2	
Nutt, Nancy	17, Apr. 1835		estate		N2	
Nutt, Nancy	7, Dec. 1837		probate		N3	
Nye, Eunice	4, Aug. 1832	1, Aug.			R3	
Nye, Gillalah	30, July 1830	July	6		N3	
Nye, James M.	26, Nov. 1830	Nov.	4m		N3	
Nye, Rowena Spencer	5, Feb. 1842	24, Jan.	45		R3	
O'Bannon, Presley N. (Major)	25, Sept 1850	12, Sept	74		Y2	
Obear, Matilda	30, July 1830	July	7m		N3	
O'Brien, (man)	1, July 1826	24, June			J2	
O'Brien, William	26, July 1850	July	7		Y2	
O'Connel, Dinnese (Mrs)	28, May 1849	27, May			L2	
O'Conner, Jeremiah	17, June 1837		probate		N2	
O'Conner, Patrick	22, Aug. 1850	Aug.	22		Y2	
Odell, Caroline Louisa	9, May 1840	7, May	2		R3	
Odell, Thomas (Rev)	8, Sept 1827	25, Aug.	80		R3	
Oder, William	12, Apr. 1849	Apr.	31		L2	
O'Ferrall, John	7, Sept 1824		probate		N3	
O'Ferrall, John	14, Dec. 1824		probate		N3	
O'Ferrall, John	9, Sept 1824		probate		E3	
O'Ferrall, John	16, Dec. 1824		probate		E3	
O'Ferrall, Rebecca	13, Feb. 1824		estate		N3	
Offinhern, Fred.	11, Nov. 1838	Nov.	2w		N3	
O'Fling, (Lt)	1, Dec. 1815	24, Nov.			S3	
Ogden, David	21, Sept 1832		estate		X3	
Ogden, David	21, Sept 1838		probate		N3	
Ogden, James E.	1, July 1828	June	7m		N3	
Ogilvie, James	21, Apr. 1821	18, Sept	45		S3	
O'Hagan, Patrick	28, June 1849	June			L2	
O'Hara, Ezra	12, May 1851	11, May			P2	
O'Hara, Ezra	14, Oct. 1851				P2	
O'Harra, James (Gen)	1, Jan. 1820	16, Dec.	66		S3	
O'Harrington, John	17, Oct. 1850	Oct.	25		Y2	
O'Lary, Daniel	14, June 1849	June	42		L2	
Olbers, (Dr)	2, May 1840	4, Mar.	81		R3	
Oldendoff, Frederick W.	13, July 1849	July	29		L2	
Oldendorff, Fred. W.	13, July 1849	July	3		L2	
Older, George	13, July 1849	July	35		L2	
Oldham, F.J.	26, Sept 1850	Sept	20		Y2	
Oldham, George	31, May 1849	30, May			L2	
Oldham, Matilda	13, Aug. 1830	Aug.	1- 2m		N3	
Olds, Jonas W. (Dr)	19, Oct. 1832	30, Sept	26		X3	
O'Leary, Ellen	1, Aug. 1850	July	13m		Y2	
Oliphant, J. (Mrs)	2, Oct. 1834	11, Sept	30	*	T2	
Oliver, Alexander (Col)	8, July 1828	July	84		N3	
Oliver, Alexander (Col)	5, July 1828	27, June			R3	
Oliver, Allen	17, Oct. 1801		estate		S3	
Oliver, Benjamin	2, Nov. 1841	30, Oct.	24		N2	
Oliver, Benjamin F.	6, Nov. 1841	30, Oct.	25		R3	
Oliver, Daniel (Dr)	14, June 1842	1, June	54		N2	
Oliver, Matthew G.	3, Jan. 1853	30, Dec.	29		P2	
Olmstead, Josephine	8, Sept 1827	Sept	4m		R3	

Name	Notice Date	Death Date	Age		Page	Maiden Name
Olmsted, Olympia	1, July 1828	June	21d		N3	
Olney, Anthony (Col)	15, Aug. 1840	25, July			R3	
O'Neal, James	11, Sept 1837		probate		N2	
O'Neal, Mary	17, May 1849	May	22		L2	
O'Neil, John	13, July 1849	July	38		L2	
Openaueo, Michael	8, Oct. 1852	Oct.			P2	
Oppenheimer, Catharine	6, July 1849	5, July	64		L2	
Oram, Robert	2, Dec. 1824	14, Nov.	74		E2	
Orange, Jane Augusta	1, June 1836	1, June	infant		T2	
Orange, Philip J.	18, June 1830	June	3		N3	
O'Reilly, P.	3, Apr. 1847		estate		K3	
Orr, (child of John)	13, Mar. 1829	Mar.	1d		N3	
Orr, (child)	9, July 1830	July	8d		N3	
Orr, (child)	26, July 1834	July	child		R3	
Orr, (child)	22, July 1834	July	child		T2	
Orr, Amelia	24, June 1828	June	1		N3	
Orr, Benjamin (Capt)	14, Jan. 1818	2, Oct.			S3	
Orr, H.	16, Dec. 1828	Dec.	28		N3	
Orr, Robert	5, Nov. 1800	30, Oct.			S3	
Orrick, Davenport	28, Aug. 1852	24, Aug.			P2	
Osborn, (child of Mrs)	17, Feb. 1829	Feb.	4m- 3d		N3	
Osborn, Abner	16, July 1830	July	30		N3	
Osborn, Eleanor	28, Nov. 1828	Nov.	40		N3	
Osborn, Elias	12, Aug. 1831	Aug.	2		A3	
Osborn, Eliza C.	20, July 1837	3, July	20		X3	
Osborn, Ezra	2, May 1840	18, Apr.	67		R3	
Osborn, Selleck	10, Nov. 1826				N3	
Osburn, Ellen	18, July 1828	July	2		N3	
Osgood, Mary	2, Aug. 1834	July	4		R3	
Osgood, Mary	29, July 1834	July	4		T2	
Otter, Jacob	19, Dec. 1826		probate		N3	
Ounaburry, Jane	1, Aug. 1828	July	28		N3	
Oustoby, William E.	5, Dec. 1840	4, Dec.	46	*	N2	
Outcalt, Ellen M.	3, Jan. 1853	1, Jan.	38		P2	Matthews
Owen, Charles	14, July 1837	12, July	15m		T2	
Owen, John	21, Dec. 1852	19, Dec.	7		P2	
Owen, Susan Pendleton	8, Aug. 1842	4, Aug.	12m- 9d		N2	
Owen, Susan Pentleton	13, Aug. 1842	4, Aug.	12m- 9d		R3	
Owen, Wash.	17, May 1849	May	30		L2	
Owens, Ellen	26, Apr. 1849	Apr.	25		L2	
Owens, Helen	1, Aug. 1851	17, July	22-11m	*	P2	McAlister
Owens, Michael	26, Apr. 1849	Apr.	32		L2	
Owens, Richard D.	28, Sept 1838	22, Sept	24		T2	
Pace, Susanna	5, Nov. 1830	Nov.	21		N3	
Pack, John N.	3, Jan. 1817		estate		S3	
Page, (child of D.)	7, May 1830	May	stillborn		N3	
Page, (child)	14, Oct. 1828	Oct.	child		N3	
Page, Joseph R.	6, Sept 1833	Sept	40		X3	
Page, Lewis	29, Mar. 1849	Mar.	24		L2	
Page, Samuel M.	9, Sept 1831	Sept	4m-19d		A3	
Pagen, Thomas	10, Dec. 1830	Dec.	23		N3	
Pain, Samuel	28, May 1814		estate		S1	
Paine, Charles	1, July 1828	June	2		N3	
Palmer, Clarissa	16, Oct. 1835	8, Sept			X3	

Name	Notice Date	Death Date	Age		Page	Maiden Name
Palmer, Dudley	27, Sept 1852	22, Sept	78	*	P2	
Palmer, Eliza	22, Aug. 1850	Aug.	3w		Y2	
Palmer, James	22, Aug. 1850	Aug.	17		Y2	
Palmer, Maria	16, Apr. 1842	11, Apr.	32		R3	
Palmore, William	2, Aug. 1834	July	14d		R3	
Palmore, William	29, July 1834	July	14d		T2	
Pancoast, Sidonias	25, Mar. 1847	23, Mar.	85		K2	
Papineau, Joseph	30, July 1841	8, July	88		N3	
Parce, Carman	31, July 1805	19, July			S3	
Parish, Elijah (Rev)	11, Nov. 1825		63		N2	
Park, Arthur	10, Mar. 1829		probate		N3	
Park, Culbertson	11, Sept 1837		probate		N2	
Park, Elizabeth	27, Jan. 1821		estate		S3	
Park, Elizabeth	19, Dec. 1826		probate		N3	
Parker, (wife & 3 children)	3, May 1838				N2	
Parker, Catharine A.	23, Jan. 1839	30, Dec.	7		T2	
Parker, Elizabeth	8, Oct. 1830	Oct.	10m		N3	
Parker, James	5, Jan. 1822		estate		S3	
Parker, Jane	21, May 1849	20, May	17- 5m		L2	
Parker, Joel	7, Apr. 1836	8, Mar.			X3	
Parker, John	22, Apr. 1835		estate		N2	
Parker, Joseph	14, Dec. 1835		probate		N2	
Parker, Robert	28, Jan. 1823		estate		N3	
Parker, Robert C.	7, Oct. 1824		estate		E3	
Parker, Robert C.	3, Aug. 1824	2, Aug.			N2	
Parker, Robert C.	5, Aug. 1824	2, Aug.			E3	
Parker, Samuel (Rev)	22, Jan. 1820	20, Dec.	48		S3	
Parker, Sarah	18, June 1830	June	10m		N3	
Parker, Stephen	13, Mar. 1829	Mar.	1- 4m		N3	
Parker, William	3, May 1838				N2	
Parker, Williard (Mrs)	23, Jan. 1839	14, Jan.	31		T2	
Parkhurst, Charles Lewis	6, Dec. 1838	4, Dec.	21m		T3	
Parkinson, Elizabeth	21, May 1830	May	30		N3	
Parks,	1, July 1850				P2	
Parks, Andrew	13, Aug. 1814		estate		S3	
Parks, Andrew	4, June 1814	2, June			S3	
Parks, Jane	30, June 1849	25, June		*	L2	
Parks, Joseph	7, Feb. 1817	21, Jan.			S2	
Parks, Martin P. (Lt)	5, July 1852	5, July			P2	
Parmele, William H.	22, Oct. 1830	Oct.	11m		N3	
Parmeter, J.F.	23, Apr. 1841	Apr.			N2	
Parrish, Elizabeth Ann F.	26, Aug. 1852	24, Aug.	26		P2	
Parrish, Jonathan	28, June 1828				R3	
Parry, Edward	25, Aug. 1841	10, Aug.	30		N2	
Parsons, Sarah	22, Nov. 1833	20, Nov.	61	*	X3	
Parvin, Holmes (Dr)	12, Feb. 1842	4, Feb.			R3	
Parvin, Josiah N.B.	18, June 1830	June	14d		N3	
Parvner, John	7, Sept 1824		probate		N3	
Parvner, John	9, Sept 1824		probate		E3	
Patch, Lizzie Rowena	27, July 1852	24, July	8- -18d		P2	
Patrick, Clara Ada	22, June 1850	21, June	18m-24d		P2	
Patrick, James DeBrette	3, July 1850	2, July	2-10m		P2	
Patson, (child of Susan)	2, Sept 1828	Aug.	9w		N3	
Pattce, William Elias	25, Dec. 1841	10, Dec.			R3	

Name	Notice Date	Death Date	Age		Page	Maiden Name
Patterson, Andrew	4, Aug. 1827	1, Aug.	45-10m	*	R3	
Patterson, Ann B.	3, Dec. 1830	Nov.	1- 6m		N3	
Patterson, Anna Sophia	14, July 1852	13, July	5m-20d		P2	
Patterson, Cynthia A.	30, July 1830	July	11m		N3	
Patterson, G.E.	28, Jan. 1837	16, Jan.			R3	
Patterson, George (Rev)	24, Dec. 1831	23, Dec.	44		R3	
Patterson, John	6, July 1849	July	6		L2	
Patterson, Josephine	22, Apr. 1847	20, Apr.	18		K2	
Patterson, Josiah	29, Oct. 1830	Oct.	4m		N3	
Patterson, Margaret	14, June 1849	June	3m		L2	
Patterson, Margaret	27, Nov. 1852	25, Nov.			P2	
Patterson, Martha	22, Aug. 1850	Aug.	23		Y2	
Patterson, Moses	21, Jan. 1848	20, Dec.	89	*	K3	
Patterson, Rebecca	25, Aug. 1827	Aug.	37		R3	
Patterson, Robert	10, Aug. 1827	5, Aug.	65		N3	
Patterson, Robert	4, Sept 1813	31, Aug.			S3	
Patterson, Robert (Col)	11, Aug. 1827	5, Aug.	65		R3	
Patterson, Samuel	25, May 1827	24, May	50		N3	
Patterson, Samuel	29, June 1827		estate		N3	
Patterson, Samuel	26, May 1827	24, May			R3	
Patterson, Samuel	17, July 1841	2, June			R3	
Patterson, Samuel	25, May 1827	24, May			Q3	
Pattison, Ezekiel Thomas	28, July 1852	26, July	17		P2	
Patton, John	6, Aug. 1850		estate		Y2	
Patton, Robert	4, Apr. 1837		probate		N2	
Patton, William	13, Nov. 1805	15, Oct.			S3	
Patton, William Humphreys	7, Jan. 1848	7, Jan.	5		K2	
Paul, Alexander	3, July 1850	2, July	28- 4m		P2	
Paul, Jacob	10, May 1849	May	48		L2	
Paul, James (Col)	26, July 1841	23, July	81		N2	
Pauline, Theodore	8, Oct. 1852	Oct.	25		P2	
Paull, Henry	7, Sept 1836		probate		N2	
Pavis, Daniel	19, July 1834	July	9m		R3	
Pawson, Percival	15, Aug. 1826	12, Aug.	13m		N3	
Pawson, Thomas	22, Aug. 1829		estate		R3	
Paxson, Robert	3, Apr. 1813	Mar.	25		S1	
Paxton, Alfred	23, Aug. 1852	20, Aug.	20		P2	
Paxton, John	1, June 1835		probate		N2	
Paytin, (child of William)	26, Nov. 1830	Nov.	1- 6m		N3	
Peabody, Elizabeth	4, Dec. 1841	28, Nov.	5w- 2d		R3	
Peabody, Elizabeth	30, Nov. 1841	28, Nov.	5w- 2d		N2	
Peacock, Wesley	19, Nov. 1830	Nov.	1		N3	
Pearce, John	19, Sept 1834	10, Aug.			X3	
Pearce, Mary French	20, Aug. 1830	Aug.	7m	*	N3	
Pearce, Thomas	9, Dec. 1828	Dec.	5		N3	
Pearce, Wilfred	7, Dec. 1852	15, Nov.			P2	
Pearce, Wilfred Lee	9, Aug. 1847	8, Aug.	8m		K2	
Pearne, George	15, May 1838	10, May	45	*	T2	
Pearson, Amanda	30, Nov. 1832	25, Nov.	31	*	X3	
Pearson, Ebenezer H.	17, Oct. 1828	10, Oct.			N2	
Pearson, Elijah	29, June 1833	21, June			R3	
Pease, Tirzah	7, June 1833	31, May	25		X3	
Peaslee, Ira	27, June 1835		estate		N2	
Peck, Amelia	11, Mar. 1823	9, Mar.	23		N3	

Name	Notice Date	Death Date	Age	Page	Maiden Name
Peckingbaugh, Frederick	20, Jan. 1821		estate	S3	
Peckinpaugh, F.	19, Aug. 1828		probate	N3	
Pedroe, S.J. (Mrs)	23, June 1851	20, June		P2	
Peeples, Burrell H.	6, Mar. 1819	9, Feb.		S3	
Peet, Truman	13, May 1836		estate	N3	
Peinter, Peter	6, July 1849	July	27	L2	
Pellbe, (child of Jarvis)	24, Feb. 1829	Feb.	3w	N3	
Pendleton, Jesse Hunt	9, Jan. 1839	7, Jan.	infant	T2	
Pendleton, Nathaniel	17, Nov. 1821	20, Oct.	64	S3	
Penniman, O.	26, Nov. 1836		estate	N2	
Penniman, Obediah	21, Sept 1838		probate	N3	
Pennington, John	8, Sept 1841	4, Sept	65	* N2	
Penny, (child of John)	24, June 1828	June	2	N3	
Penny, Edward	24, May 1816		estate	S3	
Penrose, John	5, Sept 1823	4, Sept	30	N3	
Peplow, Edward P.	29, Mar. 1849	Mar.	48	L2	
Pepper, Bridget	23, July 1850	July	35	Y2	
Percival, Calvin	27, Oct. 1810	20, Oct.		S3	
Perkins, Clement (Capt)	9, May 1823		30	N2	
Perkins, Ebenezer	2, Aug. 1834	July	1- 6m	R3	
Perkins, Ebenezer	29, July 1834	July	1- 6m	T2	
Perkins, Emily Elizabeth	10, Jan. 1838	9, Jan.	infant	N2	
Perret, P.H.	10, Mar. 1829		probate	N3	
Perret, Philip H.	25, Aug. 1829		probate	N3	
Perrin, (Capt)	3, May 1838			N2	
Perrin, Amos	17, June 1837		probate	N2	
Perrine, Matthew LaRue	10, Mar. 1836	12, Feb.	50	X3	
Perry, Ann	19, Aug. 1828	Aug.	2- 3m	N3	
Perry, Ann M.	19, Aug. 1831	Aug.	18m- 4d	A3	
Perry, Horace	20, Apr. 1835		48	T3	
Perry, Jonathan Hill	28, Apr. 1847	27, Apr.	1- 3m	K2	
Perry, Joseph	23, Sept 1852	16, Sept	70	P2	
Perry, Juliana Jane	2, Aug. 1834	23, July	18	R3	
Perry, Oliver H. (Commodore)	9, Oct. 1819	23, Aug.		S3	
Perry, William	23, Jan. 1841	Jan.	27	R3	
Perry, William	21, Jan. 1841	Jan.	27	N2	
Persons, Jane	12, July 1828			R3	
Pesicoll, Frank	13, July 1849	July	24	L2	
Peterhogan, Anna S.	26, July 1834	July	53	R3	
Peterhogan, Anna S.	22, July 1834	July	53	T2	
Peters, Augustus Benoit	8, Apr. 1847	6, Apr.	12- 3m	K2	
Peters, Mathias	13, July 1849	July		L2	
Peters, Michael	21, Apr. 1835	12, Apr.		T3	
Peters, Richard	6, Sept 1828	22, Aug.		R3	
Peterson, Mary	17, July 1841	July	34	R3	
Petit, M.S. (Dr)	22, Aug. 1817	28, July		S3	
Pettit, Jerome Seymore	6, July 1849	4, July	2- 6m	L2	
Pettit, Mary Ann	18, July 1851	17, July	36	P2	
Pettit, Samuel	1, Sept 1847	31, Aug.	84	K2	
Pettit, Sarah Bella	2, July 1849	30, June	5- 2m-13d	L2	
Pettit, Thomas	23, Apr. 1830		estate	N3	
Phares, John	15, Oct. 1830	Oct.	65	N3	
Phares, John	9, Dec. 1828		probate	N3	
Pharis, John	9, Mar. 1822	3, Mar.	86	* S2	

Name	Notice Date	Death Date	Age		Page	Maiden Name
Phelps, Harriet E.	19, Oct. 1847	10, Oct.			K2	
Phelps, John	11, July 1812		estate		S3	
Phelps, Joseph Henry	11, Mar. 1837	8, Mar.			R3	
Phelps, Joseph Henry	13, Mar. 1837	8, Mar.			T2	
Phelps, Samuel Cowdrey	17, July 1841	14, July	14m		V3	
Phelps, Samuel Cowdro	17, July 1841	14, July	14m		R3	
Phelps, Samuel W.	13, Apr. 1837	12, Apr.	54		T2	
Phelps, William Kinman	28, Sept 1820	17, Sept	infant		S3	
Philip, John D.	4, July 1840	3, July	5		R3	
Philips, Joseph	10, Dec. 1830	Dec.	2d		N3	
Philips, Richard	30, July 1830	July	37		N3	
Phillips, A.P.	10, Sept 1830	Sept	33		N3	
Phillips, Brannock	13, Aug. 1836	4, Aug.	14		T2	
Phillips, Brannock	18, Aug. 1836	4, Aug.	14		X3	
Phillips, Henry	30, Dec. 1825		estate		N3	
Phillips, Henry	27, Jan. 1826		estate		N3	
Phillips, John	24, May 1849	May	40		L2	
Phillips, Mariah	24, Sept 1842	20, Sept	26		R3	
Phillips, Mary Ann	25, Nov. 1828	Nov.	8m		N3	
Phillips, Mary Ann	28, July 1827	26, July	infant		R3	
Phillips, Richard	27, July 1833	26, July			R3	
Phillips, S.C. (Mrs)	2, Oct. 1852	26, Sept	49		P2	
Phillips, Samuel	20, Mar. 1802	10, Feb.			S3	
Phillips, Sophie M.	20, May 1837			*	R3	Barrows
Phillips, Susannah	3, Apr. 1829	Mar.	15		N2	
Phillips, William	16, June 1827		77		R3	
Phillips, William (Rev)	13, Aug. 1836	4, Aug.	39		T2	
Phillips, William (Rev)	18, Aug. 1836	4, Aug.	39		X3	
Phoends, John	3, Dec. 1830	Nov.	40		N3	
Piatt, Hannah	13, June 1818	8, June	58		S3	
Piatt, John H.	23, Feb. 1822	11, Feb.	41		S3	
Piatt, John H.	23, May 1823		estate		N3	
Piatt, John H.	13, Apr. 1824		estate		N4	
Piatt, John H.	9, Nov. 1824		estate		N4	
Piatt, John H.	3, May 1825		probate		N3	
Piatt, John H.	19, Aug. 1828		probate		N3	
Piatt, John H.	9, Dec. 1828		probate		N3	
Piatt, John H.	23, Mar. 1830		probate		N3	
Piatt, John H.	30, Mar. 1822	11, Feb.			S3	
Piatt, Martha	5, Mar. 1842	28, Feb.	76	*	R3	
Pickell, George	16, Nov. 1822		estate		S3	
Pickens, Israel	16, June 1827	23, May			R3	
Pickering, John	16, July 1850	16, July	48		P2	
Pickering, Julia	29, Nov. 1852	27, Nov.	3		P2	
Pickering, Timothy	17, Feb. 1829		84	*	N1	
Picket, John (Col)	4, Feb. 1831	21, Jan.	66		X3	
Picket, John (Col)	29, Jan. 1831	21, Jan.	67		R3	
Pickett, Esther Rockwell	15, Aug. 1829	26, July	58		R3	
Pickett, Mary C.G.	14, June 1833	8, June	11- 9m-21d		X3	
Pickle, George	16, Dec. 1825		probate		N3	
Pierce, Ann	26, July 1834	July	73		R3	
Pierce, Ann	12, July 1834		73		T2	
Pierce, Ann	22, July 1834	July	73		T2	
Pierce, Ann E.	18, June 1830	June	4m		N3	

Name	Notice Date	Death Date	Age	Page	Maiden Name
Pierce, Charles	10, July 1841	July	9m		R3	
Pierce, George	23, Sept 1831	Sept	35	A3	
Pierce, Joseph (Mrs)	9, Oct. 1841	23, Sept		* R3	
Pierce, Martha	18, July 1840	July	7m	R3	
Pierce, Mary Shreve	14, July 1849	12, July		L2	
Pierce, Sally	25, Sept 1841	25, Sept	35	R3	
Pierce, Sally	23, Sept 1841	22, Sept	55	N2	
Pierce, Samuel	22, Dec. 1829		probate	N3	
Piersin, David	4, Apr. 1837		probate	N2	
Pierson, David	9, Sept 1830	2, Sept	54	* A3	
Pierson, Ebenezer (Dr)	21, Oct. 1828	Oct.	57	N2	
Pierson, Sarah C.	20, Aug. 1847	18, Aug.		K2	
Pierson, William	8, Sept 1827	Sept	1	R3	
Pigman, Levi	30, Nov. 1822		estate	S3	
Pike, Sallie	7, Dec. 1852	5, Dec.	child	P2	
Pilkinton, Elizabeth	10, Aug. 1852	6, Aug.	1- 4m- 5d	P2	
Pinckney, Charles	26, Nov. 1824	29, Sept		N2	
Pinckney, Charles	2, Dec. 1824	9, Nov.		E2	
Pinckney, Thomas (Gen)	18, Nov. 1828	17, Nov.	79	N3	
Pindall, Joshua G.	10, Mar. 1829		probate	N3	
Pindel, Joshua G.	31, Aug. 1827		estate	Q3	
Pingree, Mary Ann	19, Dec. 1840	12, Dec.	17	R3	Halley
Pingree, Mary Ann	19, Dec. 1840	12, Dec.	17	N2	Halley
Pinney, George	30, Sept 1852	26, Sept	18	P2	
Piper, Eliza	21, Sept 1852	20, Sept	41	P2	
Pirtle, Henry	23, June 1836	18, June	infant	T2	
Pitcher, Nancy	22, Apr. 1824	14, Apr.		E3	
Pitner, Elizabeth	14, June 1849	June	53	L2	
Pitner, George	14, June 1849	June	48	L2	
Pittman, Jonathan	20, Mar. 1838		probate	N3	
Place, Ann E.	19, July 1834	July	7m	R3	
Placide, (Miss)	3, June 1835			T2	
Plater, William	7, June 1849	June	25	L2	
Plater, William	1, June 1849			* L3	
Pleasant, Peter	17, Sept 1830	Sept	22	N3	
Pleasants, Mary	14, May 1842	11, May	38	R3	
Pleasants, Mary	12, May 1842	11, May	38	N2	
Pleasants, Mary L.	13, May 1837	9, May	24	T2	
Pleasants, Zaccheus	21, July 1827	17, July		R3	
Plummer, Elizabeth G.	10, Oct. 1840	22, Sept		R3	
Poineer, John	12, Sept 1840	9, Sept	infant	R3	
Pollard, John	20, Oct. 1836	Mar.	20	* T2	
Pollock, Anna M.	27, July 1850	July	20m	Y3	
Polser, Henry	30, Mar. 1822		estate	S3	
Pomeroy, Catharine Coolidge	22, Jan. 1842	16, Jan.	1- 3m	R3	
Pomeroy, Catharine Coolidge	19, Jan. 1842	16, Jan.	1- 3m	N2	
Pomeroy, Elizabeth	17, Nov. 1852	8, Nov.		* P2	Worthington
Pomeroy, Joseph	3, Sept 1830	Aug.	32	N2	
Pomeroy, Samuel Wyllis	19, June 1841		78	R3	
Pomeroy, Samuel Wyllys	14, June 1841	4, June	77	* N2	
Ponlery, Luitlion	21, Oct. 1828	Oct.	18	N2	
Ponnell, Moses	20, Aug. 1842	16, Aug.	68	R3	
Pool, Mary	26, July 1834	July	43	R3	
Pool, Mary	22, July 1834	July	43	T2	

Name	Notice Date	Death Date	Age		Page	Maiden Name
Pool, Ruth	10, Dec. 1835	3, Aug.	97		N2	Fullerton
Poole, (Mr)	4, Mar. 1823	8, Feb.			N3	
Poor, Jacob H.	17, Dec. 1852	30, Nov.	48		P2	
Pope, Piercy (Capt)	3, Sept 1799	June			S3	
Popo, Malinda	26, Sept 1850	Sept	85		Y2	
Porer, Polly	21, Dec. 1837	30, Oct.	27	*	X3	
Porritt, Elizabeth	5, Nov. 1830	Nov.	49		N3	
Porter, Martha Ann	24, July 1841	July	2		R3	
Porter, Noah	9, Aug. 1825		92		N3	
Porter, Robert	19, Sept 1840		estate		R3	
Porter, Sidney Ida	5, Nov. 1852	1, Nov.	19		P2	
Posey, Charles	6, July 1849	July	2		L2	
Posey, Thomas	8, Aug. 1818		estate		S2	
Post, (wife & 2 children)	3, May 1838			*	N2	
Post, Josiah	27, Mar. 1805		estate		S3	
Post, Josiah	11, Dec. 1805		estate		S3	
Post, S.	3, May 1838			*	N2	
Post, Tarus	12, Aug. 1831	Aug.	29		A3	
Post, Wright (Dr)	28, June 1828	14, June	63		R3	
Postlewaite, John	21, Sept 1847	2, Sept	36	*	K2	
Pottenger, Samuel	19, May 1829		estate		N3	
Pottenger, Samuel	1, June 1835		probate		N2	
Potter, Asahel	15, Aug. 1842		estate		N2	
Potter, Joseph	22, Sept 1821		estate		S3	
Potter, Joseph	7, Sept 1824		probate		N3	
Potter, Joseph	3, May 1825		probate		N3	
Potter, Joseph	9, Sept 1824		probate		E3	
Potter, W.W.	9, Nov. 1839				R3	
Potts, Stacy	20, Jan. 1825		estate		E3	
Pouder, John	22, Mar. 1837		estate		N2	
Pouder, John	21, Sept 1838		probate		N3	
Pounds, Samuel	10, Dec. 1796		estate		F3	
Powell, Elizabeth	22, Mar. 1849	Mar.	50		L2	
Powell, Elizabeth Octavia	24, Sept 1852	22, Sept	1-8m		P2	
Powell, John E.	14, Nov. 1837	24, Oct.	23	*	T2	
Powell, Milton W.	13, July 1852	11, July	23		P2	
Powell, Nathaniel	15, Oct. 1830	Oct.	2		N3	
Powell, T.C.	3, May 1838				N2	
Powers, Catharine M.	15, Feb. 1836	25, Jan.	8-3m-9d		T3	
Powers, Edward	18, Apr. 1828	17, Apr.			Q3	
Powers, Stephen	4, Sept 1819	1, Sept	51	*	S3	
Powner, Abigail	25, Aug. 1829		probate		N3	
Prater, Henry	28, June 1849	June	26		L2	
Pratt, Thomas	30, Aug. 1833				X3	
Prazier, Magdalena	6, July 1849	July	44		L2	
Prenderil, Mary	30, July 1850	July	13m		Y3	
Prescot, Lydia C.	11, Mar. 1825	23, Feb.			N2	
Presner, Joseph	6, July 1849	July	30		L2	
Preston,	22, Aug. 1828	Aug.	1-8m		N3	
Preston, David	6, Aug. 1830	Aug.	75		N3	
Preston, James	9, June 1835		estate		N2	
Preston, John B.	4, Apr. 1837		probate		N2	
Preston, Patrick	20, Dec. 1816		estate		S3	
Preuss, Augustus W.	16, May 1840	25, Mar.	60		R3	

Name	Notice Date	Death Date	Age		Page	Maiden Name
Price, Evan	14, Oct. 1823		estate		N3	
Price, Evan	14, July 1826		estate		N3	
Price, Evan	9, Dec. 1828		probate		N3	
Price, Evan	10, Mar. 1829		probate		N3	
Price, Evan	25, Aug. 1829		probate		N3	
Price, Evan	22, Dec. 1829		probate		N3	
Price, Frances D.	12, May 1849	11, May	29- 6m		L2	
Price, Hannah F.	27, July 1850	July	57		Y3	
Price, Henry	13, Feb. 1835	10, Feb.	25	*	N2	
Price, Hezekiah	18, June 1830		estate		N3	
Price, Hezekiah	17, June 1837		probate		N2	
Price, Jacob F. (Rev)	7, June 1847	27, May			K2	
Price, James	7, Dec. 1852	4, Dec.	10		P2	
Price, James H.	22, Oct. 1830	Oct.	10m		N3	
Price, John	8, July 1825	7, July	28		N3	
Price, John	18, June 1830	June	43		N3	
Price, John	1, June 1835		probate		N2	
Price, John W.	28, Aug. 1829		estate		N3	
Price, Maria	30, Mar. 1811	30, Mar.			S3	
Price, Nancy	3, Sept 1830	Aug.	28- 2m		N2	
Price, Susan	2, Nov. 1830	31, Oct.	22		N2	Morris
Price, Susan	1, Nov. 1830	29, Oct.			A3	
Price, William	10, Oct. 1818		estate		S3	
Price, William	25, July 1818	22, July		*	S3	
Prier, Moses	17, May 1794		estate		C3	
Prince, James	3, Sept 1830	Aug.	5		N2	
Prince, John (Rev)	30, June 1836	7, June	84		X3	
Prince, Joseph (Capt)	3, Jan. 1829	24, Nov.	76	*	R3	
Prince, Sarah	30, Apr. 1808	28, Apr.			S3	Conn
Prince, Susan	8, Jan. 1836	6, Jan.	17		T3	
Prince, Susan	8, Jan. 1836	6, Jan.	17		N2	
Prince, William	24, Sept 1824	8, Sept			N3	
Prince, William	23, Apr. 1842	6, Apr.			N2	
Pringle, James R.	25, July 1840				R3	
Prior, John (minor)	17, June 1837		probate		N2	
Prisch, Daniel	6, May 1825		estate		N3	
Prisch, Daniel	11, Dec. 1827		probate		N3	
Prish, Daniel	19, Aug. 1828		probate		N3	
Pritchard, John	28, Aug. 1847	31, July			K2	
Proctor, (Mr)	22, Aug. 1834				X3	
Proffitt, George H.	11, Sept 1847	7, Sept			K2	
Provost, William	11, Dec. 1827		probate		N3	
Prudden, James	2, Dec. 1825		estate		N3	
Prudence, Leonidas	31, Dec. 1830	Dec.	7		N3	
Pryer, Andrew	3, Apr. 1829		estate		N3	
Pryer, Moses	23, Nov. 1836		estate		N4	
Pryer, Moses	21, Sept 1838		probate		N3	
Pugh, David	9, Dec. 1828		probate		N3	
Pugh, David	6, Nov. 1819	5, Nov.			S3	
Pugh, Hannah M.	31, Dec. 1836	25, Dec.	10		R3	
Pugh, John	13, June 1840	15, Apr.	82- 8m		R3	
Pugh, Nancy	29, Mar. 1816	26, Mar.			S3	
Pullan, John	19, Feb. 1842	23, Jan.	24		R3	
Pullan, John	17, Feb. 1842	23, Jan.	24		N2	

Name	Notice Date	Death Date	Age		Page	Maiden Name
Pullan, Thomas	18, 23, Jan. 1838	27, Dec.			T2	
Puller, Allen	5, Sept 1828	Sept	5- 5m		N3	
Punch, Benjamin	29, Oct. 1830	Oct.	14		N3	
Punch, John	30, July 1830	July	47		N3	
Purcell, Dennis	13, Mar. 1823		estate		J3	
Purcell, John	4, Apr. 1837		probate		N2	
Purcell, John	21, Sept 1838		probate		N3	
Purcell, John O'C.	15, Apr. 1842	14, Apr.	30		N2	
Purington, Pelatia	17, Aug. 1841		78	*	N2	
Purington, Pelatiah	21, Aug. 1841		78	*	R3	
Pursell, John	9, Dec. 1828		probate		N3	
Pursell, Miranda	29, Mar. 1847	26, Mar.	56		K2	
Putnam, Rufus (Gen)	4, June 1824	1, May	85	*	N1	
Pye, William H.H.	21, Aug. 1852	20, Aug.	13		P2	
Pyle, Levi	9, Dec. 1828		probate		N3	
Quail, Alice	24, July 1850	July	15		Y2	
Quail, Robert	24, Oct. 1850	Oct.	67		Y2	
Quarles, Letitia B.	5, July 1828				R3	
Quick, Jacob	23, Sept 1852		23		P2	
Quinn, Ellen	14, June 1849	June	3		L2	
Quinn, Francis	22, Apr. 1851	19, Apr.	36		P2	
Quinn, James	14, June 1849	June	30		L2	
Quinn, John	21, June 1849	June	1		L2	
Quinton, Esther	8, Oct. 1830	Oct.	16		N3	
Raber, George	3, May 1838				N2	
Rabun, (Governor)	27, Nov. 1819	26, Oct.			S3	
Rackett, Louisa	11, July 1849	10, July	72		L2	
Radcliff, Samuel	11, Apr. 1828		estate		N3	
Radcliff, William	21, Aug. 1852	19, Aug.			P2	
Rafinesque, C. (Professor)	3, Oct. 1840	18, Sept			R3	
Ragen, James	24, June 1850	23, June			P2	
Raguet, Claudius Morton	13, Oct. 1827	9, Oct.	infant		R3	
Raich, Adam	30, July 1850	July	16m		Y3	
Railey, Randolph (Mrs)	7, July 1836	19, June			X3	
Rain, Mary Ann	7, July 1835	2, July		*	N2	
Rainey, Walter	17, Jan. 1849	16, Jan.			B2	
Rainsworth, William	17, June 1837		probate		N2	
Ralls, George W.	1, July 1850	22, June	30		P2	
Rambo, William	3, Dec. 1830	Nov.	2		N3	
Ramer, Herman	23, July 1850	July	2- 3m		Y2	
Ramsay, Elizabeth Juliana	13, Dec. 1816	5, Dec.			S3	
Ramsay, John	7, Sept 1836		probate		N2	
Ramsay, Samuel (Dr)	12, Sept 1839		estate		T2	
Ramsay, Samuel (Dr)	8, Jan. 1831	4, Jan.			R3	
Ramsay, Thomas (Capt)	7, Nov. 1818		estate		S3	
Ramsay, William	14, Dec. 1835		probate		N2	
Ramsay, William	22, Apr. 1825	21, Apr.			N2	
Ramsey, (child of Benjamin)	30, July 1830	July	11m		N3	
Ramsey, Elizabeth	31, May 1849	29, May	77		L2	
Ramsey, John (Col)	2, Sept 1831	29, Aug.	52	*	A3	
Ramsey, Julianna Adeline	30, May 1840	30, Apr.			R3	Doddridge
Ramsey, Margaret Jane	9, Aug. 1841	Aug.	5		N2	
Ramsey, Mary	1, July 1828	June	42		N3	
Ramslery, George	8, Sept 1827	Sept	35		R3	

Name	Notice Date	Death Date	Age		Page	Maiden Name
Rand, (child)	9, July 1830	July	6m		N3	
Rand, Maria L.	24, June 1828	June	5m		N3	
Randle, William	11, Dec. 1852	9, Dec.	4		P2	
Randolph, Catharine S.	27, Dec. 1816	14, Nov.	31		S3	
Randolph, Martha	28, Oct. 1836	10, Oct.			T2	Jefferson
Randolph, Robert	14, Oct. 1825		65		N2	
Randolph, Thomas M.	12, July 1828				R3	
Randolph, Thomas Mann (Capt)	5, Oct. 1835	20, Aug.			T2	
Rands, (child of George)	14, Oct. 1828	Oct.	infant		N3	
Rankin, Robert	17, Oct. 1838	16, Oct.		*	T2	
Rankins, Robert	8, Aug. 1850	Aug.	22		Y2	
Rannels, Sarah Jane	22, Feb. 1836	19, Feb.	18	*	T3	
Rassender, Louisa	17, May 1849	May	17		L2	
Rawlins, Charles	1, Aug. 1828	July	infant		N3	
Rawlins, Charles T.	1, Oct. 1830	Sept	6d		N3	
Rawlins, John Rogers	1, Apr. 1818	4, Mar.		*	S3	
Rawlins, Thomas	18, Aug. 1815		estate		S3	
Rawlins, Thomas	28, July 1815	20, July		*	S3	
Rawlins, Thomas	29, July 1815	20, July		*	G3	
Ray, William (Major)	22, 25, Aug. 1826	30, July	54	*	N3	
Ray, William Penn	6, Oct. 1836	18, Sept	infant		X3	
Raymond, Martha H.	17, May 1849	16, May	32		L2	Macy
Raynals, John	30, Aug. 1833	14, June			X3	
Raynes, Joseph	10, May 1849	8, May	45	*	L2	
Rea, John	8, Feb. 1825	14, Sept		*	N3	
Reace, (child of John)	16, July 1830	July	stillborn		N3	
Read, (child of Alpheus)	13, Aug. 1830	Aug.	21d		N3	
Read, Francis	23, Feb. 1836	20, Feb.	37		T3	
Read, Francis	22, Feb. 1836	20, Feb.	37		N2	
Reagon, Anna	19, Sept 1828	Sept	6		N3	
Reddish, John	11, Aug. 1827	7, Aug.	infant		R3	
Reddish, Purnel Johnson	28, May 1824	Apr.			N5	
Reddish, Sarah	6, Nov. 1838		probate		N2	
Reddish, Stephenson	6, Nov. 1838		probate		N2	
Reddish, Thomas (Exec. of)	4, Apr. 1837		probate		N2	
Reddish, Thomas (heirs of)	4, Apr. 1837		probate		N2	
Redenbo, Henry	6, Oct. 1826		estate		N3	
Redinbo, Adam	10, Mar. 1829		probate		N3	
Redinbo, Adam	4, Apr. 1837		probate		N2	
Redinbo, Henry	9, Dec. 1828		probate		N3	
Redish, (child of Thomas)	23, July 1830	July	8m		N3	
Redling, Peter	6, Sept 1852	4, Sept			P2	
Reece, David	9, Aug. 1841	28, July			N2	
Reece, H.E. (Rev)	5, Nov. 1852	31, Oct.			P2	
Reed, Adam	27, Nov. 1837	25, Nov.			T2	
Reed, Catharine	24, Feb. 1829	Feb.	40		N3	
Reed, David	20, Mar. 1813		estate		S3	
Reed, Edward M.	27, July 1850	July	8m		Y3	
Reed, George	8, Aug. 1840	22, July	71		R3	
Reed, George	5, Sept 1828	Sept	9m		N3	
Reed, Henry	1, Mar. 1794		estate		C3	
Reed, Hensey	6, July 1849	July	14		L2	
Reed, Joseph	12, Aug. 1828	Aug.	8m		N3	
Reed, Julia Ann	20, July 1820	9, July	17		S3	Hailman

Name	Notice Date	Death Date	Age		Page	Maiden Name
Reed, Louis Henry	22, Feb. 1841	18, Feb.	12		N2	
Reed, Luther	26, Feb. 1814	23, Feb.			S3	
Reed, Ogden Livingston	21, Sept 1833	15, Sept	20m		R3	
Reed, Reuben	5, Sept 1840		estate		R3	
Reed, Reuben	14, Dec. 1835		probate		N2	
Reed, Rosanda P.	12, Apr. 1849	Apr.	24		L2	
Reed, Thomas	1, Sept 1852				P2	
Reed, William Skinner	11, Sept 1841	17, Aug.	7		V3	
Reede, Isaac	10, Dec. 1830	Dec.	45		N3	
Reeder, Alfred S.	1, Oct. 1839	29, Sept	37		T2	
Reeder, George McAlpin	29, Mar. 1849	28, Mar.	21m		L2	
Reeder, Jeremiah	4, Oct. 1833	26, Sept			X3	
Reeder, Mary	1, Feb. 1808	16, Jan.			S3	
Reeder, Nathaniel	31, Dec. 1831	29, Dec.	64		R3	
Reeder, Nathaniel	27, Jan. 1832		estate		A3	
Reeder, Nathaniel	7, Sept 1836		probate		N2	
Reeder, William	18, Aug. 1827	17, Aug.			R3	
Reeder, William Cleves	1, Apr. 1818	28, Mar.			S3	
Reel, Benjamin	14, May 1831		estate		R3	
Reel, John	31, Oct. 1850	Oct.	41		Y2	
Rees, George	23, July 1850	July	17d		Y2	
Rees, Hannah	1, July 1828	June	12d		N3	
Reese, David T.	15, Sept 1827	Sept	14m		R3	
Reese, Edward J.	26, Feb. 1841	Feb.	27		N2	
Reese, Granville	11, June 1842	June	34		R3	
Reese, Jacob	11, Feb. 1836	8, Feb.	2		X3	
Reese, Margaret Moran	26, July 1847	26, July	3- 8m		K2	
Reeves, W.D.	12, Aug. 1831	Aug.	4m		A3	
Reid, George	26, Jan. 1848	21, Dec.			K2	
Reid, Robert Raymond	24, July 1841	1, July	48		R3	
Reiley, Joseph H.	22, Mar. 1849	21, Mar.			L2	
Reiley, Lettice	6, Feb. 1829	Feb.	81		N2	
Reilly, Elizabeth G.	6, May 1830	29, Apr.			A3	
Reilly, Thomas	26, Sept 1838		estate		T2	
Reilly, Thomas	20, Mar. 1838		probate		N3	
Reily, Caroline	27, Sept 1816	22, Sept	3- 6m		S3	
Reily, John	17, May 1849	May	24		L2	
Reily, P.O.	1, Jan. 1836	31, Dec.	48	*	T3	
Reily, Peter	31, May 1849	27, May	27	*	L2	
Reinshagen, Amelia	23, July 1850	July	7m		Y2	
Reisch, Michael	8, Oct. 1852	Oct.	60		P2	
Relf, Samuel	18, Mar. 1823	14, Mar.	47		N3	
Remer, Ann	2, July 1852	15, June			P2	Blackmore
Renick, Jane Sterling	11, Aug. 1841	5, Aug.	34		N2	
Rensford, William Henry	31, Dec. 1852	30, Dec.	6		P2	
Resor, Edward	28, June 1849	27, June	infant		L2	
Resor, Jacob	9, Feb. 1836	8, Feb.	2		T3	
Resor, Jacob	9, Feb. 1836	8, Feb.	2		N2	
Rettig, Henry	5, July 1852	3, July	41		P2	
Reuben, Joseph	9, Aug. 1841	Aug.	35		N2	
Reville, David	24, June 1828	June	22		N3	
Reynolds, Amanda	1, Aug. 1838	31, July	10		T2	
Reynolds, Elizabeth	11, July 1826	7, July	19	*	N2	Guest
Reynolds, Jarvis	3, Oct. 1823	30, Sept	28	*	N3	

Name	Notice Date	Death Date	Age		Page	Maiden Name
Reynolds, Justus	14, July 1835	11, July	74	*	N2	
Reynolds, Laura P.	4, May 1849	3, May	54		L2	
Reynolds, Mary	22, Apr. 1823	7, Apr.	36		N2	
Reynolds, William (Lt)	9, Sept 1830	30, Aug.		*	A3	
Rheno, Lewis	16, July 1830	July	47		N3	
Rhoads, John	28, Aug. 1827		probate		N3	
Rhodes, Edward	16, Sept 1836	15, Sept	24	*	T2	
Rhomers, John	13, July 1849	July	37		L2	
Rice, (Rev)	14, Oct. 1831		54		X3	
Rice, Caesar	17, Sept 1830	Sept	42		N3	
Rice, James	8, July 1828	July	18		N3	
Rice, John	28, June 1849	June	47		L2	
Rice, John	15, Oct. 1836		estate		T2	
Rice, John	28, July 1837		estate		T2	
Rice, John G.	20, Feb. 1829		estate		N3	
Rice, John H.	30, Sept 1831	3, Sept			X3	
Rice, Mary Una	6, Oct. 1852	3, Oct.	1-11m		P2	
Rice, William B. (Rev)	4, Nov. 1840	15, Oct.	33		N2	
Richard, John A.	11, Dec. 1827		probate		N3	
Richard, John Joseph	16, Dec. 1825		estate		N3	
Richards, Caroline	13, Aug. 1830	Aug.	11m		N3	
Richards, Jennet	27, Mar. 1819	21, Mar.	21	*	S2	Gibson
Richards, John	9, July 1830	July	96		N3	
Richards, Mary	3, Sept 1830	Aug.	8m		N2	
Richards, Rebecca	3, Oct. 1837	24, Sept		*	T2	McLean
Richards, W.T.	3, Sept 1850				Y2	
Richards, William, Jr.	16, Oct. 1819		estate		S3	
Richardson, (son of Robert)	26, Jan. 1811	23, Dec.	6		S3	
Richardson, Adah Frances	9, Dec. 1852	8, Dec.	2- -8d		P2	
Richardson, Emory P.	27, July 1850	July			Y3	
Richardson, James	15, Oct. 1830	Oct.	53		N3	
Richardson, John C.	30, Mar. 1842	29, Sept	18		N2	
Richardson, John Carter (Col)	10, Sept 1847	8, Sept	53	*	K2	
Richardson, Malachiah	9, Apr. 1831		estate		R3	
Richardson, Malachiah	16, May 1823		estate		N3	
Richardson, Mary Ann	3, May 1849	May	40		L2	
Richardson, Rebecca	10, Oct. 1838		estate		N2	
Richardson, Samuel Q.	30, Mar. 1842	Sept	13		N2	
Richardson, Warren	12, Jan. 1829	Jan.	1m		N2	
Richardson, William	2, July 1830	June	30		N2	
Richey, Rebecca	7, Dec. 1835	1, Dec.			T3	
Richman, Hugh	23, July 1830	July	23		N3	
Richmond, Sarah P.	1, July 1828	June	4m		N3	
Rickett, Benjamin B.	9, Aug. 1852	6, Aug.	18m		P2	
Rickoff, Elizabeth	7, Sept 1852	5, Sept	26		P2	
Ricords, Samuel	27, Jan. 1829	Jan.	stillborn		N2	
Riddle, John	1, June 1837		estate		T2	
Riddle, John	11, Oct. 1847		estate		K2	
Riddle, John (Col)	18, June 1847	17, June	86	*	K2	
Riddle, John C.	15, Sept 1838	14, Sept	9m		T2	
Riddle, Joseph R.	24, July 1850	23, July	47		Y2	
Riddle, Mary Elizabeth	17, Oct. 1840	6, Oct.	21- 6m		R3	Newal
Riddle, Nancy	15, Sept 1810	7, Sept	28		S3	
Riddle, Tallmadge A.	16, Apr. 1849	14, Apr.	2- 3m		L2	

Name	Notice Date	Death Date	Age		Page	Maiden Name
Ridgely, Charlotte S.	23, May 1849	22, May	26		L2	
Ridgely, Frederick (Dr)	3, Dec. 1824	28, Nov.	68		N3	
Ridgely, Nicholas	22, Apr. 1830	1, Apr.	72		A3	
Rieler, Bridget	23, July 1850	July	30		Y2	
Riffenbark, Peter	9, Jan. 1841	Jan.	37		R3	
Riggle, Andrew	13, Aug. 1830		estate		N3	
Riggle, Andrew	1, June 1835		probate		N2	
Riggles, George	16, Dec. 1825		probate		N3	
Riggs, David	1, Oct. 1830		estate		N3	
Riggs, Emma	29, Sept 1850	24, Sept			Y2	
Riggs, Melville A.	5, Sept 1828	Sept	3w		N3	
Riggs, William	10, Sept 1830		estate		N3	
Riley, Erastus	7, Nov. 1826	4, Nov.	30	*	N3	
Riley, James	29, Mar. 1849	Mar.	32		L2	
Riley, Josiah	3, Aug. 1822	13, July	30	*	S3	
Riley, Thomas	13, July 1835	9, July	67		T2	
Rineer, Rhoda	27, Feb. 1829	Feb.	62		N3	
Ringgold, F.G.	14, Aug. 1850	13, Aug.	50		Y2	
Ripley, Nathaniel	18, Aug. 1826	15, Aug.	59		N3	
Riply, (Gen)	30, Nov. 1820				S3	
Risk, Charlotte C.L.	14, July 1821		50		S3	
Ritchie, Charles	29, July 1834	July	45		T2	
Ritchie, Charles	2, Aug. 1834	July	46		R3	
Rizer, Amaka	7, Dec. 1837		probate		N3	
Roadarmour,	15, Nov. 1837	13, Nov.			T2	
Roane, Archibald	30, Jan. 1819	4, Jan.			S3	
Robben, John B.	25, July 1850	July	45		Y2	
Robbins, Caroline	10, Mar. 1836	26, Jan.	43- -28d	*	X3	Tracy
Robbins, Caroline Tracy	15, Feb. 1836	26, Jan.			T3	Tracy
Robbins, Catharine	20, Oct. 1835	18, Oct.			T2	
Robbins, Cornelia	27, Oct. 1832	25, Oct.	16		R3	
Robbins, Emily	17, Jan. 1829	15, Jan.	7- 8m		R3	
Robbins, John Newton	13, Feb. 1823	9, Feb.	26	*	J2	
Robbins, L.J.	26, Oct. 1835	24, Oct.			T2	
Robbins, Rossitter	25, Dec. 1830	11, Dec.	7		R3	
Robbins, Rossitter	25, Sept 1830		estate		R3	
Robeison, Alexander	29, Dec. 1829		estate		N3	
Roberson, Jonathan	16, Aug. 1831		estate		A3	
Robert, (child)	29, July 1834	July	12d		T2	
Roberts, (child of Mary J.)	4, June 1830	June	1-10m		N3	
Roberts, (child)	2, Aug. 1834	July	12d		R3	
Roberts, David	4, Jan. 1821		estate		S3	
Roberts, Elizabeth	26, July 1834	July	21		R3	
Roberts, Elizabeth	22, July 1834	July	21		T2	
Roberts, George	19, June 1829	12, May	74		N3	
Roberts, Jesse	5, Sept 1828	Sept	23		N3	
Roberts, Ruth Ann	30, Jan. 1841	24, Jan.			R3	
Robertson, George	22, Jan. 1830		estate		N3	
Robertson, J.G.	11, Dec. 1830	5, Dec.		*	R3	
Robertson, Joshua C.	10, Dec. 1830	Dec.	24		N3	
Robertson, Thomas	17, Oct. 1840	Oct.	33		R3	
Robertson, William	9, Sept 1831	Sept	9m		A3	
Robertson, William	27, Oct. 1821		estate		S3	
Robeson, Mercy	20, Aug. 1830	Aug.	31		N3	

Name	Notice Date	Death Date	Age	Page	Maiden Name
Robins, Eliza H.	3, May 1825	28, Apr.		N3	
Robins, Emily	27, Jan. 1829	Jan.	7- 8m	N2	
Robins, Harriet Cornelia	24, Nov. 1832	25, Oct.	16	R3	
Robins, John Newton	11, Feb. 1823	9, Feb.		N3	
Robinson, (Capt)	17, Apr. 1805	23, Mar.		S2	
Robinson, (child of H.)	23, Sept 1831	Sept	7m	A3	
Robinson, (Mr)	13, Mar. 1835	15, Feb.	90	X3	
Robinson, A.C. (Dr)	28, Aug. 1850	26, Aug.		Y2	
Robinson, A.H.	19, Aug. 1828		probate	N3	
Robinson, Asa	12, July 1828		estate	R3	
Robinson, Asa H.	6, Oct. 1826		probate	N3	
Robinson, James	24, June 1828	June	9m	N3	
Robinson, John	10, May 1849	May	11	L2	
Robinson, Marshall A.	7, Sept 1832	31, Aug.	14m-10d	X3	
Robinson, Nathan	17, May 1825	9, May		N3	
Robinson, Randolph	5, Apr. 1849	Apr.	30	L2	
Robinson, S. (heirs of)	6, Nov. 1838		probate	N2	
Robinson, Samuel	14, Sept 1827		estate	N3	
Robinson, Sarah B.	24, Aug. 1811	22, Aug.		S3	
Robinson, Thomas	19, Dec. 1826		probate	N3	
Robinson, William	29, May 1823		estate	J3	
Robinson, William	3, May 1825		probate	N3	
Robinson, William	18, Aug. 1821	14, Aug.		S3	
Robson, James	23, July 1830	July	1	N3	
Robson, Thomas Fletcher	4, Sept 1852	2, Sept	4m- 9d	P2	
Rocca, John	14, May 1850	12, May		P2	
Rock, Frances	19, July 1834	July	6m	R3	
Rock, George	22, Apr. 1801		estate	S3	
Rockenfield, Abraham	11, Sept 1829		estate	N3	
Rockey, Sarah Hall	26, May 1837	25, May	infant	T2	
Rockney, Emma Frances	11, Aug. 1838	10, Aug.		T2	
Rockwell, Elizabeth	3, Feb. 1851	1, Feb.	29	P2	
Rodgers, Harriet	1, Aug. 1817	26, July		S3	
Rodney, Thomas	16, Mar. 1811	21, Jan.		S3	
Roe, Martha E.	8, Apr. 1820	5, Apr.		S3	
Roe, Mary	5, May 1826	3, May		N3	
Rogers, Alfred (Capt)	28, June 1849	10, June	30	L2	
Rogers, Amanda M.	12, Aug. 1831	Aug.	1- -7d	A3	
Rogers, Daniel R.	14, Oct. 1825		69	N2	
Rogers, David	10, June 1824		estate	E3	
Rogers, Eunice S.	20, Sept 1825	16, Sept		N3	
Rogers, George	17, May 1849	May	44	L2	
Rogers, George	12, Jan. 1837	10, Jan.		T2	
Rogers, Joseph	21, June 1828			R3	
Rogers, Josephine	12, Apr. 1838	24, Mar.		T2	Rowan
Rogers, Mary	13, Mar. 1829	Mar.	13	N3	
Rogers, Samuel	9, Sept 1825		probate	N3	
Rogers, Samuel	4, June 1836		probate	N2	
Rogers, Sceva	19, Feb. 1820	14, Feb.	43	* S2	
Rogers, Theodore	16, Apr. 1835	6, Apr.	31	T3	
Rogers, William C.	19, Nov. 1852		37	P2	
Rolfe, Zerah	25, Sept 1819		estate	S3	
Roll, Abraham	7, Sept 1830		probate	N3	
Roll, Edward	1, June 1822		estate	S3	

Name	Notice Date	Death Date	Age		Page	Maiden Name
Roll, Edward	28, Mar. 1826		estate		N3	
Roll, Edward	14, Dec. 1824		probate		N3	
Roll, Edward	3, May 1825		probate		N3	
Roll, Edward	16, Dec. 1825		probate		N3	
Roll, Edward	9, Dec. 1828		probate		N3	
Roll, Edward	6, Nov. 1838		probate		N2	
Roll, Edward	16, Dec. 1824		probate		E3	
Roll, Edward M.	19, Sept 1840	10, Sept	3- 1m		R3	
Roll, John	14, May 1808	23, Apr.	76		S3	
Roll, John	28, May 1808		estate		S3	
Roll, Wick	4, Apr. 1837		probate		N2	
Rolmitchail, Joseph	23, July 1850	July	8		Y2	
Romeril, (child of Charles)	13, Mar. 1829	Mar.	2		N3	
Romeyn, John B. (Rev)	11, Mar. 1825	22, Feb.			N2	
Roney, John D.	21, Aug. 1835	1, Aug.	47		T2	
Root, Almira	17, Aug. 1832	10, Aug.	39	*	X2	Alden
Root, David Alden	7, Sept 1832	3, Sept	8m- 2d		X3	
Root, Sophronia	1, July 1828	June	14m		N3	
Roper, William P.	24, Aug. 1833	Aug.			R3	
Ropes, Abigail Pinkman	5, Feb. 1842	1, Feb.	25d		N2	
Rorick, John	14, Aug. 1852	12, Aug.		*	P2	
Rork, Daniel	25, Aug. 1829		probate		N3	
Rorke, Daniel	2, Sept 1828		estate		N3	
Rose, Charles S.	2, Sept 1828	Aug.	3-10m		N3	
Rose, Lemuel	16, Oct. 1835	13, Sept	71		X3	
Rose, Margaret	19, Aug. 1852	18, Aug.	35	*	P2	
Rosen, Marquis	5, Aug. 1842	25, July			M2	
Rosensteil, Emanuel	31, July 1850	July	18m		Y3	
Roskin, Amelia	28, June 1849	June	7		L2	
Ross, (child of William S.)	9, Dec. 1828	Dec.	stillborn		N3	
Ross, Fleming	17, Feb. 1849	16, Feb.			L3	
Ross, Franklin	22, June 1841	20, June	1- 5m-23d		N2	
Ross, Henry	24, June 1828	June	3m		N3	
Ross, Ignatius	17, Nov. 1829		estate		N3	
Ross, Ignatius	1, June 1835		probate		N2	
Ross, Joseph	28, Sept 1820		estate		S3	
Ross, Joseph	21, Dec. 1830		probate		N3	
Ross, Mary	17, Feb. 1842	16, Feb.	2- 9m		N2	
Ross, Mary Jane	1, June 1835		probate		N2	
Ross, Mulford	25, Mar. 1837	23, Mar.			T2	
Ross, Orlando M.	30, July 1830	July	11m		N3	
Ross, Robert	29, Aug. 1804		estate		S4	
Ross, William	19, Sept 1840		estate		R3	
Ross, William	22, Aug. 1826	4, July	109	*	N3	
Ross, William	20, Mar. 1838		probate		N3	
Ross, William H.	2, Apr. 1849	31, Mar.	41		L2	
Roth, Emma Jane	11, Dec. 1852	9, Dec.	14- -20d		P2	
Roundtree, William J.	26, July 1834	July	2- 6m		R3	
Roundtree, William J.	22, July 1834	July	2- 6m		T2	
Rouse, Magdalena	6, July 1849	July	62		L2	
Roussoan, Joseph	21, May 1830	May	56		N3	
Row, Patrick	19, July 1834	July	26		R3	
Rowan, Robert	19, Dec. 1826		probate		N3	
Rowan, Robert	10, Mar. 1829		probate		N3	

Name	Notice Date	Death Date	Age	Page	Maiden Name
Rowan, William	15, June 1836	12, June	31		T2	
Rowe, James S. (Mrs)	3, June 1835			T2	
Rowe, Lazarus	16, Oct. 1829	14, Sept	104	* N2	
Rowe, Lazarus (Mrs)	31, July 1829		104	N3	
Rowekamp, Sarah	8, Sept 1852	7, Sept	31	P2	
Rowse, Margaret M.	19, July 1847	14, July	28	K2	
Rucker, Mary Jane	17, Apr. 1849	4, Apr.	34	L2	Heckewelder
Ruckman, Hannah Maria	15, Nov. 1852	11, Nov.	4m- 3d	P2	
Rude, Daniel	19, May 1815		estate	S3	
Rude, James	9, Feb. 1837	24, Jan.	23	* X3	
Rude, Samuel W.	7, Sept 1836		probate	N2	
Ruffin, (Major)	8, Sept 1834			T2	
Ruffin, Elizabeth	2, Aug. 1834	July	1- 9m	R3	
Ruffin, Elizabeth	29, July 1834	July	1- 9m	T2	
Ruffin, Elizabeth	23, Apr. 1831	16, Apr.		R3	
Ruffin, William Wilie	10, Dec. 1836	8, Dec.	33	T3	
Ruffner, Joseph (Major)	13, May 1837	10, May	69	R3	
Ruffner, Joseph (Major)	12, May 1837	10, May	69	T2	
Ruhman, Eliza	31, May 1849	27, May	16	L2	
Runeer, James	20, Sept 1833	Sept	40	X3	
Runnels, Sarah	9, July 1830	July	1	N3	
Runoun, Henry	19, July 1834	July	14d	R3	
Runsey, Mercy	1, Oct. 1830	Sept	13	N3	
Runyan, Henry	16, Apr. 1814		estate	S1	
Ruse, John	20, Sept 1833	Sept	26	X3	
Rush, Benjamin (Dr)	8, May 1813	19, Apr.		S3	
Rush, Lucy H.	1, Dec. 1852	30, Nov.		P2	
Russelar, Sarah	17, Sept 1830	Sept	55	N3	
Russell, Edmund M. (Lt)	6, Aug. 1838			T2	
Russell, Elizabeth	6, Feb. 1819	1, Feb.		S3	
Russell, Howard	26, Aug. 1850	25, Aug.	13m	P2	
Russell, James	1, Dec. 1835		estate	N1	
Russell, James	19, Dec. 1826		probate	N3	
Russell, James	11, Sept 1837		probate	N2	
Russell, John	6, July 1849	July	35	L2	
Russell, Margaret	19, Sept 1850	Sept	6w	Y2	
Russell, Margaret E.	23, July 1830	July	1	N3	
Russell, Thomas	6, Oct. 1826		probate	N3	
Russeller, Sarah	13, Sept 1830	9, Sept	70	A2	
Rutan, Ellen	4, Nov. 1828	Oct.	2- 9m	N3	
Rutar, John Quincy	28, Nov. 1828	Nov.	10m	N3	
Rutgers, Henry (Col)	5, Mar. 1830	17, Feb.	85	N2	
Rutherford, Isaac Stricker	11, May 1841	10, May	infant	N2	
Rutherford, Margaret Elizabeth	21, Feb. 1842	11, Feb.	13	N2	
Rutherford, Margaret Elizabeth	19, Feb. 1842	11, Feb.	13- 1m-15d	R3	
Rutherford, Thomas Miers B.	26, Feb. 1842	18, Feb.	5	R3	
Rutherford, Thomas Miers B.	21, Feb. 1842	18, Feb.	5	N2	
Rutter, Robert	9, June 1827	6, June		R3	
Ryan, Charles	24, May 1849	May	24	L2	
Ryan, Daniel	22, Aug. 1850	Aug.	2	Y2	
Ryan, Mariar	6, Oct. 1827	27, Sept	18	R3	
Ryan, Sarah Jane	14, Jan. 1851	12, Jan.	1- -27d	P2	
Rybolt, Jacob	14, Dec. 1835		probate	N2	
Ryland, William W.	29, May 1841	25, May	25	R3	

Name	Notice Date	Death Date	Age		Page	Maiden Name
Ryland, William W.	28, May 1841	25, May	25		N2	
Rynearson, John	21, Dec. 1830		probate		N3	
Ryon, William	14, Dec. 1835		probate		N2	
Ryon, William	4, Apr. 1837		probate		N2	
Ryon, William, Jr.	7, Sept 1836		probate		N2	
Sacks, Emma J.	10, May 1849	May	22		L2	
Sainclair, Lawrence	18, Oct. 1852	17, Oct.		*	P2	
Sale, John (Rev)	9, Feb. 1827	6, Feb.	64		N3	
Salisbury, Alexander	5, Sept 1835	22, Aug.			T2	
Salisbury, Alexander	4, Sept 1835	22, Aug.			X3	
Salisbury, James T.	12, Nov. 1835		25- -22d	*	X3	
Salmon, Ann E.	24, May 1849	May	2- 6m		L2	
Salmon, Barbara	21, June 1849	June	50		L2	
Sammons, (child of Stephen)	6, Feb. 1829	Feb.	stillborn		N2	
Sampson, Anna Maria	18, July 1840	15, July			R3	
Sampson, Dudley Andrews	12, Jan. 1833	31, Dec.	6m-13d		R3	
Sampson, Horace Holley	19, Jan. 1837	13, Jan.	7m-18d		T2	
Sampson, Horace Holly	14, Jan. 1837	13, Jan.	7m-18d		R3	
Sampson, Isabel Maria	21, May 1842	11, May	5m-15d		R3	
Sampson, Isabel Maria	20, May 1842	11, May	5m-15d		N2	
Sampson, Jane Little	14, Aug. 1841	9, Aug.	infant		R3	
Sampson, Jane Little	13, Aug. 1841	9, Aug.	infant		N2	
Sampson, Mary Ann Hastings	22, Aug. 1837	20, Aug.	8m		T2	
Sampson, Mary Elizabeth	11, Mar. 1831	9, Mar.	5		A3	
Sampson, Mary Elizabeth	11, Mar. 1831	9, Mar.	5		X3	
Sampson, S.G. Howe	14, July 1838	9, July	5m		R3	
Sampson, Stephen	9, Nov. 1824		estate		N4	
Sampson, Stephen	18, Sept 1823	16, Sept			J3	
Sampson, William	9, Jan. 1837	4, Jan.	73		T2	
Sampson, William	24, Mar. 1837				T2	
Sandburn, John	12, Aug. 1828	Aug.	2		N3	
Sanders, Amelia	18, May 1841	14, May	7- 8m		N2	
Sanders, Caroline A.	30, June 1838	26, June	14m-20d		R3	
Sanders, Caroline A.	28, June 1838	26, June	14m-29d		T2	
Sanders, Caroline N.	1, July 1837	30, June	29		T2	
Sanders, Edward A.	15, Mar. 1836	12, Mar.	3-11m		N2	
Sanders, George A.	28, June 1849	June	5m		L2	
Sanders, H.	26, Jan. 1836		estate		N3	
Sanders, Hezekiah	7, Sept 1836		probate		N2	
Sanders, Hezekiah	21, Sept 1838		probate		N3	
Sanders, John	1, June 1849	May	21		L2	
Sanders, Joseph	30, July 1830	July	22		N3	
Sanders, Mary Jane	20, Mar. 1841	Mar.	4m		N2	
Sanders, Paul R.	20, Aug. 1850	13, Aug.	25- 8m		Y2	
Sanders, Tanner	22, Mar. 1849	Mar.	24		L2	
Sanders, Thomas	12, Jan. 1829	Jan.	19		N2	
Sanders, Washington I.	16, Apr. 1842	9, Apr.	7		R3	
Sanders, Washington I.	15, Apr. 1842	9, Apr.	7		N2	
Sanders, William C.	28, Nov. 1840	16, Nov.	28	*	R3	
Sanderson, Robert	25, July 1828		24	*	N3	
Sandford, Thomas	8, June 1820		estate		S3	
Sanford, Joseph (Rev)	27, Jan. 1832	25, Dec.	34		X3	
Sanove, Nehemiah	6, Sept 1809		estate		H4	
Sanxay, Mary	16, June 1827	10, June			R3	

Name	Notice Date	Death Date	Age		Page	Maiden Name
Sarchet, Peter	24, Jan. 1817		estate		S3	
Sargeant, Daniel	15, Apr. 1842		79		N2	
Sargeant, David	20, Mar. 1838		probate		N3	
Sargeant, Michael B.	31, May 1830	19, May			A3	
Sargeant, Thomas (Dr)	18, Mar. 1834		estate		T2	
Sargent, Helena	4, Dec. 1841	1, Dec.		*	R3	
Sargent, Helena	2, Dec. 1841	1, Dec.		*	N2	
Sargent, Sallie	21, July 1852	19, July	9m		P2	
Sargent, Sarah B.	20, Nov. 1841	20, Nov.			R3	
Sargent, Sarah B.	16, Nov. 1841	15, Nov.		*	N2	
Sarle, Albert Henry	6, Oct. 1847	5, Oct.	3- 9m		K2	
Sater, Charles	21, Jan. 1815		estate		S3	
Sater, Charles	16, May 1823		estate		N3	
Satterly,	16, July 1830	July	1		N3	
Satterly, (dau. of Charles)	2, Aug. 1834	July	4		R3	
Satterly, (dau. of Charles)	29, July 1834	July	4		T2	
Saunders, William	16, May 1840		73		R3	
Savill, Martha A.	11, Aug. 1852	9, Aug.			P2	
Sawyer, (son of J.O.)	13, June 1849	11, June	12		L3	
Sax, Henry	24, July 1850	July	30		Y2	
Say, Thomas	14, Nov. 1834	10, Oct.	47		T2	
Sayre, Ananias	17, May 1816	13, May			S3	
Sayre, James	18, Nov. 1825		estate		N3	
Sayre, James	10, Mar. 1829		probate		N3	
Sayre, Leonard	26, Jan. 1822	10, Jan.	59		S3	
Sayre, Leonard	16, Feb. 1822		estate		S3	
Sayre, Levi	25, Aug. 1829		probate		N3	
Sayre, Levi	22, Dec. 1829		probate		N3	
Sayre, Lewis P. (Capt)	26, Sept 1826	15, Sept	29		N3	
Sayre, Sarah	25, June 1814	23, June			S3	
Sayre, Thomas (heirs of)	7, Sept 1836		probate		N2	
Sayre, William	11, Nov. 1828	8, Nov.	33		N3	
Sayre, William	19, Dec. 1828		estate		N3	
Schardellmann, William	20, Mar. 1838		probate		N3	
Schenck, William C. (Gen)	20, Jan. 1821	12, Jan.			S3	
Schillenger, John S.	19, Dec. 1840	15, Dec.	17		R3	
Schillinger, B.F.	26, Nov. 1835				X3	
Schillinger, Benjamin F.	21, Nov. 1835	18, Nov.			T2	
Schlanstedt, Christopher	17, May 1849	May	22		L2	
Schleick, Gertrude	6, July 1849	July	48		L2	
Schlemerdine, Samuel	23, Apr. 1841	Apr.	40		N2	
Schlonaker, John	7, Sept 1827		estate		N3	
Schmidt, Peter	23, Jan. 1841	Jan.	19		R3	
Schmidt, Peter	21, Jan. 1841	Jan.	19		N2	
Schmidt, Philip	28, July 1850	July	81		Y3	
Schneider, Catharine	14, June 1849	June	25		L2	
Schneider, William	28, June 1849	June	23		L2	
Schnencirger, Lewis H.	23, July 1850	July	14m		Y2	
Schoolcraft, Lawrence (Col)	27, June 1840	7, June	80		R3	
Schooley, Johna	20, Mar. 1838		probate		N3	
Schooley, Nathaniel S.	16, July 1847	10, July	60	*	K2	
Schoots, Jacob	7, June 1849	June	32		L2	
Schreiber, Mary	14, June 1849	June	32		L2	
Schreiner, Charles	26, Apr. 1849	Apr.	49		L2	

Name	Notice Date	Death Date	Age	Page	Maiden Name
Schrieber, John	12, Apr. 1849	Apr.	16	L2	
Schriver, Adam	10, Oct. 1840	Oct.	18	R3	
Schriver, Milchoir	10, Oct. 1840	Oct.	22	R3	
Schroeder, Charles A.	6, Aug. 1830	Aug.	17m	N3	
Schruber, Clara	24, Oct. 1840	Oct.	5	R3	
Schultz, Barnard	12, Sept 1850	Sept	28	Y2	
Schwab, Philip	14, Dec. 1835	probate		N2	
Schweine, Edward H.	26, July 1850	July	2d	Y2	
Schwinefot, B.	23, July 1850	July	25	Y2	
Schwing, Johan H.	23, July 1850	July	57	Y2	
Scime, John	3, May 1838			N2	
Scisson, James	6, July 1827	estate		Q3	
Scofield, David	10, Oct. 1838	estate		N2	
Scofield, Elnathan	7, Dec. 1841	5, Dec.		N2	
Scoggin, Elisha	2, Mar. 1822	estate		S3	
Scoggin, Elisha	16, Dec. 1825	probate		N3	
Scoggins, Reuben	5, Jan. 1822	estate		S3	
Scoley, Bridget	14, June 1849	June	21	L2	
Scott, (General)	22, Mar. 1794			C3	
Scott, Andrew	17, Sept 1835	probate		T2	
Scott, Eliza	4, Mar. 1836	2, Mar.	23	T3	
Scott, Eliza	4, Mar. 1836	2, Mar.	23	N2	
Scott, George Holmes	11, Oct. 1838	6, Oct.	19	T2	
Scott, Isabella	10, Jan. 1837	estate		N3	
Scott, James	6, Mar. 1829	Mar.	33	N2	
Scott, James	18, May 1838	probate		N2	
Scott, James Chambers	12, Sept 1817	6, Sept	22	S3	
Scott, John	26, Jan. 1816	estate		S3	
Scott, John	3, May 1825	probate		N3	
Scott, John	1, June 1835	probate		N2	
Scott, John	4, June 1836	probate		N2	
Scott, John M. (Col)	16, Jan. 1813	20, Dec.		S3	
Scott, John P.	14, Dec. 1835	probate		N2	
Scott, Margaret	8, Sept 1827	Sept	28	R3	
Scott, Mathias	9, Sept 1831	Sept	26	A3	
Scott, Michael	24, Mar. 1834	estate		T2	
Scott, Nelson	14, June 1849	June		L2	
Scott, Solomon	17, Apr. 1841	Apr.	120	R3	
Scott, Thomas	26, July 1834	July	18	R3	
Scott, Thomas	22, July 1834	July	18	T2	
Scott, Thomas	28, Oct. 1852	25, Oct.		P2	
Scott, Thomas (Rev)	21, July 1821	16, Apr.	75	S3	
Scrogin, Robert	14, Apr. 1836	1, Apr.		X3	
Scudder, Henry	21, Oct. 1823	estate		N3	
Scudder, Henry	14, Dec. 1824	probate		N3	
Scudder, Henry	19, Dec. 1826	probate		N3	
Scudder, Henry	16, Dec. 1824	probate		E3	
Scudder, John	25, Aug. 1821	7, Aug.	45	S3	
Scudder, Ruth	10, Apr. 1827	9, Apr.		N3	
Seager, (child of Dr.)	2, Aug. 1834	July	21d	R3	
Seager, (child of Dr.)	29, July 1834	July	21d	T2	
Seaman, John	24, Feb. 1820	estate		D3	
Seaman, John	16, Dec. 1825	probate		N3	
Seaman, Joseph	2, Nov. 1822	estate		S3	

Name	Notice Date	Death Date	Age		Page	Maiden Name
Seaman, -oster A.	12, Sept 1850	Sept	20		Y2	
Seaman, Thomas	12, Sept 1817		estate		S3	
Sears, Benjamin	19, Dec. 1826		probate		N3	
Secrist, Theresa A.	15, July 1852	12, July	33		P2	
Sedam, C.R.	26, Feb. 1830		estate		N3	
Sedam, Cornelius (Col)	23, May 1823	10, May	64	*	N3	
Sedam, Cornelius R.	30, Dec. 1828		estate		N3	
Sedam, Isaac	11, Dec. 1827		probate		N3	
Sedam, Isaac	9, Dec. 1828		probate		N3	
Sedenbury, Andrew T.	22, July 1834	July	1- 9m		T2	
Sederberry, A.T.	26, July 1834	July	1- 9m		R3	
See, Sarah	24, June 1828	June	6m		N3	
Seeley, Charles	20, July 1827	12, July	37	*	N3	
Seely, Charles	14, July 1827	12, July		*	R3	
Seely, Elizabeth	21, Apr. 1821	24, Mar.			S3	
Seely, George	14, Oct. 1828	Oct.	34		N3	
Seely, Mason G.	21, Apr. 1821	22, Mar.			S3	
Seemer, Jacob	9, Aug. 1841	Aug.	21		N2	
Sefton, Henry	4, June 1836		probate		N2	
Sefton, Henry	17, June 1837		probate		N2	
Segar, Nathaniel	16, Jan. 1829	Jan.	2d		N2	
Sehon, John L. (Major)	1, June 1847	17, May	77	*	K2	
Sei_er, John	17, July 1841	July	77		R3	
Seibert, Henry	6, July 1849	July	47		L2	
Seig, Mary	18, June 1849	17, June	67		L2	
Selden, Hetty	25, Oct. 1852	22, Oct.	27		P2	Gillingham
Selden, Joseph	8, July 1828	July	90		N3	
Seldon, Henry	8, Oct. 1830	Oct.	29		N3	
Sellers, John	13, Mar. 1829	Mar.	37		N3	
Sellew, John	10, Oct. 1840	Oct.	45		R3	
Sellman, Carberry J.	26, May 1838	26, May	29		T2	
Sellman, John (Dr)	5, Feb. 1828	1, Feb.			N2	
Sellors, Ann Frances	23, July 1852	21, July	2m- 2d		P2	
Semmes, Thomas	30, Aug. 1833		55		X3	
Semple, Helen M.	5, June 1849	3, June			L2	Wallace
Semple, Mary Jane	28, Aug. 1847	24, Aug.	infant		K2	
Senior, John	26, May 1827	21, May	50	*	R3	
Senior, John	23, Mar. 1830		probate		N3	
Senior, Rebecca	18, Aug. 1821	30, July	44	*	S3	
Sergeant, Margaret	17, Nov. 1836		56		X3	
Seth, Charles	14, May 1830	May	30		N3	
Settles, Francis S.	24, Jan. 1817		estate		S3	
Seward, James	3, July 1813		estate		S3	
Seward, Samuel	14, May 1814		estate		S3	
Sewards, James	9, Jan. 1818		estate		S3	
Seybold, John	1, July 1850	1, July			P2	
Seymour, Mabel	28, Apr. 1838	3, Apr.	83		R3	
Shackford, John	23, Aug. 1837				T2	
Shackler, John	3, Sept 1830	Aug.	4- 2m		N2	
Shaddows, Edward	19, July 1834	July	61		R3	
Shaebler, Maria	13, Nov. 1841	2, Nov.		*	R3	
Shaeffer, Daniel	6, Oct. 1826		probate		N3	
Shaeffer, Jacob	23, Oct. 1819	20, Oct.	infant		S3	
Shafer, Elizabeth	21, June 1849	June	28		L2	

Name	Notice Date	Death Date	Age		Page	Maiden Name
Shaffer, Henry	23, Nov. 1841	23, Nov.			N2	
Shaffler, Arnold	19, Dec. 1840	Dec.	51		R3	
Shaffler, Arnold	18, Dec. 1840	Dec.	51		N2	
Shalley, Elizabeth	21, June 1841	19, June			N2	
Shalley, Henrietta Anne	1, Dec. 1821	28, Nov.	15		S3	
Shan, William	19, Aug. 1831	Aug.	23		A3	
Shands, Frances J.	19, Sept 1840	19, Sept	19		R3	
Shands, Martha Ann Theophania	4, May 1838	2, May			T2	
Shane, Laura Winslow	27, Apr. 1837	19, Apr.	1- 8m-14d		X3	
Shanklin, John	8, Sept 1847		81		K2	
Shanklin, John	1, June 1835		probate		N2	
Shanklin, Mary Ann	24, Mar. 1838		estate		N2	
Shannon, James	26, July 1834	July	24		R3	
Shannon, James	22, July 1834	July	24		T2	
Shannon, Patrick	25, Oct. 1852	23, Oct.			P2	
Sharp, Delia Frances	17, July 1834	16, July	1- 3m-19d		T2	
Sharp, Edelia	2, Aug. 1834	July	5m		R3	
Sharp, Edelia	29, July 1834	July	5m		T2	
Sharp, Henry Clay	15, Jan. 1842	11, Jan.	5m		R3	
Sharp, James	11, Feb. 1831	6, Feb.	26		X3	
Sharp, James	4, June 1836		probate		N2	
Shaw, (Mr)	11, May 1850				P2	
Shaw, Henry	5, Apr. 1849	Apr.	27		L2	
Shaw, Henry	9, Nov. 1839	6, Nov.	28	*	R3	
Shaw, James	26, July 1834	July	24		R3	
Shaw, James	22, July 1834	July	24		T2	
Shaw, John	7, Oct. 1823	17, Sept	50		N3	
Shaw, John	3, Aug. 1803		estate		S3	
Shaw, Josiah	13, Aug. 1830	Aug.			N3	
Shaw, Thomas	9, June 1849	8, June			L2	
Shaw, William H.	30, July 1830	July	7m		N3	
Shawalton, Jacob	30, Dec. 1847				K2	
Shay, Martha Lavina	9, May 1850	5, May			P2	
Shays, Charlotte Mary	5, Mar. 1836	4, Mar.	3		T3	
Shays, Daniel (Gen)	11, Nov. 1825	29, Sept	84		N2	
Shays, Frances B.	16, Mar. 1849	15, Mar.	54		L2	
Shea, Mary	26, July 1850	July	40		Y2	
Shea, Mary Ann	25, July 1850	July	7w		Y2	
Sheardin, Thomas	12, Apr. 1849	Apr.	49		L2	
Sheed, John B.	23, Sept 1831	Sept	1- 8m		A3	
Sheehen, Thomas	1, June 1849	May	55		L2	
Sheeney, Thadeus	5, Apr. 1849	Apr.	40		L2	
Sheets, (child of T.)	5, Nov. 1830	Nov.	2d		N3	
Sheets, Eliza Ann	5, Nov. 1830	Nov.	12		N3	
Sheets, Levi	23, Apr. 1849	Apr.	21		L2	
Shehane, (child of Mary)	10, May 1849	May	stillborn		L2	
Shehane, Mary	10, May 1849	May	25		L2	
Shelby, Isaac (Governor)	25, July 1826	18, July			N3	
Shelby, Susan	24, Aug. 1833	25, July			R3	
Shellito, James	1, Sept 1852	30, Aug.	63	*	P2	
Shelmerdine, Samuel	17, Apr. 1841		50	*	R3	
Shelton, Fleming	24, Oct. 1850	Oct.	24		Y2	
Shemin, Sylvester	24, May 1849	May	17		L2	
Shepard, C.J.	25, Aug. 1852	23, Aug.	22		P2	

Name	Notice Date	Death Date	Age	Page	Maiden Name
Shepherd, (child of John)	31, Dec. 1830	Dec.	stillborn	N3	
Shepherd, Frances A.	3, July 1841	29, June		R3	
Shepherd, Frances A.	30, June 1841	29, June		N2	
Shepherd, Louisa C.	3, July 1841	20, June	6m	R3	
Shepherd, Louisa C.	28, June 1841	27, June	6m	N2	
Shepherd, Morris L.	7, Aug. 1841	1, Aug.	27	R3	
Shepherd, Morris L.	2, Aug. 1841	1, Aug.		N2	
Shepherd, Thomas	21, Sept 1830		estate	N3	
Shepherd, Zerelda	21, Aug. 1841	30, July		R3	
Shepherd, Zerelda E.	17, Aug. 1841	30, July		N2	
Shepherdson, (child of John)	18, June 1830	June	1d	N3	
Sheppard, E.	25, July 1850	July	38	Y2	
Sheppard, Edwin	25, July 1850	23, July	38 *	Y2	
Sheppard, Mary Ann Gaither	6, Apr. 1848	6, Apr.	infant	K2	
Sheridon, Mary	14, June 1849	June	40	L2	
Sherlock, John	29, May 1829		estate	N3	
Sherlock, Martha Ann	29, June 1849	28, June	10m	L2	
Sherlock, Thomas	28, July 1850	July	5m	Y3	
Sherriden, James B.	29, Mar. 1849	Mar.	30	L2	
Sherwin, Elnathan	7, Dec. 1822		estate	S3	
Sherwin, Sarah Ann	21, Aug. 1837	21, Aug.	1- 3m	T2	
Sherwin, Wellington W.	13, July 1849	July	19	L2	
Sherwood, Aris B.	20, Mar. 1849	18, Mar.	18m-15d	L2	
Sherwood, Isaac	9, May 1840	24, Apr.	72	R3	
Sherwood, Robert R.	24, July 1850	July	1	Y2	
Shield, Francis	28, Nov. 1840	25, Nov.		R3	
Shield, Thomas	20, Mar. 1829	Mar.	48	N3	
Shields, Caroline	3, Sept 1830	Aug.	7m	N2	
Shields, Elizabeth	3, Feb. 1829	Jan.	29	N3	
Shields, Melinda	26, July 1834	July	1- 3m	R3	
Shields, Melinda	22, July 1834	July	1- 3m	T2	
Shilleto, Mary	13, Aug. 1830	Aug.	15	N3	
Shillito, Jane Eliza	13, Nov. 1841	7, Nov.	infant	R3	
Shillito, Jane Eliza	9, Nov. 1841	17, Oct.		N2	
Shiner, Charles A.	17, Sept 1835		probate	T2	
Shingledecker, (child of Isaac)	9, Dec. 1828	Dec.	2m	N3	
Shingledecker, Abigail	9, Aug. 1838	8, Aug.	103-1m-16d *	T2	
Shinn, (child of Samuel)	11, June 1842	June	stillborn	R3	
Shinn, (heirs of C.A.)	14, Dec. 1835		probate	N2	
Shinn, Benjamin M.	24, June 1828	June	3	N3	
Shipman, (child of William)	12, Nov. 1830	Nov.	1- 8m	N3	
Shipman, William	9, Mar. 1836		estate	N3	
Shipman, William	4, Apr. 1837		probate	N2	
Shippen, Edward	6, May 1806	15, Apr.	78	S3	
Shires, Mary Anne	9, Aug. 1851	8, Aug.	38	P2	
Shirley, Joshua	15, May 1819	13, Apr.		S3	
Shoaad, (child of Sam.)	29, Mar. 1834	Mar.	3	R3	
Shoals, Philip	15, Jan. 1814	16, Nov.	115 *	S3	
Shober, P.K.	23, Sept 1831	Sept	1	A3	
Shoemaker, Charles	23, July 1847	22, July	20	K2	
Shores, David	1, June 1849	May	27	L2	
Shortrage, Eliza	24, Oct. 1828	Oct.	15	N2	
Shortridge, (son of John)	8, Sept 1827	Sept	12	R3	
Shortridge, Sarah	10, Dec. 1830	Dec.	41	N3	

Name	Notice Date	Death Date	Age		Page	Maiden Name
Shotwell, John T.	25, July 1850	23, July			P2	
Shotwell, John T.	25, July 1850	23, July			Y2	
Shotwell, John T.	27, July 1850	July			Y3	
Shreyer, George	4, Oct. 1838				T2	
Shriver, (Mr)	15, Sept 1826				Q3	
Shriver, Elizabeth	3, Oct. 1840	Sept	38	*	R3	
Shriver, J.	25, Aug. 1826	8, Aug.			N3	
Shriver, Margaret	3, Oct. 1840	Sept	17	*	R3	
Shroyer, George	5, Oct. 1838	28, Sept			N2	
Shryhe, James	24, Dec. 1830	Dec.	21		N3	
Shull, Lewis	27, Aug. 1830	Aug.	42		N3	
Shull, Peter	8, Aug. 1828		estate		N3	
Shultart, John	25, Nov. 1828	Nov.	31		N3	
Sidel, Henry	14, June 1849	June	25		L2	
Sigerson, Theodore M.	29, Nov. 1852	26, Nov.	10		P2	
Sill, John	12, Sept 1828	Sept	35		N3	
Silliman, Isabella	13, Nov. 1841	8, Nov.	18		R3	
Silliman, Isabella E.	11, Nov. 1841	9, Nov.	18		N2	
Sills, James	12, Aug. 1828	Aug.	55		N3	
Silsbee, Bell	27, June 1850	26, June	1		P2	
Silver, Elias	28, Feb. 1837		estate		N3	
Silver, Elias	17, June 1837		probate		N2	
Silver, James	19, Oct. 1822	6, Oct.	52		S3	
Silver, John	9, Dec. 1828		probate		N3	
Silvers, James	8, Oct. 1822	6, Oct.			J3	
Silvester, Sally	30, Apr. 1808	28, Apr.			S3	
Silvey, A.D.	10, Apr. 1847	10, Apr.	24		K2	
Simes, Charles W.	10, Oct. 1840	Oct.	24		R3	
Simmons, A.H.	31, July 1841	23, July		*	R3	
Simmons, George	20, Mar. 1838		probate		N3	
Simmons, Jane	3, Dec. 1838	23, Nov.	28	*	N2	
Simmons, John	6, July 1849	July	23		L2	
Simmons, Mordecai	9, Dec. 1828		probate		N3	
Simmons, William	18, July 1828	July	9m		N3	
Simms, James	5, Feb. 1831	3, Feb.	37	*	R3	
Simpson, Harriet	17, Sept 1835		probate		T2	
Simpson, James	3, May 1849	May	21		L2	
Simpson, John	2, Mar. 1811		estate		S3	
Simpson, William	6, Feb. 1829	Feb.	1		N2	
Sims, James	11, Feb. 1831	3, Feb.	37	*	X3	
Sims, James	9, June 1832		estate		R3	
Sims, James	1, June 1835		probate		N2	
Sims, William	12, Sept 1840	Sept	26		R3	
Sinclair, John	21, Apr. 1835	12, Apr.	40		T3	
Sinclair, William A.	31, Oct. 1850	Oct.	22		Y2	
Sine, William M.	16, Jan. 1829	Jan.	2m		N2	
Singleton, Sarah	19, Sept 1850	Sept	17d		Y2	
Sinnet, Elizabeth	2, Sept 1828	Aug.	60		N3	
Sipiard, (child of Elijah)	25, June 1830	June	8d		N3	
Sirp, Francis	13, July 1849	July	36		L2	
Sisco, Mary	6, Oct. 1827	Oct.	57		R3	
Sisson, Caroline	23, Sept 1828	19, Sept	21		N3	
Sisson, Elizabeth	1, Sept 1826	25, Aug.	64	*	N2	
Sisson, Isaac	8, June 1835	6, June	73		T2	

Name	Notice Date	Death Date	Age	Page	Maiden Name
Sisson, James	22, Aug. 1823	19, Aug.	34	N3	
Sisson, James	7, Nov. 1823		estate	N2	
Sisson, James	6, Oct. 1826		probate	N3	
Sisson, James M.	30, Dec. 1847			K2	
Sisson, Orrin	21, Sept 1838		probate	N3	
Sisson, Owen	10, Oct. 1836		estate	N2	
Skates, Abigail	6, Sept 1833	Sept	24	X3	
Skillman, Samuel	15, Sept 1821		estate	S3	
Skillman, Thomas	19, Aug. 1828		estate	N3	
Skyron, Elizabeth	5, Jan. 1833	2, Jan.		* R3	
Slack, Joshua (Rev)	24, 31, Aug. 1822	20, Aug.		* S3	
Slacum, W.A.	16, Nov. 1839	1, Nov.		T2	
Slade, Henry A.	6, Oct. 1837	20, Sept		T2	
Slade, Jane Mariah	27, Dec. 1838	9, Dec.	19	T2	
Slaughter, Abraham	2, July 1824		estate	N3	
Slayback, Abel (Mrs)	17, Nov. 1821	10, Nov.		S3	
Slayback, Ann Maria	16, July 1830	July	2- 5m	N3	
Slayback, Solomon	11, June 1814		estate	S3	
Slayback, Solomon	7, Sept 1824		probate	N3	
Slayback, Solomon	9, Sept 1824		probate	E3	
Sleeper, Oscar	3, Apr. 1849	1, Apr.	10m- 1d	L2	
Sleker, Jacob	2, Aug. 1834	July	1	R3	
Sleker, Jacob	29, July 1834	July	1	T2	
Sloan, David	2, Nov. 1811		estate	S3	
Sloan, David	13, Sept 1809		estate	H2	
Sloan, Rachel	17, May 1816		estate	S3	
Sloat, Cordelia A.	19, July 1834	July	1- 4m	R3	
Sloo, Harriett	19, May 1815	11, May		S3	
Sloo, Howell	19, Sept 1829	Aug.		* R3	
Sloo, John R.	28, Aug. 1837	28, July		T2	
Sloo, Nathaniel	19, Sept 1818	15, Sept		S3	
Sloo, William Irwin	18, June 1836	17, June	21	T2	
Sloo, William Irwin	18, June 1836	17, June	21	N2	
Sloop, Emily Frances	25, June 1842	16, June	22m- 8d	R3	
Sloop, H.	21, Oct. 1828	Oct.	18m	N2	
Sloop, John	26, Sept 1828	Sept	35	N3	
Slymer, Ellen	23, July 1850	July	55	Y2	
Smallwood, Josiah	29, Oct. 1830	Oct.	19	N3	
Smart, J.R.	3, June 1836	31, May	23	* N2	
Smead, Dedamond (Mrs)	28, Nov. 1828	Nov.	49	N3	
Smead, Diadema	29, Nov. 1828	26, Nov.		R3	
Smether, Carneal Franklin	11, Sept 1830	6, Sept	3- 3m	R3	
Smethers, Carneal F.	10, Sept 1830	Sept	3	N3	
Smilie, John	23, Jan. 1813	22, Jan.	71	* S3	
Smith,	9, Dec. 1837	1, Dec.		R3	
Smith, (child of J.)	20, Aug. 1830	Aug.	10m	N3	
Smith, (child of Peter)	9, July 1830	July	21d	N3	
Smith, (Mrs)	27, Aug. 1830	Aug.	83	N3	
Smith, (Mrs)	1, Oct. 1830	Sept		N3	
Smith, (son of Asahel)	23, Dec. 1825	14, Dec.	3	N3	
Smith, A.	17, Feb. 1829	Feb.		N3	
Smith, Abraham	4, Mar. 1828		probate	N3	
Smith, Abram	6, Oct. 1815		estate	S3	
Smith, Amos B.H.	1, Oct. 1830	Sept	5- 8m	N3	

Name	Notice Date	Death Date	Age		Page	Maiden Name
Smith, Ann	26, Sept 1840	Sept	25		R3	
Smith, Ballard (Major)	26, Apr. 1794		estate		C3	
Smith, Ballard (Major)	22, Mar. 1794	20, Mar.			C3	
Smith, Bartholomew	17, Dec. 1796		estate		F3	
Smith, Benjamin C.	27, Dec. 1828	Dec.	7		R3	
Smith, Benjamin C.	23, Dec. 1828	Dec.	7		N3	
Smith, Benjamin Y.	7, July 1838	2, July			R3	
Smith, Burrows	14, Oct. 1824		estate		E3	
Smith, Burrows (Capt)	17, Oct. 1823	9, Oct.	59	*	N2	
Smith, Casander	12, Jan. 1829	Jan.	2		N2	
Smith, Charles	19, Dec. 1812	13, Dec.	89	*	S3	
Smith, Charles	18, June 1830	June	1m		N3	
Smith, Charles Osmond	20, Dec. 1847	19, Dec.	15m- 9d		K2	
Smith, Christian	24, Oct. 1823		estate		N3	
Smith, Christian	16, Dec. 1825		probate		N3	
Smith, Clara J.	19, Aug. 1831	Aug.	2		A3	
Smith, Cyrus N.	15, May 1819				S3	
Smith, Daniel	26, July 1834	July	2		R3	
Smith, Daniel	22, July 1834	July	2		T2	
Smith, Edmund C.	24, Apr. 1847	23, Apr.	23- 4m		K2	
Smith, Elizabeth	23, Dec. 1824	19, Dec.	68		E2	
Smith, Elizabeth	21, Dec. 1824	19, Dec.	78		N3	
Smith, Frances	30, July 1850	July	23		Y3	
Smith, G.W.	31, July 1850	July			Y3	
Smith, Garret	29, July 1851	26, July			P2	
Smith, George (Capt)	8, Apr. 1828	1, Apr.	70	*	N2	
Smith, George (Capt)	28, Nov. 1840	13, Nov.	78		R3	
Smith, Hannah Miller	15, Dec. 1834	9, Dec.	10m		T2	
Smith, Henrietta A.	9, July 1842	4, July			R3	
Smith, Henry (Major)	23, Feb. 1827		90	*	N3	
Smith, Holland	20, Nov. 1819	17, Nov.	infant		S3	
Smith, Isaac	8, Oct. 1814		estate		S3	
Smith, James	30, July 1850	July	3		Y3	
Smith, James	27, Aug. 1852	26, Aug.	46		P2	
Smith, James	26, Jan. 1830		estate		N3	
Smith, James	18, Apr. 1838		estate		N2	
Smith, James	27, Apr. 1807	23, Apr.			S3	
Smith, James	14, Sept 1838	13, Sept			T2	
Smith, James B.	14, May 1830	May	7- 3m- 9d		N3	
Smith, James P. (Capt)	1, Feb. 1837	11, Jan.	41	*	T2	
Smith, James P. (Capt)	11, Feb. 1837		estate		T2	
Smith, Jesse	5, July 1838		estate		T2	
Smith, Jesse (Dr)	27, July 1833	July			R3	
Smith, Jesse H.	20, Mar. 1838		probate		N3	
Smith, John	30, June 1829	26, June	30	*	N3	
Smith, John	3, Dec. 1830	Nov.	60		N3	
Smith, John	21, Dec. 1830		probate		N3	
Smith, John	28, July 1841	27, July			N3	
Smith, John	26, Aug. 1815	6, Aug.			G3	
Smith, John (Rev)	3, Sept 1824	27, Aug.			N3	
Smith, John Armor	20, Mar. 1841	12, Mar.	3		N2	
Smith, John Broadfoot	30, Apr. 1831	23, Apr.	76		R3	
Smith, Joseph B.	10, Apr. 1829	Apr.	55		N3	
Smith, Josiah	19, July 1834	July	40		R3	

Name	Notice Date	Death Date	Age		Page	Maiden Name
Smith, Julius	7, Oct. 1823	3, Oct.	28	*	N3	
Smith, Laughlin	16, Sept 1823		100	*	N3	
Smith, Laura	6, Aug. 1831	3, Aug.	child		R3	
Smith, Lockwood W.	21, Dec. 1830		probate		N3	
Smith, Louisa P.	17, Mar. 1832		20		R3	
Smith, Lovicy	18, Aug. 1821	16, Aug.			S3	
Smith, Margaret A.	15, Aug. 1850	Aug.	8m		Y2	
Smith, Maria	8, July 1835	24, June	21		T2	
Smith, Martin Ror	3, May 1825	24, Apr.	18m- 5d		N3	
Smith, Mary	26, Sept 1850	Sept	16		Y2	
Smith, Mary	24, Feb. 1829	Feb.	49		N3	
Smith, Mary Ann	13, Sept 1838	Sept	4d		T2	
Smith, Michael	26, Sept 1850	Sept	56		Y2	
Smith, Nathan	9, Feb. 1822		estate		S3	
Smith, Oliver	6, Apr. 1837	1, Apr.	63		X3	
Smith, Oliver	25, Mar. 1837				N2	
Smith, Patrick	24, Mar. 1832		estate		R3	
Smith, Peter	9, July 1830	July	33		N3	
Smith, Peter	8, Aug. 1850	Aug.	4w		Y2	
Smith, Peter U.	3, July 1835	14, June	32		X3	
Smith, Rhoda	15, Sept 1827	Sept	38		R3	
Smith, Robert	11, Sept 1837		probate		N2	
Smith, Runous	23, Sept 1824		estate		E3	
Smith, Sampson	27, Oct. 1810	20, Oct.			S3	
Smith, Samuel Stanhope	25, Sept 1819	21, Aug.			S3	
Smith, Sarah	27, Aug. 1842	18, Aug.			R3	
Smith, Sarah L.	29, Dec. 1836	30, Sept	34		X3	Huntington
Smith, Sol (Mrs)	13, June 1838	6, June			T2	
Smith, Sophia	17, Sept 1830	Sept	15		N3	
Smith, Stephen	18, Apr. 1817	8, Apr.			S3	
Smith, T.B.	7, Dec. 1837		probate		N3	
Smith, Thomas	5, Sept 1834	15, July	46- 9m-15d	*	X3	
Smith, Thomas	27, Feb. 1819	2, Feb.			S3	
Smith, Thomas B.	10, Jan. 1837		estate		N2	
Smith, Thomas B.	28, Apr. 1836		estate		X3	
Smith, Thomas B.	6, Nov. 1838		probate		N2	
Smith, Thomas E.	31, Mar. 1834	30, Mar.		*	T2	
Smith, William	20, Dec. 1830	18, Dec.	42		A3	
Smith, William	27, Jan. 1821		estate		S3	
Smith, William	6, Oct. 1826		probate		N3	
Smith, William	7, Dec. 1837	1, Dec.			T2	
Smith, William H.	1, Aug. 1840	24, July	7m		R3	
Smith, William Henry	6, Oct. 1827	Oct.	8m		R3	
Smith, William Henry Harrison	20, Mar. 1841	7, Mar.	11m		N2	
Smith, William M. (Gen)	29, Nov. 1830	25, Nov.			A3	
Smith, William P.	1, Mar. 1816	26, Feb.			S3	
Smith, William R.	4, June 1849	3, June			L2	
Smith, William R.	4, June 1849	3, June			L3	
Smith, William Richard	24, Aug. 1852	22, Aug.	7w		P2	
Smithermon, John	16, Nov. 1835		estate		T2	
Smithu, Jacob	6, Mar. 1829	Mar.	32		N2	
Smoot, David B.	17, Dec. 1824	13, Dec.	20		N3	
Snead, Nancy W.	17, Nov. 1836	4, Nov.			X3	
Snell, Ruth	8, July 1828	July	2		N3	

Name	Notice Date	Death Date	Age		Page	Maiden Name
Snider, (child of John)	24, June 1828	June	5m		N3	
Snider, Asa S.	8, Oct. 1830	Oct.	2- 3m		N3	
Snider, C.	7, May 1824		estate		N3	
Snider, Cornelius	25, Apr. 1823		estate		N3	
Snider, Cornelius	2, Jan. 1824		estate		N3	
Snider, Cornelius	12, May 1826		estate		N3	
Snider, Cornelius	23, Mar. 1830		probate		N3	
Snider, Daniel	20, Oct. 1829		estate		N3	
Snider, Elizabeth	17, May 1849	May	68		L2	
Snider, George	12, Jan. 1829	Jan.	32		N2	
Snodgrass, James F.	16, Mar. 1830	11, Mar.	20		N3	
Snodgrass, William	10, Jan. 1837		estate		N3	
Snodgrass, William	20, July 1836	14, July			N2	
Snow, Henry Potter	18, Aug. 1852	16, Aug.		*	P2	
Snow, Lemuel	7, Sept 1824	3, Sept	65	*	N3	
Snowden, Isaac	18, Feb. 1836	14, Dec.	73		X3	
Snyder, Asa S.	8, Oct. 1830	3, Oct.			N3	
Snyder, Jacob	4, Dec. 1829	1, Dec.			N3	
Snyder, Simon	27, Nov. 1819	9, Nov.	60		S3	
Solander, Francis	12, July 1794		estate		C3	
Solauder, Francis	14, June 1794	27, May		*	C3	
Somerlot, Dorothy	31, Mar. 1826		100-10m-2d		N3	
Somerville, Archibald	7, Sept 1836		probate		N2	
Sonntagg, George (Admiral)	10, June 1841	23, May	66	*	N2	
Sorter, (child of John)	22, Oct. 1830	Oct.	stillborn		N3	
Sorton, Martin	26, July 1852	July			P2	
Sotcher, Abner	29, Sept 1826		estate		N3	
Souders, John	3, Dec. 1830	Nov.	6		N3	
Souders, William R.	6, 27, Jan. 1826		estate		N3	
Southgate, Elizabeth	1, Aug. 1834	30, July			T2	
Southgate, Jane	20, June 1840	14, June			R3	
Southgate, Maria C.	25, Mar. 1836	23, Mar.			T2	
Southgate, Robert Copland	1, Jan. 1836	27, Dec.			T3	
Sowders, Sarah	21, May 1830	May	60		N3	
Sparks, Elizabeth	7, Nov. 1840	28, Oct.	51		R3	
Sparks, Isaac	7, Dec. 1837		probate		N3	
Sparks, Samuel	28, Nov. 1828	Nov.	32		N3	
Spear, John G.	14, Dec. 1835		probate		N2	
Spear, Thomas	2, June 1827		163		R3	
Spear, William	5, Nov. 1824	23, Oct.	34	*	N1	
Spear, William	9, Dec. 1824		estate		E3	
Speck, Ann	23, July 1850	July	40		Y2	
Spelar, Thomas	22, Oct. 1830	Oct.	2m		N3	
Spence, (Rev)	10, Mar. 1836	15, Feb.			X3	
Spencer, Alexander O.	21, Oct. 1841	12, Oct.	28		N2	
Spencer, Anne Eliza	18, May 1833	12, May	18		R3	
Spencer, Elvira Elizabeth	6, Sept 1852	4, Sept	1- 7m		P2	
Spencer, Henry Evans	26, Sept 1840	20, Sept	3		R3	
Spencer, John	28, June 1849	June	22		L2	
Spencer, Noah	1, Jan. 1853	31, Dec.		*	P2	
Spencer, O.M.	2, June 1838	29, May	57		R3	
Spencer, O.M.	11, Oct. 1847		estate		K2	
Spencer, Ogden	26, June 1849	25, June	8		L2	
Spencer, Oliver	18, June 1814		estate		S3	

Name	Notice Date	Death Date	Age	Page	Maiden Name
Spencer, Oliver (Col)	26, Jan. 1811	22, Jan.	74	S3	
Spencer, Oliver M.	30, May 1838	30, May	57	T2	
Spencer, Oliver M.	31, May 1838	30, May	57	N2	
Spencer, Oliver M.	8, June 1838	30, May	57	* N2	
Spencer, Robert Halsted	17, June 1837	11, June	2	R3	
Spencer, Robert Halsted	13, June 1837	11, June	2	T2	
Spencer, William Halsted	19, Sept 1840	13, Sept	1- 3m	R3	
Spiller, Benjamin	15, Sept 1827	Sept	8m	R3	
Spinham, Arthur	12, Jan. 1829	Jan.	11	N2	
Spinning, Charles N.	26, May 1838	23, May	23	T2	
Spinning, Ichabod	16, Jan. 1819	8, Jan.	63	S3	
Spinning, John P.	14, Dec. 1835		probate	N2	
Spinning, John P.	7, Sept 1836		probate	N2	
Spinning, Newton	3, Nov. 1810	27, Sept		S3	
Spooner, Alden	16, June 1827		70	R3	
Spooner, Daniel W.	13, Sept 1833		estate	X3	
Spooner, Reed	25, Sept 1835	22, Sept	46	T2	
Spooner, Reed	17, June 1837		probate	N2	
Spooner, Reed	20, Mar. 1838		probate	N3	
Spooner, Sarah L.	1, Aug. 1850	31, July		* Y2	Leonard
Spragg, John	2, Nov. 1833		estate	R3	
Sprague, Elizabeth	10, July 1849	5, July	17	L2	
Sprigman, Eliza Louisa	10, Feb. 1836	1, Feb.	18	T3	
Spring, Clara	25, Dec. 1852	20, Dec.	1- 2m	P2	
Springer, Jacob	14, Jan. 1818		estate	S3	
Springer, Jacob	7, Sept 1824		probate	N3	
Springer, Jacob	9, Sept 1824		probate	E3	
Springer, Joseph	31, Mar. 1832	11, Mar.	94	R3	
Springer, Mary Elizabeth	9, July 1842	2, July	16m	R3	
Springfield, Henry	24, Mar. 1836	18, Mar.		X3	
Sprull, (Rev)	30, Aug. 1833			X3	
Spurrier, Thomas	11, Dec. 1827		probate	N3	
Srewer, Henry	23, July 1850	July	1	Y2	
St.Clair, A.	7, Oct. 1823		estate	N3	
St.Clair, Arthur	11, Sept 1841	24, Aug.	38	R3	
St.Clair, Arthur	8, Sept 1841	24, Aug.	38	N2	
St.Clair, Arthur	4, Sept 1841	24, Aug.	38	V3	
St.Clair, Arthur	10, Mar. 1821		estate	S1	
St.Clair, Arthur	28, Sept 1820	26, Sept		S3	
St.Clair, George	21, Apr. 1829		estate	N3	
St.Clair, George	4, Mar. 1828		probate	N3	
St.Clair, George	25, Aug. 1829		probate	N3	
St.Clair, George	22, Dec. 1829		probate	N3	
St.Clair, George (heirs of)	18, May 1838		probate	N2	
St.Clair, Hannah	8, Sept 1827	Sept	32	R3	
St.Clair, Hannah	30, Oct. 1827		estate	N3	
St.Clair, Hannah	7, Sept 1830		probate	N3	
Stabbs, Emily	28, July 1850	July	15m	Y3	
Stack, Mary	8, Oct. 1852	Oct.	26	P2	
Stackhouse, (child of Rachel)	8, July 1828	July	infant	N3	
Staebler, Maria	9, Nov. 1841	2, Nov.		* N2	
Stagemiller, James	13, July 1849	July	2- 6m	L2	
Stain, (Mr)	18, Aug. 1842	16, Aug.		N2	
Stait, John S.	7, June 1849	June	74	L2	

Name	Notice Date	Death Date	Age		Page	Maiden Name
Stakel, Matthias	7, Dec. 1827		estate		N3	
Stakel, Matthias	25, Aug. 1829		probate		N3	
Stakel, Matthias	22, Dec. 1829		probate		N3	
Stall, Edward H. (Dr)	24, Dec. 1831	17, Dec.			R3	
Stall, Edward H. (Dr)	23, Dec. 1831	17, Dec.			X3	
Stall, G.W.	28, May 1830		estate		N3	
Stall, George W. (Lt)	13, Feb. 1819	6, Feb.			S3	
Stall, John	7, May 1814		estate		S3	
Stames, William A.	29, Mar. 1834	Mar.	12		R3	
Stanbery, (Mrs)	22, Aug. 1842	11, Aug.			N2	
Stanbery, Henry	11, Nov. 1852	8, Nov.	17		P2	
Stanford, Richard	26, Apr. 1816	9, Apr.	47		S3	
Stanislaus, Anna Maria	23, Sept 1852	22, Sept	46		P2	
Stanley, John	30, Aug. 1833	3, Aug.			X3	
Stanley, Mary	3, Sept 1847	2, Sept	52		K2	
Stanley, Peter	9, Sept 1801		estate		S3	
Stanley, William	20, Aug. 1814		estate		S3	
Stanley, William (Major)	14, May 1814	8, May			S3	
Stansbury, Caroline E.	2, July 1849	24, June	24		L2	Burch
Stansbury, Mary	2, Sept 1835	15, Aug.	40		T2	
Stansbury, Thomas J.	26, Mar. 1849	24, Mar.	38		L2	
Stansbury, Wesley	2, Sept 1835	26, Aug.	3- 5m		T2	
Stanton, Loyd Coleman	10, Oct. 1840	30, Sept	1- 9m		R3	
Stanton, William F.	15, Oct. 1839	22, Sept			T2	
Stanwwood, Mehitable R.	7, Oct. 1847	3, Oct.		*	K2	
Stapleton, (child of James)	21, June 1849	June	stillborn		L2	
Starbuck, David	31, July 1827		29		N3	
Starbuck, Sarah	3, Sept 1830	Aug.	2		N2	
Starbuck, Sarah Ann	25, Nov. 1852	18, Nov.	20- 4m-16d		P2	
Stark, Sarah	2, Feb. 1803	28, Jan.	99		S3	
Starkey, Josiah	26, June 1829		estate		N3	
Starr, (child of John)	12, Aug. 1828	Aug.	3m		N3	
Starr, George	28, July 1850	July	2		Y3	
Starr, John	30, Nov. 1837	26, Oct.	64	*	X3	
Staughton, J.M.	9, Sept 1831	Sept	10m		A3	
Staughton, James	3, Sept 1831	31, Aug.	infant		R3	
Staughton, James	4, June 1836		probate		N2	
Staughton, William	24, Mar. 1832	20, Mar.	4		R3	
Stearns, Kate	14, July 1852	12, July	1-11m		P2	
Stedman, Jane Anne	26, Sept 1837	25, Sept			T2	
Steed, Thomas	15, Aug. 1812		estate		S3	
Steel, James Breckenridge	22, Sept 1836	9, Sept	5m		X3	
Steele, Andrew	25, Mar. 1815	13, Mar.		*	W3	
Steele, J.	28, Aug. 1841	21, Aug.			R3	
Steele, James	27, Aug. 1841	21, Aug.			N2	
Steele, Mary Jane	4, May 1822	26, Apr.			S3	Rowan
Steele, Peter	28, June 1849	June	22		L2	
Steer, Samuel	24, Mar. 1838	23, Mar.	45		T2	
Steidel, Margaret	26, July 1834	July	56		R3	
Steidel, Margaret	22, July 1834	July	56		T2	
Stein, Valentine	30, July 1850	July	7m		Y3	
Steinbaugh, Ernst	14, June 1849	June	28		L2	
Steinhoff, Louis	6, July 1849	July	28		L2	
Steinman, Henry	6, July 1849	July	3- 6m		L2	

Name	Notice Date	Death Date	Age	Page	Maiden Name
Steinman, John	6, July 1849	July	7	L2	
Stephens, George	25, Aug. 1829		probate	N3	
Stephens, Henry	23, May 1823		estate	N3	
Stephens, Mary	14, June 1849	June	48	L2	
Stephens, Naomi	23, July 1830	July	63	N3	
Stephens, Olive	19, Aug. 1831	Aug.	2- 8m	A3	
Stephens, Thomas	10, Mar. 1829		probate	N3	
Stephens, Willard	19, Aug. 1831	Aug.	4- 2m-10d	A3	
Stephenson, Caroline	29, June 1849	28, June	20	L2	
Stephenson, James W. (Col)	4, Sept 1838			T2	
Stephenson, John S.	14, May 1830	May	1m-20d	N3	
Stephenson, William	19, Aug. 1828		probate	N3	
Sterges, Isaac	18, Jan. 1833		51	X3	
Sterling, (child of R.)	28, July 1850	July	18d	Y3	
Sterling, Eliza	8, Oct. 1852	3, Oct.	65	P2	
Sterret, (child of Robert)	19, Aug. 1828	Aug.	infant	N3	
Sterrett, Jane B.	3, Oct. 1840	25, Sept	29	R3	Keys
Sterrett, John	26, June 1849	23, June	55	L2	
Stettinius, Mary L.	20, Jan. 1837			T2	Longworth
Stettinius, Mary L.	20, Jan. 1837			N2	Longworth
Stevens,	19, June 1849	15, June	8	L3	
Stevens, Ann	17, Sept 1835		probate	T2	
Stevens, Ann	4, June 1836		probate	N2	
Stevens, George Henry	29, Apr. 1842	21, Apr.	3- 9m	N2	
Stevens, Henry	3, Aug. 1822	28, July		S3	
Stevens, John	17, Sept 1835		probate	T2	
Stevens, John	4, June 1836		probate	N2	
Stevens, Lerana	9, Sept 1831	Sept	1- 5m	A3	
Stevens, Mary	7, May 1842	28, Apr.		R3	
Stevens, Mary Alice	24, July 1852	22, July	infant	P2	
Stevens, Sarah Catharine	10, Aug. 1837	28, July	7w	X3	
Stevens, Susan	3, Oct. 1840	28, Sept	25	R3	
Stevens, T. (heirs of)	7, Sept 1836		probate	N2	
Stevenson, Job	1, Aug. 1837	10, July	55	T2	
Stevenson, Sarah	7, Jan. 1848	6, Jan.	23	K2	Phillips
Steward, John	10, Oct. 1840	Oct.	29	R3	
Steward, John	22, Dec. 1829		probate	N3	
Stewart, Charles	17, May 1849	May	35	L2	
Stewart, Charles D.	28, Dec. 1852	26, Dec.	32	P2	
Stewart, David T.	20, Mar. 1847	17, Mar.	20	K2	
Stewart, James	8, May 1835	4, May		T2	
Stewart, James (Mrs)	8, May 1835	4, May		T2	
Stewart, Jane	28, Apr. 1841	27, Apr.		N2	
Stewart, John	9, Sept 1825		estate	N3	
Stewart, John	28, Mar. 1826		estate	N3	
Stewart, John	6, Oct. 1826		probate	N3	
Stewart, John	4, Mar. 1828		probate	N3	
Stewart, John	19, Aug. 1828		probate	N3	
Stewart, Lucinda	17, Sept 1852	15, Sept	57	P2	
Stewart, Mary	19, Aug. 1828		probate	N3	
Stewart, Mary	9, Dec. 1828		probate	N3	
Stewart, Mary	25, Mar. 1815	19, Mar.		W3	
Stewart, Mary A.	7, June 1849	June	18	L2	
Stewart, Mary P.	1, Dec. 1852	29, Nov.	38	P2	

Name	Notice Date	Death Date	Age		Page	Maiden Name
Stewart, William	9, Sept 1831	Sept	7d		A3	
Stewart, William F.	6, Nov. 1841	2, Nov.	25	*	V3	
Stewart, William Taylor	6, Feb. 1841	29, Jan.	infant		R3	
Stickerser, William	6, Feb. 1829	Feb.	23		N2	
Stickney, Evelina	19, Aug. 1830	16, Aug.	15		A3	
Stickney, Harriet Eliza	6, Dec. 1830	5, Dec.			A3	
Stickney, Harriet Eliza	11, Dec. 1830	3, Dec.			R3	
Stickney, Henrietta E.	10, Dec. 1830	Dec.	25		N3	
Stickney, Mary V.	20, Aug. 1830	Aug.	15		N3	
Stickney, Moses P.	13, July 1849	July	40		L2	
Stiles, Benjamin	14, Dec. 1822		estate		S3	
Stille, John	30, Aug. 1852	25, Aug.			P2	
Stilley, Thomas	29, Mar. 1834	Mar.	1		R3	
Stillman, Adam	13, July 1849	July	40		L2	
Stillman, Mary Ann	5, Jan. 1833	4, Jan.			R3	Pancoast
Stilson, Martha	26, Feb. 1841	Feb.			N2	
Stilwell, (child of Mrs)	17, Feb. 1829	Feb.	stillborn		N3	
Stimpson, William Hooper	12, Dec. 1814	6, Dec.	10		W3	
Stine, Daniel	5, Mar. 1814		estate		S3	
Stinson, Stephen	25, Aug. 1827	Aug.	68		R3	
Stites, Benjamin	12, Sept 1804		estate		S3	
Stites, Benjamin	20, Nov. 1805		estate		S3	
Stites, Benjamin	6, Feb. 1824		estate		N3	
Stites, Benjamin	7, Sept 1824		probate		N3	
Stites, Benjamin	19, Dec. 1826		probate		N3	
Stites, Benjamin	21, Dec. 1830		probate		N3	
Stites, Benjamin	9, Sept 1824		probate		E3	
Stites, Martha	6, Aug. 1830	Aug.	47		N3	
Stitt, Samuel	23, Aug. 1847	21, Aug.	85	*	K2	
Stocker, Olive	31, July 1827				N3	
Stockford, (2 children)	8, Sept 1827	Sept	17d		R3	
Stockman, John H.	2, Jan. 1824		estate		N3	
Stockton, Catharine	14, Mar. 1842				N2	McMurray
Stockton, Lucius Horatio	8, June 1835			*	T2	
Stocton, John H.	12, Sept 1828	Sept	10		N3	
Stoddard, (Major)	22, May 1813				S3	
Stoddard, David	11, June 1847	10, June			K2	
Stodert, Joseph	11, Sept 1852	10, Sept			P2	
Stokes, Amelia	28, July 1826	26, July			N3	
Stokes, Edward	31, July 1829		100		N3	
Stokes, Henry	3, May 1838				N2	
Stokes, John	28, May 1830	May	56		N3	
Stoll, Sasis	6, July 1849	July	37		L2	
Stoms, Peter	16, Sept 1835	8, Sept	21	*	T2	
Stoms, Peter	14, Sept 1835	8, Sept	21	*	N2	
Stone, (child of Richard L.)	2, Aug. 1834	July	1- 2m		R3	
Stone, (child of Richard L.)	29, July 1834	July	1- 2m		T2	
Stone, Calvin R.	3, May 1838			*	N2	
Stone, David	7, Nov. 1839	3, Nov.	53		T2	
Stone, Elisha	10, Feb. 1841		estate		N3	
Stone, W.S. (Rev)	19, Oct. 1837		30		X3	
Stone, Wilmot	27, July 1833	July			R3	
Stong, Elizabeth	3, Oct. 1840	Sept	26		R3	
Storch, John A.	10, Oct. 1817		estate		S2	

Name	Notice Date	Death Date	Age	Page	Maiden Name
Storch, John A.	11, Dec. 1827		probate	N3	
Storer, Margaret	10, Oct. 1840	21, Sept	75	R3	
Storrs, Charles B. (Rev)	4, Oct. 1833			X3	
Stothart, John D.	17, May 1842	15, May		* N2	
Stoughton, Thomas	20, Apr. 1835	7, Apr.	25	T3	
Stout, (child of George)	18, June 1830	June	child	N3	
Stout, Abraham	20, Oct. 1821		estate	S3	
Stout, Benijah	17, July 1823		estate	J2	
Stout, Ira	5, Dec. 1823		estate	N2	
Stout, Ira	3, May 1825		probate	N3	
Stout, John	17, Mar. 1832	11, Mar.	40	R3	
Stout, John	14, July 1832		estate	R3	
Stout, John W.	13, Aug. 1836	28, July	30	T2	
Stout, John W.	18, Aug. 1836	28, July	30	X3	
Stout, Rachel	13, Nov. 1830	1, Nov.	67	* R3	
Stout, Reuben	27, May 1836		estate	N2	
Stout, Reuben	20, Mar. 1838		probate	N3	
Stout, Samuel	1, June 1835		probate	N2	
Stout, Sarah	2, Nov. 1835	31, Oct.	50	T2	
Stoutenburg, John H.	22, July 1823	16, July	29	N3	
Stoutenburgh, John H.	16, Oct. 1823		estate	J3	
Stoutenburgh, John H.	16, Dec. 1825		probate	N3	
Stow, J.B.	30, July 1842	25, July		R3	
Stowe, (Mrs)	8, Aug. 1834	6, Aug.		X3	Tyler
Stowe, Adonijah C.	16, Nov. 1835		estate	T2	
Strader, (child of Captain)	9, Sept 1831	Sept		A3	
Strader, Abby	4, June 1841	2, June		N2	
Strader, D.P. (Dr)	31, Aug. 1852	29, Aug.	42	P2	
Straeffer, Martha Elizabeth	23, Aug. 1836	20, Aug.	18m-18d	N2	
Strait, (child of F.)	1, July 1828	June	stillborn	N3	
Straits, Andrew	10, June 1850	8, June		P2	
Stratten, Job	24, Oct. 1818		estate	S3	
Stratton, Job	7, Sept 1824		probate	N3	
Stratton, Job	9, Sept 1824		probate	E3	
Stratton, Josiah J.	9, Nov. 1850	9, Nov.	45	P2	
Street, (Mr)	15, July 1831	June		X2	
Street, George	26, Feb. 1841	Feb.	35	N2	
Street, William	11, Sept 1827		estate	N3	
Stricker, Henry	6, July 1849	July	26	L2	
Stridleburgh, (child of Jacob)	23, Dec. 1828	Dec.	stillborn	N3	
Stroas, James	29, Oct. 1830	Oct.	32	N3	
Strobridge, James Gordon	18, May 1849	16, May	23	L2	
Strong, Caleb	27, Nov. 1819	7, Oct.		S3	
Strong, Chloe	6, Apr. 1822		estate	S3	
Strong, Chloe	13, Jan. 1821			S3	
Strong, David	4, Sept 1813		estate	S3	
Strong, David (Col)	1, May 1802		estate	S3	
Strong, David (Col)	10, Oct. 1801	19, Aug.		S3	
Strong, David, Jr.	30, Nov. 1793	29, Nov.	7	C3	
Strong, Elijah	4, Feb. 1815		estate	S3	
Strong, Jebediah	1, July 1828	June	45	N3	
Strong, S.A. (Mrs)	23, May 1840	26, Apr.		R3	
Stroodles, John	10, Dec. 1830	Dec.	28	N3	
Strother, George F.	9, Dec. 1840	5, Dec.		* N2	

Name	Notice Date	Death Date	Age		Page	Maiden Name
Stroud, Daniel	7, Oct. 1828	Oct.	55		N3	
Strub, John	29, Aug. 1840	Aug.	4		R3	
Stuart, Charles	19, Mar. 1814		estate		S1	
Stubart, Mary	30, July 1830	July	3m		N3	
Stull, Adil	26, Sept 1828	Sept	7m		N3	
Stull, Matilda	7, Oct. 1828	Oct.	35		N3	
Stump, William	7, Sept 1836		probate		N2	
Sturdivant, E.A.	8, Aug. 1850	Aug.	37		Y2	
Sturges, Thomas	10, Oct. 1823		estate		N3	
Sturgis, Thomas (Capt)	4, Mar. 1823				N3	
Sublette, Milton G.	23, June 1837	5, Apr.			T2	
Sullivan, Ann	28, June 1849	June	35		L2	
Sullivan, Daniel	4, Sept 1819	1, Sept	96	*	S3	
Sullivan, Dennis	14, June 1849	June	28		L2	
Sullivan, Elizabeth	3, Apr. 1829	Mar.	2m		N2	
Sullivan, Eunice	8, Aug. 1834	1, Aug.		*	X3	Lamb
Sullivan, Giles	22, Aug. 1850	Aug.	47		Y2	
Sullivan, James	27, Feb. 1835	10, Dec.			X3	
Sullivan, John	27, Feb. 1835	22, Dec.			X3	
Sullivan, Margaret	8, Oct. 1852	Oct.	23		P2	
Sullivan, Mary	8, Oct. 1852	Oct.	91		P2	
Sullivan, Mary Ann	22, Aug. 1835	3, Aug.		*	T2	Brooks
Sultzbach, John	5, Dec. 1828		estate		N3	
Summer, William	21, May 1830	May	12		N3	
Sumner, Alexander B.	25, July 1840	22, July	52	*	R3	
Sumner, William H.	5, Sept 1840				R3	
Sumter, (Gen)	4, Nov. 1830	16, Oct.			A3	
Sute, Nathaniel	28, May 1830		estate		N3	
Suter, John J.	29, Oct. 1830	Oct.	49		N3	
Sutherland, Elizabeth	9, July 1850	6, July			P2	
Sutton, Isaac	19, Aug. 1828	Aug.	5m		N3	
Sutton, Mary	16, Oct. 1847	11, Oct.	51	*	K2	
Suwthberger, George	23, July 1850	July	50		Y2	
Swain, John	26, July 1850	July	20m		Y2	
Swan, (man)	6, Aug. 1850	3, Aug.	40		Y2	
Swan, Caleb	16, Nov. 1811		estate		S1	
Swan, Caleb	14, Nov. 1812		estate		S3	
Swan, David	8, Dec. 1826		estate		N3	
Swan, David	23, Mar. 1830		probate		N3	
Swan, Mary L.	7, June 1828	June			R3	White
Swartz, E.	21, June 1849	June	1		L2	
Swartz, Henry	21, June 1849	June	4		L2	
Swartz, James	21, June 1849	June	5		L2	
Swartz, Nicholas	21, June 1849	June	2- 6m		L2	
Swartz, Valentine	21, June 1849	June	50		L2	
Swasey, Ella Maria	16, Sept 1852	13, Sept	5- 9m-13d		P2	
Swasey, William	30, Oct. 1841	17, Oct.	23		R3	
Swasey, William B.	14, Feb. 1848	12, Feb.	3		K2	
Swasey, William B.	26, Oct. 1841	17, Oct.	23		N2	
Swazey, (child of Hazen)	25, Nov. 1828	Nov.	stillborn		N3	
Swazey, Hazen	27, Aug. 1830	Aug.	34		N3	
Swearingen, Artimas	12, Aug. 1815	16, July		*	G3	
Sweeney, (Mr)	20, May 1835	20, May		*	T2	
Sweeney, John	26, July 1850	July	55		Y2	

Name	Notice Date	Death Date	Age		Page	Maiden Name
Sweet, Benoni (Dr)	3, Oct. 1840	27, Sept	80		R3	
Sweet, Mahala	17, Sept 1842	12, Sept	31		R3	
Sweet, Stephen W.	8, Sept 1852	6, Sept	1- -28d		P2	
Swift, Calvin	28, Dec. 1824	24, Dec.	27		N3	
Swift, Calvin	22, Dec. 1826		estate		N3	
Swift, John (Gen)	9, Aug. 1814	July			W3	
Swift, Joseph	3, May 1838			*	N2	
Swift, Reuben	22, Dec. 1826		estate		N3	
Swift, Reuben	25, Aug. 1829		probate		N3	
Swinehart, Gabriel	19, Dec. 1804		estate		S3	
Swing, (child of D.)	8, Sept 1827	Sept	3m		R3	
Swing, James	7, June 1828	June			R3	
Swing, James	6, June 1828	8, May			Q3	
Sykes, Robert	25, Sept 1841	22, Sept	1- 5m		N2	
Symmes, Betsey	27, Jan. 1824	24, Jan.	10		N3	
Symmes, Daniel	16, 23, May 1817	11, May	51	*	S3	
Symmes, Daniel	26, Sept 1817		estate		S3	
Symmes, Daniel	10, Oct. 1823		estate		N3	
Symmes, Daniel	25, Aug. 1829		probate		N3	
Symmes, David Cleves	31, Dec. 1831	25, Dec.	infant		R3	
Symmes, Ethan Allen Brown	2, Mar. 1837	25, Feb.	7- 6m		T2	
Symmes, J.C.	14, Mar. 1818		estate		S1	
Symmes, John C.	7, Oct. 1824		estate		E3	
Symmes, John Cleves	12, Mar. 1814	26, Feb.	72		S3	
Symmes, John Cleves	28, Apr. 1815		estate		S3	
Symmes, John Cleves	24, Mar. 1821		estate		S3	
Symmes, John Cleves (Capt)	30, May 1829	28, May		*	R3	
Symmes, John Cleves (Capt)	2, June 1829	28, May		*	N2	
Symmes, Mercy Harker	6, June 1818	5, June		*	S3	
Symmes, Timothy	23, Sept 1823	18, Sept	27		N3	
Symmes, Timothy	28, Oct. 1823		estate		N2	
Symonds, Isaac	9, Jan. 1835		estate		T2	
Taft, Nancy M.	2, June 1847	31, May	3		K2	
Tait, Charles	1, Dec. 1835				T2	
Tait, John	1, June 1835		probate		N2	
Tait, Robert	4, Jan. 1794		estate		C3	
Talbott, Isham	30, Sept 1837	23, Sept			T2	
Talmine, Francis	3, May 1838				N2	
Talmon, Harmonious	27, Oct. 1798		estate		F4	
Talpier, Tager	7, Nov. 1804		120		S2	
Tanner, James	2, Mar. 1836		estate		N2	
Tanoise, M. Francis	15, May 1805		88		S3	
Tapley, Isaac	26, July 1834	July	30		R3	
Tapley, Isaac	22, July 1834	July	30		T2	
Tappan, Betsey	20, June 1840				R3	
Tappan, Eugene B.	20, Aug. 1830	Aug.	15m		N3	
Tappan, Eugene Barrington	26, Aug. 1830	16, Aug.	infant		A3	
Tarrant, Larkin M.	13, May 1830	20, Apr.	34		A3	
Tatem, Charles	6, May 1837	30, Apr.	8m		R3	
Tatem, Charles	12, Feb. 1835	11, Feb.			N2	
Tatem, John	21, Oct. 1837	7, Oct.	39		R3	
Tatem, John	19, Oct. 1837	7, Oct.	39		T2	
Tatem, John	20, Oct. 1837	7, Oct.	39		N2	
Tatem, Rachel	24, July 1838	23, July			T2	

Name	Notice Date	Death Date	Age	Page	Maiden Name
Tatspur, Peter	6, Sept 1833	Sept	25	X3	
Taulman, (heirs of Joseph)	19, Aug. 1828		probate	N3	
Taulman, Harmanus	16, Dec. 1825		probate	N3	
Taulman, Joseph	28, Nov. 1818		estate	S3	
Taulman, Joseph	16, Dec. 1825		probate	N3	
Taulman, Joseph	6, Oct. 1826		probate	N3	
Taulman, Joseph	4, June 1836		probate	N2	
Taulman, Peter	17, Sept 1835		probate	T2	
Taulman, Peter	4, June 1836		probate	N2	
Taylor (child)	19, July 1834	July	1d	R3	
Taylor, (child of John)	8, Oct. 1830	Oct.	stillborn	N3	
Taylor, (child of Joseph)	28, May 1830	May	stillborn	N3	
Taylor, (child of Townsend)	31, Dec. 1830	Dec.	4d	N3	
Taylor, (daughter of Col.)	23, July 1841	22, July	18m	N2	
Taylor, Benjamin	12, Sept 1795		estate	C3	
Taylor, Cornelia Florence	31, July 1841	26, July	17m-14d	R3	
Taylor, Cornelia Florence	28, July 1841	26, July	17m-14d	N3	
Taylor, Eugene A. Woodworth	18, Apr. 1840			R3	
Taylor, James	13, July 1849	July	3- 6m	L2	
Taylor, Jane	13, July 1849	July	10	L2	
Taylor, John	10, May 1816		estate	S3	
Taylor, John	10, Sept 1824	20, Aug.		N2	
Taylor, Letty Jane	20, Mar. 1829	Mar.	10m	N3	
Taylor, Maria	31, Dec. 1830	Dec.	7	N3	
Taylor, Philip	16, Apr. 1836		estate	T2	
Taylor, Philip	5, Jan. 1842		estate	N3	
Taylor, Richard A.	7, Nov. 1840	29, Oct.	23	R3	
Taylor, Robert	26, Nov. 1830	Nov.	9	N3	
Taylor, Robert	5, June 1819		estate	S3	
Taylor, Samuel	16, Jan. 1841	Jan.	24	R3	
Taylor, Samuel	16, Jan. 1841	Jan.	34	N2	
Taylor, Samuel	8, Dec. 1837		estate	N2	
Taylor, Thomas	20, Aug. 1830	Aug.	35	N3	
Taylor, William	31, May 1830	24, May	86	A3	
Taylor, William H.	26, Sept 1850	Sept	20	Y2	
Tebow, Uriah	27, Jan. 1821		estate	S3	
Templin, Agnes	28, Feb. 1826	6, Feb.	88	* N2	
Tendel, Jane B.	26, Nov. 1830	Nov.	2	N3	
Teper, Henry	27, July 1850	July	6	Y3	
Teralle, James H.	20, Aug. 1830	Aug.	11m	N3	
Terwilliger, Nathaniel	28, Oct. 1835		estate	N4	
Thane, Edwin Piatt	19, Jan. 1837	17, Jan.	4m-20d	T2	
Tharp, Andrew	21, Apr. 1834		estate	T2	
Tharp, Sarah	8, June 1835	6, June	23	T2	
Thatcher, B.B.	25, July 1840		31	R3	
Thatcher, David	22, Jan. 1820	19, Jan.		S3	
Thayer, Charles	15, Feb. 1848	14, Feb.	7- 1m	K2	
Thayer, Mary Holbrook	8, Sept 1836	27, Aug.	11m- 3d	X3	
Theising, Theod.	8, Aug. 1850	Aug.	61	Y2	
Thers, Jacob	7, June 1849	June	38	L2	
Theurer, Jacob	28, June 1849	June	30	L2	
Thew, Abraham S.	28, Aug. 1827		probate	N3	
Thew, Abraham S.	7, Oct. 1824	3, Oct.		* E3	
Thistlewaite, James	28, May 1842	20, May		N2	

Name	Notice Date	Death Date	Age		Page	Maiden Name
Thom, Isaac	11, Aug. 1827	2, Aug.			R3	
Thom, Isaac	10, Aug. 1827	2, Aug.			N3	
Thomas, (Mr)	3, May 1838				N2	
Thomas, Ann	24, Oct. 1850	Oct.			Y2	
Thomas, Catherine	31, July 1850	July	18m		Y3	
Thomas, Cathrine E.	15, Aug. 1850	Aug.	1		Y2	
Thomas, Elizabeth Andrews	28, May 1842	21, May	6- 5m		R3	
Thomas, Isaiah	19, Apr. 1831		83		A3	
Thomas, James	19, Dec. 1804	11, Apr.	134		S3	
Thomas, John S.	30, Sept 1831	28, Sept		*	X3	
Thomas, Leah	1, June 1835		probate		N2	
Thomas, Levi	11, Dec. 1827		probate		N3	
Thomas, Sarah D.	18, Aug. 1852	14, Aug.	6- 3m		P2	
Thomas, Thomas (Rev)	14, Oct. 1831	9, Oct.	50		X3	
Thomas, William	18, July 1850	18, July	71	*	P2	
Thomas, William C.	4, June 1836		probate		N2	
Thomer, Margaret	30, July 1850	July	27		Y3	
Thompson, Asa E.	12, May 1841	8, May		*	N2	
Thompson, Benjamin F.	15, May 1849	14, May	33		L2	
Thompson, Charles	3, Sept 1824	17, Aug.	95		N3	
Thompson, Charles	19, Aug. 1828		probate		N3	
Thompson, Cornelia	16, June 1849	15, June	10w		L2	
Thompson, Ellen M.	28, July 1850	July	15m		Y3	
Thompson, John	15, Aug. 1840	11, Aug.	8		R3	
Thompson, John	15, Aug. 1840	Aug.	24		R3	
Thompson, Mary Ann	22, Oct. 1830	Oct.	33		N3	
Thompson, Mary Ann	20, Aug. 1830	Aug.	15m		N3	
Thompson, Michael	5, Jan. 1822		estate		S3	
Thompson, Rebecca	19, Sept 1828	Sept	65		N3	
Thompson, Sarah Ann	29, May 1841	27, May	15- 5m		R3	
Thompson, Sarah Ann	28, May 1841	27, May	15- 5m		N2	
Thompson, Susan H.	14, Jan. 1832	11, Jan.	24		R3	
Thompson, Susan H.	27, Jan. 1832	11, Jan.	34		X3	
Thompson, Thomas	2, Aug. 1834	July	40		R3	
Thompson, Thomas	29, July 1834	July	40		T2	
Thompson, Thomas	20, Mar. 1838		probate		N3	
Thompson, Thomas	5, June 1813	31, May			S3	
Thompson, William	25, Nov. 1828	Nov.	37		N3	
Thompson, William B.	22, Sept 1827	Sept	35		R3	
Thomson, George	14, July 1849	13, July	7		L2	
Thomson, Laura Bell	10, Aug. 1852	8, Aug.	5- 8m		P2	
Thomson, Michael	14, Oct. 1823		estate		N3	
Thomson, Michael	3, Dec. 1824		estate		N3	
Thomson, Patrick	15, Aug. 1835	14, Aug.	55		T2	
Thomson, Patrick	15, Aug. 1835	14, Aug.	55		N2	
Thomson, Thomas	10, Sept 1830	Sept	5		N3	
Thonien, Mary	28, July 1850	July	53		Y3	
Thorn, Alexander	29, Mar. 1849	Mar.	25		L2	
Thorndike, William	7, Sept 1824		probate		N3	
Thorndike, William	9, Sept 1824		probate		E3	
Thorne, Milton	21, Sept 1852	20, Sept	18m		P2	
Thornley, Alice	6, July 1849	July	8m		L2	
Thornton, Henry F.	19, Sept 1829	Sept	28		R3	
Thornton, Joseph	6, Feb. 1836		estate		T3	

Name	Notice Date	Death Date	Age	Page	Maiden Name
Thornton, Joseph	5, Mar. 1836		estate	T2	
Thornton, Joseph	28, July 1821	26, July		S3	
Thornton, Martha Elizabeth	29, Mar. 1849	28, Mar.	6	L2	
Thorp, Andrew	13, Apr. 1836		estate	N2	
Thorp, Ann	17, Feb. 1821	9, Feb.		S3	
Thorp, D. (heirs of)	7, Sept 1836		probate	N2	
Thorp, Daniel	19, July 1834	July	65	R3	
Thorp, David	13, Mar. 1829	Mar.	35	N3	
Thorp, David	22, Feb. 1836		estate	N2	
Thorp, Ezekiel	1, June 1833	31, May		R3	
Thorp, Ezekiel	12, Aug. 1815	10, Aug.		G3	
Thorp, Hannah J.	2, Aug. 1834	July	2- 4m	R3	
Thorp, Hannah J.	29, July 1834	July	2- 4m	T2	
Thorp, J.D. (heirs of)	18, May 1838		probate	N2	
Thorp, James	18, June 1830	June	53	N3	
Thorp, John D.	11, Nov. 1828	8, Nov.	42	N3	
Thorp, John D.	28, Nov. 1828		estate	N3	
Thorp, Mary E.	20, Mar. 1847	19, Mar.	5- 6m	K2	
Thorpe, Mercy	26, July 1834	July	23	R3	
Thorpe, Mercy	22, July 1834	July	23	T2	
Thorwell, Henry	6, Aug. 1830	Aug.	5	N3	
Threlkeld, Caroline	8, Jan. 1842	8, Jan.	3- 3m	R3	
Throckmorton, William M.	21, Feb. 1851	20, Feb.	7m	P2	
Thrusting, Sarah	1, July 1801		27	S3	
Tibben, Elizabeth	16, Oct. 1819		estate	S3	
Tibbets, Hannah	19, Aug. 1828	Aug.	4	N3	
Tibbets, Moses	22, Aug. 1828	Aug.	35	N3	
Tibbetts, Francis D.	24, Feb. 1829	Feb.	9m	N3	
Tibbetts, Thomas	3, Mar. 1827	2, Mar.		R3	
Tibbins, Elizabeth	7, Sept 1824		probate	N3	
Tibbins, Elizabeth	9, Sept 1824		probate	E3	
Tibbits, Nathaniel (Rev)	27, Aug. 1824	23, Aug.	34	N2	
Tibbs, Samuel	2, Aug. 1834	July	77	R3	
Tibbs, Samuel	11, July 1835		estate	T2	
Tibbs, Tamuel	29, July 1834	July	77	T2	
Tieber, (child of M.C.)	20, Aug. 1830	Aug.	stillborn	N3	
Tieber, Maria Cabar	20, Aug. 1830	Aug.	43	N3	
Tierney, Barney	12, Apr. 1849	Apr.	28	L2	
Tilden, Charlie	10, Dec. 1852	9, Dec.	17m- 1d	P2	
Tilghman, William	15, May 1827	29, Apr.	71	N2	
Tillinghast, Anna	2, May 1840	15, Apr.	73	R3	
Tillotson, Edward R.	24, July 1852	22, July	32	P2	
Tillotson, Joseph	7, Sept 1830		probate	N3	
Tilly, August	18, Aug. 1847	2, Aug.		* K2	
Tilly, Clara	18, Aug. 1847	3, Aug.	18	K2	
Tilton, William	19, June 1819	7, June		* S2	
Tilton, William P. (Col)	19, Nov. 1838	16, Oct.		N2	
Timmen, Jerry	23, July 1850	July	6m	Y2	
Tindell, Charles	15, Oct. 1830	Oct.	19	N3	
Tipton, Elizabeth	19, May 1847	18, May	68	K2	
Tipton, Matilda	16, June 1827	14, June		R3	
Tipton, Matilda S.	26, June 1827	14, June	16	N3	
Titus, Daniel	19, Nov. 1830	Nov.	47	N3	
Titus, Thomas	16, May 1836		estate	N3	

Name	Notice Date	Death Date	Age		Page	Maiden Name
Titus, Thomas	11, Sept 1837		probate		N2	
Tobin, Johanna	25, July 1850	July	20m		Y2	
Toby, Eliza	13, Mar. 1819	6, Mar.		*	S2	Cleghorn
Todd, (Mr)	3, Sept 1830	Aug.	22		N2	
Todd, S.	11, Feb. 1823		estate		N3	
Todd, Samuel	19, Aug. 1828		probate		N3	
Todd, Samuel	14, Sept 1822	7, Sept			S3	
Toddhunter, Thomas	10, July 1838	7, July			T2	
Tomlinson, J.C.	15, Sept 1838	9, Aug.		*	T2	
Tompkins, Bingham Cutler	13, Apr. 1832	10, Apr.	1-11m		X3	
Tompkins, Christopher	12, Apr. 1837	5, Apr.			T2	
Tompkins, Daniel D.	28, June 1825	11, June	51		N3	
Tompkins, George F.	17, June 1837		probate		N2	
Tompkins, Lois	23, May 1840	23, May	43		R3	
Toor, James	8, July 1828	July	14m		N3	
Torbert, Ellis Lewis	25, July 1840	19, July	18	*	R3	
Torbert, Simpson (Col)	27, Feb. 1838	23, Feb.		*	N2	
Torrence, John	22, Feb. 1808		estate		S3	
Torrence, John	19, July 1809		estate		H4	
Torrence, John	8, Feb. 1808	29, Jan.			S2	
Torrey, (Lt)	5, July 1794	30, June			C3	
Totten, Ann	21, Nov. 1817		estate		S2	
Tottrel, Harriet	14, Oct. 1828	Oct.	3		N3	
Toulman, Joseph	3, May 1825		probate		N3	
Tours, Abraham	25, Aug. 1829		probate		N3	
Tourtelot, Jesse	1, June 1835		probate		N2	
Touver, Martha A.	18, June 1830	June	9m		N3	
Towler, Edward	28, Aug. 1841	23, Aug.	18m-14d		R3	
Towler, Edward	27, Aug. 1841	23, Aug.	18m-14d		N2	
Towler, James Henry	7, June 1833	30, May	2- 4m		X3	
Towles, Henry B. (Lt)	6, Sept 1794	20, Aug.			C3	
Townsend, Francis Cooper	20, Aug. 1835	5, Aug.	8		T2	
Townsend, George Henry	15, July 1852	13, July	child		P2	
Townsend, Lydia	24, Mar. 1849	23, Mar.	52		L2	
Townsend, Mary Henrietta	26, May 1849	18, May	5- 2m		L2	
Townsend, Thomas	31, Aug. 1833	24, Aug.	67	*	R3	
Townsend, Thomas	8, Oct. 1824		estate		N3	
Townsend, Thomas	14, Dec. 1835		probate		N2	
Toy, Benjamin R.	16, Dec. 1852	12, Dec.	30		P2	
Tracy, George	19, Dec. 1834	26, Oct.	30		X3	
Tracy, William D.	10, July 1849	8, July	16		L2	
Tracy, William L.	7, Dec. 1837		probate		N3	
Trautman, (child of Peter)	3, May 1838		2-6m		N2	
Traverse, Scott	8, Mar. 1794	4, Mar.			C3	
Trazy, Moses	16, July 1830	July	3m		N3	
Trimble, Robert	6, Sept 1828	25, Aug.			R3	
Trimble, Robert	2, Sept 1828	25, Aug.			N3	
Trischler, Nicholas	14, June 1849	June	59		L2	
Troscell, Elizabeth	23, Sept 1831	Sept	20		A3	
Trow, George	9, Aug. 1841	Aug.	45		N2	
Truett, David	3, Apr. 1849	1, Apr.	20		L2	
Truman, Elizabeth Hotchkiss	28, July 1841	26, July	1		N3	
Truman, Elizabeth Hotchkiss	31, July 1841	26, July	10m		R3	
Tucker, Ephraim	10, Sept 1814		estate		S3	

Name	Notice Date	Death Date	Age		Page	Maiden Name
Tucker, John	6, May 1806		131		S3	
Tucker, Martin	8, June 1849	6, June	26	*	L2	
Tucker, Sarah	30, Sept 1824	3, Sept	25		E2	
Tucker, Sarah T.	11, Aug. 1827		1- 5m		R3	
Tucker, Thomas	31, Dec. 1830	Dec.	52		N3	
Tucker, William	25, 28, May 1830	22, May	50	*	N3	
Tucker, William	19, July 1834	July	77		R3	
Tudor, Elihu (Dr)	14, Apr. 1826	6, Mar.	93	*	N3	
Tudor, Rachel Ann	22, July 1841	16, July	13m		N2	
Tudor, Thomas	19, Feb. 1841				N2	
Tuite, Alicia	4, Aug. 1850	2, Aug.	25		Y2	
Tuite, William S.	19, July 1834	July	4m		R3	
Tull, Amelia	11, Nov. 1838	Nov.	3		N3	
Tull, Isaac (Rev)	29, May 1813	26, May			S3	
Tullis, Morgan	3, Dec. 1830	Nov.	1m		N3	
Tuma, Mary Ella	25, Dec. 1852	23, Dec.	3- 1m-11d		P2	
Turland, John	14, June 1849	June	29		L2	
Turner, Ann	31, Aug. 1833		estate		R3	
Turner, Ann Eliza Parkhouse	31, Aug. 1852	29, Aug.	17m-19d		P2	
Turner, Isaac	1, June 1835		probate		N2	
Turner, James	20, Apr. 1824	14, Apr.	45		N3	
Turner, James	22, Apr. 1824	14, Apr.	45	*	E3	
Turner, James P. (Dr)	8, Dec. 1852	7, Dec.	64		P2	
Turner, Jennet	18, June 1830	June	30		N3	
Turner, Thompson	29, July 1852	26, July	44		P2	
Turner, Willem	3, Apr. 1841	Mar.	35		R3	
Turner, William	1, June 1835		probate		N2	
Turney, (Capt)	25, Sept 1819	10, Sept			S3	
Turpen, Philip	9, Feb. 1835		estate		N2	
Turpin, Phillip	11, Sept 1837		probate		N2	
Turpin, Robert C.	13, Jan. 1848	22, Dec.	27		K2	
Turplin, Caroline	11, July 1822	3, July			J3	
Turrill, Jared	4, Oct. 1833	27, Sept	72	*	X3	
Turwell, Georgiana	17, Oct. 1850	Oct.	1m		Y2	
Tuxford, William	19, Mar. 1842	16, Mar.	44		R3	
Tuxford, William	18, Mar. 1842	16, Mar.	44		N2	
Twentyman, Kate	15, June 1850	14, June	14m- 4d		P2	
Twichell, Rebecca B.	31, Oct. 1840	8, Oct.	27		R3	
Tyler, Francis C.	28, July 1850	July	2		Y3	
Tyler, John J.	19, Sept 1850	Sept	5m		Y2	
Tyre, Whitfield	17, Oct. 1840	Oct.	35		R3	
Ulm, Dieterick	6, Nov. 1838		probate		N2	
Ulmer, (Gen)	31, Mar. 1826				N3	
Underwood, James	28, Oct. 1841	2, Oct.	40		N2	
Underwood, Sophia Amelia	9, Mar. 1837	5, Mar.	9- 3m		N2	
Union, Richard B.	18, May 1820		estate		S3	
Unvergayt, Catharine	6, July 1849	July	29		L2	
Upjohn, Sarah	6, June 1826	3, June			N3	
Urner, Nathan	19, Apr. 1836	2, Apr.			T2	
Urquhart, Mary	7, June 1828	June			R3	
Usher, Jane	4, Oct. 1852	2, Oct.			P2	
Vail, Jacob Stader	30, Aug. 1852	27, Aug.	16		P2	
Valentine, Aaron	30, July 1850	July	52		Y3	
Valentine, Aaron	15, Sept 1827	Sept	22m		R3	

Name	Notice Date	Death Date	Age		Page	Maiden Name
Valiant, Hugh	18, Sept 1847	13, Sept	63	*	K2	
Vallet, Peter	11, Dec. 1827		probate		N3	
Vallet, Peter	4, Oct. 1825	3, Oct.			N3	
Vallett, Benjamin	21, May 1830	May	17- 6m		N3	
Vallette, Henrietta	23, July 1842	15, July	27		R3	
Vallette, Henrietta	16, July 1842	15, July	27		N2	
Vanate, Simon W.	28, July 1850	July	2		Y3	
VanBuren, Jane	3, July 1838	19, June	59		T2	
Vance, James	17, Apr. 1835	8, Apr.	47		X3	
Vance, James	23, Nov. 1836		estate		N2	
Vance, James	27, July 1837		estate		N3	
Vance, James	8, May 1835		estate		X3	
Vance, James	18, May 1838		probate		N2	
Vanderlippi, R.C.H.	6, July 1849	July	59		L2	
VanDike, Andrew Heuston	30, Sept 1831	9, Sept	8- 3m		X3	
Vandyke, Dominicus	18, June 1814		estate		S3	
VanDyke, Nicholas	6, June 1826	21, May			N3	
Vanhooten, Peter	12, Aug. 1831	Aug.	78		A3	
VanHorne, Thomas B. (Col)	2, Oct. 1841	24, Sept	59	*	R3	
Vanhorne, William B.	26, July 1834	July	6m		R3	
Vanhorne, William B.	22, July 1834	July	6m		T2	
VanHouten, John P.	15, Jan. 1835		estate		N2	
VanHouten, Jolin P.	14, Dec. 1835		probate		N2	
Vanice, John	19, Aug. 1828		probate		N3	
Vanleer, Francis J.	16, July 1830	July	1		N3	
Vanmater, (child of S.W.)	2, Aug. 1834	July	8m		R3	
Vanmater, (child of S.W.)	29, July 1834	July	8m		T2	
VanMatre, John Henderson	28, May 1847	27, May	13m-15d		K2	
Vanmeter, Abraham	13, Mar. 1813		estate		S3	
Vannatta, Elizabeth	10, Dec. 1830	Dec.	1m		N3	
Vannerson, William Crawford	11, Sept 1819	3, Sept			S3	
Vanness, Garret	12, Feb. 1814		estate		S3	
VanNess, William	1, Apr. 1823	28, Feb.			N2	
VanNess, William P.	22, Sept 1826				N3	
Vannice, John	19, Dec. 1826		probate		N3	
Vannice, John	11, Dec. 1827		probate		N3	
Vannice, Phebe	14, Dec. 1835		probate		N2	
Vanniel, John	3, May 1825		probate		N3	
Vanor, Jonathan	9, Dec. 1828	Dec.	32		N3	
VanPelt, Pierce	21, Dec. 1838	15, Dec.	24	*	N2	
Vansickle, Ralph	7, Sept 1836		probate		N2	
Vansickle, Ralph	7, Dec. 1837		probate		N3	
VanSickle, Sarah	19, Feb. 1835	12, Feb.	39		N2	
Vansicklen, Mary Jane	14, Dec. 1852	11, Dec.	18		P2	
Vantavoren, Jacob	14, Oct. 1828	Oct.	4		N3	
VanWaters, Isaac	15, Sept 1827	Sept	30		R3	
Vanzant, (child of R.)	24, Sept 1830	Sept	1- 6m		N3	
Varick, Richard (Col)	16, Sept 1831	30, July	79		X3	
Vatchett, Isaac	29, May 1851	23, May		*	P2	
Vattier, Charles	9, Mar. 1841	6, Mar.			N2	
Vattier, Margareta S.	19, May 1832	9, May	22		R3	
Vattier, William	20, Aug. 1850	17, Aug.	3- 6m		Y2	
Vaughn, Claiborne	27, July 1852	6, July	38		P2	
Venaman, Joseph	5, Apr. 1830	22, Mar.			A3	

Name	Notice Date	Death Date	Age		Page	Maiden Name
Vennice, Cornelius	23, Mar. 1830		probate		N3	
Vennice, John	23, Mar. 1830		probate		N3	
Vestal, John	28, Nov. 1804		estate		S3	
Veteas, Sarah	19, July 1834	July	25		R3	
Vickers, Benajmin	12, Aug. 1835	29, May		*	T2	
Vickers, James	20, Oct. 1821	19, Oct.			S3	
Vincent, Bartlet C.	23, Mar. 1830		probate		N3	
Vinton, Lucy	11, Aug. 1827	8, Aug.	27	*	R3	
Vinton, Romaine M.	24, June 1831	21, May	29		A3	Bureau
Vinton, Romaine M.	28, May 1831	21, May	29		R3	Bureau
Virgin, Thomas	1, Oct. 1830		estate		N3	
Vogel, Catharine	8, Aug. 1850	Aug.			Y2	
VonEichthal, William	28, Dec. 1847	27, Dec.			K2	
Voorhees, Abraham	4, Apr. 1837		probate		N2	
Voorhees, Jacob	1, Feb. 1828		estate		N3	
Voorhees, Sarah P.	3, July 1841	27, June	35		R3	
Voorhees, Sarah P.	29, June 1841	17, June	35		N2	
Voorhees, William Henry H.	22, Feb. 1841	18, Feb.	4m		N2	
Voorheese, Cornelius	11, Dec. 1805		estate		S3	
Voorheese, Cornelius	12, Jan. 1807		estate		S3	
Voorheese, Cornelius	27, Nov. 1805	20, Nov.			S3	
Voorheese, Ralph	7, Mar. 1828	5, Mar.			N2	
Voorheese, Ralph M.	7, Mar. 1828	5, Mar.			Q3	
Waas, Henry	13, July 1849	July	54		L2	
Wacks, Caroline	5, Sept 1828	Sept	21		N3	
Wade, David E.	30, July 1842		estate		R3	
Wade, David E. (Mrs)	4, May 1811	28, Apr.			S3	
Wade, Harriet Ramsay	4, June 1842	18, May	child		R3	
Wade, Mary C.	22, Apr. 1825	20, Apr.			N2	
Waggoner, Christina	14, June 1849	June	32		L2	
Waggoner, J.	23, Sept 1831	Sept	20		A3	
Wagner, (child of Catharine)	8, Oct. 1852	Oct.	2d		P2	
Wagner, Charles	26, July 1834	July	2		R3	
Wagner, Charles	22, July 1834	July			T2	
Wagner, Margaret	26, July 1834	July	24		R3	
Wagner, Margaret	22, July 1834	July	24		T2	
Wahlors, Rebecca	21, June 1849	June	34		L2	
Waide, Henry	28, Nov. 1826	21, Nov.	69	*	N3	
Wainwright, R.D. (Col)	16, Oct. 1841	11, Oct.			R3	
Wait, Mary	8, Mar. 1838		estate		N3	
Waitmer, Gerhard B.	23, July 1850	July	8m		Y2	
Waits, William	10, Dec. 1830	Dec.	22		N3	
Wakefield, Andrew	21, Dec. 1830		probate		N3	
Waldeck, Matthew H.	29, Oct. 1830	Oct.	6		N3	
Walden, Reuben	13, Sept 1828	27, Aug.	49	*	R3	
Walden, Reuben	5, Sept 1828	Sept	49		N3	
Walden, Reuben	25, Aug. 1837		estate		N3	
Walden, Reuben	23, Mar. 1830		probate		N3	
Waldron, Isaac	21, Jan. 1832		estate		R3	
Waldron, Joseph	8, Aug. 1818	4, Aug.			S3	
Waldsmith, Christian	16, Apr. 1814		estate		S3	
Wales, Henry H.	25, Apr. 1838	22, Apr.	2m-15d		T2	
Wales, John W.	25, Apr. 1838	22, Apr.	28		T2	
Wales, Thomas	27, Feb. 1829	Feb.	59		N3	

Name	Notice Date	Death Date	Age		Page	Maiden Name
Walker, (boy)	20, Oct. 1827	Oct.	9m		R3	
Walker, Alfred	17, June 1837		probate		N2	
Walker, Ann	18, Dec. 1819	17, Dec.			S3	
Walker, Ann Eliza	1, Nov. 1836	31, Oct.			N2	
Walker, Anna L.	1, Nov. 1834	7, Oct.	24		R3	
Walker, Anna L.	30, Oct. 1834	7, Oct.	24	*	T2	
Walker, Benjamin	19, Sept 1840	7, Sept	30		R3	
Walker, Bryant	9, Aug. 1836	6, Aug.			T2	
Walker, Christopher	13, May 1841	9, May	84	*	N2	
Walker, Christopher	15, May 1841	9, May	84	*	R3	
Walker, Dan	29, Sept 1852	27, Sept	37	*	P2	
Walker, David	9, Sept 1825		probate		N3	
Walker, Davis Lawler	1, Nov. 1834	27, Oct.	17d		R3	
Walker, Davis Lawler	30, Oct. 1834	27, Oct.	17d		T2	
Walker, George	14, July 1832		estate		R3	
Walker, George	4, June 1836		probate		N2	
Walker, James	1, Aug. 1828	July	20		N3	
Walker, James	11, Dec. 1827		probate		N3	
Walker, James (Col)	20, Jan. 1829		55		N3	
Walker, Jesse	11, Nov. 1838	Nov.	33		N3	
Walker, Jesse	31, Oct. 1828	29, Oct.	35		N2	
Walker, Louisa	24, July 1830	21, July	infant		R3	
Walker, Martha E.	30, Jan. 1841	22, Jan.			R3	
Walker, Martha E.	24, Jan. 1841	23, Jan.			N2	
Walker, Mary	6, Dec. 1831	22, Sept	8		A3	
Walker, Mary	28, June 1849	June	25		L2	
Walker, Mary	20, Aug. 1830	Aug.	84		N3	
Walker, Thomas Bryant	9, Aug. 1836	6, Aug.	4		N2	
Walker, Thomas Bryant	18, Aug. 1836	6, Aug.	4		X3	
Walker, Washington	8, Oct. 1841	Oct.	26		N2	
Wallace, Deborah	28, July 1815	19, July	33		S3	
Wallace, Edith	23, Apr. 1831	18, Apr.			R3	
Wallace, Harriet Scott	31, July 1813	24, July	16		S3	
Wallace, Helen	12, Aug. 1828	Aug.	1- 3m		N3	
Wallace, James	11, Nov. 1838	Nov.	9m		N3	
Wallace, James P. (Capt)	29, Sept 1826				Q3	
Wallace, Jane	17, Sept 1852	16, Sept	27		P2	
Wallace, Jane	18, Sept 1852	14, Sept	76		P2	
Wallace, John S.	18, Aug. 1821	15, Aug.	17		S3	
Wallace, John S. (Col)	2, Aug. 1836	1, Aug.			N2	
Wallace, Mary	9, June 1836	2, June	19		X3	
Wallace, Mary J.	12, Aug. 1831	Aug.	2- 7m		A3	
Wallace, Moses	19, July 1834	July	40		R3	
Wallace, Rebecca	14, Dec. 1835		probate		N2	
Wallace, Robert	5, Sept 1828	Sept	95		N3	
Wallace, Samuel	24, Oct. 1818	22, Oct.		*	S3	
Wallis, Casandra	1, Dec. 1821	14, Nov.		*	S3	
Wallow, Ann	23, July 1850	July	3		Y2	
Walls, Edwin Sargent	28, Dec. 1852	25, Dec.	4- 3m		P2	
Walls, John	18, Dec. 1841		estate		N2	
Walls, John	5, Jan. 1842		estate		N3	
Walsh, Barnard	31, July 1850	July	2		Y3	
Walter, Frank	1, Apr. 1847	30, Mar.	infant		K2	
Walter, Ira	1, July 1828	June	8		N3	

Name	Notice Date	Death Date	Age		Page	Maiden Name
Walter, Thomas	7, Feb. 1795	2, Feb.			C3	
Walton, Thomas	28, June 1849	27, June	37		L2	
Wandall, Julia	21, June 1833	17, June	6		X3	
Wappenburgh, Henry	7, June 1849	June	35		L2	
Ward, Asa	27, June 1849	26, June	65	*	L2	
Ward, Edward (Col)	10, Jan. 1838	22, Dec.			T2	
Ward, George	23, Oct. 1847	21, Oct.		*	K2	
Ward, Lewis B.	7, May 1830	May	27		N3	
Ward, Nathaniel	13, Aug. 1830	Aug.	2- 8m		N3	
Ward, Sarah	30, July 1830	July	7m		N3	
Ward, William	18, July 1828	July	18m		N3	
Warden, Charles Augustus	2, June 1847	1, June	7m		K2	
Ware, Emily	30, Aug. 1842	27, Aug.	21		N2	
Warner, Francis Maria	10, July 1852	8, July	17m- 2d		P2	
Warner, Sarah C.	13, Oct. 1815	4, Oct.			S3	
Warnes, Azariah C.	2, Aug. 1834	July	36		R3	
Warnes, Azariah C.	29, July 1834	July	36		T2	
Warnock, James	28, Oct. 1835		estate		N4	
Warnock, James	17, June 1837		probate		N2	
Warrior, Big	5, Apr. 1825	8, Mar.			N3	
Warwick, Robert	1, June 1835		probate		N2	
Washburn, Calvin	12, Oct. 1835	9, Oct.	58		T2	
Washburn, Calvin	10, Oct. 1835	9, Oct.	58		N2	
Washburn, Calvin	16, Dec. 1835		estate		N3	
Washburn, F.W. (Rev)	30, Oct. 1852	22, Oct.	31		P2	
Washburn, Warren	23, July 1830	July	1- 3m		N3	
Washington, (Mrs)	12, June 1802	22, May			S3	
Washington, Ann	6, July 1849	July	50		L2	
Washington, George (Gen)	7, Jan. 1800	14, Dec.			S3	
Washington, Lucinda	11, June 1842	June	31		R3	
Washington, Theodore H.	18, Jan. 1842	15, Jan.	7m-21d		N2	
Washington, William Augustine	3, Nov. 1810		53		S3	
Waters, Caroline	26, Dec. 1840	Dec.	6		R3	
Waters, Daniel	10, Sept 1830	Sept	24		N3	
Waters, Mary Ann	10, July 1829	4, July	21	*	N3	
Waters, Polly	21, May 1830	May	30- 7m		N3	
Watkins, (Mr)	3, May 1838				N2	
Watkins, Elizabeth	19, Aug. 1831	Aug.	14m		A3	
Watson, (child of Elizabeth)	25, Nov. 1828	Nov.	stillborn		N3	
Watson, Benjamin (Capt)	6, Oct. 1827	4, Oct.			R3	
Watson, Benjamin (Major)	5, Oct. 1827	4, Oct.			N3	
Watson, Charlotte	5, Sept 1828	Sept	15m		N3	
Watson, E.Y. (Dr)	20, Oct. 1847	17, Oct.		*	K2	
Watson, Francis	28, Apr. 1835	21, Apr.			T3	
Watson, James	25, Dec. 1852	19, Dec.	25		P2	
Watson, James	3, Apr. 1813		estate		S3	
Watson, John	24, June 1823		estate		N3	
Watson, John	1, July 1823		estate		N3	
Watson, John	19, Aug. 1828		probate		N3	
Watson, John	4, Aug. 1821	15, July			S3	
Watson, Luman	9, Dec. 1834		estate		T3	
Watson, Luman	4, June 1836		probate		N2	
Watson, Luman	21, Sept 1838		probate		N3	
Watson, Margaret A.	12, Aug. 1831	Aug.	1- 4m		A3	

Name	Notice Date	Death Date	Age	Page	Maiden Name
Watson, Mary	10, Apr. 1829	Apr.	20	N3	
Watson, Sarah	22, Mar. 1841	20, Mar.	44	N2	
Watson, William	9, Sept 1831	Sept	11	A3	
Watt, James	27, Nov. 1819		84	S3	
Watt, Robert	3, May 1838			N2	
Watt, Thomas	3, May 1838			N2	
Watts, William	30, July 1850	July	12	Y3	
Wauby, John	2, Jan. 1841	Dec.	28	R3	
Waver, Jacob	3, May 1838			N2	
Weakly, Luella M.	30, Mar. 1847	27, Mar.	8- 4m- 2d	K2	
Weatherby, Jane	24, Dec. 1852	22, Dec.	84	P2	
Weaver, David	4, Feb. 1835		estate	N2	
Weaver, David	18, Feb. 1837		estate	N2	
Weaver, David	1, June 1835		probate	N2	
Weaver, David	14, Dec. 1835		probate	N2	
Weaver, Isabella	21, July 1852	16, July	infant	P2	
Weaver, William	8, May 1802		estate	S3	
Webb, Cecelia E.	28, Dec. 1852	26, Dec.	22- 4m- 6d	P2	
Webb, Lucinda	1, Aug. 1828	July	15m	N3	
Webb, Stephen	7, Sept 1836		probate	N2	
Webb, Thomas S.	7, Aug. 1819			S3	
Webb, William	13, July 1849	July	24	L2	
Webb, William	17, Sept 1835		probate	T2	
Webb, William	6, Oct. 1826		probate	N3	
Webb, William H.	20, Oct. 1838	17, Oct.	9m	N2	
Webber, David	4, June 1836		probate	N2	
Weber, David	12, Dec. 1835		estate	N2	
Weber, David (Capt)	10, Oct. 1835	8, Oct.	62	T2	
Weber, David (Capt)	10, Oct. 1835	8, Oct.	62	N2	
Webster, Amelia	2, Sept 1835	20, Aug.	50	T2	
Webster, Elvira	2, Sept 1835	24, Aug.	1-11m	T2	
Webster, George	18, Mar. 1823	22, Feb.	62	N3	
Webster, Ralph	11, Dec. 1827		probate	N3	
Wechrell, Charles	21, May 1830	May	42	N3	
Wedilin, Charlotte	17, Apr. 1841	Apr.	10w	R3	
Weed, Edward Payson	17, Aug. 1837	11, Aug.	10m- 8d	X3	
Weeks, Sebastian	24, Oct. 1828	Oct.	9m	N2	
Weems, Mason L. (Rev)	22, July 1825	23, May		N3	
Weilel, Adam	13, July 1849	9, July	46	L2	
Weiner, John	25, July 1840	July	65	R3	
Weir, James	31, July 1850	30, July	86	Y2	
Weisch, John	31, Oct. 1850	Oct.	28	Y2	
Welch, Catharine	26, July 1850	July	45	Y2	
Wellen, Anna	23, July 1850	July	64	Y2	
Weller, Anna E.	26, Aug. 1836	12, Aug.	22	T2	
Weller, John (Mrs)	5, Mar. 1842	22, Feb.		R3	
Weller, John (Mrs)	26, Feb. 1842			N2	
Weller, Samuel C.	13, July 1849	July	24	L2	
Wells, (child of J.)	12, Aug. 1831	Aug.	3m	A3	
Wells, Benjamin	15, Nov. 1833	11, Nov.	22	X3	
Wells, Darius	28, Jan. 1825	24, Jan.	*	N3	
Wells, Darius	27, Jan. 1825	24, Jan.		E3	
Wells, Fredericka	17, June 1851	13, June	21	P2	
Wells, John	30, Sept 1823	7, Sept		N3	

Name	Notice Date	Death Date	Age		Page	Maiden Name
Wells, Maria B.	17, June 1835	14, June	27		T2	
Wells, Maria B.D.	18, June 1835	14, June	27		N2	Duncan
Welow, Elizabeth	23, July 1850	July	7		Y2	
Welsh, Edward	12, Sept 1850	Sept	48		Y2	
Welsh, J.	22, Aug. 1850	Aug.	23		Y2	
Welsh, James (Rev)	18, Nov. 1825	1, Nov.	50		N2	
Welsh, Michael	14, June 1849	June	2w		L2	
Welsh, Patrick	23, Apr. 1849	Apr.	25		L2	
Welsh, Patrick	13, July 1849	July	27		L2	
Wendal, Mary	27, Feb. 1829	Feb.	6m		N3	
Wentworth, John	22, Mar. 1837		estate		N3	
Wert, Elnathan	17, June 1837		probate		N2	
Wescott, James	19, Aug. 1828		probate		N3	
Wescott, William	14, Dec. 1824		probate		N3	
Wescott, William	16, Dec. 1824		probate		E3	
Wesset, Elizabeth	2, Aug. 1834	July	6m		R3	
Wesset, Elizabeth	29, July 1834	July	6m		T2	
West, (Mr)	26, Feb. 1836				T3	
West, Elisha	3, Dec. 1830	Nov.	48		N3	
West, Elisha	27, Nov. 1830	23, Nov.	50	*	R3	
West, Harriet	18, July 1828	July	33		N3	
West, Rebecca	7, June 1828	June			R3	
West, Rebecca	3, June 1828				N2	
West, Rebecca	6, June 1828	1, June			Q3	
West, William	12, Aug. 1831	Aug.	29		A3	
Westcoat, James	25, Mar. 1823		estate		N4	
Westcot, John	4, June 1830	June	63		N3	
Westcott, Hampton (Lt)	23, May 1837				T2	
Westcott, Mary	19, May 1847	25, Apr.			K2	Espy
Westerfield, Frances Jane	7, May 1842	30, Apr.	22m		R3	
Western, George	6, Dec. 1838		estate		N2	
Westlake, Robert	21, Dec. 1830		probate		N3	
Wetherbee, M.M.	23, 24, July 1850	22, July	32		Y2	
Wetherby, (child of Daniel)	21, May 1830	May	stillborn		N3	
Wetmore, Julia	23, Jan. 1835	20, Jan.			X3	Dexter
Whalin, Job	10, May 1849	May	39		L2	
Whallon, R.H.	4, June 1836		probate		N2	
Wheatcroft, William	22, July 1824	27, June			E3	
Wheeler, Arabella Julia	21, Mar. 1836	20, Mar.			N2	
Wheeler, Daniel	27, June 1840	12, June	70	*	R3	
Wheeler, George	27, Feb. 1829	Feb.			N3	
Wheeler, George N.	17, Dec. 1799		estate		S3	
Wheeler, John	21, Mar. 1818		estate		S3	
Wheeler, Julia Elizabeth	11, June 1842	11, June			R3	
Wheeler, Julia Elizabeth	9, June 1842	8, June			N2	
Wheeler, Stephen	2, Feb. 1807		estate		S3	
Wheeler, Worham	20, Aug. 1834	17, Aug.	42	*	T2	
Wheelock, Charles	26, Apr. 1831	18, Apr.	3		A3	
Wheelock, John	23, May 1817	11, Apr.	68		S3	
Whetsel, Jacob (Capt)	14, July 1827	2, July	63		R3	
Whetstone, David	18, July 1828	July	10		N3	
Whetstone, John	18, Dec. 1841	13, Dec.	43	*	R3	
Whetstone, John	14, Dec. 1841	13, Dec.	43	*	N2	
Whetstone, Mary Maria	1, Aug. 1828	July	3- 6m		N3	

Name	Notice Date	Death Date	Age		Page	Maiden Name
Whetstone, Reuben	5, Sept 1828		estate		N3	
Whetstone, Susan Prince	8, Jan. 1836	6, Jan.	17		T3	
Whieman, Catharine	28, Jan. 1832	22, Jan.			R3	
Whipple, Pardon M. (Lt)	16, June 1827		37		R3	
Whipple, Sumner	17, Sept 1830		estate		N3	
Whistler, John (Major)	23, Oct. 1829	21, Oct.			N3	
Whitaker, John	12, June 1849	10, May	29		L2	
Whitcomb, John	8, Aug. 1840	Aug.	10		R3	
White, (child of Elizabeth)	26, July 1834	July	2		R3	
White, (child of Elizabeth)	22, July 1834	July	2		T2	
White, Adelaide	2, Sept 1835	1, Sept			N2	
White, Alonzo Eliphalet	14, Jan. 1851	26, Dec.	13m		P2	
White, Amos	8, June 1820		estate		S3	
White, Clement	27, Sept 1838	26, Sept	22		T2	
White, Eleanor E.	12, Sept 1828	Sept	4m		N3	
White, Elisha	2, Dec. 1834	28, Nov.	24	*	T2	
White, Elizabeth	21, Sept 1820	16, Sept	18	*	S3	
White, Emmeline E.	6, Sept 1841	12, Aug.		*	N2	
White, Hannah	8, Feb. 1840	5, Feb.	91		R3	
White, Helen M.	5, Oct. 1837	27, Jan.	24		X3	Wells
White, Henry	27, Sept 1834	8, Sept		*	R3	
White, Henry	25, Sept 1834	8, Sept		*	T2	
White, Jacob	21, Oct. 1823		estate		N3	
White, Jacob	16, Dec. 1825		probate		N3	
White, Jacob	19, Dec. 1826		probate		N3	
White, James A.	1, Aug. 1850	July	14m		Y2	
White, Joseph	17, Sept 1835		probate		T2	
White, Joseph (Col)	9, Nov. 1839	19, Oct.			R3	
White, Kate	4, Nov. 1852	1, Nov.	4- 8m-14d		P2	
White, Margaret	19, July 1834	July	35		R3	
White, Martha	9, Aug. 1841	4, Aug.			N2	
White, Mary Elizabeth	6, June 1840		8m		R3	
White, R.H.	16, June 1849	15, June			L2,3	
White, Samuel	18, Nov. 1841	30, Oct.	84	*	N2	
White, William (Rev)	26, July 1836	25, July	88	*	N2	
White, William McClure	17, Mar. 1841	13, Mar.	7m-10d		N2	
Whiteman, Benjamin (Gen)	5, July 1852		84		P2	
Whiteman, Catharine	25, Sept 1852	21, Sept	81		P2	
Whiteman, Jane Findlay	13, May 1847	11, May	43		K2	
Whiteman, Louisa J.	3, Nov. 1832	30, Oct.			R3	
Whiteside, Marshall	31, Aug. 1847	22, Aug.	18m		K2	
Whiteside, William	31, Aug. 1847	24, Aug.	2m		K2	
Whiting, Indiana Bel	6, June 1849	25, May		*	L2	Sanford
Whitley, James	9, July 1852	8, July			P2	
Whitman, Josiah (Dr)	23, Oct. 1838	22, Oct.	42	*	T2	
Whitman, Josiah (Dr)	1, Nov. 1838	22, Oct.	44	*	N2	
Whitman, Josiah (Dr)	25, Oct. 1838	22, Oct.		*	N2	
Whitney, Ely	1, Feb. 1825	8, Jan.	59		N3	
Whitney, Lucia M.	28, June 1849	June	42		L2	
Whitney, Thomas	21, Aug. 1819	6, Aug.			S3	
Whittaker, Charles	25, June 1830	June	7		N3	
Whittemore, N.M.	14, Dec. 1835		probate		N2	
Wicker, Lawrence S.	29, June 1847	28, June	42		K2	
Wickliffe, Benjamin Howard	15, June 1838	June			T2	

Name	Notice Date	Death Date	Age		Page	Maiden Name
Wicks, Sarah Jane	12, Aug. 1828	Aug.	1- 6m		N3	
Wickwire, Jerome	12, Aug. 1831	Aug.	2- 6m		A3	
Wienhold, Henry	14, June 1849	June	51		L2	
Wier, James	1, Aug. 1850	July	85		Y2	
Wieser, Edward	30, July 1842	29, July	3m-11d		M2	
Wiggins, Thomas	24, Oct. 1823		estate		N2	
Wigham, William	19, Jan. 1827		estate		Q3	
Wigham, William	22, Dec. 1829		probate		N3	
Wigham, William	21, Dec. 1830		probate		N3	
Wight, Robert	20, June 1818		estate		S3	
Wilber, John C.	24, July 1850	July	6		Y2	
Wild, Henry	5, Sept 1836		estate		N2	
Wildon, James	21, June 1849	June	45		L2	
Wiles, William M.	25, Apr. 1837	22, Apr.	50		N2	
Wiley, Ann	9, Jan. 1841	27, Dec.			R3	
Wiley, John	9, Jan. 1841	27, Dec.			R3	
Wiley, Mary	9, Jan. 1841	3, Jan.			R3	
Wiley, William	16, July 1830	July	46		N3	
Wilkins, Andrew A.	2, Aug. 1842	1, Aug.	49	*	M3	
Wilkins, Charles	22, Sept 1827	15, Sept			R3	
Wilkins, Hannah	1, Aug. 1828	July	35		N3	
Wilkinson, Ann	3, Apr. 1807	25, Feb.			S3	
Wilkinson, Jemima	14, Aug. 1819		66	*	S4	
Wilkinson, Samuel D.	1, Jan. 1853	29, Dec.	24	*	P2	
Wilkinson, William	24, Apr. 1813	12, Feb.	28		S3	
Wilkson, Andrew	2, July 1830	June	36		N2	
Willard, Janette	19, Oct. 1850	18, Oct.			Y2	
Willard, Martin	16, Jan. 1829	Jan.	6m		N2	
Willard, Samuel	19, Feb. 1820	16, Feb.	54	*	S2	
Willard, Samuel (Dr)	17, Feb. 1820	16, Feb.	54	*	D3	
Willard, Susan	7, Dec. 1847	5, Dec.			K2	
Willcox, P.L.	4, Oct. 1794		estate		C3	
Willet, Marinus (Col)	3, Sept 1830		91		N2	
Willet, Samuel	6, Feb. 1827		estate		N3	
Willey, Allen	20, Apr. 1835	19, Apr.	75	*	T3	
Willey, Hannah	18, Dec. 1813	14, Dec.			S3	
Willey, Hosea	4, Dec. 1829		estate		N3	
Willey, Hosea	21, Dec. 1830		probate		N3	
Willey, Israel	18, Apr. 1828		estate		N3	
Willey, Israel	6, Mar. 1829		estate		N3	
Willey, Israel	21, Dec. 1830		probate		N3	
Williams,	24, Aug. 1852	23, Aug.	2		P2	
Williams, (child of E.D.)	6, Mar. 1829	Mar.	2m		N2	
Williams, (child of J.S.)	23, July 1830	July	2m		N3	
Williams, (child of James S.)	6, Feb. 1829	Feb.	stillborn		N2	
Williams, (child of S.)	26, July 1850	July	4		Y2	
Williams, (heirs of A.)	14, Dec. 1835		probate		N2	
Williams, A.	22, Jan. 1830		estate		N3	
Williams, Abraham	31, July 1829		estate		N3	
Williams, Abraham	21, Dec. 1830		probate		N3	
Williams, Adelaide	6, Sept 1833	Sept	23		X3	
Williams, Allen	28, Nov. 1828	Nov.	1- 3m		N3	
Williams, Anne	18, July 1828	13, July	52		N3	
Williams, Benjamin	15, May 1841	May	22		R3	

Name	Notice Date	Death Date	Age	Page	Maiden Name
Williams, Caroline Louise	27, Nov. 1852	25, Nov.	2-10m-13d	P2	
Williams, Catharine	15, Nov. 1816	7, Nov.		S3	
Williams, Charity	25, Jan. 1840	18, Jan.	88	* R3	
Williams, Charlotte C.	19, Aug. 1831	Aug.	21	A3	
Williams, David	9, Sept 1831	2, Sept	77	A3	
Williams, Effy	2, Oct. 1813	26, Sept		S3	
Williams, Elmore W.	24, Dec. 1830	20, Dec.	32	N3	
Williams, Elmore W.	24, Dec. 1830	Dec.	32	N3	
Williams, Ephraim L.	28, Nov. 1818	26, Nov.		* S3	
Williams, Frank Carrall	15, Mar. 1839	13, Mar.	infant	T2	
Williams, George F.	27, Aug. 1830	Aug.		N3	
Williams, Halsey	3, May 1838			N2	
Williams, Hannah	30, July 1850	July	43	Y3	
Williams, Henry M.	23, Dec. 1852	21, Dec.	2- -23d	P2	
Williams, J.	3, May 1838			N2	
Williams, Jacob	11, July 1840	8, July	66	R3	
Williams, Jacob	25, July 1840		estate	R3	
Williams, Jacob	19, Sept 1840		estate	R3	
Williams, Jacob	23, July 1842		estate	R3	
Williams, James	8, Aug. 1840	Aug.	56	R3	
Williams, Joel	2, Oct. 1829		estate	N3	
Williams, Joel	11, Dec. 1827		probate	N3	
Williams, Joel	19, Aug. 1828		probate	N3	
Williams, Joel	23, Mar. 1830		probate	N3	
Williams, Joel	4, Nov. 1824	29, Oct.		E3	
Williams, John	9, July 1830	July	34	N3	
Williams, John	9, Apr. 1814		estate	S3	
Williams, John T.	26, July 1834	July	36	R3	
Williams, John T.	22, July 1834	July	36	T2	
Williams, Joshua	15, Dec. 1836		estate	N2	
Williams, Joshua	20, Mar. 1838		probate	N3	
Williams, Laura	20, July 1852	18, July	4- 9m-19d	P2	
Williams, Lewis	10, Sept 1824	3, Sept	18	N2	
Williams, Martha Ann	27, Aug. 1836	26, Aug.		N2	
Williams, Mary	30, July 1830	July	1- 6m	N3	
Williams, Mary Jane	21, Oct. 1852	20, Oct.	2- 7m-22d	P2	
Williams, Matilda	17, May 1849	May	35	L2	
Williams, Peter	11, Mar. 1837	23, Feb.	67	R3	
Williams, Peter	9, Mar. 1837	23, Feb.	67	T2	
Williams, Peter	9, Mar. 1837	23, Feb.	67	N2	
Williams, Peter	21, Sept 1838		probate	N3	
Williams, Phoebe	6, Nov. 1819	26, Oct.		S3	
Williams, Robert (Dr)	7, Nov. 1840	12, Oct.	83	R3	
Williams, Samuel	10, Dec. 1825	3, Dec.	73	* N3	
Williams, Sarah	27, Feb. 1829	Feb.	48	N3	
Williams, Thomas	6, Nov. 1838		probate	N2	
Williams, William H.	12, Aug. 1831	Aug.	1- -6d	A3	
Williams, Zephorah	23, July 1830	July	7m	N3	
Williamson, (child of J.)	16, Jan. 1829	Jan.	stillborn	N2	
Williamson, George	29, July 1825		47	N3	
Williamson, J.D.	9, Dec. 1828		probate	N3	
Williamson, Jacob D.	22, Dec. 1829		probate	N3	
Williamson, John G.A.	12, Sept 1840	7, Aug.	50	R3	
Williamson, Martha	28, June 1828		59	R3	

Name	Notice Date	Death Date	Age		Page	Maiden Name
Williamson, Morris	28, Dec. 1820		estate		S3	
Willington, Perry	2, Jan. 1841	Dec.	24		R3	
Willis, Edwin	24, Oct. 1850	Oct.	30		Y2	
Willis, Mary	20, Aug. 1850	18, Aug.			Y2	
Willsey, Henry	14, Dec. 1836		estate		N2	
Willsey, Henry	6, Nov. 1838		probate		N2	
Willson, William	4, June 1836		probate		N2	
Wilmers, John	21, June 1849	June	32		L2	
Wilson, (child of A.)	12, Aug. 1831	Aug.	7m		A3	
Wilson, (man)	27, Nov. 1852	24, Nov.			P2	
Wilson, Abraham	6, Oct. 1826		probate		N3	
Wilson, Amanda L.	31, Oct. 1826	20, Oct.	22		N3	
Wilson, Arva (Dr)	21, June 1833	28, May		*	X3	
Wilson, Charles	15, Aug. 1850	Aug.	3		Y2	
Wilson, David	31, Aug. 1822		estate		S3	
Wilson, David	5, Sept 1823		estate		N3	
Wilson, David	9, Jan. 1824		estate		N3	
Wilson, David	4, Mar. 1828		probate		N3	
Wilson, Elizabeth	12, June 1841	June	4m		N2	
Wilson, Elsy Melvine	30, July 1831	19, July			R3	
Wilson, Emeline	9, Sept 1831	Sept	2- 7m-15d		A3	
Wilson, Frances	13, June 1836	7, June	4		T2	
Wilson, George C.	4, Aug. 1841	20, July			N2	
Wilson, George J.	25, Nov. 1828	Nov.	4w		N3	
Wilson, George M.	26, Aug. 1825	28, July			N3	
Wilson, Hugh (Capt)	12, Sept 1826	17, Sept	42		N3	
Wilson, James	13, July 1849	July	43		L2	
Wilson, James	4, Sept 1838	29, Aug.	50		T2	
Wilson, James	9, Feb. 1841	5, Feb.	78	*	N2	
Wilson, Joseph	19, Oct. 1839	13, Oct.	21	*	R3	
Wilson, Joseph J.	2, Aug. 1834	July	33		R3	
Wilson, Joseph J.	29, July 1834	July	33		T2	
Wilson, Miletus	27, Aug. 1830	Aug.	29		N3	
Wilson, Nancy Johnston	25, June 1849	23, June	29		L2	
Wilson, P. (Rev)	30, July 1799				S3	
Wilson, Peter (Rev)	3, Dec. 1799		estate		S3	
Wilson, Peter (Rev)	6, Aug. 1799	24, July			S2	
Wilson, Robert	4, Jan. 1794		estate		C3	
Wilson, Ruth	1, Aug. 1828	July	52		N3	
Wilson, Sarah	4, June 1836		probate		N2	
Wilson, Sarah Ann	21, Sept 1838		probate		N3	
Wilson, Sarah Francis	10, July 1852	4, July	7-10m		P2	
Wilson, Sarah White	13, Mar. 1841	10, Mar.	79	*	R3	
Wilson, Sarah White	13, Mar. 1841	12, Mar.	79	*	N2	
Wilson, Susan	28, May 1830	May	32		N3	
Wilson, Thomas	11, Dec. 1819	6, Nov.	57		S3	
Wilson, Thomas Q.	29, Apr. 1842	28, Apr.	48		N2	
Wilson, Timothy	17, June 1837		probate		N2	
Wilson, Virginia Annette	30, Oct. 1852	28, Oct.	5m-10d		P2	
Wilson, William	19, Nov. 1830	Nov.	54		N3	
Wilson, William	6, Oct. 1826		probate		N3	
Wilson, William	9, June 1827	28, May			R3	
Wilson, William (Major)	14, Oct. 1825			*	N2	
Wiltsee, Thomas M.	27, July 1850	July	2		Y3	

Name	Notice Date	Death Date	Age	Page	Maiden Name
Wimon, John	13, July 1849	July	22	L2	
Winchester, James	6, May 1806	5, May		S3	
Winchester, Sullivan G.	26, Sept 1850	5, Sept	20- 7m- 9d	P2	
Winden, George	18, July 1828	July	6m	N3	
Winder, Levin	17, July 1819	1, July		S3	
Windner, Thomas R.	1, Oct. 1830	Sept	1- 6m	N3	
Wing, Cornelius	3, Oct. 1823	26, Sept	58	* N3	
Wing, Cornelius	9, Oct. 1829		estate	N3	
Wing, Cornelius	11, Dec. 1827		probate	N3	
Wing, Cornelius	9, Dec. 1828		probate	N3	
Wing, Cornelius	25, Aug. 1829		probate	N3	
Wing, Cornelius	23, Mar. 1830		probate	N3	
Wing, Isaiah	6, July 1849	3, July	67	L2	
Wingfield, Laura H.	7, Sept 1837	10, Aug.	13m- 8d	X3	
Winsel, (son of W.)	27, Aug. 1808	Aug.	infant	S3	
Winship, Charles Henry	27, July 1833	25, July		R3	
Winslow, Henry	22, Dec. 1852	18, Dec.		P2	
Winslow, John	4, Oct. 1825		estate	N3	
Winslow, Thomas	11, Jan. 1837		estate	N2	
Winslow, Thomas	1, Apr. 1837		estate	N2	
Winslow, Timothy F.	5, Nov. 1830	Nov.	12	N3	
Winsor, Frederick Albert	15, July 1830		68	A3	
Winston, Marcia	19, Oct. 1837	10, Oct.	9	T2	
Winston, Marcia	21, Oct. 1837	10, Oct.	19	R3	
Winston, William (Major)	22, Apr. 1801	29, Mar.		S3	
Winter, Harriet	20, May 1837	12, May	26	R3	
Winters, Mary R.	13, July 1849	July	20	L2	
Winters, William	21, May 1830	May	4- 9m	N3	
Winthrop, Eliza Cabot	2, 9, July 1842	21, June	33	R3	Blanchard
Winton, Mary	8, Jan. 1806	3, Jan.	17	S3	
Wirt, William	13, Mar. 1834	Mar.		T2	
Wise, Amelia	13, Oct. 1852	11, Oct.	32- 2m-13d	P2	
Wise, Joanna	16, Nov. 1847	15, Nov.	24- 8m-22d	K2	Townsend
Wiseman, (child of John)	14, Oct. 1828	Oct.	infant	N3	
Wishart, John	1, Aug. 1850	July	50	Y2	
Wishart, Margaret Alice	6, Sept 1852	2, Sept	2- -26d	P2	
Wiskott, William	5, Jan. 1822	1, Jan.		S3	
Wisner, B.B. (Rev)	20, Feb. 1835	9, Feb.		X3	
Wistar, Bartholomew	14, Aug. 1841	6, Aug.	54	R3	
Withers, John Lynch	13, Apr. 1841	8, Apr.	9	N2	
Witman, Elizabeth J.	4, Feb. 1837	31, Jan.	20- 4m-25d	T2	
Wolcott, Horace	7, July 1836			X3	
Wolf, Betsey	18, July 1828	July	41	N3	
Wolf, Herman	21, June 1849	June	35	L2	
Wolf, Jane Emele	1, Sept 1827	Aug.	18m	R3	
Wolf, Jane Seymour	28, Feb. 1826	21, Feb.	28	N2	
Wolf, Phebe	22, Aug. 1828	Aug.	37- 2m	N3	
Wolf, William	13, July 1849	July	28	L2	
Wolfe, Johannes	13, July 1849	July	28	L2	
Wones, Mary Louisa	5, Aug. 1841	14, July	7	N2	
Wood, (child)	25, June 1830	June	12	N3	
Wood, Abby Ann	15, Dec. 1838	14, Dec.	31	* T2	Withington
Wood, Charlotte	11, Feb. 1836	9, Feb.		T3	
Wood, Clarissa	26, Dec. 1840	22, Dec.	21	R3	

Name	Notice Date	Death Date	Age	Page	Maiden Name
Wood, Cynthia Ann	10, Sept 1830	Sept	1m	N3	
Wood, Harriet Noel	23, Aug. 1850	23, Aug.		P2	
Wood, Harriet Noel	24, Aug. 1850	23, Aug.		Y2	
Wood, James	27, Oct. 1832	13, Oct.		* R3	
Wood, John	3, Sept 1808	26, Aug.		S3	
Wood, John (Gen)	5, July 1828			R3	
Wood, John Wrenshand	14, July 1849	10, July	15	L2	
Wood, Josiah	8, June 1850			P2	
Wood, Lewis M.	26, Aug. 1831	15, Aug.	25	X3	
Wood, Mary Jane	28, June 1849	June	22	L2	
Wood, Sally	18, June 1830	June		N3	
Wood, Spencer A.	6, May 1837	2, May		R3	
Wood, William	26, Apr. 1849	Apr.	37	L2	
Wood, William	29, Mar. 1849	Mar.	50	L2	
Wood, William	16, May 1840	14, May	53	R3	
Wood, William	23, Feb. 1827	14, Dec.	75	N3	
Wood, William A.H.	10, July 1849	9, July	infant	L2	
Wooden, John	4, Apr. 1840	15, Mar.	83	* R3	
Woodford, (child of A.)	25, June 1830	June	stillborn	N3	
Woodford, Andrew	16, Jan. 1829	Jan.	1m	N2	
Woodin, J.G. (Capt)	30, Nov. 1847	22, Nov.		* K2	
Woodman, James	14, June 1849	June	31	L2	
Woodrow, John W.	1, Aug. 1850	July	4	Y2	
Woodruff, (child of Aaron)	27, Aug. 1830	Aug.	1- 7m	N3	
Woodruff, (child of Aaron)	13, Aug. 1830	Aug.	1m-14d	N3	
Woodruff, Caroline	9, Feb. 1836	8, Feb.	52	N2	
Woodruff, Catharine	25, Aug. 1832	21, Aug.	58	R3	
Woodruff, Cornelia	9, Feb. 1836	8, Feb.	52	T3	
Woodruff, Cornelia	11, Feb. 1836	8, Feb.	52	X3	
Woodruff, Harry Percy	8, Aug. 1840	30, July	1- 3m	R3	
Woodruff, Hezekiah	1, June 1835		probate	N2	
Woodruff, Joseph	6, Sept 1833	Sept	20	X3	
Woodruff, Lewis	14, Oct. 1828	Oct.	1	N3	
Woodruff, Nathaniel	10, Nov. 1826		estate	N3	
Woodruff, Nathaniel	17, Sept 1835		probate	T2	
Woodruff, Nathaniel	11, Dec. 1827		probate	N3	
Woodruff, Nathaniel	22, Dec. 1829		probate	N3	
Woodruff, Nathaniel	21, Dec. 1830		probate	N3	
Woodruff, Walter Ferguson	22, Mar. 1841	20, Mar.	7	N2	
Woodruff, William	15, Oct. 1830	Oct.	35	N3	
Woodruff, William B.	26, May 1838	18, May	26	R3	
Woods, Ann Eliza	13, Sept 1838	Sept	3w	T2	
Woods, Micajah	25, May 1837	23, Mar.	61	X3	
Woods, Sarah	13, Aug. 1830	Aug.	46	N3	
Woodward, Augustus B.	20, July 1827	12, June		N3	
Woodward, George A.	17, Sept 1835		probate	T2	
Woodward, Huldah	5, Aug. 1841	3, Aug.	78	* N2	
Woodward, Jane	2, July 1799	26, June		S3	
Woodward, Lemuel	17, Oct. 1840	13, Oct.	21	R3	
Woodward, Lucy A.	17, Sept 1835		probate	T2	
Woodward, Samuel	13, Nov. 1852	12, Nov.		P2	
Woodward, Theodore (Dr)	7, Nov. 1840	Oct.		R3	
Woodward, William	1, June 1835		probate	N2	
Woodward, William	26, Jan. 1833	23, Jan.		R3	

Name	Notice Date	Death Date	Age	Page	Maiden Name
Woodworth, Jehiel N.	1, June 1835		probate	N2	
Wooley, Asher	10, Dec. 1852	8, Dec.	60	P2	
Woolley, (child of Sarah B.)	15, Sept 1827	Sept	22m	R3	
Woolley, George	25, Aug. 1829		probate	N3	
Woolley, John	7, Sept 1836		probate	N2	
Woolley, John (Dr)	31, Aug. 1833		estate	R3	
Woolley, John (Dr)	24, Aug. 1833	19, Aug.		R3	
Woolly, (child of Asher)	9, Dec. 1828	Dec.	stillborn	N3	
Woolsey, Hannah	19, Jan. 1828	18, Jan.	27	R3	Neave
Woolsey, Hannah	22, Jan. 1828	18, Jan.		N2	Neave
Woozencraft, Eliza	25, Aug. 1827	Aug.	18	R3	
Worchester, Noah (Dr)	6, Apr. 1847	4, Apr.	36	K2	
Worman, Jemima	19, July 1834	July	8m	R3	
Worrall, Charles A.	27, Mar. 1847	7, Mar.		K2	
Worst, Martin	17, May 1849	May		L2	
Worthington, Benjamin J.	22, Nov. 1847	20, Nov.	33	K2	
Worthington, Charles (Dr)	22, Sept 1836	18, Sept	77	T2	
Worthington, Frances B.	9, May 1840	2, May	30	R3	Wood
Worthington, Francis Anthony	19, June 1849	17, June	30	* L2	
Worthington, Mary Ann	28, Oct. 1834	25, Oct.	32	T2	Burnet
Worthington, Rebecca Burnet	28, Apr. 1836	24, Apr.	3-11m	T2	
Worthington, Thomas	6, July 1827	20, June	54	N3	
Worthington, Thomas (Gen)	7, July 1827	20, June		R3	
Worthington, William	1, June 1835		probate	N2	
Worthington, William M.	5, Mar. 1842	22, Feb.		* R3	
Worthson, Thomas	12, Feb. 1828		15	N3	
Wray, Ida	27, July 1852	26, July	10m- 2d	P2	
Wright, Ammon	6, Aug. 1830	Aug.	27	N3	
Wright, Amnon	14, Aug. 1830		estate	R3	
Wright, Barzillai	5, Aug. 1823	17, July		N3	
Wright, Benjamin T.	4, July 1840	12, May	30	R3	
Wright, Charles Franklin	6, Dec. 1852	1, Dec.	1- 3m	P2	
Wright, Christopher W.	17, Sept 1835		probate	T2	
Wright, Clarissa	19, Sept 1828	Sept	24	N3	
Wright, David	20, Aug. 1836		estate	N4	
Wright, David	11, Sept 1837		probate	N2	
Wright, Ella Frances	9, Nov. 1852	6, Nov.	3- 1m	P2	
Wright, Frances	16, Dec. 1852	13, Dec.	57	P2	
Wright, John	16, Dec. 1828	Dec.	65	N3	
Wright, John	5, Oct. 1852	28, Sept		P2	
Wright, John Marshall	11, Nov. 1839	10, Nov.		* T2	
Wright, Joseph	9, Sept 1852	8, Sept	65	P2	
Wright, Joseph L.	26, July 1834	July	10m	R3	
Wright, Joseph L.	22, July 1834	July	10m	T2	
Wright, Margaret	12, Nov. 1830	Nov.	54	N3	
Wright, Mary	29, Sept 1836	28, Sept	33	N2	
Wright, Mary	27, Oct. 1841	13, Oct.		* N2	Burns
Wright, Mary Elizabeth	15, Jan. 1842	15, Jan.	5- 4m	R3	
Wright, Mary Jane	29, Sept 1836	28, Sept	23	T2	
Wright, Mary L.	30, July 1850	July	42	Y3	
Wright, Samuel	1, June 1849	May	76	L2	
Wright, Thomas C.	18, Oct. 1839	16, Oct.	15m	T2	
Wyatt, Eliza	9, Sept 1831	Sept	10m	A3	
Wyeth, Jacob (Dr)	6, Oct. 1841	24, Aug.	42	* N2	

Name	Notice Date	Death Date	Age	Page	Maiden Name
Wyeth, Joshua	24, Jan. 1829	22, Jan.	77	R3	
Wyeth, Prentis	4, Sept 1810	27, Aug.		S3	
Wyle, James	14, Dec. 1839			R3	
Wynkoop, Elizabeth H.	6, June 1840	12, May	37	R3	Estill
Wynn, Daniel	27, Oct. 1827	Oct.		R3	
Wynn, James	12, Jan. 1828	7, Jan.	12	R3	
Wythe, Joshua	3, Feb. 1829	Jan.	77	N3	
Yaman, Sally C.	22, Jan. 1828		estate	N3	
Yardley, Mary A.	13, July 1849	11, July		L2	
Yardley, Thomas	7, June 1842	6, June	5- 6m- 4d	N2	
Yardley, William	9, Dec. 1852	2, Dec.	22- 4m	P2	
Yarger, W.H.	8, Sept 1827	Sept	10	R3	
Yarnall, Ephraim	17, June 1837		probate	N2	
Yarnell, Ephraim	9, Feb. 1836		estate	N2	
Yarwood, Joel	12, Apr. 1849	Apr.	31	L2	
Yast, Peter (Mrs)	30, Aug. 1852			P2	
Yates, Abraham	13, Aug. 1796	1, July		F3	
Yates, Joseph C.	13, Apr. 1837			X3	
Yeager, John	16, Aug. 1834	31, July	38	R3	
Yeager, John	14, Aug. 1834	31, July	38	T2	
Yeaman, Sally	13, Nov. 1827	10, Nov.	47	N3	
Yeaman, Sally C.	22, Dec. 1829		probate	N3	
Yeatman, Caroline W. Burrows	26, May 1821	22, May		S3	
Yeatman, Griffen	6, Mar. 1849	4, Mar.	79	L2	
Yeatman, Griffin (Mrs)	24, Sept 1808	23, Sept		S3	
Yeatman, Julia Graham	19, Mar. 1831	17, Mar.		R3	
Yeatman, Margaret	12, Nov. 1852	10, Nov.	71-10m	P2	
Yeatman, Mary Louisa	12, Aug. 1828	Aug.	2- 8m	N3	
Yeatman, Walker	31, Mar. 1849	22, Mar.	21	* L2	
Yeatman, Walker	6, Mar. 1841	12, Feb.		R3	
Yeatman, Walker	3, Mar. 1841	12, Feb.		N2	
Yeoman, Irene	7, Aug. 1841	3, Aug.	84	R3	
Yeomans, Irene	5, Aug. 1841	3, Aug.	84	N2	
Yocom, Emily Jane	6, July 1849	5, July	45	L2	
Yokum, Charles	6, July 1849	July	33	L2	
Yorke, Mary A.	5, July 1837	5, July		T2	
Youart, Samuel	27, Jan. 1825		estate	E3	
Youart, Samuel	11, Jan. 1828		estate	Q3	
Youart, Samuel	25, Aug. 1829		probate	N3	
Youman, Jose	20, Aug. 1830	Aug.	1- 9m	N3	
Young, (child of Jonathan)	26, July 1834	July	3	R3	
Young, (child of Jonathan)	22, July 1834	July	3	T2	
Young, Abner	14, Dec. 1833	10, Dec.		* R3	
Young, Abner	13, Dec. 1833	9, Dec.		X3	
Young, Fanny	19, Sept 1828	Sept	32	N3	
Young, George H.	28, May 1838	28, May		T2	
Young, Joseph B.	23, Apr. 1849	Apr.	28	L2	
Young, Julia	30, July 1850	July	49	Y3	
Young, Lydia Ann	22, May 1819	19, May		S3	
Young, Mary Ann	28, May 1830	May	23d	N3	
Young, Peter	6, Nov. 1838		probate	N2	
Young, Thomas	28, Nov. 1828	Nov.	43	N3	
Young, Thomas	19, Dec. 1818	11, Dec.		S3	
Younghusband, Isaac Pleasent	1, Nov. 1794	16, Oct.		C3	

Name	Notice Date	Death Date	Age		Page	Maiden Name
Yourt, Samuel	14, Mar. 1818		estate		S1	
Youtzy, (Mrs)	11, July 1822	3, July			J3	
Zeber, Jacob	22, Aug. 1850	Aug.	43		Y2	
Zebold, Louisa	10, Oct. 1840	5, Oct.		*	R3	
Zeigler, David	28, Sept 1811	24, Sept		*	S3	
Zeigler, John	13, July 1849	July	23		L2	
Zeigler, Lucy Anna	7, Dec. 1820	18, Nov.	53		S3	
Ziermann, Augustus	17, May 1849	May	23		L2	
Zimmerman, Charles	16, May 1840		39		R3	
Zimmermann, Joseph	26, Jan. 1848	21, Dec.			K2	

Maiden Name	Name	Notice Date	Death Date	Age	Page
Alden	Root, Almira	17, Aug. 1832	10, Aug.	39	X2
Armstrong	Collins, Mary Ann	3, Nov. 1836	1, Nov.	33	T2
Aydelotte	Farnham, Margaret P.	20, Apr. 1847	18, Apr.	23	K2
Bailey	Chase, Sarah S.	12, May 1836			X3
Barrows	Phillips, Sophie M.	20, May 1837			R3
Best	Barkley, Elizabeth C.	31, Dec. 1852	24, Dec.		P2
Biddle	Lytle, Sarah S.	8, June 1833	3, June	25	R3
Birdsall	Denny, Hannah E.	23, Mar. 1833	15, Mar.		R3
Bishop	Hageman, Laura D.	26, June 1841	24, June		R3
Blackmore	Remer, Ann	2, July 1852	15, June		P2
Blanchard	Winthrop, Eliza Cabot	2, 9, July 1842	21, June	33	R3
Bowman	Gossin, Catharine	9, Oct. 1847	8, Oct.		K2
Broadwell	Everett, Amanda M.	24, Oct. 1840	15, Oct.	23	R3
Brooks	Sullivan, Mary Ann	22, Aug. 1835	3, Aug.		T2
Brower	Kugler, Matilda Caroline	31, Oct. 1840	24, Oct.	32- 9m	R3
Brown	Avery, Mary Ann	14, Sept 1836	19, Aug.		N2
Burch	Stansbury, Caroline E.	2, July 1849	24, June	24	L2
Bureau	Vinton, Romaine M.	24, June 1831	21, May	29	A3
Bureau	Vinton, Romaine M.	28, May 1831	21, May	29	R3
Burnet	Worthington, Mary Ann	28, Oct. 1834	25, Oct.	32	T2
Burns	Wright, Mary	27, Oct. 1841	13, Oct.		N2
Bush	Ernst, Lydia A.	17, July 1841	13, June		R3
Cadwell	Kean, Rhoda	19, Nov. 1799	16, Sept		S3
Childs	Gooddel, Lucy C.	2, Dec. 1831	16, Oct.		X3
Clark	Meyers, Mary	13, Oct. 1852	10, Oct.		P2
Clay	Erwin, Ann	16, Dec. 1835	10, Dec.		T3
Cleghorn	Toby, Eliza	13, Mar. 1819	6, Mar.		S2
Clingman	Cady, Ann Eliza	11, Mar. 1848	11, Mar.		K2
Conn	Prince, Sarah	30, Apr. 1808	28, Apr.		S3
Cornelius	Lewis, Mary	17, Aug. 1837	17, July	38	X3
Curry	Burnet, Margaret	23, Jan. 1836	26, Dec.		T3
Decker	Eberly, Ellen	30, Dec. 1852	28, Dec.		P2
Dexter	Wetmore, Julia	23, Jan. 1835	20, Jan.		X3
Doddridge	Ramsey, Julianna Adeline	30, May 1840	30, Apr.		R3
Dorman	Brandon, Maria E.B.	18, Dec. 1838	17, Dec.		T2
Drake	Glenn, Elizabeth	23, Oct. 1819	20, Oct.		S3
Duncan	Wells, Maria B.D.	18, June 1835	14, June	27	N2
Dunham	Innes, Emeline	27, Oct. 1841	14, Oct.	28	N2
Dunseth	Merritt, Margaret Adelia	28, Nov. 1835	24, Nov.	20	T2
Espy	Westcott, Mary	19, May 1847	25, Apr.		K2
Estill	Wynkoop, Elizabeth H.	6, June 1840	12, May	37	R3
Ewing	Clark, Sarah	13, May 1835	9, May		T3
Fairbank	Morton, Sarah Ann	23, Nov. 1832	1, Nov.	20	X3
Ferris	Jewett, Mary	24, Mar. 1838	15, Mar.	23	R3
Foreman	Ferris, Harriet	10, Sept 1842	5, Sept	26	R3
Fosdick	Mason, Anna S.	25, Mar. 1824	22, Mar.	21	E3
Fullerton	Pool, Ruth	10, Dec. 1835	3, Aug.	97	N2
Gano	Anderson, Maria J.	11, Oct. 1852	29, Sept	19	P2
Garniss	Chase, S.P. (Mrs)	3, Dec. 1835	1, Dec.		X3
Gibson	Richards, Jennet	27, Mar. 1819	21, Mar.	21	S2
Gillingham	Selden, Hetty	25, Oct. 1852	22, Oct.	27	P2
Goodwin	Davidson, Nancy	23, June 1836	3, June	29	X3
Guest	Reynolds, Elizabeth	11, July 1826	7, July	19	N2
Hailman	Reed, Julia Ann	20, July 1820	9, July	17	S3

Maiden Name	Name	Notice Date	Death Date	Age	Page
Halley	Pingree, Mary Ann	19, Dec. 1840	12, Dec.	17	R3
Halley	Pingree, Mary Ann	19, Dec. 1840	12, Dec.	17	N2
Handy	Garrison, Margaret A.	10, July 1849	9, July		L2
Harrison	Este, Lucy	11, Apr. 1826	7, Apr.		N3
Haywood	McGrew, Aurelia	20, July 1820	7, July	27	S3
Heckewelder	Rucker, Mary Jane	17, Apr. 1849	4, Apr.	34	L2
Hill	Greenwood, Howard W. (Mrs)	7, Sept 1835	31, Aug.	23	T2
Hill	Greenwood, Howard W. (Mrs)	8, Sept 1835	31, Aug.	23	N2
Holmes	Browning, Martha Ann	13, Oct. 1847	11, Oct.	23	K2
Houston	Clinch, Elizabeth Bayard	11, Sept 1838	21, Aug.	38	T2
Hughes	Merrill, Mary Anne	2, June 1836	21, May		X3
Huntington	Foster, Anna Maria	24, Nov. 1847	23, Nov.	25	K2
Huntington	Smith, Sarah L.	29, Dec. 1836	30, Sept	34	X3
Irvin	January, Fanney P.	26, Nov. 1835	4, Nov.	34	X3
Jefferson	Randolph, Martha	28, Oct. 1836	10, Oct.		T2
Johnson	Dorsey, Sarah Johnson	13, Sept 1834	25, Aug.	45	R3
Jones	Black, Harriet	16, Oct. 1841	10, Oct.	27	R3
Jones	Black, Harriet	14, Oct. 1841	10, Oct.	27	N2
Jones	Elliott, Hattie	20, Nov. 1852			P2
Jones	Knight, Abby H.	25, Oct. 1850	25, Oct.		P2
Kennedy	Holland, George (Mrs)	22, Oct. 1796	18, Oct.		F3
Keys	Lardner, Mary Ann	22, Nov. 1839	8, Nov.	18	T2
Keys	Sterrett, Jane B.	3, Oct. 1840	25, Sept	29	R3
Lamb	Sullivan, Eunice	8, Aug. 1834	1, Aug.		X3
Langstroth	Brainerd, Sarah	24, June 1835	20, June	28	T2
Lawrence	Lupton, Harriet B.	8, Dec. 1836	2, Dec.	19	X3
Lawrence	Lupton, Harriet O.	5, Dec. 1836	2, Dec.	20	T2
Lee	Jones, Anne Lucinda	29, May 1835	15, May	45	T2
Leonard	Spooner, Sarah L.	1, Aug. 1850	31, July		Y2
Leslie	Lupton, Mary F.	19, May 1849	3, May	32	L2
Levassor	DeBarr, Clara Julia	27, Apr. 1849	23, Apr.	19- 9m-17d	L2
Longworth	Stettinius, Mary L.	20, Jan. 1837			T2
Longworth	Stettinius, Mary L.	20, Jan. 1837			N2
Lowry	Foulds, Elizabeth	7, Apr. 1838	17, Feb.	33	R3
Lytle	MacAlester, Eliza Ann	9, 11, Sept 1835	31, Aug.		T2
Macy	Raymond, Martha H.	17, May 1849	16, May	32	L2
Matthews	Outcalt, Ellen M.	3, Jan. 1853	1, Jan.	38	P2
McAlister	Owens, Helen	1, Aug. 1851	17, July	22-11m	P2
McLean	Hayward, Ann	21, Nov. 1840	8, Oct.	27	R3
McLean	Richards, Rebecca	3, Oct. 1837	24, Sept		T2
McMurray	Stockton, Catharine	14, Mar. 1842			N2
Morris	Price, Susan	2, Nov. 1830	31, Oct.	22	N2
Murray	Holcomb, Mary Ann	7, 10, Nov. 1834	29, Oct.	22	T2
Neave	Woolsey, Hannah	19, Jan. 1828	18, Jan.	27	R3
Neave	Woolsey, Hannah	22, Jan. 1828	18, Jan.		N2
Newal	Riddle, Mary Elizabeth	17, Oct. 1840	6, Oct.	21- 6m	R3
Nourse	McClanahan, Maria J.	23, June 1836	24, May	30	X3
Pancoast	Stillman, Mary Ann	5, Jan. 1833	4, Jan.		R3
Patterson	Findlay, Elizabeth	20, 22, July 1847	18, July	34	K2
Phillips	Stevenson, Sarah	7, Jan. 1848	6, Jan.	23	K2
Pierce	Jackson, Sarah	18, June 1838	17, June	53	T2
Pike	Harrison, Clarissa B.	17, Feb. 1837	1, Feb.		T2
Pike	Harrison, Clarissa B.	20, Mar. 1837	1, Feb.		T2
Posey	Hall, James (Mrs)	1, Sept 1832			R3

Maiden Name	Name	Notice Date	Death Date	Age	Page
Prince	McQuillen, Cynthia Holland	15, Sept 1836	14, Aug.	37	T2
Provoost	Colden, Maria	20, May 1837	10, May		T2
Reeve	Harper, Rachel	23, May 1835	16, May	38	T2
Rhoades	Hill, Alice	15, Aug. 1837	15, Aug.	24	T2
Rowan	Rogers, Josephine	12, Apr. 1838	24, Mar.		T2
Rowan	Steele, Mary Jane	4, May 1822	26, Apr.		S3
Sanford	Whiting, Indiana Bel	6, June 1849	25, May		L2
Schroeder	Moore, Barbara	4, Feb. 1841	28, Jan.	61	N2
Sellman	Conover, Julia Ann	25, Mar. 1836	24, Mar.	24- 3m	T2
Sellman	Conover, Julia Ann E.	26, Mar. 1836	24, Mar.	24- 3m	N2
Sibley	Alling, Sarah Ann	14, July 1849	8, July	30- 7m	L2
Sinclair	Cowen, (Mrs)	3, Dec. 1835	Nov.		X3
Sinclar	Cowan, (Mrs)	30, Nov. 1835			T2
Singleton	McDuffie, Mary Rebecca	7, Oct. 1830	14, Sept		A3
Snow	Ferguson, Salome	1, May 1835	6, May	30	X3
St.Clair	Dill, Eliza	28, Jan. 1825	16, Jan.	62	N3
St.Clair	Mayo, Frances M.	6, Dec. 1838	Nov.		T3
Stockbridge	Merrell, Levisa	16, Nov. 1838	14, Nov.	20	T2
Stone	Morgan, Harriet	11, July 1849	10, July		L2
Strickland	Graham, Ellen D.	8, Aug. 1834			X3
Teater	Buchanan, Susan	19, Oct. 1822	11, Oct.	31	S3
Townsend	Wise, Joanna	16, Nov. 1847	15, Nov.	24- 8m-22d	K2
Tracy	Robbins, Caroline	10, Mar. 1836	26, Jan.	43- -28d	X3
Tracy	Robbins, Caroline Tracy	15, Feb. 1836	26, Jan.		T3
Trimble	Davis, Rebecca F.	9, July 1842	30, June		R3
Trimble	Nelson, Mary L.	8, Sept 1836	9, Aug.	41	X3
Truman	Hagerman, Laura D.	26, June 1841	24, June		N2
Tyler	Stowe, (Mrs)	8, Aug. 1834	6, Aug.		X3
Wallace	Semple, Helen M.	5, June 1849	3, June		L2
Weare	Bennett, Elizabeth	13, Nov. 1838	4, Nov.		T2
Wells	White, Helen M.	5, Oct. 1837	27, Jan.	24	X3
White	Swan, Mary L.	7, June 1828	June		R3
Williams	Brown, Jane W.	4, Nov. 1852	29, Oct.	23	P2
Williams	Dunkinson, Ann B.	18, Sept 1837	1, Sept		T2
Withington	Wood, Abby Ann	15, Dec. 1838	14, Dec.	31	T2
Wood	Carlos, Sarah Ann	29, June 1833	17, June		R3
Wood	Newton, Abby B.	11, May 1830	7, May	32	N2
Wood	Worthington, Frances B.	9, May 1840	2, May	30	R3
Worthington	Macomb, Mary Tiffin	28, Mar. 1837	Mar.		T2
Worthington	Pomeroy, Elizabeth	17, Nov. 1852	8, Nov.		P2
Yeatman	Graham, Julia	18, Mar. 1831	17, Mar.		A3

Grooms	Brides	Date of Notice	Page
Abbott, William	Cooper, Mary	16, Dec. 1852	P2
Abbay, C.H.	Shorts, Maria	30, Sept 1830	A3
Abbott, Henry B.	Berry, Catharine E.	24, Dec. 1852	P2
Abraham, J.	DeYoung, Sarah	6, Sept 1841	N2
Ackerman, Richard	Mann, Catharine W.	8, June 1841	N2
Ackerson, James	Hoaps, Angeline	9, July 1814	S3
Acres, Frederick	Colby, Margery	4, Jan. 1808	S3
Adae, Charles F.	Woods, Ellen	19, Mar. 1842	R3
Adams, Alex H.	Ballard, Mary J.	11, Nov. 1837	R3
Adams, Alexander	Baird, Jane	14, Oct. 1828	N3
Adams, Elmer W.	Smith, Mary Ellen	28, Dec. 1839	R3
Adams, John	Fox, Christian	23, Sept 1812	S3
Adams, Joseph	Stockman, Susan Jane	10, June 1835	T2
Adams, T.J.	Hutchinson, Ann	5, July 1828	R3
Adams, Thomas J.	Bogie, Isabella	26, May 1821	S3
Adams, William H.	Johnson, Sarah Jane	31, Aug. 1850	P2
Adamson, Benjamin	Armstrong, Sarah B.	20, Feb. 1813	S3
Adderman, Joseph P.	Jones, Emily W.	13, Aug. 1852	P2
Adkins, Thomas O.	Ward, Martha	3, Mar. 1834	T3
Agnew, John	Chapman, Elizabeth	1, Aug. 1840	R3
Alden, Bradford R.	Coleman, Anne C.	25, June 1842	R3
Aldey, Perine	Tankesley, Ann	18, Sept 1805	S3
Aldrich, Edwin R.	Rayner, Helen M.	26, Aug. 1852	P2
Allan, Abraham W.	Kent, Martha	13, June 1829	R3
Allen, Hazen	Shaffer, Sarah	9, Oct. 1851	P2
Allen, L.S. (Dr)	Greene, Alvernon H.	25, Sept 1841	R3
Allen, L.S. (Dr)	Green, Alvernon H.	25, Sept 1841	N2
Allen, Martin	Hughes, Rachel W.	15, Nov. 1852	P2
Allen, Nathan	Spinning, Eliza Jane	11, July 1835	T2
Allen, Samuel R.	Williams, Martha	17, Jan. 1818	S3
Allen, Thomas	Russell, Ann C.	20, July 1842	N2
Allen, Thomas H.	Coleman, Eliza	3, Mar. 1827	R3
Allen, William E.	McHenry, Catharine	9, Oct. 1841	R3
Allen, William F.	McHenry, Catharine	9, Oct. 1841	N2
Allen, William H.	Mann, Mary Davis	23, Mar. 1841	N2
Alley, Samuel A.	Burnett, Anne	4, Jan. 1840	R3
Alter, Charles	Raddish, Jane Ann	28, Apr. 1827	R3
Anderson, Charles R.	Loring, Eliza B.	28, May 1842	R3
Anderson, Charles R.	Loring, Eliza B.	26, May 1842	N2
Anderson, Evan	Lumley, Mary	2, Oct. 1841	R3
Anderson, Evan	Lumley, Mary	4, Oct. 1841	N2
Anderson, George L.	Humphreys, Emiline M	25, June 1842	R3
Anderson, J.W.	McFadden, Catharine	18, Sept 1852	P2
Anderson, James	Bread, Anna	24, June 1837	T2
Anderson, James	Johnson, Catharine	30, Sept 1836	N2
Anderson, James	Alfred, Mary Ann	4, Mar. 1837	N2
Anderson, John	Clark, Mary	10, Jan. 1826	N3
Anderson, Larz	Pope, Ann	12, July 1828	R3
Anderson, Pierce B.	Luke, Ann M.	29, Nov. 1828	R3
Anderson, Robert	Bonnel, Rachel V.	22, June 1811	S3
Anderson, Samuel	Phillips, Sarah Ann	17, Nov. 1821	S3
Anderson, Samuel	English, Kezziah	23, Sept 1852	P2
Anderson, W.C.	Yeatman, Anna Maria	20, May 1837	R3
Anderson, W.C.	Yeatman, Anna Maria	19, May 1837	T2

Grooms	Brides	Date of Notice	Page
Anderson, William	Pangburn, Jemima	21, July 1827	R3
Anderson, William	Douglas, Jane	7, Oct. 1837	T2
Anderson, William C.	Winton, Sally	27, June 1812	S3
Andress, Charles	Doddsworth, Mary	19, June 1841	R3
Andress, Charles	Doddsworth, Mary	15, June 1841	N2
Andrew, John	Ewing, Eliza	20, May 1806	S3
Andrews, Charles	Maranda, Priscilla	9, Oct. 1841	R3
Andrews, Charles S.	Maranda, Priscilla	8, Oct. 1841	N2
Andrews, John W.	Gwynne, Lavinia M.	13, Oct. 1835	T2
Andrews, Rupert R.	Harvie, Cordelia M.	1, Dec. 1832	R3
Andrick, John U.	Sheidegger, Barbara	21, Apr. 1835	T3
Anthony, Charles	Evans, Elizabeth	26, Mar. 1820	S2
Antrim, Joseph	Tatspan, Eliza	24, Jan. 1829	R3
Arbigust, John	Vail, Eliza	10, Nov. 1827	R3
Armstrong, Arthur E.	Schillinger, Prisc.	28, Oct. 1837	R3
Armstrong, Charles G.	Smith, Harriet	23, Oct. 1841	R3
Armstrong, Charles G.	Smith, Harriet	18, Oct. 1841	N2
Armstrong, J.Y.	Hollingsworth, Elizabeth	24, June 1837	R3
Armstrong, J.Y.	Hollingsworth, Elizabeth	19, June 1837	T2
Armstrong, James	Smith, Sarah	15, Apr. 1820	S2
Armstrong, James	Smith, Sarah	20, Apr. 1820	D3
Armstrong, John	Willis, Susan	28, Dec. 1807	S3
Armstrong, John	Marshall, Harriet	1, Nov. 1838	N2
Armstrong, R.G.	Summons, Mary	30, Nov. 1847	K2
Armstrong, Robert	Burley, Jane	5, Oct. 1835	T2
Arnold, William	Sloop, Catharine (Mrs)	24, Oct. 1818	S3
Arons, William	Carrell, Eliza Jane	15, Sept 1827	R3
Arthur, Nicholas	Cobb, Charlotte	9, May 1836	T2
Arthur, William	Parsons, Eliza	15, Apr. 1820	S2
Arthur, William	Parsons, Elizabeth	20, Apr. 1820	D3
Arthurs, William	Wallace, Amanda C.	13, Dec. 1825	N3
Asbury, Walter	Bowman, Elizabeth	12, July 1837	T2
Ashcroft, Robert	Bruner, Mary A.	2, Nov. 1847	K2
Athearn, Prince A.	Hastings, Louisa	15, Nov. 1833	X3
Atherton, Amos	Francis, Mary	19, July 1816	S3
Atlee, S. Yorke	Williams, Mary Anna	3, May 1841	N2
AtLee, Samuel York	Edwards, Ann M.	6, June 1836	N2
AtLee, Samuel Yorke	Williams, Mary	7, June 1836	T2
Attee, Charles	Hampton, Sarah Jane	2, June 1847	K2
Attwell, Robert G.	Fones, Amanda	16, Oct. 1847	K2
Atwell, John	Ray, Mary	12, May 1838	R3
Aubery, Henry S.	Key, Cecilia	17, July 1841	R3
Augur, Daniel	See, Mary Clayton	24, Oct. 1818	S3
Aull, Conrad A.	Earley, Catharine	12, Aug. 1852	P2
Austin, Seneca	Miner, Julia A. (Mrs)	5, Sept 1840	R3
Auten, William	Wharten, Sarah	1, Jan. 1828	R3
Averel, Edward	Peers, Sarah	10, Oct. 1840	R3
Avery, Charles (Dr)	Bakewell, Martha P.	8, June 1847	K2
Avery, Dudley	Browne, Mary Ann	30, Mar. 1807	S3
Avery, John C.	Robinson, Lydia	31, Oct. 1829	R3
Avery, John C. (Lt)	Satterly, Nancy	25, Dec. 1813	S3
Avery, John L.	Sayre, Martha	10, July 1813	S3
Avinger, Frederick	Cosgrove, Mary Ann	6, Oct. 1852	P2
Aydelott, B.P. (Rev)	Fosdick, Elizabeth	26, June 1841	V3

Grooms	Brides	Date of Notice	Page
Ayer, Richard	Archer, Matilda	2, Jan. 1841	R3
Ayres, James	Roll, Abigail	13, Oct. 1815	S3
Babb, Thomas	Smith, Rachel	31, Aug. 1847	K2
Bachelor, William W.	Gogin, Rachel	29, July 1831	A3
Bachman, John J.	Sutton, Caroline	6, Nov. 1852	P2
Bacon, James H.	Eberle, Catharine	20, Dec. 1833	X3
Badeau, Silas R.	Plum, Phebe (Mrs)	10, June 1831	X3
Bailey, Andrew	McCarty, Martha	30, Apr. 1814	S3
Bailhache, John	Heath, Eliza	10, Jan. 1817	S3
Baily, Thomas	Watson, Charlotte	9, Mar. 1837	T2
Baker, Adam	Green, Nancy	27, Dec. 1825	N2
Baker, Benjamin	Blackburn, Mahala	1, May 1835	T3
Baker, Elias	Burns, Martha	22, Apr. 1830	A3
Baker, James	Carroll, Elizabeth (Mrs)	22, Mar. 1836	T2
Baker, John	Flint, Esther	4, July 1817	S3
Baker, John W.	Adams, Henrietta	15, Oct. 1839	T2
Baker, Joseph	Boyce, Lucy Ann	7, Oct. 1837	R3
Baker, Nathan	Horner, Amelia	8, Aug. 1840	R3
Baker, Nelson	Collins, Phena	19, Oct. 1836	T2
Baker, Nelson	Collins, Phena	13, Oct. 1836	X3
Baker, William W.	King, Mary	28, May 1842	R3
Baker, William W.	King, Mary	21, May 1842	N2
Bakewell, W.G.	Mathews, Alicia A.	29, Nov. 1828	R3
Bakewell, William W.	Jaudon, Elizabeth	7, Oct. 1847	K2
Baldock, Milton	Boss, Virginia	5, Feb. 1842	R3
Baldock, Milton	Boss, Virginia	3, Feb. 1842	N2
Baldwin, Arden W.	Elliott, Sophronia A	21, Dec. 1839	R3
Baldwin, Henry	Bowers, Julia A.	25, July 1835	T2
Baldwin, Henry	Clark, Mary Elizabeth	27, Sept 1852	P2
Baldwin, James H.	Spencer, Rhoda	15, May 1847	K2
Ball, B.W.	Denny, Rebecca	12, June 1827	N2
Ball, Blackall W.	Dennie, Rebecca	9, June 1827	R3
Ball, Danforth E.	Morten, Maria Ann A.	30, Aug. 1834	R3
Ball, Daniel	McCauley, Lucinda	25, Feb. 1831	X3
Ball, George W.	McNickle, Mary Jane	21, June 1841	N2
Ball, James (Capt)	Stittwell, Sarah	4, Jan. 1808	S3
Ballance, Charles	England, Elizabeth	29, Jan. 1836	T3
Ballauf, William	Storch, Josephine	12, June 1847	K2
Bamber, Thomas	Beasley, Sarah	21, July 1827	R3
Banks, Lawrence S.	James, Isabella M.	16, Aug. 1828	R3
Barber, James H.	House, Emeline	1, Nov. 1852	P2
Barbour, Charles (Dr)	Smith, Nancy E.	10, Apr. 1819	S3
Bard, John	Forshe, Mary Ann	28, Nov. 1818	S3
Bare, Martin	Caldwell, Sarah Ann	31, Aug. 1847	K2
Bargen, Otto G.	Barnett, Isabella	22, Sept 1852	P2
Barger, Andrew	Capp, Winney (Mrs)	18, Dec. 1840	N2
Barker, John	Braden, Mary Ann	2, June 1847	K2
Barker, Thomas C.	Yeatman, Julia	30, Apr. 1814	S3
Barnes, Charles (Dr)	Herringten, Harriet	1, Nov. 1834	R3
Barnes, Charles (Dr)	Herrington, Harriet	31, Oct. 1834	T2
Barnes, John	Grey, Permelia	11, Mar. 1831	X3
Barnes, John C.	Starr, Mary	9, Mar. 1849	L2
Barnet, George W.	Moore, Charlotte	17, Apr. 1819	S2

Grooms	Brides	Date of Notice	Page
Barnhart, Daniel	Williams, Anna	10, Sept 1842	R3
Barns, Samuel	Johnson, Mary	9, Nov. 1839	R3
Barnum, H.L. (Capt)	Moore, Augusta	14, Jan. 1832	R3
Barnum, H.L. (Capt)	Moore, Augusta L.	27, Jan. 1832	X3
Barrett, William D.	Conner, Eliza	16, Aug. 1834	R3
Barrett, William D.	Conner, Eliza	13, Aug. 1834	T2
Barringer, A.V.	Olmstead, Sallie E.	7, July 1852	P2
Bartlett, N.	Ward, Eliza A.	8, Nov. 1830	A3
Bartlett, William H.	Wallace, Caroline W.	13, Oct. 1832	R3
Barwise, John	Marchant, Catharine	11, Nov. 1831	X3
Barwise, Luther Y.	Morris, Mary Jane	24, Sept 1851	P2
Barwise, Thomas	Collins, Julia	16, Feb. 1822	S3
Barwise, William	Taylor, Elinor	5, Dec. 1822	J3
Bascom, H.B. (Rev)	VanAntwerp, Eliza	15, Mar. 1839	T2
Basley, William H.	Phillips, Catharine	26, Jan. 1839	T2
Basset, Jonathan	Skiff, Catharine	16, May 1818	S3
Bassford, Thomas	Singer, Mary Jane	16, Jan. 1841	R3
Bateham, M.B.	Cushman, Josephine	3, Oct. 1850	Y2
Bateman, William D.	Langdon, Mary Jane	20, Aug. 1842	R3
Bateman, William D.	Langdon, Mary Jane	17, Aug. 1842	N2
Bates, Caleb	Humphreys, E.T.	1, Feb. 1828	N3
Bates, George H.	Perry, Caroline A.	7, May 1842	R3
Bates, Henry M.	Fawcett, Mary Ann	20, Jan. 1838	R3
Bates, Henry M.	Fawcett, Mary Ann	23, Jan. 1838	T2
Bates, James L.	Kelly, Maria	4, Nov. 1837	R3
Bates, John S.	Gwathmey, Matilda G.	20, Nov. 1835	T2
Bates, Samuel R.	Grandin, Hannah M.	26, Mar. 1842	R3
Baughman, Robert A.	Armstrong, Margaret	11, June 1842	R3
Baughman, Robert A.	Armstrong, Margaret	9, June 1842	N2
Baum, D.C.	Sraff, Amanda	11, Mar. 1837	R3
Baum, D.C.	Sraff, Amanda	9, Mar. 1837	T2
Baxter, Hiram J.	Nugent, Bridget	30, Aug. 1850	Y2
Bayly, James K.	McKnight, Betsey	8, Mar. 1816	S3
Baymiller, Jacob	Pearson, Ann	18, Sept 1819	S3
Bazzle, Thomas H.	Newton, Mary E.	23, Oct. 1841	R3
Beal, Edward C.	Williams, Rebecca M.	15, Dec. 1827	R3
Beale, John	Bradford, Sarah	9, Sept 1847	K2
Beall, Edwin J. (Dr)	Smith, Lydia W.	10, May 1828	R3
Beall, William B.	Low, Mary G.	26, Oct. 1822	S3
Beans, William W.	Clark, Frances	31, May 1849	L2
Beatty, James S.	Devou, Sarah Alice	28, July 1838	R3
Beatty, James S.	Devou, Sarah Alice	27, July 1838	T2
Beatty, John A.	Briggs, Priscilla M.	28, Sept 1835	T2
Bechtle, Henry C.	Perry, Betsey	16, Feb. 1816	S3
Becker, C.F.	Thesing, Marie E.	28, Dec. 1847	K2
Beckett, Henry	Walsh, Eliza	12, Sept 1840	R3
Bedinger, B.F. (Dr)	Wade, Sarah	6, July 1820	S3
Bedinger, George M.	Fleming, Hannah M.	5, Sept 1850	Y2
Bedinger, Henry C.	Drake, Lavinia	14, Sept 1820	S3
Bee, James	Bom, Ellen	24, May 1828	R2
Beebe, Rosswell	Elliott, Clarissa	12, Oct. 1835	T2
Beeching, John	Gill, Ann	29, Mar. 1847	K2
Beekley, Eliphalet	Moore, Jane	9, Oct. 1841	N2
Beers, John R.	Stephens, Margaret M.	6, July 1847	K2

Grooms	Brides	Date of Notice	Page
Beggs, Joseph P.	Curtis, Mary	24, Aug. 1847	K2
Bell, John	Yeatman, Jane (Mrs)	4, Nov. 1835	T2
Bell, Joseph	Foley, Mary	3, Sept 1847	K2
Bell, Peter	Orr, Peggy	27, Aug. 1799	S3
Bell, Samuel L.	Masterson, Letitia	9, Aug. 1841	N2
Bell, Thomas	Hornblower, Joanna	21, July 1827	R3
Bell, Thomas	Hornblower, Joanna	20, July 1827	N3
Bell, Thomas	Hall, Jane	17, June 1851	P2
Belman, J.C.	Nichols, Clarissa	28, July 1850	Y2
Belser, Samuel	Skaates, Jane	17, Nov. 1827	R3
Belvel, James	Folger, Harriet	17, Oct. 1838	T2
Beman, Gamaliel C.	Creichton, Emilia	3, Nov. 1836	X3
Beman, I.C.	Williams, Anne S.	22, Sept 1838	R3
Beman, I.C.	Williams, Anne S.	15, Sept 1838	T2
Benbridge, Thomas	Coleman, Ann	14, Feb. 1831	A3
Benbridge, William T.	Hamilton, Curtis	19, Sept 1829	R3
Bender, George A.	Hales, Clemima	19, Aug. 1830	A3
Bender, George A.	Hales, Jemima	21, Aug. 1830	R3
Benedict, Alexander	Cleveland, Sarah	4, Aug. 1842	N2
Benedict, Alexander	Cleveland, Sarah	4, Aug. 1842	M3
Beneman, J.S.	Porter, Elizabeth	7, Nov. 1840	R3
Bennett, John	Nabs, Mary Jane	8, Oct. 1852	P2
Benson, Gabriel L.	Mills, Abigail	15, Apr. 1820	S2
Benson, Gabriel L.	Mills, Abigail	20, Apr. 1820	D3
Benson, Martin	Banks, Elizabeth J.	25, Oct. 1852	P2
Benson, Matthew	Keyser, Mary Ann	28, Dec. 1820	S3
Benton, Thomas H.	McDowell, Eliza	5, May 1821	S3
Beresford, Benjamin	Johnston, Mary Ann	9, Sept 1836	T2
Berry, Andrew	Cary, Rosetta Jane	20, Sept 1834	T2
Berry, William	Cox, Mary Elizabeth	12, July 1834	T2
Betts, Smith	Toy, Ann	15, Dec. 1827	R3
Betts, Smith	Young, Cynthia Ann	28, Jan. 1848	K2
Bickham, William	Dennison, Eliza A.	2, Sept 1826	J3
Biddecombe, D. (Rev)	Edmondson, Mary Ann	4, June 1842	R3
Biggar, G.D.	Parvin, Delia M.	30, Apr. 1842	R3
Biggar, G.D.	Parvin, Delia M.	28, Apr. 1842	N2
Biggers, James	Ernout, Mary	29, Sept 1827	R3
Billings, Charles F.	Ross, Susannah	22, Feb. 1841	N2
Billings, James A.	Canfield, Catharine	25, July 1828	Q3
Birdsal, Caleb S.	Beach, Nancy S.	4, Sept 1830	R3
Bird, John	Moore, Martha	1, Oct. 1799	S3
Birney, David B.	Case, Anna B.	11, May 1847	K2
Bishop, Samuel	Hoge, Elizabeth H.	16, Oct. 1841	R3
Bishop, Samuel P.	Hunter, Elis. (Mrs)	16, Oct. 1841	V3
Bishop, Truman (Rev)	Langdon, Mary	20, Jan. 1821	S3
Bissell, Israel M.	Clay, Margaret	20, Jan. 1826	N3
Bittle, Hezekiah	Everson, Ann	23, Nov. 1820	S3
Blachly, Joseph W.	Tuttle, Mary C.	17, May 1828	R3
Blachly, O.B.	Alden, Elizabeth	17, June 1825	N1
Black, James	Carter, Rebecca F.	19, Apr. 1828	R3
Black, Mahlon	Jones, Harriet	30, Jan. 1839	T2
Black, Robert	Bagley, Elizabeth	31, May 1825	N3
Black, Robert B.	Redish, (Mrs)	10, Sept 1852	P2
Black, Samuel H.	Mervin, Francis M.	9, June 1836	X3

Grooms	Brides	Date of Notice	Page
Blackburn, David	Spurrier, Carsa	20, Mar. 1819	S2
Blackly, Joseph W.	Tuttle, Caroline W.	19, Oct. 1822	S3
Blackwell, Robert	Stapp, Maria	8, Apr. 1820	S3
Blakely, John S.	Harvey, Anna Eveline	20, Aug. 1842	R3
Blanchard, Cary H.	Dexter, Ellen	8, Aug. 1840	R3
Blaney, Daniel T.	Moreton, Charlotte	2, Jan. 1819	S3
Bleck, R.F.	Caldwell, Ellen J.	14, June 1849	L2
Blecker, William W.	Badger, Lucretia Ann	23, May 1840	R3
Bledsoe, Abraham	Egleston, Diana	5, Sept 1834	X3
Bledsoe, Albert T.	Coxe, Harriet	26, May 1836	X3
Blinn, James	Nye, Emily C.	7, May 1842	R3
Blinn, James	Nye, Emily C.	5, May 1842	N2
Blodget, John (Capt)	Bugbee, Hannah (Mrs)	10, Jan. 1826	N3
Blount, Beverly	Davis, Nancy	20, Sept 1814	W4
Blundell, Joseph M.	Redding, Mary Ann	19, Feb. 1839	T2
Boake, John	Ball, Elvira	7, Nov. 1840	R3
Boal, Robert, Jr.	Mills, Phoebe H.	3, Jan. 1817	S3
Boddman, Hanson A.	Fisher, Eliza	14, May 1842	R3
Bogart, John E.	Lynch, Anna M.	1, Sept 1847	K2
Bohrer, Benjamin S.	Luffborough, Eliza	26, Oct. 1820	S3
Bolles, William T.	Avey, Eliza J.	8, June 1847	K2
Bolton, Samuel	Hodgson, Elizabeth	6, Mar. 1819	S3
Bolton, William C.	Lynch, Mary H.	10, June 1842	N2
Bonnel, Benjamin	Robeson, Margaret	17, Nov. 1821	S3
Bonnel, Clark	Wicoff, Elsa	14, Sept 1811	S3
Bonnel, John	Benedict, Sarah E.	15, May 1847	K2
Bonnell, Allison B.	Looker, Catharine	4, Nov. 1835	T2
Bonsol, Joseph	Chadwick, Eliza	30, Oct. 1819	S3
Borden, Samuel (Capt)	Zesline, Sarah (Mrs)	17, July 1819	S3
Boswell, G.W.	McGinnis, Ann E.	7, Dec. 1847	K2
Bourgoin, Alexis J.	Mosier, Elizabeth Y.	16, June 1849	L2
Boutell, George	Oliver, Phebe	22, Sept 1835	T3
Boutell, George W.	Oliver, Phebe	21, Sept 1835	N2
Bowdle, Daniel	Dickey, Catharine	24, Nov. 1832	R3
Bowers, Augustus	Cole, Caroline	29, Sept 1838	R3
Bowers, Augustus	Cole, Caroline	29, Sept 1838	T2
Bowers, Augustus	Cole, Caroline	29, Sept 1838	N2
Bowers, David	Brooks, Abigail	27, Nov. 1819	S3
Bowers, Henry	Cox, Hannah	12, June 1847	K2
Bowers, William	Butt, Lydia	25, July 1817	S3
Bowman, Alexander D.	Thornton, Mildred B.	28, Oct. 1836	T2
Bowman, Alexander D.	Thornton, Mildred	28, Oct. 1836	N2
Bowman, Andrew	Wallingford, Malinda	12, July 1837	T2
Bowman, William W.	Grayson, M.E.	30, Nov. 1847	K2
Boyce, John W.	Pratt, Elizabeth H.	19, Dec. 1836	T2
Boyd, Allan	McLean, Elizabeth	3, Jan. 1829	R3
Boyd, D.B.	Elliott, Caroline	29, Dec. 1852	P2
Boyer, Jacob	Hunt, Susannah	23, Nov. 1822	S3
Boylan, Julius A.	Bradley, Mary	3, Dec. 1852	P2
Bozarth, John	Gorden, Anne	22, Apr. 1830	A3
Bradbury, Cornelius	Spinning, Sarah Ann	24, Nov. 1821	S3
Bradbury, E.H. (Dr)	Lovell, Jane Ann	6, Dec. 1830	A3
Bradford, C.D.	Palmer, Louisa S.	15, Nov. 1831	A3
Bradford, James	Middleton, Hannah	14, Aug. 1841	R3

Grooms	Brides	Date of Notice	Page
Bradford, James	Middleton, Hannah	13, Aug. 1841	N2
Bradley, Samuel H.	McClure, Maria	11, Dec. 1841	R3
Bradley, William P.	Landrum, V. Minnie	27, Nov. 1852	P2
Brady, Willis	Kenyon, Caroline	5, Sept 1840	R3
Bragg, Willis N.	Legg, Jane	6, Oct. 1827	R3
Brandon, James P.	Dorman, Maria E.	22, Nov. 1838	T2
Brandon, Matthew	Austin, Louisa S.	19, Mar. 1831	R3
Brandon, Matthew	Austin, Louisa S.	11, Mar. 1831	X3
Brashears, Gassaway	Laws, Amelia	2, Jan. 1837	T2
Brashears, Gassaway	Laws, Amelia C.	31, Dec. 1836	N2
Brasher, Robert	Simmons, Hannah	20, Aug. 1799	S3
Brasher, Robert	Alter, Mary Ann	10, May 1828	R3
Brasher, Robert	Alter, Mary Ann	9, May 1828	Q3
Bray, William W.B.	Robbins, Mary A.	17, Nov. 1847	K2
Breeden, Abel	Thompson, Martha B.	23, Aug. 1830	A3
Brellsford, Timothy	Malatt, Mary	11, July 1835	T2
Briant, Silas	Harsha, Juliet	26, Aug. 1826	J3
Briddell, John A.	Langley, Margaret E.	23, Oct. 1852	P2
Brieker, David	McAnnally, Bridget	2, Sept 1852	P2
Briggs, Henry	Crowly, Jane	11, Apr. 1829	R3
Briggs, William H.	Suiter, Ellen	21, Feb. 1842	N2
Brigham, Matthias	Crossman, Caroline	8, Oct. 1821	S3
Bright, Ethelbert	Reed, Eliza M.	21, Mar. 1839	T2
Broadwell, Lewis	Penn, Harriet Ann	19, Jan. 1839	T2
Broadwell, Mahlon	Agnew, Sarah Ann	1, Mar. 1833	X3
Broadwell, Samuel	Pancoast, Mary Ann	12, Dec. 1812	S3
Broks, T.M.	McGowan, Maria	30, Nov. 1847	K2
Brooks, Daniel	Barwise, Mary Ann	28, Mar. 1823	N2
Brooks, David A.	Milligan, Jane	14, Aug. 1852	P2
Brooks, James	Randolph, Mary (Mrs)	30, July 1841	N3
Brooks, Valentine	Hoak, Margaret Ann	20, Jan. 1838	R3
Brooks, Valentine	Hoak, Margaret Ann	23, Jan. 1838	T2
Brotherton, David	Dugan, Nancy	4, Apr. 1829	R3
Brotherton, James H.	Snyder, Anne L.	14, Mar. 1849	L2
Brown, Daniel	Hubbell, Mary	30, Dec. 1823	N3
Brown, David O.	Alter, Harriet	20, Sept 1834	R3
Brown, David O.	Alter, Harriet	13, Sept 1834	T2
Brown, Edmund L.	Steele, Mary (Mrs)	25, Sept 1838	T2
Brown, Edward W.	Cres, Mary	13, July 1852	P2
Brown, Ethan	Huffman, Mary Jane	25, Aug. 1841	N2
Brown, Ira S.	Wilder, Olive	31, Oct. 1840	R3
Brown, James	Page, Maria C.	9, Dec. 1830	A3
Brown, James D.	Wilson, Margaret	23, Oct. 1852	P2
Brown, Jenks	Williams, Rachael	19, Aug. 1823	N3
Brown, John T.	Barrett, Mary Ann	2, Nov. 1852	P2
Brown, Richard F.	Smith, Elizabeth	1, Aug. 1840	R3
Brown, Robert	Galloway, Sarah A.	16, Nov. 1837	T2
Brown, Robert P.	Galloway, Sarah	11, Nov. 1837	R3
Brown, William	Foster, Eliza (Mrs)	17, Mar. 1827	R3
Brown, Wilson	Coffin, L.W.	8, Oct. 1852	P2
Browne, Thomas V.	Lee, Catharine	7, Oct. 1852	P2
Brunot, W. (Lt)	Reville, Ann T.	8, May 1819	S3
Bryan, Timothy M.	Heiskell, Frances E.	26, July 1828	R3
Bryce, Robert	Heth, Sophia	27, Sept 1852	P2

Grooms	Brides	Date of Notice	Page
Brydon, G.C.	Sweeney, Adalaide	13, June 1850	P2
Bryson, Ambrose M.	Walker, Mary	9, Jan. 1841	R3
Buchanan, Joseph	Teater, Susan	27, Nov. 1819	S3
Buchanan, Robert	Riggle, Sarah Jane	8, May 1847	K2
Buchanan, W.A.	Bryon, Sallie E.O.	26, Oct. 1852	P2
Buckingham, E.J.	Doyle, Emeline A.	18, Mar. 1851	P2
Buckingham, John S.	Ferguson, Mary	31, Aug. 1852	P2
Buckingham, Oliver P.	Wheeler, Eliza J.	29, Nov. 1852	P2
Bucknell, Thomas	Davis, Olivia	14, Dec. 1839	R3
Buckner, Thomas M.	Perry, Caroline	6, July 1820	S3
Budd, T.L.	Maffit, Eliza Jane	14, Dec. 1839	R3
Buell, George P.	Lane, Ann	25, June 1824	N2
Bullitt, Fred N.	Beckwith, Minerva E.	14, Mar. 1829	R3
Burbridge, Rowland	Madeira, Harriet	25, Nov. 1837	R3
Burdsal, Caleb L.	Beach, Nancy S.	3, Sept 1830	N2
Burdsal, Solomon B.	Denny, Elizabeth	3, May 1847	K2
Burdsal, Stephen W.	Turner, Ann Maria	25, Feb. 1836	T3
Burgess, Isaac F.	Drayton, Mary	28, Jan. 1832	R3
Burk, John	Heaslett, Mary	4, Jan. 1836	T3
Burke, Walter	Egbert, Rosalie R.	28, June 1828	R3
Burke, William (Rev)	Lane, Mary	20, Aug. 1842	R3
Burke, William W.	Rees, Mary N.	19, Sept 1818	S3
Burnap, George	Seward, Martha Maria	30, Oct. 1819	S3
Burnard, Elijah	Moore, Clara	12, Sept 1850	P2
Burnet, David S.	Gano, Mary	5, Apr. 1830	A3
Burnet, David S.	Gano, Mary	2, Apr. 1830	N2
Burnet, George	Greene, Sophia	28, May 1799	S3
Burnet, William	Clark, Susan Maria	13, Feb. 1841	R3
Burnet, William	Clark, Susan Maria	8, Feb. 1841	N2
Burns, James	Varney, Charlotte C.	16, May 1840	R3
Burns, John	Todd, Jane	14, May 1847	K2
Burr, Edward	Richey, Francis B.	21, Aug. 1852	P2
Burr, Edward M.	Ritchey, Frances B.	24, Aug. 1852	P2
Burrows, John M.D.	Gammage, Sarrah H.	15, Dec. 1836	X3
Burt, Andrew	Gano, Sarah	9, Feb. 1807	S2
Burt, John S. Gano	Magowan, Catharine T	28, Dec. 1841	N3
Burt, Moses	Jones, Mary F.	30, May 1835	T2
Burton, Robert (Capt)	Latham, Catharine A.	7, Oct. 1837	N2
Bush, John E. (Dr)	Johnson, Maria Ann	4, Sept 1819	S3
Bushnell, A. Lee	Hastings, Sarah P.	13, Apr. 1837	X3
Butler, Joseph C.	Laverty, Alice B.	2, Sept 1847	K2
Butler, Thomas C.	Wells, Clarissa	28, Dec. 1852	P2
Butler, Thomas S.	Patterson, Jane	4, Dec. 1841	R3
Butler, Thomas S.	Patterson, Jane	27, Nov. 1841	N2
Butler, William	Shrieve, Margaret	4, Oct. 1828	R3
Butterfield, James	Barker, Hannah (Mrs)	21, Aug. 1819	S3
Byrn, John	Johnston, Mary B.	28, Dec. 1852	P2
Cadwallader, Jonah	Whitaker, Priscilla	4, Dec. 1813	S3
Cadwell, George	Haskell, Elizabeth	16, Oct. 1841	R3
Cahill, James	Carroll, Dorcas	24, Sept 1847	K2
Cain, George J.	Burch, Martha M.	12, July 1828	R3
Cake, Charles T.	Hull, Louisa Jane	12, Mar. 1839	T2
Caldow, Robert	McGregor, Margaret	26, Sept 1840	R3

Grooms	Brides	Date of Notice	Page
Caldow, William	Richardson, Louisa M	11, Mar. 1841	N2
Caldwell, Robert	Avery, Ann	30, Mar. 1807	S3
Caldwell, Thomas L.	Clifford, Mary Jane	15, June 1822	S3
Calhoun, Andrew	Spining, Susan J.	21, May 1831	R3
Callahan, J.P.(Dr)	Hindle, Ann E.	11, Sept 1847	K2
Cambreleng, C.C.	Glover, Phoebe	30, Nov. 1835	T2
Cameron, Wesley	Starbuck, Eliza	16, July 1836	T2
Camnitz, Daniel F.	Richardson, Maria H.	21, Aug. 1841	R3
Camnitz, Daniel F.	Richardson, Maria M.	19, Aug. 1841	N2
Camp, Henry R.	Collins, Caroline E.	26, July 1852	P2
Campbell, Carey A.	Armstrong, Mary Ann	15, Sept 1827	R3
Campbell, Edwin R.	Wright, Sarah Jane	19, May 1849	L2
Campbell, James	Cordry, Mary (Mrs)	3, Jan. 1839	T2
Campbell, Lewis D.	Reily, Jane	9, Jan. 1836	T3
Campbell, William	Smith, Jane	5, July 1828	R3
Canaan, John	Brooks, Maria	30, Oct. 1819	S3
Candler, Samuel	Cowdrey, Sarah H.	6, Aug. 1836	T2
Cannahan, C.	Monfort, Sarah C.	11, Oct. 1838	T2
Capp, Henry	Butler, Lucy	18, Feb. 1823	N3
Capp, Henry B.	Butler, Lucy	20, Feb. 1823	J3
Card, John	Wilson, Eliza Jane	25, Oct. 1852	P2
Card, Thomas A.	Bartlett, Anna Maria	25, Oct. 1852	P2
Carel, John	Johnson, Nancy	28, Mar. 1823	N2
Carey, Samuel D.	Fenton, Louisa M.	19, Aug. 1852	P2
Carey, William W.	Smith, Hannah E.	1, May 1835	X3
Cargill, Austin	Seymour, Amelia	15, Aug. 1822	J3
Carll, Maskell (Rev)	Brewster, Hannah	12, Sept 1840	R3
Carman, Benjamin	Adamson, Catharine	19, Feb. 1820	S2
Carnahan, G.A.	Warner, Louisa	9, Oct. 1852	P2
Carneal, Thomas D.	Stanley, Sarah (Mrs)	11, Feb. 1815	S3
Carnes, Peter	Whitney, Harriet	26, Mar. 1842	R3
Caroline, Absalom	Treen, R.	28, Apr. 1815	S3
Carothers, John	Oakman, Martha	30, Aug. 1828	R3
Carpenter, Ezra	Andrews, Sarah P.	18, May 1833	R3
Carpenter, Isaac B.	Ellmaker, Susan	1, July 1837	R3
Carr, Francis (Col)	Upjohn, Mary Ann	10, Aug. 1822	S3
Carroll, Foster	Lynch, Anna M.	25, Oct. 1850	Y2
Carson, Isaac	McGarvey, Mary Ann	28, Aug. 1813	S3
Carson, William J.	Terry, Margaret	11, Aug. 1821	S3
Carter, A.G.W.	Wishart, Margaretta	9, Apr. 1842	R3
Carter, Daniel C.	Stites, Hannah (Mrs)	23, Nov. 1811	S3
Carter, James H.	Brooke, Lydia	10, Feb. 1831	A3
Carter, John W.	Collins, Mary Fanny	29, Oct. 1852	P2
Carter, John W.	Collins, Mary F.	1, Nov. 1852	P2
Carter, Joseph (Dr)	Carlyle, Margaret S.	1, Dec. 1832	R3
Carter, Lewis R.	Fleming, Ellis M.	16, June 1827	R3
Carter, Samuel	McClure, Frances S.	22, Sept 1821	S3
Carver, George W.	Fusselbaugh, Margaret	2, Dec. 1825	N3
Carver, Henry	Heffly, Mary	13, Dec. 1828	R3
Carver, Henry	Heffley, Mary	9, Dec. 1828	N2
Cary, Freeman G.	Macon, Malvina	12, Apr. 1833	X3
Cary, Robert	Jessup, Betsey	15, Jan. 1814	S3
Cary, S.F.	Stilwell, Eliza	31, May 1849	L2
Cary, Samuel F.	Allen, Maria Louisa	27, Oct. 1836	X3

Grooms	Brides	Date of Notice	Page
Case, J.T.	Purscell, Rebecca C.	13, Jan. 1831	A3
Case, John	McGuigan, Mary Ann	10, Oct. 1840	R3
Casey, John	Seebrooks, Priscilla	4, Mar. 1820	S2
Casey, John	Seebrooks, Priscilla	2, Mar. 1820	D3
Cassady, John L.	Michelson, Margaret	27, Nov. 1852	P2
Cassat, Dennis	Leach, Rebecca	4, May 1830	N3
Castleman, David	Harrison, Virginia	2, Dec. 1824	E2
Casto, Jona.	Dodge, Frances Ann	7, Dec. 1847	K2
Caswell, Daniel J.	Hay, Nancy L.	27, Nov. 1819	S3
Caswell, Daniel J.	Wilson, Mary	4, May 1822	S3
Cathcart, David	Sherwin, Charlotte	31, Jan. 1818	S3
Cathel, John	Wells, Tryphena	27, Apr. 1822	S3
Catlett, Fairfax	Laverty, Esther Ann	28, May 1838	T2
Celcher, Lewis	Greenham, Rachel	28, Feb. 1838	N2
Center, Robert H.	Conn, Maria W.	17, Nov. 1826	N2
Challen, James (Rev)	Bradford, Eliza	2, June 1827	R3
Chamberlain, J.D.	Graw, Thirza	19, Sept 1817	S3
Chamberlaine, James	Moore, Caroline	3, Oct. 1823	N3
Chamberlin, David	Reed, Nancy	28, Nov. 1835	T2
Chamberlin, John	Williams, Mary	10, Sept 1842	R3
Chamberlin, William	Bigler, Sallie T.	14, Sept 1852	P2
Chambers, John T.	Bonte, Jane Eliza	8, Oct. 1841	N2
Channing, W.E.	Fuller, Ellen	27, Sept 1841	N2
Chapman, William S.	Evens, Louisa Anna	23, Nov. 1838	T2
Charters, William M.	Seely, Cynthia D.	30, June 1827	R3
Chase, Abraham	Wheeler, Harriet	18, May 1807	S3
Chase, Pailander (Rev)	Ingraham, Sophia M.	17, July 1819	S3
Chase, Salmon P.	Garniss, Catharine J	8, Mar. 1834	R3
Chase, Salmon P.	Garniss, Catharine J	8, Mar. 1834	T2
Chase, Salmon P.	Smith, Eliza Ann	28, Sept 1839	T3
Chase, William F.	Gillespie, Mary	27, Oct. 1837	T2
Chauncey, John S.	Graham, Maria	28, Dec. 1838	T2
Cheseldine, G.R.	Phelps, Martha G.	3, Dec. 1831	R3
Chester, Joseph	McMaster, Hannah	26, May 1838	R3
Chidlaw, Benjamin	Gwilym, Hannah	2, June 1836	X3
Childress, George C.	Vance, Margaret	28, June 1828	R3
Childs, C.J. (Dr)	Baldridge, Elizabeth	18, Mar. 1847	K2
Childs, Mordecai	Gowdy, Jane	27, June 1829	R3
Chipman, W. Douglass	Longstreet, Josephin	8, Nov. 1851	P2
Chittenden, Edward	Rogers, Julia M.	11, Feb. 1836	X3
Chittenden, Edward F	Rogers, Julia M.	9, Feb. 1836	T3
Churchill, David	McKim, Frances A.	25, Feb. 1825	N2
Chute, James	Clapp, Martha H.	24, Oct. 1817	S3
Cist, Lewis J.	Renshaw, Mary S.	24, May 1847	K2
Clark, Ansel R.(Rev)	Clark, Electa P.	30, Nov. 1837	X3
Clark, Carlton	Day, Lavinia	1, June 1820	S3
Clark, Charles M.	Bonsall, Martha A.	30, Dec. 1852	P2
Clark, Francis B.	Wheat, Mary	25, Aug. 1841	N2
Clark, George	Clark, Lydia	22, May 1847	K2
Clark, Henry	Skyrin, Mary S.	7, July 1832	R3
Clark, Henry	Folger, Eliza	24, June 1824	E3
Clark, John	Abright, Sophia	2, June 1827	R3
Clark, John	Jackson, Olive	10, Nov. 1826	N3
Clark, John M.	White, Elizabeth	10, Apr. 1841	R3

Grooms	Brides	Date of Notice	Page
Clark, John M.	White, Elizabeth	13, Apr. 1841	N2
Clark, Ozro V.	Menge, Harriet	8, Sept 1847	K2
Clark, Samuel H.	VanValkenburg, Jane	15, June 1837	T2
Clark, Sumner	McInvaine, Eliza	27, June 1835	T2
Clark, Thomas	Barton, Eliza H.	21, Oct. 1825	N2
Clark, William	Hicks, Luciann	7, Jan. 1832	R3
Clarke, John	Dodge, Christiana	26, Sept 1840	R3
Clarke, William	Luke, Margaret	16, July 1834	T2
Clarkson, C.F.	Colescott, Elizabeth	21, May 1849	L2
Clarkson, E. Smith	Menzies, Caroline	1, June 1833	R3
Clarkson, John D.	Cox, Rebecca Ann	18, June 1850	P2
Clarkson, Samuel (Dr)	Dennison, Eliza Ann	10, Mar. 1827	R3
Clarkson, William	Gregory, Mary	17, May 1834	R3
Clason, Lewis W.	Rutledge, Lucy Jane	26, Oct. 1847	K2
Clay, Porter	Hardin, Elizabeth (Mrs)	22, Apr. 1830	A3
Clay, Ralph A.	Gassaway, Lucy Ann	23, Oct. 1841	R3
Clay, Ralph A.	Gassaway, Lucy Ann	16, Oct. 1841	N2
Claypoole, James T.	Allibone, Eliza	19, Aug. 1823	N3
Clayton, John	Kennedy, Bridgett	9, Nov. 1852	P2
Clemson, Thomas C.	Calhoun, Anna	27, Dec. 1838	T2
Clerc, Laurent	Boardman, Eliza C.	29, May 1819	S3
Cleveland, George P.	Scott, Henrietta E.	26, Nov. 1834	T2
Clifton, William	Weatherford, Letitia	22, Sept 1838	R3
Clingman, Enoch G.	Lyon, Sarah	16, Nov. 1839	R3
Clinton, DeWitt	Jones, Catharine	22, May 1819	S3
Cloon, Samuel	Clemons, Martha Ann	12, Aug. 1847	K2
Clowser, Andrew	Maynadr, Lucinda	25, Dec. 1852	P2
Cobb, John	Steel, Miriam	30, July 1841	N3
Coburn, John A.	Converse, Cornelia L	29, Nov. 1852	P2
Cochnower, John	Barton, Amanda	16, Sept 1852	P2
Cochran, Richard	Sisson, Emily	19, Aug. 1837	T2
Cochrill, Enoch	Davis, Mary (Mrs)	2, Oct. 1841	R3
Cochrill, Enoch	Davis, Mary	27, Sept 1841	N2
Cockerell, Francis M	Goddard, Elizabeth	23, Oct. 1841	R3
Cockrell, Francis M.	Goddard, Elizabeth M	25, Oct. 1841	N2
Coddington, G.W.	Hulbert, Mary	16, June 1849	L2
Coffin, Christopher	Gibson, Alice	5, July 1830	A3
Coffin, Henry A.	Osborn, Susan L.	14, Sept 1837	X3
Coffin, William G.	Murray, Hannah I.	2, May 1840	R3
Coffin, Zebulon B.	Justice, Catharine E	19, Oct. 1839	R3
Cogy, Joseph (Dr)	Wood, Abigail	29, June 1820	S3
Colburn, Charles L.	Symmes, Mary S.	30, July 1847	K2
Colby, George W.	Kendall, Samantha	22, Nov. 1851	P2
Colby, Samuel	Drollener, Hannah	25, Apr. 1810	H3
Colby, Zerebabal	Campbell, Sarah (Mrs)	31, July 1813	S3
Cole, Ephraim	Duffy, Lydia Ann	9, Aug. 1850	Y2
Coleman, Chapman	Crittenden, Ann Mary	2, Dec. 1830	A3
Coleman, George	Lummis, Rebecca	30, June 1827	R3
Coleman, John M.	Luster, Hannah	3, Nov. 1838	T2
Coleman, Leroy C.	Parks, Mary	1, Nov. 1825	N3
Coleman, Wesley	Thompson, Marian	16, Jan. 1815	W3
Colett, W.R.	Suydam, Eliza	17, Aug. 1833	R3
Collier, Allen	How, Susan C.	18, Sept 1852	P2
Collier, Daniel	Sampson, Lydia F.	13, July 1838	T2

Grooms	Brides	Date of Notice	Page
Collins, Edmund	Taylor, Elizabeth (Mrs)	4, Aug. 1842	N2
Collins, Edward	Taylor, Elizabeth D.	4, Aug. 1842	M3
Collins, John	Currie, Isabella	15, July 1835	T2
Collins, John	McEvoy, Elizabeth	30, Sept 1852	P2
Collins, Lewis	Peers, Mary Elinor	11, Apr. 1823	N3
Collins, William	Quail, Mary V.	29, Oct. 1852	P2
Collord, Samuel W.	Robson, Mary Ann	30, Aug. 1828	R3
Colter, Aaron A.	Burdsall, Margaret D	7, Oct. 1852	P2
Colvin, Thomas	Williamson, Matilda	19, Jan. 1837	X3
Colwell, Stephen	Caldwell, Elizabeth	9, June 1827	R3
Combs, Leslie	Man, Mary E.	21, Apr. 1849	L2
Comly, Richard N.	Sanders, Julia C.	11, May 1833	R3
Comly, Richard N.	Saunders, Julia E.	10, May 1833	X3
Comly, William F.	Judkins, Sarah R.	21, Oct. 1836	T2
Comly, William F.	Judkins, Sarah R.	22, Oct. 1836	N2
Compton, Abram	Areheart, Mary Ann	22, Apr. 1830	A3
Comstock, William H.	Foote, Catharine A.	26, May 1847	K2
Conant, E.L.	Hurdus, Maria	31, Oct. 1826	N3
Conkelon, Alexander	Shigley, Tamer	22, Apr. 1830	A3
Conklin, John T.	Gregar, Rebecca Ann	15, Dec. 1852	P2
Conn, James	Hurdus, Hannah	21, Nov. 1817	S3
Conn, John A.	Halley, Mary Ann	30, Oct. 1841	N2
Connahan, Charles	Monfort, Sarah C.	12, Oct. 1838	N2
Connell, Silas	Hotchkiss, Elizabeth	7, Mar. 1829	R3
Conover, James F.	Sellman, Julia A.E.	20, Jan. 1832	A3
Conover, James F.	Sellman, Julia A.	21, Jan. 1832	R3
Conover, James F.	Sellman, Julia E.	27, Jan. 1832	X3
Cook, Amasa	Lamb, Esther	4, May 1830	N3
Cook, Austin	Davis, Lucinda	15, Sept 1827	R3
Cook, Jesse S.	Thorp, Eliza Ann	18, Sept 1819	S3
Cook, John	Graham, Sarah	27, June 1817	S2
Cook, M. Scott	Tiffin, Ellen W.	2, May 1840	R3
Cook, Oliver	Forman, Amy Ann	11, July 1835	T2
Cook, Robert F.	Stuart, Anna L.	20, Sept 1847	K2
Cook, Samuel	Dollin, Frances	16, Nov. 1820	S3
Cooke, George	Hertzog, Rachael W.	29, Nov. 1830	A3
Cooke, William F.	Musick, Charity	2, Oct. 1847	K2
Coombes, A.D.	Smith, Sarah E.	7, June 1830	A3
Coombs, A.D.	Smith, Sarah E.	5, June 1830	R3
Coombs, Alfred D.	Frankenstein, Maria	18, May 1849	L2
Coombs, S.A.	Atlee, Margaret L.	11, Nov. 1830	A3
Coombs, S.A.	Atlee, Margaret L.	13, Nov. 1830	R3
Coonse, Frederick	Dean, Elizabeth	14, Sept 1811	S3
Cooper, D. Zeigler	Smith, Letitia C.	25, Sept 1835	T2
Cooper, Daniel C.	Burnet, Sophia (Mrs)	25, Sept 1805	S3
Cooper, James	Oliver, Frances E.	25, Apr. 1840	R3
Cooper, Jonas	Price, Elizabeth (Mrs)	29, Dec. 1821	S3
Cooper, Robert W.	Smith, Mary Ann	21, Oct. 1837	R3
Copeland, Nathaniel	Clifford, Mary	6, May 1828	N3
Coplen, Isaac C.	Bassett, Ruth	25, Sept 1819	S3
Corbin, William	Hey, Ann	27, Mar. 1819	S2
Corey, A.W.	Foote, Elizabeth A.	21, Sept 1837	X3
Cornell, John P.	Chapin, Sylvia	4, June 1842	R3
Corry, James A.	Powers, Catharine	23, Jan. 1841	R3

Grooms	Brides	Date of Notice	Page
Corry, James A.	Powers, Catharine	16, Jan. 1841	N2
Corwin, Daniel W.	Loring, Harriet W.	20, Jan. 1838	R3
Corwin, Daniel W.	Loring, Harriet W.	23, Jan. 1838	T2
Corwine, R.M.	Quinton, Mary Eliza	19, Feb. 1842	R3
Corwine, Richard M.	Quinton, Mary Eliza	17, Feb. 1842	N2
Cosper, John	Richards, Sarah	28, May 1835	T2
Cottam, Richard	Ladley, Lydia Ann	2, Oct. 1841	R3
Cottam, Richard	Ladley, Lydia Ann	27, Sept 1841	N2
Cotterel, Joseph	Gallahan, Mary	11, Mar. 1831	X3
Cottingham, Thomas	Stoms, Sarah Mills	22, Nov. 1834	R3
Cottingham, Thomas	Stoms, Sarah Mills	19, Nov. 1834	T2
Cotty, William	Leeds, Eliza	3, Mar. 1849	L2
Coulte, J.D. (Capt)	Mills, Frances	2, Dec. 1824	E2
Covert, Jeremiah	Make, Mary	9, Aug. 1814	W3
Cowgle, Tarvin (Dr)	Tarvin, Agnes	31, May 1837	T2
Cowling, Richard	Brush, Mary	17, May 1849	L2
Cox, John	Hanna, Nancy	20, Dec. 1828	R3
Cox, Richard K.	Dee, Louisa	1, Aug. 1829	R3
Cox, Rodolph	Roberts, Lucy B.	5, Oct. 1838	T2
Cozzens, Brown	Martin, Eliza	17, May 1828	R3
Craft, J.W.	Applegate, Ellen	28, May 1847	K2
Craig, Johnson	Pringle, Isabella	16, Oct. 1841	R3
Craig, William G.	Suggett, ----	7, June 1828	R3
Cramer, John	Hanes, Ann	20, Mar. 1835	N2
Crampton, Henry	Andrews, Mary	14, July 1826	N3
Cranch, Edward P.	Wood, Bertha	16, Apr. 1841	N2
Crane, (Dr)	Davis, Sarah P.	3, July 1852	P2
Crane, Andrew L.	Baker, Esther A.	9, May 1840	R3
Crane, Henry	Hanks, Zerviah	20, Dec. 1838	T2
Crane, Joseph	Elliot, Julia Ann	19, July 1809	H3
Crane, Oliver	Crane, Abigail	11, Apr. 1812	S2
Crane, Rufus	Folger, Sarah	23, May 1829	R3
Crane, Thirstin	Owens, Ann	1, June 1820	S3
Craut, Henry	Hubbert, Jannet C.	2, May 1840	R3
Craven, Thomas T.	Henderson, Emily	2, May 1840	R3
Cravens, Benjamin	Black, Sarah	11, July 1835	T2
Crawford, Robert	Lemond, Anna	20, June 1817	S3
Crawson, James	Mackey, Maria (Mrs)	24, Aug. 1811	S3
Cropper, Cyrus	Bushart, Nancy	6, Mar. 1819	S3
Crosby, B.	Madin, Rachel B.	24, Nov. 1832	R3
Crosby, Joshua E.	Stibbs, Sarah Ann	10, June 1836	T2
Crouse, Jacob S.	Hales, Isabella	17, Nov. 1827	R3
Crouse, Jacob S.	Hales, Isabella W.	16, Nov. 1827	N2
Crump, N.W. (Capt)	Bowen, Exzene M.	8, Nov. 1838	T2
Cullom, Allen	Smith, Eliza (Mrs)	25, June 1835	T2
Cullum, George	Wilson, Rebecca	5, July 1830	A3
Cumming, Edward H.	Warder, Sarah A.	2, Mar. 1833	R3
Cummings, C.P.	Campton, Cynthia Ann	5, Feb. 1842	R3
Cummings, Caleb	Campton, Cynthia Ann	5, Feb. 1842	N2
Cummings, Hamilton	Odger, Emily C.	14, May 1847	K2
Cummings, J.P.	Litherbury, Nett	8, Oct. 1852	P2
Cummings, John N.	Chapin, Olive S.	14, May 1847	K2
Cunningham, E.W.	Swift, Lucy	22, Sept 1838	R3
Cunningham, E.W.	Swift, Lucy	21, Sept 1838	T2

Grooms	Brides	Date of Notice	Page
Cuny, Richard R.	Miller, Clara	18, Apr. 1829	R3
Curd, John E.	Luster, Susan F.	9, Sept 1837	T2
Curtis, Henry J.	Fisher, Clarissa	26, Aug. 1831	A3
Curtis, Henry J.	Fisher, Clarissa	27, Aug. 1831	R3
Curtis, Henry J.	Fisher, Clarissa	26, Aug. 1831	X3
Curtis, William	Addis, Eliza	13, Nov. 1819	S3
Curtiss, L.G.	Browne, Frances M.	7, Sept 1847	K2
Cushing, Milton B.	Smith, Mary B.	1, July 1836	T2
Cushing, Milton B.	Smith, Mary B.	14, July 1836	X3
Custard, David C.	Susars, Electa Ann	29, June 1841	N2
Cutter, Alphonso	Riddle, Martha Jane	20, Aug. 1847	K2
Cutter, Amos	Harrington, Cath. M.	20, June 1840	R3
Cutter, B.G.	Valentine, Eliza Ann	14, Sept 1837	X3
Dacker, Matthias M.	Stoker, Henrietta	24, June 1837	R3
Dacker, Matthias M.	Stokes, Henrietta	19, June 1837	T2
Dagget, David	Lines, Mary	23, May 1840	R3
Daily, John	Brown, Elizabeth (Mrs)	28, May 1799	S3
Dale, James	Baughman, Sarah E.	8, Nov. 1852	P2
Dale, Richard C.	Manson, Sophiah	6, Mar. 1819	S3
Dalton, George W.	Jones, Sarah	30, Aug. 1852	P2
Dana, Charles D.	Lyman, Sarah P.	16, June 1832	R3
Dangerfield, T.A.	Ellsberry, Isabella	13, Mar. 1835	N2
Daniel, Isaac	Daniel, Lydia	26, Aug. 1824	E2
Daniels, Henry	Gale, Adelia	4, May 1830	N3
Darby, Joseph	Chafer, Mary	7, Apr. 1851	P2
Darling, George H.	Sweet, Maria A.	17, June 1850	P2
Dart, George L.	Eddy, Hannah J. (Mrs)	19, July 1852	P2
Davenport, Cyrus	Stevens, Mary Ann	9, July 1847	K2
Davenport, Darius	Burr, Emma C.	20, Apr. 1820	D3
Davidson, George	Mayhew, Rebecca	2, May 1828	N3
Davie, Melarcton O.	Wood, Frances M.	14, Apr. 1836	T2
Davies, Samuel W.	Pierson, Clarrissa	11, Mar. 1815	S3
Davis, Benjamin W.	Phillip, Louisa	11, June 1831	R3
Davis, Dan	Tremper, Elizabeth	15, Sept 1815	S3
Davis, E.P.	Lapp, Mary Ann	26, Aug. 1847	K2
Davis, George F.	Wilson, Nancy	16, July 1841	N2
Davis, Henry F.	Kellogg, Almira S.	14, Mar. 1840	R3
Davis, Jesse E.	Allen, Mary F.	19, Nov. 1847	K2
Davis, Joseph	Brown, Eliza	30, June 1821	S3
Davis, Joseph	Glasgow, Mary	28, Mar. 1823	N2
Davis, Joshua	Tilton, Mary	4, Sept 1850	Y2
Davis, Julian N.	Peticolas, Catharine	11, Oct. 1852	P2
Davis, Preston (Dr)	Sumner, Amanda C.	17, May 1828	R3
Davis, S.H.	Loury, Mary P.	7, Apr. 1834	T2
Dawson, Thomas	Cullen, Margaret	29, Sept 1827	R3
Dawson, Washington	Langeville, Jane P.	29, Apr. 1820	S3
Dayton, Eli (Dr)	Wood, Catharine	15, Feb. 1839	T2
D'Carteret, John H.	Hearington, Eliza	27, Apr. 1822	S3
Dean, Abner	Pease, Mary	15, Jan. 1814	S3
Dean, Daniel	Garniss, Emma	18, Apr. 1840	R3
Deane, William	Rickman, Adeline	15, May 1819	S3
Dearstine, John	Jolly, Elizabeth	2, Nov. 1835	T2
Decker, Josiah	Wiltberger, S. (Mrs)	18, May 1822	S3

Grooms	Brides	Date of Notice	Page
DeCoursey, Francis	Horne, Mary Ann	7, June 1828	R3
Deeds, Isaac W.	Rogers, Ann Eliza	9, May 1818	S3
Defining, Benjamin F	Rawlins, Mary	17, Oct. 1840	R3
DeForest, Delauzun	Stephenson, Mary W.	7, July 1832	R3
Defrees, Anthony	McKnight, Betsey	27, Oct. 1821	S3
DeGraw, Abraham	Cornelius, Mary	8, Jan. 1842	R3
DeGraw, Abraham	Cornelius, Mary	4, Jan. 1842	N2
DeGraw, John	Farmer, Mary D.	24, Dec. 1836	R3
Degraw, P.G.	Miller, Lizzie A.	13, Nov. 1847	K2
Delaplaine, Joseph	Levingston, Jane Ann	7, Oct. 1812	S3
Delvin, John	Cook, Elizabeth Ann	30, Aug. 1828	R3
Deming, M.R.	Barnum, Abigail	18, Aug. 1836	X3
Denier, Elijah	Nichols, Thankful	25, Apr. 1818	S3
Dennis, Benjamin (Dr)	Besson, Charlotte W.	3, Feb. 1838	R3
Denniston, Alex (Rev)	Rawlins, Ann (Mrs)	30, May 1817	S3
Dent, John T.	Smith, A.	6, Oct. 1832	R3
Derby, Thomas	Badger, Martha	18, Jan. 1841	N2
DeSerisy, Louis	Thomas, Mary Ann	20, Sept 1852	P2
DeWitt, G.V.H.	Pierson, Mary Ann	22, May 1819	S3
Dewitt, G.V.H.	Kilgour, Juliana (Mrs)	7, Jan. 1832	R3
Dick, George	Anderson, Jane	2, May 1812	S3
Dickinson, Austin	Camp, Laura W.	2, June 1836	X3
Diddle, Ingersoll	James, Catharine E.	31, Oct. 1840	R3
Diel, Jacob	Kerchner, Sarah	4, Feb. 1831	X3
Digby, Theodore	Stone, Frances F.	23, Mar. 1847	K2
Dillingham, John	McKenzie, Catharine	28, Sept 1820	S3
Dinsmoor, Silas G.	Resor, Elizabeth S.	16, Nov. 1833	R3
Disney, David T.	Carter, Sarah	2, Sept 1825	N3
Disney, William	Thatcher, Julia (Mrs)	21, June 1828	R3
Disney, William	Thatcher, Julia (Mrs)	24, June 1828	N3
Disten, William L.	Lehmanowsky, Anna S.	21, Sept 1837	X3
Distin, William L.	Lehmanowsky, Anna S.	16, Sept 1837	R3
Distin, William L.	Lehmanowsky, Ann S.	14, Sept 1837	T2
Doan, Isaac	Cook, Isabella	1, Dec. 1838	T2
Dobson, Benjamin	Leech, Sarah	22, Apr. 1847	K2
Dockstader, Nicholas	Judd, Harriet	5, July 1828	R3
Dodd, James	Gibbs, C.H.	26, Dec. 1840	R3
Dodd, John M.	Williamson, Abigail	14, July 1836	X3
Dolton, Ellis	Shields, Mary	12, June 1847	K2
Donaldson, George	Guilford, Appeline	27, May 1847	K2
Donaldson, William	Shreve, Elizabeth	5, Oct. 1838	T2
Donelson, Daniel S.	Branch, Margaret	1, Nov. 1830	A3
Donelson, Daniel S.	Branch, Margaret	2, Nov. 1830	N2
Donelson, Stackly	Lawrence, Philian	12, July 1828	R3
Donough, John P.	Mahard, Esther	7, Nov. 1835	T2
Donsee, John	Smith, Elizabeth	15, Jan. 1831	R3
Dorfeuille, J.	Davis, Janette	11, May 1824	N3
Dorfeuille, J.	Davis, Janette	13, May 1824	E3
Dorks, Joseph B.	Howard, Elizabeth J.	19, Aug. 1850	P2
Dow, Lorenzo (Rev)	Doalbear, Lucy	18, May 1820	S3
Downer, William	Wattson, Ann Delia	18, May 1841	N2
Downs, W.H.	White, Rebecca Ann	3, June 1847	K2
Doyle, Samuel	Burk, Abigail	21, Nov. 1829	R3
Doyle, Thomas A.	Turner, Elizabeth	8, Oct. 1822	J3

Grooms	Brides	Date of Notice	Page
Drake, Aaron	Scudder, Mary	19, Apr. 1816	S3
Drake, Aaron	Harrison, Ann	31, Mar. 1821	S3
Drake, Charles D.	Blow, Martha Ella T.	17, Sept 1835	T2
Drake, Edward L.	Sebree, Ann S. (Mrs)	9, July 1831	R3
Drake, Francis	Ferris, Catharine	21, Feb. 1835	R3
Drake, Francis	Ferris, Catharine	24, Feb. 1835	T2
Drake, John T.	Slocum, Oliva Eliza	23, Feb. 1828	R3
Drake, John T.	Slocum, Olivia Eliza	22, Feb. 1828	N3
Drane, A.	Ferguson, Elizabeth	13, Dec. 1828	R3
Dresbach, Charles F.	Russell, Lucinda	15, Sept 1835	T2
Drew, William C.	Armstrong, Mary G.	12, Dec. 1817	S3
Duckwall, David	Frazier, Hester	6, Oct. 1852	P2
Dudley, Ambrose	Curry, Clarissa (Mrs)	7, July 1837	T2
Dudley, F.D.	Palmer, Mary Ann	18, Oct. 1828	R3
Dudley, Moses S.	Carl, Ellen	28, Aug. 1847	K2
Duffield, Charles	Dickey, Margaret	22, Sept 1832	R3
Duffield, Charles	Cloon, Sarah E.	2, Apr. 1842	R3
Duffield, Charles	Cloon, Sarah E.	28, Mar. 1842	N2
Duffield, J.J.	Pienier, Eliza	23, May 1836	T2
Duffield, S.B.	Litchfield, Mary F.	14, May 1842	R3
Dugan, John A.	Gilliams, Susan L.	13, Oct. 1852	P2
Dumas, John P.	Hudson, Jane	3, Oct. 1850	P2
Dumass, Benjamin	Pettit, Maria	16, Oct. 1819	S3
Dun, James	Walke, Susan V.	5, Dec. 1840	R3
Dun, James	Walke, Susan Virginia	1, Dec. 1840	N2
Dunbar, Robert W.	Sampson, Harriet	13, Nov. 1835	T2
Dunbar, Seth	Mahew, Hannah	8, June 1820	S3
Duncan, Jesse S.	Patterson, Elizabeth	3, Feb. 1832	X3
Duncan, Richard G.	Bradbury, Mary P.	5, Nov. 1852	P2
Dunham, William	McLean, Eliza L.	20, Feb. 1841	R3
Dunham, William	McLean, Eliza L.	13, Feb. 1841	N2
Dunlap, Samuel	Pratt, Hannah	20, Feb. 1813	S3
Dunlap, W.H.	Trinnel, Ellen	6, Oct. 1852	P2
Dunn, John	James, Elizabeth	16, Oct. 1841	R3
Dunn, John	Gardner, Janette	29, July 1826	J3
Dunseth, John	Woodard, Patsey	20, Sept 1814	W4
Dunseth, Lewis	Hawkins, Louisa	18, Apr. 1840	R3
Durbin, John (Rev)	Cook, Frances	22, Sept 1827	R3
Durkee, Dwight	Davis, Sarah Jane	10, June 1851	P2
Durrett, R.T.	Bates, Lizzie	22, Dec. 1852	P2
Dusky, Eli	Patmor, Rachel	30, June 1827	R3
Duvall, Alexander	Elliott, Anne Elizabeth	1, Sept 1835	T2
Dyer, A.E.	Morse, Mary Jane	18, Feb. 1848	K2
Dyer, Elisha	Gregory, Frances	6, Mar. 1841	R3
Dyer, Isaac	Gregory, Frances	4, Mar. 1841	N2
Earl, Isaac F.	Carpenter, Abby	6, Oct. 1832	R3
Earnest, Andrew	Haffley, Catharine	6, June 1817	S3
Easton, E.	Kemper, Mary D.	29, Oct. 1831	R3
Easton, Shadford	Reed, Eliza	27, Nov. 1841	R3
Eaton, Charles H.	Rue, Mary Ann	25, Oct. 1838	T2
Eaton, Charles H.	Rue, Mary Ann	26, Oct. 1838	N2
Eaton, George G.	Harrison, Bessie S.	3, June 1847	K2
Eaton, John H.	Timberlake, Margaret	12, Jan. 1829	N2

Grooms	Brides	Date of Notice	Page
Ebbert, Isaac (Rev)	Easton, Eliza	29, May 1841	N2
Eberle, Richard (Dr)	Higbee, Theodosia W.	5, Dec. 1840	R3
Eberle, Richard (Dr)	Higbee, Theodosia W.	5, Dec. 1840	N2
Eccles, Henry	Johnston, Jane	1, July 1847	K2
Eddy, Dean W.	McPherrin, Margaret	1, Nov. 1833	X3
Eddy, John	Irwin, Sarah (Mrs)	12, July 1828	R3
Edmonston, Robert	Provost, M. (Mrs)	10, Mar. 1827	R3
Edwards, Abraham (Dr)	Hunt, Ruth	3, July 1805	S3
Edwards, Charles G.	Townsend, Margaretta	22, Apr. 1841	N2
Edwards, Edwin	Risinger, Sarah W.	19, May 1847	K2
Edwards, Isaac	Gorreal, Jane (Mrs)	9, Dec. 1852	P2
Edwards, Jonathan	Rice, Eliza	6, May 1847	K2
Edwards, R.E.	Goshorn, Mary Jane	21, Aug. 1852	P2
Edwards, Samuel	Parmeter, Aurelia M.	28, May 1842	R3
Edwards, William	Brown, Charlotte	28, Mar. 1812	S3
Elder, Thomas	Scott, Jane	9, Oct. 1805	S3
Elliott, Arthur	Hayford, Achsah (Mrs)	5, Nov. 1852	P2
Elliott, Michael K.	Plow, Elizabeth	29, Oct. 1838	N2
Elliott, Silas H.	Magie, Rhoda M.	23, Feb. 1835	T2
Elliott, Thomas	Florer, Phoebe C.	5, July 1841	N2
Ellis, Humphrey	Duvey, Elizabeth (Mrs)	1, Dec. 1821	S3
Ellis, Rowland	Rogers, Mary C.	20, Dec. 1828	R3
Ellis, Rowland	Rogers, Mary C.	19, Dec. 1828	N3
Elsrode, William	Hayden, Elenor	6, Oct. 1827	R3
Elstner, John	Rains, Mary	14, Mar. 1823	N3
Elston, William	McKee, Emma	28, May 1842	R3
Ely, Jonathan	Cooly, Jeanette (Mrs)	10, June 1837	R3
Ely, Jonathan	Cooley, Jeannette C.	12, June 1837	T2
Ely, Seneca W.	Delano, Mary	29, Aug. 1840	R3
Embree, Jesse	Dickinson, Mary	26, Sept 1818	S3
Emerson, Henry	Benbridge, Evelina	1, Jan. 1828	R3
Emerson, Nathan	Barber, Catharine W.	1, Sept 1837	N2
Emery, Charles	Crane, Mary	23, Mar. 1833	R3
English, Isaac B.	Hannis, Catharine	19, May 1847	K2
English, Samuel	Trout, Susan J.	11, Apr. 1812	S2
Enness, John B.	Barr, Susan	24, Aug. 1811	S3
Enyart, Thomas	Keef, Mary	16, Oct. 1819	S3
Ernest, Jacob	Swager, Elizabeth	8, June 1849	L2
Ernst, A.H.	Otis, Sarah H.	2, Oct. 1841	R3
Ernst, A.H.	Otis, Sarah H.	25, Sept 1841	N2
Ernst, Franklin	Hopper, Jemima	22, May 1841	R3
Ernst, Franklin	Hopper, Jemima	21, May 1841	N2
Ernst, Jacob	Bruce, Louisa (Mrs)	30, May 1840	R3
Esep, Edward	Smith, Sarah T.	3, Feb. 1842	N2
Este, David K.	Harrison, Lucy S.	2, Oct. 1819	S3
Este, David K.	Miller, Louisa	16, May 1829	R3
Estep, Joshua	Danison, Julia	12, Jan. 1839	T2
Estep, Richard P.	Noble, Mary F.	9, July 1842	R3
Estep, Thomas	Smith, Sarah Y.	5, Feb. 1842	R3
Evans, Daniel P.	Humphries, Nancy C.	21, July 1827	R3
Evans, Daniel T.	Atherstone, Caroline	7, Oct. 1824	E3
Evans, J. (Dr)	Schooley, Ann E.	16, Apr. 1835	T3
Evans, John	Dillon, Elizabeth	10, Oct. 1838	T2
Evans, Thomas	Sellman, Elizabeth	23, May 1836	T2

Grooms	Brides	Date of Notice	Page
Evans, William	Barkus, Martha	28, Nov. 1812	S3
Everett, William H.	Broadwell, Amanda M.	17, Mar. 1837	T2
Ewer, George W.	Coggeshall, Margaret	17, Feb. 1826	N3
Ewing, Henry	VanDyke, Phebe P.	2, Jan. 1841	R3
Ewing, James	Atkinson, Amanda	23, Dec. 1835	T3
Fairchild, Oliver (Dr)	Edson, Roxana	5, Jan. 1816	S3
Faran, James J.	Russell, Angeline	4, Apr. 1840	R3
Farnham, Charles A.	Aydelott, Margaret P.	2, July 1842	R3
Farnsworth, William	Britton, Lavinia	13, Oct. 1827	R3
Farquhar, William P.	Sampson, Mary	11, Sept 1835	T2
Farran, Charles	Kotts, Pheby	8, May 1805	S3
Farrar, Andrew S.	Cutter, Lydia Ann	21, July 1827	R3
Farrar, D.	Botley, Macbei (Mrs)	17, June 1825	N1
Farrel, James	Reagin, Sophia	17, Mar. 1821	S3
Farvin, Samuel W.	Johnston, Elizabeth Ann	12, Nov. 1836	N2
Faulkner, Jeremiah	Jacobs, Ann E.	14, Nov. 1840	R3
Febriger, George L.	Smith, Caroline A.	9, Apr. 1849	L2
Fenn, Ira I.	Pomeroy, Eunice B.	2, June 1836	X3
Ferguson, Abijah F.	Kemper, Susan M.	22, Mar. 1816	S3
Ferguson, E.A.	Moore, Agnes A.	19, Sept 1851	P2
Ferguson, James	Mellor, Emma	10, Sept 1842	R3
Ferguson, John	Ross, Sarah	15, Mar. 1833	X3
Ferris, William J.	Brown, Ann Eliza	21, Dec. 1839	R3
Field, J.M.	Riddle, Eliza	20, Nov. 1837	T2
Field, William R.	Howard, Mary Ann	15, Sept 1827	R3
Fielding, M.B.	Ridge, Anna M.	8, Oct. 1852	P2
Fields, Daniel	Cox, Minerva	4, Feb. 1831	X3
Filley, Lucius L.	Jones, Christiana	22, Mar. 1849	L2
Finch, William	Young, Frances Mary	23, June 1838	R3
Finch, William	Young, Frances Mary	22, June 1838	T2
Findlay, Samuel B.	Duncan, Elizabeth	9, Dec. 1837	R3
Fine, John	Shoyer, Mary Jane	7, Oct. 1847	K2
Finkbine, William	Delaplaine, Jane (Mrs)	23, Feb. 1828	R3
Finkbine, William	Delaplaine, Jane (Mrs)	22, Feb. 1828	N3
Finkbine, William H.	Woodward, Mary Ann	8, Oct. 1847	K2
Finley, James	Speer, Eliza	28, Oct. 1830	A3
Finley, James C.	Smith, Margaret	26, Feb. 1831	R3
Fisher, Charles	Brigham, Julia R.	9, Nov. 1833	R3
Fisher, Elwood	Smith, Julia	17, Oct. 1840	R3
Fisher, Jonathan	Titus, Eliza	26, Nov. 1835	X3
Fisher, Ludevick	Dodd, Hannah	1, Mar. 1833	X3
Fisk, Allen	Francisco, Virginia	16, Aug. 1852	P2
Fitch, M.C.	Paxson, Anna Maria	14, Apr. 1821	S3
Flagg, Jared B.	Montague, Sarah R.	18, Jan. 1842	N2
Fleming, Albert	Mires, Mary	23, June 1835	T2
Fletcher, Adolphus	Brooks, Caroline E.	14, Apr. 1836	X3
Fletcher, Lowell	Drennan, Mary R.	24, Mar. 1832	R3
Fletcher, Robert	Haines, Mary Ann	27, Dec. 1834	R3
Flinn, Jesse	Wilson, Sarah Ann	19, Apr. 1847	K2
Flint, James H.	Pike, Maria M.	16, May 1840	R3
Florer, John N.	Whittemore, Harriet	29, Mar. 1838	T2
Florer, Robert C.	Rand, Emeline	14, Feb. 1839	T2
Flowers, Michael B.	Coltier, Catharine	12, Oct. 1820	S3

Grooms	Brides	Date of Notice	Page
Floyd, Gabriel J.	Conn, Sarah M.	5, Dec. 1817	S3
Folger, Charles R.	Brown, Jane D.	3, Oct. 1840	R3
Folger, George M.	Laird, Anna G.	22, May 1847	K2
Folger, Seth	Clasby, Lydia	20, Apr. 1820	D3
Folger, Seth W.	Washburn, Mary F.	6, June 1837	N2
Folger, Thomas B.	Settlemyer, Esther	10, Dec. 1852	P2
Follin, Augustus	Reeder, Carolina A.	11, Sept 1847	K2
Folsom, S.	Davis, Sophia	30, Nov. 1847	K2
Foos, Thomas J.	Linville, Jane	3, Sept 1847	K2
Foot, Joseph	Hardesty, Rebeckah	1, Jan. 1814	S3
Foote, Andrew	Ware, Abigail	16, Sept 1837	R3
Foote, Andrew R.	Ward, Abigail	15, Sept 1837	T2
Foote, James M.	Loring, Jane	23, Nov. 1835	T2
Foote, James M.	Loring, Jane	26, Nov. 1835	X3
Foote, Samuel E.	Elliott, Elizabeth	29, Sept 1827	R3
Forbes, James C.	Peoples, Mary Ann	3, Aug. 1830	N2
Forbes, John	Sisson, Amelia S.	15, Aug. 1818	S3
Ford, Smith	Fox, Frances L.	19, June 1847	K2
Forquer, George	Cranmer, Ann	5, Apr. 1828	R3
Forquer, George	Cranmer, Ann	4, Apr. 1828	N3
Forte, Elijah C.	Watson, Annie A.	8, Sept 1852	P2
Fosdick, Samuel	Wood, Sarah Ann	14, Jan. 1836	T3
Foster, Charles	Barker, Rachel	7, June 1828	R3
Foster, David	Allen, Martha Ann	13, Sept 1852	P2
Foster, Joseph C.	Karrack, Catharine	28, June 1828	R3
Foster, Samuel	Cutter, Susannah	3, June 1806	S3
Foster, William C.	Smith, M.A.W.	5, July 1830	A3
Foster, William C.	Smith, Martha Ann W.	3, July 1830	R3
Foster, William M.	Bonnett, Eliza T.	21, Sept 1837	T2
Fougler, Seth	Clasby, Lydia	15, Apr. 1820	S2
Foulke, Thomas D.	Smith, Ann M.	28, July 1827	R3
Foulks, George W.	Maning, Jemima	26, Oct. 1847	K2
Fowler, John	Arbigust, Mary Ann	9, July 1830	N2
Fowler, John	Sharp, S.C.	26, Aug. 1847	K2
Fox, Charles	Miller, Mary	9, Dec. 1824	E2
Fox, Frederick	Bellamy, Ann	28, Sept 1850	Y2
Fox, John	Haughton, Martha	20, Oct. 1821	S3
Francis, David	Oldham, Susanna	9, July 1814	S3
Francis, Thomas	Walker, Eunice	22, Feb. 1825	N3
Francisco, A.N.	Clark, Ella M.	24, Jan. 1848	K2
Franklin, Samuel	Jester, Sarah	27, June 1829	R3
Franklin, William	Smith, Mary Eliza	18, Sept 1841	R3
Frazer, Samuel G.	Garrison, S.A.	18, Oct. 1838	T2
Freeman, Amos	Weatherford, Sarah	22, Sept 1838	R3
Freeman, Clarkson	Cassidy, Abbey	26, Mar. 1820	S2
Freeman, Edmund	Rodman, Elizabeth (Mrs)	30, July 1799	S3
French, Ezra P.	King, Eliza R.	18, Apr. 1829	R3
French, George H.	Porter, Eliza A.	18, May 1838	T2
French, John S.	House, Mary M.	30, Oct. 1852	P2
Friant, Clayton	Craig, Sarah	22, Apr. 1830	A3
Froome, Samuel	Redhead, Jane	5, Dec. 1840	R3
Froome, Samuel	Redhead, Jane	1, Dec. 1840	N2
Frost, Edward L.	Holloway, Hannah	11, Aug. 1827	R3
Fry, George M.	Meldrum, Mary B.	11, July 1836	T2

Grooms	Brides	Date of Notice	Page
Fry, J. Reese	Nevins, Cornelia	16, June 1841	N2
Frye, George B.	Young, Ann	6, June 1836	T2
Fuller, John W.	Peck, Delia A.	24, Sept 1847	K2
Fuller, Robert C.	Martin, Laura Attila	19, Apr. 1847	K2
Fuller, Robert C.	Hamilton, Laura A.	19, Apr. 1847	K2
Fullerton, Samuel W.	Davis, Martha	13, Sept 1838	T2
Fulwiler, John	Moore, Frances Ann	7, Dec. 1838	T2
Funk, Daniel	Carns, Sarah	22, Apr. 1830	A3
Furry, Daniel	Griffin, Mary	28, May 1835	T2
Furst, Joseph	Helmling, Sophia M.	9, Oct. 1850	Y2
Gabriet, Edwin T.	Patton, Philinda	3, Jan. 1839	T2
Gaines, James M.	Tousy, Elvira	25, Aug. 1827	R3
Gaines, Richard	Sisson, Mary H.	11, Feb. 1815	S3
Gale, John H.	Lawrence, Hannah	24, June 1837	R3
Gale, John H.	Lawrence, Hannah	19, June 1837	T2
Gale, John H.	Lawrence, Hannah	17, June 1837	N2
Gallagher, Francis	Madin, Sarah B.	24, Nov. 1832	R3
Gallagher, John M.	Cushing, Hannah L.	22, Oct. 1834	T3
Gallagher, William D	Adamson, E.R.	5, July 1830	A3
Gallagher, William D	Adamson, Emma R.	3, July 1830	R3
Galt, John H.	Warner, Emeline A.	10, Nov. 1852	P2
Gano, Aaron (Lt)	Burley, Frances	16, May 1818	S3
Gano, Daniel (Major)	Lawrence, Rebecca	27, Sept 1816	S3
Gano, John A.	Hubbell, Catharine	5, Oct. 1822	S3
Gano, R.M. (Gen)	Goforth, Deborah (Mrs)	15, Nov. 1814	W4
Gano, W.G.W.	Willis, Nancy	13, Oct. 1821	S3
Gant, George	Ashton, Mary Ann	27, Aug. 1852	P2
Gardiner, James	Smith, Rebecca	8, July 1852	P2
Gardner, Allen M.	Montgomery, Caroline	21, May 1842	R3
Gardner, Charles Hy.	Hunter, Sarah	2, Jan. 1830	R3
Gardner, Collin	Hemphill, Jane (Mrs)	6, July 1849	L2
Gardner, Elijah F.	Smith, Elizabeth M.	22, Sept 1852	P2
Gardner, William J.	Craig, Elizabeth J.	23, May 1849	L2
Garrard, Jeptha D.	Ludlow, Sarabella	19, Aug. 1824	E3
Garretson, Israel	Buntz, Maria	26, Aug. 1824	E2
Garretson, Samuel	Wilson, Sarah Jane	27, Dec. 1828	R3
Garrett, Ashton	Spangler, Priscilla	29, Nov. 1828	R3
Garrett, R.J.	Smith, Mary	21, May 1842	N2
Garrison, Edward	Miller, Margaret	26, Oct. 1832	X3
Garrison, William	Williamson, Eliza	29, May 1841	N2
Garwood, Nicholas	Rollin, Mary A.	10, June 1847	K2
Gavin, James	Cather, Hester	7, May 1814	S3
Gazlay, James W.	Williams, Rebecca M.	15, Apr. 1820	S2
Gazlay, James W.	Williams, Rebecca M.	20, Apr. 1820	D3
Gelvin, John	Hart, Lydia A.	11, Nov. 1852	P2
Gest, Andrew M.	Bryan, Melissa S.	22, June 1836	T2
Gest, Condui G.	Biggs, Margaretta	28, Nov. 1840	R3
Getty, Robert	Smith, Clarinda	23, May 1829	R3
Geyer, John	Jackson, Ann	7, May 1831	R3
G---hase, S.	Eichelberger, Susan	5, Sept 1840	R3
Gibbon, Leonard	Ardrey, Sarah B.	27, Dec. 1834	R3
Gibbs, Edward G.	Kelpan, Mary Jane	16, Oct. 1841	R3
Gibbs, Edward G.	Kelpan, Mary Jane	16, Oct. 1841	N2

Grooms	Brides	Date of Notice	Page
Gibbs, William F.	Eaton, Eliza Ann	17, Mar. 1836	T2
Giles, Benjamin	Longshore, Rachel C.	30, Oct. 1847	K2
Giles, George B.	Gardner, Deborah	21, July 1827	R3
Gill, Michael	Weaver, Sarah Dell	8, Aug. 1818	S3
Gillim, Isaac	McStuart, Agnes	25, Oct. 1841	N2
Gillingham, Harper	Gillingham, Eliza	28, May 1842	R3
Gillingham, Harper	Gillingham, Eliza	24, May 1842	N2
Gilmore, Gurdon R.	Butler, Malvina	8, Sept 1838	R3
Gilmore, Gurdon R.	Butler, Malvina	7, Sept 1838	T2
Gilmore, Hiram S.	Moore, Maria H.	6, June 1840	R3
Gilmore, James	Stibbs, Mary Jane	23, July 1842	R3
Gilmore, James	Stibbs, Mary Jane	19, July 1842	N2
Gilpin, Joseph H.	Scudler, Elvira	3, Jan. 1839	T2
Gimble, Henry	Doughty, Nancy	16, Apr. 1814	S3
Gist, Robert C.	Dorsey, Mary	14, Jan. 1832	R3
Glascoe, James S.	Dill, Frances Ann	12, May 1832	R3
Glasgow, William	Lane, Sarah S.	25, Apr. 1840	R3
Glen, Milton	Newell, Amanda	28, Nov. 1835	T2
Glen, Milton	Newell, Amana	3, Dec. 1835	X3
Glenn, James	Sayre, Ann	18, May 1820	S3
Glenn, John	Campbell, Elizabeth	23, July 1838	T2
Glover, Henry	Flintham, Susan D.	16, Nov. 1833	R3
Glover, Henry	Flintham, Susan D.	15, Nov. 1833	X3
Goblo, Daniel L.	Linn, Martha	4, July 1834	X3
Goddard, John F.	Daniel, Mary L.	4, Sept 1837	T2
Goddard, John F.	Daniel, Mary L.V.	7, Sept 1837	X3
Godley, John	McHenry, Mary	29, June 1820	S3
Goforth, Aaron	Winters, Debby	24, Apr. 1805	S3
Goforth, Thomas J.	Matthews, Eliza V.	17, Mar. 1826	N3
Goforth, William G.	Hay, Eulalie	18, May 1820	S3
Goldenburgh, John	Fosdick, Emeline B.	12, May 1841	N2
Golding, Aaron	Garrish, Sophia	9, Mar. 1822	S2
Gooch, Henry	Stoddart, Clarissa	29, May 1841	N2
Good, Robert	Kelly, Susan A.	2, Nov. 1839	R3
Goodhart, Richard	Hodship, Mary I.	25, Dec. 1852	P2
Goodhue, G.W.	Graves, Elizabeth S.	1, May 1847	K2
Goodin, Samuel H.	Greene, Ellen	12, Sept 1840	R3
Goodloe, James	Weaver, Myriam	13, Nov. 1819	S3
Goodman, Augustus	Grandin, Lucy A.	8, July 1847	K2
Goodman, Charles	Wiles, Catharine E.	25, Dec. 1841	R3
Goodman, Charles	Wiles, Catharine F.	23, Dec. 1841	N2
Goodman, Henry H.	Langdon, Esther Ann	5, Dec. 1840	R3
Goodman, William	Adams, Margaret Rand	16, Aug. 1828	R3
Goodrich, Jeremiah	Walker, Amelia	19, Feb. 1814	S3
Goodwin, William G.	Tucker, Eliza	1, Apr. 1806	S3
Gordon, Archibald	Hanson, Mary	18, Sept 1830	R3
Gordon, David	Sloane, Esther	24, Apr. 1830	R3
Gordon, George H.	Werner, Ellen Agnes	10, June 1836	T2
Gordon, John (Capt)	Wood, Rebecca H.	14, Jan. 1837	R3
Gordon, William J.M.	German, Anna M.	8, Sept 1850	Y2
Goshorn, George	Switzer, Belinda	15, Aug. 1840	R3
Goshorn, John M.	Jenkins, Louisa	12, Aug. 1835	T2
Goshorn, William F.	Daggett, Eliza J.	22, Apr. 1847	K2
Gosman, Richard S.	Sampson, Caroline	10, Nov. 1827	R3

Grooms	Brides	Date of Notice	Page
Gosney, Nimrod	Daniels, Nancy	9, May 1812	S3
Gossin, Jacob	Morrison, Elizabeth	19, Oct. 1852	P2
Gottshalkson, Sol.	Nancarrow, Eliza	4, Feb. 1801	S3
Goudy, James H.	Barnes, Sarah	25, Apr. 1818	S3
Gould, John	Stone, Eunice A.	30, Sept 1847	K2
Gourgas, J. Louis	Gourgas, Louisa M.	23, Dec. 1840	N2
Gouverneur, Samuel L	Munroe, Maria Hester	8, Apr. 1820	S3
Grace, Benjamin	Rhodes, Elizabeth	28, July 1827	R3
Grace, John William	Heaslett, Ruth A.	14, Aug. 1841	N2
Gradner, Richard	Sisson, Mary	6, Aug. 1817	S3
Graham, B. (Dr)	Boggs, Lilley	16, Nov. 1837	T2
Graham, George	Murdock, Ellen F.	16, Aug. 1828	R3
Graham, Samuel	Jones, Ann	7, Feb. 1829	R3
Graham, Thomas	Symmes, Elizabeth (Mrs)	2, Oct. 1819	S3
Graham, William A.	Price, Harriet D.	20, Mar. 1847	K2
Graves, Joseph S.	Kemper, Frances	18, June 1842	R3
Graves, Joseph S.	Kemper, Frances	16, June 1842	N2
Graveson, J.	Corke, Sarah	31, Dec. 1852	P2
Gray, William	Vance, A.E.	23, June 1836	X3
Greatbatch, Hamlet	Myers, Sarah	26, Nov. 1850	P2
Green, George	Hoover, Lucy	26, Dec. 1840	R3
Green, George	Hoover, Lucy	23, Dec. 1840	N2
Green, James	Frazer, Elizabeth	31, Dec. 1852	P2
Green, John	Foulk, Margaret	7, June 1828	R3
Green, Richard H.	Turney, Mary Ann S.	7, Oct. 1831	A3
Green, Robert C.	Burrows, Maria Tunis	8, Sept 1827	R3
Green, Stephen A.	Lovejoy, Mary	8, June 1847	K2
Green, Thomas J.	Bonsell, Margaret L.	16, Mar. 1837	T2
Green, Timothy	Jacobs, Julia (Mrs)	2, Dec. 1837	R3
Green, William N.	Stockwell, Elizabeth B.	21, Nov. 1840	R3
Green, William N.	Langhorne, Elizabeth	17, Nov. 1840	N2
Greene, Caleb	Tunis, Caroline B.	10, Oct. 1840	R3
Greene, John A.	Kirk, Margaret E.	14, May 1842	R3
Greene, William W.	Conn, Sarah Ann	10, Nov. 1827	R3
Greenleaf, Charles T.	Worrels, Lucretia	8, Sept 1838	R3
Greenleaf, Samuel	Hueston, Matilda	5, Oct. 1822	S3
Greenleaf, William K.	Miller, Mary Jane	9, May 1829	R3
Greenleaf, William T.	Milligan, Agnes K.	16, Aug. 1834	R3
Greenleaf, William T.	Milligan, Agnes K.	14, Aug. 1834	T2
Greenwood, Miles	Hopson, Phebe Jane	24, Mar. 1836	T2
Gregory, Thomas	Sater, Rebecca	31, Dec. 1814	S3
Gridley, E.G.	Terry, Mary A.	28, Apr. 1827	R3
Gridley, E.G.	Terry, Mary A.	27, Apr. 1827	N2
Griffin, David	Connover, Mary Ann	9, Nov. 1835	T2
Griffin, William P.	Lawrence, Mary N.	14, May 1838	T2
Griffith, David	Lawrence, Eliza	19, Dec. 1834	X3
Griffith, Romulus R.	Merriweather, Rachel	30, June 1827	R3
Griffiths, David J.	Wagner, Kate	27, Nov. 1852	P2
Grimes, Thomas	Woodward, Mary	4, July 1812	S3
Griswold, George	Douglass, Jane	1, Dec. 1840	N2
Griswold, Robert H.	Powers, Helen Maria	28, Nov. 1840	R3
Groene, Ernst	Gassman, Frederika	9, Aug. 1850	Y2
Groesbeck, Herman J.	Benoist, Rosina E.	21, Oct. 1837	R3
Groesbeck, Herman J.	Benoist, Rosina E.	13, Oct. 1837	T2

Grooms	Brides	Date of Notice	Page
Groesbeck, William	Burnet, Elizabeth	4, Nov. 1837	R3
Groesbeck, William S	Burnet, Elizabeth	3, Nov. 1837	T2
Grover, Abraham	Dunham, Zeruah	11, Aug. 1835	T2
Grover, Ira	Glanton, Elizabeth	18, Feb. 1823	N3
Grundy, R.C. (Rev)	Canfield, Hannah M.	21, Apr. 1836	X3
Guelich, Lewis	Phillips, Mary A.	16, Oct. 1852	P2
Guilford, Nathan	Farnsworth, Eliza W.	30, Oct. 1819	S3
Guinn, John K.	Pray, Ann (Mrs)	14, July 1838	R3
Gullet, A.G.	Nicholson, Sarah Ann	22, Sept 1838	R3
Guthrie, Colin	Gray, Jennet	16, Jan. 1819	S3
Guy, Alexander	Wade, Susan A.D.	5, Apr. 1830	A3
Guy, Alexander	Wade, Susan A.L.	2, Apr. 1830	N2
Guyon, James	Goodwin, Mary A.	21, Dec. 1852	P2
Gwinn, Evan	Field, Nancy	21, May 1847	K2
Gwynne, Abraham	Flagg, Cettie M.	30, May 1840	R3
Gwynne, David	McLean, Sarah	24, May 1834	T2
Hadlock, Hezekiah	Wilson, Olive	4, Oct. 1830	A3
Hadlock, James	Hill, Susannah (Mrs)	1, Dec. 1847	K2
Hafer, Henry	Schwartz, Charlotte	27, Jan. 1824	N3
Hageman, Christian	Harckless, Jane	20, July 1803	S3
Hageman, James	Swing, Kerenda	30, Oct. 1835	T2
Hagerman, Benjamin	Bishop, Laura	30, Jan. 1830	R3
Haggarty, John H.	Newkirk, Temperance	11, May 1820	S3
Haggit, J.P. (Dr)	McElroy, Mary Ann	4, Nov. 1837	R3
Haggott, John P.	McAroy, Mary B.	11, Nov. 1837	R3
Haight, Benjamin J.	Coolidge, Hetty B.	1, July 1835	T2
Haile, William	Joor, Nancy	7, July 1827	R3
Hailman, David (Dr)	Edmonds, (Miss)	14, Apr. 1821	S3
Haines, Charles G.	Stewart, Nancy	4, Sept 1852	P2
Haines, E.S.	Higbee, Charlotte	19, Nov. 1831	R3
Haines, J. (Dr)	Bailey, Eliza (Mrs)	23, Dec. 1831	X3
Haines, Josiah	Marsh, Lydia	10, Feb. 1821	S2
Hains, J. (Dr)	Bayley, Eliza (Mrs)	24, Dec. 1831	R3
Hale, Lewis	Flourngy, Letitla	28, June 1828	R3
Hales, Charles	Davis, Margaretta H.	31, May 1849	L2
Hall, Edward	Vandegriff, Frances	15, Sept 1835	T2
Hall, George	Carls, Catharine	11, Mar. 1831	X3
Hall, James	Alexander, M.L. (Mrs)	10, Sept 1839	T3
Hall, James C.	Oliver, Harriet R.	19, Aug. 1835	T2
Hall, James H.	Secuts, Matilda	5, Sept 1834	X3
Hall, James P.	Burns, Virginia L.	10, Oct. 1850	P2
Hall, John C.	Faulkner, Sarah Ann	2, Oct. 1841	R3
Hall, Joseph	Howel, Mary G.	13, Nov. 1835	T2
Hall, Joseph	Reid, Sarah	3, Nov. 1852	P2
Hall, Joseph W.	Norton, Elizabeth W.	5, Oct. 1839	R3
Halley, David J.	Betts, Mary	11, Apr. 1812	S2
Halley, Samuel B.	Hathaway, Harriet	13, Nov. 1841	R3
Halley, Samuel B.	Hathaway, Harriet	11, Nov. 1841	N2
Halley, Washington G.	Westcott, Rachel P.	27, Jan. 1827	R2
Halsey, Ichabod B.	Smith, Sally W.	5, Jan. 1803	S3
Hamar, James	Gallagher, Margaret	2, Nov. 1822	S3
Hambrock, J.H.	Martin, Maria	25, Oct. 1851	P2
Hamilton, Samuel R.	Bigger, Abigail M.	2, Nov. 1833	R3

Grooms	Brides	Date of Notice	Page
Hammit, Joseph (Rev)	James, Deborah	25, Sept 1841	R3
Hammond, C.	Moorehead, Elizabeth	8, Jan. 1836	T3
Hammond, Charles	Moorehead, Elizabeth	11, Jan. 1836	N2
Hampson, Jefferson	Foster, Epenetus	26, July 1834	T2
Hampton, William	Kain, Mary S.	15, Apr. 1847	K2
Hancinct, David	Bellows, Mary	5, Dec. 1836	T2
Hancock, J.	Brown, Isabella	4, Jan. 1851	P2
Hand, Ellis	Evans, Ellen S.	25, May 1847	K2
Hanes, Albert S.	Jungman, Anna S.	6, May 1847	K2
Hankins, William J.	Morris, Belle	17, Nov. 1852	P2
Hanks, George L.	Bunce, Julia	26, May 1836	X3
Hanselman, Charles	Gill, Mary	18, Aug. 1852	P2
Hanson, Custis A.	Butler, R.P. (Mrs)	16, Aug. 1834	R3
Hanson, Custus A.	Butler, R.P. (Mrs)	13, Aug. 1834	T2
Harbeson, Benjamin	Paxton, Mary	7, Jan. 1832	R3
Harbeson, Matthew L.	Morris, Jane	15, Oct. 1831	R3
Harbeson, Matthew L.	Morris, Jane	14, Oct. 1831	X3
Hardin, Joseph	Cottle, Susan	1, Jan. 1820	S3
Harding, Lyman	Shephard, Mary P.C.	10, Jan. 1837	T2
Hare, Jacob	Hunt, Susan	6, Mar. 1819	S3
Hargan, James	Simns, Esther Ann	23, Oct. 1850	P2
Harig, Albert	Whitaker, Harriet R.	7, Aug. 1850	Y2
Harlan, Aaron	Whiteman, Clarissa	4, Oct. 1830	A3
Harm, George W.	Robinson, Margaret B	9, Sept 1847	K2
Harman, Josiah	Lanman, Sarah C.	21, Oct. 1830	A3
Harp, David	Smith, Harriet	23, Oct. 1847	K2
Harr, William	Riser, Margaret	11, Feb. 1836	X3
Harrier, Edward	Parrish, Susannah	2, Nov. 1835	T2
Harris, Daniel	Solvin, Elizabeth T.	2, Sept 1852	P2
Harris, Horatio T.	Taylor, Keturah	25, Aug. 1821	S3
Harris, James A.	McFelch, Sarah	22, Sept 1838	R3
Harris, John W.	Jackson, Alice Ann	30, Jan. 1841	R3
Harris, John W.	Jackson, Alice Ann	24, Jan. 1841	N2
Harris, Robert S.	Reeder, Phebe H.	3, Mar. 1836	X3
Harris, William	Stuart, Mary	26, Feb. 1842	R3
Harrison, Carter B.	Southerland, Ann	22, June 1836	T2
Harrison, Carter B.	Sutherland, Anna	30, June 1836	X3
Harrison, Henry	St.Clair, Margaret	8, Oct. 1841	N2
Harrison, J.C.S.	Pike, Clarissa M.	2, Oct. 1819	S3
Harrison, John P.	Merrie, Mary Ann	19, May 1838	R3
Harrison, John Pitts	Merrie, Mary Ann	19, May 1838	T2
Harrison, John Scott	Irwin, Elizabeth R.	20, Aug. 1831	R3
Harrison, John Scott	Johnson, Lucretia K.	30, Dec. 1824	E3
Harrison, Levingston	Pierson, Mary	26, Oct. 1822	S3
Harrison, William	Looker, Eliza	3, Aug. 1830	N2
Harrison, William H.	Irwin, Jane Findlay	9, Mar. 1824	N3
Harrison, William H.	Irwin, Jane F.	11, Mar. 1824	E3
Hart, Edson P.	Nelson, Angeline	1, July 1852	P2
Hart, Henry N.	Church, Jane Elizabeth	27, Sept 1838	T2
Hart, Samuel	Pugh, Mary A.	12, June 1841	R3
Hart, Samuel	Pugh, Mary A.	8, June 1841	N2
Harter, L.F.	Williams, Catharine	11, July 1849	L2
Harthorn, Hugh B.	Bunnell, Jane	31, May 1816	S3
Hartshorn, Charles	Baum, Eleanor	4, Dec. 1841	N2

Grooms	Brides	Date of Notice	Page
Hartshorn, Warren	Wade, Ann (Mrs)	14, July 1834	T2
Hartshorne, Saunders	Burrows, Ann Eliza	7, Feb. 1831	A3
Hartwell, J.W.	Athearn, Asia B.	4, Nov. 1837	R3
Hartwell, John W.	Lee, Anna	14, Dec. 1841	N2
Hartzell, David A.	Griffin, Charlotte	13, Dec. 1825	N3
Harvey, Samuel	Gordon, Julia (Mrs)	14, July 1852	P2
Haskett, William	Hargrave, Catharine	17, May 1850	P2
Haskins, J.I.	Ruffner, Eliza	7, June 1830	A3
Hasluck, D.S.	Vandyke, Fidelia R.	4, June 1842	R3
Hasluck, D.S.	VanDyke, Fidelia R.	3, June 1842	N2
Hasson, William	Sherman, Ann	25, Mar. 1837	N2
Hastings, Royal	Gabrielson, Caroline	3, Jan. 1839	T2
Hatch, Harlan	Wright, Mary	11, Oct. 1828	R3
Hatchler, John	McCann, Rosella Ann	20, Aug. 1847	K2
Hathaway, Henry	Hubbell, Jane	10, Mar. 1827	R3
Hathaway, John	Sherzer, Frances	11, May 1841	N2
Hatton, George	Foulk, Margaret	11, Feb. 1815	S3
Hay, Andrew	Morrison, Emily	21, June 1828	R3
Hay, Benajah S.	Manfort, Anna	3, July 1813	S3
Hay, George	Hartman, Elizabeth	3, Apr. 1823	J2
Hay, William	Millburn, (Mrs)	28, Nov. 1840	R3
Hayden, Alfred	Burley, Esther P.	9, June 1827	R3
Hayden, Alfred	Burley, Esther B.	8, June 1827	N3
Hayes, R.B.	Webb, Lucy W.	3, Jan. 1853	P2
Haynes, Robert (Capt)	Tremper, Catharine	28, July 1815	S3
Hays, Nelson B.	Blackiston, Rachel A	14, May 1847	K2
Hayward, Joshua H.	McLean, Sarah A.	19, July 1830	A3
Haywood, Samuel M.	Bennett, Eliza M.	20, Mar. 1847	K2
Hazen, Alfred	Camp, Elizabeth	9, Sept 1847	K2
Hazen, Livius	Earnot, Elizabeth	21, July 1827	R3
Hazen, N.L.	Twichell, Hannah J.	1, Nov. 1834	R3
Hazen, Nathan L.	Twichell, H. Jennett	31, Oct. 1834	X3
Hazen, William L.	Mills, Julia L.	30, Oct. 1847	K2
Head, James Edward	Smith, Mary J.	23, July 1847	K2
Heap, George	Fisk, Eliza	17, May 1831	A3
Heard, John W.	McCracken, Sarah	7, Aug. 1841	R3
Heaton, George	Richardson, Mary E.	22, Sept 1852	P2
Heferman, Thomas	Zebold, Mary E.	11, Oct. 1852	P2
Heiskell, Henry Lee	Gouverneur, Elizabeth K.	25, June 1842	R3
Henderson, F.	Cullender, Jane	11, May 1822	S3
Henderson, Garden J.	White, Mary M.	1, Sept 1852	P2
Henderson, John C.S.	Northrup, Charlotte	3, Mar. 1832	R3
Henderson, Moses	Flannery, Bridget	16, Aug. 1852	P2
Henderson, William R.	Lumb, Ann	2, Nov. 1835	T2
Hendrick, Oscar C.	Clark, Mary A.	6, July 1849	L2
Hendricks, William	Paul, Nancy	24, May 1816	S3
Hennesy, Michael	Daines, Almean	4, Jan. 1841	N2
Henry, James	Krouskop, Sarah	23, May 1835	T2
Henry, John H.	Ridgely, Lucy E.S.	19, Jan. 1828	R3
Henry, S.	Fontain, Matilda	22, Mar. 1829	R3
Heron, John	Robertson, Jane	9, June 1849	L2
Hewman, C.D.	Collins, Lidia	13, Nov. 1852	P2
Hickett, Bright	Cole, Eliza	1, Apr. 1828	N3
Hickman, Jesse	Green, Eliza Ann	4, June 1842	R3

Grooms	Brides	Date of Notice	Page
Hicks, James	Hicks, Frances Mary	1, Nov. 1828	R3
Hicks, James	Harrison, Martha A.	18, June 1842	R3
Hicks, James	Hicks, Frances Mary	31, Oct. 1828	N2
Higbee, Ira B.	Leice, Jane (Mrs)	5, July 1850	P2
Higdon, Peter	Hall, Martha	6, Oct. 1827	R3
Higdon, Peter	Hall, Martha	5, Oct. 1827	N3
High, George M.	Kincade, Anna Maria	23, Oct. 1852	P2
Hight, George W.	Vance, Mary	23, Aug. 1816	S3
Hill, Frederick	Stratton, Sarah Jane	18, Oct. 1852	P2
Hill, George H.	Rhodes, Alice K.	21, Sept 1835	T2
Hill, James	Doyle, Amanda	14, Apr. 1829	N3
Hillerman, William J	Robinson, Elizabeth	3, Mar. 1849	L2
Hilton, George H.	Laverty, Honora U.	25, June 1842	R3
Hilton, George H.	Laverty, Honora U.	22, June 1842	N2
Hinch, Augustus F.	Denman, Louisa E.	9, May 1836	T2
Hine, L.A.	Chapin, Helen	16, Nov. 1847	K2
Hine, Theodore B.	Reynolds, Levina C.	20, Sept 1851	P2
Hiner, David	Hulbert, Parthina	9, May 1829	R3
Hinkle, Anthony H.	Schillinger, Frances	9, Apr. 1842	R3
Hinman, Arnold	Larison, Elizabeth	20, Sept 1814	W4
Hinsch, Augustus F.	Denman, Louisa E.	19, May 1836	X3
Hinsdale, John T.	Loring, Susan M.	5, Dec. 1836	T2
Hinsdale, John T.	Loring, Susan M.	8, Dec. 1836	X3
Hobby, Josephus	Brown, Mary L.	7, May 1841	N2
Hodge, David	Bailey, Elizabeth	11, Dec. 1819	S3
Hoe, Robert	Cregar, Jane	23, Jan. 1838	T2
Hoffman, Allen	Gilman, Barbara A.	8, Oct. 1847	K2
Hoffman, Henry	Kemper, Harriet	4, Nov. 1852	P2
Hoffman, Ogden	Southard, Virginia E.	3, Dec. 1838	N2
Hoffner, Jacob	Marsden, Elizabeth	8, June 1820	S3
Holbrook, D.B.	Ingraham, Elizabeth T.	30, June 1836	T2
Holbrook, David L.	Tuite, Maria	31, Dec. 1831	R3
Holbrook, David L.	Tute, Maria	6, Jan. 1832	X3
Holbrooks, George	Broils, (Mrs)	18, May 1836	T2
Holbrooks, George	Broils, (Mrs)	26, May 1836	X3
Holcomb, Asa H.	Sullivan, Mary	29, Mar. 1816	S3
Holcomb, Daniel H.	Mooney, Mary	15, Mar. 1828	R3
Holcomb, Horace L.	Murray, Mary Ann	13, July 1833	R3
Holcombe, Horace L.	Murray, Mary Ann	19, July 1833	X3
Holcome, William Hy.	Palmer, Rebecca	5, July 1852	P2
Holden, Amos P.	Goodman, Mary Jean	3, Aug. 1835	T2
Holdworth, Benjamin	Buckston, Mary Ann	3, Oct. 1850	Y2
Holland, Palmer	Vanausdol, Esther A.	6, Sept 1839	T2
Holland, R.C. (Dr)	Coit, Elizabeth F.C.	3, Oct. 1835	T2
Holliday, Joseph	Smith, Susan M.	22, May 1847	K2
Hollingsworth, Ed.	Kidd, Susan	29, Nov. 1852	P2
Hollis, Robert S.	Adams, Elizabeth	30, Dec. 1852	P2
Holmes, Henry	Pickering, Julia	20, Dec. 1852	P2
Holmes, Samuel D.	Frazer, Mary	25, Feb. 1831	X3
Holmes, William	Buffington, Elizabeth	6, Nov. 1847	K2
Holroyd, Edward	Tucker, Hannah	17, Nov. 1841	N2
Homan, Henry O.	Snell, Albina L.	10, Dec. 1852	P2
Hood, Jonathan N.	Dodd, Louisa M.	7, May 1842	R3
Hood, Jonathan N.	Dodd, Louisa M.	4, May 1842	N2

Grooms	Brides	Date of Notice	Page
Hood, M. James	Ross, Josephine	8, Sept 1852	P2
Hood, William	Burkett, Mary	8, Aug. 1835	T2
Hooker, Edward	Loring, Georgiana	25, Dec. 1852	P2
Hooker, John	Beecher, Isabel H.	21, Aug. 1841	R3
Hooker, John	Beecher, Isabel H.	19, Aug. 1841	N2
Hoole, Joseph	Graham, Lucy Ann	3, Mar. 1838	R3
Hoover, David (Dr)	Morrison, Isabella J	20, May 1842	N2
Hopkins, John (Rev)	Perry, Mary C.	7, Nov. 1840	R3
Hopkins, Richard R.	Baldridge, Mary L.	18, Mar. 1847	K2
Hopkins, William	Looker, Maria	24, Dec. 1824	N3
Hopkins, William H.	Ruffin, Frances	23, Apr. 1814	S3
Hopkins, William R.	Hobbs, Laura W.	23, July 1842	R3
Hopkins, William R.	Hobbs, Laura W.	18, July 1842	N2
Hopper, Jonathan	Marsh, Ann Eliza	9, Dec. 1824	E2
Hopper, Morris	Westlake, Susan	17, Mar. 1838	N3
Hopper, Morris S.	Westlake, Susan	24, Mar. 1838	R3
Horne, Daniel H.	Coffin, Anna B.	15, Feb. 1839	T2
Horne, John R.	McConnell, Amanda M.	28, May 1842	R3
Horrocks, John	Gardiner, Harriet N.	26, May 1836	X3
Horton, Benjamin	Hart, Carrie	3, Sept 1852	P2
Horton, Johiel	Horton, Caroline (Mrs)	9, Sept 1852	P2
Horton, Jonathan	Whipple, Sophia	6, Aug. 1814	S3
Horton, Lewis Y.	Rice, Caroline E.	12, Oct. 1847	K2
Horton, V.B.	Pomeroy, Clara A.	7, Dec. 1833	R3
Hoskins, Henry	Mehne, Josephine	10, Oct. 1835	T2
Hoskinson, Isaiah	Fisk, Elizabeth	12, Oct. 1820	S3
Hotchkiss, Henry O.	Sawyler, Mary Fitz	29, May 1841	R3
Hotchkiss, Henry O.	Sawyer, Mary A.F.	28, May 1841	N2
Hough, Amos (Dr)	Winfree, Eliza	7, May 1831	R3
Houston, John B.	Allen, Margaret	6, Oct. 1836	X3
Houston, Samuel	Lea, Margaret	6, June 1840	R3
How, John	Morris, Louisa H.	15, Oct. 1835	T2
Howard, James N.	Irwin, Mary M.	14, May 1842	R3
Howe, Jacob	Alley, Susan (Mrs)	14, Aug. 1841	R3
Howe, Jacob	Alley, Susan (Mrs)	13, Aug. 1841	N2
Howe, Joseph	Fulton, Martha J.	9, June 1836	X3
Howe, William T.	Whaley, Sarah Jane	12, Nov. 1847	K2
Howel, Rozel P.	Hall, Hulda (Mrs)	6, Nov. 1847	K2
Howell, Daniel G.	Lyall, Jane Eliza	29, Aug. 1818	S3
Howell, Lewis (Lt)	Mills, Mary	13, June 1812	S3
Howell, Nathan	McNicoll, Catharine	21, Oct. 1830	A3
Hubbell, Nathaniel S	McChesney, Eliza	8, Aug. 1818	S3
Hubble, Gabriel	Perry, Martha	25, Apr. 1810	H3
Hudson, Edwin	Ellstrep, Elizabeth	21, Oct. 1852	P2
Huey, George J.	Whetstone, Hannah E.	24, Oct. 1840	R3
Huffmaster, S.W.	Cottle, Sarah (Mrs)	26, Apr. 1833	X3
Hughes, John	Burt, Sarah A. (Mrs)	19, Sept 1817	S3
Hughes, Joshua	Legg, Mary Ann	22, Dec. 1847	K2
Hughs, Henry	Evans, Sarah	2, May 1840	R3
Hull, James	Cake, Martha E.	19, Feb. 1842	R3
Humble, James	Barber, Jane	23, June 1847	K2
Hume, Thomas W.	Dowd, Ann	24, July 1838	T2
Humphrey, John	Elliott, Sally	24, Aug. 1811	S3
Humphreys, Joseph	Cassiday, Mary (Mrs)	24, June 1837	R3

Grooms	Brides	Date of Notice	Page
Humphreys, Joseph	Cassidy, Mary (Mrs)	21, June 1837	T2
Hunt, Bart F.	Dodd, Cornelia Ann	15, Mar. 1834	R3
Hunt, John	Harrison, Zebulino A.	19, Dec. 1840	R3
Hunt, John	Harrison, Zebuline	10, Dec. 1840	N2
Hunt, S.H.	Williamson, Mat.	28, Oct. 1852	P2
Hunt, William	Cumming, Margaret	12, Nov. 1814	S3
Hunter, Joseph	Dalzell, Rachael	15, Sept 1835	T2
Hunter, William	Smith, Sally H.	30, Nov. 1835	T2
Hunting, Richard	Odell, Susan B.	26, Oct. 1837	T2
Hurd, Rukard	Osborn, Mary	6, Dec. 1825	N3
Hurst, Frederick	Appleby, Caroline	13, June 1837	T2
Hutchinson, Levi	Reddish, Joanna J.	3, May 1833	X3
Hutchinson, William	Smith, Sarah	11, Mar. 1825	N2
Hyler, Jeremiah	Ralphy, Mary Ann	12, Aug. 1852	P2
Iglehart, N.P.	Gano, Frances Mary	20, July 1837	T2
Ingols, Chester	Bishop, Ada	6, Feb. 1819	S3
Ingraham, Henry	Harrison, Lucinda	23, Oct. 1841	R3
Ireland, George	Vanblunby, Ann	14, Aug. 1841	R3
Ireland, George	Vanblunby, Ann	13, Aug. 1841	N2
Irvin, Thomas	Pomeroy, Mary R.	24, Dec. 1835	T3
Irvine, George	Crewson, Mary Jane	29, Dec. 1841	N2
Irwin, Archibald	Jones, Emily Albina	28, June 1828	R3
Irwin, B.J.	Hazleton, Clarissa	4, Nov. 1835	T2
Irwin, J.G.	Peck, Hannah	11, Jan. 1833	X3
Irwin, John V.	Eaton, Anna Jane	3, Oct. 1838	T2
Irwin, John V.	Eaton, Anna Jane	3, Oct. 1838	N2
Irwin, William	Smith, Mary Jane	14, Jan. 1832	R3
Irwin, William	Ramsay, Sarah L.	22, Aug. 1838	T2
Irwin, William (Major)	Ramsy, Sarah L.	25, Aug. 1838	R3
Ives, Silliman (Rev)	Hobart, Rebecca S.	11, Mar. 1825	N2
Jackson, A.	Niles, Sarah A.	3, Dec. 1838	N2
Jackson, Charles	Jocelyn, Mary H.	18, May 1822	S3
Jackson, Henry S.	Lovejoy, Ann	2, Dec. 1824	E2
Jackson, James	Craig, Charlotte E.	25, Dec. 1852	P2
Jackson, John	Jocelyn, Hannah	5, Oct. 1820	S3
Jackson, John	Tindle, Lydia Ann	23, Jan. 1827	N3
Jackson, Robert C.	Waters, Ann M.	27, Nov. 1852	P2
Jackson, T.M.	Collins, M.S.	26, May 1821	S3
Jacobs, William H.	Green, Lucy Jane	19, May 1847	K2
Jaimeson, Edward	Wallace, Mary Ann	28, Mar. 1829	R3
James, A.C.	Ernst, Mary A.	17, Oct. 1840	R3
James, Alfred	Flinn, Frances S.	11, Oct. 1852	P2
James, David A.	Bakewell, Elizabeth	5, June 1841	R3
James, David A.	Bakewell, Elizabeth	29, May 1841	N2
James, Henry	Ames, Mary	25, Dec. 1827	N3
James, Henry	Disney, Amilia Maria	14, Apr. 1836	X3
James, Joseph Junius	Keating, Margaret	7, July 1826	N3
James, U.P.	Wood, Olive H.	13, May 1847	K2
Jamison, Love H. (Rev)	Clark, Elizabeth	22, Dec. 1837	T2
Jaudon, William L.	Lea, Susan G.	28, Nov. 1823	N2
Jeffries, John C.	Vanausdal, Mary R.	16, Apr. 1842	R3
Jeffries, John C.	Vanausdol, Mary R.	15, Apr. 1842	N2

Grooms	Brides	Date of Notice	Page
Jenckes, Joseph	Greene, Isabella M.	18, May 1833	R3
Jenifer, Benjamin	Coddington, Sarah	26, Dec. 1840	R3
Jenifer, Benjamin	Coddington, Sarah	23, Dec. 1840	N2
Jenkins, Seymour	Agres, Sabra	15, Dec. 1852	P2
Jennings, Charles E.	Warner, Rebecca	12, Aug. 1835	T2
Jennings, J.S.	Monjah, Elizabeth A.	21, Aug. 1852	P2
Jewell, Henry (Rev)	Smith, Caroline E.	24, June 1851	P2
Johnson, Andrew	Harris, Sarah	25, Dec. 1813	S3
Johnson, Archibald	Ferguson, Amelia R.	10, July 1819	S3
Johnson, Benjamin W.	Gregory, Elizabeth	5, Dec. 1817	S3
Johnson, Henry A.	Hoadley, Mary R.	9, July 1841	N2
Johnson, James	Snewley, Hannah	29, June 1822	S3
Johnson, James (Dr)	Zane, Sophia	19, Apr. 1828	R3
Johnson, Leonidas N.	Childs, Mary W.	17, Oct. 1840	R3
Johnson, Lewis	Hopper, Margaret	4, Mar. 1837	R3
Johnson, Noble S.	Todd, Mary Ann (Mrs)	28, Oct. 1837	R3
Johnson, Noble S.	Todd, Mary Ann (Mrs)	28, Oct. 1837	T2
Johnson, Noble S.	Tood, Mary A. (Mrs)	2, Nov. 1837	X3
Johnson, Peter	Douglass, Mary	26, Aug. 1824	E2
Johnson, Robert D.	Moffit, Matilda	23, Oct. 1841	R3
Johnson, Robert D.	Maffit, Matilda	27, Sept 1841	N2
Johnson, Robert F.	Finkbine, Ann	21, Apr. 1829	N2
Johnson, Thomas	Barston, H. (Mrs)	30, Oct. 1838	T2
Johnston, J.W.	Patterson, Mary	6, Nov. 1841	R3
Johnston, J.W.	Patterson, Mary	30, Oct. 1841	N2
Johnston, James	Todd, Henrietta (Mrs)	28, Apr. 1838	R3
Johnston, Samuel	Wilson, Margaretta E.	7, Dec. 1820	S3
Johnston, Stephen	Anderson, Elizabeth	16, July 1838	T2
Johnston, Stephen (Lt)	Miller, Elizabeth (Mrs)	21, July 1838	R3
Johnston, Thomas	Barstow, H. (Mrs)	30, Oct. 1838	N2
Johnston, W. (Capt)	Gibson, Ellen D.	8, Nov. 1837	T2
Johnston, William S.	Barton, Clarena	3, Mar. 1821	S3
Jolly, William	Prather, Elizabeth	12, May 1838	R3
Jonas, Abraham	Seixas, Lucia	18, Mar. 1824	E2
Jones, Asa P. (Dr)	Watson, Olive V.	1, Nov. 1834	R3
Jones, Caleb	Taylor, Mary Ann	11, Oct. 1837	T2
Jones, Charles	Stewart, Laura	24, Sept 1842	R3
Jones, Charles T.	Chalfant, Margaretta	9, May 1840	R3
Jones, Ephraim	Lewis, Margaretta E.	23, Feb. 1828	R3
Jones, Ephraim	Lewis, Margaretta E.	22, Feb. 1828	N3
Jones, Ephraim	Lewis, Margaretta E.	22, Feb. 1828	Q3
Jones, George	Erickson, Sarah	25, Oct. 1852	P2
Jones, George W.	Febiger, Hannah (Mrs)	25, Aug. 1832	R3
Jones, George W.	Riske, Charlotte	6, Oct. 1832	R3
Jones, Henry	Haywood, Ann (Mrs)	3, Nov. 1827	R3
Jones, Henry	Haywood, Ann (Mrs)	2, Nov. 1827	N3
Jones, James L.	Debolt, Eliza	23, Nov. 1839	R3
Jones, John D.	Johnson, Elizabeth	30, Sept 1823	N3
Jones, John T.	Lawrence, Ann B.	30, June 1821	S3
Jones, John W.	Reynolds, Martha G.	15, Nov. 1851	P2
Jones, Joseph	Oppenheimer, Martha	21, Nov. 1838	T2
Jones, Joseph H.	Howell, Anna Maria	11, Nov. 1825	N2
Jones, L.A. (Dr)	Gaither, Almira J.G.	10, Feb. 1848	K2
Jones, Samuel R.	Pool, Eliza	4, Dec. 1841	R3

Grooms	Brides	Date of Notice	Page
Jones, Thomas	Hill, Elizabeth	9, July 1835	T2
Jones, Thomas C.	Tait, Mary	24, May 1836	T2
Jones, Thomas C.	Tait, Mary	26, May 1836	X3
Jones, William D.	Longworth, Charlotte	17, Mar. 1821	S3
Jordon, Henry	Abrams, Eliza	20, Dec. 1828	R3
Jordon, Martin	Lashley, Polly	7, July 1827	R3
Joseph, J.G.	Symonds, Rebecca	28, Dec. 1833	R3
Judkins, William (Dr)	Palmer, Mary M.	11, Sept 1841	R3
Judkins, William (Dr)	Palmer, Mary M.	11, Sept 1841	N2
Kanan, John	Glass, Sophia	21, Aug. 1835	T2
Kay, James	Newton, Rebecca	19, Dec. 1818	S3
Keating, John	Wheelwright, Mary R.	28, Apr. 1826	N2
Keckeler, Theophilus	Manser, Mary A.	15, July 1852	P2
Keech, Orlando B.	Mundy, Ophelia	3, July 1841	R3
Keech, Orlando B.	Mundy, Ophelia	28, June 1841	N2
Keen, John	Green, Mary M.	17, June 1837	R3
Keene, John	Green, Mary M.	15, June 1837	X3
Keller, Jacob	Hales, Margaret	9, Oct. 1819	S3
Keller, Thomas	Harrigan, Emily J.	22, Apr. 1847	K2
Kelley, Julius	Hitchcock, Mary A.	14, Apr. 1836	T2
Kellogg, A.	Dudgeon, E.	22, Oct. 1831	R3
Kellogg, Albert	Dudgeon, Elizabeth	21, Oct. 1831	X3
Kellogg, Charles F.	Downs, Eliza (Mrs)	14, Feb. 1829	R3
Kellogg, Charles H.	Todd, Margaret	4, Nov. 1847	K2
Kellogg, Sheldon J.	Edmands, Catharine R.	3, Nov. 1835	T2
Kellum, C.B.	Masson, Kate	30, Aug. 1850	Y2
Kelly, John	Knoblaugh, Eliza Ann	13, Nov. 1841	R3
Kelly, John	Koblaugh, Eliza Ann	12, Nov. 1841	N2
Kelsey, Naamen	Barber, Sarah Jane	21, May 1842	R3
Kemper, Charles H.	Terry, Margaret	3, Sept 1847	K2
Kemper, E.Y. (Dr)	Deeds, Joana	12, Oct. 1820	S3
Kemper, F.A. (Rev)	Sering, Mary	23, Dec. 1831	X3
Kemper, J.H.	Wood, Martha B.	5, Jan. 1833	R3
Kemper, John H.	Wood, Martha B.	4, Jan. 1833	X3
Kenna, Edward	Lewis, Margery J.	23, June 1847	K2
Kennady, James	Hudson, Sarah	14, Sept 1820	S3
Kennedy, G.W. (Rev)	Jennings, Mary Ellen	19, Jan. 1837	X3
Kennedy, John	Marshall, Louisa	18, Oct. 1837	T2
Kennedy, John	Marshall, Louisa	18, Oct. 1837	N3
Kennedy, John H.	Howard, Aurelia	7, June 1828	R3
Kenner, William B.	Riskf, Ruhamah	15, Sept 1832	R3
Kennett, John	Gassaway, Elizabeth	15, Nov. 1834	T2
Kent, Luke	Ernst, Adeline	4, July 1840	R3
Kernes, Samuel	Knox, Mary Ann	11, Oct. 1828	R3
Kerns, Robert	King, Margaret	27, Nov. 1852	P2
Kerns, Thomas	Scowden, Sarah Ann	30, Dec. 1835	T3
Kerr, Stephen F.	Riker, Margaret Ann	3, Nov. 1838	T2
Kettle, Peter	Boyd, Susan A.	26, Oct. 1852	P2
Key, Marshall	Sellman, Harriet	19, Apr. 1816	S3
Keys, William	McCoppin, Ann	17, Nov. 1827	R3
Keys, William	McCawley, Elizabeth	18, Sept 1847	K2
Kibbe, Jarvis	Clark, Eliza	22, Jan. 1820	S3
Killin, Richard S.	Cambridge, Rosa	31, July 1841	V3

Grooms	Brides	Date of Notice	Page
Killough, J. (Dr)	Brownrigg, C.	3, Aug. 1837	T2
Kimball, Warren	Cargill, Mary Seely	1, Nov. 1830	A3
Kimber, Samuel	Konigmacher, Susan	9, June 1835	N2
Kinder, William R.	Long, Agnes	16, Oct. 1852	P2
King, D. Cleaves	Dodson, Cynthia Ann	13, June 1849	L2
King, Edward	Worthington, Sarah A	31, May 1816	S3
King, Edward A.	McNaughton, Sarah M.	31, May 1841	N2
King, James	Randall, Martha Ann	30, Oct. 1852	P2
King, John	Luke, Mary	22, Nov. 1834	R3
King, John	Luke, Mary	19, Nov. 1834	T2
King, Joseph	Thompson, Mary A.	3, Dec. 1852	P2
Kingsbury, C.S.	Schenk, Mary Fannie	19, Nov. 1852	P2
Kingsbury, Obadiah	Hopkins, Julia A.	12, Jan. 1830	N2
Kinmont, A.	Eckstein, Mary	24, Jan. 1829	R3
Kinnear, Samuel	Hill, Elon	19, Apr. 1830	A3
Kinsey, Edward	Pocock, Temperance	4, Jan. 1841	N2
Kirby, Edmund	Brown, Eliza A.	11, Mar. 1825	N2
Kirby, James	Ball, Hannah	16, Oct. 1819	S3
Kirby, William	Winters, Lydia C.	11, Oct. 1852	P2
Kirkland, John T.	Cabot, Elizabeth	29, Sept 1827	R3
Kite, George	Beach, Patty	18, Sept 1819	S3
Knies, John K.	Poineer, Mary Ann	6, July 1820	S3
Knight, Albert G.	Gazlay, Delia	16, Nov. 1832	X3
Knight, Benjamin	Adamson, Frances	21, July 1838	T2
Knight, Henry	Buel, Abigail	26, Oct. 1836	T2
Knight, Henry	Buel, Abigail (Mrs)	25, Oct. 1836	N2
Knight, Henry W.	Martin, Eliza D.	5, Sept 1835	T2
Knight, Henry W.	Martin, Eliza D.	4, Sept 1835	X3
Knight, William	Muntz, Rhoda Ann	5, Dec. 1817	S3
Knowlton, Sherman	Manahan, Dorcas	15, May 1847	K2
Knox, James H.	Thomas, Adaline E.	2, Dec. 1840	N2
Kovatz, Agusta (Lt)	Wallace, Martha N.	20, Nov. 1852	P2
Kropf, G.S.	Stewart, Elizabeth A.	22, May 1850	P2
Kyes, Alvin	Elsturn, Sarah (Mrs)	2, Aug. 1828	R3
Kyzer, William	Wlliams, Nancy	27, Feb. 1819	S3
Lackey, Ira	Merrit, Catharine	29, June 1822	S3
Ladd, William H.	White, Jean M.	30, July 1847	K2
Lamb, James L.	Cranmer, Susan	16, Jan. 1824	N3
Lambdin, Robert	Farland, Caroline M.	17, July 1819	S3
Lambeth, William M.	Slocum, Georgiana	17, Aug. 1839	T2
Landis, Medry	Tunis, Susan	21, Mar. 1817	S3
Lane, Andrew	Rogers, Semor A.	26, Sept 1840	R3
Lane, William	Ashenhurst, Sarah	21, July 1827	R3
Langdon, Elam P.	Cromwell, Ann	20, Oct. 1821	S3
Langtree, C.	Farrelly, Eliza	18, Jan. 1840	R3
Langtry, Thomas	Weir, Mary	29, Apr. 1825	N3
Langtry, William	Beresford, Ann	19, Oct. 1822	S3
Langtry, William	Beresford, Ann	24, Oct. 1822	J3
Langworthy, Lucius	Reeder, Francis C.	1, May 1835	X3
Lanier, James W. (Dr)	Barcalow, Helana	14, Sept 1807	S3
Lapham, William	Beran, M.J.	18, Aug. 1852	P2
Lapse, William H.	Taylor, Martha Ann	23, June 1847	K2
Lardner, Henry (Dr)	Keys, Mary Ann	1, Sept 1838	T2

Grooms	Brides	Date of Notice	Page
Lathrop, Frank W.	Macalister, Elizabeth	7, June 1828	R3
Lathrop, Martin (Dr)	Wright, Rebecca	18, Feb. 1815	S3
Latta, Alexander B.	Parson, Elizabeth Ann	23, Oct. 1847	K2
Latta, Finley	Smith, Eliza Ann	13, Mar. 1841	N2
Latta, Samuel A.	Blackmon, Caroline	18, Mar. 1831	X3
Lauderman, David	Shaddinger, Sarah A.	20, Dec. 1836	N2
Launder, James	Stow, Eliza	1, July 1835	T2
Laurence, Robert	Suydam, Lydia (Mrs)	24, Jan. 1829	R3
Lawder, John B.	Shelden, Rebecca A.	21, May 1842	R3
Lawder, John B.	Sheldon, Rebecca A.	21, May 1842	N2
Lawrence, Alfred A.	Graham, Jenny	30, Nov. 1852	P2
Lawrence, David H.	Whitehead, Sarah	3, Aug. 1830	N2
Lawrence, Edward M.	Whitney, Mary Jane	27, Aug. 1852	P2
Lawrence, G.F.	Lloyd, Louisa Mat.	23, Oct. 1835	T2
Lawrence, George	Allen, Margaret	26, Oct. 1852	P2
Lawrence, William	Ramsay, Margaret E.	3, Aug. 1847	K2
Lawrence, William C.	Fertig, Catharine	22, May 1841	R3
Lawrence, William C.	Fertig, Catharine A.	3, May 1841	N2
Layman, S.B.	Better, Charlotte	11, May 1841	N2
Lea, James H.	Campbell, Ellen	9, May 1836	T2
Leavitt, Daniel K.	Belch, Lucinda	14, Mar. 1829	R3
Leavitt, Richard H.	McKim, Isabella F.	23, Nov. 1850	P2
Lee, Edmund F.	Addison, Meliora E.	18, May 1836	N2
Lee, Z. Collins	Jenkins, Martha Ann	23, June 1837	T2
Leeds, George	Stapleton, Henrietta	2, Sept 1836	N2
Leffingwell, Winslow	Baker, Caroline (Mrs)	9, Nov. 1850	P2
Leitch, William	Gaylord, Hannah (Mrs)	21, Apr. 1836	X3
Lemaire, Isaac K.	Kirby, Jane	13, Oct. 1847	K2
Lemmon, James	Moon, Rebecca	6, Oct. 1827	R3
Lemmon, James	Moon, Rebecca	5, Oct. 1827	N3
Leonard, Nathaniel	Looker, Rachel B.	5, Sept 1840	R3
LeRoy, S.R. Faunt	Phillips, Virginia	2, Oct. 1852	P2
Leslie, James	Marsh, Rachael A.	16, July 1852	P2
Leuba, Henry	Goddard, Catharine G	8, Jan. 1831	R3
Lewark, John	Clark, Elizabeth	22, Sept 1838	R3
Lewis, Albert	Rose, Serena Ann	22, Mar. 1829	R3
Lewis, Charles H.	Anderson, Mary C.	23, June 1838	R3
Lewis, Charles H.	Anderson, Mary C.	20, June 1838	T2
Lewis, Hickman	Lindsay, Virginia	4, Sept 1835	T2
Lewis, James	Bradford, Margaret	25, Apr. 1840	R3
Lewis, James Ewing	West, Sophronia S.	23, June 1838	R3
Lewis, John H.	Vanhouton, Phebe L.	29, Oct. 1831	R3
Lewis, Samuel	Goforth, Charlotte K.	8, Aug. 1823	N3
Lewis, William	Whetstone, Sarah	1, Dec. 1821	S3
Lewis, William G.W.	Baldwin, Virginia	22, Oct. 1847	K2
Lewis, William L.	Floyd, Letitia	12, Apr. 1837	T2
Lewisson, Charles	Joseph, Clarissa	2, July 1842	R3
L'Hommedieu, Stephen	Hammond, Alma	29, Apr. 1830	A3
L'Hommedieu, Stephen	Hammond, Alma	27, Apr. 1830	N3
Libeau, Charles	Pile, Mary	7, Dec. 1838	T2
Light, Daniel	Flinn, Nancy A.	21, Apr. 1835	T3
Lighthizer, S.F.	Budd, Elizabeth	14, Jan. 1837	R3
Lilley, John	Taylor, Mary A. (Mrs)	10, Apr. 1849	L2
Lilley, William	Forest, Josephine	11, Aug. 1850	Y2

Grooms	Brides	Date of Notice	Page
Lindley, Abraham	L'Hommedieu, Sarah	2, Mar. 1822	S3
Lindman, Lewis T.	Donaldson, Mary	22, Apr. 1847	K2
Lindslay, William L.	Easton, Mary	5, July 1828	R3
Linley, Francis	Surguy, Eliza	1, June 1841	N2
Litherbury, John	Weeks, Caroline	27, Aug. 1824	N2
Littell, Eliakim	Smith, Mary F.	1, Mar. 1828	R3
Little, George	Miles, Caroline	16, Jan. 1841	R3
Little, George	Miles, Caroline	16, Jan. 1841	N2
Little, Jacob (Rev)	Thomson, Ann D.	7, Apr. 1836	X3
Livezey, J.W.	Lee, S.	1, Jan. 1853	P2
Lloyd, Frederick	Wade, Harriett	24, Aug. 1850	Y2
Lockwood, Daniel D.	Shays, Frances C.	5, June 1837	T2
Lockwood, Henry (Rev)	Medhurst, Sarah S.	6, Oct. 1836	X3
Lodge, Caleb T.	Irwin, Sarah W.	16, Aug. 1828	R3
Lodge, John	Arion, Susanna	22, Aug. 1817	S3
Lodge, Laban	Piatt, Catharine S.	13, May 1823	N3
Logan, John W.	Wilkins, Jane	20, Apr. 1833	R3
Logan, William	Henry, Caroline	30, Jan. 1819	S3
Long, Christian	Royal, Mourning	22, Sept 1827	R3
Long, William H.	Harris, Eliza	9, Oct. 1852	P2
Longacer, Isaac N.	Steed, Selina M.	22, Sept 1852	P2
Longley, Elias	Vater, Elizabeth M.	15, May 1847	K2
Longworth, Joseph	Rives, Anna	22, May 1841	R3
Longworth, Joseph	Rives, Anna	17, May 1841	N2
Longworth, Nicholas	Conner, Susan (Mrs)	28, Dec. 1807	S3
Longworth, Thomas	Morris, Alphia	20, June 1828	Q3
Looker, James H.	Looker, Rachael H.	27, Dec. 1828	R3
Looker, James H.	Looker, Rachel (Mrs)	26, Dec. 1828	N3
Loomis, M.D.W.	Dilworth, Eliza W.	25, Mar. 1847	K2
Lord, John P.	Bogert, Mary	11, Dec. 1819	S3
Loring, Allen	Oliver, Eliza Ann	25, May 1841	N2
Lovejoy, Henry B.	Nebblett, Sarah S.	7, July 1841	N2
Lovejoy, Thatcher	Tindall, Eliza Ann	8, May 1819	S3
Lovelace, Seneca	Kendall, Susan Ann	25, Dec. 1841	R3
Lowe, Peter P.	Bomberger, Ann	17, May 1830	A3
Lowndes, John	Howell, Catharine	3, Jan. 1817	S3
Lowry, James	Phillips, Henrietta	28, July 1832	R3
Lucas, Edward	Meline, Catharine A.	19, Feb. 1838	T2
Lucas, Edward	Meline, Catharine A.	20, Feb. 1838	N2
Luce, Elijah	McKoy, Angeline	6, Jan. 1832	X3
Luce, Elijah W.	McKoy, Angeline	6, Jan. 1832	A3
Ludlow, Benjamin W.	McLaughlin, Elizabeth A.	14, Oct. 1852	P2
Ludlow, Israel L.	Slacum, Helena Adela	1, July 1830	A3
Ludlow, Israel L.	Slacum, Helen A.	3, July 1830	R3
Ludlow, S.L.	Ustick, Jane Harris	23, Jan. 1841	R3
Ludlow, S.T.	Ustick, Jane H.	13, Jan. 1841	N2
Lumley, Robert	Shipley, Mary A. (Mrs)	7, May 1841	N2
Lupton, D.B.	Lawrence, Harriet O.	4, Feb. 1836	T3
Lupton, Thomas	Nedy, Elizabeth	22, Nov. 1838	T2
Lusk, Thomas	Wartman, Elizabeth	17, Nov. 1838	T2
Lusk, Uzal B.	Meady, Eliza (Mrs)	27, Mar. 1847	K2
Lynch, Micajah T.	Lorimer, Virginia (Mrs)	29, Oct. 1841	N2
Lynes, William (Rev)	Forsha, Deborah	7, July 1827	R3
Lynes, William (Rev)	Forsha, Deborah (Mrs)	6, July 1827	N3

Grooms	Brides	Date of Notice	Page
Lyon, Edward	Langton, M.M. (Mrs)	15, July 1835	T2
Lyon, James M.	Kent, Elizabeth	5, Jan. 1833	R3
Lyon, John F.	Barker, Maria C.	15, May 1829	N3
Lyon, Richard	Lamb, Aravesta	29, Sept 1829	N3
Lyon, Stephen	Lamb, Rebecca	7, Mar. 1817	S2
Lyons, William	Mears, Mary	24, Aug. 1811	S3
Lytle, Edward H.	Shoenberger, Elizabeth	27, Sept 1838	T2
Lytle, John S.	Biddle, Sarah S.	31, Mar. 1832	R3
Lytle, Robert T.	Haines, Elizabeth S.	6, Dec. 1825	N3
MacAlester, Charles	Lytle, Eliza Ann	21, Oct. 1824	E3
Macalester, Edward	Brand, Eliza	25, Feb. 1832	R3
MacCracken, John	Brooks, Elise	23, Apr. 1847	K2
Mack, Samuel E.	Robins, Rebecca A.	11, Sept 1841	N2
Mackintosh, Robert J	Appleton, Mary	18, Jan. 1840	R3
Maddox, Thomas (Dr)	Miller, Delia	21, Mar. 1836	T2
Madeira, J.	Dashiell, Mary Y.	23, Nov. 1824	N2
Madeira, J.	Dashiell, Mary Y.	25, Nov. 1824	E2
Madison, Ransil A.	McKim, Margaret	4, Feb. 1825	N2
Madison, Ransil A.	McKimm, Margaret	27, Jan. 1825	E3
Magee, Jacob	Nicholas, Margaret	29, Aug. 1817	S3
Mager, John	Kieth, Sarah Jane	11, Nov. 1852	P2
Magill, Wesley W.	Cooke, Mary S.	18, Mar. 1847	K2
Magness, Benjamin	Anderson, Mary	2, Mar. 1820	D3
Magness, Benjamin B.	Anderson, Mary	4, Mar. 1820	S2
Magurk, Michael J.	McOliff, Mary C.	4, May 1841	N2
Mahaffey, Robert	Kellogg, Frances A.	8, Sept 1852	P2
Mahard, John	Patterson, Mary K.	17, Jan. 1829	R3
Mahard, John	Patterson, Mary E.	20, Jan. 1829	N3
Mahew, Alexander	Hawthorn, Rhoda	9, Dec. 1824	E2
Maitland, Peter I.	Alden, Josephine N.	23, Nov. 1832	X3
Maker, Thomas S.	Robbins, Abby	21, July 1852	P2
Mallard, Henry (Capt)	Cross, Esther	12, June 1841	N2
Malone, Michael	Rafferty, Hannah	16, July 1852	P2
Mann, Hartley	Cobb, Mary E.	6, July 1838	T2
Mann, Lowell A.	Folger, Eunice	27, Mar. 1841	N2
Mann, Marshall	Bartlett, Elizabeth	19, Feb. 1814	S3
Mann, William C.	Patterson, Adeline E.	14, Nov. 1840	R3
Manser, William	Barrett, Mary Elizabeth	20, Aug. 1831	R3
Mansfield, Edward D.	Peck, Mary	12, May 1827	R3
Mapes, Joel M.	Spinks, E.J.	23, Nov. 1847	K2
Marchant, Johnson	Dozier, Thursday	25, June 1842	R3
Marsh, Anderson	Ware, Harriet (Mrs)	28, Nov. 1835	T2
Marsh, David	Little, Mary	5, Sept 1840	R3
Marsh, Ebenezer	Caldwell, ----	25, Apr. 1840	R3
Marsh, George A.	Jones, C.A.	24, Sept 1847	K2
Marshall, Benjamin	Sellers, Caroline	14, Jan. 1831	X3
Marshall, Edward C.	Chalfant, Josephine	30, Nov. 1852	P2
Marshall, James	Moore, Mary Ann R.	10, Oct. 1829	R3
Marshall, N.B. (Dr)	Ewing, Sallie M.	11, Aug. 1852	P2
Marshall, Peter	Boyd, Ellen	11, May 1842	N2
Marshall, Robert M.	Davey, Mary A.	20, Nov. 1852	P2
Marshall, Vincent C.	Pugh, Leah	27, July 1820	S3
Marshall, Vincent C.	Cassilly, Ann S.	27, Dec. 1825	N2

Grooms	Brides	Date of Notice	Page
Marshall, William H.	Perry, Elizabeth E.	2, Nov. 1835	T2
Martin, A.	Saunders, Harriet	5, July 1828	R3
Martin, Alexander	Schoonmaker, Mary	6, June 1840	R3
Martin, Alfred	Daniels, Elizabeth	14, Nov. 1840	R3
Martin, George	Easton, Sophia H.	5, July 1852	P2
Martin, H.G.	Cornelius, Mary A.	3, Jan. 1853	P2
Martin, Hiram	Tenner, Nancy T.	28, Apr. 1815	S3
Martin, Oliver	Coffin, Sarah	24, Oct. 1817	S3
Martin, Samuel	Wood, Amanda	2, Jan. 1839	T2
Martin, Thomas B.	Perkins, L.B.	10, Sept 1831	R3
Martin, William	Bowen, Dulcinia	27, July 1835	T2
Marvin, Charles	Price, Emily	24, Nov. 1827	R3
Mason, A.C.	Biles, Hester M.	15, Apr. 1847	K2
Mason, Edwin	Smith, Henrietta S.	16, Sept 1852	P2
Mason, John W.	Weir, Priscilla R.	28, Nov. 1823	N2
Mason, Thomas J.	Sherman, Mary A.	4, Nov. 1852	P2
Massaliki, Joseph	Deed, Frances	1, July 1836	T2
Massalski, Joseph	Powers, Frances	1, July 1836	N2
Massie, Henrie	Smith, Sarah W.	5, Mar. 1842	R3
Massie, Wallar (Dr)	Brann, Nancy A.	22, Mar. 1851	P2
Maston, William D.	Rice, Eliza A.	18, Nov. 1837	T2
Mather, Bartholomew	Hartman, Sophia C.	21, Aug. 1819	S3
Mathias, Jacob	Grooms, Emily	29, Mar. 1828	R3
Matthews, James	Ellis, Jane	23, Oct. 1847	K2
Matthews, W.	Orr, Eliza (Mrs)	18, July 1840	R3
Matthews, William	Emerson, Clarissa	7, May 1841	N2
Mauk, Jacob	Thomas, Amanda	28, May 1850	P2
Maxwell, Hugh B.	Henderson, Sophia	6, Oct. 1832	R3
May, William L.	Rodney, Caroline	8, Jan. 1838	T2
Maynard, William W.	VanLiew, Margaret	10, July 1852	P2
Mayo, A.F.	St.Clair, Frances M.	9, Sept 1831	X3
Mayo, Benjamin	Mayo, Ann (Mrs)	21, Sept 1837	T2
Mayo, D.	Daughty, Harriet	30, May 1835	T2
Mayronne, O.F.	Eberle, Margaret	31, Oct. 1840	R3
McAffee, Daniel	Small, Rachel	23, Feb. 1837	T2
McAffee, Daniel	Small, Rachel	21, Feb. 1837	N2
McBride, Henry R.W.	Ewing, Sarah V.	10, July 1852	P2
McCall, Edward R.	Hardenberger, Eliza	4, Oct. 1837	T2
McCammon, William	McGinnis, Ellen	5, Apr. 1828	R3
McCandless, James	Benbridge, Sarah T.	13, Dec. 1830	A3
McCandless, James	Benbridge, Sarah T.	11, Dec. 1830	R3
McCane, John	Strawbridge, Jane	11, Apr. 1812	S2
McClave, Robert	Taylor, Susan	31, Oct. 1840	R3
McClean, John	Edwards, Rebecca	3, Apr. 1807	S3
McClellan, Alexander	Smith, Eliza A. (Mrs)	21, Dec. 1835	T3
McClelland, Thomas	Bird, Patience	9, May 1812	S3
McClintock, Andrew T.	Cist, Augusta	29, May 1841	R3
McClure, Alex	Sweet, Martha	24, July 1838	T2
McClure, James	Lewis, Mary H.	10, Nov. 1826	N3
McCormick, Thomas	Allen, Sarah	7, Dec. 1811	S3
McCracken, J.B.	McCandles, Mary	13, Oct. 1835	T2
McCreary, James K.	Howell, Elizabeth C.	13, Jan. 1838	R3
McCulloch, Robert	Merrie, Jane	31, July 1819	S3
McCulloch, Robert	Bowshear, Ann	3, Nov. 1827	R3

Grooms	Brides	Date of Notice	Page
McCullough, John	Lawrence, Margaret	26, Sept 1840	R3
McCullough, William	Piatt, Arabella S.	19, May 1826	N2
McDonald, Alexander	Richardson, Annie J.	29, Dec. 1852	P2
McDonald, D.	Hardin, Mary B.	8, Aug. 1835	T2
McDonald, Isaac	Owens, Jane	26, Dec. 1840	R3
McDonald, Isaac	Owen, Jane	28, Dec. 1840	N2
McDonald, John S.	McLean, Nancy	25, Oct. 1830	A3
McDonough, James T.	Hitchcock, Laura	23, May 1840	R3
McDowell, J.H.	Rhodes, Belle	27, Dec. 1852	P2
McDowell, John	Achey, M. Ella	22, Sept 1852	P2
McDowell, Joseph	Whitehill, Margaret	13, Dec. 1833	X3
McDowell, Joseph N.	Drake, Amanda V.	14, Apr. 1827	R3
McDowell, William S.	Barr, Sarah Ann	7, Sept 1832	X3
McDuffie, George	Singleton, Mary R.	23, June 1829	N3
McElevy, Ezekiel	Stevens, Louisa C.	4, Sept 1841	R3
McElroy, George	Allen, Sabina	29, Sept 1836	X3
McElroy, Solon	Rush, Mary Jane	11, Dec. 1852	P2
McGaughy, D.S. (Dr)	Handy, Amelia C.	16, Mar. 1837	X3
McGraw, William C.	Osburn, Mary Ann	5, Feb. 1841	N2
McGregor, Alexander	Eads, Margaret	3, Jan. 1829	R3
McGrew, Alex	Hall, Carolina C.B.	10, Dec. 1840	N2
McGrew, Alexander	Heywood, Aurelia	14, Sept 1811	S3
McGrew, Alexander	Fisher, Alvira L.	12, Jan. 1822	S3
McGrew, Alexander	Bartlett, Caroline	12, Dec. 1840	R3
McGrew, Alexander	Woods, Martha M.	8, Sept 1847	K2
McGrew, James	Lundy, Nancy (Mrs)	19, Mar. 1849	L2
McGrew, William C.	Osborn, Mary A.	6, Feb. 1841	R3
McGrew, Wilson	Gallagher, Sarah	27, Aug. 1831	R3
McGrew, Wilson	Powell, Margaret R.	9, May 1840	R3
McGroarty, Patrick	Buckner, Elizabeth	1, Nov. 1850	Y2
McKenner, James C.	Snider, Mary	2, July 1852	P2
McKenny, J. Smith	O'Connor, Susan E.	9, Aug. 1841	N2
McKensie, John	See, Jane	4, Feb. 1832	R3
McKeown, Michael	Kilgallen, Mary	30, Aug. 1850	Y2
McKim, Charles S.	Savage, Mary E.	13, July 1852	P2
McKinney, John (Col)	Taylor, Polly (Mrs)	21, Mar. 1817	S3
McKinsey, C.	Shepard, Matilda	3, Feb. 1838	R3
McKnight, John	Loring, Jerusha	15, Nov. 1833	X3
McLain, James A.	Wilson, Jane	26, May 1836	X3
McLaughlin, William	Robinson, Mary Ann	6, Jan. 1825	E3
McLean, James	Smith, Amanda	1, Mar. 1828	R3
McLean, Nathaniel	Burnet, Caroline	8, Sept 1838	R3
McLean, Nathaniel	Burnet, Caroline	10, Sept 1838	T2
McMaken, M.C.	Clark, Elizabeth	20, July 1852	P2
McMaster, William	Smith, Clarissa	25, Oct. 1814	W3
McMicken, Andrew	McDowell, Anna R.	3, May 1847	K2
McMillan, Andrew	Littleford, Mary	7, June 1828	R3
McMillan, Gavin (Rev)	Ronalds, Rosanna	16, Mar. 1824	N2
McMinn, Joseph	Williams, Nancy (Mrs)	20, Sept 1816	S3
McNabb, William	Holmes, Sally	18, Mar. 1831	X3
McNeely, Cyrus	Donaldson, Jane	20, May 1837	R3
McPike, John	Guest, Lydia Jane	11, Mar. 1820	S3
McPike, John	Guest, Lydia Jane	16, Mar. 1820	D3
McQuesten, John	Scott, Margaret	22, Sept 1827	R3

Grooms	Brides	Date of Notice	Page
Mears, Daniel H.	Huston, Deborah H.	16, Oct. 1841	R3
Mears, Isaac	Raymond, Abigail	8, Nov. 1828	R3
Mears, Isaac	Raymond, Abigail	11, Nov. 1828	N3
Medaris, John	Perry, Martha	3, Mar. 1849	L2
Medary, William	Walker, Mary	27, Nov. 1819	S3
Meeker, Hervey	Lawrence, Amanda R.	25, Oct. 1825	N3
Meeker, John C.	Miller, Amanda	3, Oct. 1840	R3
Meeker, Jotham	Richardson, Elenor D	4, Oct. 1830	A3
Meeks, John (Lt)	Maxwell, Ann	14, May 1814	S3
Meeks, Simeon	Moody, Elizabeth	21, Aug. 1838	T2
Meguier, William	Smith, Jane E.	1, Sept 1834	T2
Meigs, Montgomery C.	Rodgers, Louisa	15, May 1841	R3
Meikleham, David S.	Randolph, Septimia	24, Aug. 1838	T2
Meley, Jonathan	Carson, Jane	17, Mar. 1841	N2
Melish, Thomas J.	Bromwell, Maria V.	17, May 1849	L2
Melony, Daniel	Turner, Sarah	16, Oct. 1819	S3
Mendenhall, James	Williams, Sarah T.	17, Nov. 1827	R3
Meriweather, James H	Iuppenlatz, Louisa M.	23, Sept 1835	T2
Merrell, William S.	Poor, M.T.	11, Mar. 1831	X3
Merry, Nathaniel A.	Hunt, Sarah M.	12, June 1847	K2
Merwic, Anson W.	Charters, Anna	8, June 1841	N2
Merwin, Anson W.	Chartres, Anna	12, June 1841	R3
Messenger, Asa	Lightfoot, Ann	14, Jan. 1836	T3
Mieure, William	Shelmire, Sarah	14, Jan. 1831	X3
Milford, James	Broadwell, Sarah Ann	3, Sept 1831	R3
Miller, Adolphus	Orr, Louisa	13, Sept 1850	Y2
Miller, Arthur	Morgan, Ellen	23, Sept 1852	P2
Miller, David F.	Gasten, Sarah	15, Sept 1827	R3
Miller, George A.	Brownings, Virginia	25, July 1851	P2
Miller, Henry B.	Reeves, Mary	12, June 1841	R3
Miller, Henry F.	Stainfield, Elizabeth	8, Sept 1852	P2
Miller, J.W.	Brooks, Caroline	3, Jan. 1839	T2
Miller, Jacob	Plugh, Lydia	19, Feb. 1814	S3
Miller, Jacob	Bingle, Elizabeth	9, Aug. 1814	W3
Miller, James R.	Bonte, Sarah	11, May 1847	K2
Miller, Richard	O'Ferral, Catharine	22, Nov. 1825	N3
Miller, William	Ford, Henrietta	5, July 1828	R3
Milligan, (Prof)	Russell, Ellen B.	29, Jan. 1842	R3
Mills, James R.	Thornton, Elvira	21, July 1852	P2
Mills, Marsh	Turrell, Charlana	26, Feb. 1820	S3
Mills, Thornton A.	Gazlay, Huldah	14, Sept 1837	X3
Mills, Thornton (Rev)	Gazlay, Huldah	16, Sept 1837	R3
Milne, George	Grunnell, Helen Elizabeth	13, Sept 1847	K2
Miner, John L.	Wright, Mary	4, Nov. 1837	R3
Miner, John L.	Wright, Mary	31, Oct. 1837	T2
Miner, Lawrence W.	Morris, Maria F.	11, Nov. 1852	P2
Minett, Julius C.	Thomson, Sarah	19, July 1837	T2
Minnear, John W.	Bowman, Margaret P.	23, Mar. 1847	K2
Mitchell, J.W.	Whitehead, Mary	6, Jan. 1848	K2
Mitchell, John S.	Black, Nancy	31, Oct. 1837	T2
Mitchell, Philip H.	Allen, Sarah Ann	5, July 1828	R3
Mitchell, Roland G.	Post, Cornelia	24, June 1837	R3
Mitchell, William	Miller, Maggie W.	29, Oct. 1852	P2
Mixer, William	Burnet, Julia Ann	15, Nov. 1828	R3

Grooms	Brides	Date of Notice	Page
Mixer, William	Burnet, Julia Ann	18, Nov. 1828	N3
Molin, James	Lucas, Mary Ann	9, July 1838	T2
Monsarrat, David T.	Ruffin, Harriet O.	31, May 1834	T2
Montague, Thomas	Bacon, Sarah	14, Dec. 1847	K2
Montgomery, A. (Lt)	Taylor, Elizabeth F.	12, Sept 1840	R3
Montgomery, Henry J.	Smith, Thomasina	16, Sept 1852	P2
Moodie, Thomas	Ashwell, Jane	14, Nov. 1838	T2
Moon, William	Cragg, Mary Jane	17, Nov. 1827	R3
Moore, Alfred L.	Shipley, Ann G.	20, Oct. 1827	R3
Moore, Augustus O.	Hulburd, Mary Eliza	8, Sept 1841	N2
Moore, F.	Smith, Catharine	2, Oct. 1839	T2
Moore, Hugh	Symmes, Polly	4, Dec. 1805	S2
Moore, Hugh M.	Crane, Margaretta	23, July 1842	R3
Moore, Hugh M.	Crane, Margaretta	19, July 1842	N2
Moore, Isaac	Baird, Martha	31, Oct. 1828	N2
Moore, James S.	Vater, Harriet A.	27, Dec. 1852	P2
Moore, Jesse A.	Swager, Mary A.	19, Nov. 1852	P2
Moore, Joseph M.	Palmer, Deborah D.	24, Apr. 1835	X3
Moore, Richard M.	Haman, Esther Ann	22, Oct. 1831	R3
Moore, Samuel	Worthington, Eliza	7, June 1828	R3
Moore, T.S.	Regor, Prudence Ann	5, Dec. 1840	R3
Moore, T.S.	Regor, Prudence A.	2, Dec. 1840	N2
Moore, William	Winter, Anne	27, Apr. 1824	N3
Moore, William	Winter, Anne	29, Apr. 1824	E3
Moore, William (Rev)	Forbes, Elizabeth W.	19, Oct. 1847	K2
Moore, Wilson	Smith, Jane	8, Aug. 1850	Y2
Moorhead, John (Dr)	Humphreys, Susan (Mrs)	18, Dec. 1830	R3
More, Amos	Devit, Mary	30, Dec. 1823	N3
More, William	Anderson, Margaret	1, Aug. 1817	S3
Morgan, Edward S.	Smith, Lizzy G.	1, June 1847	K2
Morgan, Hugh	Smith, Ann B.	4, June 1842	R3
Morgan, Isaac	Wood, Eliza F.	14, Nov. 1817	S2
Morgan, John M.	Dobson, Martha E.	28, Aug. 1852	P2
Morgan, Milton H.	Stute, Mary E.	17, July 1852	P2
Morland, L.F.	Guy, Elizabeth	16, May 1837	T2
Morrey, Joseph	Cox, Elizabeth	17, Dec. 1852	P2
Morrill, Onslow H.	Haskill, Sarah Eliza	9, Oct. 1841	V3
Morrill, H.E. (Dr)	Langdon, Cynthia	13, Nov. 1841	R3
Morrill, H.E. (Dr)	Langdon, Cynthia	13, Nov. 1841	N2
Morrill, Nahum	Barnard, Mary	26, Sept 1840	R3
Morrill, Onslow	Haskell, Sarah Eliza	16, Oct. 1841	R3
Morris, George P.	Hopkins, Mary W.	5, Apr. 1825	N3
Morris, Isaiah	Corwin, Rhoda	21, Nov. 1840	R3
Morris, John C.	Bauman, Mary	22, May 1847	K2
Morris, Tompson (Lt)	Upham, Martha	21, Feb. 1835	R3
Morris, William R.	Powers, Lydia S.	13, May 1823	N3
Morris, William R.	Powers, Lydia S.	15, May 1823	J3
Morrison, Thomas G.	Brown, Janet M.	2, Nov. 1852	P2
Morrow, Jeremiah	Johnson, Sarah	6, Jan. 1836	T3
Morrow, John H.	Roberts, Margaret A.	30, Oct. 1852	P2
Morrow, R.A.	Jones, Maria A.	17, Nov. 1852	P2
Morrow, Robert A.	Jones, Marie A.	15, Nov. 1852	P2
Morse, Benjamin F.	House, Elizabeth	5, Apr. 1838	T2
Morsell, James C.	Johnson, Amelia (Mrs)	19, Dec. 1823	N3

Grooms	Brides	Date of Notice	Page
Morten, Henry	Forman, Amanda	20, Jan. 1835	T2
Morton, Henry	Armstrong, Catharine	12, Oct. 1811	S3
Morton, Joseph	Armstrong, Ann	12, Oct. 1811	S3
Morton, Phineas	Fairbank, Sarah A.	16, Sept 1831	X3
Morton, Thomas	Booth, Eliza	19, Nov. 1847	K2
Morton, Wellington	Calling, Jane Ann	3, Mar. 1841	N2
Morton, Wellington L.	Calling, Jane Ann	6, Mar. 1841	R3
Moses, Benjamin	Block, Esther	16, Jan. 1836	T3
Moses, Benjamin	Block, Esther	15, Jan. 1836	N2
Moses, Morris	Oppenheim, Maria	14, Oct. 1847	K2
Moses, S.	Levi, Sarah	22, Oct. 1836	N2
Moses, Simpson P.	Tucker, Lizzie C.	14, July 1849	L2
Moses, Solomon	Levi, Sarah	25, Oct. 1836	T2
Moss, Madison R.	Porter, Mary	15, Aug. 1835	T2
Mott, Jonathan	Hunt, Susanna	24, Feb. 1820	D3
Mount, William (Dr)	McMurry, Eliza	9, Mar. 1824	N3
Mulford, William	Shane, Amanda F.	15, Dec. 1827	R3
Mullen, Jonathan	Kimball, Fanny	30, June 1832	R3
Mullen, Jonathan	Kimball, Fanny	29, June 1832	X3
Mulvany, John	Ellison, Polly	22, Sept 1838	R3
Munday, Benjamin	Riggett, Esther	27, Oct. 1827	R3
Munday, William	McQuead, Mary	27, July 1835	T2
Mundy, William (Dr)	Holcomb, Lorana A.	14, May 1847	K2
Murdock, Granville T.	Sutton, Charlotte	16, May 1840	R3
Murdock, Thomas S.	Ross, Julia Ann	24, Mar. 1832	R3
Murphy, Archibald	McCane, Sarah	4, Feb. 1825	N2
Murphy, Lewis	Yeatman, Sally T.	10, Oct. 1839	T2
Murphy, Peter	Kelly, Jane	1, Dec. 1815	S3
Murray, William	Barnes, Esther	27, Dec. 1828	R3
Musselman, Samuel	Newell, Rosalinda	14, Mar. 1829	R3
Myers, (Mr)	Phillips, Mary (Mrs)	13, Mar. 1819	S2
Myers, Abraham	Moses, Sarah Ann	28, June 1838	T2
Myers, Elkunah	Owens, Mary Ann Jane	6, July 1849	L2
Myers, George	Galloway, Rebecca	13, Mar. 1835	N2
Myers, Henry (Col)	Noble, Eliza	1, Oct. 1838	T2
Myers, Henry W.	Pehleisen, Matildey	8, Oct. 1852	P2
Myers, William W.	Nash, Anna E.	29, Oct. 1852	P2
Nashee, George	Kelly, Jane	14, Aug. 1819	S3
Neave, Charles	Caldwell, Jane R.	9, June 1827	R3
Neave, Charles	Caldwell, Jane R.	8, June 1827	N3
Neave, Thompson	Martin, Elizabeth	25, Oct. 1816	S3
Neff, George W.	White, Maria	20, Oct. 1827	R3
Neighbours, James S.	Hopkins, Caroline	2, Sept 1825	N1
Nelson, James A.	Kemper, Judith E.	3, Nov. 1836	X3
Nelson, William A.	Burdsal, Zada Emily	7, Sept 1835	T2
Nevers, Edward	Worden, Sarah F.	18, Dec. 1838	T2
Neville, John (Lt)	Hayes, Charlotte	29, Jan. 1842	R3
Neville, Julian	Dorsey, Frances H.	19, Dec. 1835	T3
Newcomb, Harvey	Wells, Alithea	7, June 1830	A3
Newcomb, Harvey	Wells, Alithea	5, June 1830	R3
Newell, Augustus	Moore, Sylvia	5, Apr. 1830	A3
Newell, Augustus	Moore, Sylvia	2, Apr. 1830	N2
Newell, James	Attenborough, Eliza	9, Apr. 1842	R3

Grooms	Brides	Date of Notice	Page
Newkirk, Matthew	St.Clair, Nancy M.	4, Mar. 1837	R3
Newkirk, Nathan	St.Clair, Nancy M.	4, Mar. 1837	T2
Newman, Joseph	Brooks, Dolly	11, June 1799	S3
Newton, C.L.	O'Roakh, D. (Mrs)	29, July 1852	P2
Newton, Henry S.	Brown, Maria Louise	20, Nov. 1841	R3
Newton, Henry T.	Brown, Maria Louise	13, Nov. 1841	N2
Nichols, John D.	Rice, Frances S.	3, Sept 1831	R3
Nichols, John D.	Rice, Frances S.	2, Sept 1831	X3
Nichols, Samuel S.	Atlee, Elizabeth J.	26, Feb. 1841	N2
Nicholson, Thomas	Goble, Elizabeth	1, Oct. 1847	K2
Niles, Paul C.	Bills, Ruth	14, July 1827	R3
Nimmo, Edward L.	Henderson, Ellen G.	21, May 1842	R3
Nimmo, Edward L.	Henderson, Ellen G.	21, May 1842	N2
Noah, M.M.	Jackson, Rebecca	18, Dec. 1827	N3
Noble, Daniel W.	Brood, Harriet M.	3, Oct. 1840	R3
Noble, William P.	Carter, Matilda L.	29, July 1828	N3
Norris, John H.	Briscoe, Jane A.	21, May 1836	T2
North, David	Fair, Susan	11, July 1835	T2
Norvell, Joseph	Walker, Agnes	11, Apr. 1823	N3
Nourse, Michael	Gibson, Sarah C.	4, Dec. 1835	T3
Nuckols, William W.	McConn, Mary E.	30, Dec. 1852	P2
Nut, James M.	Case, Sarah	8, Dec. 1827	R3
Oblinger, Christian	Horne, Mary	14, Jan. 1831	X3
O'Brian, Edward D.	Conn, Mary Ann	10, Mar. 1827	R3
O'connor, Michael	Bayless, Sophronia	26, June 1835	T2
Odell, James	Cutter, Maria	11, Aug. 1841	N2
O'Donnell, Hugh	Pitcher, Laura	7, Oct. 1837	R3
O'Donnell, Hugh	Pitcher, Laura	5, Oct. 1837	T2
Ogden, Henry T.	Rosa, Nannie Holley	9, Sept 1850	P2
Ogden, James	Hall, (Miss)	2, Jan. 1818	S3
Ogden, Jonathan	Gorham, Mary Elizabeth	27, Dec. 1834	R3
Ogden, Lewis B.	Hardy, Isabella	12, June 1847	K2
Ogden, Thomas	Loder, Hannah	15, Dec. 1815	S3
Ogg, Joel	Kugler, Sarah	29, Sept 1836	T2
Oglesby, Willis	Glore, Zorilda	2, Sept 1847	K2
O'Hara, William A.	Hughes, Jane	16, May 1840	R3
Olcott, E.K.	Gosman, Elizabeth (Mrs)	15, July 1852	P2
Olds, Chauncey N.	Woodruff, Caroline S	24, Mar. 1838	R3
Oliver, Alexander P.	Pearce, Jane	28, July 1841	N3
Oliver, David (Dr)	Wade, Mary	16, Feb. 1816	S3
Oliver, Robert	Hoops, Sarah Maria	25, Mar. 1823	N3
Oliver, William	Ruffin, Eliza	23, Apr. 1814	S3
Oliver, William B.	Baker, Sarah	26, Jan. 1816	S3
Orange, Benjamin	Beresford, Elizabeth	28, June 1828	R3
Orange, Benjamin	Beresford, Elizabeth	27, June 1828	Q3
Orr, James	Powers, Rebecca	27, June 1829	R3
Orr, Thomas G. (Dr)	Grandin, Mary E.	22, Dec. 1837	T2
Orr, William M.	Dixon, Elizabeth	26, Dec. 1817	S3
Orth, Godlove S.	Ayers, Mary Ann	3, Sept 1850	Y2
Osborn, Lewis	Corwin, Amelia	9, June 1827	R3
Osborne, Thomas (Rev)	Allibone, Mary	26, Oct. 1822	S3
Ott, Adam	Nagle, Ann	28, Sept 1852	P2
Ott, Otho C.	Crossman, H.S.	6, May 1837	R3

Grooms	Brides	Date of Notice	Page
Overman, Zebulon	Small, Elizabeth	16, June 1827	R3
Owen, Allison	Miller, Caroline	29, Dec. 1832	R3
Owen, John	Murray, Isabella	8, Feb. 1838	N2
Owens, Patrick	Gridley, Mary	26, Apr. 1833	X3
Paddock, W.R.	Hodgson, Mary Abby	10, Sept 1850	P2
Page, John (Capt)	Blaney, Mary E.	28, May 1838	T2
Paige, A.L.	Anderson, Jane W.	2, Oct. 1841	R3
Paine, Thomas L.	Chipman, Mary	17, Oct. 1817	S3
Palmer, Lewis H.	Huff, Sarah Jane	6, Aug. 1852	P2
Palmer, Solon	Beckett, Mary A.	10, July 1851	P2
Pancoast, Joseph	Whippy, Margaret	12, May 1815	S3
Pangburn, Oliver	Lanphear, Roda Ann	28, Dec. 1852	P2
Parker, Franklin	Carr, Catharine	28, Oct. 1834	T2
Parker, J.A. (Dr)	Lindley, Joanna	17, Oct. 1823	N2
Parker, Samuel	Harton, Margaret	8, Oct. 1852	P2
Parker, William	Woodruff, Catharine	1, Nov. 1838	T2
Parks, Arthur	Williams, Sally	14, Mar. 1812	S2
Parks, James	Longbrake, Elizabeth	22, Apr. 1830	A3
Parks, Robert	Diad, Celia	2, June 1838	R3
Parmele, Hervy	Fernival, Martha	17, May 1816	S3
Parmerton, A.B.	Scott, Fanny	16, Dec. 1852	P2
Parsell, George	Gibbs, Mary P.	8, Sept 1838	R3
Parson, Enoch	Horner, Sarah A.E.	28, Oct. 1852	P2
Partridge, Alden	Swasey, Ann Elizabeth	10, June 1837	R3
Partridge, Alden	Swasey, Ann Eliza	12, June 1837	T2
Parvin, H. (Dr)	Thompson, Phebe	9, June 1832	R3
Parvin, H. (Dr)	Thompson, Phebe	15, June 1832	X3
Patmore, John	Satcher, Marian	7, Sept 1847	K2
Patterson, Abraham	Neely, Nancy	4, Dec. 1813	S3
Patterson, Andrew	Nelson, Bridget	27, Feb. 1819	S3
Patterson, John K.	Bliss, Sarah S.	24, Jan. 1829	R3
Patterson, John S.	Ball, Emily A.	12, Dec. 1835	T3
Patterson, William	Porter, Mary	18, Apr. 1840	R3
Pawson, T.	Weeks, Rebecca	6, Nov. 1847	K2
Peabody, Ephraim (Rev)	Derby, Mary Jane	17, Aug. 1833	R3
Peacock, Frederick	McKee, Isabella	24, Sept 1852	P2
Peacock, William H.	Browner, Sophia J.	10, June 1847	K2
Peak, William J.	Hughes, Harriet	23, Oct. 1852	P2
Pearce, Christopher	Sackett, Jane Ann	17, Oct. 1840	R3
Pearce, Henry	Owens, Elizabeth	12, Aug. 1847	K2
Pearce, John	Bagott, Alice	9, Aug. 1841	N2
Peck, Charles A.	Potter, Adeline E.	12, Mar. 1842	R3
Peckenpaugh, M.S.	Hathorn, Susan	3, June 1847	K2
Peebles, Daniel M.	Wise, Maria	1, Jan. 1842	R3
Peebles, William S.	Stephenson, Lucy	6, Nov. 1841	R3
Peebles, William S.	Stephenson, Lucy	30, Oct. 1841	N2
Pendery, Goodloe	Davis, Clarissa	10, Nov. 1838	T2
Pendleton, N.G.	James, Anne	22, May 1841	R3
Pendleton, N.G.	James, Anne	17, May 1841	N2
Pendleton, Nathaniel	Hunt, Jane F.	18, May 1820	S3
Pendry, John L.	Rockey, Catharine O.	11, June 1847	K2
Pepper, Andrew J.	Rankins, M.A.H.	8, Oct. 1841	N2
Perdicaris, Gregory	Hanford, M.E.	17, June 1837	R3

Grooms	Brides	Date of Notice	Page
Perdicaris, Gregory	Hanford, M.E.	8, June 1837	T2
Perin, Ira	Edwards, Elizabeth	20, Dec. 1852	P2
Perin, Lyman	Wilson, Maria Louisa	16, Apr. 1849	L2
Perkins, Joseph	Thomas, Mary Ellin	4, Feb. 1831	X3
Perret, Phillip H.	Pernet, Cecilia	15, June 1824	N3
Perrin, Amos	Dee, Jerusha	26, Jan. 1833	R3
Perrin, Joseph J.	Riddle, Melissa E.	31, Aug. 1852	P2
Perrine, Isaac B.	Hathhorne, Sarah	19, July 1833	X3
Perry, George H.	Johnson, Margaret A.	18, Aug. 1852	P2
Perry, James	English, Mary	13, Mar. 1819	S2
Perry, Joshua H.	Paddock, Lydia	18, Oct. 1816	S3
Perry, Samuel	Thew, Mary B.	16, Aug. 1816	S3
Perry, William	Davis, Eliza	15, July 1830	A3
Peters, Joseph	Rogers, Lucretia	5, Sept 1834	X3
Peters, William	Taft, Serveign	1, Jan. 1828	R3
Petit, Charles V.E.	Stephan, Marie Jos.	5, Mar. 1839	T2
Petty, William C.	Redding, Eleatora	18, Dec. 1841	R3
Pharis, Washington	Looker, Pamela C.	11, Apr. 1812	S2
Phelps, Benjamin R.	Cowdry, Elizabeth	30, May 1835	T2
Phelps, Samuel W.	Ball, Anne (Mrs)	24, Feb. 1835	T2
Phillips, Asher	Ormsby, Sarah	14, Apr. 1827	R3
Phillips, Elias	Ormsby, Mary	8, Oct. 1831	R3
Phillips, Henry	Conklin, Mary	21, Oct. 1825	N2
Phillips, Isaac	Martin, Mary Ann	30, Nov. 1852	P2
Phillips, Thomas	Davis, Ruhamah	12, Jan. 1830	N2
Phillips, William	Dwyer, Elizabeth	28, June 1828	R3
Phillips, William	Symmonds, Esther E.	24, Sept 1842	R3
Piatt, Donn	Kirby, Louise	15, Oct. 1847	K2
Piatt, J.W.	Lanman, Harriet	22, Nov. 1831	A3
Piatt, J.W.	DeValcourt, Martha E	5, Sept 1837	T2
Piatt, James A.	Ford, Jemima	22, Dec. 1815	S3
Piatt, John H.	Willis, Martha Ann	24, July 1813	S3
Picket, Albert	Reser, Ann Eliza	18, Mar. 1831	X3
Picket, Charles (Dr)	Lyman, Nancy	12, Feb. 1820	S3
Pierce, Thomas	Neave, Eliza	26, May 1815	S3
Pierson, George W.	Hanker, Margaret	1, Feb. 1839	T2
Pierson, Henry A.	Waring, Ellen	19, Apr. 1831	A3
Pierson, Moses (Rev)	Riggs, Eunice	8, Sept 1827	R3
Pilling, Matthias J.	King, Mary	29, Oct. 1852	P2
Pindall, Daniel	Sterling, Elizabeth	16, Oct. 1841	N2
Pindell, Daniel	Sterling, Elizabeth	23, Oct. 1841	R3
Pinglee, E.M. (Rev)	Hally, Mary Ann	17, Oct. 1840	R3
Pitman, Jonathan	Argadine, Jane	6, Dec. 1825	N3
Platt, Jacob	Perry, Martha (Mrs)	8, May 1819	S3
Pleasants, Samuel E.	Biggs, Mary	19, May 1821	S3
Poland,	McChisne, Helen	2, Jan. 1818	S3
Polhamus, John J.	Pierce, Amanda	9, Nov. 1852	P2
Pomeroy, Charles R.	Worthington, Elizabeth	13, Nov. 1835	T2
Pomroy, R.E.	Armstrong, Fannie	28, Dec. 1852	P2
Pond, Augustus	Blaique, Sophia	20, May 1842	N2
Porter, Henry (Dr)	David, Mary	20, Sept 1852	P2
Porter, J.H.	Bonsall, L.T.	24, Mar. 1849	L2
Porter, John	Drake, Mary A.	8, Aug. 1850	Y2
Porter, John J.	Lockwood, Missouri M.	20, Jan. 1826	N1

Grooms	Brides	Date of Notice	Page
Porter, Patrick E.	Lancaster, C. Jane	18, Aug. 1852	P2
Porter, Thomas (Capt)	Towsey, Myra	1, Dec. 1821	S3
Post, Joseph	Brown, Eleanor	8, Dec. 1832	R3
Potter, Aaron	Ramsdale, Emeline	4, Oct. 1830	A3
Potts, Alfred (Dr)	Jordan, M. (Mrs)	25, Sept 1852	P2
Pounsford, William	Sisson, Sarah	28, July 1815	S3
Powell, David A.	Newell, Selina W.	13, Dec. 1833	X3
Powell, Ellick	Merrick, Elizabeth (Mrs)	22, Sept 1821	S3
Powell, Henry	Berrall, Susan	14, Aug. 1852	P2
Powell, Palemon	Fish, Susannah	29, Jan. 1836	T3
Powell, William B.	Wallace, Nancy (Mrs)	10, Aug. 1837	X3
Powers, Benjamin F.	Bosson, Catharine M.	28, Nov. 1818	S3
Powers, Henry	Bechtel, Lydia Ann	8, Sept 1832	R3
Prather, James	Martin, Louisa	2, Dec. 1824	E2
Pratt, Daniel D.	James, Sophia Jane	14, Dec. 1839	R3
Prescott, Edward F.	Mellor, Margaret G.	29, July 1852	P2
Prescott, T.O. (Rev)	Mackie, Jessie	13, July 1849	L2
Preston, E.J.	Bryant, Lydia	10, Dec. 1847	K2
Preston, William (Rev)	Cory, Maria A.	31, May 1830	A3
Preto, Francis	Griffith, Mary B.	23, Feb. 1828	R3
Price, David	Reese, Sarah	3, Jan. 1829	R3
Price, David	Reese, Sarah	6, Jan. 1829	N3
Price, J.W.	McDowell, Ann	13, Dec. 1828	R3
Price, Walter	Graham, Louisa	6, Dec. 1852	P2
Prideham, Lawrence S.	Manning, Ellen	20, Nov. 1852	P2
Prince, Joseph W.	Washburn, Harriet J.	24, May 1849	L2
Pritchard, James	McArthur, Elizabeth	2, May 1840	R3
Pritchard, Richard	Howe, Martha (Mrs)	11, Jan. 1836	T3
Probasco, Henry	Carrington, Julia A.	5, Sept 1840	R3
Proctor, Newton L.	King, Elizabeth	1, Jan. 1828	R3
Proctor, Newton T.	King, Elizabeth	25, Dec. 1827	N3
Proud, Thomas	Berry, Elizabeth	6, Oct. 1850	Y2
Prout, Hiram	Crowley, Elizabeth	14, Mar. 1829	R3
Pruden, Andrew J.	Powell, Mary Ann	21, Aug. 1841	N2
Pugh, Job	Martin, Sarah	19, Sept 1818	S3
Pugh, Jordan A.	Miller, Sarah Belle	4, June 1842	R3
Pugh, Lot	Anthony, Rachel	9, July 1814	S3
Pullan, Richard E.	Donaldson, Jessie	28, Apr. 1849	L2
Pulliam, John D.	Brown, Helen	17, Sept 1852	P2
Pursel, Joseph	Ross, Mary	12, Sept 1818	S3
Pursell, George	Fenton, Mary L.	19, May 1832	R3
Putnam, Rufus	Heiskell, Mary D.	9, Sept 1830	A3
Quarles, William	Walpole, Harriet	28, June 1828	R3
Quinlan, Thomas	Smitherner, Virgina	1, Sept 1847	K2
Quinn, J.J. (Dr)	Slevin, Maria L.	8, July 1852	P2
Quinn, James (Rev)	Witten, Elenor	2, Dec. 1824	E2
Quinn, William M.P.	Russell, Maria	23, Nov. 1820	S3
Racine, James F.	Kantz, Barbara E.	15, Oct. 1847	K2
Rager, Jeremiah	Johnson, Dorcas Ann	9, July 1852	P2
Rammelsberg, Fred.	Lape, Sarah M.	23, Apr. 1842	R3
Rammelsberg, Fred.	Lape, Sarah M.	28, Apr. 1842	N2
Ramsay, Cunningham	Bagley, Ann H.	17, May 1825	N3

Grooms	Brides	Date of Notice	Page
Ramsey, C. Sample	Peters, Anna Maria	11, Sept 1841	N2
Ramsey, William E.	Punshon, Mary E.	2, Sept 1847	K2
Randall, John	Lawrence, Mary Ann	27, Oct. 1852	P2
Randolph, Joseph F.	Cooper, Sarah Ann	3, Oct. 1840	R3
Rankin, William	Laing, Matilda	3, Nov. 1847	K2
Rannells, Charles S.	Wardnour, Mary A.	28, May 1842	R3
Rannells, D.W.	Clarkson, Mary E.	22, Jan. 1839	T2
Rannels, Charles S.	Werder, Mary A.	24, May 1842	N2
Ranney, Moses	Lucky, Catharine M.	11, Mar. 1837	R3
Ranney, Moses	Luckey, Catharine M.	11, Mar. 1837	N2
Rawson, Joseph	Richards, Mary W.	1, Dec. 1838	T2
Ray, James B.	Riddle, Mary	12, Dec. 1818	S3
Ray, Joseph (Dr)	Burt, Catharine G.	20, Aug. 1831	R3
Ray, Thomas	Molstee, Josephine	3, Nov. 1836	X3
Rayner, Kenneth	Polk, Susan	30, July 1842	R3
Reddenbough, Henry	Shanklin, Mary	1, Sept 1815	S3
Reddick, Thomas	Carson, Polly	2, July 1799	S3
Reddish, Thomas	Waters, Phebe (Mrs)	4, Feb. 1825	N2
Redington, Asa	Sherwin, Caroline F.	22, Aug. 1817	S3
Reed, Robert	Abbott, Elizabeth	31, July 1819	S3
Reed, Samuel	Mills, Jane	6, Mar. 1819	S3
Reeder, Charles A.	McCullough, Ellen	30, Jan. 1841	N2
Reeder, Jacob	Crane, Frances	16, Feb. 1816	S3
Reeder, Jeremiah	Symmes, Julia	28, Dec. 1811	S3
Reeder, Jesse	Kennedy, Mary	18, May 1807	S3
Reeder, Jesse	McKnight, Mary	12, Apr. 1816	S3
Reeder, Joseph A.	Langdon, Olive	4, Apr. 1818	S3
Reemelin, Charles	Marks, Louisa	6, Oct. 1837	T2
Rees, Charles L.	Slater, Julia	6, Aug. 1852	P2
Reeves, Edward J.	Powers, Joshufan	30, Nov. 1852	P2
Reeves, James E.	Cornell, Isabella	20, Aug. 1842	R3
Reilly, Thomas	Haines, Joanna	14, Jan. 1832	R3
Reily, John W.	Rede, Mary	2, Oct. 1835	N2
Reily, Robert	Gano, Belle	15, Aug. 1850	Y2
Reynolds, Benjamin B.	Dennison, Julia Ann	10, Mar. 1827	R3
Reynolds, Benjamin B.	Guest, Elizabeth	10, Mar. 1826	N3
Reynolds, Giles K.	Bassett, Zipporah	13, Apr. 1837	X3
Reynolds, James	Israel, E.R. (Mrs)	26, May 1835	T3
Reynolds, Lemuel	Fisher, Emmeline P.	23, Apr. 1824	N3
Reynolds, R.S.	Lansdale, Martha	12, Sept 1823	N3
Reynolds, Sackett	Guest, Mary Ann	23, Oct. 1819	S3
Reynolds, William	Johnston, Rachel	6, June 1836	T2
Reynolds, William A.	Johnston, Rachel	9, June 1836	X3
Rhoads, Charles H.	Fisher, Sarah	15, Mar. 1828	R3
Rice, Amzi	Musgrave, Sarah	15, Oct. 1850	Y2
Rice, Eliphalet L.	Harrison, Sallie P.	31, Dec. 1847	K2
Rice, John	Putnam, Lucretia	30, Mar. 1822	S3
Rich, Virtulon	Bush, Sarah C.	28, Sept 1835	T2
Richard, George	Quin, Eliza	30, Apr. 1838	T2
Richards, Channing	Williamson, Lydia H.	11, Mar. 1837	R3
Richards, Channing	Williamson, Lydia H.	13, Mar. 1837	T2
Richards, Giles	Lloyd, Eleanor H.	2, Nov. 1820	S3
Richards, Warren	Cook, Mary Elizabeth	6, Dec. 1828	R3
Richards, William	Gibson, Jennette	7, Feb. 1818	S3

Grooms	Brides	Date of Notice	Page
Richards, Wolcott	Strong, Susan (Mrs)	3, June 1841	N2
Richardson, Francis	Conclin, Louisa	19, Apr. 1847	K2
Richardson, J.	Little, Rachel	22, Apr. 1830	A3
Richardson, James	Robinson, M.A.	13, Aug. 1851	P2
Richardson, Joseph A	Buckingham, Maria	8, Oct. 1841	N2
Richardson, Robert	Richardson, Cath.	24, Aug. 1820	S3
Richardson, Samuel	Eppley, Mary	23, Aug. 1852	P2
Richardson, Samuel	Lawrence, Mary Elizabeth	22, Sept 1847	K2
Riddle, Adam N.	Cook, Elizabeth	1, May 1835	T3
Riddle, Hiram B.	Tuttle, Mary Ann	13, Mar. 1835	N2
Ridgway, Joseph	Tatem, Janett S.	1, Dec. 1827	R3
Rigdon, Charles	Dolton, Ann	22, Jan. 1820	S3
Rigdon, Isaac	Auchey, Emma	15, Dec. 1852	P2
Riggs, Samuel J.	Cheatham, Medora	3, Oct. 1835	T2
Rinear, William	Jones, Marian	15, Dec. 1827	R3
Rinehart, Joseph H.	Myers, Caroline	27, June 1851	P2
Ringer, John T.	Patton, Elenor T.	29, Oct. 1852	P2
Ringham, John	McDonald, Mary Ann	7, July 1852	P2
Rippey, William	Bliss, Caroline	9, June 1836	X3
Ritchie, James (Dr)	Martin, Charlotte S.	13, Aug. 1831	R3
Rittenhouse, Eli F.	Harsha, Lydia	21, Nov. 1818	S3
Rivers, Robert J.	Chatham, Amanda	5, July 1828	R3
Rlake, A. (Rev)	Leonard, Ann J.	11, Sept 1841	V3
Roach, Steven F.	Smith, D. (Mrs)	17, Aug. 1841	N2
Roark, James	Yates, Margaret	31, July 1852	P2
Robacamp, Frederick	Fieldden, Sarah Jane	30, Jan. 1839	T2
Robb, James M. (Dr)	Stevenson, Eleanor	15, July 1852	P2
Robb, John H.	Smith, Nancy S.	28, June 1828	R3
Robb, Thomas B.	Moore, Ann	11, Aug. 1835	T2
Robbins, Daniel P.	Leverett, Charlotte (Mrs)	19, June 1819	S2
Roberts, Edward	Boltazar, Caroline	31, July 1852	P2
Robertson, Alfred	Tappan, Jane D.	8, Dec. 1836	X3
Robins, Ephraim	Huzzey, Jane	14, Jan. 1832	R3
Robinson, A.F.	Lincoln, Louisa	16, Aug. 1830	A3
Robinson, Conway	Leigh, Mary Susan	26, July 1836	T2
Robinson, D.	Stackhouse, Emeline	9, May 1840	R3
Robinson, Gabriel J.	Jacks, Matilda	26, July 1836	T2
Robinson, Henry H.	Glancy, Josephine	6, Jan. 1848	K2
Robinson, Jeremiah	Boyden, Julia M.	25, May 1832	X3
Robinson, John A.	Bond, Ellen J.	23, Oct. 1852	P2
Robinson, John C.	Martin, Almira	19, Mar. 1849	L2
Robinson, Robert	Plew, Athea	5, Jan. 1816	S3
Robinson, Solon	Evans, M. (Mrs)	17, May 1828	R3
Robinson, Thaddius P	Zane, Mary	7, Mar. 1829	R3
Robinson, Thomas	Morrow, Rachel Ann	15, Mar. 1828	R3
Robinson, Thomas G.	Lovejoy, Mary E.	30, July 1852	P2
Robinson, William E.	Epply, Julia M.	14, May 1847	K2
Rockey, Henry	Ruffin, Mary	16, Nov. 1820	S3
Roe, Daniel	Longly, Patty	28, Dec. 1807	S3
Roe, Daniel	Smith, Emily	3, Nov. 1821	S3
Roe, Francis	Drayton, Malinda	20, Sept 1834	R3
Rogers, Hiram	Harding, Cordelia	24, Aug. 1833	R3
Rogers, M. (Dr)	Lane, Margaret	23, Apr. 1831	R3
Rogers, Nathaniel	Foulke, Elizabeth	14, Mar. 1829	R3

Grooms	Brides	Date of Notice	Page
Romeril, Charles E.	Looker, Emmeline	14, Apr. 1826	N3
Ropes, Nathaniel	Brown, Sarah E.	14, July 1826	N3
Rose, Erasmus (Dr)	Kuhn, Sarah (Mrs)	10, Apr. 1849	L2
Rose, Timothy	Price, Harriett	1, Apr. 1818	S3
Ross, David A.	Perry, Diadama	23, Jan. 1827	N3
Ross, Frederick F.	Dicks, Catharine A.	5, Apr. 1834	R3
Ross, J.W.	Waters, Henrietta	7, June 1842	N2
Ross, S.R.	Kinney, Elizabeth	11, Sept 1847	K2
Row, Conrad	Lambdin, Eliza	23, Mar. 1822	S3
Row, George T.	Fenton, Louisa	11, Mar. 1824	E3
Rowan, John A.	Perrine, Jane C.	24, Apr. 1835	X3
Rowan, Matthew B.	Osborn, Ann	22, Oct. 1847	K2
Rowe, Stanhope S.	Thomas, Frances Mary	31, July 1841	V3
Rowland, George E.	Sheeler, Kate	31, May 1849	L2
Roye, John H.	Spicer, Pamela Ann	14, July 1827	R3
Rucker, Henry L.	Heckwelder, Mary J.	20, Apr. 1833	R3
Rue, Benjamin	Row, Mary	29, Sept 1827	R3
Ruffner, Sylvester	Wilson, Alice Jane	9, July 1838	T2
Ruggles, Benjamin	Atwood, Clarissa (Mrs)	2, Dec. 1825	N3
Rush, Jacob	Irwin, Elizabeth	4, Jan. 1836	T3
Rusk, Baltis	Gibson, Elizabeth W.	11, Feb. 1837	T2
Russel, Samuel	Crane, Mary	1, Nov. 1825	N3
Russell, H.W. (Dr)	French, Eliza (Mrs)	24, July 1847	K2
Russell, Henry W.	Tait, Jane	8, Sept 1841	N2
Russell, Joseph	Hammitt, Hephziba	2, June 1827	R3
Rust, John	West, Susan	19, Sept 1840	R3
Rust, Joseph G.	Morris, Jane	9, June 1836	T2
Rust, William B.	Winston, Mary	20, Sept 1852	P2
Rutherford, John	Bailey, Sylvia C.	24, Sept 1852	P2
Rynearson, William	Brown, Mahala	25, Aug. 1835	T2
Ryon, Theodore	Byrne, Mary Helen	23, Nov. 1835	N2
Sage, Samuel	Fleming, Mary	29, Dec. 1832	R3
Salmon, Samuel M.	Palmer, Elizabeth S.	25, Nov. 1825	N3
Sambert, James	Leach, Sarah (Mrs)	29, Apr. 1831	X3
Sampson, Calvin	Lethbridge, Hepsy	8, Aug. 1818	S3
Sampson, Joseph S.	Perry, Mary F.	7, Nov. 1840	R3
Sampson, William S.	Coolidge, Ann Maria	2, Sept 1831	A3
Sampson, William S.	Coolidge, Ann Maria	3, Sept 1831	R3
Sanders, David	Douglass, Hannah	3, Oct. 1818	S3
Sanders, John	Wilkins, Maria D.	7, Jan. 1839	T2
Sanders, Ravid A.	Wright, Lucy	16, Aug. 1838	T2
Sands, J.R.	Crook, Eleanor Ann	31, Aug. 1847	K2
Sanxay, Theodore	Perry, Hetty A.	4, June 1842	R3
Sargeant, C.H.	Lawson, Hannah	17, June 1842	N2
Sargent, George B.	Perrin, Mary	5, Oct. 1839	R3
Saunders, David M.	Dwyer, Jane	12, July 1828	R3
Saunders, William	Richardson, Elizabeth F.	28, Nov. 1812	S3
Sayre, William	Hamilton, Juliana	17, Feb. 1821	S1
Schell, Lewis T.	Gowers, Angeline	24, Jan. 1835	T2
Schenck, Aaron L.	Wood, Maria P.	3, Aug. 1822	S3
Schenck, John	Wood, Lucy	9, Mar. 1837	T2
Schenck, John	Wood, Lucy	8, Mar. 1837	N2
Schenck, O.H.	Lang, Mary J.	9, June 1835	T2

Grooms	Brides	Date of Notice	Page
Schenck, Obadiah	Freeman, Abigail	27, May 1806	S3
Schenck, Woodhull S.	Miller, Jeanette A.	15, Oct. 1841	N2
Schillinger, William	Cones, Frances Mary	5, June 1841	R3
Schillinger, William	Lovejoy, Mary (Mrs)	28, Oct. 1836	N2
Schillinger, William	Cones, Frances Mary	28, May 1841	N2
Schoolfield, Joseph	Clark, Sarah	13, Sept 1852	P2
Schultz, Charles	Bowers, Ann Elizabeth	13, Feb. 1827	N3
Schwartze, Augustus	Moore, Maria	7, Feb. 1818	S3
Schwartze, F.W.	Vattier, Parmelia A.	14, Nov. 1851	P2
Schwartze, F.W.	Weatherby, Mary G.	15, Apr. 1847	K2
Scot, John L.	Stevens, Jane M.	23, Oct. 1841	R3
Scott, Chasteen	Ramcey, Martha (Mrs)	21, Oct. 1837	R3
Scott, Edgar W.	Armstrong, Martha A.	21, May 1842	R3
Scott, Isaac M.	Mitchel, Susan B.	26, May 1838	R3
Scott, John L.	Stevens, Jane M.	22, Oct. 1841	N2
Scott, William	Frizzle, Nancy	10, May 1833	X3
Scudder, William	Brewster, Ruth	28, Apr. 1821	S3
Searing, Robert	Britt, Lydia Ann	27, May 1824	E3
Sedam, David Z.	Percipall, Amanda M.	13, June 1829	R3
Sedam, David Z.	Percefull, Amanda M.	20, June 1829	R3
Sefton, John	Strouder, Mary	26, Apr. 1842	N2
Seichrest, William H.	Woods, Eliza A.	17, Aug. 1852	P2
Selden, Alanson D.	Johnson, Louisa D.	21, Sept 1822	S3
Selden, Alvinson D.	Johnson, Louisa D.	26, Sept 1822	J3
Sellman, Carberry J.	Smith, Mary Ann	22, Oct. 1831	R3
Sells, Walter	Briggs, Kate (Mrs)	7, Aug. 1850	Y2
Selmon, Garret	Howell, Alice	11, Dec. 1841	R3
Selmon, Garrit	Howell, Alice	7, Dec. 1841	N2
Semmes, Raphael	Spencer, Ann E.	5, May 1837	T2
Sewell, John W.	Perkins, Harriet M.	6, Sept 1852	P2
Sexton, Horatio (Dr)	Pugh, Hannah	23, Nov. 1820	S3
Seymour, Jeffrey	Bagg, Clarissa	10, Oct. 1818	S3
Shaffer, David Henry	Robinson, Jane C.	14, Oct. 1835	T2
Shane, Charles (Dr)	Mulford, Hannah F.	21, Dec. 1832	X3
Shane, Charles G. (Dr)	Mulford, Hannah F.	22, Dec. 1832	R3
Shane, William	Lawson, Maria	2, June 1827	R3
Sharland, Edward H.	Dunham, (Miss)	5, May 1821	S3
Sharp, James	Huff, Sarah	17, Jan. 1829	R3
Sharpless, Thomas	Sayre, Margaretta	23, Nov. 1822	S3
Shattuck, William B.	Richardson, Elizabeth C.	22, May 1850	P2
Shaw, Ira	Huff, Ann	21, July 1827	R3
Shaw, John	Wright, Elizabeth	9, Apr. 1814	S3
Shaw, John	Hiler, Nancy	27, Aug. 1850	Y2
Shelden, Moses	Hanford, Mary H.	7, May 1842	R3
Shelden, Moses	Hanford, Mary H.	4, May 1842	N2
Shepard, Charles	Donnell, Mary	2, May 1840	R3
Shepherd, Chauncey B	Armstrong, Eliza (Mrs)	9, Apr. 1841	N2
Shepherd, M.L.	O'Reilly, Catharine	13, Jan. 1838	R3
Shepherd, Stephen	Smith, Sarah	4, Oct. 1841	N2
Sheppard, B.R.	Hinkle, Elizabeth	1, Apr. 1836	N2
Sheppard, Isaac D.	Tull, Theresa (Mrs)	22, Sept 1836	X3
Sheppard, J.W.	Offley, Rachael	9, Oct. 1852	P2
Sherburne, John H.	Devens, Frances P.	25, June 1842	R3
Sherer, John	Cordingley, Marcian	30, July 1842	R3

Grooms	Brides	Date of Notice	Page
Sherlock, Thomas	Turpin, Nancy C.	25, Sept 1852	P2
Sherlock, Thomas	Redhead, Martha Ann	26, Mar. 1847	K2
Sherrods, Calvin G.	Hoffman, Olympia	5, Sept 1840	R3
Shields, Timothy S.	Law, Hannah	29, Dec. 1838	T2
Shillito, John	Wallace, Mary	23, May 1836	T2
Shimer, Edward	Dupant, Martha (Mrs)	10, Aug. 1852	P2
Shipley, Joseph	Kiles, Sarah Ann	26, Aug. 1825	N3
Shires, William	Kent, Imogene	22, Oct. 1852	P2
Shively, John	Flood, Clarissa	4, Feb. 1825	N2
Shively, John	Flood, Clarissa	20, Jan. 1825	E3
Shoemaker, R.M.	Steiner, Mary C.	25, Jan. 1840	R3
Short, J. Cleves	Harrison, Betsey B.	2, July 1814	S3
Shorthill, Thomas	Harris, Rebecca	28, May 1842	R3
Shorthill, Thomas	Harris, Rebecca	24, May 1842	N2
Shotwell, George H.	Tudor, Elizabeth A.	10, Nov. 1836	T2
Shotwell, John (Dr)	Foote, Mary Ward	27, Oct. 1832	R3
Shotwrdl, John	Pucas, Sallie S.	7, July 1852	P2
Shourt, John	Davee, Mary	24, Aug. 1811	S3
Shultz, William J.	Spencer, Maria T.	10, June 1842	N2
Shumard, John	Miller, Caroline	7, Sept 1852	P2
Shumard, Richard	Shields, Susan	21, Apr. 1835	T3
Sidener, Samuel	Miller, Elizabeth M.	3, Oct. 1835	T2
Sidle, John	Todd, Nancy	23, Nov. 1832	X3
Sigerson, John	Schillinger, Philom.	28, Oct. 1836	N2
Sill, Shadrach	Lytle, Mary	26, Aug. 1830	A3
Silrerman, D.	Lepel, Josephine	28, Sept 1852	P2
Silsbee, Samuel (Dr)	Whipple, Hanna	5, July 1841	N2
Silsbee, William (Rev)	Lyman, Charlotte	24, Mar. 1838	R3
Silvers, Aaron	Buchanan, Eliza	20, Oct. 1815	S3
Silvers, F.G.	Matson, Fredonia M.	20, June 1840	R3
Simcox, James	Finkbine, Mary	20, Jan. 1835	T2
Simonton, William	Wilson, Maria	6, Sept 1816	S3
Sinks, Randolph M.	Frazer, Mary	8, Sept 1852	P2
Slade, Henry August	Pace, Laura H.	4, Nov. 1835	T2
Slane, Alexander	Bradford, Ann	23, July 1847	K2
Slayback, Abel (Dr)	Coleman, Maria (Mrs)	13, May 1823	N3
Sloan, Samuel	Dawson, Mary	2, June 1847	K2
Smead, Wesley	McKinnon, Amelia C.	12, May 1832	R3
Smead, Wesley	Gardner, Mary Jane	8, Aug. 1823	N3
Smiley, William	Strickler, Eliza	15, Sept 1838	R3
Smith, Abial	Hall, Ann	24, May 1828	R2
Smith, Charles M.	Highland, Cedonia	27, Dec. 1828	R3
Smith, Charles P.	Addis, Amelia	15, Aug. 1822	J3
Smith, Chester	Preston, Mary Ann E.	7, Apr. 1849	L2
Smith, Daniel J.	Brickley, Sarah E.	7, Apr. 1849	L2
Smith, DeWitt Clint.	Getz, Elizabeth	22, Oct. 1847	K2
Smith, E.G.	Weir, Ellen	1, Aug. 1840	R3
Smith, F.	Rice, Lucy	11, May 1822	S3
Smith, Franklin C.	Kountz, Martha A.	31, Dec. 1852	P2
Smith, Fred A. (Capt)	Mechlin, Agnes Maria	23, May 1840	R3
Smith, George	Byare, Mary	14, May 1847	K2
Smith, George W.	Dodson, Cynthia Anne	25, Dec. 1827	N3
Smith, J.H.	Arnold, Mary Jane	17, Mar. 1849	L2
Smith, James B.	German, Rebecca	10, Apr. 1819	S3

Grooms	Brides	Date of Notice	Page
Smith, James H.	Miller, Harriet	3, Aug. 1850	P2
Smith, James R.	Nixon, Elizabeth A.	9, Apr. 1847	K2
Smith, John	Scamahorne, Elizabeth	8, Apr. 1823	N3
Smith, John C.	Ritter, Maria	27, June 1835	T2
Smith, Joseph K.	Bell, Melinda	4, June 1824	N5
Smith, Joseph K.	Bell, Melinda	10, June 1824	E3
Smith, Julius H.	Carroll, Elizabeth	24, Mar. 1836	T2
Smith, Lemuel	Winship, Francis M.	7, July 1826	N3
Smith, Moses	Kilgour, Jemima	15, Mar. 1831	A3
Smith, Patrick	Sisson, Eliza	10, Aug. 1822	S3
Smith, Richard P.	Gray, Amanda	4, Oct. 1830	A3
Smith, Samuel	Stewart, Mary Ann	1, Jan. 1828	R3
Smith, Samuel S.	McCormick, Margery	2, Sept 1826	J3
Smith, Spencer	Wainwright, Ruth	4, June 1841	N2
Smith, Thomas	Prince, Mannette	3, Apr. 1819	S3
Smith, Thomas	Dollin, Jane	16, Nov. 1820	S3
Smith, Thomas B.	Ripley, Amelia (Mrs)	25, July 1840	R3
Smith, William	Allen, Nancy	20, Feb. 1841	R3
Smith, William	Allen, Nancy	15, Feb. 1841	N2
Smith, William H.	Lamb, Elizabeth	22, Mar. 1849	L2
Smith, William J.	Young, Julia S.	21, Aug. 1847	K2
Smith, William M.	Carter, Harriet S.	19, Aug. 1852	P2
Smith, William R.	Watson, Caroline	21, Dec. 1838	T2
Smith, William S.	Lovell, Clarissa	18, Oct. 1828	R3
Smith, Wilson	Cane, Margaret	9, Aug. 1852	P2
Smith, Winthrop B.	Sargeant, Mary	7, Nov. 1834	X3
Smith, Wright	Walker, Matilda H.	14, Nov. 1835	T2
Smizer, Henry (Dr)	Armstrong, Ruth Jane	14, Apr. 1847	K2
Snowden, Sidney	Mitchell, Eliza	26, Aug. 1837	T2
Snowden, Sydney	Mitchel, Eliza	31, Aug. 1837	X3
Snyder, Isaac	Hastings, Mercy	31, Mar. 1821	S1
Snyder, Jacob	Williams, Rebecca	25, Aug. 1821	S3
Snyder, M.J.	Hayslip, S.A.	3, June 1847	K2
Souder, John	Rose, Henrietta	9, June 1827	R3
Soule, Charles	Mead, Elizabeth	11, Mar. 1831	X3
Southgate, George M.	Scott, Gertrude V.	18, May 1836	T2
Southgate, Henry H.	Smith, Maria C.	4, Oct. 1834	R3
Southgate, James	Brigham, Cornelia S.	13, May 1831	A3
Southgate, James	Brigham, Cornelia	14, May 1831	R3
Sovereign, Daniel L.	Hampton, Martha A.	1, Sept 1852	P2
Spahr, Benjamin	Lemens, Elizabeth	25, July 1850	P2
Spalding, Henry P.	----, ----	14, Aug. 1841	N2
Spangenberg, L.A.	Mason, E.S.	23, June 1847	K2
Spark, Benjamin	Morrison, Matilda	7, Sept 1832	X3
Spark, John	Green, Clara	2, Dec. 1830	A3
Sparks, William	Weggins, Jane	16, Oct. 1819	S3
Spatz, Bernard	Marks, Miriam	22, Jan. 1842	R3
Spear, Samuel B.	Carey, Rachel	23, July 1842	R3
Spear, Samuel B.	Barret, Lucy D.	16, May 1836	T2
Spear, Samuel B.	Barret, Lucy D.	14, May 1836	N2
Spear, Samuel B.	Carey, Rachel	20, July 1842	N2
Spear, William	Love, Mary Ann (Mrs)	29, Oct. 1814	S3
Speed, James	Cochran, Jane L.	2, May 1840	R3
Speed, W.P.	Phillips, Margaret D.	25, Jan. 1840	R3

Grooms	Brides	Date of Notice	Page
Speer, Burnet V.	Grapevine, Eliza	15, Mar. 1831	A3
Spencer, Alexander O.	Workman, Catharine	28, Nov. 1838	T2
Spencer, John C.	Barr, Susan S.	21, Aug. 1835	T2
Spencer, O.M.	Coombs, Emily	30, Sept 1837	R3
Spencer, O.M.	Coombs, Emily	30, Sept 1837	T2
Spencer, Oliver	Oliver, Electa	16, Jan. 1805	S2
Spencer, Oliver M.	Barton, Ann Eliza	1, Dec. 1832	R3
Spencer, Samuel A.	Keating, Maria	24, Feb. 1841	N2
Spilman, G.	Richards, S.L.	5, July 1852	P2
Spinning, John	Ingram, Hannah	1, Jan. 1828	R3
Spinning, William	Worley, Margaret E.	24, May 1849	L2
Spofford, A.R.	Partridge, Sarah F.	23, Sept 1852	P2
Spooner, Thomas	Leonard, Sarah	17, Sept 1842	R3
Spooner, William L.	Smith, Catharine	31, Oct. 1840	R3
Sprague, Andrew W.	Watkins, Lydia	17, Feb. 1842	N2
Sprague, Darius	Linsley, Phoebe Ann	8, Nov. 1852	P2
Springer, Charles G.	Kilgour, Catharine	9, May 1840	R3
Squire, William B.	Barnard, Elizabeth M	10, Apr. 1841	R3
St.Clair, John	Crooker, Ann	22, Sept 1827	R3
St.John, Job	Newbury, Lydia (Mrs)	23, Dec. 1840	N2
St.Johns, Job	Newbury, Lydia (Mrs)	26, Dec. 1840	R3
Stanbery, Henry	Bond, Cecilia Key	20, July 1841	N2
Stanbery, Henry	Bond, Cecilia	17, July 1841	V3
Stanfield, Thomas S.	Peebles, Nancy H.	1, Jan. 1842	R3
Stanley, George S.	Maywood, Mary	22, June 1849	L2
Stannus, Richard G.	Walker, Margaret M.	28, Dec. 1847	K2
Stansbury, John C.	Coffin, Mary F.	8, Sept 1837	N2
Starbuck, John	Horton, Sophia (Mrs)	27, July 1820	S3
Stark, William T.	Miby, Lydia	28, Apr. 1815	S3
Starkweather, Samuel	Judd, Julia	5, July 1828	R3
Starr, David L.	Harper, Sarah J.	24, May 1849	L2
Starr, Henry	Morsell, Amelia (Mrs)	1, Dec. 1836	X3
Steavison, Jolett	Boon, Hester	30, Oct. 1841	R3
Steavison, Joseph	Boon, Hester	29, Oct. 1841	N2
Steel, ----	Pierce, Phebe	28, Nov. 1812	S3
Steel, David	Danforth, Mary	29, Mar. 1828	R3
Steel, John	Baker, Elizabeth	23, Feb. 1827	N3
Stephens, Ephraim M.	Mayhew, Aceneth	9, June 1827	R3
Stephens, Ephraim M.	Mayhew, Aceneth	8, June 1827	N3
Stephens, Isaac	Middleton, Lydia	26, Oct. 1847	K2
Stephens, Marcus	Butler, Charlotte	20, Feb. 1823	J3
Stephenson, Andrew C	Davis, Harriet Ann	15, Oct. 1847	K2
Stephenson, H.W.	Dorman, Sarah Ann	16, Feb. 1839	T2
Sterns, R.	Baldwin, H.	26, June 1841	R3
Sterns, R.	Baldwin, H.	23, June 1841	N2
Sterrett, A.	McCreary, Elizabeth	3, Aug. 1847	K2
Sterrett, Benjamin	Keys, Jane B.	7, June 1830	A3
Sterrett, Benjamin	Keys, Jane B.	5, June 1830	R3
Sterrett, Robert	Duke, Eugenia	15, Sept 1827	R3
Stettinius, John	Longworth, Mary	22, July 1830	A3
Steuart, Hugh C.	Allibone, Sarah	4, Oct. 1828	R3
Stevens, Elijah	Ramsay, Hannah	14, Mar. 1829	R3
Stevens, John	Arnold, Mary	26, Oct. 1836	T2
Stevens, Marcus	Butler, Charlotte	18, Feb. 1823	N3

Grooms	Brides	Date of Notice	Page
Stevenson, Hugh	Williamson, Marian	28, Jan. 1832	R3
Stevenson, Hugh	Williamson, Marian	3, Feb. 1832	X3
Stewart, Benjamin	Barlow, Hannah	25, Sept 1819	S3
Stewart, Benjamin M.	Parker, Mary	25, Sept 1852	P2
Stewart, William B.	Warner, Margaret L.	20, Sept 1852	P2
Stewart, William S.	Guilford, Belle E.	22, Nov. 1852	P2
Stickney, Daniel	Lewis, Sarah A.	1, June 1847	K2
Stickney, J. Charles	Clifford, Abby Anna	15, June 1836	T2
Stickney, Paul	Shield, Emeline	28, Aug. 1841	R3
Stille, J.	Hamilton, Caroline	20, May 1842	N2
Stilli, John	Hamilton, Caroline T.	21, May 1842	R3
Stillman, O.D.	Talbott, Hester Ann	18, July 1838	T2
Stillwill, T. Neal	Conwell, Winnie K.	25, Oct. 1852	P2
Stinson, Charles	Graham, Rachel	21, Oct. 1837	R3
Stinson, Charles	Graham, Rachel	16, Oct. 1837	T2
Stith, Townsend D.	Spence, Martha A.	7, Nov. 1838	T2
Stockton, T.B.W.	Smith, Maria	5, Apr. 1830	A3
Stockwell, Allen M.	Langhorne, Elizabeth	9, Apr. 1836	T2
Stokes, Benjamin M.	Cadwell, Prudence	13, Aug. 1799	S3
Stokes, John M.	Ward, Sophia	6, June 1828	Q3
Stoms, William	Mears, Eliza L.	14, Oct. 1837	T2
Stone, B.T.	Williams, Hannah M.	15, Sept 1838	T2
Stone, C.T.	Williams, Hannah M.	22, Sept 1838	R3
Stone, Daniel	Farnsworth, Augusta	10, Dec. 1824	N3
Stone, Daniel	Farnsworth, Augusta	9, Dec. 1824	E2
Stone, F.H.	Fairchild, Catharine	15, Aug. 1840	R3
Stone, John E.	McMillen, Olive	15, Dec. 1852	P2
Stonehill, Joseph	Newberger, Rebecca	17, Nov. 1852	P2
Stonestreet, Thomas	Swinam, Sarah (Mrs)	28, Sept 1835	T2
Stonfer, Henry	Dellon, Eliza Ann	15, Sept 1827	R3
Storer, Belamy	Barton, Euretta L.	5, Oct. 1820	S3
Stoughton, Samuel	Hearne, Netor	25, Apr. 1818	S3
Stout, Isaiah M.	Hardesty, Lucinda	7, Nov. 1840	R3
Stout, Moses	Platt, Eulalie (Mrs)	29, Nov. 1830	A3
Stout, Nathaniel R.	Peck, Emily P.	6, May 1847	K2
Strader, D.P. (Dr)	Ritchey, Abbey G.	11, Mar. 1841	N2
Strickler, George W.	Dicks, Mary Ellen	26, Feb. 1842	R3
Strickler, George W.	Johnson, M.B.	16, Nov. 1847	K2
Strickler, John	Ruckle, Catharine C.	20, Aug. 1842	R3
Strickler, John	Ruckle, Catharine C.	17, Aug. 1842	N2
Strodtbeck, Jacob	Crisman, Mary	1, Dec. 1827	R3
Strong, Edward K.	Fine, Elizabeth	15, July 1852	P2
Strothers, Thomas	Gibson, Jane	15, July 1835	T2
Stuart, Ewing T.	Adams, Roberta C.	8, June 1849	L2
Studyvan, Thomas	Stewart, Nancy	14, Jan. 1831	X3
Sullivan, C.W.	Smith, S.S.	23, Nov. 1852	P2
Sumwall, William	Parsons, Jane	27, Jan. 1825	E3
Sumwalt, William	Parsons, Jane	4, Feb. 1825	N2
Sutton, Joseph M.	Nicholas, Lydia Ann	17, May 1849	L2
Swaim, S.B.	Noble, Mary N.	20, May 1837	R3
Swain, Alonzo	----, Elvina	2, Jan. 1841	R3
Swain, Frederick C.	Barnard, Lucretia	25, Apr. 1836	T2
Swasey, Moses	Martin, Maria (Mrs)	31, Oct. 1840	R3
Swift, Abiol	Frazier, Sarah	7, July 1827	R3

Grooms	Brides	Date of Notice	Page
Swift, Milton	Whitney, Eliza	24, Nov. 1827	R3
Swing, David	Gazlay, Kerendah	19, Aug. 1825	N3
Swing, Jeremiah	Erwin, Olivia	28, July 1827	R3
Swormsted, Leroy (Rev)	Cummins, Ann (Mrs)	13, Jan. 1825	E3
Sykes, Charles	Jones, Martha Ann	29, Mar. 1849	L2
Symmes, Americus	Scott, Frances	26, Sept 1840	R3
Symmes, Daniel	Oliver, Elizabeth	16, Apr. 1796	C2
Symmes, Peyton S.	Close, Hannah B.	22, May 1819	S3
Symmes, Timothy	Spurrier, Ruth	3, Oct. 1818	S3
Taber, William B.	Hopper, Hester Jane	9, Dec. 1830	A3
Taber, William B.	Hopper, Hester Jane	4, Dec. 1830	R3
Tabor, Elisha	Britton, Ellenor	6, May 1806	S3
Tagart, Mathew	Lowry, Martha	26, May 1832	R3
Talbert, Joseph	Tudor, Alice	17, Sept 1831	R3
Talbott, David L.	Hildreth, Silvia	26, Dec. 1829	R3
Talbott, John	Conklin, Phebe	2, Dec. 1824	E2
Taliaferro, John N.	Southgate, Frances M.	2, Dec. 1830	A3
Talliaferro, John N.	McKinney, Mary Ann	20, Feb. 1819	S3
Tannebill, Wilkins	Mullikin, Eliza A.	6, Oct. 1837	T2
Tarquary, Isaac P.	Baily, Angeline	17, Oct. 1840	R3
Tarrance, John	Urton, Esther	15, Sept 1827	R3
Tarrant, Larkin M.	Tunis, Emmeline	20, Jan. 1826	N3
Taulman, P.J.	Sweignhart, Caroline	10, Oct. 1836	T3
Taylor, Calvin	Crary, Almira	12, Nov. 1841	N2
Taylor, E.	Marsh, Hannah M.	25, Dec. 1835	T3
Taylor, Edward	Brown, Annis (Mrs)	11, Dec. 1819	S3
Taylor, Eli	Marsh, Hannah M.	24, Dec. 1835	X3
Taylor, Gabriel A.	Miller, Sarah Jane	22, Sept 1847	K2
Taylor, George	Porter, Elizabeth	18, Sept 1819	S3
Taylor, Griffin	Thomas, Mary S.	11, Sept 1819	S3
Taylor, J.P. (Capt)	McLean, Eveline A.	8, Dec. 1827	R3
Taylor, John Drake	Reid, Elizabeth	20, Sept 1828	R3
Taylor, Mahlon R.	Lyon, Elizabeth W.	5, Dec. 1836	T2
Taylor, Mahlon R.	Lyon, Elizabeth W.	4, Dec. 1836	N2
Taylor, Mahlon R.	Williams, Elisabeth	8, Dec. 1836	X3
Taylor, Thomas	Calvert, (Mrs)	2, Dec. 1824	E2
Taylor, W.H.H.	Harrison, Anna J.	30, June 1836	X3
Taylor, Wesley	Carrick, Louisa Jane	29, Nov. 1837	T2
Taylor, William H.H.	Harrison, Anna T.	24, June 1836	T2
Taylor, William R.	Silliman, Caroline A.	23, May 1840	R3
Teal, Samuel R.	Revill, Amelia	7, July 1827	R3
Tealen, Robert	Parker, Ann	3, Jan. 1839	T2
Teasdale, William	Cook, Eliza	24, Feb. 1838	R3
Teator, Henry	Buchanan, Christina	16, Aug. 1816	S3
Teesdale, John	Dulty, Mary	19, June 1837	N2
Terry, John	Harvay, Martha	11, Sept 1819	S3
Terry, Washington	Mix, Catharine	1, Mar. 1833	X3
Thatcher, David	Flint, Julia	12, Mar. 1814	S3
Thatcher, David	Yeazee, Mary Jane	26, Aug. 1850	P2
Thatcher, Woodbridge	Swearingen, Sarah B.	7, Mar. 1840	R3
Thayer, Henry	Wood, Susan M.	25, Apr. 1840	R3
Thistlewaite, James	Punshon, Rachel	15, Feb. 1837	N2
Thomas, Alexander J.	Shepperson, Mary	2, June 1847	K2

Grooms	Brides	Date of Notice	Page
Thomas, Alexander S.	Ball, Elizabeth J.	10, Oct. 1850	P2
Thomas, Benjamin	Jones, Louisa	4, Oct. 1852	P2
Thomas, C. Walen	Wade, Harriet C.	12, Aug. 1852	P2
Thomas, George	Jackson, Elizabeth	19, Feb. 1814	S3
Thomas, Isaiah	Reeder, Mary Ann	4, June 1831	R3
Thomas, Israel	Chambers, Hannah	2, May 1812	S3
Thomas, John	Lattimore, Isabella	15, Oct. 1852	P2
Thomas, John	Bennett, Mary	31, July 1850	Y2
Thomas, John R.	Hayer, Abigail	29, Dec. 1821	S3
Thomas, John S.	Burley, Margaret	24, Oct. 1817	S3
Thomas, Joseph W.	Hopple, Mary	23, Oct. 1841	R3
Thomas, Joseph W.	Hopple, Mary	29, Oct. 1841	N2
Thomas, Robert	Whitney, Elizabeth (Mrs)	15, May 1847	K2
Thomas, Washington	Rochafeller, Charlotte	26, Nov. 1835	X3
Thompson, Francis R.	Norris, Martha	8, Sept 1847	K2
Thompson, J.J. (Rev)	Pool, Henrietta B.	26, July 1852	P2
Thompson, James K.	Hartley, Rachel M.	11, Sept 1841	N2
Thompson, Jesse W.	Sanders, Mary	2, June 1827	R3
Thompson, John	Ross, Maria	2, June 1827	R3
Thompson, John	Langlands, Janet	24, Mar. 1837	T2
Thompson, Samuel	Bragg, Mary	2, May 1812	S3
Thompson, Samuel G.	Smith, Mary Ann	26, Mar. 1847	K2
Thompson, Smith	Livingston, Eliza D.	17, Dec. 1836	T2
Thompson, Thomas	Nancarrow, Polly	25, Feb. 1806	S3
Thompson, William	Browne, Mary A.	15, July 1852	P2
Thoms, James	Summerfield, Marion	15, Mar. 1828	R3
Thomson, James	Oliver, Eliza Ann	24, Mar. 1838	R3
Thornton, Benjamin	Howell, Elizabeth	18, May 1833	R3
Thornton, Joseph	West, Mary	27, Dec. 1825	N2
Thornton, Tyrrel	Carey, Rosetta Jane	21, Dec. 1835	T3
Thorp, F.S. (Dr)	Kilbourne, Mary R.	2, Apr. 1842	R3
Thorp, John P.	Tiley, Emma	12, July 1836	N2
Thorp, Milton	Covert, Hannah	7, Mar. 1829	R3
Thorpe, Charles W.	Ernst, Catharine M.	15, June 1836	N2
Thorpe, George S.	Mlller, Fanny B.	20, Sept 1852	P2
Thorpe, John	Robinson, Lucy	15, July 1852	P2
Thorpe, John D.	Flintham, Margaret	22, July 1847	K2
Thurston, William H.	Miller, Delela	15, Sept 1827	R3
Tibbatts, John W.	Taylor, Ann	4, Jan. 1825	N3
Tibbatts, John W.	Taylor, Ann	13, Jan. 1825	E3
Tibbetts, Robert	Pangburn, Martha Ann	14, Mar. 1823	N3
Tidball, John (Rev)	Hunter, Nancy	5, July 1828	R3
Tiley, Francis	Hughes, Sarah (Mrs)	14, Oct. 1841	N2
Timberman, Isaiah	Cook, Elizabeth M.	29, Nov. 1852	P2
Timmons, Elisha	Williams, Elizabeth	24, May 1828	R2
Tizzard, William B.	Hice, Amelia	20, Mar. 1847	K2
Todd, James M.	Rennick, Alisonia B.	28, May 1847	K2
Todd, John P.	Smith, Frances (Mrs)	22, Nov. 1837	T2
Todd, P.G.	Reynolds, Minerva	19, Jan. 1822	S3
Todd, Thomas	Smith, Jane	25, Jan. 1841	N2
Todhunter, Thomas	Handley, Margaret	16, Feb. 1816	S3
Tomlinson, J.C.	Rogers, Charlotte	4, May 1833	R3
Torbet, N.H. (Dr)	Lewis, Eliza W.	1, Dec. 1832	R3
Torrence, James F.	Finley, Ann Rebecca	16, Oct. 1841	R3

Grooms	Brides	Date of Notice	Page
Totten, George M.	Gamble, Julia Rusk	6, Aug. 1842	R3
Tounly, Major J.	Allen, Harriet	17, Nov. 1838	T2
Townley, Asa H.	Reed, Catharine M.	4, May 1847	K2
Townsend, Louis	Warren, Elizabeth A.	3, Dec. 1852	P2
Trafton, Lysander B.	Hill, Joanna	31, July 1841	V3
Trainer, Lewis	Wolf, Rosina	7, Aug. 1841	R3
Tranter, James	Worchester, Lucy	28, Apr. 1849	L2
Tratobas, Maurice	Hawkins, Maria	17, Mar. 1832	R3
Treadwell, Alexander	Williams, Caroline	15, Nov. 1828	R3
Treat, Isaac	North, Jane (Mrs)	25, Aug. 1841	N2
Trimble, Cary A.	McArthur, Mary	6, Jan. 1838	R3
Trimble, Cary A.	McArthur, Mary	5, Jan. 1838	T2
Triplett, Robert	Pegram, Virginia	17, May 1828	R3
Trotter, Daniel	Hamilton, Maria L.	6, Oct. 1832	R3
Tucker, Daniel E.	Monroe, Maria	24, Nov. 1821	S3
Tucker, George W.	Colthar, Sarah Ann	4, May 1833	R3
Tufts, Servetus	Dudley, Emily	28, June 1834	R3
Tuite, Aaron G.	Howard, Mary Elizabeth	1, Mar. 1848	K2
Turner, Evan	Fleming, Ann (Mrs)	20, Sept 1839	T3
Turner, James	Tribby, Rebecca	27, Dec. 1828	R3
Turner, T.	McMillan, Diana	22, Apr. 1830	A3
Turner, William (Capt)	Morris, Maria	25, Nov. 1825	N3
Tuttle, G.P.	Clark, Sarah Jane	7, Sept 1847	K2
Tuttle, John F.	Gilman, Mary	21, Apr. 1849	L2
Tuttle, Oliver S.	LeBerteaux, Frances	14, Apr. 1836	X3
Tuttle, Samuel (Rev)	Camp, Amelia	12, June 1841	R3
Tuttle, Samuel L.	Camp, Amelia	10, June 1841	N2
Twichell, John W.	Holms, Frances Ellen	4, Oct. 1836	T2
Twichell, T.	Greene, Rebecca B.	6, Sept 1834	R3
Twichell, T.	Greene, Rebecca B.	4, Sept 1834	T2
Twitchell, Sophron.	Spencer, Julia W.	17, Nov. 1837	T2
Twornely, Israel S.	Neal, Mary A.	9, July 1852	P2
Ulrey, Stephen	McDonald, Cassandra	30, Apr. 1842	R3
Underhill, Abner H.	Bartow, Eugenia M.	28, July 1835	T2
Underwood, J.	Smith, Eve	21, May 1842	N2
Urner, Benjamin	Keyser, Elizabeth	11, Nov. 1825	N2
Utley, Hasting	Thompson, Sarah	7, June 1830	A3
Utley, Hasting	Thompson, Sarah	4, June 1830	N2
Vail, Aaron	Salles, Emily L.	20, Oct. 1835	T2
Vail, Daniel H.	Todd, Harriet	2, Nov. 1822	S3
Valentine, Lewis	Dunn, Elizabeth	15, Apr. 1842	N2
Valiant, William A.	Higgins, Levisa	6, Sept 1852	P2
Vallentine, Lewis	Dunn, Elizabeth	16, Apr. 1842	R3
Vallet, Henry	Carley, Sarah Julia	4, Oct. 1828	R3
VanBuren, Abraham	Singleton, Sarah A.	26, Dec. 1838	T2
VanBuren, Abraham	Singleton, Sarah A.	24, Dec. 1838	N2
Vance, Alex F.	Ward, Mary Rebecca	11, Aug. 1835	T2
Vandegriff, D.C.	Kemper, Martha Ann	13, June 1840	R3
Vandegriff, William	Douglass, Margaret	17, Apr. 1819	S2
VanDyke, Henry (Rev)	Soule, Maria L.	2, June 1836	X3
VanEaton, Isaac	Martin, Sarah Ellen	29, Aug. 1835	T2
VanEaton, James	Cox, Hannah	22, June 1833	R3

Grooms	Brides	Date of Notice	Page
VanHorn, Thomas B.	Chapeze, Elizabeth	4, Feb. 1831	X3
VanHorn, William	Barr, Margaret R.	26, Sept 1828	N3
VanHorne, Thomas B.	Chapeze, Elizabeth (Mrs)	29, Jan. 1831	R3
VanHorne, W.J.	Barr, Margaret R.	27, Sept 1828	R3
VanKuren, Edward	Duncan, Susan M.	12, June 1849	L2
VanMatre, Daniel	Henderson, Maria	4, May 1833	R3
VanPelt, George	Cuppuck, Janet R.	3, Oct. 1835	T2
VanTuyl, Charles	Hansell, Jane W.	14, June 1847	K2
Vanwey, Henry	Grant, Laura	26, Aug. 1831	X3
Vattier, John L.	Fouzatte, Margaretta	27, Sept 1828	R3
Vawse, Isaac	Broadrick, Betsy	27, Oct. 1798	F3
Veach, Charles	Collard, Catharine	5, Oct. 1820	S3
Vennemann, Anthony	Biedenhorn, Lezette	1, Feb. 1837	T2
Victor, Henry C.	Edwards, Jane	6, Nov. 1852	P2
Vogdes, J. (Lt)	Berard, Georgiana	2, May 1840	R3
Voorhees, Abram P.	Holcomb, Delia S.	21, Apr. 1836	X3
Voorhees, Ralph M.	Kirker, Mary	20, Apr. 1824	N3
Voorhees, Ralph M.	Kirker, Mary	22, Apr. 1824	E3
Voorhes, Daniel B.	Barnwerl, Mary M.	17, Nov. 1852	P2
Vorhes, Isaac	Grigg, Harriet	10, Apr. 1841	R3
Waddell, John W.	Porter, Lucia C.	4, Sept 1835	T2
Wade, David	Mansfield, Mary C.	20, June 1812	S3
Wade, Eben	Clifford, Sarah S.	11, Oct. 1831	A3
Wade, Joseph	McCormick, Jane	17, Oct. 1840	R3
Wade, Stephen J.	Ramsay, Harriet S.	31, Jan. 1835	N2
Waggoner, Conrod	Rambo, Malinda	29, Mar. 1828	R3
Walden, Baltzer C.	Streeter, Julia Ann	30, Oct. 1838	N2
Walden, William	Rohrman, Charlote	27, Mar. 1841	N2
Waldo, F.A. (Dr)	Lawrence, Arabella	18, Jan. 1833	X3
Waldo, Fred. Aug. (Dr)	Lawrence, Arabella H	19, Jan. 1833	R3
Waldo, Frederick	Egelston, Martha	17, Dec. 1852	P2
Walker, Benjamin	Reese, Hester Ann	3, Jan. 1829	R3
Walker, Benjamin	Reese, Hester Ann	6, Jan. 1829	N3
Walker, Charles C.	Wood, Jane H.	10, Nov. 1827	R3
Walker, George B.	Clark, Elizabeth	27, June 1835	T2
Walker, George W.	Ward, Mary L.	13, Mar. 1841	N2
Walker, Henry	Langhorn, Sarah Bell	13, May 1837	T2
Walker, James	Turner, Eleanor	8, Dec. 1821	S3
Walker, James H.	Trainer, Sarah M.	12, Oct. 1839	R3
Walker, Jesse	Hedden, Esther C.	18, July 1822	J3
Walker, John	Turnpaw, Elizabeth (Mrs)	11, July 1835	T2
Walker, Joseph	Orr, Martha E.	19, Oct. 1836	T2
Walker, Joseph	Orr, Martha E.	13, Oct. 1836	X3
Walker, Lewis S.	Taylor, Mary	13, Nov. 1841	R3
Walker, Lewis S.	Taylor, Mary	12, Nov. 1841	N2
Walker, S.S.	Fowles, H.N.	26, Nov. 1835	X3
Walker, Samuel	Smith, Emily H.	5, Feb. 1831	R3
Walker, T.	Bryant, Anna L.	12, May 1832	R3
Walker, William H.	Spinning, Frances M.	26, May 1836	T2
Wall, David	Neimerick, Eliza	18, June 1835	T3
Wallace, David	Sanders, Zerelda	9, Jan. 1837	T2
Wallace, J.G.	Whitacre, Mary Jane	29, Dec. 1852	P2
Wallace, Nicholas	Gatts, Sarah	21, July 1827	R3

Grooms	Brides	Date of Notice	Page
Wallam, John	Conrad, Priscilla	18, Mar. 1831	X3
Walsh, Robert F	Chandler, Eliza R.	13, Aug. 1838	T2
Walter, William	McCall, Mary A.	25, June 1842	R3
Walton, Charles	Blake, Sarah N.	7, Mar. 1839	T2
Walton, Elias J.	Carter, Susan B.	4, Nov. 1837	R3
Walton, Elias T.	Carter, Susan B.	2, Nov. 1837	T2
Wandell, William	Hailman, Leah	30, Aug. 1825	N2
Ward, Charles (Lt)	Lindsay, Catharine	8, May 1819	S3
Ward, Frederick E.	Merry, Susan A.	10, June 1842	N2
Ward, James	Artus, Mary	10, Oct. 1840	R3
Ward, Moses	Willace, Jane	21, May 1842	R3
Ward, Moses	Wallack, Jane	20, May 1842	N2
Ward, William M.	Yeatman, Caroline	31, May 1849	L2
Ware, Henry	Johnson, Isabella	9, Oct. 1847	K2
Ware, Samuel	Wells, Marietta	12, June 1847	K2
Ware, Samuel W.	Martin, Charlotte C.	4, Feb. 1832	R3
Warfield, Thomas	Carneal, Alice D.	18, July 1838	T2
Warfield, Thomas B.	Carneal, Alice	21, July 1838	R3
Warner, George	Ware, Abigail	21, Aug. 1819	S3
Warren, John Borlase	Bussey, Julia	9, Oct. 1835	T2
Warren, John Borlase	Bussey, Julia	8, Oct. 1835	N2
Washburn, Elihu	Trotter, Zarelda	11, Sept 1835	T2
Washington, George	Wharton, Mary E.	12, Oct. 1837	T2
Waterhouse, Josiah	Sloop, Elizabeth	16, Feb. 1822	S3
Waterman, James	Fountain, Hannah	1, Aug. 1804	S3
Waters, John	Clark, Florilla	7, May 1842	R3
Watson, Robert B.	McDiarmid, Jane	5, Nov. 1851	P2
Watt, Anthony	Murphy, Malinda	12, Oct. 1852	P2
Watt, James	Thomas, Frances Ann	13, June 1836	T2
Wayne, Charles	Quinten, Sarah Ann	24, May 1828	R2
Wayne, J.S.	Palmer, Eliza C.	16, July 1831	R3
Wayne, J.S.	Palmer, Eliza C.	15, July 1831	X3
Wayne, Joseph W.	Gove, Mary F.	6, Aug. 1852	P2
Wear, John H.	Harper, Eliza Jane	6, June 1835	T2
Weatherby, Philip G.	Jackson, Mary Jane	2, Sept 1847	K2
Weaver, William	Woodman, Eliza (Mrs)	2, Dec. 1830	A3
Webb, Alexander	Wheeling, Minerva	25, Dec. 1841	R3
Webb, Alexander	Wheeling, Minerva	22, Dec. 1841	N2
Webb, Henry	Stratton, Mary P.	4, Nov. 1847	K2
Webb, Joseph	Moland, Louisa	22, Aug. 1817	S3
Webb, Thaddeus R.	Farmer, Sarah	29, Mar. 1838	N2
Webb, William H.	Wallace, Phebe F.	1, July 1837	R3
Webb, William H.	Wallace, Phebe Fran.	1, July 1837	T2
Webber, George H.	Stuart, Jane M.	23, Mar. 1849	L2
Webster, Taylor	DeCamp, Mary H.	22, Apr. 1830	A3
Weed, E.J.	McClean, Arabella E.	14, Apr. 1827	R3
Weeks, Henry	Cox, Rebecca	21, Feb. 1823	N3
Weld, Theodore D.	Grimke, Angelina E.	2, June 1838	R3
Weller, John B.	Bryan, Cornelia A.	8, Aug. 1840	R3
Weller, Tobias	Higgins, Sarah	11, Mar. 1831	X3
Wells, Charles	Hoadley, Elizabeth	8, May 1850	P2
Wells, Henry	Vandervoort, Ann E.	26, Apr. 1828	R3
Wells, Hiram K.	Sankay, Emily	19, Sept 1840	R3
Wells, Horace	Whipple, Sarah H.	23, Mar. 1822	S3

Grooms	Brides	Date of Notice	Page
Wells, L.T.	Pococke, Ann	19, Nov. 1838	N2
Wells, Oliver	Marsh, Miranda	2, Sept 1826	J3
Wells, Romanto	Morgan, Mary Ann	9, Jan. 1830	R3
Wells, William	Dutton, A.L.	30, Dec. 1837	R3
Welton, L.A.	Morris, Mary A. Penn	29, Sept 1852	P2
Wertsvern, Johannes	Schweizerhoff, Joh.	2, Nov. 1850	Y2
Wesbay, Samuel	Alcocke, Lavina	27, Dec. 1828	R3
Wescott, Leonard Wm.	Miller, Ann	14, Mar. 1849	L2
Wesel, Francis	Hepp, Mary Ann	15, Jan. 1838	T2
West, Francies	Chapman, Fanny	21, Aug. 1819	S3
West, Isaac	Morris, Nancy	3, Nov. 1835	T2
West, Isaac	Norris, Nancy	5, Nov. 1835	X3
West, Samuel (Rev)	Allison, Rebecca (Mrs)	29, Aug. 1817	S3
Westcott, John	Espy, Mary	12, Aug. 1824	E3
Wetherbee, A.	Steffens, Nettie D.	24, Dec. 1852	P2
Wetherby, Luther	Brown, Julia Ann	7, Dec. 1820	S3
Wetmore, M.W.	Dexter, Julia	29, Apr. 1834	T2
Whan, Jame	Gorham, Julia	16, Jan. 1836	T3
Wharton, Clifton	Camsby, Oliveretta	25, Aug. 1838	T2
Wheeler, G.W.	Titcob, M.F.	13, Sept 1852	P2
Wheeler, George	Hurdus, Ann	17, Sept 1814	S3
Wheeler, George	Hurdus, Nancy	20, Sept 1814	W4
Wheeler, Wilber B.	Gordon, Julia M.	29, Dec. 1847	K2
Wheelock, Daniel W.	Pierce, Eunice	31, Oct. 1817	S3
Wheelock, Samuel L.	Ashton, Sarah S.	7, Apr. 1821	S3
Whetstone, Jacob V.	Coolidge, Sophy	23, Nov. 1852	P2
Whetstone, Reuben	Collard, Jane Ann	22, Aug. 1818	S3
Whetstone, Richard A.	Smith, Marion G.	6, May 1847	K2
Whetstone, Thomas H.	Mears, Esther B.	26, Sept 1840	R3
Whetten, John B.	Sherwood, Jane A.	24, Dec. 1831	R3
Whipple, A. (Dr)	Matson, Mary A.	19, Oct. 1836	T2
Whipple, A. (Dr)	Matson, Mary A.	13, Oct. 1836	X3
Whipple, Samuel D.	Conklin, Eliza	16, Oct. 1819	S3
Whitaker, Daniel H.	Bennet, Ann Maria	21, Apr. 1836	X3
Whitaker, J.B.	Vinsell, Sarah A.	14, Feb. 1851	P2
White, Caleb	Catlett, Elizabeth	18, Apr. 1829	R3
White, Charles R.	Wirk, Hannah	20, Aug. 1852	P2
White, George L.	Utley, Almira	16, May 1829	R3
White, Henry	Duckworth, Keziah C.	10, Dec. 1847	K2
White, Isaac	Ballard, Olive	27, Apr. 1822	S3
White, Israel	Meeks, Sophia	9, July 1824	N2
White, Israel	Meeks, Sophia	8, July 1824	E3
White, John	Wilson, Nancy	25, Feb. 1815	S3
White, John	Dews, Nancy (Mrs)	9, Apr. 1836	T2
White, William	Seymour, Amelia	3, Mar. 1821	S3
Whiteman, Benjamin	Cassilly, Henrietta	15, Sept 1838	R3
Whiteman, Benjamin	Cassilly, Henrietta	15, Sept 1838	T2
Whiteman, James F.	Johnston, Rebecca	23, May 1840	R3
Whiteman, Lewis	Harrison, Jane F.	9, July 1842	R3
Whiteman, Lewis	Irwin, Louisa	14, May 1824	N2
Whiteman, Lewis	Harrison, Jane	6, July 1842	N2
Whiticar, James	Walters, Ann	12, Oct. 1820	S3
Whiting, D.P. (Lt)	Sandford, Indiana	10, Jan. 1835	R3
Whiting, D.P. (Lt)	Sandford, Indiana B.	6, Jan. 1835	T2

Grooms	Brides	Date of Notice	Page
Whiting, Isaac N.	Kilbourne, Orril	15, Sept 1835	T2
Whiting, William B.	Nicholls, Mary Lee	14, Dec. 1839	R3
Whittaker, Joseph	Wunder, Mary Ann	27, Aug. 1852	P2
Wiggins, Eli	Brockly, Ann	10, Aug. 1835	T2
Wilby, Thomas J.	Coppuck, Mary M.	3, Oct. 1835	T2
Wiley, John (Dr)	Crookshank, Jane	24, Dec. 1824	N3
Wiley, Joseph H.	Hinman, Mary H.	2, Sept 1847	K2
Wilkens, Benjamin	Overton, Sarah Brown	6, Oct. 1832	R3
Wilkinson, John	Slayback, Dianna	22, Apr. 1815	W3
Wilkinson, Walter	Jefferson, Hepsey	15, Jan. 1814	S3
Willard, R. (Dr)	Borland, Elizabeth S	7, July 1832	R3
Willey, George	Hiler, Rebecca	27, Aug. 1850	Y2
Williams, B.F. (Dr)	Addison, Sarah D.	18, May 1836	N2
Williams, Benjamin F	Ward, Rebecca	19, Apr. 1836	T2
Williams, C.H. (Rev)	Langdon, Harrette	31, Aug. 1852	P2
Williams, Chester	Baker, Mary	9, Feb. 1837	X3
Williams, Curus M.	Pollard, Mary Eliza	16, Aug. 1852	P2
Williams, Cyrus M.	Neff, Jane B.	17, June 1847	K2
Williams, David	Ward, Clarisa	15, Nov. 1828	R3
Williams, David	Ward, Clarissa	14, Nov. 1828	N3
Williams, David	Phillips, Ann	5, Jan. 1830	N2
Williams, David G.	Phillips, Ann	2, Jan. 1830	R3
Williams, David R.	Estell, Nancy	4, Nov. 1824	E3
Williams, Elmore	Harrison, Isabella	20, Sept 1816	S3
Williams, George W.	Clemens, Sarah	22, Oct. 1831	R3
Williams, H.C.	Chapman, Frances A.	30, Nov. 1835	T2
Williams, H.L.	Howe, Fanny T.	11, Apr. 1840	R3
Williams, Harbert S.	Weekly, Mary Ann	31, May 1830	A3
Williams, Isaac P.	Bernard, Louisa	16, Aug. 1834	R3
Williams, Isaac P.	Bernard, Louisa	13, Aug. 1834	T2
Williams, Jacob	Conover, Margaret	9, Jan. 1830	R3
Williams, Jacob	Conover, Margaret	12, Jan. 1830	N2
Williams, James P.	Mayhew, Harriet	24, Mar. 1829	N2
Williams, Jesse L.	Creighton, Susan	3, Dec. 1831	R3
Williams, John	Spinning, Martha Ann	10, Nov. 1827	R3
Williams, John	Barker, Esther B.	25, Dec. 1850	P2
Williams, John E.	Brokow, Catharine	13, Feb. 1819	S3
Williams, M.G.	Hamilton, Adelaide	27, June 1829	R3
Williams, Miles	Hudson, Eunice Elizabeth	6, Dec. 1838	T3
Williams, Minot	Ballard, Hannah E.	15, Jan. 1820	S3
Williams, Minot	Ballard, Hannah E.	13, Jan. 1820	D2
Williams, Noah	Lingo, Mary	19, Nov. 1831	R3
Williams, Thomas T.	Hasselton, Rebecca	1, Oct. 1850	Y2
Williams, Vachel	White, Sophronia E.	27, Dec. 1852	P2
Williams, Victor	Allen, Sarah	25, July 1851	P2
Williams, William L.	Applegate, Clarinda	8, Jan. 1830	N2
Williamson, Alex. W.	Corry, Susan Ann	4, Jan. 1840	R3
Williamson, Alex. W.	Shane, Araminta E.	20, Oct. 1847	K2
Williamson, Garret H	Arons, Rebecca	7, July 1827	R3
Williamson, George T.	Taylor, Jane M.	17, Feb. 1831	A3
Williamson, George T.	Taylor, Jane M.	19, Feb. 1831	R3
Williamson, Samuel	Beresford, Anna	28, June 1847	K2
Willing, Charles (Dr)	Tillinghast, Rebecca	4, Apr. 1840	R3
Wills, Thomas Edward	Veacock, Martha	9, June 1835	N2

Grooms	Brides	Date of Notice	Page
Wilmouth, Thomas	Evatt, Jane	15, Sept 1815	S3
Wilson, Allan	Christie, Janet	11, June 1836	T2
Wilson, George	Foster, Mary E.	25, Nov. 1852	P2
Wilson, J. Plume	James, Amanda M.	5, Feb. 1848	K2
Wilson, J.B.	Kelsey, Rosetta C.	17, Oct. 1840	R3
Wilson, J.C. (Dr)	Kinkead, Prudence B.	9, Sept 1835	T2
Wilson, James W.	Smith, Harriet C.	22, May 1847	K2
Wilson, Jefferson	Utz, Sarah Regina	13, July 1852	P2
Wilson, John L.	Eden, Rebecca	2, Dec. 1825	N3
Wilson, Joseph	Resor, Elizabeth	30, Mar. 1824	N3
Wilson, Joseph B.	Gilman, Catharine	21, Mar. 1839	T2
Wilson, Lewis	Parker, Henrietta	4, Feb. 1851	P2
Wilson, Noah L.	Waters, Kezia R.	13, June 1840	R3
Wilson, Oliver	Barlow, Eliza F.	16, July 1842	R3
Wilson, Samuel R.	Johnston, Nancy	27, Mar. 1841	N2
Wilson, Timothy H.	Lewis, Rosana T.	22, Mar. 1829	R3
Wilson, Vacter	Curtis, Anna	6, Nov. 1852	P2
Wilson, William B.	Keys, Mary	14, Apr. 1827	R3
Wilson, William D.	Eckert, Elizabeth	5, Nov. 1835	T2
Wiltberger, Jacob	Horton, Susan	6, June 1818	S3
Winall, George W.	Medarea, Susanna	18, July 1840	R3
Winchell, George D.	Weeks, Susan Ann	1, May 1847	K2
Winchester, C.C.	Kelly, Susan H.	23, Nov. 1852	P2
Winder, Thomas	Rod, Olive	21, Aug. 1819	S3
Winston, John P.	Smith, Julia S.	30, Aug. 1837	T2
Winston, Samuel	Martin, Mary	4, May 1822	S3
Winter, C.F.	Pennington, Harriet	17, Nov. 1832	R3
Winter, Edwin	Owens, Lucy Marian	8, Nov. 1852	P2
Winter, Henry	Moore, Margaret	24, June 1831	A3
Winter, John	McDonnel, Margaret	8, Oct. 1822	J3
Winter, Thomas	Wingert, Mary Ann	26, Sept 1823	N2
Winters, Edward	Owens, Lucy M.	19, Nov. 1852	P2
Winters, William	Willis, Jane F.	5, Feb. 1835	N2
Wirtz, J.B.	Ludlow, Eliza H.	16, May 1840	R3
Wise, John T.	Perry, Mary Ann	20, Nov. 1852	P2
Wise, Theodore N.	McGill, Kate B.	11, Nov. 1852	P2
Wiseman, John A.	Mankey, Mary	24, Oct. 1835	T2
Wiseman, John A.	Harrison, Mary	3, Jan. 1826	N3
Wiseman, John A.	Mankey, Sarah	26, Oct. 1835	N2
Witham, Jefferson C.	Hunt, Elizabeth J.	1, Dec. 1852	P2
Witt, George	Gosling, Rachel	4, May 1850	P2
Witt, William B.	Penny, Mary Ann	24, Feb. 1851	P2
Witterman, Fred.	Ost, Catharine	7, July 1852	P2
Wood, Alfred	Clark, Ann	22, Oct. 1836	T2
Wood, Alfred	Clark, Ann	22, Oct. 1836	N2
Wood, Clarkson F.	Gillespie, Clara B.	14, May 1842	R3
Wood, D.M.	Swift, Mary L.	10, Oct. 1840	R3
Wood, John H.	Gibson, Mary B.	31, Jan. 1831	A3
Wood, John H.	Gibson, Mary B.	5, Feb. 1831	R3
Wood, John H.	Gibson, Mary B.	4, Feb. 1831	X3
Wood, Seely	Burnet, Nancy	23, Apr. 1842	R3
Wood, William (Dr)	Morgan, M. Virginia	1, Apr. 1834	T2
Wood, William B.	Withington, Abby Ann	5, Nov. 1835	T2
Woodfin, Rutland H.	Allen, Frances M.	12, July 1828	R3

Grooms	Brides	Date of Notice	Page
Woodman, John	Long, Elizabeth	31, Aug. 1820	S3
Woodrow, David T.	Cromwell, Louisa	10, Oct. 1840	R3
Woodruff, A.P.	Hoops, Catharine	2, Aug. 1834	T2
Woodruff, Charles S.	Jenks, Charlotte R.	9, Aug. 1841	N2
Woodruff, Leonard	Jackson, Josephine	28, Sept 1850	Y2
Woods, John R.	Morrison, Sarah W.	24, Apr. 1835	X3
Woods, William	Sharp, Elizabeth M.	25, Dec. 1841	R3
Woodward, Robert C.	Spangler, Sarah E.	22, Aug. 1838	T2
Woolcott, William G.	Ewing, Juliet (Mrs)	19, Jan. 1833	R3
Woolley, A.R. (Col)	Preston, Carolina L.	22, Sept 1827	R3
Woolley, Aaron K.	Wickliffe, Sarah H.	20, Oct. 1827	R3
Woolley, Asher	Nelson, Carsey	31, Jan. 1815	W3
Woolley, John (Dr)	Drake, Lydia	5, Apr. 1816	S3
Woolsey, William M.	Hall, Hannah C.	8, Jan. 1830	N2
Worsham, William	Carl, Frances Julia	26, Nov. 1838	T2
Worthington, Amos	Wood, Frances B.	12, Nov. 1831	R3
Worthington, Amos	Wilson, Jane C.	16, July 1842	R3
Worthington, J.G.	Phillips, Elizabeth	5, July 1830	A3
Worthington, James T.	Galloway, Julia A.	13, Dec. 1828	R3
Worthington, John G.	Phillips, Elizabeth	3, July 1830	R3
Worthington, Lewis	Pierce, Sally Ann	7, Oct. 1837	R3
Worthington, Lewis	Pierce, Sally Ann	5, Oct. 1837	T2
Worthington, Vachel	Wiggins, Julia	11, Jan. 1839	T2
Worthington, Vachel	Burnet, Mary Ann	31, May 1825	N3
Wrag, George	Stickney, Mary Eliza	4, Aug. 1832	R3
Wrenn, George L.	Duffield, Mary Jane	7, Sept 1833	R3
Wright, Charles A.	Doerrer, Paulina	15, May 1847	K2
Wright, Henry W.	Cox, Sarah (Mrs)	25, June 1842	R3
Wright, Isaac	Wright, Mary	16, June 1827	R3
Wright, Isaac H.	Cobb, Harriet	10, Aug. 1837	X3
Wright, John F.	Reynolds, Maria	12, Apr. 1825	N3
Wright, Sylvanus	Goodman, Frances P.	4, Feb. 1825	N2
Wurts, W.A. (Lt)	Steele, Matilda	25, May 1837	T2
Wygant, Martin	Comstock, Cath. E.	4, Sept 1841	R3
Wynn, Daniel	Johnson, Nancy	29, Oct. 1814	S3
Wynne, John	Barnard, Sarah	24, May 1849	L2
Yates, C.C. (Dr)	Willard, Emma (Mrs)	29, Sept 1838	R3
Yeatman, Thomas H.	Hartzell, Elizabeth	13, Feb. 1827	N3
Yeatman, Walker	Burrows, Caroline W.	12, Dec. 1818	S3
Yeatman, Walker	Burrows, Frances M.	9, Mar. 1822	S2
Young, Henry	Morgan, Pallas	18, Feb. 1815	S3
Young, John	Robbins, Emily	4, Nov. 1837	R3
Young, John N.	Waters, Eliza	16, Aug. 1834	R3
Young, John N.	Waters, Eliza	14, Aug. 1834	T2
Young, Joseph G.	Langdon, Mary Jane	6, Feb. 1841	N2
Young, Samuel A.	Nichols, Frances	2, May 1840	R3

Brides	Grooms	Date of Notice	Page
----, Elvina	Swain, Alonzo	2, Jan. 1841	R3
Abbott, Elizabeth	Reed, Robert	31, July 1819	S3
Abrams, Eliza	Jordon, Henry	20, Dec. 1828	R3
Abright, Sophia	Clark, John	2, June 1827	R3
Achey, M. Ella	McDowell, John	22, Sept 1852	P2
Adams, Elizabeth	Hollis, Robert S.	30, Dec. 1852	P2
Adams, Henrietta	Baker, John W.	15, Oct. 1839	T2
Adams, Margaret Rand	Goodman, William	16, Aug. 1828	R3
Adams, Roberta C.	Stuart, Ewing T.	8, June 1849	L2
Adamson, Catharine	Carman, Benjamin	19, Feb. 1820	S2
Adamson, E.R.	Gallagher, William D	5, July 1830	A3
Adamson, Emma R.	Gallagher, William D	3, July 1830	R3
Adamson, Frances	Knight, Benjamin	21, July 1838	T2
Addis, Amelia	Smith, Charles P.	15, Aug. 1822	J3
Addis, Eliza	Curtis, William	13, Nov. 1819	S3
Addison, Meliora E.	Lee, Edmund F.	18, May 1836	N2
Addison, Sarah D.	Williams, B.F. (Dr)	18, May 1836	N2
Agnew, Sarah Ann	Broadwell, Mahlon	1, Mar. 1833	X3
Agres, Sabra	Jenkins, Seymour	15, Dec. 1852	P2
Alcocke, Lavina	Wesbay, Samuel	27, Dec. 1828	R3
Alden, Elizabeth	Blachly, O.B.	17, June 1825	N1
Alden, Josephine N.	Maitland, Peter I.	23, Nov. 1832	X3
Alexander, M.L. (Mrs)	Hall, James	10, Sept 1839	T3
Alfred, Mary Ann	Anderson, James	4, Mar. 1837	N2
Allen, Frances M.	Woodfin, Rutland H.	12, July 1828	R3
Allen, Harriet	Tounly, Major J.	17, Nov. 1838	T2
Allen, Margaret	Houston, John B.	6, Oct. 1836	X3
Allen, Margaret	Lawrence, George	26, Oct. 1852	P2
Allen, Maria Louisa	Cary, Samuel F.	27, Oct. 1836	X3
Allen, Martha Ann	Foster, David	13, Sept 1852	P2
Allen, Mary F.	Davis, Jesse E.	19, Nov. 1847	K2
Allen, Nancy	Smith, William	20, Feb. 1841	R3
Allen, Nancy	Smith, William	15, Feb. 1841	N2
Allen, Sabina	McElroy, George	29, Sept 1836	X3
Allen, Sarah	McCormick, Thomas	7, Dec. 1811	S3
Allen, Sarah	Williams, Victor	25, July 1851	P2
Allen, Sarah Ann	Mitchell, Philip H.	5, July 1828	R3
Alley, Susan (Mrs)	Howe, Jacob	14, Aug. 1841	R3
Alley, Susan (Mrs)	Howe, Jacob	13, Aug. 1841	N2
Allibone, Eliza	Claypoole, James T.	19, Aug. 1823	N3
Allibone, Mary	Osborne, Thomas (Rev)	26, Oct. 1822	S3
Allibone, Sarah	Steuart, Hugh C.	4, Oct. 1828	R3
Allison, Rebecca (Mrs)	West, Samuel (Rev)	29, Aug. 1817	S3
Alter, Harriet	Brown, David O.	20, Sept 1834	R3
Alter, Harriet	Brown, David O.	13, Sept 1834	T2
Alter, Mary Ann	Brasher, Robert	10, May 1828	R3
Alter, Mary Ann	Brasher, Robert	9, May 1828	Q3
Ames, Mary	James, Henry	25, Dec. 1827	N3
Anderson, Elizabeth	Johnston, Stephen	16, July 1838	T2
Anderson, Jane	Dick, George	2, May 1812	S3
Anderson, Jane W.	Paige, A.L.	2, Oct. 1841	R3
Anderson, Margaret	More, William	1, Aug. 1817	S3
Anderson, Mary	Magness, Benjamin	2, Mar. 1820	D3
Anderson, Mary	Magness, Benjamin B.	4, Mar. 1820	S2

Brides	Grooms	Date of Notice	Page
Anderson, Mary C.	Lewis, Charles H.	23, June 1838	R3
Anderson, Mary C.	Lewis, Charles H.	20, June 1838	T2
Andrews, Mary	Crampton, Henry	14, July 1826	N3
Andrews, Sarah P.	Carpenter, Ezra	18, May 1833	R3
Anthony, Rachel	Pugh, Lot	9, July 1814	S3
Appleby, Caroline	Hurst, Frederick	13, June 1837	T2
Applegate, Clarinda	Williams, William L.	8, Jan. 1830	N2
Applegate, Ellen	Craft, J.W.	28, May 1847	K2
Appleton, Mary	Mackintosh, Robert J	18, Jan. 1840	R3
Arbigust, Mary Ann	Fowler, John	9, July 1830	N2
Archer, Matilda	Ayer, Richard	2, Jan. 1841	R3
Ardrey, Sarah B.	Gibbon, Leonard	27, Dec. 1834	R3
Areheart, Mary Ann	Compton, Abram	22, Apr. 1830	A3
Argadine, Jane	Pitman, Jonathan	6, Dec. 1825	N3
Arion, Susanna	Lodge, John	22, Aug. 1817	S3
Armstrong, Ann	Morton, Joseph	12, Oct. 1811	S3
Armstrong, Catharine	Morton, Henry	12, Oct. 1811	S3
Armstrong, Eliza (Mrs)	Shepherd, Chauncey B	9, Apr. 1841	N2
Armstrong, Fannie	Pomroy, R.E.	28, Dec. 1852	P2
Armstrong, Margaret	Baughman, Robert A.	11, June 1842	R3
Armstrong, Margaret	Baughman, Robert A.	9, June 1842	N2
Armstrong, Martha A.	Scott, Edgar W.	21, May 1842	R3
Armstrong, Mary Ann	Campbell, Carey A.	15, Sept 1827	R3
Armstrong, Mary G.	Drew, William C.	12, Dec. 1817	S3
Armstrong, Ruth Jane	Smizer, Henry (Dr)	14, Apr. 1847	K2
Armstrong, Sarah B.	Adamson, Benjamin	20, Feb. 1813	S3
Arnold, Mary	Stevens, John	26, Oct. 1836	T2
Arnold, Mary Jane	Smith, J.H.	17, Mar. 1849	L2
Arons, Rebecca	Williamson, Garret H	7, July 1827	R3
Artus, Mary	Ward, James	10, Oct. 1840	R3
Ashenhurst, Sarah	Lane, William	21, July 1827	R3
Ashton, Mary Ann	Gant, George	27, Aug. 1852	P2
Ashton, Sarah S.	Wheelock, Samuel L.	7, Apr. 1821	S3
Ashwell, Jane	Moodie, Thomas	14, Nov. 1838	T2
Athearn, Asia B.	Hartwell, J.W.	4, Nov. 1837	R3
Atherstone, Caroline	Evans, Daniel T.	7, Oct. 1824	E3
Atkinson, Amanda	Ewing, James	23, Dec. 1835	T3
Atlee, Elizabeth J.	Nichols, Samuel S.	26, Feb. 1841	N2
Atlee, Margaret L.	Coombs, S.A.	11, Nov. 1830	A3
Atlee, Margaret L.	Coombs, S.A.	13, Nov. 1830	R3
Attenborough, Eliza	Newell, James	9, Apr. 1842	R3
Atwood, Clarissa (Mrs)	Ruggles, Benjamin	2, Dec. 1825	N3
Auchey, Emma	Rigdon, Isaac	15, Dec. 1852	P2
Austin, Louisa S.	Brandon, Matthew	19, Mar. 1831	R3
Austin, Louisa S.	Brandon, Matthew	11, Mar. 1831	X3
Avery, Ann	Caldwell, Robert	30, Mar. 1807	S3
Avey, Eliza J.	Bolles, William T.	8, June 1847	K2
Aydelott, Margaret P.	Farnham, Charles A.	2, July 1842	R3
Ayers, Mary Ann	Orth, Godlove S.	3, Sept 1850	Y2
Bacon, Sarah	Montague, Thomas	14, Dec. 1847	K2
Badger, Lucretia Ann	Blecker, William W.	23, May 1840	R3
Badger, Martha	Derby, Thomas	18, Jan. 1841	N2
Bagg, Clarissa	Seymour, Jeffrey	10, Oct. 1818	S3

Brides	Grooms	Date of Notice	Page
Bagley, Ann H.	Ramsay, Cunningham	17, May 1825	N3
Bagley, Elizabeth	Black, Robert	31, May 1825	N3
Bagott, Alice	Pearce, John	9, Aug. 1841	N2
Bailey, Eliza (Mrs)	Haines, J. (Dr)	23, Dec. 1831	X3
Bailey, Elizabeth	Hodge, David	11, Dec. 1819	S3
Bailey, Sylvia C.	Rutherford, John	24, Sept 1852	P2
Baily, Angeline	Tarquary, Isaac P.	17, Oct. 1840	R3
Baird, Jane	Adams, Alexander	14, Oct. 1828	N3
Baird, Martha	Moore, Isaac	31, Oct. 1828	N2
Baker, Caroline (Mrs)	Leffingwell, Winslow	9, Nov. 1850	P2
Baker, Elizabeth	Steel, John	23, Feb. 1827	N3
Baker, Esther A.	Crane, Andrew L.	9, May 1840	R3
Baker, Mary	Williams, Chester	9, Feb. 1837	X3
Baker, Sarah	Oliver, William B.	26, Jan. 1816	S3
Bakewell, Elizabeth	James, David A.	5, June 1841	R3
Bakewell, Elizabeth	James, David A.	29, May 1841	N2
Bakewell, Martha P.	Avery, Charles (Dr)	8, June 1847	K2
Baldridge, Elizabeth	Childs, C.J. (Dr)	18, Mar. 1847	K2
Baldridge, Mary L.	Hopkins, Richard R.	18, Mar. 1847	K2
Baldwin, H.	Sterns, R.	26, June 1841	R3
Baldwin, H.	Sterns, R.	23, June 1841	N2
Baldwin, Virginia	Lewis, William G.W.	22, Oct. 1847	K2
Ball, Anne (Mrs)	Phelps, Samuel W.	24, Feb. 1835	T2
Ball, Elizabeth J.	Thomas, Alexander S.	10, Oct. 1850	P2
Ball, Elvira	Boake, John	7, Nov. 1840	R3
Ball, Emily A.	Patterson, John S.	12, Dec. 1835	T3
Ball, Hannah	Kirby, James	16, Oct. 1819	S3
Ballard, Hannah E.	Williams, Minot	15, Jan. 1820	S3
Ballard, Hannah E.	Williams, Minot	13, Jan. 1820	D2
Ballard, Mary J.	Adams, Alex H.	11, Nov. 1837	R3
Ballard, Olive	White, Isaac	27, Apr. 1822	S3
Banks, Elizabeth J.	Benson, Martin	25, Oct. 1852	P2
Barber, Catharine W.	Emerson, Nathan	1, Sept 1837	N2
Barber, Jane	Humble, James	23, June 1847	K2
Barber, Sarah Jane	Kelsey, Naamen	21, May 1842	R3
Barcalow, Helana	Lanier, James W. (Dr)	14, Sept 1807	S3
Barker, Esther B.	Williams, John	25, Dec. 1850	P2
Barker, Hannah (Mrs)	Butterfield, James	21, Aug. 1819	S3
Barker, Maria C.	Lyon, John F.	15, May 1829	N3
Barker, Rachel	Foster, Charles	7, June 1828	R3
Barkus, Martha	Evans, William	28, Nov. 1812	S3
Barlow, Eliza F.	Wilson, Oliver	16, July 1842	R3
Barlow, Hannah	Stewart, Benjamin	25, Sept 1819	S3
Barnard, Elizabeth M	Squire, William B.	10, Apr. 1841	R3
Barnard, Lucretia	Swain, Frederick C.	25, Apr. 1836	T2
Barnard, Mary	Morrill, Nahum	26, Sept 1840	R3
Barnard, Sarah	Wynne, John	24, May 1849	L2
Barnes, Esther	Murray, William	27, Dec. 1828	R3
Barnes, Sarah	Goudy, James H.	25, Apr. 1818	S3
Barnett, Isabella	Bargen, Otto G.	22, Sept 1852	P2
Barnum, Abigail	Deming, M.R.	18, Aug. 1836	X3
Barnwerl, Mary M.	Voorhes, Daniel B.	17, Nov. 1852	P2
Barr, Margaret R.	VanHorn, William	26, Sept 1828	N3
Barr, Margaret R.	VanHorne, W.J.	27, Sept 1828	R3

Brides	Grooms	Date of Notice	Page
Barr, Sarah Ann	McDowell, William S.	7, Sept 1832	X3
Barr, Susan	Enness, John B.	24, Aug. 1811	S3
Barr, Susan S.	Spencer, John C.	21, Aug. 1835	T2
Barret, Lucy D.	Spear, Samuel B.	16, May 1836	T2
Barret, Lucy D.	Spear, Samuel B.	14, May 1836	N2
Barrett, Mary Ann	Brown, John T.	2, Nov. 1852	P2
Barrett, Mary Elizabeth	Manser, William	20, Aug. 1831	R3
Barston, H. (Mrs)	Johnson, Thomas	30, Oct. 1838	T2
Barstow, H. (Mrs)	Johnston, Thomas	30, Oct. 1838	N2
Bartlett, Anna Maria	Card, Thomas A.	25, Oct. 1852	P2
Bartlett, Caroline	McGrew, Alexander	12, Dec. 1840	R3
Bartlett, Elizabeth	Mann, Marshall	19, Feb. 1814	S3
Barton, Amanda	Cochnower, John	16, Sept 1852	P2
Barton, Ann Eliza	Spencer, Oliver M.	1, Dec. 1832	R3
Barton, Clarena	Johnston, William S.	3, Mar. 1821	S3
Barton, Eliza H.	Clark, Thomas	21, Oct. 1825	N2
Barton, Euretta L.	Storer, Belamy	5, Oct. 1820	S3
Bartow, Eugenia M.	Underhill, Abner H.	28, July 1835	T2
Barwise, Mary Ann	Brooks, Daniel	28, Mar. 1823	N2
Bassett, Ruth	Coplen, Isaac C.	25, Sept 1819	S3
Bassett, Zipporah	Reynolds, Giles K.	13, Apr. 1837	X3
Bates, Lizzie	Durrett, R.T.	22, Dec. 1852	P2
Baughman, Sarah E.	Dale, James	8, Nov. 1852	P2
Baum, Eleanor	Hartshorn, Charles	4, Dec. 1841	N2
Bauman, Mary	Morris, John C.	22, May 1847	K2
Bayless, Sophronia	O'connor, Michael	26, June 1835	T2
Bayley, Eliza (Mrs)	Hains, J. (Dr)	24, Dec. 1831	R3
Beach, Nancy S.	Birdsal, Caleb S.	4, Sept 1830	R3
Beach, Nancy S.	Burdsal, Caleb L.	3, Sept 1830	N2
Beach, Patty	Kite, George	18, Sept 1819	S3
Beasley, Sarah	Bamber, Thomas	21, July 1827	R3
Bechtel, Lydia Ann	Powers, Henry	8, Sept 1832	R3
Beckett, Mary A.	Palmer, Solon	10, July 1851	P2
Beckwith, Minerva E.	Bullitt, Fred N.	14, Mar. 1829	R3
Beecher, Isabel H.	Hooker, John	21, Aug. 1841	R3
Beecher, Isabel H.	Hooker, John	19, Aug. 1841	N2
Belch, Lucinda	Leavitt, Daniel K.	14, Mar. 1829	R3
Bell, Melinda	Smith, Joseph K.	4, June 1824	N5
Bell, Melinda	Smith, Joseph K.	10, June 1824	E3
Bellamy, Ann	Fox, Frederick	28, Sept 1850	Y2
Bellows, Mary	Hancinct, David	5, Dec. 1836	T2
Benbridge, Evelina	Emerson, Henry	1, Jan. 1828	R3
Benbridge, Sarah T.	McCandless, James	13, Dec. 1830	A3
Benbridge, Sarah T.	McCandless, James	11, Dec. 1830	R3
Benedict, Sarah E.	Bonnel, John	15, May 1847	K2
Bennet, Ann Maria	Whitaker, Daniel H.	21, Apr. 1836	X3
Bennett, Eliza M.	Haywood, Samuel M.	20, Mar. 1847	K2
Bennett, Mary	Thomas, John	31, July 1850	Y2
Benoist, Rosina E.	Groesbeck, Herman J.	21, Oct. 1837	R3
Benoist, Rosina E.	Groesbeck, Herman J.	13, Oct. 1837	T2
Beran, M.J.	Lapham, William	18, Aug. 1852	P2
Berard, Georgiana	Vogdes, J. (Lt)	2, May 1840	R3
Beresford, Ann	Langtry, William	19, Oct. 1822	S3
Beresford, Ann	Langtry, William	24, Oct. 1822	J3

Brides	Grooms	Date of Notice	Page
Beresford, Anna	Williamson, Samuel	28, June 1847	K2
Beresford, Elizabeth	Orange, Benjamin	28, June 1828	R3
Beresford, Elizabeth	Orange, Benjamin	27, June 1828	Q3
Bernard, Louisa	Williams, Isaac P.	16, Aug. 1834	R3
Bernard, Louisa	Williams, Isaac P.	13, Aug. 1834	T2
Berrall, Susan	Powell, Henry	14, Aug. 1852	P2
Berry, Catharine E.	Abbott, Henry B.	24, Dec. 1852	P2
Berry, Elizabeth	Proud, Thomas	6, Oct. 1850	Y2
Besson, Charlotte W.	Dennis, Benjamin (Dr)	3, Feb. 1838	R3
Better, Charlotte	Layman, S.B.	11, May 1841	N2
Betts, Mary	Halley, David J.	11, Apr. 1812	S2
Biddle, Sarah S.	Lytle, John S.	31, Mar. 1832	R3
Biedenhorn, Lezette	Vennemann, Anthony	1, Feb. 1837	T2
Bigger, Abigail M.	Hamilton, Samuel R.	2, Nov. 1833	R3
Biggs, Margaretta	Gest, Condui G.	28, Nov. 1840	R3
Biggs, Mary	Pleasants, Samuel E.	19, May 1821	S3
Bigler, Sallie T.	Chamberlin, William	14, Sept 1852	P2
Biles, Hester M.	Mason, A.C.	15, Apr. 1847	K2
Bills, Ruth	Niles, Paul C.	14, July 1827	R3
Bingle, Elizabeth	Miller, Jacob	9, Aug. 1814	W3
Bird, Patience	McClelland, Thomas	9, May 1812	S3
Bishop, Ada	Ingols, Chester	6, Feb. 1819	S3
Bishop, Laura	Hagerman, Benjamin	30, Jan. 1830	R3
Black, Nancy	Mitchell, John S.	31, Oct. 1837	T2
Black, Sarah	Cravens, Benjamin	11, July 1835	T2
Blackburn, Mahala	Baker, Benjamin	1, May 1835	T3
Blackiston, Rachel A	Hays, Nelson B.	14, May 1847	K2
Blackmon, Caroline	Latta, Samuel A.	18, Mar. 1831	X3
Blaique, Sophia	Pond, Augustus	20, May 1842	N2
Blake, Sarah N.	Walton, Charles	7, Mar. 1839	T2
Blaney, Mary E.	Page, John (Capt)	28, May 1838	T2
Bliss, Caroline	Rippey, William	9, June 1836	X3
Bliss, Sarah S.	Patterson, John K.	24, Jan. 1829	R3
Block, Esther	Moses, Benjamin	16, Jan. 1836	T3
Block, Esther	Moses, Benjamin	15, Jan. 1836	N2
Blow, Martha Ella T.	Drake, Charles D.	17, Sept 1835	T2
Boardman, Eliza C.	Clerc, Laurent	29, May 1819	S3
Bogert, Mary	Lord, John P.	11, Dec. 1819	S3
Boggs, Lilley	Graham, B. (Dr)	16, Nov. 1837	T2
Bogie, Isabella	Adams, Thomas J.	26, May 1821	S3
Boltazar, Caroline	Roberts, Edward	31, July 1852	P2
Bom, Ellen	Bee, James	24, May 1828	R2
Bomberger, Ann	Lowe, Peter P.	17, May 1830	A3
Bond, Cecilia	Stanbery, Henry	17, July 1841	V3
Bond, Cecilia Key	Stanbery, Henry	20, July 1841	N2
Bond, Ellen J.	Robinson, John A.	23, Oct. 1852	P2
Bonnel, Rachel V.	Anderson, Robert	22, June 1811	S3
Bonnett, Eliza T.	Foster, William M.	21, Sept 1837	T2
Bonsall, L.T.	Porter, J.H.	24, Mar. 1849	L2
Bonsall, Martha A.	Clark, Charles M.	30, Dec. 1852	P2
Bonsell, Margaret L.	Green, Thomas J.	16, Mar. 1837	T2
Bonte, Jane Eliza	Chambers, John T.	8, Oct. 1841	N2
Bonte, Sarah	Miller, James R.	11, May 1847	K2
Boon, Hester	Steavison, Jolett	30, Oct. 1841	R3

Brides	Grooms	Date of Notice	Page
Boon, Hester	Steavison, Joseph	29, Oct. 1841	N2
Booth, Eliza	Morton, Thomas	19, Nov. 1847	K2
Borland, Elizabeth S	Willard, R. (Dr)	7, July 1832	R3
Boss, Virginia	Baldock, Milton	5, Feb. 1842	R3
Boss, Virginia	Baldock, Milton	3, Feb. 1842	N2
Bosson, Catharine M.	Powers, Benjamin F.	28, Nov. 1818	S3
Botley, Macbei (Mrs)	Farrar, D.	17, June 1825	N1
Bowen, Dulcinia	Martin, William	27, July 1835	T2
Bowen, Exzene M.	Crump, N.W. (Capt)	8, Nov. 1838	T2
Bowers, Ann Elizabeth	Schultz, Charles	13, Feb. 1827	N3
Bowers, Julia A.	Baldwin, Henry	25, July 1835	T2
Bowman, Elizabeth	Asbury, Walter	12, July 1837	T2
Bowman, Margaret P.	Minnear, John W.	23, Mar. 1847	K2
Bowshear, Ann	McCulloch, Robert	3, Nov. 1827	R3
Boyce, Lucy Ann	Baker, Joseph	7, Oct. 1837	R3
Boyd, Ellen	Marshall, Peter	11, May 1842	N2
Boyd, Susan A.	Kettle, Peter	26, Oct. 1852	P2
Boyden, Julia M.	Robinson, Jeremiah	25, May 1832	X3
Bradbury, Mary P.	Duncan, Richard G.	5, Nov. 1852	P2
Braden, Mary Ann	Barker, John	2, June 1847	K2
Bradford, Ann	Slane, Alexander	23, July 1847	K2
Bradford, Eliza	Challen, James (Rev)	2, June 1827	R3
Bradford, Margaret	Lewis, James	25, Apr. 1840	R3
Bradford, Sarah	Beale, John	9, Sept 1847	K2
Bradley, Mary	Boylan, Julius A.	3, Dec. 1852	P2
Bragg, Mary	Thompson, Samuel	2, May 1812	S3
Branch, Margaret	Donelson, Daniel S.	1, Nov. 1830	A3
Branch, Margaret	Donelson, Daniel S.	2, Nov. 1830	N2
Brand, Eliza	Macalester, Edward	25, Feb. 1832	R3
Brann, Nancy A.	Massie, Wallar (Dr)	22, Mar. 1851	P2
Bread, Anna	Anderson, James	24, June 1837	T2
Brewster, Hannah	Carll, Maskell (Rev)	12, Sept 1840	R3
Brewster, Ruth	Scudder, William	28, Apr. 1821	S3
Brickley, Sarah E.	Smith, Daniel J.	7, Apr. 1849	L2
Briggs, Kate (Mrs)	Sells, Walter	7, Aug. 1850	Y2
Briggs, Priscilla M.	Beatty, John A.	28, Sept 1835	T2
Brigham, Cornelia	Southgate, James	14, May 1831	R3
Brigham, Cornelia S.	Southgate, James	13, May 1831	A3
Brigham, Julia R.	Fisher, Charles	9, Nov. 1833	R3
Briscoe, Jane A.	Norris, John H.	21, May 1836	T2
Britt, Lydia Ann	Searing, Robert	27, May 1824	E3
Britton, Ellenor	Tabor, Elisha	6, May 1806	S3
Britton, Lavinia	Farnsworth, William	13, Oct. 1827	R3
Broadrick, Betsy	Vawse, Isaac	27, Oct. 1798	F3
Broadwell, Amanda M.	Everett, William H.	17, Mar. 1837	T2
Broadwell, Sarah Ann	Milford, James	3, Sept 1831	R3
Brockly, Ann	Wiggins, Eli	10, Aug. 1835	T2
Broils, (Mrs)	Holbrooks, George	18, May 1836	T2
Broils, (Mrs)	Holbrooks, George	26, May 1836	X3
Brokow, Catharine	Williams, John E.	13, Feb. 1819	S3
Bromwell, Maria V.	Melish, Thomas J.	17, May 1849	L2
Brood, Harriet M.	Noble, Daniel W.	3, Oct. 1840	R3
Brooke, Lydia	Carter, James H.	10, Feb. 1831	A3
Brooks, Abigail	Bowers, David	27, Nov. 1819	S3

Brides	Grooms	Date of Notice	Page
Brooks, Caroline	Miller, J.W.	3, Jan. 1839	T2
Brooks, Caroline E.	Fletcher, Adolphus	14, Apr. 1836	X3
Brooks, Dolly	Newman, Joseph	11, June 1799	S3
Brooks, Elise	MacCracken, John	23, Apr. 1847	K2
Brooks, Maria	Canaan, John	30, Oct. 1819	S3
Brown, Ann Eliza	Ferris, William J.	21, Dec. 1839	R3
Brown, Annis (Mrs)	Taylor, Edward	11, Dec. 1819	S3
Brown, Charlotte	Edwards, William	28, Mar. 1812	S3
Brown, Eleanor	Post, Joseph	8, Dec. 1832	R3
Brown, Eliza	Davis, Joseph	30, June 1821	S3
Brown, Eliza A.	Kirby, Edmund	11, Mar. 1825	N2
Brown, Elizabeth (Mrs)	Daily, John	28, May 1799	S3
Brown, Helen	Pulliam, John D.	17, Sept 1852	P2
Brown, Isabella	Hancock, J.	4, Jan. 1851	P2
Brown, Jane D.	Folger, Charles R.	3, Oct. 1840	R3
Brown, Janet M.	Morrison, Thomas G.	2, Nov. 1852	P2
Brown, Julia Ann	Wetherby, Luther	7, Dec. 1820	S3
Brown, Mahala	Rynearson, William	25, Aug. 1835	T2
Brown, Maria Louise	Newton, Henry S.	20, Nov. 1841	R3
Brown, Maria Louise	Newton, Henry T.	13, Nov. 1841	N2
Brown, Mary L.	Hobby, Josephus	7, May 1841	N2
Brown, Sarah E.	Ropes, Nathaniel	14, July 1826	N3
Browne, Frances M.	Curtiss, L.G.	7, Sept 1847	K2
Browne, Mary A.	Thompson, William	15, July 1852	P2
Browne, Mary Ann	Avery, Dudley	30, Mar. 1807	S3
Browner, Sophia J.	Peacock, William H.	10, June 1847	K2
Brownings, Virginia	Miller, George A.	25, July 1851	P2
Brownrigg, C.	Killough, J. (Dr)	3, Aug. 1837	T2
Bruce, Louisa (Mrs)	Ernst, Jacob	30, May 1840	R3
Bruner, Mary A.	Ashcroft, Robert	2, Nov. 1847	K2
Brush, Mary	Cowling, Richard	17, May 1849	L2
Bryan, Cornelia A.	Weller, John B.	8, Aug. 1840	R3
Bryan, Melissa S.	Gest, Andrew M.	22, June 1836	T2
Bryant, Anna L.	Walker, T.	12, May 1832	R3
Bryant, Lydia	Preston, E.J.	10, Dec. 1847	K2
Bryon, Sallie E.O.	Buchanan, W.A.	26, Oct. 1852	P2
Buchanan, Christina	Teator, Henry	16, Aug. 1816	S3
Buchanan, Eliza	Silvers, Aaron	20, Oct. 1815	S3
Buckingham, Maria	Richardson, Joseph A	8, Oct. 1841	N2
Buckner, Elizabeth	McGroarty, Patrick	1, Nov. 1850	Y2
Buckston, Mary Ann	Holdworth, Benjamin	3, Oct. 1850	Y2
Budd, Elizabeth	Lighthizer, S.F.	14, Jan. 1837	R3
Buel, Abigail	Knight, Henry	26, Oct. 1836	T2
Buel, Abigail (Mrs)	Knight, Henry	25, Oct. 1836	N2
Buffington, Elizabeth	Holmes, William	6, Nov. 1847	K2
Bugbee, Hannah (Mrs)	Blodget, John (Capt)	10, Jan. 1826	N3
Bunce, Julia	Hanks, George L.	26, May 1836	X3
Bunnell, Jane	Harthorn, Hugh B.	31, May 1816	S3
Buntz, Maria	Garretson, Israel	26, Aug. 1824	E2
Burch, Martha M.	Cain, George J.	12, July 1828	R3
Burdsal, Zada Emily	Nelson, William A.	7, Sept 1835	T2
Burdsall, Margaret D	Colter, Aaron A.	7, Oct. 1852	P2
Burk, Abigail	Doyle, Samuel	21, Nov. 1829	R3
Burkett, Mary	Hood, William	8, Aug. 1835	T2

Brides	Grooms	Date of Notice	Page
Burley, Esther B.	Hayden, Alfred	8, June 1827	N3
Burley, Esther P.	Hayden, Alfred	9, June 1827	R3
Burley, Frances	Gano, Aaron (Lt)	16, May 1818	S3
Burley, Jane	Armstrong, Robert	5, Oct. 1835	T2
Burley, Margaret	Thomas, John S.	24, Oct. 1817	S3
Burnet, Caroline	McLean, Nathaniel	8, Sept 1838	R3
Burnet, Caroline	McLean, Nathaniel	10, Sept 1838	T2
Burnet, Elizabeth	Groesbeck, William	4, Nov. 1837	R3
Burnet, Elizabeth	Groesbeck, William S	3, Nov. 1837	T2
Burnet, Julia Ann	Mixer, William	15, Nov. 1828	R3
Burnet, Julia Ann	Mixer, William	18, Nov. 1828	N3
Burnet, Mary Ann	Worthington, Vachel	31, May 1825	N3
Burnet, Nancy	Wood, Seely	23, Apr. 1842	R3
Burnet, Sophia (Mrs)	Cooper, Daniel C.	25, Sept 1805	S3
Burnett, Anne	Alley, Samuel A.	4, Jan. 1840	R3
Burns, Martha	Baker, Elias	22, Apr. 1830	A3
Burns, Virginia L.	Hall, James P.	10, Oct. 1850	P2
Burr, Emma C.	Davenport, Darius	20, Apr. 1820	D3
Burrows, Ann Eliza	Hartshorne, Saunders	7, Feb. 1831	A3
Burrows, Caroline W.	Yeatman, Walker	12, Dec. 1818	S3
Burrows, Frances M.	Yeatman, Walker	9, Mar. 1822	S2
Burrows, Maria Tunis	Green, Robert C.	8, Sept 1827	R3
Burt, Catharine G.	Ray, Joseph (Dr)	20, Aug. 1831	R3
Burt, Sarah A. (Mrs)	Hughes, John	19, Sept 1817	S3
Bush, Sarah C.	Rich, Virtulon	28, Sept 1835	T2
Bushart, Nancy	Cropper, Cyrus	6, Mar. 1819	S3
Bussey, Julia	Warren, John Borlase	9, Oct. 1835	T2
Bussey, Julia	Warren, John Borlase	8, Oct. 1835	N2
Butler, Charlotte	Stephens, Marcus	20, Feb. 1823	J3
Butler, Charlotte	Stevens, Marcus	18, Feb. 1823	N3
Butler, Lucy	Capp, Henry	18, Feb. 1823	N3
Butler, Lucy	Capp, Henry B.	20, Feb. 1823	J3
Butler, Malvina	Gilmore, Gurdon R.	8, Sept 1838	R3
Butler, Malvina	Gilmore, Gurdon R.	7, Sept 1838	T2
Butler, R.P. (Mrs)	Hanson, Custis A.	16, Aug. 1834	R3
Butler, R.P. (Mrs)	Hanson, Custus A.	13, Aug. 1834	T2
Butt, Lydia	Bowers, William	25, July 1817	S3
Byare, Mary	Smith, George	14, May 1847	K2
Byrne, Mary Helen	Ryon, Theodore	23, Nov. 1835	N2
Cabot, Elizabeth	Kirkland, John T.	29, Sept 1827	R3
Cadwell, Prudence	Stokes, Benjamin M.	13, Aug. 1799	S3
Cake, Martha E.	Hull, James	19, Feb. 1842	R3
Caldwell, ----	Marsh, Ebenezer	25, Apr. 1840	R3
Caldwell, Elizabeth	Colwell, Stephen	9, June 1827	R3
Caldwell, Ellen J.	Bleck, R.F.	14, June 1849	L2
Caldwell, Jane R.	Neave, Charles	9, June 1827	R3
Caldwell, Jane R.	Neave, Charles	8, June 1827	N3
Caldwell, Sarah Ann	Bare, Martin	31, Aug. 1847	K2
Calhoun, Anna	Clemson, Thomas C.	27, Dec. 1838	T2
Calling, Jane Ann	Morton, Wellington	3, Mar. 1841	N2
Calling, Jane Ann	Morton, Wellington L.	6, Mar. 1841	R3
Calvert, (Mrs)	Taylor, Thomas	2, Dec. 1824	E2
Cambridge, Rosa	Killin, Richard S.	31, July 1841	V3

Brides	Grooms	Date of Notice	Page
Camp, Amelia	Tuttle, Samuel (Rev)	12, June 1841	R3
Camp, Amelia	Tuttle, Samuel L.	10, June 1841	N2
Camp, Elizabeth	Hazen, Alfred	9, Sept 1847	K2
Camp, Laura W.	Dickinson, Austin	2, June 1836	X3
Campbell, Elizabeth	Glenn, John	23, July 1838	T2
Campbell, Ellen	Lea, James H.	9, May 1836	T2
Campbell, Sarah (Mrs)	Colby, Zerebabal	31, July 1813	S3
Campton, Cynthia Ann	Cummings, C.P.	5, Feb. 1842	R3
Campton, Cynthia Ann	Cummings, Caleb	5, Feb. 1842	N2
Camsby, Oliveretta	Wharton, Clifton	25, Aug. 1838	T2
Cane, Margaret	Smith, Wilson	9, Aug. 1852	P2
Canfield, Catharine	Billings, James A.	25, July 1828	Q3
Canfield, Hannah M.	Grundy, R.C. (Rev)	21, Apr. 1836	X3
Capp, Winney (Mrs)	Barger, Andrew	18, Dec. 1840	N2
Carey, Rachel	Spear, Samuel B.	23, July 1842	R3
Carey, Rachel	Spear, Samuel B.	20, July 1842	N2
Carey, Rosetta Jane	Thornton, Tyrrel	21, Dec. 1835	T3
Cargill, Mary Seely	Kimball, Warren	1, Nov. 1830	A3
Carl, Ellen	Dudley, Moses S.	28, Aug. 1847	K2
Carl, Frances Julia	Worsham, William	26, Nov. 1838	T2
Carley, Sarah Julia	Vallet, Henry	4, Oct. 1828	R3
Carls, Catharine	Hall, George	11, Mar. 1831	X3
Carlyle, Margaret S.	Carter, Joseph (Dr)	1, Dec. 1832	R3
Carneal, Alice	Warfield, Thomas B.	21, July 1838	R3
Carneal, Alice D.	Warfield, Thomas	18, July 1838	T2
Carns, Sarah	Funk, Daniel	22, Apr. 1830	A3
Carpenter, Abby	Earl, Isaac F.	6, Oct. 1832	R3
Carr, Catharine	Parker, Franklin	28, Oct. 1834	T2
Carrell, Eliza Jane	Arons, William	15, Sept 1827	R3
Carrick, Louisa Jane	Taylor, Wesley	29, Nov. 1837	T2
Carrington, Julia A.	Probasco, Henry	5, Sept 1840	R3
Carroll, Dorcas	Cahill, James	24, Sept 1847	K2
Carroll, Elizabeth	Smith, Julius H.	24, Mar. 1836	T2
Carroll, Elizabeth (Mrs)	Baker, James	22, Mar. 1836	T2
Carson, Jane	Meley, Jonathan	17, Mar. 1841	N2
Carson, Polly	Reddick, Thomas	2, July 1799	S3
Carter, Harriet S.	Smith, William M.	19, Aug. 1852	P2
Carter, Matilda L.	Noble, William P.	29, July 1828	N3
Carter, Rebecca F.	Black, James	19, Apr. 1828	R3
Carter, Sarah	Disney, David T.	2, Sept 1825	N3
Carter, Susan B.	Walton, Elias J.	4, Nov. 1837	R3
Carter, Susan B.	Walton, Elias T.	2, Nov. 1837	T2
Cary, Rosetta Jane	Berry, Andrew	20, Sept 1834	T2
Case, Anna B.	Birney, David B.	11, May 1847	K2
Case, Sarah	Nut, James M.	8, Dec. 1827	R3
Cassiday, Mary (Mrs)	Humphreys, Joseph	24, June 1837	R3
Cassidy, Abbey	Freeman, Clarkson	26, Mar. 1820	S2
Cassidy, Mary (Mrs)	Humphreys, Joseph	21, June 1837	T2
Cassilly, Ann S.	Marshall, Vincent C.	27, Dec. 1825	N2
Cassilly, Henrietta	Whiteman, Benjamin	15, Sept 1838	R3
Cassilly, Henrietta	Whiteman, Benjamin	15, Sept 1838	T2
Cather, Hester	Gavin, James	7, May 1814	S3
Catlett, Elizabeth	White, Caleb	18, Apr. 1829	R3
Chadwick, Eliza	Bonsol, Joseph	30, Oct. 1819	S3

Brides	Grooms	Date of Notice	Page
Chafer, Mary	Darby, Joseph	7, Apr. 1851	P2
Chalfant, Josephine	Marshall, Edward C.	30, Nov. 1852	P2
Chalfant, Margaretta	Jones, Charles T.	9, May 1840	R3
Chambers, Hannah	Thomas, Israel	2, May 1812	S3
Chandler, Eliza R.	Walsh, Robert F	13, Aug. 1838	T2
Chapeze, Elizabeth	VanHorn, Thomas B.	4, Feb. 1831	X3
Chapeze, Elizabeth (Mrs)	VanHorne, Thomas B.	29, Jan. 1831	R3
Chapin, Helen	Hine, L.A.	16, Nov. 1847	K2
Chapin, Olive S.	Cummings, John N.	14, May 1847	K2
Chapin, Sylvia	Cornell, John P.	4, June 1842	R3
Chapman, Elizabeth	Agnew, John	1, Aug. 1840	R3
Chapman, Fanny	West, Francies	21, Aug. 1819	S3
Chapman, Frances A.	Williams, H.C.	30, Nov. 1835	T2
Charters, Anna	Merwic, Anson W.	8, June 1841	N2
Chartres, Anna	Merwin, Anson W.	12, June 1841	R3
Chatham, Amanda	Rivers, Robert J.	5, July 1828	R3
Cheatham, Medora	Riggs, Samuel J.	3, Oct. 1835	T2
Childs, Mary W.	Johnson, Leonidas N.	17, Oct. 1840	R3
Chipman, Mary	Paine, Thomas L.	17, Oct. 1817	S3
Christie, Janet	Wilson, Allan	11, June 1836	T2
Church, Jane Elizabeth	Hart, Henry N.	27, Sept 1838	T2
Cist, Augusta	McClintock, Andrew T.	29, May 1841	R3
Clapp, Martha H.	Chute, James	24, Oct. 1817	S3
Clark, Ann	Wood, Alfred	22, Oct. 1836	T2
Clark, Ann	Wood, Alfred	22, Oct. 1836	N2
Clark, Electa P.	Clark, Ansel R.(Rev)	30, Nov. 1837	X3
Clark, Eliza	Kibbe, Jarvis	22, Jan. 1820	S3
Clark, Elizabeth	Jamison, Love H. (Rev)	22, Dec. 1837	T2
Clark, Elizabeth	Lewark, John	22, Sept 1838	R3
Clark, Elizabeth	McMaken, M.C.	20, July 1852	P2
Clark, Elizabeth	Walker, George B.	27, June 1835	T2
Clark, Ella M.	Francisco, A.N.	24, Jan. 1848	K2
Clark, Florilla	Waters, John	7, May 1842	R3
Clark, Frances	Beans, William W.	31, May 1849	L2
Clark, Lydia	Clark, George	22, May 1847	K2
Clark, Mary	Anderson, John	10, Jan. 1826	N3
Clark, Mary A.	Hendrick, Oscar C.	6, July 1849	L2
Clark, Mary Elizabeth	Baldwin, Henry	27, Sept 1852	P2
Clark, Sarah	Schoolfield, Joseph	13, Sept 1852	P2
Clark, Sarah Jane	Tuttle, G.P.	7, Sept 1847	K2
Clark, Susan Maria	Burnet, William	13, Feb. 1841	R3
Clark, Susan Maria	Burnet, William	8, Feb. 1841	N2
Clarkson, Mary E.	Rannells, D.W.	22, Jan. 1839	T2
Clasby, Lydia	Folger, Seth	20, Apr. 1820	D3
Clasby, Lydia	Fougler, Seth	15, Apr. 1820	S2
Clay, Margaret	Bissell, Israel M.	20, Jan. 1826	N3
Clemens, Sarah	Williams, George W.	22, Oct. 1831	R3
Clemons, Martha Ann	Cloon, Samuel	12, Aug. 1847	K2
Cleveland, Sarah	Benedict, Alexander	4, Aug. 1842	N2
Cleveland, Sarah	Benedict, Alexander	4, Aug. 1842	M3
Clifford, Abby Anna	Stickney, J. Charles	15, June 1836	T2
Clifford, Mary	Copeland, Nathaniel	6, May 1828	N3
Clifford, Mary Jane	Caldwell, Thomas L.	15, June 1822	S3
Clifford, Sarah S.	Wade, Eben	11, Oct. 1831	A3

Brides	Grooms	Date of Notice	Page
Cloon, Sarah E.	Duffield, Charles	2, Apr. 1842	R3
Cloon, Sarah E.	Duffield, Charles	28, Mar. 1842	N2
Close, Hannah B.	Symmes, Peyton S.	22, May 1819	S3
Cobb, Charlotte	Arthur, Nicholas	9, May 1836	T2
Cobb, Harriet	Wright, Isaac H.	10, Aug. 1837	X3
Cobb, Mary E.	Mann, Hartley	6, July 1838	T2
Cochran, Jane L.	Speed, James	2, May 1840	R3
Coddington, Sarah	Jenifer, Benjamin	26, Dec. 1840	R3
Coddington, Sarah	Jenifer, Benjamin	23, Dec. 1840	N2
Coffin, Anna B.	Horne, Daniel H.	15, Feb. 1839	T2
Coffin, L.W.	Brown, Wilson	8, Oct. 1852	P2
Coffin, Mary F.	Stansbury, John C.	8, Sept 1837	N2
Coffin, Sarah	Martin, Oliver	24, Oct. 1817	S3
Coggeshall, Margaret	Ewer, George W.	17, Feb. 1826	N3
Coit, Elizabeth F.C.	Holland, R.C. (Dr)	3, Oct. 1835	T2
Colby, Margery	Acres, Frederick	4, Jan. 1808	S3
Cole, Caroline	Bowers, Augustus	29, Sept 1838	R3
Cole, Caroline	Bowers, Augustus	29, Sept 1838	T2
Cole, Caroline	Bowers, Augustus	29, Sept 1838	N2
Cole, Eliza	Hickett, Bright	1, Apr. 1828	N3
Coleman, Ann	Benbridge, Thomas	14, Feb. 1831	A3
Coleman, Anne C.	Alden, Bradford R.	25, June 1842	R3
Coleman, Eliza	Allen, Thomas H.	3, Mar. 1827	R3
Coleman, Maria (Mrs)	Slayback, Abel (Dr)	13, May 1823	N3
Colescott, Elizabeth	Clarkson, C.F.	21, May 1849	L2
Collard, Catharine	Veach, Charles	5, Oct. 1820	S3
Collard, Jane Ann	Whetstone, Reuben	22, Aug. 1818	S3
Collins, Caroline E.	Camp, Henry R.	26, July 1852	P2
Collins, Julia	Barwise, Thomas	16, Feb. 1822	S3
Collins, Lidia	Hewman, C.D.	13, Nov. 1852	P2
Collins, M.S.	Jackson, T.M.	26, May 1821	S3
Collins, Mary F.	Carter, John W.	1, Nov. 1852	P2
Collins, Mary Fanny	Carter, John W.	29, Oct. 1852	P2
Collins, Phena	Baker, Nelson	19, Oct. 1836	T2
Collins, Phena	Baker, Nelson	13, Oct. 1836	X3
Colthar, Sarah Ann	Tucker, George W.	4, May 1833	R3
Coltier, Catharine	Flowers, Michael B.	12, Oct. 1820	S3
Comstock, Cath. E.	Wygant, Martin	4, Sept 1841	R3
Conclin, Louisa	Richardson, Francis	19, Apr. 1847	K2
Cones, Frances Mary	Schillinger, William	5, June 1841	R3
Cones, Frances Mary	Schillinger, William	28, May 1841	N2
Conklin, Eliza	Whipple, Samuel D.	16, Oct. 1819	S3
Conklin, Mary	Phillips, Henry	21, Oct. 1825	N2
Conklin, Phebe	Talbott, John	2, Dec. 1824	E2
Conn, Maria W.	Center, Robert H.	17, Nov. 1826	N2
Conn, Mary Ann	O'Brian, Edward D.	10, Mar. 1827	R3
Conn, Sarah Ann	Greene, William W.	10, Nov. 1827	R3
Conn, Sarah M.	Floyd, Gabriel J.	5, Dec. 1817	S3
Conner, Eliza	Barrett, William D.	16, Aug. 1834	R3
Conner, Eliza	Barrett, William D.	13, Aug. 1834	T2
Conner, Susan (Mrs)	Longworth, Nicholas	28, Dec. 1807	S3
Connover, Mary Ann	Griffin, David	9, Nov. 1835	T2
Conover, Margaret	Williams, Jacob	9, Jan. 1830	R3
Conover, Margaret	Williams, Jacob	12, Jan. 1830	N2

Brides	Grooms	Date of Notice	Page
Conrad, Priscilla	Wallam, John	18, Mar. 1831	X3
Converse, Cornelia L	Coburn, John A.	29, Nov. 1852	P2
Conwell, Winnie K.	Stillwill, T. Neal	25, Oct. 1852	P2
Cook, Eliza	Teasdale, William	24, Feb. 1838	R3
Cook, Elizabeth	Riddle, Adam N.	1, May 1835	T3
Cook, Elizabeth Ann	Delvin, John	30, Aug. 1828	R3
Cook, Elizabeth M.	Timberman, Isaiah	29, Nov. 1852	P2
Cook, Frances	Durbin, John (Rev)	22, Sept 1827	R3
Cook, Isabella	Doan, Isaac	1, Dec. 1838	T2
Cook, Mary Elizabeth	Richards, Warren	6, Dec. 1828	R3
Cooke, Mary S.	Magill, Wesley W.	18, Mar. 1847	K2
Cooley, Jeannette C.	Ely, Jonathan	12, June 1837	T2
Coolidge, Ann Maria	Sampson, William S.	2, Sept 1831	A3
Coolidge, Ann Maria	Sampson, William S.	3, Sept 1831	R3
Coolidge, Hetty B.	Haight, Benjamin J.	1, July 1835	T2
Coolidge, Sophy	Whetstone, Jacob V.	23, Nov. 1852	P2
Cooly, Jeanette (Mrs)	Ely, Jonathan	10, June 1837	R3
Coombs, Emily	Spencer, O.M.	30, Sept 1837	R3
Coombs, Emily	Spencer, O.M.	30, Sept 1837	T2
Cooper, Mary	Abbott, William	16, Dec. 1852	P2
Cooper, Sarah Ann	Randolph, Joseph F.	3, Oct. 1840	R3
Coppuck, Mary M.	Wilby, Thomas J.	3, Oct. 1835	T2
Cordingley, Marcian	Sherer, John	30, July 1842	R3
Cordry, Mary (Mrs)	Campbell, James	3, Jan. 1839	T2
Corke, Sarah	Graveson, J.	31, Dec. 1852	P2
Cornelius, Mary	DeGraw, Abraham	8, Jan. 1842	R3
Cornelius, Mary	DeGraw, Abraham	4, Jan. 1842	N2
Cornelius, Mary A.	Martin, H.G.	3, Jan. 1853	P2
Cornell, Isabella	Reeves, James E.	20, Aug. 1842	R3
Corry, Susan Ann	Williamson, Alex. W.	4, Jan. 1840	R3
Corwin, Amelia	Osborn, Lewis	9, June 1827	R3
Corwin, Rhoda	Morris, Isaiah	21, Nov. 1840	R3
Cory, Maria A.	Preston, William (Rev)	31, May 1830	A3
Cosgrove, Mary Ann	Avinger, Frederick	6, Oct. 1852	P2
Cottle, Sarah (Mrs)	Huffmaster, S.W.	26, Apr. 1833	X3
Cottle, Susan	Hardin, Joseph	1, Jan. 1820	S3
Covert, Hannah	Thorp, Milton	7, Mar. 1829	R3
Cowdrey, Sarah H.	Candler, Samuel	6, Aug. 1836	T2
Cowdry, Elizabeth	Phelps, Benjamin R.	30, May 1835	T2
Cox, Elizabeth	Morrey, Joseph	17, Dec. 1852	P2
Cox, Hannah	Bowers, Henry	12, June 1847	K2
Cox, Hannah	VanEaton, James	22, June 1833	R3
Cox, Mary Elizabeth	Berry, William	12, July 1834	T2
Cox, Minerva	Fields, Daniel	4, Feb. 1831	X3
Cox, Rebecca	Weeks, Henry	21, Feb. 1823	N3
Cox, Rebecca Ann	Clarkson, John D.	18, June 1850	P2
Cox, Sarah (Mrs)	Wright, Henry W.	25, June 1842	R3
Coxe, Harriet	Bledsoe, Albert T.	26, May 1836	X3
Cragg, Mary Jane	Moon, William	17, Nov. 1827	R3
Craig, Charlotte E.	Jackson, James	25, Dec. 1852	P2
Craig, Elizabeth J.	Gardner, William J.	23, May 1849	L2
Craig, Sarah	Friant, Clayton	22, Apr. 1830	A3
Crane, Abigail	Crane, Oliver	11, Apr. 1812	S2
Crane, Frances	Reeder, Jacob	16, Feb. 1816	S3

Brides	Grooms	Date of Notice	Page
Crane, Margaretta	Moore, Hugh M.	23, July 1842	R3
Crane, Margaretta	Moore, Hugh M.	19, July 1842	N2
Crane, Mary	Emery, Charles	23, Mar. 1833	R3
Crane, Mary	Russel, Samuel	1, Nov. 1825	N3
Cranmer, Ann	Forquer, George	5, Apr. 1828	R3
Cranmer, Ann	Forquer, George	4, Apr. 1828	N3
Cranmer, Susan	Lamb, James L.	16, Jan. 1824	N3
Crary, Almira	Taylor, Calvin	12, Nov. 1841	N2
Cregar, Jane	Hoe, Robert	23, Jan. 1838	T2
Creichton, Emilia	Beman, Gamaliel C.	3, Nov. 1836	X3
Creighton, Susan	Williams, Jesse L.	3, Dec. 1831	R3
Cres, Mary	Brown, Edward W.	13, July 1852	P2
Crewson, Mary Jane	Irvine, George	29, Dec. 1841	N2
Crisman, Mary	Strodtbeck, Jacob	1, Dec. 1827	R3
Crittenden, Ann Mary	Coleman, Chapman	2, Dec. 1830	A3
Cromwell, Ann	Langdon, Elam P.	20, Oct. 1821	S3
Cromwell, Louisa	Woodrow, David T.	10, Oct. 1840	R3
Crook, Eleanor Ann	Sands, J.R.	31, Aug. 1847	K2
Crooker, Ann	St.Clair, John	22, Sept 1827	R3
Crookshank, Jane	Wiley, John (Dr)	24, Dec. 1824	N3
Cross, Esther	Mallard, Henry (Capt)	12, June 1841	N2
Crossman, Caroline	Brigham, Matthias	8, Oct. 1821	S3
Crossman, H.S.	Ott, Otho C.	6, May 1837	R3
Crowley, Elizabeth	Prout, Hiram	14, Mar. 1829	R3
Crowly, Jane	Briggs, Henry	11, Apr. 1829	R3
Cullen, Margaret	Dawson, Thomas	29, Sept 1827	R3
Cullender, Jane	Henderson, F.	11, May 1822	S3
Cumming, Margaret	Hunt, William	12, Nov. 1814	S3
Cummins, Ann (Mrs)	Swormsted, Leroy (Rev)	13, Jan. 1825	E3
Cuppuck, Janet R.	VanPelt, George	3, Oct. 1835	T2
Currie, Isabella	Collins, John	15, July 1835	T2
Curry, Clarissa (Mrs)	Dudley, Ambrose	7, July 1837	T2
Curtis, Anna	Wilson, Vacter	6, Nov. 1852	P2
Curtis, Mary	Beggs, Joseph P.	24, Aug. 1847	K2
Cushing, Hannah L.	Gallagher, John M.	22, Oct. 1834	T3
Cushman, Josephine	Bateham, M.B.	3, Oct. 1850	Y2
Cutter, Lydia Ann	Farrar, Andrew S.	21, July 1827	R3
Cutter, Maria	Odell, James	11, Aug. 1841	N2
Cutter, Susannah	Foster, Samuel	3, June 1806	S3
Daggett, Eliza J.	Goshorn, William F.	22, Apr. 1847	K2
Daines, Almean	Hennesy, Michael	4, Jan. 1841	N2
Dalzell, Rachael	Hunter, Joseph	15, Sept 1835	T2
Danforth, Mary	Steel, David	29, Mar. 1828	R3
Daniel, Lydia	Daniel, Isaac	26, Aug. 1824	E2
Daniel, Mary L.	Goddard, John F.	4, Sept 1837	T2
Daniel, Mary L.V.	Goddard, John F.	7, Sept 1837	X3
Daniels, Elizabeth	Martin, Alfred	14, Nov. 1840	R3
Daniels, Nancy	Gosney, Nimrod	9, May 1812	S3
Danison, Julia	Estep, Joshua	12, Jan. 1839	T2
Dashiell, Mary Y.	Madeira, J.	23, Nov. 1824	N2
Dashiell, Mary Y.	Madeira, J.	25, Nov. 1824	E2
Daughty, Harriet	Mayo, D.	30, May 1835	T2
Davee, Mary	Shourt, John	24, Aug. 1811	S3

Brides	Grooms	Date of Notice	Page
Davey, Mary A.	Marshall, Robert M.	20, Nov. 1852	P2
David, Mary	Porter, Henry (Dr)	20, Sept 1852	P2
Davis, Clarissa	Pendery, Goodloe	10, Nov. 1838	T2
Davis, Eliza	Perry, William	15, July 1830	A3
Davis, Harriet Ann	Stephenson, Andrew C	15, Oct. 1847	K2
Davis, Janette	Dorfeuille, J.	11, May 1824	N3
Davis, Janette	Dorfeuille, J.	13, May 1824	E3
Davis, Lucinda	Cook, Austin	15, Sept 1827	R3
Davis, Margaretta H.	Hales, Charles	31, May 1849	L2
Davis, Martha	Fullerton, Samuel W.	13, Sept 1838	T2
Davis, Mary	Cochrill, Enoch	27, Sept 1841	N2
Davis, Mary (Mrs)	Cochrill, Enoch	2, Oct. 1841	R3
Davis, Nancy	Blount, Beverly	20, Sept 1814	W4
Davis, Olivia	Bucknell, Thomas	14, Dec. 1839	R3
Davis, Ruhamah	Phillips, Thomas	12, Jan. 1830	N2
Davis, Sarah Jane	Durkee, Dwight	10, June 1851	P2
Davis, Sarah P.	Crane, (Dr)	3, July 1852	P2
Davis, Sophia	Folsom, S.	30, Nov. 1847	K2
Dawson, Mary	Sloan, Samuel	2, June 1847	K2
Day, Lavinia	Clark, Carlton	1, June 1820	S3
Dean, Elizabeth	Coonse, Frederick	14, Sept 1811	S3
Debolt, Eliza	Jones, James L.	23, Nov. 1839	R3
DeCamp, Mary H.	Webster, Taylor	22, Apr. 1830	A3
Dee, Jerusha	Perrin, Amos	26, Jan. 1833	R3
Dee, Louisa	Cox, Richard K.	1, Aug. 1829	R3
Deed, Frances	Massaliki, Joseph	1, July 1836	T2
Deeds, Joana	Kemper, E.Y. (Dr)	12, Oct. 1820	S3
Delano, Mary	Ely, Seneca W.	29, Aug. 1840	R3
Delaplaine, Jane (Mrs)	Finkbine, William	23, Feb. 1828	R3
Delaplaine, Jane (Mrs)	Finkbine, William	22, Feb. 1828	N3
Dellon, Eliza Ann	Stonfer, Henry	15, Sept 1827	R3
Denman, Louisa E.	Hinch, Augustus F.	9, May 1836	T2
Denman, Louisa E.	Hinsch, Augustus F.	19, May 1836	X3
Dennie, Rebecca	Ball, Blackall W.	9, June 1827	R3
Dennison, Eliza A.	Bickham, William	2, Sept 1826	J3
Dennison, Eliza Ann	Clarkson, Samuel (Dr)	10, Mar. 1827	R3
Dennison, Julia Ann	Reynolds, Benjamin B.	10, Mar. 1827	R3
Denny, Elizabeth	Burdsal, Solomon B.	3, May 1847	K2
Denny, Rebecca	Ball, B.W.	12, June 1827	N2
Derby, Mary Jane	Peabody, Ephraim (Rev)	17, Aug. 1833	R3
DeValcourt, Martha E	Piatt, J.W.	5, Sept 1837	T2
Devens, Frances P.	Sherburne, John H.	25, June 1842	R3
Devit, Mary	More, Amos	30, Dec. 1823	N3
Devou, Sarah Alice	Beatty, James S.	28, July 1838	R3
Devou, Sarah Alice	Beatty, James S.	27, July 1838	T2
Dews, Nancy (Mrs)	White, John	9, Apr. 1836	T2
Dexter, Ellen	Blanchard, Cary H.	8, Aug. 1840	R3
Dexter, Julia	Wetmore, M.W.	29, Apr. 1834	T2
DeYoung, Sarah	Abraham, J.	6, Sept 1841	N2
Diad, Celia	Parks, Robert	2, June 1838	R3
Dickey, Catharine	Bowdle, Daniel	24, Nov. 1832	R3
Dickey, Margaret	Duffield, Charles	22, Sept 1832	R3
Dickinson, Mary	Embree, Jesse	26, Sept 1818	S3
Dicks, Catharine A.	Ross, Frederick F.	5, Apr. 1834	R3

Brides	Grooms	Date of Notice	Page
Dicks, Mary Ellen	Strickler, George W.	26, Feb. 1842	R3
Dill, Frances Ann	Glascoe, James S.	12, May 1832	R3
Dillon, Elizabeth	Evans, John	10, Oct. 1838	T2
Dilworth, Eliza W.	Loomis, M.D.W.	25, Mar. 1847	K2
Disney, Amilia Maria	James, Henry	14, Apr. 1836	X3
Dixon, Elizabeth	Orr, William M.	26, Dec. 1817	S3
Doalbear, Lucy	Dow, Lorenzo (Rev)	18, May 1820	S3
Dobson, Martha E.	Morgan, John M.	28, Aug. 1852	P2
Dodd, Cornelia Ann	Hunt, Bart F.	15, Mar. 1834	R3
Dodd, Hannah	Fisher, Ludevick	1, Mar. 1833	X3
Dodd, Louisa M.	Hood, Jonathan N.	7, May 1842	R3
Dodd, Louisa M.	Hood, Jonathan N.	4, May 1842	N2
Doddsworth, Mary	Andress, Charles	19, June 1841	R3
Doddsworth, Mary	Andress, Charles	15, June 1841	N2
Dodge, Christiana	Clarke, John	26, Sept 1840	R3
Dodge, Frances Ann	Casto, Jona.	7, Dec. 1847	K2
Dodson, Cynthia Ann	King, D. Cleaves	13, June 1849	L2
Dodson, Cynthia Anne	Smith, George W.	25, Dec. 1827	N3
Doerrer, Paulina	Wright, Charles A.	15, May 1847	K2
Dollin, Frances	Cook, Samuel	16, Nov. 1820	S3
Dollin, Jane	Smith, Thomas	16, Nov. 1820	S3
Dolton, Ann	Rigdon, Charles	22, Jan. 1820	S3
Donaldson, Jane	McNeely, Cyrus	20, May 1837	R3
Donaldson, Jessie	Pullan, Richard E.	28, Apr. 1849	L2
Donaldson, Mary	Lindman, Lewis T.	22, Apr. 1847	K2
Donnell, Mary	Shepard, Charles	2, May 1840	R3
Dorman, Maria E.	Brandon, James P.	22, Nov. 1838	T2
Dorman, Sarah Ann	Stephenson, H.W.	16, Feb. 1839	T2
Dorsey, Frances H.	Neville, Julian	19, Dec. 1835	T3
Dorsey, Mary	Gist, Robert C.	14, Jan. 1832	R3
Doughty, Nancy	Gimble, Henry	16, Apr. 1814	S3
Douglas, Jane	Anderson, William	7, Oct. 1837	T2
Douglass, Hannah	Sanders, David	3, Oct. 1818	S3
Douglass, Jane	Griswold, George	1, Dec. 1840	N2
Douglass, Margaret	Vandegriff, William	17, Apr. 1819	S2
Douglass, Mary	Johnson, Peter	26, Aug. 1824	E2
Dowd, Ann	Hume, Thomas W.	24, July 1838	T2
Downs, Eliza (Mrs)	Kellogg, Charles F.	14, Feb. 1829	R3
Doyle, Amanda	Hill, James	14, Apr. 1829	N3
Doyle, Emeline A.	Buckingham, E.J.	18, Mar. 1851	P2
Dozier, Thursday	Marchant, Johnson	25, June 1842	R3
Drake, Amanda V.	McDowell, Joseph N.	14, Apr. 1827	R3
Drake, Lavinia	Bedinger, Henry C.	14, Sept 1820	S3
Drake, Lydia	Woolley, John (Dr)	5, Apr. 1816	S3
Drake, Mary A.	Porter, John	8, Aug. 1850	Y2
Drayton, Malinda	Roe, Francis	20, Sept 1834	R3
Drayton, Mary	Burgess, Isaac F.	28, Jan. 1832	R3
Drennan, Mary R.	Fletcher, Lowell	24, Mar. 1832	R3
Drollener, Hannah	Colby, Samuel	25, Apr. 1810	H3
Duckworth, Keziah C.	White, Henry	10, Dec. 1847	K2
Dudgeon, E.	Kellogg, A.	22, Oct. 1831	R3
Dudgeon, Elizabeth	Kellogg, Albert	21, Oct. 1831	X3
Dudley, Emily	Tufts, Servetus	28, June 1834	R3
Duffield, Mary Jane	Wrenn, George L.	7, Sept 1833	R3

Brides	Grooms	Date of Notice	Page
Duffy, Lydia Ann	Cole, Ephraim	9, Aug. 1850	Y2
Dugan, Nancy	Brotherton, David	4, Apr. 1829	R3
Duke, Eugenia	Sterrett, Robert	15, Sept 1827	R3
Dulty, Mary	Teesdale, John	19, June 1837	N2
Duncan, Elizabeth	Findlay, Samuel B.	9, Dec. 1837	R3
Duncan, Susan M.	VanKuren, Edward	12, June 1849	L2
Dunham, (Miss)	Sharland, Edward H.	5, May 1821	S3
Dunham, Zeruah	Grover, Abraham	11, Aug. 1835	T2
Dunn, Elizabeth	Valentine, Lewis	15, Apr. 1842	N2
Dunn, Elizabeth	Vallentine, Lewis	16, Apr. 1842	R3
Dupant, Martha (Mrs)	Shimer, Edward	10, Aug. 1852	P2
Dutton, A.L.	Wells, William	30, Dec. 1837	R3
Duvey, Elizabeth (Mrs)	Ellis, Humphrey	1, Dec. 1821	S3
Dwyer, Elizabeth	Phillips, William	28, June 1828	R3
Dwyer, Jane	Saunders, David M.	12, July 1828	R3
Eads, Margaret	McGregor, Alexander	3, Jan. 1829	R3
Earley, Catharine	Aull, Conrad A.	12, Aug. 1852	P2
Earnot, Elizabeth	Hazen, Livius	21, July 1827	R3
Easton, Eliza	Ebbert, Isaac (Rev)	29, May 1841	N2
Easton, Mary	Lindslay, William L.	5, July 1828	R3
Easton, Sophia H.	Martin, George	5, July 1852	P2
Eaton, Anna Jane	Irwin, John V.	3, Oct. 1838	T2
Eaton, Anna Jane	Irwin, John V.	3, Oct. 1838	N2
Eaton, Eliza Ann	Gibbs, William F.	17, Mar. 1836	T2
Eberle, Catharine	Bacon, James H.	20, Dec. 1833	X3
Eberle, Margaret	Mayronne, O.F.	31, Oct. 1840	R3
Eckert, Elizabeth	Wilson, William D.	5, Nov. 1835	T2
Eckstein, Mary	Kinmont, A.	24, Jan. 1829	R3
Eddy, Hannah J. (Mrs)	Dart, George L.	19, July 1852	P2
Eden, Rebecca	Wilson, John L.	2, Dec. 1825	N3
Edmands, Catharine R.	Kellogg, Sheldon J.	3, Nov. 1835	T2
Edmonds, (Miss)	Hailman, David (Dr)	14, Apr. 1821	S3
Edmondson, Mary Ann	Biddecombe, D. (Rev)	4, June 1842	R3
Edson, Roxana	Fairchild, Oliver (Dr)	5, Jan. 1816	S3
Edwards, Ann M.	AtLee, Samuel York	6, June 1836	N2
Edwards, Elizabeth	Perin, Ira	20, Dec. 1852	P2
Edwards, Jane	Victor, Henry C.	6, Nov. 1852	P2
Edwards, Rebecca	McClean, John	3, Apr. 1807	S3
Egbert, Rosalie R.	Burke, Walter	28, June 1828	R3
Egelston, Martha	Waldo, Frederick	17, Dec. 1852	P2
Egleston, Diana	Bledsoe, Abraham	5, Sept 1834	X3
Eichelberger, Susan	G---hase, S.	5, Sept 1840	R3
Elliot, Julia Ann	Crane, Joseph	19, July 1809	H3
Elliott, Anne Elizabeth	Duvall, Alexander	1, Sept 1835	T2
Elliott, Caroline	Boyd, D.B.	29, Dec. 1852	P2
Elliott, Clarissa	Beebe, Rosswell	12, Oct. 1835	T2
Elliott, Elizabeth	Foote, Samuel E.	29, Sept 1827	R3
Elliott, Sally	Humphrey, John	24, Aug. 1811	S3
Elliott, Sophronia A	Baldwin, Arden W.	21, Dec. 1839	R3
Ellis, Jane	Matthews, James	23, Oct. 1847	K2
Ellison, Polly	Mulvany, John	22, Sept 1838	R3
Ellmaker, Susan	Carpenter, Isaac B.	1, July 1837	R3
Ellsberry, Isabella	Dangerfield, T.A.	13, Mar. 1835	N2

Brides	Grooms	Date of Notice	Page
Ellstrep, Elizabeth	Hudson, Edwin	21, Oct. 1852	P2
Elsturn, Sarah (Mrs)	Kyes, Alvin	2, Aug. 1828	R3
Emerson, Clarissa	Matthews, William	7, May 1841	N2
England, Elizabeth	Ballance, Charles	29, Jan. 1836	T3
English, Kezziah	Anderson, Samuel	23, Sept 1852	P2
English, Mary	Perry, James	13, Mar. 1819	S2
Eppley, Mary	Richardson, Samuel	23, Aug. 1852	P2
Epply, Julia M.	Robinson, William E.	14, May 1847	K2
Erickson, Sarah	Jones, George	25, Oct. 1852	P2
Ernout, Mary	Biggers, James	29, Sept 1827	R3
Ernst, Adeline	Kent, Luke	4, July 1840	R3
Ernst, Catharine M.	Thorpe, Charles W.	15, June 1836	N2
Ernst, Mary A.	James, A.C.	17, Oct. 1840	R3
Erwin, Olivia	Swing, Jeremiah	28, July 1827	R3
Espy, Mary	Westcott, John	12, Aug. 1824	E3
Estell, Nancy	Williams, David R.	4, Nov. 1824	E3
Evans, Elizabeth	Anthony, Charles	26, Mar. 1820	S2
Evans, Ellen S.	Hand, Ellis	25, May 1847	K2
Evans, M. (Mrs)	Robinson, Solon	17, May 1828	R3
Evans, Sarah	Hughs, Henry	2, May 1840	R3
Evatt, Jane	Wilmouth, Thomas	15, Sept 1815	S3
Evens, Louisa Anna	Chapman, William S.	23, Nov. 1838	T2
Everson, Ann	Bittle, Hezekiah	23, Nov. 1820	S3
Ewing, Eliza	Andrew, John	20, May 1806	S3
Ewing, Juliet (Mrs)	Woolcott, William G.	19, Jan. 1833	R3
Ewing, Sallie M.	Marshall, N.B. (Dr)	11, Aug. 1852	P2
Ewing, Sarah V.	McBride, Henry R.W.	10, July 1852	P2
Fair, Susan	North, David	11, July 1835	T2
Fairbank, Sarah A.	Morton, Phineas	16, Sept 1831	X3
Fairchild, Catharine	Stone, F.H.	15, Aug. 1840	R3
Farland, Caroline M.	Lambdin, Robert	17, July 1819	S3
Farmer, Mary D.	DeGraw, John	24, Dec. 1836	R3
Farmer, Sarah	Webb, Thaddeus R.	29, Mar. 1838	N2
Farnsworth, Augusta	Stone, Daniel	10, Dec. 1824	N3
Farnsworth, Augusta	Stone, Daniel	9, Dec. 1824	E2
Farnsworth, Eliza W.	Guilford, Nathan	30, Oct. 1819	S3
Farrelly, Eliza	Langtree, C.	18, Jan. 1840	R3
Faulkner, Sarah Ann	Hall, John C.	2, Oct. 1841	R3
Fawcett, Mary Ann	Bates, Henry M.	20, Jan. 1838	R3
Fawcett, Mary Ann	Bates, Henry M.	23, Jan. 1838	T2
Febiger, Hannah (Mrs)	Jones, George W.	25, Aug. 1832	R3
Fenton, Louisa	Row, George T.	11, Mar. 1824	E3
Fenton, Louisa M.	Carey, Samuel D.	19, Aug. 1852	P2
Fenton, Mary L.	Pursell, George	19, May 1832	R3
Ferguson, Amelia R.	Johnson, Archibald	10, July 1819	S3
Ferguson, Elizabeth	Drane, A.	13, Dec. 1828	R3
Ferguson, Mary	Buckingham, John S.	31, Aug. 1852	P2
Fernival, Martha	Parmele, Hervy	17, May 1816	S3
Ferris, Catharine	Drake, Francis	21, Feb. 1835	R3
Ferris, Catharine	Drake, Francis	24, Feb. 1835	T2
Fertig, Catharine	Lawrence, William C.	22, May 1841	R3
Fertig, Catharine A.	Lawrence, William C.	3, May 1841	N2
Field, Nancy	Gwinn, Evan	21, May 1847	K2

Brides	Grooms	Date of Notice	Page
Fieldden, Sarah Jane	Robacamp, Frederick	30, Jan. 1839	T2
Fine, Elizabeth	Strong, Edward K.	15, July 1852	P2
Finkbine, Ann	Johnson, Robert F.	21, Apr. 1829	N2
Finkbine, Mary	Simcox, James	20, Jan. 1835	T2
Finley, Ann Rebecca	Torrence, James F.	16, Oct. 1841	R3
Fish, Susannah	Powell, Palemon	29, Jan. 1836	T3
Fisher, Alvira L.	McGrew, Alexander	12, Jan. 1822	S3
Fisher, Clarissa	Curtis, Henry J.	26, Aug. 1831	A3
Fisher, Clarissa	Curtis, Henry J.	27, Aug. 1831	R3
Fisher, Clarissa	Curtis, Henry J.	26, Aug. 1831	X3
Fisher, Eliza	Boddman, Hanson A.	14, May 1842	R3
Fisher, Emmeline P.	Reynolds, Lemuel	23, Apr. 1824	N3
Fisher, Sarah	Rhoads, Charles H.	15, Mar. 1828	R3
Fisk, Eliza	Heap, George	17, May 1831	A3
Fisk, Elizabeth	Hoskinson, Isaiah	12, Oct. 1820	S3
Flagg, Cettie M.	Gwynne, Abraham	30, May 1840	R3
Flannery, Bridget	Henderson, Moses	16, Aug. 1852	P2
Fleming, Ann (Mrs)	Turner, Evan	20, Sept 1839	T3
Fleming, Ellis M.	Carter, Lewis R.	16, June 1827	R3
Fleming, Hannah M.	Bedinger, George M.	5, Sept 1850	Y2
Fleming, Mary	Sage, Samuel	29, Dec. 1832	R3
Flinn, Frances S.	James, Alfred	11, Oct. 1852	P2
Flinn, Nancy A.	Light, Daniel	21, Apr. 1835	T3
Flint, Esther	Baker, John	4, July 1817	S3
Flint, Julia	Thatcher, David	12, Mar. 1814	S3
Flintham, Margaret	Thorpe, John D.	22, July 1847	K2
Flintham, Susan D.	Glover, Henry	16, Nov. 1833	R3
Flintham, Susan D.	Glover, Henry	15, Nov. 1833	X3
Flood, Clarissa	Shively, John	4, Feb. 1825	N2
Flood, Clarissa	Shively, John	20, Jan. 1825	E3
Florer, Phoebe C.	Elliott, Thomas	5, July 1841	N2
Flourngy, Letitia	Hale, Lewis	28, June 1828	R3
Floyd, Letitia	Lewis, William L.	12, Apr. 1837	T2
Foley, Mary	Bell, Joseph	3, Sept 1847	K2
Folger, Eliza	Clark, Henry	24, June 1824	E3
Folger, Eunice	Mann, Lowell A.	27, Mar. 1841	N2
Folger, Harriet	Belvel, James	17, Oct. 1838	T2
Folger, Sarah	Crane, Rufus	23, May 1829	R3
Fones, Amanda	Attwell, Robert G.	16, Oct. 1847	K2
Fontain, Matilda	Henry, S.	22, Mar. 1829	R3
Foote, Catharine A.	Comstock, William H.	26, May 1847	K2
Foote, Elizabeth A.	Corey, A.W.	21, Sept 1837	X3
Foote, Mary Ward	Shotwell, John (Dr)	27, Oct. 1832	R3
Forbes, Elizabeth W.	Moore, William (Rev)	19, Oct. 1847	K2
Ford, Henrietta	Miller, William	5, July 1828	R3
Ford, Jemima	Piatt, James A.	22, Dec. 1815	S3
Forest, Josephine	Lilley, William	11, Aug. 1850	Y2
Forman, Amanda	Morten, Henry	20, Jan. 1835	T2
Forman, Amy Ann	Cook, Oliver	11, July 1835	T2
Forsha, Deborah	Lynes, William (Rev)	7, July 1827	R3
Forsha, Deborah (Mrs)	Lynes, William (Rev)	6, July 1827	N3
Forshe, Mary Ann	Bard, John	28, Nov. 1818	S3
Fosdick, Elizabeth	Aydelott, B.P. (Rev)	26, June 1841	V3
Fosdick, Emeline B.	Goldenburgh, John	12, May 1841	N2

Brides	Grooms	Date of Notice	Page
Foster, Eliza (Mrs)	Brown, William	17, Mar. 1827	R3
Foster, Epenetus	Hampson, Jefferson	26, July 1834	T2
Foster, Mary E.	Wilson, George	25, Nov. 1852	P2
Foulk, Margaret	Green, John	7, June 1828	R3
Foulk, Margaret	Hatton, George	11, Feb. 1815	S3
Foulke, Elizabeth	Rogers, Nathaniel	14, Mar. 1829	R3
Fountain, Hannah	Waterman, James	1, Aug. 1804	S3
Fouzatte, Margaretta	Vattier, John L.	27, Sept 1828	R3
Fowles, H.N.	Walker, S.S.	26, Nov. 1835	X3
Fox, Christian	Adams, John	23, Sept 1812	S3
Fox, Frances L.	Ford, Smith	19, June 1847	K2
Francis, Mary	Atherton, Amos	19, July 1816	S3
Francisco, Virginia	Fisk, Allen	16, Aug. 1852	P2
Frankenstein, Maria	Coombs, Alfred D.	18, May 1849	L2
Frazer, Elizabeth	Green, James	31, Dec. 1852	P2
Frazer, Mary	Holmes, Samuel D.	25, Feb. 1831	X3
Frazer, Mary	Sinks, Randolph M.	8, Sept 1852	P2
Frazier, Hester	Duckwall, David	6, Oct. 1852	P2
Frazier, Sarah	Swift, Abiol	7, July 1827	R3
Freeman, Abigail	Schenck, Obadiah	27, May 1806	S3
French, Eliza (Mrs)	Russell, H.W. (Dr)	24, July 1847	K2
Frizzle, Nancy	Scott, William	10, May 1833	X3
Fuller, Ellen	Channing, W.E.	27, Sept 1841	N2
Fulton, Martha J.	Howe, Joseph	9, June 1836	X3
Fusselbaugh, Margaret	Carver, George W.	2, Dec. 1825	N3
Gabrielson, Caroline	Hastings, Royal	3, Jan. 1839	T2
Gaither, Almira J.G.	Jones, L.A. (Dr)	10, Feb. 1848	K2
Gale, Adelia	Daniels, Henry	4, May 1830	N3
Gallagher, Margaret	Hamar, James	2, Nov. 1822	S3
Gallagher, Sarah	McGrew, Wilson	27, Aug. 1831	R3
Gallahan, Mary	Cotterel, Joseph	11, Mar. 1831	X3
Galloway, Julia A.	Worthington, James T.	13, Dec. 1828	R3
Galloway, Rebecca	Myers, George	13, Mar. 1835	N2
Galloway, Sarah	Brown, Robert P.	11, Nov. 1837	R3
Galloway, Sarah A.	Brown, Robert	16, Nov. 1837	T2
Gamble, Julia Rusk	Totten, George M.	6, Aug. 1842	R3
Gammage, Sarrah H.	Burrows, John M.D.	15, Dec. 1836	X3
Gano, Belle	Reily, Robert	15, Aug. 1850	Y2
Gano, Frances Mary	Iglehart, N.P.	20, July 1837	T2
Gano, Mary	Burnet, David S.	5, Apr. 1830	A3
Gano, Mary	Burnet, David S.	2, Apr. 1830	N2
Gano, Sarah	Burt, Andrew	9, Feb. 1807	S2
Gardiner, Harriet N.	Horrocks, John	26, May 1836	X3
Gardner, Deborah	Giles, George B.	21, July 1827	R3
Gardner, Janette	Dunn, John	29, July 1826	J3
Gardner, Mary Jane	Smead, Wesley	8, Aug. 1823	N3
Garniss, Catharine J	Chase, Salmon P.	8, Mar. 1834	R3
Garniss, Catharine J	Chase, Salmon P.	8, Mar. 1834	T2
Garniss, Emma	Dean, Daniel	18, Apr. 1840	R3
Garrish, Sophia	Golding, Aaron	9, Mar. 1822	S2
Garrison, S.A.	Frazer, Samuel G.	18, Oct. 1838	T2
Gassaway, Elizabeth	Kennett, John	15, Nov. 1834	T2
Gassaway, Lucy Ann	Clay, Ralph A.	23, Oct. 1841	R3

Brides	Grooms	Date of Notice	Page
Gassaway, Lucy Ann	Clay, Ralph A.	16, Oct. 1841	N2
Gassman, Frederika	Groene, Ernst	9, Aug. 1850	Y2
Gasten, Sarah	Miller, David F.	15, Sept 1827	R3
Gatts, Sarah	Wallace, Nicholas	21, July 1827	R3
Gaylord, Hannah (Mrs)	Leitch, William	21, Apr. 1836	X3
Gazlay, Delia	Knight, Albert G.	16, Nov. 1832	X3
Gazlay, Huldah	Mills, Thornton A.	14, Sept 1837	X3
Gazlay, Huldah	Mills, Thornton (Rev)	16, Sept 1837	R3
Gazlay, Kerendah	Swing, David	19, Aug. 1825	N3
German, Anna M.	Gordon, William J.M.	8, Sept 1850	Y2
German, Rebecca	Smith, James B.	10, Apr. 1819	S3
Getz, Elizabeth	Smith, DeWitt Clint.	22, Oct. 1847	K2
Gibbs, C.H.	Dodd, James	26, Dec. 1840	R3
Gibbs, Mary P.	Parsell, George	8, Sept 1838	R3
Gibson, Alice	Coffin, Christopher	5, July 1830	A3
Gibson, Elizabeth W.	Rusk, Baltis	11, Feb. 1837	T2
Gibson, Ellen D.	Johnston, W. (Capt)	8, Nov. 1837	T2
Gibson, Jane	Strothers, Thomas	15, July 1835	T2
Gibson, Jennette	Richards, William	7, Feb. 1818	S3
Gibson, Mary B.	Wood, John H.	31, Jan. 1831	A3
Gibson, Mary B.	Wood, John H.	5, Feb. 1831	R3
Gibson, Mary B.	Wood, John H.	4, Feb. 1831	X3
Gibson, Sarah C.	Nourse, Michael	4, Dec. 1835	T3
Gill, Ann	Beeching, John	29, Mar. 1847	K2
Gill, Mary	Hanselman, Charles	18, Aug. 1852	P2
Gillespie, Clara B.	Wood, Clarkson F.	14, May 1842	R3
Gillespie, Mary	Chase, William F.	27, Oct. 1837	T2
Gilliams, Susan L.	Dugan, John A.	13, Oct. 1852	P2
Gillingham, Eliza	Gillingham, Harper	28, May 1842	R3
Gillingham, Eliza	Gillingham, Harper	24, May 1842	N2
Gilman, Barbara A.	Hoffman, Allen	8, Oct. 1847	K2
Gilman, Catharine	Wilson, Joseph B.	21, Mar. 1839	T2
Gilman, Mary	Tuttle, John F.	21, Apr. 1849	L2
Glancy, Josephine	Robinson, Henry H.	6, Jan. 1848	K2
Glanton, Elizabeth	Grover, Ira	18, Feb. 1823	N3
Glasgow, Mary	Davis, Joseph	28, Mar. 1823	N2
Glass, Sophia	Kanan, John	21, Aug. 1835	T2
Glore, Zorilda	Oglesby, Willis	2, Sept 1847	K2
Glover, Phoebe	Cambreleng, C.C.	30, Nov. 1835	T2
Goble, Elizabeth	Nicholson, Thomas	1, Oct. 1847	K2
Goddard, Catharine G	Leuba, Henry	8, Jan. 1831	R3
Goddard, Elizabeth	Cockerell, Francis M	23, Oct. 1841	R3
Goddard, Elizabeth M	Cockrell, Francis M.	25, Oct. 1841	N2
Goforth, Charlotte K.	Lewis, Samuel	8, Aug. 1823	N3
Goforth, Deborah (Mrs)	Gano, R.M. (Gen)	15, Nov. 1814	W4
Gogin, Rachel	Bachelor, William W.	29, July 1831	A3
Goodman, Frances P.	Wright, Sylvanus	4, Feb. 1825	N2
Goodman, Mary Jean	Holden, Amos P.	3, Aug. 1835	T2
Goodwin, Mary A.	Guyon, James	21, Dec. 1852	P2
Gorden, Anne	Bozarth, John	22, Apr. 1830	A3
Gordon, Julia (Mrs)	Harvey, Samuel	14, July 1852	P2
Gordon, Julia M.	Wheeler, Wilber B.	29, Dec. 1847	K2
Gorham, Julia	Whan, Jame	16, Jan. 1836	T3
Gorham, Mary Elizabeth	Ogden, Jonathan	27, Dec. 1834	R3

Brides	Grooms	Date of Notice	Page
Gorreal, Jane (Mrs)	Edwards, Isaac	9, Dec. 1852	P2
Goshorn, Mary Jane	Edwards, R.E.	21, Aug. 1852	P2
Gosling, Rachel	Witt, George	4, May 1850	P2
Gosman, Elizabeth (Mrs)	Olcott, E.K.	15, July 1852	P2
Gourgas, Louisa M.	Gourgas, J. Louis	23, Dec. 1840	N2
Gouverneur, Elizabeth K.	Heiskell, Henry Lee	25, June 1842	R3
Gove, Mary F.	Wayne, Joseph W.	6, Aug. 1852	P2
Gowdy, Jane	Childs, Mordecai	27, June 1829	R3
Gowers, Angeline	Schell, Lewis T.	24, Jan. 1835	T2
Graham, Jenny	Lawrence, Alfred A.	30, Nov. 1852	P2
Graham, Louisa	Price, Walter	6, Dec. 1852	P2
Graham, Lucy Ann	Hoole, Joseph	3, Mar. 1838	R3
Graham, Maria	Chauncey, John S.	28, Dec. 1838	T2
Graham, Rachel	Stinson, Charles	21, Oct. 1837	R3
Graham, Rachel	Stinson, Charles	16, Oct. 1837	T2
Graham, Sarah	Cook, John	27, June 1817	S2
Grandin, Hannah M.	Bates, Samuel R.	26, Mar. 1842	R3
Grandin, Lucy A.	Goodman, Augustus	8, July 1847	K2
Grandin, Mary E.	Orr, Thomas G. (Dr)	22, Dec. 1837	T2
Grant, Laura	Vanwey, Henry	26, Aug. 1831	X3
Grapevine, Eliza	Speer, Burnet V.	15, Mar. 1831	A3
Graves, Elizabeth S.	Goodhue, G.W.	1, May 1847	K2
Graw, Thirza	Chamberlain, J.D.	19, Sept 1817	S3
Gray, Amanda	Smith, Richard P.	4, Oct. 1830	A3
Gray, Jennet	Guthrie, Colin	16, Jan. 1819	S3
Grayson, M.E.	Bowman, William W.	30, Nov. 1847	K2
Green, Alvernon H.	Allen, L.S. (Dr)	25, Sept 1841	N2
Green, Clara	Spark, John	2, Dec. 1830	A3
Green, Eliza Ann	Hickman, Jesse	4, June 1842	R3
Green, Lucy Jane	Jacobs, William H.	19, May 1847	K2
Green, Mary M.	Keen, John	17, June 1837	R3
Green, Mary M.	Keene, John	15, June 1837	X3
Green, Nancy	Baker, Adam	27, Dec. 1825	N2
Greene, Alvernon H.	Allen, L.S. (Dr)	25, Sept 1841	R3
Greene, Ellen	Goodin, Samuel H.	12, Sept 1840	R3
Greene, Isabella M.	Jenckes, Joseph	18, May 1833	R3
Greene, Rebecca B.	Twichell, T.	6, Sept 1834	R3
Greene, Rebecca B.	Twichell, T.	4, Sept 1834	T2
Greene, Sophia	Burnet, George	28, May 1799	S3
Greenham, Rachel	Celcher, Lewis	28, Feb. 1838	N2
Gregar, Rebecca Ann	Conklin, John T.	15, Dec. 1852	P2
Gregory, Elizabeth	Johnson, Benjamin W.	5, Dec. 1817	S3
Gregory, Frances	Dyer, Elisha	6, Mar. 1841	R3
Gregory, Frances	Dyer, Isaac	4, Mar. 1841	N2
Gregory, Mary	Clarkson, William	17, May 1834	R3
Grey, Permelia	Barnes, John	11, Mar. 1831	X3
Gridley, Mary	Owens, Patrick	26, Apr. 1833	X3
Griffin, Charlotte	Hartzell, David A.	13, Dec. 1825	N3
Griffin, Mary	Furry, Daniel	28, May 1835	T2
Griffith, Mary B.	Preto, Francis	23, Feb. 1828	R3
Grigg, Harriet	Vorhes, Isaac	10, Apr. 1841	R3
Grimke, Angelina E.	Weld, Theodore D.	2, June 1838	R3
Grooms, Emily	Mathias, Jacob	29, Mar. 1828	R3
Grunnell, Helen Elizabeth	Milne, George	13, Sept 1847	K2

Brides	Grooms	Date of Notice	Page
Guest, Elizabeth	Reynolds, Benjamin B.	10, Mar. 1826	N3
Guest, Lydia Jane	McPike, John	11, Mar. 1820	S3
Guest, Lydia Jane	McPike, John	16, Mar. 1820	D3
Guest, Mary Ann	Reynolds, Sackett	23, Oct. 1819	S3
Guilford, Appeline	Donaldson, George	27, May 1847	K2
Guilford, Belle E.	Stewart, William S.	22, Nov. 1852	P2
Guy, Elizabeth	Morland, L.F.	16, May 1837	T2
Gwathmey, Matilda G.	Bates, John S.	20, Nov. 1835	T2
Gwilym, Hannah	Chidlaw, Benjamin	2, June 1836	X3
Gwynne, Lavinia M.	Andrews, John W.	13, Oct. 1835	T2
Haffley, Catharine	Earnest, Andrew	6, June 1817	S3
Hailman, Leah	Wandell, William	30, Aug. 1825	N2
Haines, Elizabeth S.	Lytle, Robert T.	6, Dec. 1825	N3
Haines, Joanna	Reilly, Thomas	14, Jan. 1832	R3
Haines, Mary Ann	Fletcher, Robert	27, Dec. 1834	R3
Hales, Clemima	Bender, George A.	19, Aug. 1830	A3
Hales, Isabella	Crouse, Jacob S.	17, Nov. 1827	R3
Hales, Isabella W.	Crouse, Jacob S.	16, Nov. 1827	N2
Hales, Jemima	Bender, George A.	21, Aug. 1830	R3
Hales, Margaret	Keller, Jacob	9, Oct. 1819	S3
Hall, (Miss)	Ogden, James	2, Jan. 1818	S3
Hall, Ann	Smith, Abial	24, May 1828	R2
Hall, Carolina C.B.	McGrew, Alex	10, Dec. 1840	N2
Hall, Hannah C.	Woolsey, William M.	8, Jan. 1830	N2
Hall, Hulda (Mrs)	Howel, Rozel P.	6, Nov. 1847	K2
Hall, Jane	Bell, Thomas	17, June 1851	P2
Hall, Martha	Higdon, Peter	6, Oct. 1827	R3
Hall, Martha	Higdon, Peter	5, Oct. 1827	N3
Halley, Mary Ann	Conn, John A.	30, Oct. 1841	N2
Hally, Mary Ann	Pinglee, E.M. (Rev)	17, Oct. 1840	R3
Haman, Esther Ann	Moore, Richard M.	22, Oct. 1831	R3
Hamilton, Adelaide	Williams, M.G.	27, June 1829	R3
Hamilton, Caroline	Stille, J.	20, May 1842	N2
Hamilton, Caroline T.	Stilli, John	21, May 1842	R3
Hamilton, Curtis	Benbridge, William T.	19, Sept 1829	R3
Hamilton, Juliana	Sayre, William	17, Feb. 1821	S1
Hamilton, Laura A.	Fuller, Robert C.	19, Apr. 1847	K2
Hamilton, Maria L.	Trotter, Daniel	6, Oct. 1832	R3
Hammitt, Hephziba	Russell, Joseph	2, June 1827	R3
Hammond, Alma	L'Hommedieu, Stephen	29, Apr. 1830	A3
Hammond, Alma	L'Hommedieu, Stephen	27, Apr. 1830	N3
Hampton, Martha A.	Sovereign, Daniel L.	1, Sept 1852	P2
Hampton, Sarah Jane	Attee, Charles	2, June 1847	K2
Handley, Margaret	Todhunter, Thomas	16, Feb. 1816	S3
Handy, Amelia C.	McGaughy, D.S. (Dr)	16, Mar. 1837	X3
Hanes, Ann	Cramer, John	20, Mar. 1835	N2
Hanford, M.E.	Perdicaris, Gregory	17, June 1837	R3
Hanford, M.E.	Perdicaris, Gregory	8, June 1837	T2
Hanford, Mary H.	Shelden, Moses	7, May 1842	R3
Hanford, Mary H.	Shelden, Moses	4, May 1842	N2
Hanker, Margaret	Pierson, George W.	1, Feb. 1839	T2
Hanks, Zerviah	Crane, Henry	20, Dec. 1838	T2
Hanna, Nancy	Cox, John	20, Dec. 1828	R3

Brides	Grooms	Date of Notice	Page
Hannis, Catharine	English, Isaac B.	19, May 1847	K2
Hansell, Jane W.	VanTuyl, Charles	14, June 1847	K2
Hanson, Mary	Gordon, Archibald	18, Sept 1830	R3
Harckless, Jane	Hageman, Christian	20, July 1803	S3
Hardenberger, Eliza	McCall, Edward R.	4, Oct. 1837	T2
Hardesty, Lucinda	Stout, Isaiah M.	7, Nov. 1840	R3
Hardesty, Rebeckah	Foot, Joseph	1, Jan. 1814	S3
Hardin, Elizabeth (Mrs)	Clay, Porter	22, Apr. 1830	A3
Hardin, Mary B.	McDonald, D.	8, Aug. 1835	T2
Harding, Cordelia	Rogers, Hiram	24, Aug. 1833	R3
Hardy, Isabella	Ogden, Lewis B.	12, June 1847	K2
Hargrave, Catharine	Haskett, William	17, May 1850	P2
Harper, Eliza Jane	Wear, John H.	6, June 1835	T2
Harper, Sarah J.	Starr, David L.	24, May 1849	L2
Harrigan, Emily J.	Keller, Thomas	22, Apr. 1847	K2
Harrington, Cath. M.	Cutter, Amos	20, June 1840	R3
Harris, Eliza	Long, William H.	9, Oct. 1852	P2
Harris, Rebecca	Shorthill, Thomas	28, May 1842	R3
Harris, Rebecca	Shorthill, Thomas	24, May 1842	N2
Harris, Sarah	Johnson, Andrew	25, Dec. 1813	S3
Harrison, Ann	Drake, Aaron	31, Mar. 1821	S3
Harrison, Anna J.	Taylor, W.H.H.	30, June 1836	X3
Harrison, Anna T.	Taylor, William H.H.	24, June 1836	T2
Harrison, Bessie S.	Eaton, George G.	3, June 1847	K2
Harrison, Betsey B.	Short, J. Cleves	2, July 1814	S3
Harrison, Isabella	Williams, Elmore	20, Sept 1816	S3
Harrison, Jane	Whiteman, Lewis	6, July 1842	N2
Harrison, Jane F.	Whiteman, Lewis	9, July 1842	R3
Harrison, Lucinda	Ingraham, Henry	23, Oct. 1841	R3
Harrison, Lucy S.	Este, David K.	2, Oct. 1819	S3
Harrison, Martha A.	Hicks, James	18, June 1842	R3
Harrison, Mary	Wiseman, John A.	3, Jan. 1826	N3
Harrison, Sallie P.	Rice, Eliphalet L.	31, Dec. 1847	K2
Harrison, Virginia	Castleman, David	2, Dec. 1824	E2
Harrison, Zebuline	Hunt, John	10, Dec. 1840	N2
Harrison, Zebulino A.	Hunt, John	19, Dec. 1840	R3
Harsha, Juliet	Briant, Silas	26, Aug. 1826	J3
Harsha, Lydia	Rittenhouse, Eli F.	21, Nov. 1818	S3
Hart, Carrie	Horton, Benjamin	3, Sept 1852	P2
Hart, Lydia A.	Gelvin, John	11, Nov. 1852	P2
Hartley, Rachel M.	Thompson, James K.	11, Sept 1841	N2
Hartman, Elizabeth	Hay, George	3, Apr. 1823	J2
Hartman, Sophia C.	Mather, Bartholomew	21, Aug. 1819	S3
Harton, Margaret	Parker, Samuel	8, Oct. 1852	P2
Hartzell, Elizabeth	Yeatman, Thomas H.	13, Feb. 1827	N3
Harvay, Martha	Terry, John	11, Sept 1819	S3
Harvey, Anna Eveline	Blakely, John S.	20, Aug. 1842	R3
Harvie, Cordelia M.	Andrews, Rupert R.	1, Dec. 1832	R3
Haskell, Elizabeth	Cadwell, George	16, Oct. 1841	R3
Haskell, Sarah Eliza	Morrill, Onslow	16, Oct. 1841	R3
Haskill, Sarah Eliza	Morrill, Onslow H.	9, Oct. 1841	V3
Hasselton, Rebecca	Williams, Thomas T.	1, Oct. 1850	Y2
Hastings, Louisa	Athearn, Prince A.	15, Nov. 1833	X3
Hastings, Mercy	Snyder, Isaac	31, Mar. 1821	S1

Brides	Grooms	Date of Notice	Page
Hastings, Sarah P.	Bushnell, A. Lee	13, Apr. 1837	X3
Hathaway, Harriet	Halley, Samuel B.	13, Nov. 1841	R3
Hathaway, Harriet	Halley, Samuel B.	11, Nov. 1841	N2
Hathhorne, Sarah	Perrine, Isaac B.	19, July 1833	X3
Hathorn, Susan	Peckenpaugh, M.S.	3, June 1847	K2
Haughton, Martha	Fox, John	20, Oct. 1821	S3
Hawkins, Louisa	Dunseth, Lewis	18, Apr. 1840	R3
Hawkins, Maria	Tratobas, Maurice	17, Mar. 1832	R3
Hawthorn, Rhoda	Mahew, Alexander	9, Dec. 1824	E2
Hay, Eulalie	Goforth, William G.	18, May 1820	S3
Hay, Nancy L.	Caswell, Daniel J.	27, Nov. 1819	S3
Hayden, Elenor	Elsrode, William	6, Oct. 1827	R3
Hayer, Abigail	Thomas, John R.	29, Dec. 1821	S3
Hayes, Charlotte	Neville, John (Lt)	29, Jan. 1842	R3
Hayford, Achsah (Mrs)	Elliott, Arthur	5, Nov. 1852	P2
Hayslip, S.A.	Snyder, M.J.	3, June 1847	K2
Haywood, Ann (Mrs)	Jones, Henry	3, Nov. 1827	R3
Haywood, Ann (Mrs)	Jones, Henry	2, Nov. 1827	N3
Hazleton, Clarissa	Irwin, B.J.	4, Nov. 1835	T2
Hearington, Eliza	D'Carteret, John H.	27, Apr. 1822	S3
Hearne, Netor	Stoughton, Samuel	25, Apr. 1818	S3
Heaslett, Mary	Burk, John	4, Jan. 1836	T3
Heaslett, Ruth A.	Grace, John William	14, Aug. 1841	N2
Heath, Eliza	Bailhache, John	10, Jan. 1817	S3
Heckwelder, Mary J.	Rucker, Henry L.	20, Apr. 1833	R3
Hedden, Esther C.	Walker, Jesse	18, July 1822	J3
Heffley, Mary	Carver, Henry	9, Dec. 1828	N2
Heffly, Mary	Carver, Henry	13, Dec. 1828	R3
Heiskell, Frances E.	Bryan, Timothy M.	26, July 1828	R3
Heiskell, Mary D.	Putnam, Rufus	9, Sept 1830	A3
Helmling, Sophia M.	Furst, Joseph	9, Oct. 1850	Y2
Hemphill, Jane (Mrs)	Gardner, Collin	6, July 1849	L2
Henderson, Ellen G.	Nimmo, Edward L.	21, May 1842	R3
Henderson, Ellen G.	Nimmo, Edward L.	21, May 1842	N2
Henderson, Emily	Craven, Thomas T.	2, May 1840	R3
Henderson, Maria	VanMatre, Daniel	4, May 1833	R3
Henderson, Sophia	Maxwell, Hugh B.	6, Oct. 1832	R3
Henry, Caroline	Logan, William	30, Jan. 1819	S3
Hepp, Mary Ann	Wesel, Francis	15, Jan. 1838	T2
Herringten, Harriet	Barnes, Charles (Dr)	1, Nov. 1834	R3
Herrington, Harriet	Barnes, Charles (Dr)	31, Oct. 1834	T2
Hertzog, Rachael W.	Cooke, George	29, Nov. 1830	A3
Heth, Sophia	Bryce, Robert	27, Sept 1852	P2
Hey, Ann	Corbin, William	27, Mar. 1819	S2
Heywood, Aurelia	McGrew, Alexander	14, Sept 1811	S3
Hice, Amelia	Tizzard, William B.	20, Mar. 1847	K2
Hicks, Frances Mary	Hicks, James	1, Nov. 1828	R3
Hicks, Frances Mary	Hicks, James	31, Oct. 1828	N2
Hicks, Luciann	Clark, William	7, Jan. 1832	R3
Higbee, Charlotte	Haines, E.S.	19, Nov. 1831	R3
Higbee, Theodosia W.	Eberle, Richard (Dr)	5, Dec. 1840	R3
Higbee, Theodosia W.	Eberle, Richard (Dr)	5, Dec. 1840	N2
Higgins, Levisa	Valiant, William A.	6, Sept 1852	P2
Higgins, Sarah	Weller, Tobias	11, Mar. 1831	X3

Brides	Grooms	Date of Notice	Page
Highland, Cedonia	Smith, Charles M.	27, Dec. 1828	R3
Hildreth, Silvia	Talbott, David L.	26, Dec. 1829	R3
Hiler, Nancy	Shaw, John	27, Aug. 1850	Y2
Hiler, Rebecca	Willey, George	27, Aug. 1850	Y2
Hill, Elizabeth	Jones, Thomas	9, July 1835	T2
Hill, Elon	Kinnear, Samuel	19, Apr. 1830	A3
Hill, Joanna	Trafton, Lysander B.	31, July 1841	V3
Hill, Susannah (Mrs)	Hadlock, James	1, Dec. 1847	K2
Hindle, Ann E.	Callahan, J.P.(Dr)	11, Sept 1847	K2
Hinkle, Elizabeth	Sheppard, B.R.	1, Apr. 1836	N2
Hinman, Mary H.	Wiley, Joseph H.	2, Sept 1847	K2
Hitchcock, Laura	McDonough, James T.	23, May 1840	R3
Hitchcock, Mary A.	Kelley, Julius	14, Apr. 1836	T2
Hoadley, Elizabeth	Wells, Charles	8, May 1850	P2
Hoadley, Mary R.	Johnson, Henry A.	9, July 1841	N2
Hoak, Margaret Ann	Brooks, Valentine	20, Jan. 1838	R3
Hoak, Margaret Ann	Brooks, Valentine	23, Jan. 1838	T2
Hoaps, Angeline	Ackerson, James	9, July 1814	S3
Hobart, Rebecca S.	Ives, Silliman (Rev)	11, Mar. 1825	N2
Hobbs, Laura W.	Hopkins, William R.	23, July 1842	R3
Hobbs, Laura W.	Hopkins, William R.	18, July 1842	N2
Hodgson, Elizabeth	Bolton, Samuel	6, Mar. 1819	S3
Hodgson, Mary Abby	Paddock, W.R.	10, Sept 1850	P2
Hodship, Mary I.	Goodhart, Richard	25, Dec. 1852	P2
Hoffman, Olympia	Sherrods, Calvin G.	5, Sept 1840	R3
Hoge, Elizabeth H.	Bishop, Samuel	16, Oct. 1841	R3
Holcomb, Delia S.	Voorhees, Abram P.	21, Apr. 1836	X3
Holcomb, Lorana A.	Mundy, William (Dr)	14, May 1847	K2
Hollingsworth, Elizabeth	Armstrong, J.Y.	24, June 1837	R3
Hollingsworth, Elizabeth	Armstrong, J.Y.	19, June 1837	T2
Holloway, Hannah	Frost, Edward L.	11, Aug. 1827	R3
Holmes, Sally	McNabb, William	18, Mar. 1831	X3
Holms, Frances Ellen	Twichell, John W.	4, Oct. 1836	T2
Hoops, Catharine	Woodruff, A.P.	2, Aug. 1834	T2
Hoops, Sarah Maria	Oliver, Robert	25, Mar. 1823	N3
Hoover, Lucy	Green, George	26, Dec. 1840	R3
Hoover, Lucy	Green, George	23, Dec. 1840	N2
Hopkins, Caroline	Neighbours, James S.	2, Sept 1825	N1
Hopkins, Julia A.	Kingsbury, Obadiah	12, Jan. 1830	N2
Hopkins, Mary W.	Morris, George P.	5, Apr. 1825	N3
Hopper, Hester Jane	Taber, William B.	9, Dec. 1830	A3
Hopper, Hester Jane	Taber, William B.	4, Dec. 1830	R3
Hopper, Jemima	Ernst, Franklin	22, May 1841	R3
Hopper, Jemima	Ernst, Franklin	21, May 1841	N2
Hopper, Margaret	Johnson, Lewis	4, Mar. 1837	R3
Hopple, Mary	Thomas, Joseph W.	23, Oct. 1841	R3
Hopple, Mary	Thomas, Joseph W.	29, Oct. 1841	N2
Hopson, Phebe Jane	Greenwood, Miles	24, Mar. 1836	T2
Hornblower, Joanna	Bell, Thomas	21, July 1827	R3
Hornblower, Joanna	Bell, Thomas	20, July 1827	N3
Horne, Mary	Oblinger, Christian	14, Jan. 1831	X3
Horne, Mary Ann	DeCoursey, Francis	7, June 1828	R3
Horner, Amelia	Baker, Nathan	8, Aug. 1840	R3
Horner, Sarah A.E.	Parson, Enoch	28, Oct. 1852	P2

Brides	Grooms	Date of Notice	Page
Horton, Caroline (Mrs)	Horton, Johiel	9, Sept 1852	P2
Horton, Sophia (Mrs)	Starbuck, John	27, July 1820	S3
Horton, Susan	Wiltberger, Jacob	6, June 1818	S3
Hotchkiss, Elizabeth	Connell, Silas	7, Mar. 1829	R3
House, Elizabeth	Morse, Benjamin F.	5, Apr. 1838	T2
House, Emeline	Barber, James H.	1, Nov. 1852	P2
House, Mary M.	French, John S.	30, Oct. 1852	P2
How, Susan C.	Collier, Allen	18, Sept 1852	P2
Howard, Aurelia	Kennedy, John H.	7, June 1828	R3
Howard, Elizabeth J.	Dorks, Joseph B.	19, Aug. 1850	P2
Howard, Mary Ann	Field, William R.	15, Sept 1827	R3
Howard, Mary Elizabeth	Tuite, Aaron G.	1, Mar. 1848	K2
Howe, Fanny T.	Williams, H.L.	11, Apr. 1840	R3
Howe, Martha (Mrs)	Pritchard, Richard	11, Jan. 1836	T3
Howel, Mary G.	Hall, Joseph	13, Nov. 1835	T2
Howell, Alice	Selmon, Garret	11, Dec. 1841	R3
Howell, Alice	Selmon, Garrit	7, Dec. 1841	N2
Howell, Anna Maria	Jones, Joseph H.	11, Nov. 1825	N2
Howell, Catharine	Lowndes, John	3, Jan. 1817	S3
Howell, Elizabeth	Thornton, Benjamin	18, May 1833	R3
Howell, Elizabeth C.	McCreary, James K.	13, Jan. 1838	R3
Hubbell, Catharine	Gano, John A.	5, Oct. 1822	S3
Hubbell, Jane	Hathaway, Henry	10, Mar. 1827	R3
Hubbell, Mary	Brown, Daniel	30, Dec. 1823	N3
Hubbert, Jannet C.	Craut, Henry	2, May 1840	R3
Hudson, Eunice Elizabeth	Williams, Miles	6, Dec. 1838	T3
Hudson, Jane	Dumas, John P.	3, Oct. 1850	P2
Hudson, Sarah	Kennady, James	14, Sept 1820	S3
Hueston, Matilda	Greenleaf, Samuel	5, Oct. 1822	S3
Huff, Ann	Shaw, Ira	21, July 1827	R3
Huff, Sarah	Sharp, James	17, Jan. 1829	R3
Huff, Sarah Jane	Palmer, Lewis H.	6, Aug. 1852	P2
Huffman, Mary Jane	Brown, Ethan	25, Aug. 1841	N2
Hughes, Harriet	Peak, William J.	23, Oct. 1852	P2
Hughes, Jane	O'Hara, William A.	16, May 1840	R3
Hughes, Rachel W.	Allen, Martin	15, Nov. 1852	P2
Hughes, Sarah (Mrs)	Tiley, Francis	14, Oct. 1841	N2
Hulbert, Mary	Coddington, G.W.	16, June 1849	L2
Hulbert, Parthina	Hiner, David	9, May 1829	R3
Hulburd, Mary Eliza	Moore, Augustus O.	8, Sept 1841	N2
Hull, Louisa Jane	Cake, Charles T.	12, Mar. 1839	T2
Humphreys, E.T.	Bates, Caleb	1, Feb. 1828	N3
Humphreys, Emiline M	Anderson, George L.	25, June 1842	R3
Humphreys, Susan (Mrs)	Moorhead, John (Dr)	18, Dec. 1830	R3
Humphries, Nancy C.	Evans, Daniel P.	21, July 1827	R3
Hunt, Elizabeth J.	Witham, Jefferson C.	1, Dec. 1852	P2
Hunt, Jane F.	Pendleton, Nathaniel	18, May 1820	S3
Hunt, Ruth	Edwards, Abraham (Dr)	3, July 1805	S3
Hunt, Sarah M.	Merry, Nathaniel A.	12, June 1847	K2
Hunt, Susan	Hare, Jacob	6, Mar. 1819	S3
Hunt, Susanna	Mott, Jonathan	24, Feb. 1820	D3
Hunt, Susannah	Boyer, Jacob	23, Nov. 1822	S3
Hunter, Elis. (Mrs)	Bishop, Samuel P.	16, Oct. 1841	V3
Hunter, Nancy	Tidball, John (Rev)	5, July 1828	R3

Brides	Grooms	Date of Notice	Page
Hunter, Sarah	Gardner, Charles Hy.	2, Jan. 1830	R3
Hurdus, Ann	Wheeler, George	17, Sept 1814	S3
Hurdus, Hannah	Conn, James	21, Nov. 1817	S3
Hurdus, Maria	Conant, E.L.	31, Oct. 1826	N3
Hurdus, Nancy	Wheeler, George	20, Sept 1814	W4
Huston, Deborah H.	Mears, Daniel H.	16, Oct. 1841	R3
Hutchinson, Ann	Adams, T.J.	5, July 1828	R3
Huzzey, Jane	Robins, Ephraim	14, Jan. 1832	R3
Ingraham, Elizabeth T.	Holbrook, D.B.	30, June 1836	T2
Ingraham, Sophia M.	Chase, Pailander (Rev)	17, July 1819	S3
Ingram, Hannah	Spinning, John	1, Jan. 1828	R3
Irwin, Elizabeth	Rush, Jacob	4, Jan. 1836	T3
Irwin, Elizabeth R.	Harrison, John Scott	20, Aug. 1831	R3
Irwin, Jane F.	Harrison, William H.	11, Mar. 1824	E3
Irwin, Jane Findlay	Harrison, William H.	9, Mar. 1824	N3
Irwin, Louisa	Whiteman, Lewis	14, May 1824	N2
Irwin, Mary M.	Howard, James N.	14, May 1842	R3
Irwin, Sarah (Mrs)	Eddy, John	12, July 1828	R3
Irwin, Sarah W.	Lodge, Caleb T.	16, Aug. 1828	R3
Israel, E.R. (Mrs)	Reynolds, James	26, May 1835	T3
Iuppenlatz, Louisa M.	Meriweather, James H	23, Sept 1835	T2
Jacks, Matilda	Robinson, Gabriel J.	26, July 1836	T2
Jackson, Alice Ann	Harris, John W.	30, Jan. 1841	R3
Jackson, Alice Ann	Harris, John W.	24, Jan. 1841	N2
Jackson, Ann	Geyer, John	7, May 1831	R3
Jackson, Elizabeth	Thomas, George	19, Feb. 1814	S3
Jackson, Josephine	Woodruff, Leonard	28, Sept 1850	Y2
Jackson, Mary Jane	Weatherby, Philip G.	2, Sept 1847	K2
Jackson, Olive	Clark, John	10, Nov. 1826	N3
Jackson, Rebecca	Noah, M.M.	18, Dec. 1827	N3
Jacobs, Ann E.	Faulkner, Jeremiah	14, Nov. 1840	R3
Jacobs, Julia (Mrs)	Green, Timothy	2, Dec. 1837	R3
James, Amanda M.	Wilson, J. Plume	5, Feb. 1848	K2
James, Anne	Pendleton, N.G.	22, May 1841	R3
James, Anne	Pendleton, N.G.	17, May 1841	N2
James, Catharine E.	Diddle, Ingersoll	31, Oct. 1840	R3
James, Deborah	Hammit, Joseph (Rev)	25, Sept 1841	R3
James, Elizabeth	Dunn, John	16, Oct. 1841	R3
James, Isabella M.	Banks, Lawrence S.	16, Aug. 1828	R3
James, Sophia Jane	Pratt, Daniel D.	14, Dec. 1839	R3
Jaudon, Elizabeth	Bakewell, William W.	7, Oct. 1847	K2
Jefferson, Hepsey	Wilkinson, Walter	15, Jan. 1814	S3
Jenkins, Louisa	Goshorn, John M.	12, Aug. 1835	T2
Jenkins, Martha Ann	Lee, Z. Collins	23, June 1837	T2
Jenks, Charlotte R.	Woodruff, Charles S.	9, Aug. 1841	N2
Jennings, Mary Ellen	Kennedy, G.W. (Rev)	19, Jan. 1837	X3
Jessup, Betsey	Cary, Robert	15, Jan. 1814	S3
Jester, Sarah	Franklin, Samuel	27, June 1829	R3
Jocelyn, Hannah	Jackson, John	5, Oct. 1820	S3
Jocelyn, Mary H.	Jackson, Charles	18, May 1822	S3
Johnson, Amelia (Mrs)	Morsell, James C.	19, Dec. 1823	N3
Johnson, Catharine	Anderson, James	30, Sept 1836	N2

Brides	Grooms	Date of Notice	Page
Johnson, Dorcas Ann	Rager, Jeremiah	9, July 1852	P2
Johnson, Elizabeth	Jones, John D.	30, Sept 1823	N3
Johnson, Isabella	Ware, Henry	9, Oct. 1847	K2
Johnson, Louisa D.	Selden, Alanson D.	21, Sept 1822	S3
Johnson, Louisa D.	Selden, Alvinson D.	26, Sept 1822	J3
Johnson, Lucretia K.	Harrison, John Scott	30, Dec. 1824	E3
Johnson, M.B.	Strickler, George W.	16, Nov. 1847	K2
Johnson, Margaret A.	Perry, George H.	18, Aug. 1852	P2
Johnson, Maria Ann	Bush, John E. (Dr)	4, Sept 1819	S3
Johnson, Mary	Barns, Samuel	9, Nov. 1839	R3
Johnson, Nancy	Carel, John	28, Mar. 1823	N2
Johnson, Nancy	Wynn, Daniel	29, Oct. 1814	S3
Johnson, Sarah	Morrow, Jeremiah	6, Jan. 1836	T3
Johnson, Sarah Jane	Adams, William H.	31, Aug. 1850	P2
Johnston, Elizabeth Ann	Farvin, Samuel W.	12, Nov. 1836	N2
Johnston, Jane	Eccles, Henry	1, July 1847	K2
Johnston, Mary Ann	Beresford, Benjamin	9, Sept 1836	T2
Johnston, Mary B.	Byrn, John	28, Dec. 1852	P2
Johnston, Nancy	Wilson, Samuel R.	27, Mar. 1841	N2
Johnston, Rachel	Reynolds, William	6, June 1836	T2
Johnston, Rachel	Reynolds, William A.	9, June 1836	X3
Johnston, Rebecca	Whiteman, James F.	23, May 1840	R3
Jolly, Elizabeth	Dearstine, John	2, Nov. 1835	T2
Jones, Ann	Graham, Samuel	7, Feb. 1829	R3
Jones, C.A.	Marsh, George A.	24, Sept 1847	K2
Jones, Catharine	Clinton, DeWitt	22, May 1819	S3
Jones, Christiana	Filley, Lucius L.	22, Mar. 1849	L2
Jones, Emily Albina	Irwin, Archibald	28, June 1828	R3
Jones, Emily W.	Adderman, Joseph P.	13, Aug. 1852	P2
Jones, Harriet	Black, Mahlon	30, Jan. 1839	T2
Jones, Louisa	Thomas, Benjamin	4, Oct. 1852	P2
Jones, Maria A.	Morrow, R.A.	17, Nov. 1852	P2
Jones, Marian	Rinear, William	15, Dec. 1827	R3
Jones, Marie A.	Morrow, Robert A.	15, Nov. 1852	P2
Jones, Martha Ann	Sykes, Charles	29, Mar. 1849	L2
Jones, Mary F.	Burt, Moses	30, May 1835	T2
Jones, Sarah	Dalton, George W.	30, Aug. 1852	P2
Joor, Nancy	Haile, William	7, July 1827	R3
Jordan, M. (Mrs)	Potts, Alfred (Dr)	25, Sept 1852	P2
Joseph, Clarissa	Lewisson, Charles	2, July 1842	R3
Judd, Harriet	Dockstader, Nicholas	5, July 1828	R3
Judd, Julia	Starkweather, Samuel	5, July 1828	R3
Judkins, Sarah R.	Comly, William F.	21, Oct. 1836	T2
Judkins, Sarah R.	Comly, William F.	22, Oct. 1836	N2
Jungman, Anna S.	Hanes, Albert S.	6, May 1847	K2
Justice, Catharine E	Coffin, Zebulon B.	19, Oct. 1839	R3
Kain, Mary S.	Hampton, William	15, Apr. 1847	K2
Kantz, Barbara E.	Racine, James F.	15, Oct. 1847	K2
Karrack, Catharine	Foster, Joseph C.	28, June 1828	R3
Keating, Margaret	James, Joseph Junius	7, July 1826	N3
Keating, Maria	Spencer, Samuel A.	24, Feb. 1841	N2
Keef, Mary	Enyart, Thomas	16, Oct. 1819	S3
Kellogg, Almira S.	Davis, Henry F.	14, Mar. 1840	R3

Brides	Grooms	Date of Notice	Page
Kellogg, Frances A.	Mahaffey, Robert	8, Sept 1852	P2
Kelly, Jane	Murphy, Peter	1, Dec. 1815	S3
Kelly, Jane	Nashee, George	14, Aug. 1819	S3
Kelly, Maria	Bates, James L.	4, Nov. 1837	R3
Kelly, Susan A.	Good, Robert	2, Nov. 1839	R3
Kelly, Susan H.	Winchester, C.C.	23, Nov. 1852	P2
Kelpan, Mary Jane	Gibbs, Edward G.	16, Oct. 1841	R3
Kelpan, Mary Jane	Gibbs, Edward G.	16, Oct. 1841	N2
Kelsey, Rosetta C.	Wilson, J.B.	17, Oct. 1840	R3
Kemper, Frances	Graves, Joseph S.	18, June 1842	R3
Kemper, Frances	Graves, Joseph S.	16, June 1842	N2
Kemper, Harriet	Hoffman, Henry	4, Nov. 1852	P2
Kemper, Judith E.	Nelson, James A.	3, Nov. 1836	X3
Kemper, Martha Ann	Vandegriff, D.C.	13, June 1840	R3
Kemper, Mary D.	Easton, E.	29, Oct. 1831	R3
Kemper, Susan M.	Ferguson, Abijah F.	22, Mar. 1816	S3
Kendall, Samantha	Colby, George W.	22, Nov. 1851	P2
Kendall, Susan Ann	Lovelace, Seneca	25, Dec. 1841	R3
Kennedy, Bridgett	Clayton, John	9, Nov. 1852	P2
Kennedy, Mary	Reeder, Jesse	18, May 1807	S3
Kent, Elizabeth	Lyon, James M.	5, Jan. 1833	R3
Kent, Imogene	Shires, William	22, Oct. 1852	P2
Kent, Martha	Allan, Abraham W.	13, June 1829	R3
Kenyon, Caroline	Brady, Willis	5, Sept 1840	R3
Kerchner, Sarah	Diel, Jacob	4, Feb. 1831	X3
Key, Cecilia	Aubery, Henry S.	17, July 1841	R3
Keys, Jane B.	Sterrett, Benjamin	7, June 1830	A3
Keys, Jane B.	Sterrett, Benjamin	5, June 1830	R3
Keys, Mary	Wilson, William B.	14, Apr. 1827	R3
Keys, Mary Ann	Lardner, Henry (Dr)	1, Sept 1838	T2
Keyser, Elizabeth	Urner, Benjamin	11, Nov. 1825	N2
Keyser, Mary Ann	Benson, Matthew	28, Dec. 1820	S3
Kidd, Susan	Hollingsworth, Ed.	29, Nov. 1852	P2
Kieth, Sarah Jane	Mager, John	11, Nov. 1852	P2
Kilbourne, Mary R.	Thorp, F.S. (Dr)	2, Apr. 1842	R3
Kilbourne, Orril	Whiting, Isaac N.	15, Sept 1835	T2
Kiles, Sarah Ann	Shipley, Joseph	26, Aug. 1825	N3
Kilgallen, Mary	McKeown, Michael	30, Aug. 1850	Y2
Kilgour, Catharine	Springer, Charles G.	9, May 1840	R3
Kilgour, Jemima	Smith, Moses	15, Mar. 1831	A3
Kilgour, Juliana (Mrs)	Dewitt, G.V.H.	7, Jan. 1832	R3
Kimball, Fanny	Mullen, Jonathan	30, June 1832	R3
Kimball, Fanny	Mullen, Jonathan	29, June 1832	X3
Kincade, Anna Maria	High, George M.	23, Oct. 1852	P2
King, Eliza R.	French, Ezra P.	18, Apr. 1829	R3
King, Elizabeth	Proctor, Newton L.	1, Jan. 1828	R3
King, Elizabeth	Proctor, Newton T.	25, Dec. 1827	N3
King, Margaret	Kerns, Robert	27, Nov. 1852	P2
King, Mary	Baker, William W.	28, May 1842	R3
King, Mary	Baker, William W.	21, May 1842	N2
King, Mary	Pilling, Matthias J.	29, Oct. 1852	P2
Kinkead, Prudence B.	Wilson, J.C. (Dr)	9, Sept 1835	T2
Kinney, Elizabeth	Ross, S.R.	11, Sept 1847	K2
Kirby, Jane	Lemaire, Isaac K.	13, Oct. 1847	K2

Brides	Grooms	Date of Notice	Page
Kirby, Louise	Piatt, Donn	15, Oct. 1847	K2
Kirk, Margaret E.	Greene, John A.	14, May 1842	R3
Kirker, Mary	Voorhees, Ralph M.	20, Apr. 1824	N3
Kirker, Mary	Voorhees, Ralph M.	22, Apr. 1824	E3
Knoblaugh, Eliza Ann	Kelly, John	13, Nov. 1841	R3
Knox, Mary Ann	Kernes, Samuel	11, Oct. 1828	R3
Koblaugh, Eliza Ann	Kelly, John	12, Nov. 1841	N2
Konigmacher, Susan	Kimber, Samuel	9, June 1835	N2
Kotts, Pheby	Farran, Charles	8, May 1805	S3
Kountz, Martha A.	Smith, Franklin C.	31, Dec. 1852	P2
Krouskop, Sarah	Henry, James	23, May 1835	T2
Kugler, Sarah	Ogg, Joel	29, Sept 1836	T2
Kuhn, Sarah (Mrs)	Rose, Erasmus (Dr)	10, Apr. 1849	L2
Ladley, Lydia Ann	Cottam, Richard	2, Oct. 1841	R3
Ladley, Lydia Ann	Cottam, Richard	27, Sept 1841	N2
Laing, Matilda	Rankin, William	3, Nov. 1847	K2
Laird, Anna G.	Folger, George M.	22, May 1847	K2
Lamb, Aravesta	Lyon, Richard	29, Sept 1829	N3
Lamb, Elizabeth	Smith, William H.	22, Mar. 1849	L2
Lamb, Esther	Cook, Amasa	4, May 1830	N3
Lamb, Rebecca	Lyon, Stephen	7, Mar. 1817	S2
Lambdin, Eliza	Row, Conrad	23, Mar. 1822	S3
Lancaster, C. Jane	Porter, Patrick E.	18, Aug. 1852	P2
Landrum, V. Minnie	Bradley, William P.	27, Nov. 1852	P2
Lane, Ann	Buell, George P.	25, June 1824	N2
Lane, Margaret	Rogers, M. (Dr)	23, Apr. 1831	R3
Lane, Mary	Burke, William (Rev)	20, Aug. 1842	R3
Lane, Sarah S.	Glasgow, William	25, Apr. 1840	R3
Lang, Mary J.	Schenck, O.H.	9, June 1835	T2
Langdon, Cynthia	Morrill, H.E. (Dr)	13, Nov. 1841	R3
Langdon, Cynthia	Morrill, H.E. (Dr)	13, Nov. 1841	N2
Langdon, Esther Ann	Goodman, Henry H.	5, Dec. 1840	R3
Langdon, Harrette	Williams, C.H. (Rev)	31, Aug. 1852	P2
Langdon, Mary	Bishop, Truman (Rev)	20, Jan. 1821	S3
Langdon, Mary Jane	Bateman, William D.	20, Aug. 1842	R3
Langdon, Mary Jane	Bateman, William D.	17, Aug. 1842	N2
Langdon, Mary Jane	Young, Joseph G.	6, Feb. 1841	N2
Langdon, Olive	Reeder, Joseph A.	4, Apr. 1818	S3
Langeville, Jane P.	Dawson, Washington	29, Apr. 1820	S3
Langhorn, Sarah Bell	Walker, Henry	13, May 1837	T2
Langhorne, Elizabeth	Green, William N.	17, Nov. 1840	N2
Langhorne, Elizabeth	Stockwell, Allen M.	9, Apr. 1836	T2
Langlands, Janet	Thompson, John	24, Mar. 1837	T2
Langley, Margaret E.	Briddell, John A.	23, Oct. 1852	P2
Langton, M.M. (Mrs)	Lyon, Edward	15, July 1835	T2
Lanman, Harriet	Piatt, J.W.	22, Nov. 1831	A3
Lanman, Sarah C.	Harman, Josiah	21, Oct. 1830	A3
Lanphear, Roda Ann	Pangburn, Oliver	28, Dec. 1852	P2
Lansdale, Martha	Reynolds, R.S.	12, Sept 1823	N3
Lape, Sarah M.	Rammelsberg, Fred.	23, Apr. 1842	R3
Lape, Sarah M.	Rammelsberg, Fred.	28, Apr. 1842	N2
Lapp, Mary Ann	Davis, E.P.	26, Aug. 1847	K2
Larison, Elizabeth	Hinman, Arnold	20, Sept 1814	W4

Brides	Grooms	Date of Notice	Page
Lashley, Polly	Jordon, Martin	7, July 1827	R3
Latham, Catharine A.	Burton, Robert (Capt)	7, Oct. 1837	N2
Lattimore, Isabella	Thomas, John	15, Oct. 1852	P2
Laverty, Alice B.	Butler, Joseph C.	2, Sept 1847	K2
Laverty, Esther Ann	Catlett, Fairfax	28, May 1838	T2
Laverty, Honora U.	Hilton, George H.	25, June 1842	R3
Laverty, Honora U.	Hilton, George H.	22, June 1842	N2
Law, Hannah	Shields, Timothy S.	29, Dec. 1838	T2
Lawrence, Amanda R.	Meeker, Hervey	25, Oct. 1825	N3
Lawrence, Ann B.	Jones, John T.	30, June 1821	S3
Lawrence, Arabella	Waldo, F.A. (Dr)	18, Jan. 1833	X3
Lawrence, Arabella H	Waldo, Fred. Aug. (Dr)	19, Jan. 1833	R3
Lawrence, Eliza	Griffith, David	19, Dec. 1834	X3
Lawrence, Hannah	Gale, John H.	24, June 1837	R3
Lawrence, Hannah	Gale, John H.	19, June 1837	T2
Lawrence, Hannah	Gale, John H.	17, June 1837	N2
Lawrence, Harriet O.	Lupton, D.B.	4, Feb. 1836	T3
Lawrence, Margaret	McCullough, John	26, Sept 1840	R3
Lawrence, Mary Ann	Randall, John	27, Oct. 1852	P2
Lawrence, Mary Elizabeth	Richardson, Samuel	22, Sept 1847	K2
Lawrence, Mary N.	Griffin, William P.	14, May 1838	T2
Lawrence, Philian	Donelson, Stackly	12, July 1828	R3
Lawrence, Rebecca	Gano, Daniel (Major)	27, Sept 1816	S3
Laws, Amelia	Brashears, Gassaway	2, Jan. 1837	T2
Laws, Amelia C.	Brashears, Gassaway	31, Dec. 1836	N2
Lawson, Hannah	Sargeant, C.H.	17, June 1842	N2
Lawson, Maria	Shane, William	2, June 1827	R3
Lea, Margaret	Houston, Samuel	6, June 1840	R3
Lea, Susan G.	Jaudon, William L.	28, Nov. 1823	N2
Leach, Rebecca	Cassat, Dennis	4, May 1830	N3
Leach, Sarah (Mrs)	Sambert, James	29, Apr. 1831	X3
LeBerteaux, Frances	Tuttle, Oliver S.	14, Apr. 1836	X3
Lee, Anna	Hartwell, John W.	14, Dec. 1841	N2
Lee, Catharine	Browne, Thomas V.	7, Oct. 1852	P2
Lee, S.	Livezey, J.W.	1, Jan. 1853	P2
Leech, Sarah	Dobson, Benjamin	22, Apr. 1847	K2
Leeds, Eliza	Cotty, William	3, Mar. 1849	L2
Legg, Jane	Bragg, Willis N.	6, Oct. 1827	R3
Legg, Mary Ann	Hughes, Joshua	22, Dec. 1847	K2
Lehmanowsky, Ann S.	Distin, William L.	14, Sept 1837	T2
Lehmanowsky, Anna S.	Disten, William L.	21, Sept 1837	X3
Lehmanowsky, Anna S.	Distin, William L.	16, Sept 1837	R3
Leice, Jane (Mrs)	Higbee, Ira B.	5, July 1850	P2
Leigh, Mary Susan	Robinson, Conway	26, July 1836	T2
Lemens, Elizabeth	Spahr, Benjamin	25, July 1850	P2
Lemond, Anna	Crawford, Robert	20, June 1817	S3
Leonard, Ann J.	Rlake, A. (Rev)	11, Sept 1841	V3
Leonard, Sarah	Spooner, Thomas	17, Sept 1842	R3
Lepel, Josephine	Silrerman, D.	28, Sept 1852	P2
Lethbridge, Hepsy	Sampson, Calvin	8, Aug. 1818	S3
Leverett, Charlotte (Mrs)	Robbins, Daniel P.	19, June 1819	S2
Levi, Sarah	Moses, S.	22, Oct. 1836	N2
Levi, Sarah	Moses, Solomon	25, Oct. 1836	T2
Levingston, Jane Ann	Delaplaine, Joseph	7, Oct. 1812	S3

Brides	Grooms	Date of Notice	Page
Lewis, Eliza W.	Torbet, N.H. (Dr)	1, Dec. 1832	R3
Lewis, Margaretta E.	Jones, Ephraim	23, Feb. 1828	R3
Lewis, Margaretta E.	Jones, Ephraim	22, Feb. 1828	N3
Lewis, Margaretta E.	Jones, Ephraim	22, Feb. 1828	Q3
Lewis, Margery J.	Kenna, Edward	23, June 1847	K2
Lewis, Mary H.	McClure, James	10, Nov. 1826	N3
Lewis, Rosana T.	Wilson, Timothy H.	22, Mar. 1829	R3
Lewis, Sarah A.	Stickney, Daniel	1, June 1847	K2
L'Hommedieu, Sarah	Lindley, Abraham	2, Mar. 1822	S3
Lightfoot, Ann	Messenger, Asa	14, Jan. 1836	T3
Lincoln, Louisa	Robinson, A.F.	16, Aug. 1830	A3
Lindley, Joanna	Parker, J.A. (Dr)	17, Oct. 1823	N2
Lindsay, Catharine	Ward, Charles (Lt)	8, May 1819	S3
Lindsay, Virginia	Lewis, Hickman	4, Sept 1835	T2
Lines, Mary	Dagget, David	23, May 1840	R3
Lingo, Mary	Williams, Noah	19, Nov. 1831	R3
Linn, Martha	Goblo, Daniel L.	4, July 1834	X3
Linsley, Phoebe Ann	Sprague, Darius	8, Nov. 1852	P2
Linville, Jane	Foos, Thomas J.	3, Sept 1847	K2
Litchfield, Mary F.	Duffield, S.B.	14, May 1842	R3
Litherbury, Nett	Cummings, J.P.	8, Oct. 1852	P2
Little, Mary	Marsh, David	5, Sept 1840	R3
Little, Rachel	Richardson, J.	22, Apr. 1830	A3
Littleford, Mary	McMillan, Andrew	7, June 1828	R3
Livingston, Eliza D.	Thompson, Smith	17, Dec. 1836	T2
Lloyd, Eleanor H.	Richards, Giles	2, Nov. 1820	S3
Lloyd, Louisa Mat.	Lawrence, G.F.	23, Oct. 1835	T2
Lockwood, Missouri M.	Porter, John J.	20, Jan. 1826	N1
Loder, Hannah	Ogden, Thomas	15, Dec. 1815	S3
Long, Agnes	Kinder, William R.	16, Oct. 1852	P2
Long, Elizabeth	Woodman, John	31, Aug. 1820	S3
Longbrake, Elizabeth	Parks, James	22, Apr. 1830	A3
Longly, Patty	Roe, Daniel	28, Dec. 1807	S3
Longshore, Rachel C.	Giles, Benjamin	30, Oct. 1847	K2
Longstreet, Josephin	Chipman, W. Douglass	8, Nov. 1851	P2
Longworth, Charlotte	Jones, William D.	17, Mar. 1821	S3
Longworth, Mary	Stettinius, John	22, July 1830	A3
Looker, Catharine	Bonnell, Allison B.	4, Nov. 1835	T2
Looker, Eliza	Harrison, William	3, Aug. 1830	N2
Looker, Emmeline	Romeril, Charles E.	14, Apr. 1826	N3
Looker, Maria	Hopkins, William	24, Dec. 1824	N3
Looker, Pamela C.	Pharis, Washington	11, Apr. 1812	S2
Looker, Rachael H.	Looker, James H.	27, Dec. 1828	R3
Looker, Rachel (Mrs)	Looker, James H.	26, Dec. 1828	N3
Looker, Rachel B.	Leonard, Nathaniel	5, Sept 1840	R3
Lorimer, Virginia (Mrs)	Lynch, Micajah T.	29, Oct. 1841	N2
Loring, Eliza B.	Anderson, Charles R.	28, May 1842	R3
Loring, Eliza B.	Anderson, Charles R.	26, May 1842	N2
Loring, Georgiana	Hooker, Edward	25, Dec. 1852	P2
Loring, Harriet W.	Corwin, Daniel W.	20, Jan. 1838	R3
Loring, Harriet W.	Corwin, Daniel W.	23, Jan. 1838	T2
Loring, Jane	Foote, James M.	23, Nov. 1835	T2
Loring, Jane	Foote, James M.	26, Nov. 1835	X3
Loring, Jerusha	McKnight, John	15, Nov. 1833	X3

Brides	Grooms	Date of Notice	Page
Loring, Susan M.	Hinsdale, John T.	5, Dec. 1836	T2
Loring, Susan M.	Hinsdale, John T.	8, Dec. 1836	X3
Loury, Mary P.	Davis, S.H.	7, Apr. 1834	T2
Love, Mary Ann (Mrs)	Spear, William	29, Oct. 1814	S3
Lovejoy, Ann	Jackson, Henry S.	2, Dec. 1824	E2
Lovejoy, Mary	Green, Stephen A.	8, June 1847	K2
Lovejoy, Mary (Mrs)	Schillinger, William	28, Oct. 1836	N2
Lovejoy, Mary E.	Robinson, Thomas G.	30, July 1852	P2
Lovell, Clarissa	Smith, William S.	18, Oct. 1828	R3
Lovell, Jane Ann	Bradbury, E.H. (Dr)	6, Dec. 1830	A3
Low, Mary G.	Beall, William B.	26, Oct. 1822	S3
Lowry, Martha	Tagart, Mathew	26, May 1832	R3
Lucas, Mary Ann	Molin, James	9, July 1838	T2
Luckey, Catharine M.	Ranney, Moses	11, Mar. 1837	N2
Lucky, Catharine M.	Ranney, Moses	11, Mar. 1837	R3
Ludlow, Eliza H.	Wirtz, J.B.	16, May 1840	R3
Ludlow, Sarabella	Garrard, Jeptha D.	19, Aug. 1824	E3
Luffborough, Eliza	Bohrer, Benjamin S.	26, Oct. 1820	S3
Luke, Ann M.	Anderson, Pierce B.	29, Nov. 1828	R3
Luke, Margaret	Clarke, William	16, July 1834	T2
Luke, Mary	King, John	22, Nov. 1834	R3
Luke, Mary	King, John	19, Nov. 1834	T2
Lumb, Ann	Henderson, William R.	2, Nov. 1835	T2
Lumley, Mary	Anderson, Evan	2, Oct. 1841	R3
Lumley, Mary	Anderson, Evan	4, Oct. 1841	N2
Lummis, Rebecca	Coleman, George	30, June 1827	R3
Lundy, Nancy (Mrs)	McGrew, James	19, Mar. 1849	L2
Luster, Hannah	Coleman, John M.	3, Nov. 1838	T2
Luster, Susan F.	Curd, John E.	9, Sept 1837	T2
Lyall, Jane Eliza	Howell, Daniel G.	29, Aug. 1818	S3
Lyman, Charlotte	Silsbee, William (Rev)	24, Mar. 1838	R3
Lyman, Nancy	Picket, Charles (Dr)	12, Feb. 1820	S3
Lyman, Sarah P.	Dana, Charles D.	16, June 1832	R3
Lynch, Anna M.	Bogart, John E.	1, Sept 1847	K2
Lynch, Anna M.	Carroll, Foster	25, Oct. 1850	Y2
Lynch, Mary H.	Bolton, William C.	10, June 1842	N2
Lyon, Elizabeth W.	Taylor, Mahlon R.	5, Dec. 1836	T2
Lyon, Elizabeth W.	Taylor, Mahlon R.	4, Dec. 1836	N2
Lyon, Sarah	Clingman, Enoch G.	16, Nov. 1839	R3
Lytle, Eliza Ann	MacAlester, Charles	21, Oct. 1824	E3
Lytle, Mary	Sill, Shadrach	26, Aug. 1830	A3
Macalister, Elizabeth	Lathrop, Frank W.	7, June 1828	R3
Mackey, Maria (Mrs)	Crawson, James	24, Aug. 1811	S3
Mackie, Jessie	Prescott, T.O. (Rev)	13, July 1849	L2
Macon, Malvina	Cary, Freeman G.	12, Apr. 1833	X3
Madeira, Harriet	Burbridge, Rowland	25, Nov. 1837	R3
Madin, Rachel B.	Crosby, B.	24, Nov. 1832	R3
Madin, Sarah B.	Gallagher, Francis	24, Nov. 1832	R3
Maffit, Eliza Jane	Budd, T.L.	14, Dec. 1839	R3
Maffit, Matilda	Johnson, Robert D.	27, Sept 1841	N2
Magie, Rhoda M.	Elliott, Silas H.	23, Feb. 1835	T2
Magowan, Catharine T	Burt, John S. Gano	28, Dec. 1841	N3
Mahard, Esther	Donough, John P.	7, Nov. 1835	T2

Brides	Grooms	Date of Notice	Page
Mahew, Hannah	Dunbar, Seth	8, June 1820	S3
Make, Mary	Covert, Jeremiah	9, Aug. 1814	W3
Malatt, Mary	Brellsford, Timothy	11, July 1835	T2
Man, Mary E.	Combs, Leslie	21, Apr. 1849	L2
Manahan, Dorcas	Knowlton, Sherman	15, May 1847	K2
Manfort, Anna	Hay, Benajah S.	3, July 1813	S3
Maning, Jemima	Foulks, George W.	26, Oct. 1847	K2
Mankey, Mary	Wiseman, John A.	24, Oct. 1835	T2
Mankey, Sarah	Wiseman, John A.	26, Oct. 1835	N2
Mann, Catharine W.	Ackerman, Richard	8, June 1841	N2
Mann, Mary Davis	Allen, William H.	23, Mar. 1841	N2
Manning, Ellen	Prideham, Lawrence S.	20, Nov. 1852	P2
Manser, Mary A.	Keckeler, Theophilus	15, July 1852	P2
Mansfield, Mary C.	Wade, David	20, June 1812	S3
Manson, Sophiah	Dale, Richard C.	6, Mar. 1819	S3
Maranda, Priscilla	Andrews, Charles	9, Oct. 1841	R3
Maranda, Priscilla	Andrews, Charles S.	8, Oct. 1841	N2
Marchant, Catharine	Barwise, John	11, Nov. 1831	X3
Marks, Louisa	Reemelin, Charles	6, Oct. 1837	T2
Marks, Miriam	Spatz, Bernard	22, Jan. 1842	R3
Marsden, Elizabeth	Hoffner, Jacob	8, June 1820	S3
Marsh, Ann Eliza	Hopper, Jonathan	9, Dec. 1824	E2
Marsh, Hannah M.	Taylor, E.	25, Dec. 1835	T3
Marsh, Hannah M.	Taylor, Eli	24, Dec. 1835	X3
Marsh, Lydia	Haines, Josiah	10, Feb. 1821	S2
Marsh, Miranda	Wells, Oliver	2, Sept 1826	J3
Marsh, Rachael A.	Leslie, James	16, July 1852	P2
Marshall, Harriet	Armstrong, John	1, Nov. 1838	N2
Marshall, Louisa	Kennedy, John	18, Oct. 1837	T2
Marshall, Louisa	Kennedy, John	18, Oct. 1837	N3
Martin, Almira	Robinson, John C.	19, Mar. 1849	L2
Martin, Charlotte C.	Ware, Samuel W.	4, Feb. 1832	R3
Martin, Charlotte S.	Ritchie, James (Dr)	13, Aug. 1831	R3
Martin, Eliza	Cozzens, Brown	17, May 1828	R3
Martin, Eliza D.	Knight, Henry W.	5, Sept 1835	T2
Martin, Eliza D.	Knight, Henry W.	4, Sept 1835	X3
Martin, Elizabeth	Neave, Thompson	25, Oct. 1816	S3
Martin, Laura Attila	Fuller, Robert C.	19, Apr. 1847	K2
Martin, Louisa	Prather, James	2, Dec. 1824	E2
Martin, Maria	Hambrock, J.H.	25, Oct. 1851	P2
Martin, Maria (Mrs)	Swasey, Moses	31, Oct. 1840	R3
Martin, Mary	Winston, Samuel	4, May 1822	S3
Martin, Mary Ann	Phillips, Isaac	30, Nov. 1852	P2
Martin, Sarah	Pugh, Job	19, Sept 1818	S3
Martin, Sarah Ellen	VanEaton, Isaac	29, Aug. 1835	T2
Mason, E.S.	Spangenberg, L.A.	23, June 1847	K2
Masson, Kate	Kellum, C.B.	30, Aug. 1850	Y2
Masterson, Letitia	Bell, Samuel L.	9, Aug. 1841	N2
Mathews, Alicia A.	Bakewell, W.G.	29, Nov. 1828	R3
Matson, Fredonia M.	Silvers, F.G.	20, June 1840	R3
Matson, Mary A.	Whipple, A. (Dr)	19, Oct. 1836	T2
Matson, Mary A.	Whipple, A. (Dr)	13, Oct. 1836	X3
Matthews, Eliza V.	Goforth, Thomas J.	17, Mar. 1826	N3
Maxwell, Ann	Meeks, John (Lt)	14, May 1814	S3

Brides	Grooms	Date of Notice	Page
Mayhew, Aceneth	Stephens, Ephraim M.	9, June 1827	R3
Mayhew, Aceneth	Stephens, Ephraim M.	8, June 1827	N3
Mayhew, Harriet	Williams, James P.	24, Mar. 1829	N2
Mayhew, Rebecca	Davidson, George	2, May 1828	N3
Maynadr, Lucinda	Clowser, Andrew	25, Dec. 1852	P2
Mayo, Ann (Mrs)	Mayo, Benjamin	21, Sept 1837	T2
Maywood, Mary	Stanley, George S.	22, June 1849	L2
McAnnally, Bridget	Brieker, David	2, Sept 1852	P2
McAroy, Mary B.	Haggott, John P.	11, Nov. 1837	R3
McArthur, Elizabeth	Pritchard, James	2, May 1840	R3
McArthur, Mary	Trimble, Cary A.	6, Jan. 1838	R3
McArthur, Mary	Trimble, Cary A.	5, Jan. 1838	T2
McCall, Mary A.	Walter, William	25, June 1842	R3
McCandles, Mary	McCracken, J.B.	13, Oct. 1835	T2
McCane, Sarah	Murphy, Archibald	4, Feb. 1825	N2
McCann, Rosella Ann	Hatchler, John	20, Aug. 1847	K2
McCarty, Martha	Bailey, Andrew	30, Apr. 1814	S3
McCauley, Lucinda	Ball, Daniel	25, Feb. 1831	X3
McCawley, Elizabeth	Keys, William	18, Sept 1847	K2
McChesney, Eliza	Hubbell, Nathaniel S	8, Aug. 1818	S3
McChisne, Helen	Poland,	2, Jan. 1818	S3
McClean, Arabella E.	Weed, E.J.	14, Apr. 1827	R3
McClure, Frances S.	Carter, Samuel	22, Sept 1821	S3
McClure, Maria	Bradley, Samuel H.	11, Dec. 1841	R3
McConn, Mary E.	Nuckols, William W.	30, Dec. 1852	P2
McConnell, Amanda M.	Horne, John R.	28, May 1842	R3
McCoppin, Ann	Keys, William	17, Nov. 1827	R3
McCormick, Jane	Wade, Joseph	17, Oct. 1840	R3
McCormick, Margery	Smith, Samuel S.	2, Sept 1826	J3
McCracken, Sarah	Heard, John W.	7, Aug. 1841	R3
McCreary, Elizabeth	Sterrett, A.	3, Aug. 1847	K2
McCullough, Ellen	Reeder, Charles A.	30, Jan. 1841	N2
McDiarmid, Jane	Watson, Robert B.	5, Nov. 1851	P2
McDonald, Cassandra	Ulrey, Stephen	30, Apr. 1842	R3
McDonald, Mary Ann	Ringham, John	7, July 1852	P2
McDonnel, Margaret	Winter, John	8, Oct. 1822	J3
McDowell, Ann	Price, J.W.	13, Dec. 1828	R3
McDowell, Anna R.	McMicken, Andrew	3, May 1847	K2
McDowell, Eliza	Benton, Thomas H.	5, May 1821	S3
McElroy, Mary Ann	Haggit, J.P. (Dr)	4, Nov. 1837	R3
McEvoy, Elizabeth	Collins, John	30, Sept 1852	P2
McFadden, Catharine	Anderson, J.W.	18, Sept 1852	P2
McFelch, Sarah	Harris, James A.	22, Sept 1838	R3
McGarvey, Mary Ann	Carson, Isaac	28, Aug. 1813	S3
McGill, Kate B.	Wise, Theodore N.	11, Nov. 1852	P2
McGinnis, Ann E.	Boswell, G.W.	7, Dec. 1847	K2
McGinnis, Ellen	McCammon, William	5, Apr. 1828	R3
McGowan, Maria	Broks, T.M.	30, Nov. 1847	K2
McGregor, Margaret	Caldow, Robert	26, Sept 1840	R3
McGuigan, Mary Ann	Case, John	10, Oct. 1840	R3
McHenry, Catharine	Allen, William E.	9, Oct. 1841	R3
McHenry, Catharine	Allen, William F.	9, Oct. 1841	N2
McHenry, Mary	Godley, John	29, June 1820	S3
McInvaine, Eliza	Clark, Sumner	27, June 1835	T2

Brides	Grooms	Date of Notice	Page
McKee, Emma	Elston, William	28, May 1842	R3
McKee, Isabella	Peacock, Frederick	24, Sept 1852	P2
McKenzie, Catharine	Dillingham, John	28, Sept 1820	S3
McKim, Frances A.	Churchill, David	25, Feb. 1825	N2
McKim, Isabella F.	Leavitt, Richard H.	23, Nov. 1850	P2
McKim, Margaret	Madison, Ransil A.	4, Feb. 1825	N2
McKimm, Margaret	Madison, Ransil A.	27, Jan. 1825	E3
McKinney, Mary Ann	Talliaferro, John N.	20, Feb. 1819	S3
McKinnon, Amelia C.	Smead, Wesley	12, May 1832	R3
McKnight, Betsey	Bayly, James K.	8, Mar. 1816	S3
McKnight, Betsey	Defrees, Anthony	27, Oct. 1821	S3
McKnight, Mary	Reeder, Jesse	12, Apr. 1816	S3
McKoy, Angeline	Luce, Elijah	6, Jan. 1832	X3
McKoy, Angeline	Luce, Elijah W.	6, Jan. 1832	A3
McLaughlin, Elizabeth A.	Ludlow, Benjamin W.	14, Oct. 1852	P2
McLean, Eliza L.	Dunham, William	20, Feb. 1841	R3
McLean, Eliza L.	Dunham, William	13, Feb. 1841	N2
McLean, Elizabeth	Boyd, Allan	3, Jan. 1829	R3
McLean, Eveline A.	Taylor, J.P. (Capt)	8, Dec. 1827	R3
McLean, Nancy	McDonald, John S.	25, Oct. 1830	A3
McLean, Sarah	Gwynne, David	24, May 1834	T2
McLean, Sarah A.	Hayward, Joshua H.	19, July 1830	A3
McMaster, Hannah	Chester, Joseph	26, May 1838	R3
McMillan, Diana	Turner, T.	22, Apr. 1830	A3
McMillen, Olive	Stone, John E.	15, Dec. 1852	P2
McMurry, Eliza	Mount, William (Dr)	9, Mar. 1824	N3
McNaughton, Sarah M.	King, Edward A.	31, May 1841	N2
McNickle, Mary Jane	Ball, George W.	21, June 1841	N2
McNicoll, Catharine	Howell, Nathan	21, Oct. 1830	A3
McOliff, Mary C.	Magurk, Michael J.	4, May 1841	N2
McPherrin, Margaret	Eddy, Dean W.	1, Nov. 1833	X3
McQuead, Mary	Munday, William	27, July 1835	T2
McStuart, Agnes	Gillim, Isaac	25, Oct. 1841	N2
Mead, Elizabeth	Soule, Charles	11, Mar. 1831	X3
Meady, Eliza (Mrs)	Lusk, Uzal B.	27, Mar. 1847	K2
Mears, Eliza L.	Stoms, William	14, Oct. 1837	T2
Mears, Esther B.	Whetstone, Thomas H.	26, Sept 1840	R3
Mears, Mary	Lyons, William	24, Aug. 1811	S3
Mechlin, Agnes Maria	Smith, Fred A. (Capt)	23, May 1840	R3
Medarea, Susanna	Winall, George W.	18, July 1840	R3
Medhurst, Sarah S.	Lockwood, Henry (Rev)	6, Oct. 1836	X3
Meeks, Sophia	White, Israel	9, July 1824	N2
Meeks, Sophia	White, Israel	8, July 1824	E3
Mehne, Josephine	Hoskins, Henry	10, Oct. 1835	T2
Meldrum, Mary B.	Fry, George M.	11, July 1836	T2
Meline, Catharine A.	Lucas, Edward	19, Feb. 1838	T2
Meline, Catharine A.	Lucas, Edward	20, Feb. 1838	N2
Mellor, Emma	Ferguson, James	10, Sept 1842	R3
Mellor, Margaret G.	Prescott, Edward F.	29, July 1852	P2
Menge, Harriet	Clark, Ozro V.	8, Sept 1847	K2
Menzies, Caroline	Clarkson, E. Smith	1, June 1833	R3
Merrick, Elizabeth (Mrs)	Powell, Ellick	22, Sept 1821	S3
Merrie, Jane	McCulloch, Robert	31, July 1819	S3
Merrie, Mary Ann	Harrison, John P.	19, May 1838	R3

Brides	Grooms	Date of Notice	Page
Merrie, Mary Ann	Harrison, John Pitts	19, May 1838	T2
Merrit, Catharine	Lackey, Ira	29, June 1822	S3
Merriweather, Rachel	Griffith, Romulus R.	30, June 1827	R3
Merry, Susan A.	Ward, Frederick E.	10, June 1842	N2
Mervin, Francis M.	Black, Samuel H.	9, June 1836	X3
Miby, Lydia	Stark, William T.	28, Apr. 1815	S3
Michelson, Margaret	Cassady, John L.	27, Nov. 1852	P2
Middleton, Hannah	Bradford, James	14, Aug. 1841	R3
Middleton, Hannah	Bradford, James	13, Aug. 1841	N2
Middleton, Lydia	Stephens, Isaac	26, Oct. 1847	K2
Miles, Caroline	Little, George	16, Jan. 1841	R3
Miles, Caroline	Little, George	16, Jan. 1841	N2
Millburn, (Mrs)	Hay, William	28, Nov. 1840	R3
Miller, Amanda	Meeker, John C.	3, Oct. 1840	R3
Miller, Ann	Wescott, Leonard Wm.	14, Mar. 1849	L2
Miller, Caroline	Owen, Allison	29, Dec. 1832	R3
Miller, Caroline	Shumard, John	7, Sept 1852	P2
Miller, Clara	Cuny, Richard R.	18, Apr. 1829	R3
Miller, Delela	Thurston, William H.	15, Sept 1827	R3
Miller, Delia	Maddox, Thomas (Dr)	21, Mar. 1836	T2
Miller, Elizabeth (Mrs)	Johnston, Stephen (Lt)	21, July 1838	R3
Miller, Elizabeth M.	Sidener, Samuel	3, Oct. 1835	T2
Miller, Fanny B.	Thorpe, George S.	20, Sept 1852	P2
Miller, Harriet	Smith, James H.	3, Aug. 1850	P2
Miller, Jeanette A.	Schenck, Woodhull S.	15, Oct. 1841	N2
Miller, Lizzie A.	Degraw, P.G.	13, Nov. 1847	K2
Miller, Louisa	Este, David K.	16, May 1829	R3
Miller, Maggie W.	Mitchell, William	29, Oct. 1852	P2
Miller, Margaret	Garrison, Edward	26, Oct. 1832	X3
Miller, Mary	Fox, Charles	9, Dec. 1824	E2
Miller, Mary Jane	Greenleaf, William K.	9, May 1829	R3
Miller, Sarah Belle	Pugh, Jordan A.	4, June 1842	R3
Miller, Sarah Jane	Taylor, Gabriel A.	22, Sept 1847	K2
Milligan, Agnes K.	Greenleaf, William T	16, Aug. 1834	R3
Milligan, Agnes K.	Greenleaf, William T	14, Aug. 1834	T2
Milligan, Jane	Brooks, David A.	14, Aug. 1852	P2
Mills, Abigail	Benson, Gabriel L.	15, Apr. 1820	S2
Mills, Abigail	Benson, Gabriel L.	20, Apr. 1820	D3
Mills, Frances	Coulte, J.D. (Capt)	2, Dec. 1824	E2
Mills, Jane	Reed, Samuel	6, Mar. 1819	S3
Mills, Julia L.	Hazen, William L.	30, Oct. 1847	K2
Mills, Mary	Howell, Lewis (Lt)	13, June 1812	S3
Mills, Phoebe H.	Boal, Robert, Jr.	3, Jan. 1817	S3
Miner, Julia A. (Mrs)	Austin, Seneca	5, Sept 1840	R3
Mires, Mary	Fleming, Albert	23, June 1835	T2
Mitchel, Eliza	Snowden, Sydney	31, Aug. 1837	X3
Mitchel, Susan B.	Scott, Isaac M.	26, May 1838	R3
Mitchell, Eliza	Snowden, Sidney	26, Aug. 1837	T2
Mix, Catharine	Terry, Washington	1, Mar. 1833	X3
Moffit, Matilda	Johnson, Robert D.	23, Oct. 1841	R3
Moland, Louisa	Webb, Joseph	22, Aug. 1817	S3
Molstee, Josephine	Ray, Thomas	3, Nov. 1836	X3
Monfort, Sarah C.	Cannahan, C.	11, Oct. 1838	T2
Monfort, Sarah C.	Connahan, Charles	12, Oct. 1838	N2

Brides	Grooms	Date of Notice	Page
Monjah, Elizabeth A.	Jennings, J.S.	21, Aug. 1852	P2
Monroe, Maria	Tucker, Daniel E.	24, Nov. 1821	S3
Montague, Sarah R.	Flagg, Jared B.	18, Jan. 1842	N2
Montgomery, Caroline	Gardner, Allen M.	21, May 1842	R3
Moody, Elizabeth	Meeks, Simeon	21, Aug. 1838	T2
Moon, Rebecca	Lemmon, James	6, Oct. 1827	R3
Moon, Rebecca	Lemmon, James	5, Oct. 1827	N3
Mooney, Mary	Holcomb, Daniel H.	15, Mar. 1828	R3
Moore, Agnes A.	Ferguson, E.A.	19, Sept 1851	P2
Moore, Ann	Robb, Thomas B.	11, Aug. 1835	T2
Moore, Augusta	Barnum, H.L. (Capt)	14, Jan. 1832	R3
Moore, Augusta L.	Barnum, H.L. (Capt)	27, Jan. 1832	X3
Moore, Caroline	Chamberlaine, James	3, Oct. 1823	N3
Moore, Charlotte	Barnet, George W.	17, Apr. 1819	S2
Moore, Clara	Burnard, Elijah	12, Sept 1850	P2
Moore, Frances Ann	Fulwiler, John	7, Dec. 1838	T2
Moore, Jane	Beekley, Eliphalet	9, Oct. 1841	N2
Moore, Margaret	Winter, Henry	24, June 1831	A3
Moore, Maria	Schwartze, Augustus	7, Feb. 1818	S3
Moore, Maria H.	Gilmore, Hiram S.	6, June 1840	R3
Moore, Martha	Bird, John	1, Oct. 1799	S3
Moore, Mary Ann R.	Marshall, James	10, Oct. 1829	R3
Moore, Sylvia	Newell, Augustus	5, Apr. 1830	A3
Moore, Sylvia	Newell, Augustus	2, Apr. 1830	N2
Moorehead, Elizabeth	Hammond, C.	8, Jan. 1836	T3
Moorehead, Elizabeth	Hammond, Charles	11, Jan. 1836	N2
Moreton, Charlotte	Blaney, Daniel T.	2, Jan. 1819	S3
Morgan, Ellen	Miller, Arthur	23, Sept 1852	P2
Morgan, M. Virginia	Wood, William (Dr)	1, Apr. 1834	T2
Morgan, Mary Ann	Wells, Romanto	9, Jan. 1830	R3
Morgan, Pallas	Young, Henry	18, Feb. 1815	S3
Morris, Alphia	Longworth, Thomas	20, June 1828	Q3
Morris, Belle	Hankins, William J.	17, Nov. 1852	P2
Morris, Jane	Harbeson, Matthew L.	15, Oct. 1831	R3
Morris, Jane	Harbeson, Matthew L.	14, Oct. 1831	X3
Morris, Jane	Rust, Joseph G.	9, June 1836	T2
Morris, Louisa H.	How, John	15, Oct. 1835	T2
Morris, Maria	Turner, William (Capt)	25, Nov. 1825	N3
Morris, Maria F.	Miner, Lawrence W.	11, Nov. 1852	P2
Morris, Mary A. Penn	Welton, L.A.	29, Sept 1852	P2
Morris, Mary Jane	Barwise, Luther Y.	24, Sept 1851	P2
Morris, Nancy	West, Isaac	3, Nov. 1835	T2
Morrison, Elizabeth	Gossin, Jacob	19, Oct. 1852	P2
Morrison, Emily	Hay, Andrew	21, June 1828	R3
Morrison, Isabella J	Hoover, David (Dr)	20, May 1842	N2
Morrison, Matilda	Spark, Benjamin	7, Sept 1832	X3
Morrison, Sarah W.	Woods, John R.	24, Apr. 1835	X3
Morrow, Rachel Ann	Robinson, Thomas	15, Mar. 1828	R3
Morse, Mary Jane	Dyer, A.E.	18, Feb. 1848	K2
Morsell, Amelia (Mrs)	Starr, Henry	1, Dec. 1836	X3
Morten, Maria Ann A.	Ball, Danforth E.	30, Aug. 1834	R3
Moses, Sarah Ann	Myers, Abraham	28, June 1838	T2
Mosier, Elizabeth Y.	Bourgoin, Alexis J.	16, June 1849	L2
Mulford, Hannah F.	Shane, Charles (Dr)	21, Dec. 1832	X3

Brides	Grooms	Date of Notice	Page
Mulford, Hannah F.	Shane, Charles G. (Dr)	22, Dec. 1832	R3
Mullikin, Eliza A.	Tannebill, Wilkins	6, Oct. 1837	T2
Mundy, Ophelia	Keech, Orlando B.	3, July 1841	R3
Mundy, Ophelia	Keech, Orlando B.	28, June 1841	N2
Munroe, Maria Hester	Gouverneur, Samuel L	8, Apr. 1820	S3
Muntz, Rhoda Ann	Knight, William	5, Dec. 1817	S3
Murdock, Ellen F.	Graham, George	16, Aug. 1828	R3
Murphy, Malinda	Watt, Anthony	12, Oct. 1852	P2
Murray, Hannah I.	Coffin, William G.	2, May 1840	R3
Murray, Isabella	Owen, John	8, Feb. 1838	N2
Murray, Mary Ann	Holcomb, Horace L.	13, July 1833	R3
Murray, Mary Ann	Holcombe, Horace L.	19, July 1833	X3
Musgrave, Sarah	Rice, Amzi	15, Oct. 1850	Y2
Musick, Charity	Cooke, William F.	2, Oct. 1847	K2
Myers, Caroline	Rinehart, Joseph H.	27, June 1851	P2
Myers, Sarah	Greatbatch, Hamlet	26, Nov. 1850	P2
Nabs, Mary Jane	Bennett, John	8, Oct. 1852	P2
Nagle, Ann	Ott, Adam	28, Sept 1852	P2
Nancarrow, Eliza	Gottshalkson, Sol.	4, Feb. 1801	S3
Nancarrow, Polly	Thompson, Thomas	25, Feb. 1806	S3
Nash, Anna E.	Myers, William W.	29, Oct. 1852	P2
Neal, Mary A.	Twornely, Israel S.	9, July 1852	P2
Neave, Eliza	Pierce, Thomas	26, May 1815	S3
Nebblett, Sarah S.	Lovejoy, Henry B.	7, July 1841	N2
Nedy, Elizabeth	Lupton, Thomas	22, Nov. 1838	T2
Neely, Nancy	Patterson, Abraham	4, Dec. 1813	S3
Neff, Jane B.	Williams, Cyrus M.	17, June 1847	K2
Neimerick, Eliza	Wall, David	18, June 1835	T3
Nelson, Angeline	Hart, Edson P.	1, July 1852	P2
Nelson, Bridget	Patterson, Andrew	27, Feb. 1819	S3
Nelson, Carsey	Woolley, Asher	31, Jan. 1815	W3
Nevins, Cornelia	Fry, J. Reese	16, June 1841	N2
Newberger, Rebecca	Stonehill, Joseph	17, Nov. 1852	P2
Newbury, Lydia (Mrs)	St.John, Job	23, Dec. 1840	N2
Newbury, Lydia (Mrs)	St.Johns, Job	26, Dec. 1840	R3
Newell, Amana	Glen, Milton	3, Dec. 1835	X3
Newell, Amanda	Glen, Milton	28, Nov. 1835	T2
Newell, Rosalinda	Musselman, Samuel	14, Mar. 1829	R3
Newell, Selina W.	Powell, David A.	13, Dec. 1833	X3
Newkirk, Temperance	Haggarty, John H.	11, May 1820	S3
Newton, Mary E.	Bazzle, Thomas H.	23, Oct. 1841	R3
Newton, Rebecca	Kay, James	19, Dec. 1818	S3
Nicholas, Lydia Ann	Sutton, Joseph M.	17, May 1849	L2
Nicholas, Margaret	Magee, Jacob	29, Aug. 1817	S3
Nicholls, Mary Lee	Whiting, William B.	14, Dec. 1839	R3
Nichols, Clarissa	Belman, J.C.	28, July 1850	Y2
Nichols, Frances	Young, Samuel A.	2, May 1840	R3
Nichols, Thankful	Denier, Elijah	25, Apr. 1818	S3
Nicholson, Sarah Ann	Gullet, A.G.	22, Sept 1838	R3
Niles, Sarah A.	Jackson, A.	3, Dec. 1838	N2
Nixon, Elizabeth A.	Smith, James R.	9, Apr. 1847	K2
Noble, Eliza	Myers, Henry (Col)	1, Oct. 1838	T2
Noble, Mary F.	Estep, Richard P.	9, July 1842	R3

Brides	Grooms	Date of Notice	Page
Noble, Mary N.	Swaim, S.B.	20, May 1837	R3
Norris, Martha	Thompson, Francis R.	8, Sept 1847	K2
Norris, Nancy	West, Isaac	5, Nov. 1835	X3
North, Jane (Mrs)	Treat, Isaac	25, Aug. 1841	N2
Northrup, Charlotte	Henderson, John C.S.	3, Mar. 1832	R3
Norton, Elizabeth W.	Hall, Joseph W.	5, Oct. 1839	R3
Nugent, Bridget	Baxter, Hiram J.	30, Aug. 1850	Y2
Nye, Emily C.	Blinn, James	7, May 1842	R3
Nye, Emily C.	Blinn, James	5, May 1842	N2
Oakman, Martha	Carothers, John	30, Aug. 1828	R3
O'Connor, Susan E.	McKenny, J. Smith	9, Aug. 1841	N2
Odell, Susan B.	Hunting, Richard	26, Oct. 1837	T2
Odger, Emily C.	Cummings, Hamilton	14, May 1847	K2
O'Ferral, Catharine	Miller, Richard	22, Nov. 1825	N3
Offley, Rachael	Sheppard, J.W.	9, Oct. 1852	P2
Oldham, Susanna	Francis, David	9, July 1814	S3
Oliver, Electa	Spencer, Oliver	16, Jan. 1805	S2
Oliver, Eliza Ann	Loring, Allen	25, May 1841	N2
Oliver, Eliza Ann	Thomson, James	24, Mar. 1838	R3
Oliver, Elizabeth	Symmes, Daniel	16, Apr. 1796	C2
Oliver, Frances E.	Cooper, James	25, Apr. 1840	R3
Oliver, Harriet R.	Hall, James C.	19, Aug. 1835	T2
Oliver, Phebe	Boutell, George	22, Sept 1835	T3
Oliver, Phebe	Boutell, George W.	21, Sept 1835	N2
Olmstead, Sallie E.	Barringer, A.V.	7, July 1852	P2
Oppenheim, Maria	Moses, Morris	14, Oct. 1847	K2
Oppenheimer, Martha	Jones, Joseph	21, Nov. 1838	T2
O'Reilly, Catharine	Shepherd, M.L.	13, Jan. 1838	R3
Ormsby, Mary	Phillips, Elias	8, Oct. 1831	R3
Ormsby, Sarah	Phillips, Asher	14, Apr. 1827	R3
O'Roakh, D. (Mrs)	Newton, C.L.	29, July 1852	P2
Orr, Eliza (Mrs)	Matthews, W.	18, July 1840	R3
Orr, Louisa	Miller, Adolphus	13, Sept 1850	Y2
Orr, Martha E.	Walker, Joseph	19, Oct. 1836	T2
Orr, Martha E.	Walker, Joseph	13, Oct. 1836	X3
Orr, Peggy	Bell, Peter	27, Aug. 1799	S3
Osborn, Ann	Rowan, Matthew B.	22, Oct. 1847	K2
Osborn, Mary	Hurd, Rukard	6, Dec. 1825	N3
Osborn, Mary A.	McGrew, William C.	6, Feb. 1841	R3
Osborn, Susan L.	Coffin, Henry A.	14, Sept 1837	X3
Osburn, Mary Ann	McGraw, William C.	5, Feb. 1841	N2
Ost, Catharine	Witterman, Fred.	7, July 1852	P2
Otis, Sarah H.	Ernst, A.H.	2, Oct. 1841	R3
Otis, Sarah H.	Ernst, A.H.	25, Sept 1841	N2
Overton, Sarah Brown	Wilkens, Benjamin	6, Oct. 1832	R3
Owen, Jane	McDonald, Isaac	28, Dec. 1840	N2
Owens, Ann	Crane, Thirstin	1, June 1820	S3
Owens, Elizabeth	Pearce, Henry	12, Aug. 1847	K2
Owens, Jane	McDonald, Isaac	26, Dec. 1840	R3
Owens, Lucy M.	Winters, Edward	19, Nov. 1852	P2
Owens, Lucy Marian	Winter, Edwin	8, Nov. 1852	P2
Owens, Mary Ann Jane	Myers, Elkunah	6, July 1849	L2

Brides	Grooms	Date of Notice	Page
Pace, Laura H.	Slade, Henry August	4, Nov. 1835	T2
Paddock, Lydia	Perry, Joshua H.	18, Oct. 1816	S3
Page, Maria C.	Brown, James	9, Dec. 1830	A3
Palmer, Deborah D.	Moore, Joseph M.	24, Apr. 1835	X3
Palmer, Eliza C.	Wayne, J.S.	16, July 1831	R3
Palmer, Eliza C.	Wayne, J.S.	15, July 1831	X3
Palmer, Elizabeth S.	Salmon, Samuel M.	25, Nov. 1825	N3
Palmer, Louisa S.	Bradford, C.D.	15, Nov. 1831	A3
Palmer, Mary Ann	Dudley, F.D.	18, Oct. 1828	R3
Palmer, Mary M.	Judkins, William (Dr)	11, Sept 1841	R3
Palmer, Mary M.	Judkins, William (Dr)	11, Sept 1841	N2
Palmer, Rebecca	Holcome, William Hy.	5, July 1852	P2
Pancoast, Mary Ann	Broadwell, Samuel	12, Dec. 1812	S3
Pangburn, Jemima	Anderson, William	21, July 1827	R3
Pangburn, Martha Ann	Tibbetts, Robert	14, Mar. 1823	N3
Parker, Ann	Tealen, Robert	3, Jan. 1839	T2
Parker, Henrietta	Wilson, Lewis	4, Feb. 1851	P2
Parker, Mary	Stewart, Benjamin M.	25, Sept 1852	P2
Parks, Mary	Coleman, Leroy C.	1, Nov. 1825	N3
Parmeter, Aurelia M.	Edwards, Samuel	28, May 1842	R3
Parrish, Susannah	Harrier, Edward	2, Nov. 1835	T2
Parson, Elizabeth Ann	Latta, Alexander B.	23, Oct. 1847	K2
Parsons, Eliza	Arthur, William	15, Apr. 1820	S2
Parsons, Elizabeth	Arthur, William	20, Apr. 1820	D3
Parsons, Jane	Sumwall, William	27, Jan. 1825	E3
Parsons, Jane	Sumwalt, William	4, Feb. 1825	N2
Partridge, Sarah F.	Spofford, A.R.	23, Sept 1852	P2
Parvin, Delia M.	Biggar, G.D.	30, Apr. 1842	R3
Parvin, Delia M.	Biggar, G.D.	28, Apr. 1842	N2
Patmor, Rachel	Dusky, Eli	30, June 1827	R3
Patterson, Adeline E.	Mann, William C.	14, Nov. 1840	R3
Patterson, Elizabeth	Duncan, Jesse S.	3, Feb. 1832	X3
Patterson, Jane	Butler, Thomas S.	4, Dec. 1841	R3
Patterson, Jane	Butler, Thomas S.	27, Nov. 1841	N2
Patterson, Mary	Johnston, J.W.	6, Nov. 1841	R3
Patterson, Mary	Johnston, J.W.	30, Oct. 1841	N2
Patterson, Mary E.	Mahard, John	20, Jan. 1829	N3
Patterson, Mary K.	Mahard, John	17, Jan. 1829	R3
Patton, Elenor T.	Ringer, John T.	29, Oct. 1852	P2
Patton, Philinda	Gabriet, Edwin T.	3, Jan. 1839	T2
Paul, Nancy	Hendricks, William	24, May 1816	S3
Paxson, Anna Maria	Fitch, M.C.	14, Apr. 1821	S3
Paxton, Mary	Harbeson, Benjamin	7, Jan. 1832	R3
Pearce, Jane	Oliver, Alexander P.	28, July 1841	N3
Pearson, Ann	Baymiller, Jacob	18, Sept 1819	S3
Pease, Mary	Dean, Abner	15, Jan. 1814	S3
Peck, Delia A.	Fuller, John W.	24, Sept 1847	K2
Peck, Emily P.	Stout, Nathaniel R.	6, May 1847	K2
Peck, Hannah	Irwin, J.G.	11, Jan. 1833	X3
Peck, Mary	Mansfield, Edward D.	12, May 1827	R3
Peebles, Nancy H.	Stanfield, Thomas S.	1, Jan. 1842	R3
Peers, Mary Elinor	Collins, Lewis	11, Apr. 1823	N3
Peers, Sarah	Averel, Edward	10, Oct. 1840	R3
Pegram, Virginia	Triplett, Robert	17, May 1828	R3

Brides	Grooms	Date of Notice	Page
Pehleisen, Matildey	Myers, Henry W.	8, Oct. 1852	P2
Penn, Harriet Ann	Broadwell, Lewis	19, Jan. 1839	T2
Pennington, Harriet	Winter, C.F.	17, Nov. 1832	R3
Penny, Mary Ann	Witt, William B.	24, Feb. 1851	P2
Peoples, Mary Ann	Forbes, James C.	3, Aug. 1830	N2
Percefull, Amanda M.	Sedam, David Z.	20, June 1829	R3
Percipall, Amanda M.	Sedam, David Z.	13, June 1829	R3
Perkins, Harriet M.	Sewell, John W.	6, Sept 1852	P2
Perkins, L.B.	Martin, Thomas B.	10, Sept 1831	R3
Pernet, Cecilia	Perret, Phillip H.	15, June 1824	N3
Perrin, Mary	Sargent, George B.	5, Oct. 1839	R3
Perrine, Jane C.	Rowan, John A.	24, Apr. 1835	X3
Perry, Betsey	Bechtle, Henry C.	16, Feb. 1816	S3
Perry, Caroline	Buckner, Thomas M.	6, July 1820	S3
Perry, Caroline A.	Bates, George H.	7, May 1842	R3
Perry, Diadama	Ross, David A.	23, Jan. 1827	N3
Perry, Elizabeth E.	Marshall, William H.	2, Nov. 1835	T2
Perry, Hetty A.	Sanxay, Theodore	4, June 1842	R3
Perry, Martha	Hubble, Gabriel	25, Apr. 1810	H3
Perry, Martha	Medaris, John	3, Mar. 1849	L2
Perry, Martha (Mrs)	Platt, Jacob	8, May 1819	S3
Perry, Mary Ann	Wise, John T.	20, Nov. 1852	P2
Perry, Mary C.	Hopkins, John (Rev)	7, Nov. 1840	R3
Perry, Mary F.	Sampson, Joseph S.	7, Nov. 1840	R3
Peters, Anna Maria	Ramsey, C. Sample	11, Sept 1841	N2
Peticolas, Catharine	Davis, Julian N.	11, Oct. 1852	P2
Pettit, Maria	Dumass, Benjamin	16, Oct. 1819	S3
Phelps, Martha G.	Cheseldine, G.R.	3, Dec. 1831	R3
Phillip, Louisa	Davis, Benjamin W.	11, June 1831	R3
Phillips, Ann	Williams, David	5, Jan. 1830	N2
Phillips, Ann	Williams, David G.	2, Jan. 1830	R3
Phillips, Catharine	Basley, William H.	26, Jan. 1839	T2
Phillips, Elizabeth	Worthington, J.G.	5, July 1830	A3
Phillips, Elizabeth	Worthington, John G.	3, July 1830	R3
Phillips, Henrietta	Lowry, James	28, July 1832	R3
Phillips, Margaret D.	Speed, W.P.	25, Jan. 1840	R3
Phillips, Mary (Mrs)	Myers, (Mr)	13, Mar. 1819	S2
Phillips, Mary A.	Guelich, Lewis	16, Oct. 1852	P2
Phillips, Sarah Ann	Anderson, Samuel	17, Nov. 1821	S3
Phillips, Virginia	LeRoy, S.R. Faunt	2, Oct. 1852	P2
Piatt, Arabella S.	McCullough, William	19, May 1826	N2
Piatt, Catharine S.	Lodge, Laban	13, May 1823	N3
Pickering, Julia	Holmes, Henry	20, Dec. 1852	P2
Pienier, Eliza	Duffield, J.J.	23, May 1836	T2
Pierce, Amanda	Polhamus, John J.	9, Nov. 1852	P2
Pierce, Eunice	Wheelock, Daniel W.	31, Oct. 1817	S3
Pierce, Phebe	Steel, ----	28, Nov. 1812	S3
Pierce, Sally Ann	Worthington, Lewis	7, Oct. 1837	R3
Pierce, Sally Ann	Worthington, Lewis	5, Oct. 1837	T2
Pierson, Clarrissa	Davies, Samuel W.	11, Mar. 1815	S3
Pierson, Mary	Harrison, Levingston	26, Oct. 1822	S3
Pierson, Mary Ann	DeWitt, G.V.H.	22, May 1819	S3
Pike, Clarissa M.	Harrison, J.C.S.	2, Oct. 1819	S3
Pike, Maria M.	Flint, James H.	16, May 1840	R3

Brides	Grooms	Date of Notice	Page
Pile, Mary	Libeau, Charles	7, Dec. 1838	T2
Pitcher, Laura	O'Donnell, Hugh	7, Oct. 1837	R3
Pitcher, Laura	O'Donnell, Hugh	5, Oct. 1837	T2
Platt, Eulalie (Mrs)	Stout, Moses	29, Nov. 1830	A3
Plew, Athea	Robinson, Robert	5, Jan. 1816	S3
Plow, Elizabeth	Elliott, Michael K.	29, Oct. 1838	N2
Plugh, Lydia	Miller, Jacob	19, Feb. 1814	S3
Plum, Phebe (Mrs)	Badeau, Silas R.	10, June 1831	X3
Pocock, Temperance	Kinsey, Edward	4, Jan. 1841	N2
Pococke, Ann	Wells, L.T.	19, Nov. 1838	N2
Poineer, Mary Ann	Knies, John K.	6, July 1820	S3
Polk, Susan	Rayner, Kenneth	30, July 1842	R3
Pollard, Mary Eliza	Williams, Curus M.	16, Aug. 1852	P2
Pomeroy, Clara A.	Horton, V.B.	7, Dec. 1833	R3
Pomeroy, Eunice B.	Fenn, Ira I.	2, June 1836	X3
Pomeroy, Mary R.	Irvin, Thomas	24, Dec. 1835	T3
Pool, Eliza	Jones, Samuel R.	4, Dec. 1841	R3
Pool, Henrietta B.	Thompson, J.J. (Rev)	26, July 1852	P2
Poor, M.T.	Merrell, William S.	11, Mar. 1831	X3
Pope, Ann	Anderson, Larz	12, July 1828	R3
Porter, Eliza A.	French, George H.	18, May 1838	T2
Porter, Elizabeth	Beneman, J.S.	7, Nov. 1840	R3
Porter, Elizabeth	Taylor, George	18, Sept 1819	S3
Porter, Lucia C.	Waddell, John W.	4, Sept 1835	T2
Porter, Mary	Moss, Madison R.	15, Aug. 1835	T2
Porter, Mary	Patterson, William	18, Apr. 1840	R3
Post, Cornelia	Mitchell, Roland G.	24, June 1837	R3
Potter, Adeline E.	Peck, Charles A.	12, Mar. 1842	R3
Powell, Margaret R.	McGrew, Wilson	9, May 1840	R3
Powell, Mary Ann	Pruden, Andrew J.	21, Aug. 1841	N2
Powers, Catharine	Corry, James A.	23, Jan. 1841	R3
Powers, Catharine	Corry, James A.	16, Jan. 1841	N2
Powers, Frances	Massalski, Joseph	1, July 1836	N2
Powers, Helen Maria	Griswold, Robert H.	28, Nov. 1840	R3
Powers, Joshufan	Reeves, Edward J.	30, Nov. 1852	P2
Powers, Lydia S.	Morris, William R.	13, May 1823	N3
Powers, Lydia S.	Morris, William R.	15, May 1823	J3
Powers, Rebecca	Orr, James	27, June 1829	R3
Prather, Elizabeth	Jolly, William	12, May 1838	R3
Pratt, Elizabeth H.	Boyce, John W.	19, Dec. 1836	T2
Pratt, Hannah	Dunlap, Samuel	20, Feb. 1813	S3
Pray, Ann (Mrs)	Guinn, John K.	14, July 1838	R3
Preston, Carolina L.	Woolley, A.R. (Col)	22, Sept 1827	R3
Preston, Mary Ann E.	Smith, Chester	7, Apr. 1849	L2
Price, Elizabeth (Mrs)	Cooper, Jonas	29, Dec. 1821	S3
Price, Emily	Marvin, Charles	24, Nov. 1827	R3
Price, Harriet D.	Graham, William A.	20, Mar. 1847	K2
Price, Harriett	Rose, Timothy	1, Apr. 1818	S3
Prince, Mannette	Smith, Thomas	3, Apr. 1819	S3
Pringle, Isabella	Craig, Johnson	16, Oct. 1841	R3
Provost, M. (Mrs)	Edmonston, Robert	10, Mar. 1827	R3
Pucas, Sallie S.	Shotwrdl, John	7, July 1852	P2
Pugh, Hannah	Sexton, Horatio (Dr)	23, Nov. 1820	S3
Pugh, Leah	Marshall, Vincent C.	27, July 1820	S3

Brides	Grooms	Date of Notice	Page
Pugh, Mary A.	Hart, Samuel	12, June 1841	R3
Pugh, Mary A.	Hart, Samuel	8, June 1841	N2
Punshon, Mary E.	Ramsey, William E.	2, Sept 1847	K2
Punshon, Rachel	Thistlewaite, James	15, Feb. 1837	N2
Purscell, Rebecca C.	Case, J.T.	13, Jan. 1831	A3
Putnam, Lucretia	Rice, John	30, Mar. 1822	S3
Quail, Mary V.	Collins, William	29, Oct. 1852	P2
Quin, Eliza	Richard, George	30, Apr. 1838	T2
Quinten, Sarah Ann	Wayne, Charles	24, May 1828	R2
Quinton, Mary Eliza	Corwine, R.M.	19, Feb. 1842	R3
Quinton, Mary Eliza	Corwine, Richard M.	17, Feb. 1842	N2
Raddish, Jane Ann	Alter, Charles	28, Apr. 1827	R3
Rafferty, Hannah	Malone, Michael	16, July 1852	P2
Rains, Mary	Elstner, John	14, Mar. 1823	N3
Ralphy, Mary Ann	Hyler, Jeremiah	12, Aug. 1852	P2
Rambo, Malinda	Waggoner, Conrod	29, Mar. 1828	R3
Ramcey, Martha (Mrs)	Scott, Chasteen	21, Oct. 1837	R3
Ramsay, Hannah	Stevens, Elijah	14, Mar. 1829	R3
Ramsay, Harriet S.	Wade, Stephen J.	31, Jan. 1835	N2
Ramsay, Margaret E.	Lawrence, William	3, Aug. 1847	K2
Ramsay, Sarah L.	Irwin, William	22, Aug. 1838	T2
Ramsdale, Emeline	Potter, Aaron	4, Oct. 1830	A3
Ramsy, Sarah L.	Irwin, William (Major)	25, Aug. 1838	R3
Rand, Emeline	Florer, Robert C.	14, Feb. 1839	T2
Randall, Martha Ann	King, James	30, Oct. 1852	P2
Randolph, Mary (Mrs)	Brooks, James	30, July 1841	N3
Randolph, Septimia	Meikleham, David S.	24, Aug. 1838	T2
Rankins, M.A.H.	Pepper, Andrew J.	8, Oct. 1841	N2
Rawlins, Ann (Mrs)	Denniston, Alex (Rev)	30, May 1817	S3
Rawlins, Mary	Defining, Benjamin F	17, Oct. 1840	R3
Ray, Mary	Atwell, John	12, May 1838	R3
Raymond, Abigail	Mears, Isaac	8, Nov. 1828	R3
Raymond, Abigail	Mears, Isaac	11, Nov. 1828	N3
Rayner, Helen M.	Aldrich, Edwin R.	26, Aug. 1852	P2
Reagin, Sophia	Farrel, James	17, Mar. 1821	S3
Redding, Eleatora	Petty, William C.	18, Dec. 1841	R3
Redding, Mary Ann	Blundell, Joseph M.	19, Feb. 1839	T2
Reddish, Joanna J.	Hutchinson, Levi	3, May 1833	X3
Rede, Mary	Reily, John W.	2, Oct. 1835	N2
Redhead, Jane	Froome, Samuel	5, Dec. 1840	R3
Redhead, Jane	Froome, Samuel	1, Dec. 1840	N2
Redhead, Martha Ann	Sherlock, Thomas	26, Mar. 1847	K2
Redish, (Mrs)	Black, Robert B.	10, Sept 1852	P2
Reed, Catharine M.	Townley, Asa H.	4, May 1847	K2
Reed, Eliza	Easton, Shadford	27, Nov. 1841	R3
Reed, Eliza M.	Bright, Ethelbert	21, Mar. 1839	T2
Reed, Nancy	Chamberlin, David	28, Nov. 1835	T2
Reeder, Carolina A.	Follin, Augustus	11, Sept 1847	K2
Reeder, Francis C.	Langworthy, Lucius	1, May 1835	X3
Reeder, Mary Ann	Thomas, Isaiah	4, June 1831	R3
Reeder, Phebe H.	Harris, Robert S.	3, Mar. 1836	X3
Rees, Mary N.	Burke, William W.	19, Sept 1818	S3

Brides	Grooms	Date of Notice	Page
Reese, Hester Ann	Walker, Benjamin	3, Jan. 1829	R3
Reese, Hester Ann	Walker, Benjamin	6, Jan. 1829	N3
Reese, Sarah	Price, David	3, Jan. 1829	R3
Reese, Sarah	Price, David	6, Jan. 1829	N3
Reeves, Mary	Miller, Henry B.	12, June 1841	R3
Regor, Prudence A.	Moore, T.S.	2, Dec. 1840	N2
Regor, Prudence Ann	Moore, T.S.	5, Dec. 1840	R3
Reid, Elizabeth	Taylor, John Drake	20, Sept 1828	R3
Reid, Sarah	Hall, Joseph	3, Nov. 1852	P2
Reily, Jane	Campbell, Lewis D.	9, Jan. 1836	T3
Rennick, Alisonia B.	Todd, James M.	28, May 1847	K2
Renshaw, Mary S.	Cist, Lewis J.	24, May 1847	K2
Reser, Ann Eliza	Picket, Albert	18, Mar. 1831	X3
Resor, Elizabeth	Wilson, Joseph	30, Mar. 1824	N3
Resor, Elizabeth S.	Dinsmoor, Silas G.	16, Nov. 1833	R3
Revill, Amelia	Teal, Samuel R.	7, July 1827	R3
Reville, Ann T.	Brunot, W. (Lt)	8, May 1819	S3
Reynolds, Levina C.	Hine, Theodore B.	20, Sept 1851	P2
Reynolds, Maria	Wright, John F.	12, Apr. 1825	N3
Reynolds, Martha G.	Jones, John W.	15, Nov. 1851	P2
Reynolds, Minerva	Todd, P.G.	19, Jan. 1822	S3
Rhodes, Alice K.	Hill, George H.	21, Sept 1835	T2
Rhodes, Belle	McDowell, J.H.	27, Dec. 1852	P2
Rhodes, Elizabeth	Grace, Benjamin	28, July 1827	R3
Rice, Caroline E.	Horton, Lewis Y.	12, Oct. 1847	K2
Rice, Eliza	Edwards, Jonathan	6, May 1847	K2
Rice, Eliza A.	Maston, William D.	18, Nov. 1837	T2
Rice, Frances S.	Nichols, John D.	3, Sept 1831	R3
Rice, Frances S.	Nichols, John D.	2, Sept 1831	X3
Rice, Lucy	Smith, F.	11, May 1822	S3
Richards, Mary W.	Rawson, Joseph	1, Dec. 1838	T2
Richards, S.L.	Spilman, G.	5, July 1852	P2
Richards, Sarah	Cosper, John	28, May 1835	T2
Richardson, Annie J.	McDonald, Alexander	29, Dec. 1852	P2
Richardson, Cath.	Richardson, Robert	24, Aug. 1820	S3
Richardson, Elenor D	Meeker, Jotham	4, Oct. 1830	A3
Richardson, Elizabeth C.	Shattuck, William B.	22, May 1850	P2
Richardson, Elizabeth F.	Saunders, William	28, Nov. 1812	S3
Richardson, Louisa M	Caldow, William	11, Mar. 1841	N2
Richardson, Maria H.	Camnitz, Daniel F.	21, Aug. 1841	R3
Richardson, Maria M.	Camnitz, Daniel F.	19, Aug. 1841	N2
Richardson, Mary E.	Heaton, George	22, Sept 1852	P2
Richey, Francis B.	Burr, Edward	21, Aug. 1852	P2
Rickman, Adeline	Deane, William	15, May 1819	S3
Riddle, Eliza	Field, J.M.	20, Nov. 1837	T2
Riddle, Martha Jane	Cutter, Alphonso	20, Aug. 1847	K2
Riddle, Mary	Ray, James B.	12, Dec. 1818	S3
Riddle, Melissa E.	Perrin, Joseph J.	31, Aug. 1852	P2
Ridge, Anna M.	Fielding, M.B.	8, Oct. 1852	P2
Ridgely, Lucy E.S.	Henry, John H.	19, Jan. 1828	R3
Riggett, Esther	Munday, Benjamin	27, Oct. 1827	R3
Riggle, Sarah Jane	Buchanan, Robert	8, May 1847	K2
Riggs, Eunice	Pierson, Moses (Rev)	8, Sept 1827	R3
Riker, Margaret Ann	Kerr, Stephen F.	3, Nov. 1838	T2

Brides	Grooms	Date of Notice	Page
Ripley, Amelia (Mrs)	Smith, Thomas B.	25, July 1840	R3
Riser, Margaret	Harr, William	11, Feb. 1836	X3
Risinger, Sarah W.	Edwards, Edwin	19, May 1847	K2
Riske, Charlotte	Jones, George W.	6, Oct. 1832	R3
Riskf, Ruhamah	Kenner, William B.	15, Sept 1832	R3
Ritchey, Abbey G.	Strader, D.P. (Dr)	11, Mar. 1841	N2
Ritchey, Frances B.	Burr, Edward M.	24, Aug. 1852	P2
Ritter, Maria	Smith, John C.	27, June 1835	T2
Rives, Anna	Longworth, Joseph	22, May 1841	R3
Rives, Anna	Longworth, Joseph	17, May 1841	N2
Robbins, Abby	Maker, Thomas S.	21, July 1852	P2
Robbins, Emily	Young, John	4, Nov. 1837	R3
Robbins, Mary A.	Bray, William W.B.	17, Nov. 1847	K2
Roberts, Lucy B.	Cox, Rodolph	5, Oct. 1838	T2
Roberts, Margaret A.	Morrow, John H.	30, Oct. 1852	P2
Robertson, Jane	Heron, John	9, June 1849	L2
Robeson, Margaret	Bonnel, Benjamin	17, Nov. 1821	S3
Robins, Rebecca A.	Mack, Samuel E.	11, Sept 1841	N2
Robinson, Elizabeth	Hillerman, William J	3, Mar. 1849	L2
Robinson, Jane C.	Shaffer, David Henry	14, Oct. 1835	T2
Robinson, Lucy	Thorpe, John	15, July 1852	P2
Robinson, Lydia	Avery, John C.	31, Oct. 1829	R3
Robinson, M.A.	Richardson, James	13, Aug. 1851	P2
Robinson, Margaret B	Harm, George W.	9, Sept 1847	K2
Robinson, Mary Ann	McLaughlin, William	6, Jan. 1825	E3
Robson, Mary Ann	Collord, Samuel W.	30, Aug. 1828	R3
Rochafeller, Charlotte	Thomas, Washington	26, Nov. 1835	X3
Rockey, Catharine O.	Pendry, John L.	11, June 1847	K2
Rod, Olive	Winder, Thomas	21, Aug. 1819	S3
Rodgers, Louisa	Meigs, Montgomery C.	15, May 1841	R3
Rodman, Elizabeth (Mrs)	Freeman, Edmund	30, July 1799	S3
Rodney, Caroline	May, William L.	8, Jan. 1838	T2
Rogers, Ann Eliza	Deeds, Isaac W.	9, May 1818	S3
Rogers, Charlotte	Tomlinson, J.C.	4, May 1833	R3
Rogers, Julia M.	Chittenden, Edward	11, Feb. 1836	X3
Rogers, Julia M.	Chittenden, Edward F	9, Feb. 1836	T3
Rogers, Lucretia	Peters, Joseph	5, Sept 1834	X3
Rogers, Mary C.	Ellis, Rowland	20, Dec. 1828	R3
Rogers, Mary C.	Ellis, Rowland	19, Dec. 1828	N3
Rogers, Semor A.	Lane, Andrew	26, Sept 1840	R3
Rohrman, Charlote	Walden, William	27, Mar. 1841	N2
Roll, Abigail	Ayres, James	13, Oct. 1815	S3
Rollin, Mary A.	Garwood, Nicholas	10, June 1847	K2
Ronalds, Rosanna	McMillan, Gavin (Rev)	16, Mar. 1824	N2
Rosa, Nannie Holley	Ogden, Henry T.	9, Sept 1850	P2
Rose, Henrietta	Souder, John	9, June 1827	R3
Rose, Serena Ann	Lewis, Albert	22, Mar. 1829	R3
Ross, Josephine	Hood, M. James	8, Sept 1852	P2
Ross, Julia Ann	Murdock, Thomas S.	24, Mar. 1832	R3
Ross, Maria	Thompson, John	2, June 1827	R3
Ross, Mary	Pursel, Joseph	12, Sept 1818	S3
Ross, Sarah	Ferguson, John	15, Mar. 1833	X3
Ross, Susannah	Billings, Charles F.	22, Feb. 1841	N2
Row, Mary	Rue, Benjamin	29, Sept 1827	R3

Brides	Grooms	Date of Notice	Page
Royal, Mourning	Long, Christian	22, Sept 1827	R3
Ruckle, Catharine C.	Strickler, John	20, Aug. 1842	R3
Ruckle, Catharine C.	Strickler, John	17, Aug. 1842	N2
Rue, Mary Ann	Eaton, Charles H.	25, Oct. 1838	T2
Rue, Mary Ann	Eaton, Charles H.	26, Oct. 1838	N2
Ruffin, Eliza	Oliver, William	23, Apr. 1814	S3
Ruffin, Frances	Hopkins, William H.	23, Apr. 1814	S3
Ruffin, Harriet O.	Monsarrat, David T.	31, May 1834	T2
Ruffin, Mary	Rockey, Henry	16, Nov. 1820	S3
Ruffner, Eliza	Haskins, J.I.	7, June 1830	A3
Rush, Mary Jane	McElroy, Solon	11, Dec. 1852	P2
Russell, Angeline	Faran, James J.	4, Apr. 1840	R3
Russell, Ann C.	Allen, Thomas	20, July 1842	N2
Russell, Ellen B.	Milligan, (Prof)	29, Jan. 1842	R3
Russell, Lucinda	Dresbach, Charles F.	15, Sept 1835	T2
Russell, Maria	Quinn, William M.P.	23, Nov. 1820	S3
Rutledge, Lucy Jane	Clason, Lewis W.	26, Oct. 1847	K2
Sackett, Jane Ann	Pearce, Christopher	17, Oct. 1840	R3
Salles, Emily L.	Vail, Aaron	20, Oct. 1835	T2
Sampson, Caroline	Gosman, Richard S.	10, Nov. 1827	R3
Sampson, Harriet	Dunbar, Robert W.	13, Nov. 1835	T2
Sampson, Lydia F.	Collier, Daniel	13, July 1838	T2
Sampson, Mary	Farquhar, William P.	11, Sept 1835	T2
Sanders, Julia C.	Comly, Richard N.	11, May 1833	R3
Sanders, Mary	Thompson, Jesse W.	2, June 1827	R3
Sanders, Zerelda	Wallace, David	9, Jan. 1837	T2
Sandford, Indiana	Whiting, D.P. (Lt)	10, Jan. 1835	R3
Sandford, Indiana B.	Whiting, D.P. (Lt)	6, Jan. 1835	T2
Sankay, Emily	Wells, Hiram K.	19, Sept 1840	R3
Sargeant, Mary	Smith, Winthrop B.	7, Nov. 1834	X3
Satcher, Marian	Patmore, John	7, Sept 1847	K2
Sater, Rebecca	Gregory, Thomas	31, Dec. 1814	S3
Satterly, Nancy	Avery, John C. (Lt)	25, Dec. 1813	S3
Saunders, Harriet	Martin, A.	5, July 1828	R3
Saunders, Julia E.	Comly, Richard N.	10, May 1833	X3
Savage, Mary E.	McKim, Charles S.	13, July 1852	P2
Sawyer, Mary A.F.	Hotchkiss, Henry O.	28, May 1841	N2
Sawyler, Mary Fitz	Hotchkiss, Henry O.	29, May 1841	R3
Sayre, Ann	Glenn, James	18, May 1820	S3
Sayre, Margaretta	Sharpless, Thomas	23, Nov. 1822	S3
Sayre, Martha	Avery, John L.	10, July 1813	S3
Scamahorne, Elizabeth	Smith, John	8, Apr. 1823	N3
Schenk, Mary Fannie	Kingsbury, C.S.	19, Nov. 1852	P2
Schillinger, Frances	Hinkle, Anthony H.	9, Apr. 1842	R3
Schillinger, Philom.	Sigerson, John	28, Oct. 1836	N2
Schillinger, Prisc.	Armstrong, Arthur E.	28, Oct. 1837	R3
Schooley, Ann E.	Evans, J. (Dr)	16, Apr. 1835	T3
Schoonmaker, Mary	Martin, Alexander	6, June 1840	R3
Schwartz, Charlotte	Hafer, Henry	27, Jan. 1824	N3
Schweizerhoff, Joh.	Wertsvern, Johannes	2, Nov. 1850	Y2
Scott, Fanny	Parmerton, A.B.	16, Dec. 1852	P2
Scott, Frances	Symmes, Americus	26, Sept 1840	R3
Scott, Gertrude V.	Southgate, George M.	18, May 1836	T2

Brides	Grooms	Date of Notice	Page
Scott, Henrietta E.	Cleveland, George P.	26, Nov. 1834	T2
Scott, Jane	Elder, Thomas	9, Oct. 1805	S3
Scott, Margaret	McQuesten, John	22, Sept 1827	R3
Scowden, Sarah Ann	Kerns, Thomas	30, Dec. 1835	T3
Scudder, Mary	Drake, Aaron	19, Apr. 1816	S3
Scudler, Elvira	Gilpin, Joseph H.	3, Jan. 1839	T2
Sebree, Ann S. (Mrs)	Drake, Edward L.	9, July 1831	R3
Secuts, Matilda	Hall, James H.	5, Sept 1834	X3
See, Jane	McKensie, John	4, Feb. 1832	R3
See, Mary Clayton	Augur, Daniel	24, Oct. 1818	S3
Seebrooks, Priscilla	Casey, John	4, Mar. 1820	S2
Seebrooks, Priscilla	Casey, John	2, Mar. 1820	D3
Seely, Cynthia D.	Charters, William M.	30, June 1827	R3
Seixas, Lucia	Jonas, Abraham	18, Mar. 1824	E2
Sellers, Caroline	Marshall, Benjamin	14, Jan. 1831	X3
Sellman, Elizabeth	Evans, Thomas	23, May 1836	T2
Sellman, Harriet	Key, Marshall	19, Apr. 1816	S3
Sellman, Julia A.	Conover, James F.	21, Jan. 1832	R3
Sellman, Julia A.E.	Conover, James F.	20, Jan. 1832	A3
Sellman, Julia E.	Conover, James F.	27, Jan. 1832	X3
Sering, Mary	Kemper, F.A. (Rev)	23, Dec. 1831	X3
Settlemyer, Esther	Folger, Thomas B.	10, Dec. 1852	P2
Seward, Martha Maria	Burnap, George	30, Oct. 1819	S3
Seymour, Amelia	Cargill, Austin	15, Aug. 1822	J3
Seymour, Amelia	White, William	3, Mar. 1821	S3
Shaddinger, Sarah A.	Lauderman, David	20, Dec. 1836	N2
Shaffer, Sarah	Allen, Hazen	9, Oct. 1851	P2
Shane, Amanda F.	Mulford, William	15, Dec. 1827	R3
Shane, Araminta E.	Williamson, Alex. W.	20, Oct. 1847	K2
Shanklin, Mary	Reddenbough, Henry	1, Sept 1815	S3
Sharp, Elizabeth M.	Woods, William	25, Dec. 1841	R3
Sharp, S.C.	Fowler, John	26, Aug. 1847	K2
Shays, Frances C.	Lockwood, Daniel D.	5, June 1837	T2
Sheeler, Kate	Rowland, George E.	31, May 1849	L2
Sheidegger, Barbara	Andrick, John U.	21, Apr. 1835	T3
Shelden, Rebecca A.	Lawder, John B.	21, May 1842	R3
Sheldon, Rebecca A.	Lawder, John B.	21, May 1842	N2
Shelmire, Sarah	Mieure, William	14, Jan. 1831	X3
Shepard, Matilda	McKinsey, C.	3, Feb. 1838	R3
Shephard, Mary P.C.	Harding, Lyman	10, Jan. 1837	T2
Shepperson, Mary	Thomas, Alexander J.	2, June 1847	K2
Sherman, Ann	Hasson, William	25, Mar. 1837	N2
Sherman, Mary A.	Mason, Thomas J.	4, Nov. 1852	P2
Sherwin, Caroline F.	Redington, Asa	22, Aug. 1817	S3
Sherwin, Charlotte	Cathcart, David	31, Jan. 1818	S3
Sherwood, Jane A.	Whetten, John B.	24, Dec. 1831	R3
Sherzer, Frances	Hathaway, John	11, May 1841	N2
Shield, Emeline	Stickney, Paul	28, Aug. 1841	R3
Shields, Mary	Dolton, Ellis	12, June 1847	K2
Shields, Susan	Shumard, Richard	21, Apr. 1835	T3
Shigley, Tamer	Conkelon, Alexander	22, Apr. 1830	A3
Shipley, Ann G.	Moore, Alfred L.	20, Oct. 1827	R3
Shipley, Mary A. (Mrs)	Lumley, Robert	7, May 1841	N2
Shoenberger, Elizabeth	Lytle, Edward H.	27, Sept 1838	T2

Brides	Grooms	Date of Notice	Page
Shorts, Maria	Abbay, C.H.	30, Sept 1830	A3
Shoyer, Mary Jane	Fine, John	7, Oct. 1847	K2
Shreve, Elizabeth	Donaldson, William	5, Oct. 1838	T2
Shrieve, Margaret	Butler, William	4, Oct. 1828	R3
Silliman, Caroline A.	Taylor, William R.	23, May 1840	R3
Simmons, Hannah	Brasher, Robert	20, Aug. 1799	S3
Simns, Esther Ann	Hargan, James	23, Oct. 1850	P2
Singer, Mary Jane	Bassford, Thomas	16, Jan. 1841	R3
Singleton, Mary R.	McDuffie, George	23, June 1829	N3
Singleton, Sarah A.	VanBuren, Abraham	26, Dec. 1838	T2
Singleton, Sarah A.	VanBuren, Abraham	24, Dec. 1838	N2
Sisson, Amelia S.	Forbes, John	15, Aug. 1818	S3
Sisson, Eliza	Smith, Patrick	10, Aug. 1822	S3
Sisson, Emily	Cochran, Richard	19, Aug. 1837	T2
Sisson, Mary	Gradner, Richard	6, Aug. 1817	S3
Sisson, Mary H.	Gaines, Richard	11, Feb. 1815	S3
Sisson, Sarah	Pounsford, William	28, July 1815	S3
Skaates, Jane	Belser, Samuel	17, Nov. 1827	R3
Skiff, Catharine	Basset, Jonathan	16, May 1818	S3
Skyrin, Mary S.	Clark, Henry	7, July 1832	R3
Slacum, Helen A.	Ludlow, Israel L.	3, July 1830	R3
Slacum, Helena Adela	Ludlow, Israel L.	1, July 1830	A3
Slater, Julia	Rees, Charles L.	6, Aug. 1852	P2
Slayback, Dianna	Wilkinson, John	22, Apr. 1815	W3
Slevin, Maria L.	Quinn, J.J. (Dr)	8, July 1852	P2
Sloane, Esther	Gordon, David	24, Apr. 1830	R3
Slocum, Georgiana	Lambeth, William M.	17, Aug. 1839	T2
Slocum, Oliva Eliza	Drake, John T.	23, Feb. 1828	R3
Slocum, Olivia Eliza	Drake, John T.	22, Feb. 1828	N3
Sloop, Catharine (Mrs)	Arnold, William	24, Oct. 1818	S3
Sloop, Elizabeth	Waterhouse, Josiah	16, Feb. 1822	S3
Small, Elizabeth	Overman, Zebulon	16, June 1827	R3
Small, Rachel	McAffee, Daniel	23, Feb. 1837	T2
Small, Rachel	McAffee, Daniel	21, Feb. 1837	N2
Smith, A.	Dent, John T.	6, Oct. 1832	R3
Smith, Amanda	McLean, James	1, Mar. 1828	R3
Smith, Ann B.	Morgan, Hugh	4, June 1842	R3
Smith, Ann M.	Foulke, Thomas D.	28, July 1827	R3
Smith, Caroline A.	Febriger, George L.	9, Apr. 1849	L2
Smith, Caroline E.	Jewell, Henry (Rev)	24, June 1851	P2
Smith, Catharine	Moore, F.	2, Oct. 1839	T2
Smith, Catharine	Spooner, William L.	31, Oct. 1840	R3
Smith, Clarinda	Getty, Robert	23, May 1829	R3
Smith, Clarissa	McMaster, William	25, Oct. 1814	W3
Smith, D. (Mrs)	Roach, Steven F.	17, Aug. 1841	N2
Smith, Eliza (Mrs)	Cullom, Allen	25, June 1835	T2
Smith, Eliza A. (Mrs)	McClellan, Alexander	21, Dec. 1835	T3
Smith, Eliza Ann	Chase, Salmon P.	28, Sept 1839	T3
Smith, Eliza Ann	Latta, Finley	13, Mar. 1841	N2
Smith, Elizabeth	Brown, Richard F.	1, Aug. 1840	R3
Smith, Elizabeth	Donsee, John	15, Jan. 1831	R3
Smith, Elizabeth M.	Gardner, Elijah F.	22, Sept 1852	P2
Smith, Emily	Roe, Daniel	3, Nov. 1821	S3
Smith, Emily H.	Walker, Samuel	5, Feb. 1831	R3

Brides	Grooms	Date of Notice	Page
Smith, Eve	Underwood, J.	21, May 1842	N2
Smith, Frances (Mrs)	Todd, John P.	22, Nov. 1837	T2
Smith, Hannah E.	Carey, William W.	1, May 1835	X3
Smith, Harriet	Armstrong, Charles G.	23, Oct. 1841	R3
Smith, Harriet	Armstrong, Charles G.	18, Oct. 1841	N2
Smith, Harriet	Harp, David	23, Oct. 1847	K2
Smith, Harriet C.	Wilson, James W.	22, May 1847	K2
Smith, Henrietta S.	Mason, Edwin	16, Sept 1852	P2
Smith, Jane	Campbell, William	5, July 1828	R3
Smith, Jane	Moore, Wilson	8, Aug. 1850	Y2
Smith, Jane	Todd, Thomas	25, Jan. 1841	N2
Smith, Jane E.	Meguier, William	1, Sept 1834	T2
Smith, Julia	Fisher, Elwood	17, Oct. 1840	R3
Smith, Julia S.	Winston, John P.	30, Aug. 1837	T2
Smith, Letitia C.	Cooper, D. Zeigler	25, Sept 1835	T2
Smith, Lizzy G.	Morgan, Edward S.	1, June 1847	K2
Smith, Lydia W.	Beall, Edwin J. (Dr)	10, May 1828	R3
Smith, M.A.W.	Foster, William C.	5, July 1830	A3
Smith, Margaret	Finley, James C.	26, Feb. 1831	R3
Smith, Maria	Stockton, T.B.W.	5, Apr. 1830	A3
Smith, Maria C.	Southgate, Henry H.	4, Oct. 1834	R3
Smith, Marion G.	Whetstone, Richard A.	6, May 1847	K2
Smith, Martha Ann W.	Foster, William C.	3, July 1830	R3
Smith, Mary	Garrett, R.J.	21, May 1842	N2
Smith, Mary Ann	Cooper, Robert W.	21, Oct. 1837	R3
Smith, Mary Ann	Sellman, Carberry J.	22, Oct. 1831	R3
Smith, Mary Ann	Thompson, Samuel G.	26, Mar. 1847	K2
Smith, Mary B.	Cushing, Milton B.	1, July 1836	T2
Smith, Mary B.	Cushing, Milton B.	14, July 1836	X3
Smith, Mary Eliza	Franklin, William	18, Sept 1841	R3
Smith, Mary Ellen	Adams, Elmer W.	28, Dec. 1839	R3
Smith, Mary F.	Littell, Eliakim	1, Mar. 1828	R3
Smith, Mary J.	Head, James Edward	23, July 1847	K2
Smith, Mary Jane	Irwin, William	14, Jan. 1832	R3
Smith, Nancy E.	Barbour, Charles (Dr)	10, Apr. 1819	S3
Smith, Nancy S.	Robb, John H.	28, June 1828	R3
Smith, Rachel	Babb, Thomas	31, Aug. 1847	K2
Smith, Rebecca	Gardiner, James	8, July 1852	P2
Smith, S.S.	Sullivan, C.W.	23, Nov. 1852	P2
Smith, Sally H.	Hunter, William	30, Nov. 1835	T2
Smith, Sally W.	Halsey, Ichabod B.	5, Jan. 1803	S3
Smith, Sarah	Armstrong, James	15, Apr. 1820	S2
Smith, Sarah	Armstrong, James	20, Apr. 1820	D3
Smith, Sarah	Hutchinson, William	11, Mar. 1825	N2
Smith, Sarah	Shepherd, Stephen	4, Oct. 1841	N2
Smith, Sarah E.	Coombes, A.D.	7, June 1830	A3
Smith, Sarah E.	Coombs, A.D.	5, June 1830	R3
Smith, Sarah T.	Esep, Edward	3, Feb. 1842	N2
Smith, Sarah W.	Massie, Henrie	5, Mar. 1842	R3
Smith, Sarah Y.	Estep, Thomas	5, Feb. 1842	R3
Smith, Susan M.	Holliday, Joseph	22, May 1847	K2
Smith, Thomasina	Montgomery, Henry J.	16, Sept 1852	P2
Smitherner, Virgina	Quinlan, Thomas	1, Sept 1847	K2
Snell, Albina L.	Homan, Henry O.	10, Dec. 1852	P2

Brides	Grooms	Date of Notice	Page
Snewley, Hannah	Johnson, James	29, June 1822	S3
Snider, Mary	McKenner, James C.	2, July 1852	P2
Snyder, Anne L.	Brotherton, James H.	14, Mar. 1849	L2
Solvin, Elizabeth T.	Harris, Daniel	2, Sept 1852	P2
Soule, Maria L.	VanDyke, Henry (Rev)	2, June 1836	X3
Southard, Virginia E.	Hoffman, Ogden	3, Dec. 1838	N2
Southerland, Ann	Harrison, Carter B.	22, June 1836	T2
Southgate, Frances M.	Taliaferro, John N.	2, Dec. 1830	A3
Spangler, Priscilla	Garrett, Ashton	29, Nov. 1828	R3
Spangler, Sarah E.	Woodward, Robert C.	22, Aug. 1838	T2
Speer, Eliza	Finley, James	28, Oct. 1830	A3
Spence, Martha A.	Stith, Townsend D.	7, Nov. 1838	T2
Spencer, Ann E.	Semmes, Raphael	5, May 1837	T2
Spencer, Julia W.	Twitchell, Sophron.	17, Nov. 1837	T2
Spencer, Maria T.	Shultz, William J.	10, June 1842	N2
Spencer, Rhoda	Baldwin, James H.	15, May 1847	K2
Spicer, Pamela Ann	Roye, John H.	14, July 1827	R3
Spining, Susan J.	Calhoun, Andrew	21, May 1831	R3
Spinks, E.J.	Mapes, Joel M.	23, Nov. 1847	K2
Spinning, Eliza Jane	Allen, Nathan	11, July 1835	T2
Spinning, Frances M.	Walker, William H.	26, May 1836	T2
Spinning, Martha Ann	Williams, John	10, Nov. 1827	R3
Spinning, Sarah Ann	Bradbury, Cornelius	24, Nov. 1821	S3
Spurrier, Carsa	Blackburn, David	20, Mar. 1819	S2
Spurrier, Ruth	Symmes, Timothy	3, Oct. 1818	S3
Sraff, Amanda	Baum, D.C.	11, Mar. 1837	R3
Sraff, Amanda	Baum, D.C.	9, Mar. 1837	T2
St.Clair, Frances M.	Mayo, A.F.	9, Sept 1831	X3
St.Clair, Margaret	Harrison, Henry	8, Oct. 1841	N2
St.Clair, Nancy M.	Newkirk, Matthew	4, Mar. 1837	R3
St.Clair, Nancy M.	Newkirk, Nathan	4, Mar. 1837	T2
Stackhouse, Emeline	Robinson, D.	9, May 1840	R3
Stainfield, Elizabeth	Miller, Henry F.	8, Sept 1852	P2
Stanley, Sarah (Mrs)	Carneal, Thomas D.	11, Feb. 1815	S3
Stapleton, Henrietta	Leeds, George	2, Sept 1836	N2
Stapp, Maria	Blackwell, Robert	8, Apr. 1820	S3
Starbuck, Eliza	Cameron, Wesley	16, July 1836	T2
Starr, Mary	Barnes, John C.	9, Mar. 1849	L2
Steed, Selina M.	Longacer, Isaac N.	22, Sept 1852	P2
Steel, Miriam	Cobb, John	30, July 1841	N3
Steele, Mary (Mrs)	Brown, Edmund L.	25, Sept 1838	T2
Steele, Matilda	Wurts, W.A. (Lt)	25, May 1837	T2
Steffens, Nettie D.	Wetherbee, A.	24, Dec. 1852	P2
Steiner, Mary C.	Shoemaker, R.M.	25, Jan. 1840	R3
Stephan, Marie Jos.	Petit, Charles V.E.	5, Mar. 1839	T2
Stephens, Margaret M.	Beers, John R.	6, July 1847	K2
Stephenson, Lucy	Peebles, William S.	6, Nov. 1841	R3
Stephenson, Lucy	Peebles, William S.	30, Oct. 1841	N2
Stephenson, Mary W.	DeForest, Delauzun	7, July 1832	R3
Sterling, Elizabeth	Pindall, Daniel	16, Oct. 1841	N2
Sterling, Elizabeth	Pindell, Daniel	23, Oct. 1841	R3
Stevens, Jane M.	Scot, John L.	23, Oct. 1841	R3
Stevens, Jane M.	Scott, John L.	22, Oct. 1841	N2
Stevens, Louisa C.	McElevy, Ezekiel	4, Sept 1841	R3

Brides	Grooms	Date of Notice	Page
Stevens, Mary Ann	Davenport, Cyrus	9, July 1847	K2
Stevenson, Eleanor	Robb, James M. (Dr)	15, July 1852	P2
Stewart, Elizabeth A.	Kropf, G.S.	22, May 1850	P2
Stewart, Laura	Jones, Charles	24, Sept 1842	R3
Stewart, Mary Ann	Smith, Samuel	1, Jan. 1828	R3
Stewart, Nancy	Haines, Charles G.	4, Sept 1852	P2
Stewart, Nancy	Studyvan, Thomas	14, Jan. 1831	X3
Stibbs, Mary Jane	Gilmore, James	23, July 1842	R3
Stibbs, Mary Jane	Gilmore, James	19, July 1842	N2
Stibbs, Sarah Ann	Crosby, Joshua E.	10, June 1836	T2
Stickney, Mary Eliza	Wrag, George	4, Aug. 1832	R3
Stilwell, Eliza	Cary, S.F.	31, May 1849	L2
Stites, Hannah (Mrs)	Carter, Daniel C.	23, Nov. 1811	S3
Stittwell, Sarah	Ball, James (Capt)	4, Jan. 1808	S3
Stockman, Susan Jane	Adams, Joseph	10, June 1835	T2
Stockwell, Elizabeth B.	Green, William N.	21, Nov. 1840	R3
Stoddart, Clarissa	Gooch, Henry	29, May 1841	N2
Stoker, Henrietta	Dacker, Matthias M.	24, June 1837	R3
Stokes, Henrietta	Dacker, Matthias M.	19, June 1837	T2
Stoms, Sarah Mills	Cottingham, Thomas	22, Nov. 1834	R3
Stoms, Sarah Mills	Cottingham, Thomas	19, Nov. 1834	T2
Stone, Eunice A.	Gould, John	30, Sept 1847	K2
Stone, Frances F.	Digby, Theodore	23, Mar. 1847	K2
Storch, Josephine	Ballauf, William	12, June 1847	K2
Stow, Eliza	Launder, James	1, July 1835	T2
Stratton, Mary P.	Webb, Henry	4, Nov. 1847	K2
Stratton, Sarah Jane	Hill, Frederick	18, Oct. 1852	P2
Strawbridge, Jane	McCane, John	11, Apr. 1812	S2
Streeter, Julia Ann	Walden, Baltzer C.	30, Oct. 1838	N2
Strickler, Eliza	Smiley, William	15, Sept 1838	R3
Strong, Susan (Mrs)	Richards, Wolcott	3, June 1841	N2
Strouder, Mary	Sefton, John	26, Apr. 1842	N2
Stuart, Anna L.	Cook, Robert F.	20, Sept 1847	K2
Stuart, Jane M.	Webber, George H.	23, Mar. 1849	L2
Stuart, Mary	Harris, William	26, Feb. 1842	R3
Stute, Mary E.	Morgan, Milton H.	17, July 1852	P2
Suggett, ----	Craig, William G.	7, June 1828	R3
Suiter, Ellen	Briggs, William H.	21, Feb. 1842	N2
Sullivan, Mary	Holcomb, Asa H.	29, Mar. 1816	S3
Summerfield, Marion	Thoms, James	15, Mar. 1828	R3
Summons, Mary	Armstrong, R.G.	30, Nov. 1847	K2
Sumner, Amanda C.	Davis, Preston (Dr)	17, May 1828	R3
Surguy, Eliza	Linley, Francis	1, June 1841	N2
Susars, Electa Ann	Custard, David C.	29, June 1841	N2
Sutherland, Anna	Harrison, Carter B.	30, June 1836	X3
Sutton, Caroline	Bachman, John J.	6, Nov. 1852	P2
Sutton, Charlotte	Murdock, Granville T.	16, May 1840	R3
Suydam, Eliza	Colett, W.R.	17, Aug. 1833	R3
Suydam, Lydia (Mrs)	Laurence, Robert	24, Jan. 1829	R3
Swager, Elizabeth	Ernest, Jacob	8, June 1849	L2
Swager, Mary A.	Moore, Jesse A.	19, Nov. 1852	P2
Swasey, Ann Eliza	Partridge, Alden	12, June 1837	T2
Swasey, Ann Elizabeth	Partridge, Alden	10, June 1837	R3
Swearingen, Sarah B.	Thatcher, Woodbridge	7, Mar. 1840	R3

Brides	Grooms	Date of Notice	Page
Sweeney, Adalaide	Brydon, G.C.	13, June 1850	P2
Sweet, Maria A.	Darling, George H.	17, June 1850	P2
Sweet, Martha	McClure, Alex	24, July 1838	T2
Sweignhart, Caroline	Taulman, P.J.	10, Oct. 1836	T3
Swift, Lucy	Cunningham, E.W.	22, Sept 1838	R3
Swift, Lucy	Cunningham, E.W.	21, Sept 1838	T2
Swift, Mary L.	Wood, D.M.	10, Oct. 1840	R3
Swinam, Sarah (Mrs)	Stonestreet, Thomas	28, Sept 1835	T2
Swing, Kerenda	Hageman, James	30, Oct. 1835	T2
Switzer, Belinda	Goshorn, George	15, Aug. 1840	R3
Symmes, Elizabeth (Mrs)	Graham, Thomas	2, Oct. 1819	S3
Symmes, Julia	Reeder, Jeremiah	28, Dec. 1811	S3
Symmes, Mary S.	Colburn, Charles L.	30, July 1847	K2
Symmes, Polly	Moore, Hugh	4, Dec. 1805	S2
Symmonds, Esther E.	Phillips, William	24, Sept 1842	R3
Symonds, Rebecca	Joseph, J.G.	28, Dec. 1833	R3
Taft, Serveign	Peters, William	1, Jan. 1828	R3
Tait, Jane	Russell, Henry W.	8, Sept 1841	N2
Tait, Mary	Jones, Thomas C.	24, May 1836	T2
Tait, Mary	Jones, Thomas C.	26, May 1836	X3
Talbott, Hester Ann	Stillman, O.D.	18, July 1838	T2
Tankesley, Ann	Aldey, Perine	18, Sept 1805	S3
Tappan, Jane D.	Robertson, Alfred	8, Dec. 1836	X3
Tarvin, Agnes	Cowgle, Tarvin (Dr)	31, May 1837	T2
Tatem, Janett S.	Ridgway, Joseph	1, Dec. 1827	R3
Tatspan, Eliza	Antrim, Joseph	24, Jan. 1829	R3
Taylor, Ann	Tibbatts, John W.	4, Jan. 1825	N3
Taylor, Ann	Tibbatts, John W.	13, Jan. 1825	E3
Taylor, Elinor	Barwise, William	5, Dec. 1822	J3
Taylor, Elizabeth (Mrs)	Collins, Edmund	4, Aug. 1842	N2
Taylor, Elizabeth D.	Collins, Edward	4, Aug. 1842	M3
Taylor, Elizabeth F.	Montgomery, A. (Lt)	12, Sept 1840	R3
Taylor, Jane M.	Williamson, George T.	17, Feb. 1831	A3
Taylor, Jane M.	Williamson, George T.	19, Feb. 1831	R3
Taylor, Keturah	Harris, Horatio T.	25, Aug. 1821	S3
Taylor, Martha Ann	Lapse, William H.	23, June 1847	K2
Taylor, Mary	Walker, Lewis S.	13, Nov. 1841	R3
Taylor, Mary	Walker, Lewis S.	12, Nov. 1841	N2
Taylor, Mary A. (Mrs)	Lilley, John	10, Apr. 1849	L2
Taylor, Mary Ann	Jones, Caleb	11, Oct. 1837	T2
Taylor, Polly (Mrs)	McKinney, John (Col)	21, Mar. 1817	S3
Taylor, Susan	McClave, Robert	31, Oct. 1840	R3
Teater, Susan	Buchanan, Joseph	27, Nov. 1819	S3
Tenner, Nancy T.	Martin, Hiram	28, Apr. 1815	S3
Terry, Margaret	Carson, William J.	11, Aug. 1821	S3
Terry, Margaret	Kemper, Charles H.	3, Sept 1847	K2
Terry, Mary A.	Gridley, E.G.	28, Apr. 1827	R3
Terry, Mary A.	Gridley, E.G.	27, Apr. 1827	N2
Thatcher, Julia (Mrs)	Disney, William	21, June 1828	R3
Thatcher, Julia (Mrs)	Disney, William	24, June 1828	N3
Thesing, Marie E.	Becker, C.F.	28, Dec. 1847	K2
Thew, Mary B.	Perry, Samuel	16, Aug. 1816	S3
Thomas, Adaline E.	Knox, James H.	2, Dec. 1840	N2

Brides	Grooms	Date of Notice	Page
Thomas, Amanda	Mauk, Jacob	28, May 1850	P2
Thomas, Frances Ann	Watt, James	13, June 1836	T2
Thomas, Frances Mary	Rowe, Stanhope S.	31, July 1841	V3
Thomas, Mary Ann	DeSerisy, Louis	20, Sept 1852	P2
Thomas, Mary Ellin	Perkins, Joseph	4, Feb. 1831	X3
Thomas, Mary S.	Taylor, Griffin	11, Sept 1819	S3
Thompson, Marian	Coleman, Wesley	16, Jan. 1815	W3
Thompson, Martha B.	Breeden, Abel	23, Aug. 1830	A3
Thompson, Mary A.	King, Joseph	3, Dec. 1852	P2
Thompson, Phebe	Parvin, H. (Dr)	9, June 1832	R3
Thompson, Phebe	Parvin, H. (Dr)	15, June 1832	X3
Thompson, Sarah	Utley, Hasting	7, June 1830	A3
Thompson, Sarah	Utley, Hasting	4, June 1830	N2
Thomson, Ann D.	Little, Jacob (Rev)	7, Apr. 1836	X3
Thomson, Sarah	Minett, Julius C.	19, July 1837	T2
Thornton, Elvira	Mills, James R.	21, July 1852	P2
Thornton, Mildred	Bowman, Alexander D.	28, Oct. 1836	N2
Thornton, Mildred B.	Bowman, Alexander D.	28, Oct. 1836	T2
Thorp, Eliza Ann	Cook, Jesse S.	18, Sept 1819	S3
Tiffin, Ellen W.	Cook, M. Scott	2, May 1840	R3
Tiley, Emma	Thorp, John P.	12, July 1836	N2
Tillinghast, Rebecca	Willing, Charles (Dr)	4, Apr. 1840	R3
Tilton, Mary	Davis, Joshua	4, Sept 1850	Y2
Timberlake, Margaret	Eaton, John H.	12, Jan. 1829	N2
Tindall, Eliza Ann	Lovejoy, Thatcher	8, May 1819	S3
Tindle, Lydia Ann	Jackson, John	23, Jan. 1827	N3
Titcob, M.F.	Wheeler, G.W.	13, Sept 1852	P2
Titus, Eliza	Fisher, Jonathan	26, Nov. 1835	X3
Todd, Harriet	Vail, Daniel H.	2, Nov. 1822	S3
Todd, Henrietta (Mrs)	Johnston, James	28, Apr. 1838	R3
Todd, Jane	Burns, John	14, May 1847	K2
Todd, Margaret	Kellogg, Charles H.	4, Nov. 1847	K2
Todd, Mary Ann (Mrs)	Johnson, Noble S.	28, Oct. 1837	R3
Todd, Mary Ann (Mrs)	Johnson, Noble S.	28, Oct. 1837	T2
Todd, Nancy	Sidle, John	23, Nov. 1832	X3
Tood, Mary A. (Mrs)	Johnson, Noble S.	2, Nov. 1837	X3
Tousy, Elvira	Gaines, James M.	25, Aug. 1827	R3
Townsend, Margaretta	Edwards, Charles G.	22, Apr. 1841	N2
Towsey, Myra	Porter, Thomas (Capt)	1, Dec. 1821	S3
Toy, Ann	Betts, Smith	15, Dec. 1827	R3
Trainer, Sarah M.	Walker, James H.	12, Oct. 1839	R3
Treen, R.	Caroline, Absalom	28, Apr. 1815	S3
Tremper, Catharine	Haynes, Robert (Capt)	28, July 1815	S3
Tremper, Elizabeth	Davis, Dan	15, Sept 1815	S3
Tribby, Rebecca	Turner, James	27, Dec. 1828	R3
Trinnel, Ellen	Dunlap, W.H.	6, Oct. 1852	P2
Trotter, Zarelda	Washburn, Elihu	11, Sept 1835	T2
Trout, Susan J.	English, Samuel	11, Apr. 1812	S2
Tucker, Eliza	Goodwin, William G.	1, Apr. 1806	S3
Tucker, Hannah	Holroyd, Edward	17, Nov. 1841	N2
Tucker, Lizzie C.	Moses, Simpson P.	14, July 1849	L2
Tudor, Alice	Talbert, Joseph	17, Sept 1831	R3
Tudor, Elizabeth A.	Shotwell, George H.	10, Nov. 1836	T2
Tuite, Maria	Holbrook, David L.	31, Dec. 1831	R3

Brides	Grooms	Date of Notice	Page
Tull, Theresa (Mrs)	Sheppard, Isaac D.	22, Sept 1836	X3
Tunis, Caroline B.	Greene, Caleb	10, Oct. 1840	R3
Tunis, Emmeline	Tarrant, Larkin M.	20, Jan. 1826	N3
Tunis, Susan	Landis, Medry	21, Mar. 1817	S3
Turner, Ann Maria	Burdsal, Stephen W.	25, Feb. 1836	T3
Turner, Eleanor	Walker, James	8, Dec. 1821	S3
Turner, Elizabeth	Doyle, Thomas A.	8, Oct. 1822	J3
Turner, Sarah	Melony, Daniel	16, Oct. 1819	S3
Turney, Mary Ann S.	Green, Richard H.	7, Oct. 1831	A3
Turnpaw, Elizabeth (Mrs)	Walker, John	11, July 1835	T2
Turpin, Nancy C.	Sherlock, Thomas	25, Sept 1852	P2
Turrell, Charlana	Mills, Marsh	26, Feb. 1820	S3
Tute, Maria	Holbrook, David L.	6, Jan. 1832	X3
Tuttle, Caroline W.	Blackly, Joseph W.	19, Oct. 1822	S3
Tuttle, Mary Ann	Riddle, Hiram B.	13, Mar. 1835	N2
Tuttle, Mary C.	Blachly, Joseph W.	17, May 1828	R3
Twichell, H. Jennett	Hazen, Nathan L.	31, Oct. 1834	X3
Twichell, Hannah J.	Hazen, N.L.	1, Nov. 1834	R3
Upham, Martha	Morris, Tompson (Lt)	21, Feb. 1835	R3
Upjohn, Mary Ann	Carr, Francis (Col)	10, Aug. 1822	S3
Urton, Esther	Tarrance, John	15, Sept 1827	R3
Ustick, Jane H.	Ludlow, S.T.	13, Jan. 1841	N2
Ustick, Jane Harris	Ludlow, S.L.	23, Jan. 1841	R3
Utley, Almira	White, George L.	16, May 1829	R3
Utz, Sarah Regina	Wilson, Jefferson	13, July 1852	P2
Vail, Eliza	Arbigust, John	10, Nov. 1827	R3
Valentine, Eliza Ann	Cutter, B.G.	14, Sept 1837	X3
VanAntwerp, Eliza	Bascom, H.B. (Rev)	15, Mar. 1839	T2
Vanausdal, Mary R.	Jeffries, John C.	16, Apr. 1842	R3
Vanausdol, Esther A.	Holland, Palmer	6, Sept 1839	T2
Vanausdol, Mary R.	Jeffries, John C.	15, Apr. 1842	N2
Vanblunby, Ann	Ireland, George	14, Aug. 1841	R3
Vanblunby, Ann	Ireland, George	13, Aug. 1841	N2
Vance, A.E.	Gray, William	23, June 1836	X3
Vance, Margaret	Childress, George C.	28, June 1828	R3
Vance, Mary	Hight, George W.	23, Aug. 1816	S3
Vandegriff, Frances	Hall, Edward	15, Sept 1835	T2
Vandervoort, Ann E.	Wells, Henry	26, Apr. 1828	R3
Vandyke, Fidelia R.	Hasluck, D.S.	4, June 1842	R3
VanDyke, Fidelia R.	Hasluck, D.S.	3, June 1842	N2
VanDyke, Phebe P.	Ewing, Henry	2, Jan. 1841	R3
Vanhouton, Phebe L.	Lewis, John H.	29, Oct. 1831	R3
VanLiew, Margaret	Maynard, William W.	10, July 1852	P2
VanValkenburg, Jane	Clark, Samuel H.	15, June 1837	T2
Varney, Charlotte C.	Burns, James	16, May 1840	R3
Vater, Elizabeth M.	Longley, Elias	15, May 1847	K2
Vater, Harriet A.	Moore, James S.	27, Dec. 1852	P2
Vattier, Parmelia A.	Schwartze, F.W.	14, Nov. 1851	P2
Veacock, Martha	Wills, Thomas Edward	9, June 1835	N2
Vinsell, Sarah A.	Whitaker, J.B.	14, Feb. 1851	P2
Wade, Ann (Mrs)	Hartshorn, Warren	14, July 1834	T2

Brides	Grooms	Date of Notice	Page
Wade, Harriet C.	Thomas, C. Walen	12, Aug. 1852	P2
Wade, Harriett	Lloyd, Frederick	24, Aug. 1850	Y2
Wade, Mary	Oliver, David (Dr)	16, Feb. 1816	S3
Wade, Sarah	Bedinger, B.F. (Dr)	6, July 1820	S3
Wade, Susan A.D.	Guy, Alexander	5, Apr. 1830	A3
Wade, Susan A.L.	Guy, Alexander	2, Apr. 1830	N2
Wagner, Kate	Griffiths, David J.	27, Nov. 1852	P2
Wainwright, Ruth	Smith, Spencer	4, June 1841	N2
Walke, Susan V.	Dun, James	5, Dec. 1840	R3
Walke, Susan Virginia	Dun, James	1, Dec. 1840	N2
Walker, Agnes	Norvell, Joseph	11, Apr. 1823	N3
Walker, Amelia	Goodrich, Jeremiah	19, Feb. 1814	S3
Walker, Eunice	Francis, Thomas	22, Feb. 1825	N3
Walker, Margaret M.	Stannus, Richard G.	28, Dec. 1847	K2
Walker, Mary	Bryson, Ambrose M.	9, Jan. 1841	R3
Walker, Mary	Medary, William	27, Nov. 1819	S3
Walker, Matilda H.	Smith, Wright	14, Nov. 1835	T2
Wallace, Amanda C.	Arthurs, William	13, Dec. 1825	N3
Wallace, Caroline W.	Bartlett, William H.	13, Oct. 1832	R3
Wallace, Martha N.	Kovatz, Agusta (Lt)	20, Nov. 1852	P2
Wallace, Mary	Shillito, John	23, May 1836	T2
Wallace, Mary Ann	Jaimeson, Edward	28, Mar. 1829	R3
Wallace, Nancy (Mrs)	Powell, William B.	10, Aug. 1837	X3
Wallace, Phebe F.	Webb, William H.	1, July 1837	R3
Wallace, Phebe Fran.	Webb, William H.	1, July 1837	T2
Wallack, Jane	Ward, Moses	20, May 1842	N2
Wallingford, Malinda	Bowman, Andrew	12, July 1837	T2
Walpole, Harriet	Quarles, William	28, June 1828	R3
Walsh, Eliza	Beckett, Henry	12, Sept 1840	R3
Walters, Ann	Whiticar, James	12, Oct. 1820	S3
Ward, Abigail	Foote, Andrew R.	15, Sept 1837	T2
Ward, Clarisa	Williams, David	15, Nov. 1828	R3
Ward, Clarissa	Williams, David	14, Nov. 1828	N3
Ward, Eliza A.	Bartlett, N.	8, Nov. 1830	A3
Ward, Martha	Adkins, Thomas O.	3, Mar. 1834	T3
Ward, Mary L.	Walker, George W.	13, Mar. 1841	N2
Ward, Mary Rebecca	Vance, Alex F.	11, Aug. 1835	T2
Ward, Rebecca	Williams, Benjamin F	19, Apr. 1836	T2
Ward, Sophia	Stokes, John M.	6, June 1828	Q3
Warder, Sarah A.	Cumming, Edward H.	2, Mar. 1833	R3
Wardnour, Mary A.	Rannells, Charles S.	28, May 1842	R3
Ware, Abigail	Foote, Andrew	16, Sept 1837	R3
Ware, Abigail	Warner, George	21, Aug. 1819	S3
Ware, Harriet (Mrs)	Marsh, Anderson	28, Nov. 1835	T2
Waring, Ellen	Pierson, Henry A.	19, Apr. 1831	A3
Warner, Emeline A.	Galt, John H.	10, Nov. 1852	P2
Warner, Louisa	Carnahan, G.A.	9, Oct. 1852	P2
Warner, Margaret L.	Stewart, William B.	20, Sept 1852	P2
Warner, Rebecca	Jennings, Charles E.	12, Aug. 1835	T2
Warren, Elizabeth A.	Townsend, Louis	3, Dec. 1852	P2
Wartman, Elizabeth	Lusk, Thomas	17, Nov. 1838	T2
Washburn, Harriet J.	Prince, Joseph W.	24, May 1849	L2
Washburn, Mary F.	Folger, Seth W.	6, June 1837	N2
Waters, Ann M.	Jackson, Robert C.	27, Nov. 1852	P2

Brides	Grooms	Date of Notice	Page
Waters, Eliza	Young, John N.	16, Aug. 1834	R3
Waters, Eliza	Young, John N.	14, Aug. 1834	T2
Waters, Henrietta	Ross, J.W.	7, June 1842	N2
Waters, Kezia R.	Wilson, Noah L.	13, June 1840	R3
Waters, Phebe (Mrs)	Reddish, Thomas	4, Feb. 1825	N2
Watkins, Lydia	Sprague, Andrew W.	17, Feb. 1842	N2
Watson, Annie A.	Forte, Elijah C.	8, Sept 1852	P2
Watson, Caroline	Smith, William R.	21, Dec. 1838	T2
Watson, Charlotte	Baily, Thomas	9, Mar. 1837	T2
Watson, Olive V.	Jones, Asa P. (Dr)	1, Nov. 1834	R3
Wattson, Ann Delia	Downer, William	18, May 1841	N2
Weatherby, Mary G.	Schwartze, F.W.	15, Apr. 1847	K2
Weatherford, Letitia	Clifton, William	22, Sept 1838	R3
Weatherford, Sarah	Freeman, Amos	22, Sept 1838	R3
Weaver, Myriam	Goodloe, James	13, Nov. 1819	S3
Weaver, Sarah Dell	Gill, Michael	8, Aug. 1818	S3
Webb, Lucy W.	Hayes, R.B.	3, Jan. 1853	P2
Weekly, Mary Ann	Williams, Harbert S.	31, May 1830	A3
Weeks, Caroline	Litherbury, John	27, Aug. 1824	N2
Weeks, Rebecca	Pawson, T.	6, Nov. 1847	K2
Weeks, Susan Ann	Winchell, George D.	1, May 1847	K2
Weggins, Jane	Sparks, William	16, Oct. 1819	S3
Weir, Ellen	Smith, E.G.	1, Aug. 1840	R3
Weir, Mary	Langtry, Thomas	29, Apr. 1825	N3
Weir, Priscilla R.	Mason, John W.	28, Nov. 1823	N2
Wells, Alithea	Newcomb, Harvey	7, June 1830	A3
Wells, Alithea	Newcomb, Harvey	5, June 1830	R3
Wells, Clarissa	Butler, Thomas C.	28, Dec. 1852	P2
Wells, Marietta	Ware, Samuel	12, June 1847	K2
Wells, Tryphena	Cathel, John	27, Apr. 1822	S3
Werder, Mary A.	Rannels, Charles S.	24, May 1842	N2
Werner, Ellen Agnes	Gordon, George H.	10, June 1836	T2
West, Mary	Thornton, Joseph	27, Dec. 1825	N2
West, Sophronia S.	Lewis, James Ewing	23, June 1838	R3
West, Susan	Rust, John	19, Sept 1840	R3
Westcott, Rachel P.	Halley, Washington G.	27, Jan. 1827	R2
Westlake, Susan	Hopper, Morris	17, Mar. 1838	N3
Westlake, Susan	Hopper, Morris S.	24, Mar. 1838	R3
Whaley, Sarah Jane	Howe, William T.	12, Nov. 1847	K2
Wharten, Sarah	Auten, William	1, Jan. 1828	R3
Wharton, Mary E.	Washington, George	12, Oct. 1837	T2
Wheat, Mary	Clark, Francis B.	25, Aug. 1841	N2
Wheeler, Eliza J.	Buckingham, Oliver P.	29, Nov. 1852	P2
Wheeler, Harriet	Chase, Abraham	18, May 1807	S3
Wheeling, Minerva	Webb, Alexander	25, Dec. 1841	R3
Wheeling, Minerva	Webb, Alexander	22, Dec. 1841	N2
Wheelwright, Mary R.	Keating, John	28, Apr. 1826	N2
Whetstone, Hannah E.	Huey, George J.	24, Oct. 1840	R3
Whetstone, Sarah	Lewis, William	1, Dec. 1821	S3
Whipple, Hanna	Silsbee, Samuel (Dr)	5, July 1841	N2
Whipple, Sarah H.	Wells, Horace	23, Mar. 1822	S3
Whipple, Sophia	Horton, Jonathan	6, Aug. 1814	S3
Whippy, Margaret	Pancoast, Joseph	12, May 1815	S3
Whitacre, Mary Jane	Wallace, J.G.	29, Dec. 1852	P2

Brides	Grooms	Date of Notice	Page
Whitaker, Harriet R.	Harig, Albert	7, Aug. 1850	Y2
Whitaker, Priscilla	Cadwallader, Jonah	4, Dec. 1813	S3
White, Elizabeth	Clark, John M.	10, Apr. 1841	R3
White, Elizabeth	Clark, John M.	13, Apr. 1841	N2
White, Jean M.	Ladd, William H.	30, July 1847	K2
White, Maria	Neff, George W.	20, Oct. 1827	R3
White, Mary M.	Henderson, Garden J.	1, Sept 1852	P2
White, Rebecca Ann	Downs, W.H.	3, June 1847	K2
White, Sophronia E.	Williams, Vachel	27, Dec. 1852	P2
Whitehead, Mary	Mitchell, J.W.	6, Jan. 1848	K2
Whitehead, Sarah	Lawrence, David H.	3, Aug. 1830	N2
Whitehill, Margaret	McDowell, Joseph	13, Dec. 1833	X3
Whiteman, Clarissa	Harlan, Aaron	4, Oct. 1830	A3
Whitney, Eliza	Swift, Milton	24, Nov. 1827	R3
Whitney, Elizabeth (Mrs)	Thomas, Robert	15, May 1847	K2
Whitney, Harriet	Carnes, Peter	26, Mar. 1842	R3
Whitney, Mary Jane	Lawrence, Edward M.	27, Aug. 1852	P2
Whittemore, Harriet	Florer, John N.	29, Mar. 1838	T2
Wickliffe, Sarah H.	Woolley, Aaron K.	20, Oct. 1827	R3
Wicoff, Elsa	Bonnel, Clark	14, Sept 1811	S3
Wiggins, Julia	Worthington, Vachel	11, Jan. 1839	T2
Wilder, Olive	Brown, Ira S.	31, Oct. 1840	R3
Wiles, Catharine E.	Goodman, Charles	25, Dec. 1841	R3
Wiles, Catharine F.	Goodman, Charles	23, Dec. 1841	N2
Wilkins, Jane	Logan, John W.	20, Apr. 1833	R3
Wilkins, Maria D.	Sanders, John	7, Jan. 1839	T2
Willace, Jane	Ward, Moses	21, May 1842	R3
Willard, Emma (Mrs)	Yates, C.C. (Dr)	29, Sept 1838	R3
Williams, Anna	Barnhart, Daniel	10, Sept 1842	R3
Williams, Anne S.	Beman, I.C.	22, Sept 1838	R3
Williams, Anne S.	Beman, I.C.	15, Sept 1838	T2
Williams, Caroline	Treadwell, Alexander	15, Nov. 1828	R3
Williams, Catharine	Harter, L.F.	11, July 1849	L2
Williams, Elisabeth	Taylor, Mahlon R.	8, Dec. 1836	X3
Williams, Elizabeth	Timmons, Elisha	24, May 1828	R2
Williams, Hannah M.	Stone, B.T.	15, Sept 1838	T2
Williams, Hannah M.	Stone, C.T.	22, Sept 1838	R3
Williams, Martha	Allen, Samuel R.	17, Jan. 1818	S3
Williams, Mary	AtLee, Samuel Yorke	7, June 1836	T2
Williams, Mary	Chamberlin, John	10, Sept 1842	R3
Williams, Mary Anna	Atlee, S. Yorke	3, May 1841	N2
Williams, Nancy	Kyzer, William	27, Feb. 1819	S3
Williams, Nancy (Mrs)	McMinn, Joseph	20, Sept 1816	S3
Williams, Rachael	Brown, Jenks	19, Aug. 1823	N3
Williams, Rebecca	Snyder, Jacob	25, Aug. 1821	S3
Williams, Rebecca M.	Beal, Edward C.	15, Dec. 1827	R3
Williams, Rebecca M.	Gazlay, James W.	15, Apr. 1820	S2
Williams, Rebecca M.	Gazlay, James W.	20, Apr. 1820	D3
Williams, Sally	Parks, Arthur	14, Mar. 1812	S2
Williams, Sarah T.	Mendenhall, James	17, Nov. 1827	R3
Williamson, Abigail	Dodd, John M.	14, July 1836	X3
Williamson, Eliza	Garrison, William	29, May 1841	N2
Williamson, Lydia H.	Richards, Channing	11, Mar. 1837	R3
Williamson, Lydia H.	Richards, Channing	13, Mar. 1837	T2

Brides	Grooms	Date of Notice	Page
Williamson, Marian	Stevenson, Hugh	28, Jan. 1832	R3
Williamson, Marian	Stevenson, Hugh	3, Feb. 1832	X3
Williamson, Mat.	Hunt, S.H.	28, Oct. 1852	P2
Williamson, Matilda	Colvin, Thomas	19, Jan. 1837	X3
Willis, Jane F.	Winters, William	5, Feb. 1835	N2
Willis, Martha Ann	Piatt, John H.	24, July 1813	S3
Willis, Nancy	Gano, W.G.W.	13, Oct. 1821	S3
Willis, Susan	Armstrong, John	28, Dec. 1807	S3
Wilson, Alice Jane	Ruffner, Sylvester	9, July 1838	T2
Wilson, Eliza Jane	Card, John	25, Oct. 1852	P2
Wilson, Jane	McLain, James A.	26, May 1836	X3
Wilson, Jane C.	Worthington, Amos	16, July 1842	R3
Wilson, Margaret	Brown, James D.	23, Oct. 1852	P2
Wilson, Margaretta E.	Johnston, Samuel	7, Dec. 1820	S3
Wilson, Maria	Simonton, William	6, Sept 1816	S3
Wilson, Maria Louisa	Perin, Lyman	16, Apr. 1849	L2
Wilson, Mary	Caswell, Daniel J.	4, May 1822	S3
Wilson, Nancy	Davis, George F.	16, July 1841	N2
Wilson, Nancy	White, John	25, Feb. 1815	S3
Wilson, Olive	Hadlock, Hezekiah	4, Oct. 1830	A3
Wilson, Rebecca	Cullum, George	5, July 1830	A3
Wilson, Sarah Ann	Flinn, Jesse	19, Apr. 1847	K2
Wilson, Sarah Jane	Garretson, Samuel	27, Dec. 1828	R3
Wiltberger, S. (Mrs)	Decker, Josiah	18, May 1822	S3
Winfree, Eliza	Hough, Amos (Dr)	7, May 1831	R3
Wingert, Mary Ann	Winter, Thomas	26, Sept 1823	N2
Winship, Francis M.	Smith, Lemuel	7, July 1826	N3
Winston, Mary	Rust, William B.	20, Sept 1852	P2
Winter, Anne	Moore, William	27, Apr. 1824	N3
Winter, Anne	Moore, William	29, Apr. 1824	E3
Winters, Debby	Goforth, Aaron	24, Apr. 1805	S3
Winters, Lydia C.	Kirby, William	11, Oct. 1852	P2
Winton, Sally	Anderson, William C.	27, June 1812	S3
Wirk, Hannah	White, Charles R.	20, Aug. 1852	P2
Wise, Maria	Peebles, Daniel M.	1, Jan. 1842	R3
Wishart, Margaretta	Carter, A.G.W.	9, Apr. 1842	R3
Withington, Abby Ann	Wood, William B.	5, Nov. 1835	T2
Witten, Elenor	Quinn, James (Rev)	2, Dec. 1824	E2
Wolf, Rosina	Trainer, Lewis	7, Aug. 1841	R3
Wood, Abigail	Cogy, Joseph (Dr)	29, June 1820	S3
Wood, Amanda	Martin, Samuel	2, Jan. 1839	T2
Wood, Bertha	Cranch, Edward P.	16, Apr. 1841	N2
Wood, Catharine	Dayton, Eli (Dr)	15, Feb. 1839	T2
Wood, Eliza F.	Morgan, Isaac	14, Nov. 1817	S2
Wood, Frances B.	Worthington, Amos	12, Nov. 1831	R3
Wood, Frances M.	Davie, Melarcton O.	14, Apr. 1836	T2
Wood, Jane H.	Walker, Charles C.	10, Nov. 1827	R3
Wood, Lucy	Schenck, John	9, Mar. 1837	T2
Wood, Lucy	Schenck, John	8, Mar. 1837	N2
Wood, Maria P.	Schenck, Aaron L.	3, Aug. 1822	S3
Wood, Martha B.	Kemper, J.H.	5, Jan. 1833	R3
Wood, Martha B.	Kemper, John H.	4, Jan. 1833	X3
Wood, Olive H.	James, U.P.	13, May 1847	K2
Wood, Rebecca H.	Gordon, John (Capt)	14, Jan. 1837	R3

Brides	Grooms	Date of Notice	Page
Wood, Sarah Ann	Fosdick, Samuel	14, Jan. 1836	T3
Wood, Susan M.	Thayer, Henry	25, Apr. 1840	R3
Woodard, Patsey	Dunseth, John	20, Sept 1814	W4
Woodman, Eliza (Mrs)	Weaver, William	2, Dec. 1830	A3
Woodruff, Caroline S	Olds, Chauncey N.	24, Mar. 1838	R3
Woodruff, Catharine	Parker, William	1, Nov. 1838	T2
Woods, Eliza A.	Seichrest, William H.	17, Aug. 1852	P2
Woods, Ellen	Adae, Charles F.	19, Mar. 1842	R3
Woods, Martha M.	McGrew, Alexander	8, Sept 1847	K2
Woodward, Mary	Grimes, Thomas	4, July 1812	S3
Woodward, Mary Ann	Finkbine, William H.	8, Oct. 1847	K2
Worchester, Lucy	Tranter, James	28, Apr. 1849	L2
Worden, Sarah F.	Nevers, Edward	18, Dec. 1838	T2
Workman, Catharine	Spencer, Alexander O.	28, Nov. 1838	T2
Worley, Margaret E.	Spinning, William	24, May 1849	L2
Worrels, Lucretia	Greenleaf, Charles T.	8, Sept 1838	R3
Worthington, Eliza	Moore, Samuel	7, June 1828	R3
Worthington, Elizabeth	Pomeroy, Charles R.	13, Nov. 1835	T2
Worthington, Sarah A	King, Edward	31, May 1816	S3
Wright, Elizabeth	Shaw, John	9, Apr. 1814	S3
Wright, Lucy	Sanders, Ravid A.	16, Aug. 1838	T2
Wright, Mary	Hatch, Harlan	11, Oct. 1828	R3
Wright, Mary	Miner, John L.	4, Nov. 1837	R3
Wright, Mary	Miner, John L.	31, Oct. 1837	T2
Wright, Mary	Wright, Isaac	16, June 1827	R3
Wright, Rebecca	Lathrop, Martin (Dr)	18, Feb. 1815	S3
Wright, Sarah Jane	Campbell, Edwin R.	19, May 1849	L2
Wunder, Mary Ann	Whittaker, Joseph	27, Aug. 1852	P2
Yates, Margaret	Roark, James	31, July 1852	P2
Yeatman, Anna Maria	Anderson, W.C.	20, May 1837	R3
Yeatman, Anna Maria	Anderson, W.C.	19, May 1837	T2
Yeatman, Caroline	Ward, William M.	31, May 1849	L2
Yeatman, Jane (Mrs)	Bell, John	4, Nov. 1835	T2
Yeatman, Julia	Barker, Thomas C.	30, Apr. 1814	S3
Yeatman, Sally T.	Murphy, Lewis	10, Oct. 1839	T2
Yeazee, Mary Jane	Thatcher, David	26, Aug. 1850	P2
Young, Ann	Frye, George B.	6, June 1836	T2
Young, Cynthia Ann	Betts, Smith	28, Jan. 1848	K2
Young, Frances Mary	Finch, William	23, June 1838	R3
Young, Frances Mary	Finch, William	22, June 1838	T2
Young, Julia S.	Smith, William J.	21, Aug. 1847	K2
Zane, Mary	Robinson, Thaddius P	7, Mar. 1829	R3
Zane, Sophia	Johnson, James (Dr)	19, Apr. 1828	R3
Zebold, Mary E.	Heferman, Thomas	11, Oct. 1852	P2
Zesline, Sarah (Mrs)	Borden, Samuel (Capt)	17, July 1819	S3

Name	Type of Notice	Date of Notice	Page
Abbot, Aaron & Mary	Divorce/abandonment	7, Nov. 1795	C3
Abbott, George	Runaway apprentice	9, Oct. 1823	J3
Abercrombia, Hugh & Mary	Divorce/abandonment	22, Oct. 1830	N3
Ackerson, James & Angeline	Divorce/abandonment	21, Mar. 1817	S3
Adams, Abraham	Horse found	6, Sept 1809	H4
Adams, Alexander	Insolvent debtor	23, July 1830	N3
Adams, Caleb	Debt relief	27, Jan. 1821	S3
Adams, J.M.	Missing child case	15, Aug. 1836	T2
Adams, Margaret	Information wanted	28, Jan. 1823	N3
Adams, Sally	Poor house inmate	14, Nov. 1851	P2
Addleman, Joseph & Telney	Divorce/abandonment	6, Nov. 1851	P2
Adkins, Timothy	Horse found	5, Jan. 1815	S3
Agnew, Samuel	Run away apprentice	8, Jan. 1814	S3
Agniel, Isaure	Female school award	28, July 1835	N2
Agniel, Louisa	Female school award	28, July 1835	N2
Alair, William	Deserter from army	30, Nov. 1793	C3
Alberger, Adam	Insolvent debtor	27, Jan. 1829	N3
Alcorn, William	Horse lost	14, Jan. 1818	S2
Aldrige, Joseph	Horse found	19, July 1809	H3
Alexander, Sarah	Horse found	29, Aug. 1817	S3
Alger, Skillman	Horse found	1, June 1811	S3
Alison, Richard	Departure notice	5, Nov. 1799	S3
Allaire, Peter A.	Run away notice	16, Jan. 1827	N3
Allen, Davisson	Deposition given	4, Oct. 1842	Z4
Allen, James	Run away slave	13, Apr. 1820	D3
Allen, John	Horse found	21, Feb. 1810	H4
Alling, Jared	Partition petition	22, Mar. 1837	N3
Alling, Julia S.	Partition petition	22, Mar. 1837	N3
Allison, Archibald	Run away apprentice	21, Aug. 1813	S1
Allison, James	Court sentencing	4, Nov. 1836	N2
Allison, Richard	Cow found	12, Mar. 1800	S3
Alloway, Archelaus	Run away	16, Jan. 1802	S3
Allsworth, Josiah	Escaped prisoner	26, Sept 1795	C3
Alverson, Oliver W. & Nancy	Divorce/abandonment	4, Oct. 1834	R3
Ambrose, James & Priscilla	Divorce/abandonment	16, Feb. 1848	K3
Anderson, Andrew	Horse found	7, July 1821	S3
Anderson, Benjamin	Land for sale	29, Jan. 1806	S1
Anderson, Cornelius W.	Land partition	29, Apr. 1828	N3
Anderson, Elijah	Horse stolen	27, June 1823	N2
Anderson, Enoch	Horse found	14, Dec. 1827	N3
Anderson, Enos & Jerusha	Divorce/abandonment	2, Apr. 1824	N3
Anderson, George	Court sentencing	4, Nov. 1836	N2
Anderson, Henry	Notice	8, Oct. 1799	S3
Anderson, Isaac	Horse lost	1, July 1801	S3
Anderson, John	Horse found	27, June 1812	S3
Anderson, John	Escaped convict	3, Oct. 1818	S2
Anderson, John	Court sentencing	4, Nov. 1836	N2
Anderson, John G. & Sarah	Divorce/abandonment	17, Nov. 1815	S3
Anderson, Parmela	Land partition	29, Apr. 1828	N3
Anderson, Warfield & Mary	Divorce/abandonment	3, Jan. 1851	P2
Andrews, Dudley	Chancery case	9, Nov. 1824	N4
Andrews, Hepza Dana	Chancery case	9, Nov. 1824	N4
Andrews, Silas	Horse found	16, Feb. 1816	S3
Anthony, McKinney	Chancery case	10, Oct. 1823	N3

Name	Type of Notice	Date of Notice	Page
Applegate, William	Horse found	11, July 1826	N3
Arbot, Thomas	Horse found	27, June 1812	S3
Archer, Benjamin	Horse lost	5, Nov. 1796	F3
Archeson, David	Debt notice	5, Nov. 1796	F3
Archibald, Hugh	Partition petition	23, Jan. 1837	N3
Archibald, Robert	Partition petition	23, Jan. 1837	N3
Archibald, Robert & Elizabeth	Divorce/abandonment	15, Aug. 1818	S3
Armor, James	Inquiry	1, June 1822	S3
Armstrong, Abby	Partition petition	25, Aug. 1837	N3
Armstrong, Andrew	Horse lost	13, Dec. 1794	C3
Armstrong, Archibald	Horse lost	27, July 1803	S3
Armstrong, J.S.	Committee member	15, Nov. 1838	N2
Armstrong, James	Notice	5, Oct. 1803	S3
Armstrong, James	Horse found	6, Aug. 1817	S3
Armstrong, John	Horse lost	16, Nov. 1807	S3
Armstrong, John	Horse stolen	1, Mar. 1794	C3
Armstrong, John	Land for sale	17, Sept 1796	F3
Armstrong, John	Deposition given	13, Sept 1842	Z4
Armstrong, Nathaniel	Partition petition	25, Aug. 1837	N3
Armstrong, Robert	Horse found	19, Dec. 1812	S1
Armstrong, Robert & Elizabeth	Divorce/abandonment	11, July 1795	C3
Armstrong, Stephen & Ruth	Divorce/abandonment	11, July 1818	S3
Arnel, George	Horse found	6, Oct. 1815	S2
Arnold, (son of Montgomery)	Birth notice	7, Mar. 1849	L2
Arnold, William	Horse found	10, Nov. 1815	S3
Arnold, William & Catharine	Divorce/abandonment	7, Mar. 1826	N3
Arral, Thomas	Horse found	5, Nov. 1796	F3
Arthur, Isom	Run away	11, May 1811	S3
Arthur, William	Debt inquiry	18, Dec. 1819	S3
Arthurs, John	Horse lost	15, July 1806	S3
Arthurs, John	Horse found	29, July 1806	S1
Asa, John	Run away notice	25, Dec. 1827	N3
Ashburn, Thomas	Notice	29, Sept 1815	S3
Ashburn, Thomas	Horse found	21, Feb. 1810	H4
Askew, David & Mary	Guardianship	20, Sept 1816	S1
Atherton, Aaron	Horse found	22, June 1820	S3
Atherton, David	Horse found	30, June 1815	S3
Atherton, David	Horse found	25, July 1818	S3
Atherton, Peter	Horse found	20, Aug. 1814	S3
Attee, William	Chancery case	15, July 1835	N3
Aupperle, David	Horse lost	25, Nov. 1823	J3
Auter, Leah & Thomas	Divorce/abandonment	20, Feb. 1819	S1
Auter, Thomas & Leah	Divorce/abandonment	6, Feb. 1819	S3
Avery, Charles	Horse lost	13, Mar. 1802	S3
Avery, Charles	Horse lost	18, May 1803	S4
Avery, John C.	Debt relief	20, June 1818	S3
Ayer, John	Horse found	7, Aug. 1819	S3
Ayers, Thomas & Rosanna	Divorce/abandonment	3, Sept 1808	S2
Bachelor, Robertson	Deserter from army	2, Oct. 1813	S3
Backley, Isaac	Run away notice	4, Jan. 1837	T2
Bacon, David	Horse found	6, Aug. 1817	S3
Bacon, Horace	Chancery case	21, Mar. 1838	N2
Bacon, John	Horse found	7, July 1821	S3

Name	Type of Notice	Date of Notice	Page
Bacon, John & Elizabeth	Divorce/abandonment	31, Jan. 1823	N3
Badger, Daniel	Horse found	25, Sept 1802	S3
Badgley, William	Horse found	13, July 1822	S2
Baird, Paul	Horse found	8, May 1813	S3
Baker, Elizabeth	Stealing charge	25, Mar. 1796	C3
Baker, Horace E. & Mary A.	Divorce/abandonment	6, Sept 1831	A3
Balch, William	Horse found	5, June 1813	S2
Baldwin, Eleazer	Horse found	23, May 1828	Q3
Baldwin, Philander	Horse found	14, July 1821	S3
Balem, Thomas	Horse found	21, Feb. 1817	S4
Banister, John	Horse found	25, July 1818	S3
Banta, Peter	Horse lost	31, July 1805	S3
Barcalow, Derick	Horse found	23, Jan. 1813	S3
Barcelow, Cerick	Horse found	17, Oct. 1812	S3
Barker, Abial & Rosana	Divorce/abandonment	15, Jan. 1820	S3
Barker, John	Horse found	28, Nov. 1812	S3
Barker, Stephen A. & Sarah	Divorce/abandonment	6, Nov. 1805	S3
Barker, Thomas	Horse lost	18, May 1807	S3
Barlew, Robert	Horse found	27, Mar. 1819	S3
Barnes, Charles C.	Insolvent debtor	11, Nov. 1828	N1
Barnes, Euphemia A.	Female school award	28, July 1835	N2
Barnett, Abraham	Horse found	26, Oct. 1807	S1
Barns, Thomas	Cow found	31, Dec. 1796	F3
Barr, John M.	Horse found	11, Dec. 1819	S3
Barr, John T.	Chancery case	21, Dec. 1830	N3
Barret, John	Horse lost	16, Mar. 1803	S3
Barrett, James	Cow found	3, Dec. 1796	F3
Barry, John	Deserter from army	12, Sept 1795	C3
Bartine, David & Elizabeth	Chancery case	21, Mar. 1838	N2
Bartlett, Richard	Runaway - 17 yrs.	7, Mar. 1817	S3
Bartmess, Joseph & Lucy	Divorce/abandonment	5, Mar. 1824	N3
Bartmiss, Joseph & Lucy	Divorce/abandonment	3, Feb. 1825	E3
Basset, Michael	Horse found	24, Mar. 1821	S3
Basset, Michael	Horse found	20, Jan. 1826	N3
Bateman, Aaron	Horse lost	9, Oct. 1819	S3
Bates, Clark	Horse found	22, May 1813	S3
Bates, Clarke	Cow found	26, Dec. 1801	S3
Bates, Isaac	Horse lost	28, May 1800	S3
Bates, Isaac	Cow found	23, Apr. 1796	C2
Bates, Isaac (Lt)	Hamilton Co militia	28, Nov. 1801	S3
Battell, William	Information wanted	21, Aug. 1835	N2
Bavis, Ann	Horse found	23, Apr. 1814	S1
Baxter, James	Horse found	28, Nov. 1801	S3
Baxter, John	Guardian	21, Sept 1838	N3
Bazadon, Laurence	Court case	19, Nov. 1800	S3
Beach, Samuel	Estate case	18, Oct. 1816	S3
Beall, Benjamin	Run away	26, Mar. 1800	S3
Beamish, Henry	Inquiry	10, July 1819	S3
Beard, John B.	Chancery case	20, Jan. 1829	N3
Beard, Joseph	Horse found	3, Oct. 1812	S3
Beasly, Susan D.	Real estate sale	17, June 1825	N3
Beaty, David	Horse found	26, Oct. 1807	S1
Beaty, John	Horse lost	4, June 1800	S3
Beavor, William	Murdered	4, Nov. 1836	N2

Name	Type of Notice	Date of Notice	Page
Beazley, John	Horse lost	13, July 1803	S3
Beazley, Joseph	Horse lost	9, Oct. 1805	S3
Bedford, John	Run away	27, Feb. 1802	S3
Bedinger, B.F.	Committee member	15, Nov. 1838	N2
Beekett, John	Horse lost	6, Aug. 1799	S3
Beeler, Samuel	Horse found	9, Feb. 1811	S3
Behyner, Nathaniel	Horse found	13, June 1817	S3
Belding, Thomas	Escaped convict	3, Oct. 1818	S2
Bell, Adam	Run away notice	19, June 1837	T2
Bell, Ann	Horse found	11, Feb. 1815	S3
Bell, Isabella	Guardianship	8, Oct. 1830	N3
Bell, James	Guardianship	8, Oct. 1830	N3
Bell, Jane	Guardianship	8, Oct. 1830	N3
Bell, John	Guardianship	8, Oct. 1830	N3
Bell, Michael	Horse found	7, Dec. 1827	N3
Bell, Miller	Horse found	21, Apr. 1826	N3
Bell, Miller	Horse found	30, Nov. 1830	N3
Bell, Obed	Horse found	20, Feb. 1813	S3
Bell, Peter	Horse found	3, Dec. 1814	S3
Bell, Sheba	Guardianship	8, Oct. 1830	N3
Bell, Thomas	Chancery case	21, Dec. 1830	N3
Belles, Isaac & Elizabeth	Partition case	28, Sept 1827	Q3
Benefiel, John	Horse lost	21, Dec. 1803	S3
Benefield, Robert	Horse found	1, Oct. 1830	N3
Bennet, Jacob	Estate case	31, May 1816	S1
Bennet, James	Court case	19, July 1809	H4
Bennet, John	Horse found	8, Oct. 1814	S3
Bennet, Samuel	Horse found	21, May 1814	S3
Bennett, James	Horse lost	14, Aug. 1805	S3
Bennett, John	Deserter from army	15, Oct. 1814	S1
Bennett, John	Horse found	5, May 1815	S3
Bennett, Samuel	Horse found	18, Jan. 1808	S3
Bennett, Samuel	Runaway apprentice	10, Oct. 1817	S3
Bennett, William	Horse stolen	5, June 1819	S2
Bentley, A.W.	Committee member	15, Nov. 1838	N2
Bently, John & Mary	Divorce/abandonment	3, Dec. 1799	S3
Berch, Daniel	Horse found	17, Apr. 1813	S3
Bercount, John	Horse found	8, June 1807	S3
Beresford, Richard	Cow lost	18, May 1824	N3
Bernard, Charles T.	Insolvent debtor	27, Jan. 1829	N3
Besewick, George	Information wanted	24, Apr. 1834	T2
Best, Thomas	Horse lost	18, May 1807	S3
Betts, John	Horse found	29, May 1819	S3
Bevins, Jesse	Horse found	17, Sept 1814	S3
Bevis, Jesse	Horse found	17, July 1819	S3
Bickham, George	Court case	19, Nov. 1800	S3
Bigerton, Benjamin	Horse found	18, Dec. 1829	N3
Biggadike, John & Martha	Divorce/abandonment	16, Oct. 1852	P2
Bigger, John	Horse lost	28, May 1800	S3
Biggs, Dorrington	Guardian	21, Sept 1838	N3
Bird, John & Martha	Divorce/abandonment	24, July 1805	S1
Birdsal, Aaron	Horse found	11, Jan. 1837	N2
Bishop, James	Land purchase	23, July 1814	S3
Bishop, Joel	Cow found	24, Dec. 1819	S3

Name	Type of Notice	Date of Notice	Page
Black, Alexander	Horse stolen	16, Feb. 1816	S3
Black, James W.	Court case witness	20, June 1850	P2
Blackburn, Bryson	Horse lost	12, Sept 1804	S3
Blackburn, George (Soldier)	Letter at P.O.	18, Oct. 1794	C3
Blackburn, James	Cow found	5, Nov. 1796	F3
Blackford, William	Deserter from army	31, Dec. 1800	S3
Blair, Greenville & Martha	Divorce/abandonment	30, Jan. 1841	N2
Blake, Francis A.	Escaped from city	29, Aug. 1822	J3
Blanchard, Famde	Estate case	4, July 1826	N3
Blanchard, Joshua	Insolvent debtor	27, Jan. 1829	N3
Blanchard, Josiah	Estate case	4, July 1826	N3
Bland, (Mrs)	Pioneer incident	27, Mar. 1848	K2
Blasdel, Jacob	Cow found	1, Apr. 1801	S3
Blew, Joseph & Hannah	Divorce/abandonment	6, Mar. 1802	S3
Blue, Elizabeth	Administratrix	11, Jan. 1828	Q3
Blue, Henry & Rebecca	Divorce/abandonment	26, Oct. 1838	T2
Blum, Richard & Hannah	Divorce/abandonment	6, Nov. 1851	P2
Boal, Phebe H.	Chancery case	4, Mar. 1828	N3
Boal, Robert	Horse lost	14, June 1816	S3
Boal, Robert	Chancery case	4, Mar. 1828	N3
Boden, Andrew	Horse lost	25, Nov. 1806	S3
Bodine, Elisha & Sally	Divorce/abandonment	4, July 1818	S2
Boes, Anthony	Run away apprentice	29, Sept 1815	S3
Bolender, Stephen	Horse found	9, Feb. 1811	S3
Bond, Richard & Mary	Chancery case	21, Mar. 1838	N2
Boner, William & Katharine	Divorce/abandonment	12, Mar. 1796	C3
Bonsall, Joseph	Committee member	15, Nov. 1838	N2
Boothby, Timothy & Catherine	Divorce/abandonment	21, Oct. 1806	S4
Boots, Samuel	Insolvent debtor	23, July 1830	N3
Borough, Joseph	Horse lost	12, Nov. 1800	S3
Boswell, John	Horse found	26, Jan. 1816	S1
Botton, Joseph	Horse found	8, Aug. 1818	S3
Boudinot, Elias	Estate sale	11, Jan. 1837	N2
Bough, French	Pioneer incident	17, Dec. 1847	K2
Bourns, James	Letter at P.O.	18, Oct. 1794	C3
Bouyer, John & Margaret	Divorce/abandonment	27, Apr. 1803	S3
Bowman, ---- & ----	Divorce/abandonment	16, Oct. 1852	P2
Bowman, Anna	Notice	30, Oct. 1827	N3
Bowman, Henry	Horse found	25, June 1824	N3
Bowman, Henry	Insolvent debtor	23, July 1830	N3
Bowman, Jacob	Notice	30, Oct. 1827	N3
Bowman, John	Chancery case	4, Mar. 1828	N3
Bowman, Richard	Horse found	27, June 1812	S3
Boyd, Allen	Insolvent debtor	23, July 1830	N3
Boyd, Isabella	Partition petition	23, Jan. 1837	N3
Boyer, Abraham	Horse found	13, Nov. 1819	S3
Boyer, Abraham	Notice	7, Sept 1820	S3
Boyer, John	Debt relief	5, Mar. 1824	N3
Boyer, John & Eleanor	Divorce/abandonment	16, Sept 1823	J3
Boyes, Robert & James	Notice	27, Feb. 1805	S4
Bracken, Hugh	Debt relief	11, May 1811	S3
Bracken, Hugh & Margaret R.	Divorce/abandonment	11, July 1812	S1
Bradburn, John	Horse lost	24, Sept 1808	S4
Bradbury, G.W.	Committee member	15, Nov. 1838	N2

Name	Type of Notice	Date of Notice	Page
Bradford, David	Horse found	3, July 1813	S3
Bradford, James & Jane	Divorce/abandonment	27, July 1822	S3
Bradley, Thomas	Run away	22, Dec. 1821	S3
Brady, James	Horse lost	15, Aug. 1795	C3
Brandriff, David	Guardianship	20, Apr. 1830	N3
Brandriff, Eliza	Guardianship	20, Apr. 1830	N3
Brandriff, James	Guardianship	20, Apr. 1830	N3
Brandriff, John	Guardianship	20, Apr. 1830	N3
Brandriff, Lydia Ann	Guardianship	20, Apr. 1830	N3
Brasher, Robert	Cow lost	11, Mar. 1801	S3
Bray, Wiliam George	Notice	19, July 1809	H1
Brecount, John	Horse found	18, Mar. 1815	S3
Brees, Timothy	Horse found	3, Dec. 1814	S3
Breese, Eleanor	Partition petition	28, Dec. 1838	N2
Brewer, Peter	Horse lost	20, May 1806	S3
Brewster, Samuel	Letter at P.O.	18, Oct. 1794	C3
Brice, Richard Henry	Insolvent debtor	27, Jan. 1829	N3
Bridge, John T.	Horse found	2, Nov. 1811	S3
Bridges, John	Horse found	14, May 1814	S3
Briggs, Eliza	Poor house inmate	14, Nov. 1851	P2
Briggs, Marcus D. & Highly	Divorce/abandonment	30, Dec. 1825	N3
Brinton, Thomas	Escaped prisoner	7, Nov. 1795	C3
Brisbin, James	Horse found	18, Dec. 1829	N3
Britton, Nathan	Horse lost	26, July 1816	S3
Broadbury, David	Horse lost	8, Oct. 1799	S3
Broadwell, Baxter	Debt relief	17, Apr. 1819	S3
Broadwell, Charles	Court case witness	20, June 1850	P2
Broadwell, Moses	Cow lost	15, Jan. 1800	S3
Broadwell, Silas	Chancery case	28, May 1830	N3
Broadwell, William	Run away apprentice	10, Dec. 1814	S3
Brooks, James	Deserter from army	5, July 1794	C3
Browder, John	Court sentencing	4, Nov. 1836	N2
Brown, Daniel	Chancery case	6, May 1828	N3
Brown, David	Horse found	17, July 1819	S3
Brown, Ephm.	Horse found	9, Jan. 1796	C3
Brown, Ethan	Land partition	9, July 1835	N2
Brown, Euphamia	Horse lost	17, Dec. 1824	N3
Brown, Israel	Horse found	4, Dec. 1805	S3
Brown, Jacob	Tavern for sale	26, Nov. 1796	F4
Brown, James	Escaped convict	3, Oct. 1818	S2
Brown, James	Chancery case	6, May 1828	N3
Brown, James	Court sentencing	4, Nov. 1836	N2
Brown, John	Deserter from army	12, Sept 1795	C3
Brown, Joseph	Horse lost	15, May 1802	S3
Brown, Mary	Administratrix	21, May 1830	N3
Brown, Nancy	Land partition	9, July 1835	N2
Brown, Robert	Horse found	7, Nov. 1812	S3
Brown, Samuel	Cow lost	4, Feb. 1815	W3
Brown, William	Horse found	10, Dec. 1799	S3
Brown, William	Public notice	17, May 1794	C3
Browne, Henry	Chancery case	10, May 1831	A3
Browne, Samuel J.	Chancery case	10, May 1831	A3
Browne, William	Chancery case	10, May 1831	A3
Brownson, John	Land petition	25, June 1830	N3

Name	Type of Notice	Date of Notice	Page
Bruharde, George	Cow lost	21, Aug. 1802	S3
Bruner, Jacob	Horse found	17, Jan. 1817	S4
Bruner, Jacob	Deserter from army	12, Sept 1795	C3
Buchanan, James	Hogs found	5, Mar. 1800	S3
Buchanan, Robert	Chancery case	1, Jan. 1842	N2
Buchanon, John	Horse stolen	5, Oct. 1807	S3
Buck, William & Mary	Divorce/abandonment	15, Oct. 1814	S3
Buckingham, Levi	Horse found	16, Sept 1828	N3
Buckingham, William	Horse lost	14, May 1830	N3
Budd, John C.	Petition filed	6, Apr. 1803	S3
Buell, John (Major)	Letter at P.O.	18, Oct. 1794	C3
Bump, Ansel	Horse found	11, July 1818	S3
Bump, Ansel & Elizabeth	Divorce/abandonment	13, Feb. 1838	T2
Bundy, Benjamin	Horse lost	12, Aug. 1801	S3
Bunnell, Benjamin	Horse found	4, Sept 1813	S3
Burch, Daniel	Horse found	16, Jan. 1813	S3
Burdsal, Elijah	Deposition given	17, Sept 1842	Z3
Burger, Adam	Horse found	20, June 1812	S3
Burges, C. & Elizabeth	Divorce/abandonment	4, Sept 1813	S3
Burk, Thomas & Hannah	Divorce/abandonment	3, Oct. 1804	S3
Burk, Thomas & Hannah	Divorce/abandonment	30, Oct. 1805	S3
Burk, Ulick	Horse found	18, Mar. 1815	S3
Burnet, David	Petition filed	6, Apr. 1803	S3
Burnet, George W.	Deposition given	4, Oct. 1842	Z4
Burnet, Isaac G.	Petition filed	6, Apr. 1803	S3
Burnet, Jacob	Horse lost	7, Jan. 1800	S3
Burnet, Jacob	Horse lost	19, Aug. 1801	S3
Burnet, Jacob	Petition filed	6, Apr. 1803	S3
Burnet, John	Petition filed	6, Apr. 1803	S3
Burnet, R.W.	Committee member	15, Nov. 1838	N2
Burnet, Statis	Petition filed	6, Apr. 1803	S3
Burns, John	Runaway apprentice	1, Aug. 1817	S3
Burns, Matilda	Run away	27, Mar. 1805	S3
Burnsides, John	Insolvent debtor	11, Nov. 1828	N1
Burrett, Solomon & Nancy	Divorce/abandonment	21, Feb. 1818	S3
Burrowes, Israel	Horse found	19, July 1809	H1
Burrowes, Walters	Inquiry	29, Apr. 1820	S3
Burrows, Joseph	Debt relief	4, Oct. 1816	S1
Burt, Andrew	Attachment	19, July 1809	H1
Burtch, Darius & Mary	Divorce/abandonment	21, Oct. 1825	N2
Burtch, William	Horse lost	3, Dec. 1814	S3
Burton, Samuel	Runaway apprentice	9, Nov. 1820	S3
Burton, Washington	Insolvent debtor	23, July 1830	N3
Bush, Isaac & Elizabeth	Divorce/abandonment	14, Jan. 1801	S3
Bustard, John	Debt notice	11, Mar. 1797	F4
Butler, Isaac	Indian prisoner	28, Nov. 1801	S1
Butler, James	Indian prisoner	28, Nov. 1801	S1
Butler, Mary	Indian prisoner	28, Nov. 1801	S1
Butler, Samuel	Indian prisoner	28, Nov. 1801	S1
Butler, William	Horse lost	7, Nov. 1818	S2
Butter, Joshua	Cow found	10, Dec. 1799	S3
Butterfield, Betsy	Chancery case	10, June 1824	E3
Butterfield, Jeremiah	Horse lost	24, Sept 1808	S4
Butterfield, Jeremiah	Horse found	16, Feb. 1827	N3

Name	Type of Notice	Date of Notice	Page
Buxton, Charles	Horse lost	21, Mar. 1818	S3
Buxton, Edmon	Horse lost	24, Oct. 1804	S3
Bywaters, Robert	Debt relief	31, Jan. 1817	S3
Cade, Elisha W.	Insolvent debtor	27, Jan. 1829	N3
Cadwell, Aaron	Land for sale	2, July 1799	S3
Cady, Polly	Insolvent debtor	23, July 1830	N3
Cafe, Joseph	Notice	5, Oct. 1803	S3
Cairin, Margaret	Female school award	28, July 1835	N2
Caldwell, Henry	Run away	17, Oct. 1801	S3
Caldwell, James	Horse found	4, Apr. 1812	S3
Caldwell, James (Lt)	Hamilton Co militia	28, Nov. 1801	S3
Caldwell, John W.	Inquiry	8, Sept 1821	S3
Caldwell, Joseph	Horse found	15, Feb. 1808	S3
Caldwell, Thomas	Deserter from army	6, Aug. 1799	S4
Cale, James	Run away	27, Mar. 1805	S3
Calvin, Joseph	Horse found	5, Sept 1817	S2
Cameron, James	Horse found	28, June 1816	S3
Cammins, John N.	Petition filed	6, Apr. 1803	S3
Campbell, Alexander	Inquiry -15 yrs old	26, Feb. 1820	S3
Campbell, Alexander	Insolvent debtor	27, Jan. 1829	N3
Campbell, James	Horse lost	3, June 1806	S3
Campbell, James	Horse lost	17, Aug. 1807	S3
Campbell, John	Cow found	4, Mar. 1801	S3
Campbell, John	Horse found	16, Feb. 1827	N3
Campbell, Thomas	Run away	27, Aug. 1800	S3
Campbell, William	Letter at P.O.	18, Oct. 1794	C3
Candor, Joseph	Debt relief	22, Jan. 1820	S4
Cannon, James	Horse lost	28, May 1800	S3
Cannutt, William	Horse found	8, Feb. 1808	S3
Careman, Reuben	Horse found	23, July 1814	S3
Carharr, Seth	Letter at P.O.	18, Oct. 1794	C3
Carleton, Jonathan	Removal	25, Feb. 1815	S1
Carley, James S.	Horse found	21, Jan. 1815	S3
Carlisle, John	Attachment	19, July 1809	H3
Carlisle, William	Chancery case	21, Dec. 1830	N3
Carno, John	Horse found	28, May 1814	S3
Carpenter, J.	Horse lost	8, Dec. 1810	S3
Carpenter, John	Deserter from army	7, Mar. 1795	C3
Carpenter, Joseph	Cow lost	1, Jan. 1806	S4
Carr, John	Chancery case	19, Jan. 1811	S3
Carr, Samuel	Horse found	16, Oct. 1819	S3
Carrel, Bar	Horse found	9, Aug. 1794	C3
Carrol, William	Deserter from army	21, June 1794	C3
Carson, David	Run away	19, July 1809	H3
Carson, Enoch W.	Horse lost	17, June 1825	N3
Carson, John	Horse found	3, June 1836	N2
Carter, Daniel C. & Hannah	Divorce/abandonment	11, Feb. 1815	S3
Carter, Daniel C. & Hannah	Divorce/abandonment	19, Jan. 1816	S3
Carter, Elijah	Chancery case	29, Sept 1829	N3
Carter, Elisha	Horse found	5, June 1813	S3
Carter, George	Horse lost	17, Jan. 1817	S4
Carter, John	Insolvent debtor	23, July 1830	N3
Carter, Thomas & Thankful	Divorce/abandonment	17, Oct. 1812	S3

Name	Type of Notice	Date of Notice	Page
Cary, Abraham	Horse lost	25, Jan. 1804	S2
Case, Jacob	Horse found	4, Apr. 1812	S1
Case, Jacob	Horse found	17, Jan. 1818	S3
Case, Jacob	Horse found	8, Dec. 1821	S3
Case, Lewis H.	Horse found	6, July 1827	Q3
Case, William	Deserter from army	9, Oct. 1813	S3
Casey, Ann	Poor house inmate	14, Nov. 1851	P2
Cassat, David C.	Horse found	4, May 1824	N3
Casson, John	Inquiry	2, Jan. 1818	S3
Casterline, Silas & Mary	Divorce/abandonment	6, Oct. 1832	R3
Castle, George V.	Horse found	13, Nov. 1819	S3
Castle, Nicholas	Deposition given	17, Sept 1842	Z3
Castner, Michael	Reward notice	28, Nov. 1795	C3
Casto, James	Run away apprentice	27, Apr. 1803	S3
Catterlin, Hiram	Insolvent debtor	11, Nov. 1828	N1
Cavanaugh, Mary	Poor house inmate	14, Nov. 1851	P2
Cavenagh, Garrett & Nancy	Divorce/abandonment	27, Aug. 1796	F3
Cavenagh, Nathaniel	Chancery case	10, May 1831	A3
Chace, Abraham	Horse found	29, Feb. 1812	S3
Chamberlan, William	Horse found	8, Nov. 1816	S3
Chapman, Charles	Runaway apprentice	2, Oct. 1823	J3
Chapman, Zachariah	Horse found	28, May 1808	S3
Chase, Seth	Horse found	26, Feb. 1820	S3
Cheek, James	Horse found	29, May 1813	S3
Cherry, Aaron & Mary	Divorce/abandonment	5, Feb. 1800	S3
Chesterson, George	Horse found	15, Jan. 1800	S3
Chicks, George	Horse found	26, May 1815	S3
Chribbs, Elizabeth	Cow lost	12, Mar. 1800	S3
Chribe, Daniel	Land purchase	23, July 1814	S3
Christman, Adam	Guardian	6, Nov. 1838	N2
Christy, Andrew	Sale notice	12, Nov. 1796	F1
Christy, James & Alice	Divorce/abandonment	26, Jan. 1836	N3
Clapp, Lucretia	Cow lost	2, May 1818	S3
Clark, George	Cow found	8, Apr. 1820	S1
Clark, George (Soldier)	Letter at P.O.	18, Oct. 1794	C3
Clark, George Rogers	Court case	19, Nov. 1800	S3
Clark, Jeremiah & Catharine	Estate case	20, Sept 1816	S1
Clark, John	Horse stealing	20, Aug. 1808	S3
Clark, John	Deserter from army	13, Feb. 1813	S3
Clark, Joseph	Horse found	19, July 1809	H3
Clark, Josiah	Horse found	4, July 1818	S3
Clark, Josiah	Horse found	19, June 1819	S3
Clark, Mary	Poor house inmate	14, Nov. 1851	P2
Clark, Silas (Soldier)	Letter at P.O.	18, Oct. 1794	C3
Clark, Thomas	Horse found	25, Apr. 1810	H3
Clark, William	Deserter from army	30, July 1814	S3
Clark, William B.	Insolvent debtor	27, Jan. 1829	N3
Clarke, James	Deserter from army	15, June 1807	S3
Clarke, Matthias	Horse found	21, Dec. 1827	N3
Clarke, N.B.	Deposition given	17, Sept 1842	Z4
Clements, Alexander & Sarah	Divorce/abandonment	1, Oct. 1799	S3
Clifton, Nathan	Deserter from army	9, Oct. 1813	S3
Clifton, Thomas	Horse found	13, Feb. 1829	N3
Clyde, ---- & ----	Divorce/abandonment	16, Oct. 1852	P2

Name	Type of Notice	Date of Notice	Page
Cochran, Thomas	Trespass action	13, Mar. 1802	S3
Coen, Thomas & Nancy	Divorce/abandonment	4, Dec. 1813	S3
Coffin, Eliza S.	Female school award	28, July 1835	N2
Coffin, Nancy B.	Female school award	28, July 1835	N2
Coldwell, James	Horse lost	11, June 1808	S3
Cole, John	Horse found	6, Aug. 1817	S3
Cole, Robert & Sina	Divorce/abandonment	13, Mar. 1813	S3
Coleman, Adbeel	Horse found	14, July 1815	S3
Coleman, Henry	Runaway slave	9, July 1796	F3
Coleman, James & Mary	Divorce/abandonment	21, May 1814	S3
Coleman, John W. & Eve	Divorce/abandonment	27, Jan. 1824	N3
Coleman, Thomas B.	Debt relief	20, Oct. 1821	S3
Colemun, James & Mary	Divorce/abandonment	29, June 1820	S3
Collier, James	Pioneer incident	21, Dec. 1847	K2
Collins, Elisha	Information wanted	15, Apr. 1825	N3
Collins, Joseph	Trespass action	13, Mar. 1802	S3
Collins, Robert	Horse found	28, Nov. 1812	S3
Collins, Robert & Sarah	Divorce/abandonment	24, June 1825	N3
Collom, George	Horse found	8, Jan. 1806	S3
Colshear, Peter	Horse found	13, Nov. 1819	S3
Colwell, Martin	Escaped prisoner	27, Nov. 1805	S3
Conclin, Isaac	Horse lost	24, Dec. 1830	N3
Cone, Charles	Chancery court case	17, June 1823	N3
Congreves, Thomas	Horse found	15, Aug. 1823	N3
Conklin, Stephen	Horse found	17, Oct. 1812	S3
Conklin, Stephen	Horse found	13, Aug. 1814	S3
Conkling, Eliza	Guardianship	8, Oct. 1830	N3
Conkling, Joseph	Horse lost	26, Aug. 1806	S3
Conley, William	Horse found	9, Feb. 1811	S3
Conn, James	Guardian	9, Dec. 1828	N3
Conn, James	Guardian	25, Aug. 1829	N3
Conn, Joseph	Guardian	9, Dec. 1828	N3
Conn, Sarah Ann	Guardian	9, Dec. 1828	N3
Conn, Sarah Ann	Guardian	25, Aug. 1829	N3
Connel, ---- & ----	Divorce/abandonment	16, Oct. 1852	P2
Conor, William	Horse found	12, Jan. 1822	S3
Conway, Barney & Catharine	Divorce/abandonment	21, Feb. 1851	P2
Conway, John	Court sentencing	4, Nov. 1836	N2
Cook, Charles	Horse found	12, June 1813	S3
Cook, George	Horse found	7, Nov. 1817	S3
Cook, George	Horse found	3, July 1819	S3
Cook, John	Horse found	19, July 1809	H3
Cook, Thomas	Horse lost	1, May 1802	S3
Coons, Frederick	Horse found	24, Jan. 1818	S3
Coons, Frederick	Horse found	19, Dec. 1818	S3
Coonse, Frederick	Cow found	25, Mar. 1797	F4
Cooper, Abner M.	Insolvent debtor	23, July 1830	N3
Cooper, Christian & Rachel	Divorce/abandonment	19, Sept 1804	S4
Cooper, Daniel C.	Land for sale	13, Aug. 1796	F1
Cooper, Daniel C.	Tavern for sale	12, Nov. 1796	F3
Cooper, Isaac	Guardian	23, Mar. 1830	N3
Cooper, James	Horse found	20, June 1812	S3
Cooper, James	Horse found	19, July 1809	H3
Cooper, James	Guardian	23, Mar. 1830	N3

Name	Type of Notice	Date of Notice	Page
Cooper, John	Horse found	1, Dec. 1815	S3
Cooper, John	Guardian	23, Mar. 1830	N3
Cooper, Samuel	Guardian	23, Mar. 1830	N3
Cooper, Stephen	Guardian	23, Mar. 1830	N3
Cooper, Thomas	Horse found	9, Mar. 1811	S3
Cooper, Thomas	Horse found	3, Sept 1814	S3
Cooper, Thomas & Jane M.	Divorce/abandonment	7, Feb. 1837	N2
Cooper, William	Run away notice	6, Sept 1809	H4
Cooper, William	Chancery case	10, Oct. 1823	N3
Cope, Samuel	Deserter from army	15, June 1807	S3
Copeland, Abram	Horse found	22, May 1819	S3
Corbin, George	Deserter from army	30, Oct. 1813	S2
Corbin, Lewis	Theft notice	13, Apr. 1827	Q3
Corder, Elizabeth	Inquiry	23, May 1817	S2
Corder, James	Inquiry	23, May 1817	S2
Cornelius, William	Court sentencing	4, Nov. 1836	N2
Cornthwaite, Thomas & Elizabeth	Divorce/abandonment	27, May 1824	E3
Corry, William	Chancery case	10, Oct. 1823	N3
Corry, William M.	Committee member	15, Nov. 1838	N2
Cortney, John	Runaway apprentice	4, Oct. 1816	S4
Cory, Elnathon	Horse found	11, May 1809	H3
Coryell, John	Horse found	4, June 1824	N3
Cottingham, Daniel	Court sentencing	4, Nov. 1836	N2
Cotton, John	Run away prisoner	17, Feb. 1820	D3
Cotton, William	Horse found	29, Apr. 1820	S3
Courtnay, William	Escaped prisoner	27, Sept 1794	C3
Couse, John	Court sentencing	4, Nov. 1836	N2
Covert, Jeremiah	Horse found	25, July 1817	S4
Cowan, John W.	Murder case	3, Nov. 1835	N2
Cox, Jacob	Letter at P.O.	18, Oct. 1794	C3
Cox, James	House to rent	12, Nov. 1796	F1
Cox, Joseph & Elizabeth	Divorce/abandonment	14, Nov. 1836	T3
Cox, Samuel	Horse found	21, Feb. 1810	H4
Cox, Samuel M.	Reward notice	23, Sept 1823	N3
Cox, Thomas	Horse found	17, June 1825	N3
Cox, William	Horse found	25, July 1817	S4
Crain, Aaron	Partition petition	24, Apr. 1837	N2
Crain, David	Partition petition	24, Apr. 1837	N2
Crain, Elias	Partition petition	24, Apr. 1837	N2
Crain, Elihu	Horse lost	1, July 1801	S3
Crain, Hiram	Partition petition	24, Apr. 1837	N2
Crain, Jonathan	Partition petition	24, Apr. 1837	N2
Crain, Mary	Partition petition	24, Apr. 1837	N2
Crain, Rachel	Partition petition	24, Apr. 1837	N2
Crain, Sarah Jane	Partition petition	24, Apr. 1837	N2
Crain, Stephen	Insolvent debtor	23, July 1830	N3
Cramer, John G. & Rebecca	Partition petition	22, Mar. 1837	N3
Crane, Abigail	Estate case	17, May 1816	S3
Crane, David B.	Estate case	17, May 1816	S3
Crane, Elias	Horse lost	29, May 1805	S3
Crane, Moses	Estate case	17, May 1816	S3
Crane, Oliver	Estate case	17, May 1816	S3
Crane, Stephen	Estate case	17, May 1816	S3
Crane, William	Estate case	17, May 1816	S3

Name	Type of Notice	Date of Notice	Page
Crary, Benjamin	Horse found	22, May 1819	S3
Crawford, Hazard	Court sentencing	4, Nov. 1836	N2
Crawford, Hugh	Horse found	28, Feb. 1810	H3
Crawford, John H.	Horse lost	6, Jan. 1807	S3
Creary, John	Horse found	16, Feb. 1816	S3
Cresswell, Samuel	Notice	6, Feb. 1796	C3
Crippin, Thomas	Runaway	14, Nov. 1822	J2
Crippin, William	Insolvent debtor	27, Jan. 1829	N3
Crisman, James	Insolvent debtor	27, Jan. 1829	N3
Crissey, William T.	Chancery case	10, Oct. 1823	N3
Crissman, Elias	Horse found	27, May 1825	N3
Crist, Catharine	Chancery case	4, Mar. 1828	N3
Crist, Cornelius	Horse found	18, Oct. 1816	S3
Crist, Moses	Chancery case	4, Mar. 1828	N3
Cristman, Peter James	Run away notice	13, Oct. 1836	N2
Crocket, Kendall	Inquiry	15, Aug. 1828	Q3
Crosley, Ross	Horse lost	13, July 1803	S3
Cross, Charles & Rachel	Divorce/abandonment	13, May 1850	P3
Crossley, Ross	Cow found	20, Aug. 1799	S3
Croxton, Abraham	Escaped prisoner	9, July 1796	F4
Crum, John	Horse lost	8, Aug. 1804	S3
Crump, Allen & Mary	Divorce/abandonment	23, Jan. 1835	N2
Cullom, Francis	Horse found	14, May 1808	S3
Cullom, George	Horse found	24, Aug. 1830	N3
Cullum, William T. (Lt)	Hamilton Co militia	28, Nov. 1801	S3
Cumming, John N.	Horse found	28, Aug. 1829	N3
Cummings, John (Lt)	Hamilton Co militia	28, Nov. 1801	S3
Cummins, David	Chancery case	2, Jan. 1829	N3
Cummins, Sarah	Chancery case	20, Jan. 1825	E3
Cummis, Joseph	Horse found	2, Apr. 1796	C3
Cunningham, Fred. & Mary A.	Divorce/abandonment	6, Nov. 1851	P2
Cunningham, Jennet	Horse found	25, Nov. 1825	N3
Cunningham, John	Horse found	25, July 1817	S4
Cunningham, Samuel	Horse found	26, June 1827	N3
Current, Hannah	Notice	6, Feb. 1796	C3
Cutter, Seth	Horse lost	3, May 1794	C3
Cutter, William	Runaway apprentice	7, Nov. 1817	S3
Dailey, John	Chancery case	25, May 1830	N3
Daily, John & Elizabeth	Divorce/abandonment	28, Jan. 1815	S3
Danford, Thomas	Run away apprentice	1, Feb. 1812	S3
Dannely, William	Horse found	19, Dec. 1812	S1
Darby, ---- & ----	Divorce/abandonment	16, Oct. 1852	P2
Darr, Abraham F.	Debt relief	14, Feb. 1818	S3
Darrel, Hulda	Dower petition	21, Jan. 1837	N3
Dary, George & Elizabeth	Divorce/abandonment	24, Mar. 1835	N2
Daugherty, ----	Escaped prisoner	30, Jan. 1796	C1
Daughterty, James	Debt relief	30, Sept 1828	N3
Davidson, Moses	Horse found	27, June 1812	S3
Davies, Samuel W.	Committee member	15, Nov. 1838	N2
Davis, (Mrs)	Pioneer incident	27, Mar. 1848	K2
Davis, Baxter	Chancery case	6, May 1828	N3
Davis, Isaac	Horse found	18, July 1823	N3
Davis, James	Cows found	29, Jan. 1800	S3

Name	Type of Notice	Date of Notice	Page
Davis, James Handy	Lost child notice	13, May 1837	T2
Davis, John	Information wanted	21, Aug. 1835	N2
Davis, John	Court sentencing	4, Nov. 1836	N2
Davis, Joseph F.	Insolvent debtor	11, Nov. 1828	N1
Davis, Peter & Elizabeth	Divorce/abandonment	14, June 1794	C3
Davis, Thomas	Lost child notice	13, May 1837	T2
Davis, Thomas	Guardian	8, Oct. 1830	N3
Davis, William	Horse found	25, Apr. 1810	H4
Davison, John	Deserter from army	2, Feb. 1807	S3
Daviss, David	Horse lost	19, Nov. 1800	S3
Dawson, Nathaniel	Insolvent debtor	11, Nov. 1828	N1
Dawson, Samuel J.	Run away apprentice	31, July 1802	S4
Day, Abigail	Guardian	11, Sept 1837	N2
Day, Jane	Guardian	11, Sept 1837	N2
Day, Rosanna	Guardian	11, Sept 1837	N2
Day, W.L.	Guardian	11, Sept 1837	N2
Dayton, Susan	Real estate sale	17, June 1825	N3
Dean, James	Debt relief notice	21, Feb. 1823	N3
Dean, Levi	Horse found	18, June 1814	S3
Dearmond, John	Horse lost	14, May 1796	C3
Debetaz, Daniel & Margaret	Divorce/abandonment	11, Oct. 1814	W3
Decatur, Stephen	Biography	11, May 1820	S1
Deen, Levi	Horse found	23, June 1826	N3
Deford, William & Sarah	Divorce/abandonment	6, June 1817	S3
Degolar, Anthony	Horse found	11, Apr. 1812	S3
Delafield, J.	Committee member	15, Nov. 1838	N2
Delaplane, Joshua	Cow lost	1, Oct. 1799	F2
Dellino, Richard	Horse found	20, May 1825	N3
DeLong, Eliza	Land petition	25, June 1830	N3
DeLong, Joseph	Land petition	25, June 1830	N3
DeLong, Mary	Land petition	25, June 1830	N3
DeLong, Sarah	Land petition	25, June 1830	N3
DeLong, William	Land petition	25, June 1830	N3
Delvin, John	Insolvent debtor	27, Jan. 1829	N3
Demint, James & Elizabeth	Divorce/abandonment	14, May 1796	C3
Demler, F. George (Lt)	Letter at P.O.	18, Oct. 1794	C3
Demoss, Charles	Horse found	22, June 1811	S3
Deneen, Samuel	Inquiry	16, Jan. 1819	S3
Denham, Edmund Harvey	Notice	8, June 1827	Q2
Denham, Obed	Notice	27, Aug. 1799	S3
Denham, Obed	Land for sale	30, July 1796	F3
Denman, Abraham	Dower petition	21, Jan. 1837	N3
Denman, Effee	Dower petition	21, Jan. 1837	N3
Denman, Jacob	Notice	8, June 1827	Q2
Denman, John	Dower petition	21, Jan. 1837	N3
Denman, Mary	Dower petition	21, Jan. 1837	N3
Denman, Matthew	Chancery case	25, May 1830	N3
Denman, Morris	Dower petition	21, Jan. 1837	N3
Denman, Nathaniel	Dower petition	21, Jan. 1837	N3
Denman, Susan	Dower petition	21, Jan. 1837	N3
Denning, James	Horse lost	7, Sept 1803	S3
Dennison, Daniel	Horse found	14, Dec. 1822	S3
Denny, John	Attachment	8, Nov. 1809	H1
Derling, Andrew	Run away notice	8, July 1828	N3

Name	Type of Notice	Date of Notice	Page
Derrough, Amos	Horse lost	18, May 1803	S3
Devers, John	Insolvent debtor	27, Jan. 1829	N3
Devore, John	Inquiry	2, Oct. 1819	S3
Dewitt, Thomas	Deserter from army	9, Apr. 1814	S3
Dewitt, Zachariah P.	Horse found	7, Mar. 1808	S3
Dexter, Isaac	Debt notice	21, Feb. 1810	H3
Dey, Anthony	Chancery case	20, Jan. 1825	E3
Dickey, Adam	Horse found	22, Dec. 1802	S3
Dickey, Margaret	Gold medal	19, Feb. 1830	N3
Dickey, P.	Horse lost	12, Sept 1804	S3
Dickey, Patrick	Chancery case	19, Jan. 1811	S3
Dickinson, William	Insolvent debtor	11, Nov. 1828	N1
Dickson, John	Horse lost	11, Feb. 1801	S3
Diddip, Archibald	Escaped prisoner	30, Jan. 1796	C1
Digbey, William & Catharine	Divorce/abandonment	24, June 1795	C3
Dill, John	Attachment	19, July 1809	H1
Dillon, John	Escaped prisoner	28, Mar. 1795	C3
Dillon, Samuel	Horse found	15, Sept 1810	S3
Dingman, James	Land purchase	23, July 1814	S3
Disney, D.T.	Committee member	15, Nov. 1838	N2
Disney, Mary Frances	Gold medal	19, Feb. 1830	N3
Dlashmutt, William	Letter at P.O.	18, Oct. 1794	C3
Dobbins, George	Horse found	28, June 1816	S3
Dodd, John	Deposition given	1, Oct. 1842	Z4
Dodson, John	Horse found	27, Oct. 1798	F3
Doherty, ----	Escaped prisoner	24, Oct. 1795	C3
Dolaheide, James	Runaway apprentice	15, Sept 1821	S3
Dolby, Stephen	Inquiry	31, July 1819	S3
Dolson, Matthew	Horse found	9, Nov. 1820	S3
Donaldson, John	Attachment	8, Nov. 1809	H1
Donally, Patrick	Attachment	19, July 1809	H3
Doneldson, William	Court sentencing	4, Nov. 1836	N2
Donesbergel, Anthony	Horse lost	21, July 1827	R3
Doolittle, Sarah	Real estate case	9, Jan. 1838	N3
Dorfeuille, Amanda	Female school award	28, July 1835	N2
Dorsey, James	Escaped prisoner	4, July 1795	C3
Dorton, Ephraim & Mary	Chancery court case	17, June 1823	N3
Doty, George	Horse found	9, Aug. 1814	W4
Doty, Jacob & Mary	Estate case	1, Nov. 1816	S2
Doty, Jesse	Inquiry	31, Aug. 1822	S3
Dougherty, James	Escaped from jail	28, May 1808	S3
Dougherty, John	Deserter from army	15, June 1807	S3
Douglass, Ann Eliza	Chancery case	14, Oct. 1836	N2
Douglass, William	Chancery case	14, Oct. 1836	N2
Dowden, Clemmenhouse	Horse found	18, June 1799	S3
Downey, Patrick	Horse lost	18, Mar. 1823	N3
Downing, Edward & Betsey	Divorce/abandonment	4, Dec. 1813	S3
Doyeal, Edward	Horse found	19, July 1809	H3
Doyle, Thomas	Horse lost	28, May 1800	S3
Drake, B.	Committee member	15, Nov. 1838	N2
Drake, Dan	Horse lost	20, Oct. 1815	S3
Drake, Daniel	Chancery case	10, Oct. 1823	N3
Drake, Jesse	Inquiry	12, May 1821	S1
Drum, Philip	Run away apprentice	16, July 1799	S3

Name	Type of Notice	Date of Notice	Page
Ducks, George	Deserter from army	19, Feb. 1814	S3
Dudley, Benjamin	Chancery case	25, May 1830	N3
Dudley, Catharine	Chancery case	25, May 1830	N3
Duffey, Daniel	Debt notice	18, July 1795	C3
Duffey, Daniel	Debt notice	5, Nov. 1796	F3
Duffey, Rachel	Debt notice	12, Nov. 1796	F3
Duffield, Johnston E.	Debt relief	26, May 1821	S3
Duffy, Christopher & Susan	Divorce/abandonment	6, Jan. 1851	P3
Duffy, Daniel	Debt notice	9, July 1796	F1
Dugan, Henry	Horse found	28, Jan. 1823	N3
Dugen, Robert	Run away apprentice	18, Mar. 1815	W4
Dukes, George & Martha	Divorce/abandonment	7, Sept 1820	S3
Duncan, John	Run away prisoner	17, Feb. 1820	D3
Dunham, Henry	Run away apprentice	30, Apr. 1814	S3
Dunkin, Jesse	Horse lost	31, July 1805	S3
Dunlap, Agnes	Guardian	20, Mar. 1838	N3
Dunlap, Ephraim & Mary	Divorce/abandonment	23, May 1828	Q3
Dunlap, John	Land notice	14, Dec. 1793	C3
Dunlap, R.A.	Guardian	20, Mar. 1838	N3
Dunlap, William John	Guardian	20, Mar. 1838	N3
Dunlavy, Francis	Horse lost	5, Nov. 1796	F3
Dunlop, John	Notice	27, Sept 1794	C3
Dunlop, John	Notice	31, Dec. 1796	F3
Dunn, John	Horse found	4, July 1818	S3
Dunn, John C.	Guardian	19, Dec. 1826	N3
Dunn, Samuel	Hogs found	15, Jan. 1800	S3
Dunn, Samuel	Horse found	5, Dec. 1812	S3
Dunn, Samuel W.	Guardian	19, Dec. 1826	N3
Dunseth, Andrew	Apprentice wanted	14, Aug. 1802	S3
Dunseth, David	Chancery case	19, Jan. 1811	S3
Dunseth, James	Cow found	12, Mar. 1800	S3
Dwinell, Seneca S.	Attachment case	12, Aug. 1825	N3
Dyer, George & Polly	Divorce/abandonment	12, May 1815	S3
Earp, George	Chancery case	6, May 1828	N3
Earp, Robert	Chancery case	6, May 1828	N3
Earp, Thomas	Chancery case	6, May 1828	N3
Eastwood, John	Horse lost	20, Nov. 1805	S3
Easy, Charles	Notice	27, Mar. 1805	S3
Eaverson, Richard	Horse lost	23, Apr. 1808	S3
Edwards, Isaac	Horse found	29, Sept 1815	S3
Edwards, Isaac	Horse found	17, Jan. 1817	S4
Edwards, Polly	Estate case	17, May 1816	S3
Edwards, Thomas	Cows found	29, Jan. 1800	S3
Efau, Alexander (Capt)	Hamilton Co militia	28, Nov. 1801	S3
Egnew, William	Debt notice	12, Oct. 1827	N3
Eidee, Samuel	Escaped prisoner	28, Mar. 1795	C3
Ellery, William	Escaped prisoner	9, May 1795	C3
Elliot, Joshua	Horse found	28, Nov. 1812	S3
Elliot, Rufus	Caution on a note	27, Oct. 1798	F4
Elliot, William	Deserter from army	9, Aug. 1814	W3
Elliott, John	Horse lost	1, Oct. 1799	F2
Elliott, Rufus	Trespass action	13, Mar. 1802	S3
Ellis, James	Land partition	29, Apr. 1828	N3

Name	Type of Notice	Date of Notice	Page
Ellis, Thomas	Horse found	26, Jan. 1811	S4
Ely, Jacob	Cow lost	13, Dec. 1816	S3
Ely, Joseph	Deserter from army	23, Apr. 1814	S1
Emberson, John	Horse found	7, Nov. 1812	S3
Embree, Elijah	Horse lost	31, July 1805	S3
Emerick, Jacob	Attachment case	30, Dec. 1825	N3
Emerson, Bailey	Chancery case	10, June 1824	E3
Emerson, Calista	Chancery case	10, June 1824	E3
Emerson, Henry	Chancery case	21, Mar. 1838	N2
Emerson, Jonathan	Chancery case	10, June 1824	E3
Emerson, Paul	Chancery case	10, June 1824	E3
Emery, Keziah	Female school award	28, July 1835	N2
Emmett, Abraham	Inquiry	26, May 1821	S1
Endicott, Joseph	Insolvent debtor	27, Jan. 1829	N3
Enesworth, John	Deserter from army	30, Nov. 1793	C3
Engle, Joshua	Debtor	4, Feb. 1815	S3
Enness, John B.	Inquiry	7, Sept 1822	S3
Epperly, Nancy	Insolvent debtor	27, Jan. 1829	N3
Erwin, Andrew	Horse found	3, Oct. 1812	S3
Erwin, John	Runaway apprentice	28, Aug. 1819	S3
Erwin, Joseph & Mary Maria	Divorce/abandonment	20, Mar. 1819	S3
Este, David K.	Chancery case	20, Jan. 1829	N3
Este, David K.	Estate case	23, Dec. 1841	N2
Este, Lucy	Estate case	23, Dec. 1841	N2
Evans, Ann	Partition petition	28, Dec. 1838	N2
Evans, David	Partition petition	28, Dec. 1838	N2
Evans, Griffith	Partition petition	28, Dec. 1838	N2
Evans, John	Horse found	3, Nov. 1815	S3
Evans, Sarah	Land petition	25, June 1830	N3
Evans, William	Horse found	8, Jan. 1814	S3
Evatt, William	Horse found	9, Nov. 1811	S3
Evens, Daniel T. & Caroline	Divorce/abandonment	3, Mar. 1829	N3
Evens, P.	Committee member	15, Nov. 1838	N2
Everingham, Abigail	Partition case	28, Sept 1827	Q3
Everingham, Enoch	Partition case	28, Sept 1827	Q3
Everingham, John	Partition case	28, Sept 1827	Q3
Everingham, Joseph	Partition case	28, Sept 1827	Q3
Everingham, Mary	Partition case	28, Sept 1827	Q3
Everingham, Nancy	Partition case	28, Sept 1827	Q3
Everingham, Rhoda Ann	Partition case	28, Sept 1827	Q3
Everingham, Tryphena	Partition case	28, Sept 1827	Q3
Everly, Christian	Runaway apprentice	25, Apr. 1818	S2
Eversole, Jacob	Horse found	10, Aug. 1820	S3
Ewing, A.H.	Committee member	15, Nov. 1838	N2
Ewing, Henry	Run away apprentice	15, Jan. 1800	S3
Ewing, Samuel	Horse lost	8, Nov. 1809	H4
Eynon, (Mr)	Cow found	11, July 1795	C3
Eynon, Zebulon	Letter at P.O.	18, Oct. 1794	C3
Fagin, Abner & Barbery	Divorce/abandonment	15, Aug. 1795	C3
Falkener, Jacob	Horse found	5, July 1816	S3
Faran, James J.	Committee member	15, Nov. 1838	N2
Fares, John	Horse found	8, Feb. 1808	S3
Farnum, Russel	Horse lost	29, Nov. 1794	C3

Name	Type of Notice	Date of Notice	Page
Farraday, Charles & Mary A.	Divorce/abandonment	8, Nov. 1851	P2
Farrall, Jane	Inquiry	21, Aug. 1819	S1
Farren, Charles & Malentha	Divorce/abandonment	20, Jan. 1825	E3
Fee, Elijah	Horse found	8, Feb. 1808	S3
Fee, James	Horse found	23, Apr. 1808	S3
Felter, Jacob	Guardian	8, Oct. 1830	N3
Felton, James	Deserter from army	19, Feb. 1814	S3
Fenton, Roswel	Horse found	18, June 1814	S3
Fenton, Roswell	Horse found	28, Aug. 1829	N3
Ferguson, Arthur	Partition petition	23, Jan. 1837	N3
Ferguson, David	Horse Lost	2, Nov. 1827	N3
Ferguson, James	Horse lost	17, June 1806	S3
Ferguson, James	Payment request	27, Oct. 1798	F4
Ferral, Moses	Cow found	27, Feb. 1805	S3
Ferral, Moses	Horse lost	29, July 1806	S3
Ferral, Moses	Cow found	11, June 1808	S3
Ferrell, James	Escaped prisoner	4, June 1796	C3
Ferril, Abner	Horse found	23, Apr. 1814	S1
Ferril, James	Inquiry	14, Aug. 1819	S3
Ferrill, Richard	Escaped prisoner	9, July 1796	F4
Ferris, Abram	Horse stolen	2, July 1830	N2
Ferris, John	Horse found	21, Feb. 1817	S4
Ferris, John	Guardian	8, Oct. 1830	N3
Ferris, Solomon	Horse found	3, Aug. 1827	N3
Field, Jacob	Horse found	16, July 1830	N3
Field, Seth	Cow found	22, Oct. 1796	F1
Fields, Alpheus	Chancery case	10, June 1824	E3
Fields, John	Runaway apprentice	16, May 1818	S2
Fields, Rhoda	Chancery case	10, June 1824	E3
Fifer, Catharine	Guardian	22, Dec. 1829	N3
Fifer, David	Guardian	22, Dec. 1829	N3
Figg, James	Insolvent debtor	27, Jan. 1829	N3
Figg, Thomas	Runaway apprentice	30, May 1818	S1
Filsworth, William	Deserter from army	21, June 1794	C3
Finch, John	Horse found	23, May 1817	S2
Finch, William	Horse found	17, Nov. 1826	N3
Findlay, Robert & Martha	Divorce/abandonment	8, Nov. 1851	P2
Finnehon, John	Debt notice	4, July 1795	C3
Finney, John	Horse lost	19, May 1815	S3
Finnie, James	Horse lost	27, July 1803	S3
Fisher, David	Inquiry	8, Dec. 1821	S4
Fisher, David	Inquiry	12, Jan. 1822	S4
Fisher, Fanny	Inquiry	8, Dec. 1821	S4
Fisher, Fanny	Inquiry	12, Jan. 1822	S4
Fisher, John	Cow lost	15, Jan. 1800	S3
Flagg, Jacob J.	Chancery case	29, Sept 1829	N3
Flanagen, Barton	Run away notice	18, Aug. 1829	N3
Fleek, Gasham	Run away notice	6, Sept 1809	H4
Fleek, John & Ann	Chancery court case	17, June 1823	N3
Fleming, Samuel	Horse found	11, July 1812	S3
Flemming, Robert & Elizabeth	Divorce/abandonment	21, Aug. 1813	S3
Fletcher, John R.	Swindler	15, Apr. 1818	S3
Fletcher, William	Horse found	28, Dec. 1807	S3
Fletcher, William	Horse found	25, July 1817	S4

Name	Type of Notice	Date of Notice	Page
Flin, William	Run away apprentice	16, July 1799	S3
Flinn, Benjamin	Horse lost	24, Sept 1800	S3
Flinn, William	Horse found	12, Dec. 1814	W4
Flint, Eli	Estate case	4, July 1826	N3
Flint, Esther	Estate case	4, July 1826	N3
Flint, Famde	Estate case	4, July 1826	N3
Flint, Fanny	Estate case	4, July 1826	N3
Flint, Hezekiah	Horse lost	27, Oct. 1810	S4
Flint, Rebecca	Estate case	4, July 1826	N3
Flournoy, Matthew	Run away	13, May 1801	S3
Flowlers, Aaron	Horse lost	1, July 1806	S3
Foley, Isaac	Horse found	21, June 1816	S3
Foor, Joseph	Horse found	21, Feb. 1810	H4
Foot, Joseph & Rebecca	Divorce/abandonment	22, Sept 1815	S3
Foote, J.P.	Committee member	15, Nov. 1838	N2
Ford, Catharine B.	Guardianship	8, Oct. 1830	N3
Ford, Mordecai S.	Horse stealing	20, Aug. 1808	S3
Forden, John	Horse found	26, May 1821	S3
Forden, John	Horse found	23, Jan. 1821	S3
Foreman, James M.	Partition petition	24, Mar. 1838	N2
foreman, John	Partition petition	24, Mar. 1838	N2
Foreman, Jonathan	Partition petition	24, Mar. 1838	N2
Forguson, James	Departure notice	10, Sept 1799	S3
Forman, Jonathan	Horse found	6, July 1822	S3
Forrest, George	Deserter from army	22, July 1801	S3
Forrest, Reason	Insolvent debtor	23, July 1830	N3
Forte, Henry B.	Deceased	25, June 1830	N3
Foster, Luke	Horse found	11, July 1812	S3
Foster, Luke	Horse found	13, Jan. 1821	S3
Foster, Robert	Horse found	13, Mar. 1813	S3
Foster, Salmon H.	Horse found	6, Mar. 1819	S3
Foster, Samuel	Apprentice wanted	8, Aug. 1804	S3
Foster, Samuel	Horse lost	31, July 1805	S3
Foster, Thomas	Horse found	16, May 1828	N3
Foster, W.R.	Committee member	15, Nov. 1838	N2
Foulke, Levi	Insolvent debtor	11, Nov. 1828	N1
Fowler, Jacob & Sarah	Partition petition	23, Jan. 1837	N3
Fowler, John	Horse found	21, Mar. 1818	S2
Fox, Jacob	Horse found	9, Nov. 1811	S3
Fox, Stephen	Horse found	24, Oct. 1812	S3
Frakes, Robert	Escaped prisoner	7, Mar. 1795	C3
Frame, Thomas	Notice	20, Feb. 1796	C3
Frances, John	Horse found	7, Dec. 1811	S3
Frank, Leonard & Lydia Ann	Divorce/abandonment	1, Aug. 1851	P3
Franklin, Ahasel	Horse found	8, Sept 1815	S3
Frazee, Benjamin	Horse found	19, Sept 1812	S1
Frazee, Joseph	Horse lost	6, Aug. 1800	S3
Frazer, Levi & Mary	Divorce/abandonment	18, July 1812	S3
Frazer, Thomas	Horse found	21, Nov. 1804	S3
Fream, Thomas	Cow lost	10, Dec. 1796	F3
Freelinghope, Theodore	Chancery case	20, Jan. 1825	E3
Freeman, Abraham	Horse lost	7, Nov. 1801	S3
Freeman, Ezra Fitz	Land for sale	17, Sept 1796	F3
Freeman, John H. & Sarah	Divorce/abandonment	20, Jan. 1825	E3

Name	Type of Notice	Date of Notice	Page
Freeman, Samuel	Debt notice	3, Sept 1796	F3
Freeman, William	Horse lost	27, Oct. 1798	F4
Freidlein, George & Angel.	Divorce/abandonment	6, Nov. 1851	P2
French, George & Eliza Ann	Divorce/abandonment	20, Nov. 1838	N3
French, Jeremiah	Horse found	25, Apr. 1812	S3
French, Ralph	Horse lost	1, Aug. 1804	S4
Frost, Isaac	Horse found	19, Oct. 1820	S3
Fulcher, George	Horse found	11, Aug. 1815	S3
Fuller, Isaac	Horse found	26, Feb. 1814	S3
Fuller, Lucius Q. & Charity	Divorce/abandonment	28, Feb. 1818	S3
Fuller, Solomon	Horse found	12, Oct. 1811	S3
Fuller, Zekiel & Elizabeth	Divorce/abandonment	18, Apr. 1795	C3
Fullerton, John	Debt relief	8, Oct. 1821	S3
Fulton, ---- & ----	Divorce/abandonment	16, Oct. 1852	P2
Funk, Conrad	Horse found	23, Apr. 1814	S1
Furney, Anthony & Elizabeth	Divorce/abandonment	9, May 1795	C3
Fury, Bidy	Poor house inmate	14, Nov. 1851	P2
Galbraith, John	Debt notice	28, Mar. 1795	C3
Gall, Jacob	Insolvent debtor	27, Jan. 1829	N3
Gallaway, James	Horse lost	24, June 1806	S3
Galloway, Albert	Deposition given	22, Sept 1842	Z3
Galloway, James	Horse lost	28, May 1800	S3
Galt, John	Biography article	28, Mar. 1848	K2
Gamble, Joseph	Cow lost	16, June 1821	S3
Gano, Daniel	Committee member	15, Nov. 1838	N2
Gano, John S.	Cow lost	7, May 1796	C3
Gard, Job	Lost pocket book	9, Nov. 1793	C4
Gardner, George	Escaped prisoner	9, May 1795	C3
Gardner, George & Maria	Divorce/abandonment	1, May 1823	J3
Garner, Henry	Land partition	10, June 1828	N3
Garner, Vica	Land partition	10, June 1828	N3
Garrigus, Abner	Estate case	1, Nov. 1816	S2
Garrigus, Jacob	Estate case	1, Nov. 1816	S2
Garrigus, Jeptha	Estate case	1, Nov. 1816	S2
Garrigus, Silas	Estate case	1, Nov. 1816	S2
Garrigus, Timothy	Estate case	1, Nov. 1816	S2
Garrish, Francis B.	Insolvent debtor	23, July 1830	N3
Garrison, Abraham	Sale of lots notice	12, Sept 1795	C3
Garrison, Abraham	Cow found	30, Apr. 1796	C3
Garrison, Jonathan	Deserter from army	23, Apr. 1814	S1
Garvey, Joseph	Run away	27, Aug. 1800	S3
Gates, Uriah & Rebecca	Divorce/abandonment	24, Dec. 1800	S3
Gates, Uriah & Rebecca	Divorce/abandonment	15, Jan. 1806	S3
Gates, Uriah & Rebecca	Divorce/abandonment	26, Oct. 1807	S3
Gatz, John & Joseph	Run away apprentice	6, Aug. 1799	S4
Gavin, Elizabeth	Chancery court case	17, June 1823	N3
Gavin, John	Chancery court case	17, June 1823	N3
Gay, Harvey	Run away notice	26, Sept 1823	N3
Gazlay, James W.	Case dismissed	1, Aug. 1822	J3
Gazlay, James W.	Biography	5, Sept 1822	J2
Gentle, William T.	Guardian	20, Apr. 1830	N3
George, Reuben	Horse found	20, Dec. 1816	S3
German, Caleb	Horse lost	22, Dec. 1802	S3

Name	Type of Notice	Date of Notice	Page
Gerrard, Reece A.P.	Debtor	19, Sept 1812	S3
Gest, Clarissa	Female Institution	19, Feb. 1830	N3
Gest, Reuben & Rachael	Divorce/abandonment	22, Jan. 1830	N3
Gibb, John	Debt relief	3, Apr. 1819	S3
Gibbins, Hannah	Real estate sale	17, June 1825	N3
Gibbs, John	Runaway -17 yrs old	18, Mar. 1820	S3
Gibbs, Justice	Horse lost	11, June 1799	S3
Gibbs, Justus	Horse found	26, Jan. 1811	S4
Gibbs, Justus	Horse found	14, Sept 1811	S3
Gibbs, Justus	Horse found	27, June 1812	S3
Gibbs, Justus	Horse found	8, Sept 1815	S3
Gibbs, Justus	Horse found	28, June 1816	S3
Gibbs, Justus	Horse found	28, Feb. 1810	H3
Gibbs, Justus	Horse found	22, Aug. 1826	N3
Gibson, James A.	Deserter from army	15, Oct. 1814	S1
Gibson, Thomas	Debt notice	11, July 1795	C3
Gibson, Thomas	Land for sale	13, Aug. 1796	F1
Gibson, Thomas	Debt notice	18, Mar. 1797	F4
Gibson, William	Deserter from army	18, Jan. 1794	C3
Giles, David B. & Lidya H.	Divorce/abandonment	20, Jan. 1825	E3
Gillespia, George	Cow found	26, Nov. 1796	F3
Gillespie, James	Horse lost	27, Oct. 1802	S3
Gillespie, James	Brew house notice	5, Sept 1795	C3
Gilman, Ann	Dower petition	21, Jan. 1837	N3
Gilman, Daniel	Horse found	7, Mar. 1808	S3
Gilman, John	Horse lost	12, Jan. 1803	S3
Gilman, John	Dower petition	21, Jan. 1837	N3
Gilmore, William	Horse found	24, Aug. 1811	S3
Glancy, John	horse found	28, Nov. 1823	N2
Glenn, Isaac & Elizabeth	Divorce/abandonment	26, Oct. 1836	N2
Glenn, James	Tavern for sale	3, Sept 1796	F3
Glenn, James	Notice to public	17, Sept 1796	F3
Glenn, James	Committee member	15, Nov. 1838	N2
Glisson, Thomas	Horse found	12, Nov. 1814	S3
Goble, Daniel	Horse found	24, Jan. 1817	S3
Goble, Daniel & Margaret	Divorce/abandonment	3, Sept 1799	S3
Golding, Aaron	Insolvent debtor	27, Jan. 1829	N3
Goldtrap, John	Horse found	2, Feb. 1822	S3
Goodrich, Jeremiah	Horse found	13, Feb. 1813	S3
Goodrich, William & Polly	Divorce/abandonment	1, May 1819	S3
Goodrich, William & Polly	Divorce/abandonment	24, Feb. 1821	S3
Goodwin, Asa	Horse found	16, Aug. 1816	S3
Gordon, John	Horse found	28, May 1814	S3
Gordon, Riley W. & Fanny	Divorce/abandonment	13, Aug. 1836	T2
Gottshalk, Eliza (Mrs)	Birth notice	23, Jan. 1802	S3
Goucher, Samuel	Inquiry	17, Apr. 1819	S3
Goudy, James	Horse found	1, Aug. 1804	S4
Goudy, Samuel & Elizabeth	Divorce/abandonment	15, June 1803	S3
Goudy, Thomas	Lost goods	23, Nov. 1793	C4
Goudy, Thomas (Capt)	Hamilton Co militia	28, Nov. 1801	S3
Goudy, William	Land for sale	25, Mar. 1797	F4
Gowdy, William	Horse lost	18, Mar. 1797	F3
Grage, Samuel	Horse found	25, Dec. 1813	S3
Graham, Elizabeth	Chancery case	10, Oct. 1823	N3

Name	Type of Notice	Date of Notice	Page
Graham, George	Chancery case	1, Jan. 1842	N2
Graham, James	Chancery case	21, Dec. 1830	N3
Graham, Joseph	Committee member	15, Nov. 1838	N2
Graham, Patrick	Hogs found	16, Apr. 1796	C3
Graham, Patrick	Horse lost	27, Aug. 1796	F3
Graham, Thomas	Chancery case	10, Oct. 1823	N3
Grandbeck, Daniel & Amelia	Divorce/abandonment	10, Mar. 1842	N3
Granger, Ephraim & Dolly	Divorce/abandonment	14, Feb. 1818	S3
Graves, Bartlett	Land partition	29, Apr. 1828	N3
Graves, Betsy	Land partition	29, Apr. 1828	N3
Graves, Franky	Run away	14, Nov. 1801	S3
Graves, James Hudson	Run away apprentice	22, Apr. 1815	W3
Graves, Zachariah	Horse found	29, Aug. 1817	S3
Gray, Daniel	Notice	26, Oct. 1827	Q3
Gray, Franklin	Deserter from army	30, July 1814	S3
Gray, George & Ann	Chancery case	6, Dec. 1838	N2
Gray, Henry	Insolvent debtor	27, Jan. 1829	N3
Gray, Jacob	Notice	3, July 1805	S3
Gray, John M.	Horse lost	7, May 1808	S3
Gray, Robert	Horse found	18, June 1814	S3
Gray, Robert	Inquiry	20, Nov. 1819	S3
Gray, Robert	Horse found	25, Apr. 1810	H4
Gray, William	Horse found	28, Sept 1811	S3
Greagry, Jonathan	Horse found	14, May 1808	S3
Greasy, James	Court sentencing	4, Nov. 1836	N2
Green, Daniel A. & Frances	Divorce/abandonment	6, Sept 1831	A3
Green, James	Court sentencing	4, Nov. 1836	N2
Green, Jo	Run away slave	13, Apr. 1820	D3
Green, John	Chancery case	10, June 1824	E3
Green, Peter	Run away notice	23, July 1796	F3
Greene, W.	Committee member	15, Nov. 1838	N2
Greene, William	Chancery case	28, May 1830	N3
Greenwell, Caroline	Guardianship	20, Apr. 1830	N3
Greenwell, John	Guardianship	20, Apr. 1830	N3
Greenwell, Robert	Guardianship	20, Apr. 1830	N3
Greer, James	Horse found	18, Mar. 1815	S3
Greer, John & Eleanor	Divorce/abandonment	27, Feb. 1813	S3
Greer, William	Runaway apprentice	25, July 1817	S4
Gregory, J. Rebecca	Chancery court case	17, June 1823	N3
Gregory, Samuel	Horse lost	29, May 1802	S3
Gregory, Samuel	Deserter from army	10, Oct. 1812	S3
Gregory, Thomas	Chancery court case	17, June 1823	N3
Griffin, Ebenezer	Horse lost	12, Sept 1804	S3
Griffin, William	Adultry	2, Jan. 1802	S3
Griffith, Elias	Letter at P.O.	18, Oct. 1794	C3
Grigg, James	Horse found	17, July 1813	S3
Grimes, John	Deserter from army	9, Oct. 1813	S3
Griswold, George	Chancery case	20, Jan. 1825	E3
Grole, William	Run away apprentice	15, June 1803	S4
Grose, Jacob	Run away	25, Jan. 1808	S3
Grummons, David	Horse lost	12, Sept 1804	S4
Guess, Hercules & Eliza	Chancery case	14, Dec. 1838	N2
Guess, Reuben & Rachael	Divorce/abandonment	30, Jan. 1829	N3
Guest, Sarah A.	Guardianship	20, Apr. 1830	N3

Name	Type of Notice	Date of Notice	Page
Guilford, N.	Committee member	15, Nov. 1838	N2
Guinn, Benjamin	Horse found	3, Oct. 1818	S3
Gunn, Daniel	Deserter from army	10, Sept 1814	S1
Gunning, David	Horse found	27, July 1820	S3
Gwinup, Isaac L. & Sarah	Divorce/abandonment	16, Feb. 1827	Q3
Gwynne, David	Chancery case	11, Oct. 1847	K2
Hacket, Peter & Rachel	Divorce/abandonment	12, Feb. 1820	S1
Hafer, Henry	Horse lost	20, Aug. 1808	S3
Hafer, Henry	Horse lost	20, Feb. 1819	S3
Hafer, Henry	Horse lost	28, Dec. 1820	S1
Hageman, Simon	Horse found	26, Sept 1828	N3
Hagerman, Charlotte	Guardian	28, Aug. 1827	N3
Hagerman, Christian	Horse found	28, Feb. 1817	S4
Hagerman, Levina	Guardian	28, Aug. 1827	N3
Hagerman, Lucinda	Guardian	28, Aug. 1827	N3
Hail, James	Deserter from army	15, Aug. 1795	C3
Haily, Timothy	Escaped prisoner	26, Sept 1795	C3
Haines, Josiah & Lydia	Divorce notice	4, Jan. 1828	N3
Hall, James	Committee member	15, Nov. 1838	N2
Hall, John T.	Cow lost	19, Nov. 1800	S3
Hall, William	Horse lost	28, Feb. 1810	H3
Halstead, Nicholas	Horse found	23, Oct. 1819	S3
Halstead, Nick & Jerusha	Divorce/abandonment	28, Apr. 1826	N3
Hamar, James & Margaret	Divorce/abandonment	7, Feb. 1823	N3
Hamel, Andrew & Martha	Divorce/abandonment	23, Jan. 1838	N2
Hamel, James & Catharine	Divorce/abandonment	10, Feb. 1836	T3
Hamilton, Andrew	Cow lost	9, Oct. 1802	S3
Hamilton, Charles J.	Swindler notice	24, July 1829	N3
Hamilton, Jabez	Debt relief	2, June 1821	S3
Hamilton, John	Horse lost	17, Nov. 1802	S3
Hamilton, William J.	Court sentencing	4, Nov. 1836	N2
Hammond, Solomon	Horse lost	17, Sept 1808	S2
Hampton, James	Runaway slave	10, Feb. 1821	S2
Hancock, Joseph	Cow found	16, Sept 1801	S3
Hand, William	Horse found	4, May 1811	S3
Handley, John & Sophia	Divorce/abandonment	20, Jan. 1821	S1
Hanes, Daniel S.	Horse found	12, Mar. 1814	S3
Haney, James	Land purchase	23, July 1814	S3
Hanlen, Demas	Horse found	2, July 1814	S3
Hanlen, George	Horse found	2, June 1815	S3
Hanly, Thomas	Horse found	26, Sept 1818	S3
Hanna, Thomas	Horse found	27, July 1811	S3
Hannaman, Christopher	Horse found	16, Apr. 1808	S3
Hansel, David & Rachel	Divorce/abandonment	11, July 1812	S1
Hansell, Lawrence	Horse found	21, Feb. 1810	H4
Hany, James	Info wanted	14, Mar. 1812	S3
Hardford, Thaddeus	Horse found	4, Jan. 1808	S3
Hardin, James	Horse found	12, Jan. 1822	S3
Hardin, John	Horse found	1, Dec. 1829	N3
Hardin, John (Col)	Pioneer incident	23, Dec. 1847	K2
Hardin, Mark	Run away notice	17, Dec. 1796	F3
Hardy, David	Run away apprentice	30, Sept 1801	S3
Hargraves, Hercules & Amy E	Divorce/abandonment	31, Aug. 1847	K2

Name	Type of Notice	Date of Notice	Page
Hariman, Moses	Horse found	4, July 1817	S3
Harker, Amanda	Insolvent debtor	27, Jan. 1829	N3
Harlam, Edward	Horse found	28, Feb. 1810	H3
Harlan, George	Horse found	1, Feb. 1808	S3
Harlan, George	Debt relief	20, June 1817	S1
Harper, Garret	Horse found	25, Aug. 1821	S3
Harper, John M.	Guardian	17, June 1837	N2
Harper, Mathew	Guardian	17, June 1837	N2
Harper, Robert	Horse found	2, July 1799	S3
Harper, Thomas	Horse lost	6, July 1803	S3
Harper, William	Horse lost	29, Apr. 1801	S3
Harpham, Jon & Priscilla	Divorce/abandonment	15, Jan. 1814	S3
Harred, Samuel	Horse found	6, Feb. 1802	S3
Harriman, David	Horse lost	20, June 1812	S3
Harris, Abner	cow lost	9, Mar. 1803	S3
Harris, Baptist	Run away notice	8, Nov. 1809	H4
Harris, John	Chancery court case	17, June 1823	N4
Harris, John & Rosanna	Divorce/abandonment	10, Dec. 1814	S3
Harris, Samuel	Horse found	17, Jan. 1818	S3
Harris, Walter	Run away notice	8, Nov. 1809	H4
Harris, William	Deserter from army	2, July 1814	S3
Harrison, Ann	Chancery case	7, Oct. 1824	E3
Harrison, Ann	Chancery case	20, Jan. 1825	E3
Harrison, Anna	Estate case	23, Dec. 1841	N2
Harrison, Anna Carter	Estate case	23, Dec. 1841	N2
Harrison, Benjamin	Estate case	23, Dec. 1841	N2
Harrison, Clarissa	Estate case	23, Dec. 1841	N2
Harrison, James Findley	Estate case	23, Dec. 1841	N2
Harrison, John C.	Estate case	23, Dec. 1841	N2
Harrison, John J.	Estate case	23, Dec. 1841	N2
Harrison, John Scott	Estate case	23, Dec. 1841	N2
Harrison, John Symmes	Estate case	23, Dec. 1841	N2
Harrison, Montgomery Pike	Estate case	23, Dec. 1841	N2
Harrison, Obed & Sally	Divorce/abandonment	1, Mar. 1816	S3
Harrison, William (Lt)	Letter at P.O.	18, Oct. 1794	C3
Harrison, William H.	Estate case	23, Dec. 1841	N2
Harrison, William H.	Chancery case	7, Oct. 1824	E3
Harrison, William H. (Gen)	Estate case	23, Dec. 1841	N2
Harrison, William Henry	Petition filed	6, Apr. 1803	S3
Harrison, William Henry	Chancery case	20, Jan. 1825	E3
Harrold, Jonathan & Betsey	Divorce/abandonment	17, Oct. 1829	R3
Hars, Robert	Chancery case	14, Oct. 1823	N3
Hart, Edward	Notice of theft	2, Aug. 1794	C3
Hartley, John	Horse lost	9, July 1796	F1
Hartman, Christopher	Horse found	28, Dec. 1807	S3
Hartman, William	Horse found	14, Feb. 1818	S3
Hartzell, Elizabeth	Attachment case	17, June 1825	N3
Harvey, Asa	Horse lost	20, Aug. 1799	S3
Harvey, John	Horse found	25, Apr. 1810	H3
Haseltine, David	Run away notice	15, July 1825	N2
Haskill, Joseph	Deposition given	27, Sept 1842	Z4
Hatch, Harlan	Insolvent debtor	23, July 1830	N3
Hatch, William S.	Chancery case	14, Oct. 1836	N2
Hatfield, Aaron	Insolvent debtor	27, Jan. 1829	N3

Name	Type of Notice	Date of Notice	Page
Hathaway, Elijah & Ruth	Divorce/abandonment	18, Feb. 1825	N3
Hathner, George	Horse found	17, Apr. 1813	S3
Hatt, Lewis	Horse found	16, Nov. 1827	N3
Hatt, William & Sarah	Divorce/abandonment	8, Oct. 1850	P2
Havens, Benjamin	Horse found	5, June 1819	S2
Hawkins, James B.	Escaped convict	3, Oct. 1818	S2
Hawkins, William	Run away slave	18, Sept 1805	S3
Haynes, Josiah & Lydia	Divorce/abandonment	27, Jan. 1829	N3
Hays, Abiah	Horse stolen	25, Nov. 1825	N3
Hays, Joseph	Horse found	17, Aug. 1811	S3
Hays, Thomas	Escaped prisoner	26, Sept 1795	C3
Hayt, E.	Cow lost	4, Jan. 1837	N3
Heald, Ebenezer	Horse found	27, Sept 1816	S3
Hearley, Henry	Notice	15, Feb. 1825	N3
Heckewelder, Th.	Horse lost	17, Jan. 1817	S4
Hedges, John	Horse found	20, Sept 1816	S3
Heffner, Frederick	Horse found	10, Feb. 1826	N3
Henderson, Henry	Court sentencing	4, Nov. 1836	N2
Henderson, John	Deserter from army	30, July 1814	S3
Hendley, John	Horse found	27, July 1811	S3
Hendrickson, Henry & Betsy	Divorce/abandonment	7, Dec. 1811	S3
Henne, F.H. & Catharine F.	Divorce/abandonment	6, Nov. 1851	P2
Henne, Frederick W. & Cath.	Divorce/abandonment	8, Nov. 1851	P2
Henning, William	Insolvent debtor	27, Jan. 1829	N3
Henry, Joseph	Horse lost	1, July 1806	S3
Hercules, William	Pig found	25, Mar. 1797	F4
Herndon, Richard W.	Horse stolen	19, Dec. 1818	S3
Herrell, William	Horse found	26, July 1816	S3
Herren, Jesse	Horse found	21, Nov. 1817	S2
Heuston, David	Horse found	24, Oct. 1812	S3
Heuston, Thomas	Horse found	13, Feb. 1813	S3
Hewitt, Moses	Frontier life bio	24, Nov. 1847	K3
Hick, John	Horse lost	7, May 1808	S3
Hickman, George	Insolvent debtor	23, July 1830	N3
Hickman, James C.	Runaway apprentice	26, Sept 1818	S3
Hickman, William	Horse found	7, Aug. 1819	S3
Higbee, Nehemiah	Horse found	11, Nov. 1828	N3
Higdon, Hezekiah	Run away notice	9, Sept 1823	N3
Higgins, John V.	Horse found	12, Sept 1817	S3
Higgins, John V.	Horse found	20, Jan. 1826	N3
Higgins, Thomas	Horse found	12, Sept 1817	S3
Hilderbrand, Laurence & El.	Divorce/abandonment	15, Apr. 1801	S3
Hilditch, Hannah	Notice	18, Dec. 1813	S3
Hiley, Abraham	Boar found	22, Oct. 1796	F3
Hill, Andrew	Horse lost	27, Apr. 1803	S3
Hill, Andrew	Horse found	23, Feb. 1816	S3
Hill, Daniel	Deserter from army	30, Nov. 1793	C3
Hill, Elsea	Horse found	28, Feb. 1837	N3
Hill, James	Debt notice	7, May 1796	C3
Hill, John	Horse found	28, Nov. 1812	S3
Hill, Philip A.	Horse found	8, Aug. 1828	N3
Hill, Thomas	Horse lost	1, July 1801	S3
Hiller, Richard	Chancery case	21, Mar. 1838	N2
Hilton, Theophius	Horse stolen	23, Nov. 1827	N3

Name	Type of Notice	Date of Notice	Page
Hinds, Ethan & Susanna	Chancery case	21, Mar. 1838	N2
Hiner, James	Deposition given	17, Sept 1842	Z4
Hinkle, Asa	Horse lost	10, Sept 1808	S2
Hinkle, Asa	Horse found	20, June 1818	S3
Hirons, Samuel	Horse found	19, July 1809	H1
Hockett, Moses	Horse lost	5, Dec. 1817	S3
Hodger, John	Horse found	2, June 1815	S3
Hodges, Rufus	Committee member	15, Nov. 1838	N2
Hodgson, Samuel	Chancery court case	17, June 1823	N4
Hoff, Isaac	Horse lost	13, July 1803	S3
Hoffman, George	Bull found	2, Sept 1801	S3
Hoffman, George W.	Guardian	11, Sept 1837	N2
Hoffman, John	Debt relief	29, June 1820	S3
Hoffman, John	Guardian	11, Sept 1837	N2
Hoffman, Sarah Ann	Guardian	11, Sept 1837	N2
Hogan, Francis T.	Information wanted	18, Jan. 1838	T2
Hogan, Martha	Information wanted	18, Jan. 1838	T2
Hogan, William	Deserter from army	4, June 1814	S3
Hogue, William	Deposition given	13, Sept 1842	Z3
Holabird, Amos B.	Chancery case	14, Dec. 1838	N2
Holcomb, Amanda	Female school award	28, July 1835	N2
Hole, John	Debt notice	26, Apr. 1794	C3
Holfield, Joseph	Notice	5, Oct. 1803	S3
Holinshade, John	Insolvent debtor	23, July 1830	N3
Holland, James	Deserter from army	2, May 1795	C3
Holland, John & Katharine	Divorce/abandonment	14, May 1796	C3
Holland, Zachariah	Horse found	4, Sept 1805	S3
Hollenshade, John	Insolvent debtor	27, Jan. 1829	N3
Holly, Josiah	Run away	27, Mar. 1805	S3
Holman, George & Mary	Chancery case	11, Oct. 1847	K2
Holston, Andrew	Horse found	20, Feb. 1813	S3
Hood, John	Attachment case	12, Aug. 1825	N3
Hook, Henry	Debt relief	20, Sept 1816	S1
Hopkins, Conrad & Mary Eliz	Divorce/abandonment	8, Nov. 1851	P2
Hopkins, Solomon	Notice	25, Feb. 1815	S2
Hopkins, Solomon	Notice	25, Feb. 1815	W3
Hopkins, William H.	Debt relief	9, May 1817	S4
Hopple, Casper	Chancery case	10, Oct. 1823	N3
Horner, Samuel D.	Debtor	23, June 1815	S3
Horom, Timothy	Horse found	2, June 1815	S3
Hosier, Abraham & Polly	Divorce/abandonment	22, June 1803	S3
Hotchkiss, Harvey	Partition petition	22, Mar. 1837	N3
Hotchkiss, Sally	Partition petition	22, Mar. 1837	N3
Houck, John	Horse found	11, Aug. 1826	N3
Hough, Joseph	Horse lost	16, Apr. 1808	S3
Howard, Benjamin	Horse found	21, July 1815	S3
Howard, Benjamin	Horse found	14, Mar. 1817	S3
Howard, George	Horse stolen	30, July 1814	S3
Howell, Lewis	Chancery case	4, Mar. 1828	N3
Howell, Mary R.	Chancery case	4, Mar. 1828	N3
Hubbard, John & Asenath	Divorce/abandonment	4, May 1803	S3
Hubbell, Gabriel	Chancery case	10, Oct. 1823	N3
Hubbis, Abijah	Horse found	13, Feb. 1813	S3
Hubble, Maria R.	Female Institution	19, Feb. 1830	N3

Name	Type of Notice	Date of Notice	Page
Huddard, George	Chancery case	1, Dec. 1826	Q3
Huddard, Joseph	Chancery case	1, Dec. 1826	Q3
Hudson, Mary	Land partition	10, June 1828	N3
Hueston, Robert	Run away apprentice	30, Mar. 1811	S3
Hueston, Thomas	Horse found	14, May 1808	S3
Hughes, Ann	Partition petition	28, Dec. 1838	N2
Hughes, Levi	Horse found	21, Jan. 1823	N3
Hughes, William	Partition petition	28, Dec. 1838	N2
Hughs, George	Horse lost	4, Dec. 1805	S3
Hulbert, Stephen & Mercy	Divorce/abandonment	23, Feb. 1816	S3
Hulingsiner, William	Horse found	4, July 1817	S3
Hull, Eliakim	Deserter from army	31, May 1794	C3
Huls, William	Horse found	4, July 1818	S3
Humes, John	Horse found	29, Mar. 1816	S3
Humes, John	Notice	10, Oct. 1795	C3
Hunt, Abijah	Court case	21, Jan. 1801	S3
Hunt, Abijah	Partnership notice	25, July 1795	C3
Hunt, Isaac	Horse found	20, Mar. 1811	S3
Hunt, Jeremiah	Chancery case	19, Jan. 1811	S3
Hunt, Jesse	Horse lost	29, May 1813	S3
Hunt, John	Estate case	23, Dec. 1841	N2
Hunt, John R.	Estate sale	11, Jan. 1837	N2
Hunt, John R.	Administrator	21, Mar. 1838	N2
Hunt, Joshua & Mary	Divorce/abandonment	18, Mar. 1820	S3
Hunt, Ralph W.	Sale notice	27, Oct. 1798	F3
Hunt, Robert & Frances	Divorce/abandonment	19, Jan. 1816	S3
Hunt, Thomas	Horse found	11, Feb. 1815	S3
Hunt, William	Horse lost	1, Apr. 1815	S3
Hunt, William B.	Court case	20, Sept 1816	S1
Hunt, Zebuline	Estate case	23, Dec. 1841	N2
Hunter, John & Mary	Divorce/abandonment	6, Sept 1809	H4
Hunter, Jon	Horse found	12, Jan. 1816	S1
Hunter, Thomas	Horse found	26, Jan. 1811	S4
Hunter, Thomas	Horse found	4, May 1809	H4
Hunter, William	Horse found	6, Mar. 1813	S3
Hurdus, Adam	Debt relief	29, June 1822	S3
Hutchinson, Abigail	Guardian	21, Sept 1838	N3
Hutchinson, Amos	Guardian	21, Sept 1838	N3
Hutchinson, David	Horse found	14, Apr. 1829	N3
Hutchinson, Ezekiel	Horse found	9, Mar. 1811	S3
Hutchinson, Ezekiel	Horse found	21, Mar. 1818	S2
Hutchinson, John & Charlotte	Divorce/abandonment	18, July 1826	N3
Hutchinson, Nancy	Guardian	21, Sept 1838	N3
Hutchinson, Naomi	Guardian	21, Sept 1838	N3
Ingels, James	Run away slave	24, Feb. 1820	D3
Ireland, Aaron	Cow found	27, Oct. 1798	F4
Ireland, Japhet	Debt relief	5, Sept 1817	S3
Irvine, Christopher (Capt)	Pioneer incident	11, Jan. 1848	K2
Irvine, William (Col)	Pioneer incident	11, Jan. 1848	K2
Irwin, James	Horse found	11, Aug. 1815	S1
Irwin, John	Horse lost	11, Feb. 1806	S3
Irwin, John	Horse found	22, Jan. 1814	S3
Irwin, Mary	Guardian	20, Mar. 1838	N3

Name	Type of Notice	Date of Notice	Page
Irwin, William & Catharine	Divorce/abandonment	8, Sept 1821	S3
Isgrig, Daniel	Horse found	8, Jan. 1814	S3
Isgrigg, John	Horse found	1, Dec. 1815	S3
Iupenlatz, George & Elizabeth	Divorce/abandonment	19, Jan. 1816	S3
Jacklin, Isaac	Missing child	7, July 1821	S2
Jackson, Charles	Debt relief	10, Nov. 1821	S3
Jackson, Ebenezer	Horse lost	17, Apr. 1819	S3
Jackson, John	Horse lost	18, Feb. 1806	S3
Jackson, William	Insolvent debtor	27, Jan. 1829	N3
James, Samuel	Run away notice	5, May 1834	T2
Jamison, John	Deserter from army	30, Oct. 1813	S2
Jardan, Jacob	Horse found	25, Jan. 1812	S3
Jaudin, Charle & Elizabeth	Divorce/abandonment	7, June 1795	C3
Jeans, Zachariah	Horse found	31, Jan. 1817	S3
Jenkins, Aaron	Horse lost	17, Aug. 1803	S3
Jenkins, Southward & Anna	Divorce/abandonment	17, Jan. 1818	S2
Jennings, Benjamin	Sale notice	27, Oct. 1798	F3
Jennings, Elnathan	Horse found	19, Mar. 1814	S3
Jennings, Henry	Horse lost	5, Feb. 1800	S3
Jennings, Levi	Cow found	24, Dec. 1796	F3
Jennings, Solomon	Horse found	9, Nov. 1811	S3
Jessup, Daniel	Guardian	8, Oct. 1830	N3
Jinks, Scott	Horse found	8, Oct. 1824	N3
Jocelyn, Luther F.B.	Real estate case	9, Jan. 1838	N3
Jocelyn, Mary Ann	Real estate case	9, Jan. 1838	N3
John, Abijah	Guardian	17, June 1837	N2
John, William	Insolvent debtor	27, Jan. 1829	N3
Johnson, Abner	Horse found	12, Nov. 1814	S3
Johnson, Caroline A.	Gold medal	19, Feb. 1830	N3
Johnson, Daniel	Horse found	18, Jan. 1812	S3
Johnson, Deborah	Inquiry	26, Sept 1818	S3
Johnson, Ebenezer & Elenor	Partition petition	22, Mar. 1837	N3
Johnson, James	Horse borrowed	18, Aug. 1815	S3
Johnson, James	Court case witness	20, June 1850	P2
Johnson, John	Deserter from army	30, Nov. 1793	C3
Johnson, John & Harriet S.	Divorce/abandonment	16, Feb. 1848	K2
Johnson, Orson & Mary Jane	Divorce/abandonment	6, Nov. 1851	P2
Johnson, Robert	Deserter from army	2, Feb. 1807	S3
Johnson, Wilford	Horse found	9, Jan. 1813	S3
Johnson, Wilford	Horse found	29, Jan. 1814	S3
Johnson, William	Court sentencing	4, Nov. 1836	N2
Johnson, William & Mary	Divorce/abandonment	21, July 1827	R3
Johnson, William & Mary	Divorce/abandonment	5, July 1828	R3
Johnson, Zenas	Insolvent debtor	23, July 1830	N3
Johnston, Isaac	Escaped prisoner	30, Jan. 1796	C1
Johnston, John	Deserter from army	22, Mar. 1794	C3
Johnston, John	Deserter from army	7, Feb. 1795	C3
Johnston, William	Escaped prisoner	1, Jan. 1806	S4
Jones, Benjamin	Insolvent debtor	27, Jan. 1829	N3
Jones, David & Elizabeth	Divorce/abandonment	16, Feb. 1822	S3
Jones, George W.	Chancery case	10, Oct. 1823	N3
Jones, George W.	Chancery case	28, May 1830	N3
Jones, Isaac	Horse found	2, May 1817	S2

Name	Type of Notice	Date of Notice	Page
Jones, James	Land partition	10, June 1828	N3
Jones, John D.	Committee member	15, Nov. 1838	N2
Jones, Kinneth	Horse found	10, Dec. 1814	S3
Jones, Mary	Land partition	10, June 1828	N3
Jones, Mary	Partition petition	28, Dec. 1838	N2
Jones, Moses	Cow found	1, Apr. 1801	S3
Jones, Reuben	Horse found	28, June 1816	S3
Jones, Reuben	Horse found	22, June 1820	S3
Jones, Reuben	Horse found	13, Jan. 1821	S3
Jones, Robertson	Land partition	10, June 1828	N3
Jones, William	Partition petition	28, Dec. 1838	N2
Jones, William & Elizabeth	Divorce/abandonment	20, Feb. 1802	S3
Jordan, John & Nancy	Divorce/abandonment	8, Sept 1836	N2
Junge, Henry W. & Amelia	Divorce/abandonment	23, May 1823	N3
Justice, Catherine E.	Female school award	28, July 1835	N2
Kain, James	Cow found	12, Mar. 1800	S3
Kain, Richard	Horse found	17, Nov. 1815	S3
Kain, William	Insolvent debtor	11, Nov. 1828	N1
Kamper, James	Horse lost	10, Jan. 1795	C3
Kautz, Jacob	Horse found	10, Aug. 1807	S3
Kavenagh, James	Debt notice	25, Mar. 1796	C3
Kavenagh, James	Lost cow	23, July 1796	F4
Keasby, Delzil	In prison	3, Apr. 1805	S3
Kedey, Moses	Chancery case	19, Jan. 1811	S3
Kelly, David	Horse lost	7, Jan. 1801	S3
Kelly, David	Horse found	16, Apr. 1796	C3
Kelly, Dennis	Horse found	24, Apr. 1819	S3
Kelly, George	Horse lost	7, Nov. 1804	S3
Kelly, George	Horse found	4, Jan. 1808	S3
Kelly, John	Deserter from army	30, July 1814	S3
Kelly, Joseph	Escaped prisoner	4, July 1795	C3
Kelly, William	Cow found	25, Mar. 1797	F4
Kelly, William & Jane	Divorce/abandonment	26, Nov. 1796	F3
Kelsey, Isaac	Deserter from army	22, Mar. 1794	C3
Kelsey, Thomas C.	Debt relief	14, Feb. 1818	S3
Kelsey, Thomas C.	Debt relief	1, June 1820	S3
Kemper, E.	Horse found	18, Oct. 1816	S3
Kemper, E.Y. & Joann	Divorce/abandonment	24, Oct. 1823	N2
Kemper, Elnathan	Horse found	13, July 1827	N3
Kemper, Peter	Horse found	24, Dec. 1799	S3
Kemper, Stephen	Horse found	19, Oct. 1827	N3
Kemton, Seth	Horse found	4, July 1818	S3
Kenison, James & Margaret	Divorce/abandonment	7, Mar. 1823	N3
Kennedy, Francis	Horse found	3, Apr. 1819	S3
Kennedy, Francis	Deceased	9, July 1796	F3
Kennedy, James	Horse found	11, Jan. 1837	N2
Kennedy, Rebecca	Petition	22, Aug. 1795	C3
Kennedy, Rebecca	Widow	9, July 1796	F3
Kennedy, Thomas D.	Chancery case	4, Mar. 1828	N3
Kenny, Thomas	Petition filed	6, Apr. 1803	S3
Kenyon, John	Horse found	1, Dec. 1810	S3
Kerner, Joseph & Ann Maria	Divorce/abandonment	8, Nov. 1851	P2
Kerr, Jacob	Notice	31, Dec. 1796	F3

Name	Type of Notice	Date of Notice	Page
Kerr, Joseph	Court case	19, Nov. 1800	S3
Kestler, John	Deserter from army	10, July 1813	S3
Ketchum, Andrew	Horse found	28, May 1808	S3
Ketchum, Andrew	Horse found	23, July 1814	S3
Ketchum, Ira	Horse found	9, Sept 1823	N3
Keyes, George	Run away notice	19, Nov. 1824	N3
Kibby, Joseph	Horse lost	20, Feb. 1805	S3
Kiger, Christopher	Horse found	19, Dec. 1817	S3
Kilbarber, Barbara	Notice	15, Feb. 1825	N3
Killgore, Charles	Horse lost	7, Nov. 1804	S3
Kilmer, Peter W. & Eunice	Partition petition	22, Mar. 1837	N3
Kimball, Ansel	Guardian	20, Apr. 1830	N3
Kimball, Syrus	Run away notice	23, Dec. 1834	T2
Kimble, Caleb	Inquiry	26, May 1821	S1
King, James	Escaped prisoner	18, Dec. 1813	S3
King, Sarah Jane	Run away notice	24, Sept 1830	N3
King, William H.	Insolvent debtor	23, July 1830	N3
Kingsbury, Henry L.	Horse found	29, Feb. 1812	S3
Kinney, Abraham & Hannah	Petition filed	6, Apr. 1803	S3
Kirby, James	Chancery case	10, Oct. 1823	N3
Kirk, Amelia	Chancery case	31, Jan. 1835	N2
Kitchell, Arena	Guardianship	20, Sept 1816	S1
Kitchell, Jemima	Guardianship	20, Sept 1816	S1
Kitchell, Joseph	Horse found	13, June 1812	S3
Kitchell, Matilda	Guardianship	20, Sept 1816	S1
Kitchell, Moses	Guardianship	20, Sept 1816	S1
Kitchell, Moses	Horse found	1, Jan. 1830	N3
Kitchell, Nathaniel	Guardianship	20, Sept 1816	S1
Kleiber, Frederick & Gottlieba	Divorce/abandonment	23, Jan. 1837	N3
Knapp, Adam	Estate case	18, June 1824	N4
Knapp, Eliza	Estate case	18, June 1824	N4
Knapp, Noah	Estate case	18, June 1824	N4
Knapp, Phebe	Widow	18, June 1824	N4
Knees, Peter	Horse found	22, June 1811	S3
Knight, James	Horse found	2, July 1799	S3
Knight, James & Mary Ann	Chancery case	14, Dec. 1838	N2
Knowleton, Sidney A.	Horse found	22, Dec. 1826	N3
Koenigs, John J. & Barbara	Divorce/abandonment	3, May 1850	P3
Koffman, Joseph	Runaway apprentice	11, July 1818	S3
Konig, Frederick	Chancery case	20, Jan. 1829	N3
Kramer, Abraham	Notice	27, July 1827	Q3
Kramer, Catharine	Notice	27, July 1827	Q3
Krider, (Sargeant)	Letter at P.O.	18, Oct. 1794	C3
Kyle, Samuel B.	Expelled from mason	19, Dec. 1822	J1
LaBoyteaux, John G. & Phebe	Divorce/abandonment	18, Apr. 1826	N3
Laboyteaux, Joseph	Horse found	25, July 1822	J3
Lacy, Thomas	Insolvent debtor	11, Nov. 1828	N1
Lacy, Thomas & Sally	Divorce/abandonment	27, Jan. 1831	A3
Lafferty, Patrick	Cow found	25, Mar. 1797	F4
Lamar, Mark	Escaped prisoner	26, Sept 1795	C3
Lancaster, John	Biography article	28, Mar. 1848	K2
Langdon, E.P.	Committee member	15, Nov. 1838	N2
Langdon, Oliver	Horse lost	24, Oct. 1817	S3

Name	Type of Notice	Date of Notice	Page
Langley, Thomas	Horse found	10, Aug. 1807	S3
Larew, John & Ann	Partition petition	23, Jan. 1837	N3
Larew, Samuel & Margaret	Divorce/abandonment	18, Feb. 1837	N2
Larue, Isaac	Horse found	2, Feb. 1822	S3
Lash, John	Horse found	16, July 1814	S3
Latham, David	Insolvent debtor	27, Jan. 1829	N3
Laughlin, Moses	Horse found	28, Dec. 1811	S3
Law, Almira Ann	Guardian	20, Mar. 1838	N3
Law, Daniel	Horse found	25, July 1818	S3
Lawrence, Arabella H.	Gold medal	19, Feb. 1830	N3
Lawrence, George	Real estate case	9, Jan. 1838	N3
Lawrence, James & Margery	Divorce/abandonment	23, Jan. 1829	N4
Lawrence, Louisa	Real estate case	9, Jan. 1838	N3
Lawrence, Randolph W.	Insolvent debtor	23, July 1830	N3
Laycock, Nathan	Horse found	16, May 1817	S3
Layman, Jeremiah	Chancery case	4, Mar. 1828	N3
Leach, Esom	Horse found	5, Jan. 1816	S3
Leard, John & Elizabeth	Divorce/abandonment	19, Oct. 1833	R3
Leatherer, Antros	Runaway apprentice	25, Apr. 1818	S2
Leathers, Angelina	Land partition	29, Apr. 1828	N3
Leathers, B.W.	Land partition	29, Apr. 1828	N3
Leathers, Hiram	Land partition	29, Apr. 1828	N3
Leathers, John	Runaway slave	9, July 1796	F4
Leathers, John	Land partition	29, Apr. 1828	N3
Leathers, Joshua	Land partition	29, Apr. 1828	N3
Leathers, Lavina	Land partition	29, Apr. 1828	N3
Leathers, Paul	Land partition	29, Apr. 1828	N3
Leathers, Thomas	Land partition	29, Apr. 1828	N3
Leathers, William	Land partition	29, Apr. 1828	N3
Lee, David	Horse found	15, July 1825	N2
Lee, David & Anne	Divorce/abandonment	18, Dec. 1837	N3
Lee, John	Horse lost	7, Jan. 1800	S3
Leeds, James	Horse found	7, Nov. 1812	S3
Leeper, Allen	Horse found	30, Oct. 1813	S3
Leeper, Esther	Run away notice	25, Apr. 1810	H1
Leeper, John	Run away notice	25, Apr. 1810	H1
Leeper, Rachel	Run away notice	25, Apr. 1810	H1
Lees, Samuel	Horse found	11, Dec. 1813	S3
Leever, George	Horse found	15, Aug. 1812	S3
Lefeber, William	Run away notice	17, July 1827	N3
Lefever, Peter & Nancy	Divorce/abandonment	16, Oct. 1830	R3
Lefever, Peter & Rachel	Divorce/abandonment	24, June 1806	S3
Lefevre, Peter & Nancy	Divorce/abandonment	18, July 1812	S2
Lefler, David	Insolvent debtor	23, July 1830	N3
Legg, John	Horse found	28, May 1814	S3
Lemaire, Nicholas L.	Horse lost	27, Dec. 1816	S3
Lemming, Samuel	Horse found	17, Oct. 1812	S3
Lemmon, William	Chancery case	25, May 1830	N3
Lemon, Alexander	Horse found	4, Dec. 1819	S3
Lemon, John	Notice	5, June 1805	S3
Lemon, John	Insolvent debtor	11, Nov. 1828	N1
Lemond, William	Horse found	10, Oct. 1801	S3
Lemond, William & Marthew	Divorce/abandonment	25, Mar. 1796	C3
Lendon, William	Court sentencing	4, Nov. 1836	N2

Name	Type of Notice	Date of Notice	Page
Leonard, Barton	Pig found	12, Nov. 1799	S2
Leonard, Barton & Mary	Court case	21, Jan. 1801	S3
Leonard, David	Horse found	10, Sept 1808	S4
Leonhard, Jacob	Information wanted	22, Aug. 1836	N2
Leppincott, John	Deserter from army	20, Dec. 1814	W3
Lewis, Amous	Deserter from army	22, Mar. 1794	C3
Lewis, Andrew	Horse found	25, Apr. 1810	H4
Lewis, Clark	Insolvent debtor	27, Jan. 1829	N3
Lewis, James	Run away apprentice	7, Sept 1803	S4
Lewis, James	Run away apprentice	22, May 1805	S3
Lewis, Jehiel	Horse found	30, Dec. 1823	N3
Lewis, John	Horse lost	5, Feb. 1800	S3
Lewis, John	Horse found	28, Jan. 1815	S3
Lewis, John	Horse found	21, Feb. 1817	S4
Lewis, Lathrop	Insolvent debtor	11, Nov. 1828	N1
Lewis, Thomas (Capt)	Letter at P.O.	18, Oct. 1794	C3
Leyman, Christopher	Horse found	4, Feb. 1815	W3
L'Hommedieu, S.S.	Committee member	15, Nov. 1838	N2
Liganier, Ruth Ann	Convicted	27, Apr. 1807	S3
Lightner, Lucy	Convicted	27, Apr. 1807	S3
Lind, Andrew	Horse found	26, Dec. 1828	N3
Lindley, Abraham	Horse lost	15, Jan. 1800	S3
Lindley, Abraham	Horse found	26, May 1815	S3
Lindsey, Theophilus	Escaped prisoner	26, Sept 1795	C3
Lindsey, William	Horse found	20, Nov. 1813	S3
Line, David	Horse found	28, Dec. 1807	S3
Linning, Jeremiah	Horse lost	6, Sept 1809	H3
Linscot, Benjamin	Horse found	19, Mar. 1814	S3
Lipman, Solomon J. & Sarah	Divorce/abandonment	11, Jan. 1849	B1
Liston, Edmund	Attachment	6, Sept 1809	H1
Liston, Joseph	Attachment	6, Sept 1809	H1
Littell, David	Horse lost	24, Nov. 1802	S3
Littigan, Michael & Rachel	Divorce/abandonment	16, Oct. 1852	P2
Little, David & Sarah	Divorce/abandonment	16, Feb. 1803	S3
Little, George	Chancery case	21, Mar. 1838	N2
Little, Peter	Notice	8, Nov. 1809	H4
Livingston, John	Partition petition	22, Mar. 1837	N3
Lloyd, Richard & Peggy	Divorce/abandonment	23, Mar. 1822	S3
Lock, Andrew	Horse lost	8, May 1802	S3
Lock, Andrew & Sally	Divorce/abandonment	9, Feb. 1803	S3
Lock, Andrew & Sarah	Divorce/abandonment	1, Oct. 1799	F2
Lockwood, Daniel	Insolvent debtor	27, Jan. 1829	N3
Loder, Daniel	Horse found	23, June 1815	S3
Loder, Daniel	Horse found	9, Feb. 1816	S1
Loder, Daniel	Horse found	25, July 1817	S4
Loder, Daniel	Horse found	30, Jan. 1819	S3
Lodge, John	Court case witness	20, June 1850	P2
Lofland, Brownson	Deserter from army	2, Oct. 1813	S3
Lofland, William	Deserter from army	19, Feb. 1814	S3
Lofthouse, William	Chancery case	15, July 1835	N3
Logan, Benjamin (Col)	Pioneer incident	16, Dec. 1847	K2
Logan, John	Chancery case	19, Jan. 1811	S3
Logan, John	Horse found	11, Jan. 1812	S3
Logan, Mary M.	Female school award	28, July 1835	N2

Name	Type of Notice	Date of Notice	Page
Logan, William	Cow found	5, Mar. 1800	S3
Logsdon, Joseph	Horse lost	5, Feb. 1800	S3
Long, James	Horse lost	17, Aug. 1803	S3
Long, John	Horse stolen	21, Aug. 1805	S3
Long, John	Horse found	25, Mar. 1815	S3
Long, Richard	Horse found	15, Feb. 1812	S3
Long, William	Horse found	21, Feb. 1818	S3
Longworth, Nicholas	Attachment case	13, Apr. 1824	N4
Longworth, Nicholas	Chancery case	29, Sept 1829	N3
Looker, Amelia	Gold medal	19, Feb. 1830	N3
Looker, J.H.	Committee member	15, Nov. 1838	N2
Looker, James & Lorenna	Divorce/abandonment	14, Feb. 1823	N3
Looker, James H.	Chancery case	10, Oct. 1823	N3
Looker, O.	Committee member	15, Nov. 1838	N2
Looker, Silas C.	Cow lost	4, May 1820	S3
Loper, Enoch	Insolvent debtor	23, July 1830	N3
Lorah, John	Chancery case	21, Dec. 1830	N3
Lord, John	Horse found	13, Nov. 1813	S1
Lorer, Francis	Insolvent debtor	11, Nov. 1828	N1
Louckry, Patrick	Inquiry	19, Jan. 1816	S3
Louge, Edward	Insolvent debtor	23, July 1830	N3
Loukes, Abraham	Deserter from army	2, Feb. 1807	S3
Love, George	Horse found	6, Aug. 1799	S3
Love, Hiram	Run away apprentice	3, Apr. 1813	S3
Love, Peter	Horse lost	7, Oct. 1806	S3
Love, William	Horse lost	29, May 1805	S4
Lovejoy, Richard	Insolvent debtor	11, Nov. 1828	N1
Low, Francis	Horse found	5, June 1813	S2
Low, Stephen	Horse found	14, June 1816	S3
Lowe, Jacob D.	Court case	21, Jan. 1801	S3
Lowman, John (Soldier)	Letter at P.O.	18, Oct. 1794	C3
Lowry, Martha Jane	Gold medal	19, Feb. 1830	N3
Lucas, John	Escaped prisoner	3, Aug. 1827	N3
Lucas, William	Escaped prisoner	27, Feb. 1796	C3
Ludlam, Smith	Cow lost	13, Feb. 1802	S3
Ludlow, Israel	Horse found	9, Feb. 1803	S3
Ludlow, Israel	Chancery case	25, May 1830	N3
Ludlow, James C.	Chancery case	1, Dec. 1826	Q3
Ludlow, John	Horse lost	15, Jan. 1800	S3
Ludlow, John	Horse lost	23, Nov. 1793	C4
Ludlow, John	Cow found	22, Oct. 1796	F3
Ludlow, Maxfield	Horse lost	8, Aug. 1804	S3
Ludlow, William	Horse found	26, Mar. 1808	S3
Ludwick, William	Chancery case	21, Dec. 1830	N3
Luke, Samuel	Deserter from army	15, June 1807	S3
Lummis, Joseph	Horse found	30, Jan. 1796	C3
Lynch, Charles	Run away	7, Nov. 1801	S3
Lynch, George	Court sentencing	4, Nov. 1836	N2
Lynch, Richard J.	Court sentencing	4, Nov. 1836	N2
Lynes, William	Notice	19, Sept 1804	S3
Lynes, William	Debt relief	19, Jan. 1816	S3
Lyon, Jane	Horse found	5, Nov. 1814	S3
Lyon, Stephen	Forgery note	22, Oct. 1796	F4
Lyons, Alexander	Insolvent debtor	11, Nov. 1828	N1

Name	Type of Notice	Date of Notice	Page
Lyons, Bogardus	Deserter from army	2, Feb. 1807	S3
Lyons, James	Public notice	17, May 1794	C3
Lyons, Joseph	Inquiry	22, Jan. 1820	S3
Lyst, John	Horse found	4, May 1809	H3
Lytle, Edward	Horse found	7, Mar. 1808	S3
Lytle, Samuel	Run away notice	23, Mar. 1836	N2
Lytle, William	Chancery case	20, Jan. 1829	N3
MacConnel, James	Debt notice	24, May 1794	C4
Mack, Andrew (Col)	Horse lost	4, Apr. 1818	S3
Mack, Erastus	Horse found	16, Jan. 1827	N3
Mackelwaine, William	Deserter from army	5, July 1794	C3
Mackey, John & Mary G.	Divorce/abandonment	2, Nov. 1824	N3
Macky, Henson & Mary	Divorce/abandonment	1, Apr. 1837	N2
Madeary, Benjamin	Deserter from army	2, Feb. 1807	S3
Madison, Channing	Chancery case	28, May 1830	N3
Madison, James	Inquiry	14, Feb. 1817	S4
Mahany, John	Notice to public	17, Sept 1796	F3
Majars, James	Horse found	10, Nov. 1821	S3
Mallory, Daniel	Chancery case	10, Feb. 1824	N3
Malot, Josephus & Lucinda	Divorce/abandonment	21, Jan. 1825	N3
Maloy, William	Deposition given	17, Sept 1842	Z4
Malson, Jacob	Horse lost	23, Dec. 1806	S3
Malson, James	Horse found	13, Feb. 1813	S3
Maltbie, Benjamin	Horse lost	18, May 1803	S4
Mansfield, E.D.	Committee member	15, Nov. 1838	N2
Mapes, James	Horse lost	28, Sept 1803	S3
Maphet, John	Horse found	23, Feb. 1811	S3
Maranda, James	Notice	5, Oct. 1803	S3
Markelin, George	Horse found	7, Mar. 1808	S3
Markland, Bryson	Horse found	29, Apr. 1818	S4
Markland, Eliza	Information wanted	2, Sept 1835	N2
Markland, Joshua	Insolvent debtor	27, Jan. 1829	N3
Marklane, Bryson	Horse found	31, July 1819	S3
Markward, Charles	Insolvent debtor	23, July 1830	N3
Marsh, Baker & L.	Divorce/abandonment	21, Feb. 1851	P2
Marsh, Jeffrey	Run away	27, Aug. 1800	S3
Marsh, Samuel	Horse lost	26, Aug. 1806	S3
Marsh, William	Run away apprentice	18, Mar. 1815	W4
Marshall, Hanson	Run away notice	11, Nov. 1828	N1
Marshall, Lebeus	Horse found	15, Oct. 1799	S3
Marshell, Charles	Estate case	27, June 1826	N3
Marshell, Cynthia	Estate case	27, June 1826	N3
Marshell, Lebeus	Horse lost	31, Dec. 1814	S3
Marten, Joseph	Horse found	8, Oct. 1814	S3
Martin, Arthur	Chancery case	6, May 1828	N3
Martin, David	Horse found	22, June 1811	S3
Martin, Evi	Debt relief	5, Oct. 1807	S3
Martin, Francis D.	Guardian	11, Sept 1837	N2
Martin, Francis D.	Guardian	21, Sept 1838	N3
Martin, G.W.	Guardian	11, Sept 1837	N2
Martin, Jacob O.	Guardian	11, Sept 1837	N2
Martin, James, Jr.	Horse found	4, July 1818	S3
Martin, John	Horse found	14, Nov. 1812	S3

Name	Type of Notice	Date of Notice	Page
Martin, John & Lois	Divorce/abandonment	5, May 1821	S3
Martin, Josiah	Court sentencing	4, Nov. 1836	N2
Martin, Nathaniel	Debtor	19, Sept 1812	S3
Martin, Samuel (Capt)	Hamilton Co militia	28, Nov. 1801	S3
Martin, William	Horse found	22, May 1819	S3
Mason, George	Cow lost	19, Apr. 1816	S3
Mason, George & Mary	Indian prisoner	28, Nov. 1801	S1
Mason, Nancy	Indian prisoner	28, Nov. 1801	S1
Mason, William	Horse lost	5, Aug. 1801	S3
Mathews, Joseph	Horse lost	2, Oct. 1819	S3
Mathews, Thomas J.	Committee member	15, Nov. 1838	N2
Matson, John	Horse found	2, Feb. 1816	S1
Matthews, James	Run away notice	8, Dec. 1826	N3
Matthews, William	Runaway apprentice	1, Aug. 1818	S3
Mayham, Samuel	Horse found	27, Dec. 1816	S3
Mayhew, Alexander	Land petition	19, Mar. 1836	N2
Mayhew, Arven & Catharine	Divorce/abandonment	28, Feb. 1842	N3
McAdams, John	Horse lost	30, Oct. 1805	S3
McAfee, Matthew	Horse found	6, Feb. 1827	N3
McAuley, Ezekiel	Horse found	31, May 1816	S3
McAuley, William	Horse found	20, Jan. 1824	N3
McAuly, Ezekiel	Horse found	3, Oct. 1812	S3
McBride, Lyman & Jane	Divorce/abandonment	4, Jan. 1842	N3
McBroom, Robert	Information wanted	9, May 1823	N3
McCabe, Archibald	Horse found	4, June 1796	C2
McCance, David	Horse lost	22, May 1802	S3
McCance, Samuel	Horse found	16, Aug. 1816	S3
McCandlish, George	Inquiry	11, Apr. 1818	S4
McCardell, Thomas	Debt notice	14, June 1794	C3
McClain, Levi	Debt notice	28, May 1799	S3
McClane, John	Run away notice	2, May 1837	T2
McClean, William	Horse found	28, Feb. 1817	S4
McClelland, Andrew	Notice	21, Feb. 1810	H4
McClelland, Robert W.	Horse found	11, Aug. 1826	N3
McClintock, John	Horse lost	1, July 1801	S3
McClure, Hugh	Notice	28, Nov. 1795	C3
McClure, John & Catharine	Divorce/abandonment	18, Aug. 1827	R3
McClure, Richard	Horse found	15, Aug. 1812	S3
McClure, Robert	Horse lost	4, June 1800	S3
McClure, Robert	Horse lost	27, Apr. 1803	S3
McClure, Robert	Horse lost	30, Nov. 1803	S3
McClure, Robert	Cow lost	1, Nov. 1794	C3
McClure, Robert	Debt notice	25, Mar. 1797	F4
McClure, William	Deserter from army	23, Apr. 1814	S1
McCollom, Hugh	Horse lost	27, Apr. 1803	S3
McCollough, Adam	Debt relief	5, Jan. 1816	S4
McCorckle, John	Chancery case	14, Oct. 1823	N3
McCorkle, Alexander	Land purchase	23, July 1814	S3
McCormic, John	Horse found	28, Mar. 1817	S3
McCormick, James	Horse found	6, June 1818	S3
McCormick, John	Horse stolen	25, Mar. 1796	C3
McCoy, William D.	Insolvent debtor	27, Jan. 1829	N3
McCray, Martin	Horse found	17, Dec. 1799	S3
McCrea, Gilbert	Horse lost	10, July 1802	S3

Name	Type of Notice	Date of Notice	Page
McCrea, Gilbert	Horse found	29, Feb. 1812	S3
McCullach, John	Debt notice	3, Dec. 1796	F1
McCullagh, John	Run away apprentice	6, Aug. 1799	S4
McCullagh, John	Payment request	27, Oct. 1798	F4
McCulloch, Jane	Female school award	28, July 1835	N2
McCullom, Hugh	Horse lost	7, Dec. 1803	S3
McCullough, Adam	Debt relief	10, Nov. 1815	S3
McCullough, Elizabeth	Notice	21, Aug. 1813	S3
McCullough, John	Notice	24, June 1795	C3
McDaniel, James	Horse found	10, Sept 1808	S4
McDonald, Ann	Poor house inmate	14, Nov. 1851	P2
McDonald, Archibald	Run away notice	15, Aug. 1795	C3
McDonald, George & Ruth	Divorce/abandonment	22, July 1834	T2
McDonald, James	Debt relief	23, May 1817	S2
McDonald, John	Letter at P.O.	18, Oct. 1794	C3
McDonald, O.	Run away notice	5, May 1834	T2
McDonnald, Rhodah	Run away notice	15, Aug. 1795	C3
McElheny, Robert	Land for sale	20, Aug. 1796	F3
McFarland, Andrew	Land petition	25, June 1830	N3
McFarland, Anne	Land petition	25, June 1830	N3
McFarland, Thomas	Horse lost	7, Jan. 1800	S3
McGarvin, (Sargeant)	Letter at P.O.	18, Oct. 1794	C3
McGary, Joel G.	Deserter from army	19, Aug. 1836	N2
McGee, Eliza	Chancery case	4, Mar. 1828	N3
McGee, Isabella	Chancery case	4, Mar. 1828	N3
McGee, William W.	Chancery case	4, Mar. 1828	N3
McGehan, Barney & Tempy	Divorce/abandonment	2, Sept 1801	S3
McGennis, Robert	Run away apprentice	16, July 1799	S3
McGibbons, Samuel	Horse found	9, Nov. 1820	S3
McGinnes, Barnard Robert	Escaped prisoner	4, Mar. 1797	F3
McGirr, John	Insolvent debtor	23, July 1830	N3
McGoarty, Mary A.	Female school award	28, July 1835	N2
McGrew, Andrew	Partition petition	24, Apr. 1837	N2
McGrew, Henrietta	Partition petition	24, Apr. 1837	N2
McGuire, Louisa	Partition petition	25, Aug. 1837	N3
McGuire, Thomas	Partition petition	25, Aug. 1837	N3
McHenry, Enoch	Notice	3, Feb. 1825	E3
McHenry, Joseph	Horse found	4, June 1796	C3
McHenry, Samuel	Cow lost	20, June 1817	S3
McHenry, Van	Horse found	1, Feb. 1812	S3
McIntire, Thomas	Horse found	13, Oct. 1815	S3
McIntire, Thomas	Horse lost	9, May 1795	C3
McKean, Daniel	Stealing charge	25, Mar. 1796	C3
McKean, Thomas	Run away apprentice	21, Aug. 1813	S3
McKee, John	Guardian	26, Oct. 1835	N3
McKee, William & Sarah	Divorce/abandonment	27, Oct. 1810	S3
McKim, John	Chancery case	19, Jan. 1811	S3
McKirble, James	Horse found	21, June 1816	S1
McKoy, John	Court sentencing	4, Nov. 1836	N2
McKune, John	Information wanted	12, Oct. 1838	T2
McLean, James & Mary Ann	Chancery case	14, Dec. 1838	N2
McLean, Milton N.	Committee member	15, Nov. 1838	N2
McMahan, Joseph	Horse found	27, Oct. 1798	F4
McMain, William	Chancery case	6, May 1828	N3

Name	Type of Notice	Date of Notice	Page
McMeen, Josiah E.	Horse found	15, Dec. 1829	N3
McMeker, Patrick & Polly	Divorce/abandonment	6, Nov. 1805	S3
McMillan, William	Horse lost	17, July 1802	S3
McMillan, William	Petition filed	6, Apr. 1803	S3
McNaughton, Pat	Letter at P.O.	18, Oct. 1794	C3
McNeely, James & Sarah	Divorce/abandonment	21, Oct. 1806	S3
McNutt, Alexander	Deserter from army	25, Apr. 1812	S3
McNutt, John	Horse found	6, Oct. 1810	S3
McQuade, John & Elizabeth	Divorce/abandonment	29, Oct. 1851	P3
McVicker, Duncan	Horse lost	12, June 1802	S3
Meaneck, Peter	Horse found	19, July 1809	H3
Medes, Peter	Horse found	19, June 1813	S3
Meek, Samuel	Horse found	7, Aug. 1819	S3
Meeker, Enoch	Information wanted	6, Jan. 1825	E3
Meeker, John	Horse found	14, June 1794	C3
Meeker, John & Elizabeth	Divorce/abandonment	8, Mar. 1794	C3
Meeker, Joseph	Run away notice	16, Nov. 1827	N3
Meeker, William	Run away notice	16, Nov. 1827	N3
Meldrum, William	Inquiry	24, Feb. 1821	S1
Melony, Patrick	Deserter from army	25, Apr. 1795	C3
Menex, Ezekiel	Run away notice	7, Oct. 1828	N3
Mennessieur, Francis	Pioneer history	24, Jan. 1848	K2
Mercer, John	Horse lost	19, Dec. 1804	S4
Mercer, John	Horse stolen	1, Nov. 1794	C4
Merril, Adam	Deserter from army	15, May 1813	S3
Merril, John	Horse found	20, Nov. 1819	S3
Merritt, John	Run away notice	16, Jan. 1827	N3
Mershal, Henry	Letter at P.O.	18, Oct. 1794	C3
Messeck, Covington & Eliza	Divorce/abandonment	12, Feb. 1836	T3
Messer, Jacob	Horse found	23, Feb. 1811	S3
Messick, Jacob	Deserter from army	28, May 1800	S3
Metcalf, Elizabeth	Female school award	28, July 1835	N2
Meyncke, John & Catharine	Divorce/abandonment	2, Feb. 1822	S3
Michel, Joseph & Kisiah	Divorce/abandonment	22, Jan. 1806	S3
Miles, Elizabeth	Inquiry	23, May 1817	S2
Miles, Pearson	Real estate case	9, Jan. 1838	N3
Miles, William	Inquiry	23, May 1817	S2
Miley, Abraham	Horse found	29, Jan. 1814	S3
Miley, William	Horse found	10, Oct. 1812	S3
Milholland, John	Horse found	30, May 1817	S3
Mill, Richard	Inquiry	29, Apr. 1820	S3
Miller, Daniel	Horse lost	6, Nov. 1805	S3
Miller, David	Land purchase	23, July 1814	S3
Miller, David	Run away notice	10, Feb. 1824	N3
Miller, Edward	Horse found	1, July 1801	S3
Miller, Frederick	Deserter from army	23, Aug. 1794	C3
Miller, Frederick & Susan	Divorce/abandonment	12, Feb. 1814	S3
Miller, George	Horse lost	5, Nov. 1800	S3
Miller, George	Horse found	17, Nov. 1815	S3
Miller, Henry W.	Horse found	20, June 1817	S2
Miller, Henry W.	Horse found	17, Apr. 1819	S3
Miller, I.B.	Horse stolen	8, Feb. 1794	C3
Miller, I.B.	Debt notice	23, Aug. 1794	C4
Miller, Jacob	Debt relief	13, June 1817	S3

Name	Type of Notice	Date of Notice	Page
Miller, Jacob	Horse found	5, Sept 1817	S2
Miller, Jacob	Horse found	6, Sept 1809	H3
Miller, Jacob S.	Horse found	17, Aug. 1820	S3
Miller, James	Ox lost	19, Dec. 1795	C3
Miller, John	Horse found	2, May 1812	S3
Miller, John	Run away apprentice	28, Aug. 1813	S1
Miller, John	Land purchase	23, July 1814	S3
Miller, John	Horse found	18, Oct. 1816	S3
Miller, John	Horse found	25, July 1817	S4
Miller, John & Sarah	Divorce/abandonment	31, Aug. 1807	S3
Miller, Joseph	Insolvent debtor	23, July 1830	N3
Miller, Philip	Court case witness	20, June 1850	P2
Miller, Samuel R.	Guardian	14, Apr. 1829	N3
Miller, Sebastian & Catherine	Divorce/abandonment	6, Nov. 1851	P2
Miller, Thomas E.	Insolvent debtor	27, Jan. 1829	N3
Miller, William	Land purchase	23, July 1814	S3
Millholland, John	Horse found	18, Aug. 1815	S1
Mills, Azur Reed	Horse found	24, Oct. 1812	S3
Mills, Elijah	Horse found	14, Nov. 1812	S3
Mills, Isaac	Horse found	11, Apr. 1812	S3
Mills, Isaac	Horse lost	7, May 1796	C3
Mills, John R.	Horse found	17, Dec. 1799	S4
Mills, William	Horse found	12, June 1813	S3
Mininger, John & Mary	Divorce/abandonment	3, Jan. 1851	P2
Minshall, Elias	Partition petition	24, Mar. 1838	N2
Minshall, Jacob	Partition petition	24, Mar. 1838	N2
Minshall, Mary	Partition petition	24, Mar. 1838	N2
Mirick, Moses & Elizabeth	Divorce/abandonment	5, Jan. 1822	S3
Misener, Jacob	Horse found	29, May 1819	S3
Misner, Henry	Horse found	3, Dec. 1814	S3
Misner, Henry	Horse found	20, July 1820	S3
Mitchell, Enos	Land petition	19, Mar. 1836	N2
Mitchell, James	Horse found	6, Mar. 1827	N3
Mitchell, Robert	Debt notice	28, Mar. 1795	C4
Mitchell, Timothy	Land petition	19, Mar. 1836	N2
Mixer, Harriet	Gold medal	19, Feb. 1830	N3
Moke, Christian	Horse found	11, Oct. 1814	W4
Mollyneaux, Thomas	Insolvent debtor	23, July 1830	N3
Molson, Sedan	Horse found	11, Aug. 1815	S3
Montfort, Henry	Horse found	7, Aug. 1805	S3
Montgomery, David & Juliet	Divorce/abandonment	7, Mar. 1840	R3
Mooney, Samuel & Mary	Divorce/abandonment	12, Dec. 1795	C3
Moor, Abner	Horse found	31, May 1816	S3
Moore, Charles	Runaway apprentice	5, Dec. 1817	S3
Moore, Hugh	Debt relief	11, May 1811	S3
Moore, Hugh	Attachment	19, July 1809	H1
Moore, Jacob	Chancery case	19, Jan. 1811	S3
Moore, James	Horse lost	28, Nov. 1804	S3
Moore, James	Horse lost	16, Apr. 1808	S3
Moore, James	Run away apprentice	1, Sept 1832	R3
Moore, Joseph	Horse found	25, Jan. 1812	S3
Moore, Levi	Horse lost	21, Nov. 1801	S3
Moore, Montgomery	Information wanted	11, June 1838	T1
Moore, Patrick	Cow found	13, Feb. 1796	C3

Name	Type of Notice	Date of Notice	Page
Moore, Patrick	Cow found	17, Dec. 1796	F3
Moore, Robert	Caution on a note	9, July 1796	F1
Moore, Samuel	Cow lost	15, Jan. 1800	S3
Moore, Samuel	Run away apprentice	27, May 1801	S3
Moore, Samuel	Horse found	30, June 1815	S3
Moore, Samuel & Hannah	Divorce/abandonment	7, Dec. 1803	S3
Moore, Stanfield	Escaped convict	3, Oct. 1818	S2
Moore, William	Court sentencing	4, Nov. 1836	N2
Moorhead, John	Bull found	26, Mar. 1820	S3
Moorhead, Josiah	Horse found	11, Dec. 1819	S3
More, Arthur	Partition petition	23, Jan. 1837	N3
More, Caroline	Partition petition	23, Jan. 1837	N3
More, Charles	Partition petition	23, Jan. 1837	N3
More, Eliza	Partition petition	23, Jan. 1837	N3
More, Harriet	Partition petition	23, Jan. 1837	N3
More, Missouri Jane	Partition petition	23, Jan. 1837	N3
Morehead, John	Insolvent debtor	27, Jan. 1829	N3
Morfoot, George & Catharine	Divorce/abandonment	14, Nov. 1795	C3
Morfoot, George & Katharine	Divorce/abandonment	25, Mar. 1796	C3
Morison, Ephraim	Notice	13, Aug. 1799	S4
Morrel, Calvin	Letter at P.O.	18, Oct. 1794	C3
Morris, G. Helen	Chancery court case	17, June 1823	N3
Morris, Jesse	Chancery court case	17, June 1823	N3
Morris, John	Horse found	13, Aug. 1814	S3
Morris, William R.	Committee member	15, Nov. 1838	N2
Morrison, James	Debt notice	26, Apr. 1794	C3
Morrison, Joseph	Run away apprentice	17, Nov. 1827	R3
Morrow, James	Run away aprentice	28, May 1808	S3
Morton, James T.	Run away	19, July 1809	H3
Moss, Lemuel	Horse lost	7, Nov. 1817	S3
Moss, William	Horse lost	10, Aug. 1807	S3
Moss, William	Horse lost	16, Nov. 1807	S3
Mostyn, George P. & Mary	Divorce/abandonment	7, Mar. 1840	R3
Mott, Josiah	Horse found	10, Dec. 1796	F3
Moudy, Henry	Horse found	26, Sept 1812	S3
Moules, Walter	Run away apprentice	18, Feb. 1806	S3
Mounts, Providence	Land purchase	23, July 1814	S3
Mounts, Thomas	Horse found	29, July 1806	S3
Moyer, Lewis	Chancery case	20, Jan. 1829	N3
Muchmore, Samuel	Cow lost	9, Oct. 1802	S3
Muggridge, Richard	Chancery case	10, June 1824	E3
Muggridge, Sally	Chancery case	10, June 1824	E3
Muir, William	Land sale notice	24, Jan. 1795	C3
Mulford, Caleb	Horse lost	12, Aug. 1801	S3
Mulford, Daniel	Horse found	15, June 1820	S3
Mulford, Daniel	Horse found	24, Feb. 1821	S1
Mullen, Robert	Horse found	16, Aug. 1816	S3
Mullin, Arthur	Insolvent debtor	23, July 1830	N3
Mundell, James	Deserter from army	20, Feb. 1813	S3
Munger, Edmund	Hogs lost	24, Dec. 1799	S3
Munsell, Levi	Letter at P.O.	18, Oct. 1794	C3
Munsell, Levi	Notice	26, Nov. 1796	F3
Murdach, James	Horse lost	17, Sept 1796	F3
Murfey, William	Escaped prisoner	4, Oct. 1794	C3

Name	Type of Notice	Date of Notice	Page
Murfy, Samuel & Levina	Divorce/abandonment	19, Mar. 1808	S3
Murray, Eliza Ann	Gold medal	19, Feb. 1830	N3
Musgrove, John	Horse found	26, Oct. 1807	S3
Musgrove, Moses	Horse found	8, Feb. 1808	S3
Myer, Christian	Horse lost	8, Aug. 1804	S3
Myers, George	Horse lost	6, Sept 1809	H4
Naffe, Abram	Horse lost	29, Mar. 1816	S3
Nain, John	Horse lost	18, Sept 1805	S3
Neave, Thompson	Chancery case	14, Oct. 1823	N3
Need, George	Horse lost	16, Mar. 1803	S3
Neel, James	Debt action	13, Mar. 1802	S3
Nefe, Abraham	Horse found	5, June 1813	S2
Nelson, Cato	Run away slaves	24, Jan. 1810	H4
Nelson, Jane	Cow lost	9, Mar. 1803	S3
Nelson, Simon	Run away slaves	24, Jan. 1810	H4
Nelson, William D.	Run away slaves	24, Jan. 1810	H4
Nesbit, William	Horse found	7, Aug. 1805	S3
Nesmith, James & Harriet	Divorce/abandonment	2, Sept 1830	A3
Nevill, William	Horse found	20, Feb. 1819	S3
Neville, Cornelia	Chancery case	1, Jan. 1842	N2
Neville, Eugene	Chancery case	1, Jan. 1842	N2
Neville, John	Chancery case	1, Jan. 1842	N2
Neville, Julian	Chancery case	1, Jan. 1842	N2
Neville, Morgan	Committee member	15, Nov. 1838	N2
Neville, Morgan Lafayette	Chancery case	1, Jan. 1842	N2
Neville, William	Chancery case	1, Jan. 1842	N2
Newcomb, John	Run away apprentice	23, Mar. 1827	Q3
Newell, Thomas	Chancery case	10, Feb. 1824	N3
Newhouse, John C.	Debt relief	27, June 1817	S3
Newman, Joseph	Run away apprentice	27, May 1801	S3
Newman, William	Deserter from army	18, Jan. 1794	C3
Nichols, Charles	Inquiry	14, Feb. 1817	S4
Nichols, David	Horse found	7, Jan. 1800	S3
Nichols, John	Horse stolen	30, July 1814	S3
Nixon, John	Horse found	3, Oct. 1812	S3
Noble, Elizabeth	Chancery case	21, Dec. 1830	N3
Noble, William	Deceased	21, Dec. 1830	N3
Norris, Abraham	Horse found	19, July 1809	H1
Norris, James	Run away slave	26, Oct. 1836	T2
Norris, John C.	Run away notice	6, Nov. 1834	T2
Norris, Martha	Female school award	28, July 1835	N2
Northway, Ozias	Insolvent debtor	27, Jan. 1829	N3
Norton, Philo	Chancery case	19, Jan. 1811	S3
Nuts, Frederick & Elizabeth	Divorce/abandonment	24, Oct. 1801	S3
Nutts, Frederick	Horse lost	15, Jan. 1806	S3
Oakie, Abraham	Chancery case	21, Dec. 1830	N3
Oakman, John & Martha	Divorce/abandonment	23, Jan. 1827	N3
Obear, Ebenezer	Notice	31, Aug. 1827	Q3
O'Bryan, James	Deserter from army	10, Sept 1814	S1
Ocheltree, Michael	Horse lost	24, Dec. 1799	S3
Oden, Richard & Elizabeth	Divorce/abandonment	9, Feb. 1807	S1
O'Donnell, James & Anne	Divorce/abandonment	4, Mar. 1851	P2

Name	Type of Notice	Date of Notice	Page
Ogg, Loyd	Notice	10, Apr. 1802	S3
Ogg, Reuben	Insolvent debtor	27, Jan. 1829	N3
Ogle, Alexander	Horse found	13, Apr. 1809	H3
O'Hara, Hugh	Escaped prisoner	28, Mar. 1795	C3
O'Hara, Patrick	Deserter from army	30, Nov. 1793	C3
O'Hara, Patrick	Escaped prisoner	7, Mar. 1795	C3
O'Harra, Hugh	Escaped prisoner	30, Jan. 1796	C1
Oldwine, Barnabas	Deserter from army	28, Feb. 1795	C3
Olney, Ethan	Escaped convict	3, Oct. 1818	S2
Olney, Sylvenus	Letter at P.O.	18, Oct. 1794	C3
Orbison, John	Horse lost	26, June 1805	S3
Orcutt, Darius C.	Public notice	17, May 1794	C3
Orey, James	Horse found	5, July 1816	S3
Ormsby, Oliver	Guardianship	26, Oct. 1835	N3
Orr, David & Margaret	Information wanted	28, Jan. 1823	N3
Orr, Isaiah	Horse lost	17, Aug. 1803	S3
Orr, Samuel	Horse found	29, Apr. 1818	S4
Orr, William	Horse lost	8, May 1805	S3
Orsburn, Samuel & Margaret	Divorce/abandonment	4, July 1795	C3
Osborn, Barzella	Notice	17, Sept 1799	S3
Osborn, Benjamin	Insolvent debtor	27, Jan. 1829	N3
Osborn, Cyrus	Horse found	17, Sept 1796	F3
Osborn, Samuel	Tavern for sale	3, Sept 1796	F3
Osborn, Thomas J.	Insolvent debtor	27, Jan. 1829	N3
Owen, Daniel & Polly	Divorce/abandonment	12, May 1829	N3
Owens, Patrick & Nancy	Divorce/abandonment	27, Feb. 1830	R3
Owens, Peter	Horse lost	13, June 1795	C3
Owing, Nimrod	Chancery case	19, Jan. 1811	S3
Paddock, Samuel	Horse found	2, May 1817	S2
Paine, Thomas L.	Chancery case	9, Nov. 1824	N4
Paist, Charles	Chancery case	14, Oct. 1823	N3
Palmer, James H.	Insolvent debtor	23, July 1830	N3
Palmer, Peter	Horse found	29, Aug. 1812	S3
Palmer, Seneca	Committee member	15, Nov. 1838	N2
Palmer, Thomas	Murder charge	7, Mar. 1837	T2
Parker, Daniel & Deborah	Divorce/abandonment	19, Apr. 1831	A3
Parker, Isaac	Horse lost	28, Aug. 1805	S3
Parker, John & Nancy	Divorce/abandonment	1, Jan. 1806	S4
Parker, Randolph	Run away notice	29, July 1828	N3
Parker, Stephen	Cow found	27, Oct. 1798	F4
Parks, Joseph	Horse lost	5, Nov. 1800	S3
Parks, Joseph	Horse found	29, May 1819	S3
Parks, Thomas	Horse found	14, Feb. 1818	S1
Patmor, Mathias F. & Elizabeth	Divorce/abandonment	2, July 1830	N3
Patmore, Abraham	Chancery case	20, Jan. 1825	E3
Patterson, Abraham	Horse found	11, June 1814	S3
Patterson, James & Deriah	Chancery case	6, Dec. 1838	N2
Patterson, Moses	Deserter from army	26, Dec. 1812	S3
Patterson, R.	Horse lost	1, Aug. 1804	S4
Patterson, Robert	Chancery case	25, May 1830	N3
Patterson, Samuel	Horse stolen	11, Oct. 1814	W4
Patton, John	Horse found	16, Aug. 1816	S3
Patton, John	Horse found	10, Oct. 1817	S3

Name	Type of Notice	Date of Notice	Page
Patton, William R.	Horse found	26, June 1813	S3
Patton, William R.	Horse found	8, June 1822	S3
Paxton, Robert D.	Run away apprentice	9, Jan. 1829	N3
Payn, Daken & Margaret	Divorce/abandonment	5, Aug. 1801	S3
Payne, Daniel	Debt relief	14, Feb. 1817	S3
Payne, Daniel	Debt relief	20, June 1817	S1
Peak, Henry	Horse found	2, July 1814	S3
Pearce, Levi	Deserter from army	15, June 1807	S3
Pearson, David	Horse lost	28, Dec. 1811	S3
Pease, Horace & Lucretia	Divorce/abandonment	1, Nov. 1836	N2
Peck, James	Horse found	3, Jan. 1831	A3
Peckenbaugh, Elizabeth	Horse found	4, July 1817	S3
Pecker, John	Court case	19, July 1809	H4
Peers, William & Mercy Ann	Divorce/abandonment	8, Feb. 1837	N2
Pell, Abner W.	Court case witness	20, June 1850	P2
Pence, Elijah	Promissory note	19, Feb. 1830	N3
Pendleton, N.G.	Committee member	15, Nov. 1838	N2
Pendree, Alexander	Guardian	20, Apr. 1830	N3
Pendree, James	Guardianship	20, Apr. 1830	N3
Penrose, Robert	Inquiry	19, Jan. 1816	S3
Penton, John G.	Horse found	12, Oct. 1827	N3
Perce, Stephen	Letter at P.O.	18, Oct. 1794	C3
Perlieu, Benjamin (Lt)	Hamilton Co militia	28, Nov. 1801	S3
Perry, Joshua H.	Chancery court case	17, June 1823	N3
Perry, William	Horse found	28, Sept 1807	S3
Perry, William	Run away apprentice	16, June 1815	S3
Perry, William	Chancery court case	17, June 1823	N3
Pettit, Samuel & Mary	Divorce/abandonment	30, Jan. 1841	N2
Pettit, Thomas	Debt relief	5, Sept 1817	S3
Pfeil, George	Information wanted	8, Dec. 1834	T2
Phaeton, Cyrus	Horse found	8, Nov. 1816	S3
Phares, Joseph	Horse found	29, Feb. 1812	S3
Pharres, Samuel	Horse found	4, July 1828	N3
Philbrook, John	Murdered	4, Nov. 1836	N2
Philips, Horatio G.	Horse lost	25, Jan. 1808	S3
Phillips, John & Elmira	Divorce/abandonment	6, Apr. 1827	Q3
Phillips, Richard	Horse found	29, Aug. 1818	S3
Phillips, Samuel & Mary	Divorce/abandonment	3, Feb. 1825	E3
Phinney, Joseph	Horse found	11, Jan. 1828	N2
Piatt, Benjamin M.	Attachment case	13, Apr. 1824	N4
Piatt, Benjamin M.	Chancery case	9, Nov. 1824	N4
Piatt, John H.	Chancery case	3, Nov. 1829	N1
Pierce, Nathaniel & Elizabeth	Divorce/abandonment	3, Sept 1814	S1
Pierce, Thomas	Chancery case	14, Oct. 1823	N3
Pierce, William	Committee member	15, Nov. 1838	N2
Pierlon, Wyllys	Horse found	28, May 1799	S3
Pierson, Mathias	Horse lost	3, Jan. 1795	C3
Piggle, George	Horse found	15, June 1811	S3
Pittman, Calvin	Horse found	2, Nov. 1811	S3
Pittman, Jonathan	Horse found	25, May 1811	S3
Plough, Elias	Horse found	9, Aug. 1814	W4
Polk, (Mrs)	Pioneer incident	27, Mar. 1848	K2
Pollock, Cyrus & Matilda	Divorce/abandonment	31, July 1829	N3
Pollock, Ezekiel	Horse found	22, Jan. 1814	S3

Name	Type of Notice	Date of Notice	Page
Pomeroy, Joseph	Insolvent debtor	23, July 1830	N3
Pon, Stephen	Run away	17, Apr. 1813	S3
Ponta, Petrus	Horse lost	11, June 1799	S3
Poor, David J.	Horse lost	20, Aug. 1808	S3
Poor, David J. & Rachel	Divorce/abandonment	2, Jan. 1802	S3
Pope, Pearly	Estate case	4, July 1826	N3
Pope, Rebecca	Estate case	4, July 1826	N3
Port, William	Promissory note	19, Feb. 1830	N3
Porter, George	Run away apprentice	23, Mar. 1827	Q3
Porter, James	Deserter from army	4, June 1814	S3
Porter, Thomas & Sarah	Divorce/abandonment	12, July 1816	S3
Pottenger, Samuel	Horse lost	5, Aug. 1801	S3
Pottinger, Samuel	Horse found	25, July 1818	S3
Potts, Ann	Chancery case	20, Jan. 1825	E3
Potts, Joseph	Chancery case	20, Jan. 1825	E3
Potts, Rebecca	Chancery case	20, Jan. 1825	E3
Potts, Stacey	Chancery case	20, Jan. 1825	E3
Potts, William	Chancery case	20, Jan. 1825	E3
Pounds, Samuel & Matilda	Divorce/abandonment	27, June 1836	T2
Powel, William	Letter at P.O.	18, Oct. 1794	C3
Powell, Ellick	Chancery case	10, June 1824	E3
Powell, Ellick & Elizabeth	Attachment case	17, June 1825	N3
Powell, Joseph	Inquiry notice	16, July 1830	N3
Powell, William	Inquiry notice	16, July 1830	N3
Powers, Thomas	Horse found	17, Jan. 1818	S3
Powers, William	Run away apprentice	13, June 1812	S3
Presley, Isaac	Horse found	23, Nov. 1811	S3
Preston, Patrick	Horse lost	28, Nov. 1812	S3
Price, Hezekiah	Horse found	24, Oct. 1812	S3
Priest, Obediah	Horse found	28, May 1808	S3
Primos, Adam & Molly	Divorce/abandonment	17, Dec. 1814	S3
Prince, John	Land for sale	13, Aug. 1796	F3
Prince, Joseph	Horse lost	25, Mar. 1801	S3
Prince, Joseph	Horse lost	18, Nov. 1806	S3
Prince, Joseph	Insolvent debtor	27, Jan. 1829	N3
Prior, Andrew	Guardian	17, June 1837	N2
Prior, William	Guardian	17, June 1837	N2
Prisch, Daniel	Horse found	14, Nov. 1812	S3
Pritchett, Winget	Deserter from army	2, July 1800	S3
Probis, Alexander	Theft	20, Apr. 1807	S3
Provost, Samuel	Insolvent debtor	27, Jan. 1829	N3
Pruden, Isaac	Horse found	30, May 1817	S3
Pucket, Benjamin	Horse found	4, July 1812	S3
Pugh, Job	Debt relief notice	6, June 1823	N3
Purdy, Robert (Ensign)	Letter at P.O.	18, Oct. 1794	C3
Pursel, John	Guardianship	20, Apr. 1830	N3
Pursel, William & Mary	Guardian	20, Apr. 1830	N3
Puttman, John	Estate case	18, June 1824	N4
Quick, Cornelius	Horse found	11, June 1814	S3
Quick, John	Horse lost	15, Oct. 1799	S3
Rabb, John & Elizabeth	Divorce/abandonment	27, Nov. 1805	S3
Rafferty, Clarissa	Chancery case	15, July 1835	N3

Name	Type of Notice	Date of Notice	Page
Rafferty, James	Chancery case	15, July 1835	N3
Rains, James	Deserter from army	2, Feb. 1807	S3
Ramsay, G.R.	Committee member	15, Nov. 1838	N2
Ramsay, Lesley	Escaped convict	3, Oct. 1818	S2
Ramsey, William	Deposition given	4, Oct. 1842	Z4
Randolph, Edmund	Chancery case	21, Dec. 1830	N3
Randolph, Thomas	Pioneer incident	27, Mar. 1848	K2
Rassman, Frederick & Rebeca	Divorce/abandonment	8, Jan. 1814	S3
Raverty, Clarissa	Pioneer history	24, Jan. 1848	K2
Raymond, William	Chancery case	31, Jan. 1835	N2
Rea, Henry	Inquiry	7, Dec. 1820	S3
Read, Francis	Runaway apprentice	14, Mar. 1818	S3
Ready, Lain	Horse found	4, Aug. 1815	S3
Ready, Lane	Horse found	23, May 1828	Q3
Reagan, Wilkes	Debt relief	13, Nov. 1819	S3
Reagan, Wilkes	Debt relief	5, Oct. 1820	S3
Redburn, Ames T.	Cow lost	10, Apr. 1813	S3
Reddick, James	Insane	21, Nov. 1804	S3
Redding, George	Cow lost	30, Sept 1824	E3
Reddington, Daniel	Escaped convict	3, Oct. 1818	S2
Redingbough, Adam	Horse found	11, Dec. 1813	S3
Reed, Christopher	Horse found	19, June 1813	S3
Reed, Henry	Run away apprentice	25, Apr. 1812	S3
Reed, John	Horse found	9, Jan. 1813	S3
Reed, John	Horse stolen	21, Nov. 1795	C3
Reed, N.C.	Committee member	15, Nov. 1838	N2
Reed, William	Horse found	10, Aug. 1820	S3
Reed, William & Mary	Divorce/abandonment	6, Sept 1794	C3
Reeder, David	Horse found	25, Dec. 1827	N3
Reeder, Jacob	Cow found	10, Dec. 1796	F3
Reeder, Stephen (Capt)	Hamilton Co militia	28, Nov. 1801	S3
Reedy, William	Horse found	4, July 1818	S3
Reese, Jacob	Court case	19, Nov. 1800	S3
Reeves, Dolly	Run away notice	10, June 1825	N3
Reeves, Gust.	Cow found	9, Jan. 1802	S3
Reid, Hannah	Inquiry	26, Sept 1818	S3
Reilly, Margaret	Female school award	28, July 1835	N2
Reily, John	Public notice	17, May 1794	C3
Reiser, Jacob	Horse found	17, May 1816	S3
Repsher, John	Chancery case	9, Dec. 1824	E3
Resor, Jacob	Horse found	19, Feb. 1814	S3
Reynolds, John	Deserter from army	9, Oct. 1813	S3
Reynolds, John	Deserter from army	10, Sept 1814	S1
Reynolds, Sacket	Guardian	20, Apr. 1830	N3
Rice, Hubbard	Run away apprentice	3, Jan. 1815	W4
Rice, John & Frances	Divorce/abandonment	2, Nov. 1830	N3
Richard, Ralph P.	Attachment	10, Oct. 1823	N3
Richards, George	Chancery case	28, May 1830	N3
Richards, Mark	Chancery court case	20, June 1823	N3
Richards, Mark	Chancery case	28, May 1830	N3
Richards, Thomas	Chancery case	28, May 1830	N3
Richardson, Benjamin & Mary	Divorce/abandonment	27, Jan. 1824	N3
Richardson, David	Horse found	30, May 1817	S3
Richardson, David	Horse found	27, July 1820	S3

Name	Type of Notice	Date of Notice	Page
Richardson, David	Chancery court case	17, June 1823	N3
Richardson, Eleanor	Chancery court case	17, June 1823	N3
Richardson, Emeline	Chancery court case	17, June 1823	N3
Richardson, James	Horse found	28, Dec. 1807	S3
Richardson, Malachiah	Deceased	17, June 1823	N3
Rickcreek, Caspar	Deserter from army	31, May 1794	C3
Riddle, A.N.	Committee member	15, Nov. 1838	N2
Riddle, Andrew & Levina	Divorce/abandonment	8, Nov. 1851	P2
Riddle, Henry & Louisa	Divorce/abandonment	30, Jan. 1830	R3
Riddle, James	Chancery case	11, Oct. 1847	K2
Riddle, John	Chancery case	11, Oct. 1847	K2
Riddle, John (Capt)	Hamilton Co militia	28, Nov. 1801	S3
Rigel, Mathias	Horse lost	26, Aug. 1806	S1
Riorson, John	Horse found	24, Sept 1808	S4
Risk, Thomas	Chancery case	1, Dec. 1826	Q3
Ritter, Jacob	Chancery case	28, May 1830	N3
Roads, Samuel	Land purchase	23, July 1814	S3
Roas, David & Peggy	Divorce/abandonment	9, Apr. 1796	C3
Robb, Matthias	Ox lost	13, Dec. 1804	S4
Robb, Samuel	Horse lost	17, Oct. 1801	S3
Robbins, William	Horse found	16, June 1826	N3
Roberson, Robert	Horse found	4, July 1818	S3
Roberts, Anna Maria	Estate case	23, Dec. 1841	N2
Roberts, Asa	Notice	19, June 1805	S3
Roberts, James	Estate case	23, Dec. 1841	N2
Roberts, John	Chancery case	14, Oct. 1823	N3
Roberts, Mirrew	Horse found	25, July 1812	S3
Robertson, Martha Ann	Guardian	11, Sept 1837	N2
Robertson, Samuel & Dorcus	Divorce/abandonment	21, July 1815	S3
Robertson, Walter & Patty	Divorce/abandonment	21, Aug. 1805	S3
Robinson, Amos	Notice	10, June 1828	N3
Robinson, Edward	Horse lost	21, Dec. 1803	S3
Robinson, Ellen	Guardian	19, Dec. 1826	N3
Robinson, Frederic	Information wanted	31, Dec. 1836	N2
Robinson, Jane C.	Guardian	19, Dec. 1826	N3
Robinson, John	Horse lost	2, Jan. 1805	S2
Robinson, John	Horse found	26, May 1815	S3
Robinson, John	Run away apprentice	9, June 1815	S3
Robinson, John	Attachment	19, July 1809	H1
Robinson, Lucian	Guardian	19, Dec. 1826	N3
Robinson, Robert	Horse lost	15, Jan. 1806	S3
Robison, Robert	Horse lost	29, May 1805	S3
Rochenfield, Aaron	Horse lost	27, Nov. 1805	S3
Rock, Patrick	Horse lost	5, Sept 1804	S3
Rockenfield, A.A.	Guardian	21, Sept 1838	N3
Rodgers, Andrew	Horse stolen	28, Oct. 1823	N2
Roe, Daniel	Cow lost	12, Nov. 1817	S3
Rogers, Coleman	Horse stolen	10, Aug. 1820	S3
Rogers, Levi	Horse found	24, Sept 1808	S4
Rogers, Philip	Deserter from army	2, Feb. 1807	S3
Rogers, Philip & Trypheny	Divorce/abandonment	24, July 1805	S3
Rogers, Seva	Deserter from army	2, Oct. 1813	S3
Rogers, Thomas	Horse stolen	29, June 1824	N3
Rogers, William	Notice	23, Oct. 1829	N3

Name	Type of Notice	Date of Notice	Page
Rolff, Asa	Horse found	18, Dec. 1813	S3
Roll, Edward & Sally	Divorce/abandonment	3, July 1805	S3
Roll, John	Horse found	18, Mar. 1801	S3
Roll, John	Suit	7, Nov. 1804	S3
Roll, John M.	Horse found	6, June 1817	S3
Roll, John M.	Horse found	24, Oct. 1818	S3
Roll, Matthias	Ox lost	19, Dec. 1804	S4
Roll, Wick & Nancy F.	Divorce/abandonment	8, Nov. 1851	P2
Rolton, William	Freedom petition	8, June 1820	S3
Rolton, William & Judy	Divorce/abandonment	28, Oct. 1823	J3
Rook, Nancy	Run away wife	27, Aug. 1796	F3
Rose, John	Deposition given	15, Sept 1842	Z4
Rosecrance, Benjamin	Horse found	11, Aug. 1815	S3
Rosendale, Sarah A.	Female school award	28, July 1835	N2
Ross, Daniel	Debt relief	13, Feb. 1824	N3
Ross, Hugh	Escaped prisoner	24, Oct. 1795	C3
Ross, Ignatius	Public notice	17, May 1794	C3
Ross, James	Horse found	6, Nov. 1827	N3
Ross, John	Horse found	13, Oct. 1815	S3
Ross, Mary Jane	Guardianship	4, Feb. 1835	N2
Ross, William F.	Insolvent debtor	23, July 1830	N3
Roudebush, Daniel	Horse lost	16, Mar. 1803	S4
Rowe, George T.	Insolvent debtor	23, July 1830	N3
Rowe, John	Escaped prisoner	31, Aug. 1803	S3
Rue, Thomas	Chancery case	19, Jan. 1811	S3
Ruffin, John B.	Insolvent debtor	23, July 1830	N3
Ruffin, William (Lt)	Hamilton Co militia	28, Nov. 1801	S3
Runyan, Henry	Horse found	28, Dec. 1820	S3
Runyan, Samuel	Run away apprentice	2, Feb. 1807	S3
Rush, Jacob	Horse found	5, June 1813	S2
Rusk, Isaac	Horse found	1, Aug. 1812	S3
Russ, William	Run away	25, July 1838	T2
Russel, George	Horse lost	19, Nov. 1800	S3
Russel, Hugh	Horse found	16, May 1817	S3
Russell, Archibald	Run away apprentice	17, Nov. 1827	R3
Russell, Thomas	Guardian	25, Aug. 1829	N3
Rutan, John D.	Insolvent debtor	27, Jan. 1829	N3
Sallady, Jacob	Horse lost	17, Oct. 1804	S4
Sallman, Christopher	Cow found	19, Nov. 1799	S3
Salyers, John	Horse found	20, July 1827	N3
Sampson, Calvin	Chancery case	9, Nov. 1824	N4
Sampson, Caroline	Chancery case	9, Nov. 1824	N4
Sampson, Charles	Chancery case	9, Nov. 1824	N4
Sampson, George	Chancery case	9, Nov. 1824	N4
Sampson, Harriet	Chancery case	9, Nov. 1824	N4
Sampson, Henry	Chancery case	9, Nov. 1824	N4
Sampson, Hepza Dana	Chancery case	9, Nov. 1824	N4
Sampson, James	Chancery case	9, Nov. 1824	N4
Sampson, James	Run away notice	16, Jan. 1827	N3
Sampson, John	Chancery case	9, Nov. 1824	N4
Sampson, Joseph Stacy	Chancery case	9, Nov. 1824	N4
Sampson, Mary	Chancery case	9, Nov. 1824	N4
Sampson, Nathan	Chancery case	9, Nov. 1824	N4

Name	Type of Notice	Date of Notice	Page
Sampson, Phill, J.	Horse lost	22, Mar. 1816	S3
Sampson, Stephen	Chancery case	9, Nov. 1824	N4
Sampson, Stephen	Guardian	7, Dec. 1837	N3
Sampson, William Strong	Chancery case	9, Nov. 1824	N4
Sanders, D.A.	Committee member	15, Nov. 1838	N2
Sanders, Philip	Horse found	19, July 1809	H1
Sarber, Abraham	Insolvent debtor	23, July 1830	N3
Sargeant, Emery	Partition petition	22, Mar. 1837	N3
Sargent, Winthrop	Debt notice	4, Mar. 1797	F3
Sater, Charles	Chancery court case	17, June 1823	N3
Sater, Dorcas	Chancery court case	17, June 1823	N3
Sater, Sarah	Chancery court case	17, June 1823	N3
Savage, Samuel & Jane	Divorce/adandonment	9, Feb. 1839	T2
Sawyer, Amos	Escaped prisoner	15, Sept 1826	N3
Sawyer, William	Horse lost	13, Dec. 1804	S4
Sawyers, Joseph	Horse lost	1, Aug. 1804	S3
Say, James	Insolvent debtor	23, July 1830	N3
Sayre, Leonard	Land purchase	23, July 1814	S3
Sayre, Pierson	Horse found	25, Apr. 1810	H3
Sayres, Benjamin	Horse found	25, July 1812	S2
Scannell, Timothy	Apprentice wanted	31, Jan. 1795	C3
Schenck, Daniel	Horse found	3, June 1811	S3
Schenck, W.C.	Horse lost	3, Sept 1799	S3
Schenck, W.C.	Horse lost	29, Apr. 1801	S3
Schenck, W.C.	Land for sale	13, Aug. 1796	F1
Schenk, Obediah	Horse found	5, Sept 1817	S2
Schnebly, James H.	Deposition given	4, Oct. 1842	Z4
Schott, Conrad	Insolvent debtor	23, July 1830	N3
Schultz, Conrad	Chancery case	20, Jan. 1829	N3
Scofield, Isaac	Chancery case	19, Jan. 1811	S3
Scoggin, Elisha	Horse found	23, July 1814	S3
Scoggin, Solomon	Horse found	3, Dec. 1814	S3
Scoggins, Thomas	Horse found	26, Feb. 1814	S3
Scott, Alexander	Court case	19, Nov. 1800	S3
Scott, Obadiah	Advertisement	9, July 1796	F1
Scott, Obediah	Horse notice	14, Dec. 1793	C3
Scribner, Azan	Land purchase	23, July 1814	S3
Scudder, Aaron	Debtor	2, Feb. 1807	S3
Scull, John	Horse found	29, Aug. 1818	S3
Scull, John	Horse found	12, Dec. 1814	W4
Seaman, John	Horse found	12, Oct. 1807	S1
Seaman, William	Horse found	25, June 1824	N3
Seamans, John	Horse found	16, Nov. 1811	S3
Seamon, John	Horse found	11, June 1808	S3
Searcy, Robert	Runaway slave	18, Aug. 1821	S3
Searles, Daniel	Horse lost	17, Oct. 1804	S3
Sears, John	Horse found	24, Oct. 1812	S3
Sedam, Cornelius R.	Horse lost	22, Jan. 1806	S3
Sedam, Cornelius R.	Horse found	31, Oct. 1812	S3
Sedam, Cornelius R.	Horse found	19, Sept 1818	S3
Seelyne, Joseph	Horse found	2, Feb. 1822	S3
Sellman, John & Mary Ellen	Divorce/abandonment	16, Oct. 1852	P2
Semmes, Raphael & Anne	Chancery case	11, Oct. 1847	K2
Semor, William	Horse found	24, Mar. 1826	N3

Name	Type of Notice	Date of Notice	Page
Setons, Thomas	Deserter from army	13, Mar. 1813	S3
Settle, Francis	Notice	17, Oct. 1804	S4
Settle, Joseph	Attachment case	30, Dec. 1825	N3
Seward, G.W.	Guardian	22, Dec. 1829	N3
Seward, George W.	Guardian	6, Oct. 1826	N3
Seward, Jackson	Guardian	6, Oct. 1826	N3
Seward, Jackson	Guardian	22, Dec. 1829	N3
Seward, Louisa	Guardian	22, Dec. 1829	N3
Seward, Samuel	Horse found	1, Aug. 1804	S4
Seymore, Jeffrey	Committee member	15, Nov. 1838	N2
Shanabarger, Henry & Magdalena	Divorce/abandonment	28, Oct. 1825	N2
Shanklin, John	Partition petition	24, Mar. 1838	N2
Shannon, Thomas	Run away	14, Jan. 1801	S3
Sharp, Harvey	Horse found	22, June 1820	S3
Sharp, Matthias	Horse found	19, Feb. 1830	N3
Sharp, Sarah	Female school award	28, July 1835	N2
Shattrick, William	Horse found	19, Mar. 1808	S3
Shaw, Esther & Ann	Divorce/abandonment	6, Nov. 1851	P2
Shaw, Joseph	Court sentencing	4, Nov. 1836	N2
Shaw, Knoles & Catharine	Divorce/abandonment	20, Aug. 1814	S3
Shaw, Knowles & Catharine	Divorce/abandonment	20, Jan. 1829	N3
Shaylor, Joseph & Mary	Divorce/abandonment	24, Sept 1799	S3
Shays, John	Debt relief	26, Feb. 1820	S3
Shays, John	Cow lost	29, May 1823	J3
Shearer, James	Insolvent debtor	27, Jan. 1829	N3
Sheets, George	Horse found	9, Nov. 1811	S3
Shepherd, Thomas	Run away apprentice	12, Sept 1804	S3
Sherkey, Samuel & Agnes	Divorce/abandonment	13, Sept 1816	S3
Sherman, George	Chancery case	20, Jan. 1825	E3
Sherman, Rebecca	Chancery case	20, Jan. 1825	E3
Shingles, Philip John	Cow found	27, Aug. 1799	S3
Shirk, Andrew	Cow lost	22, Apr. 1801	S3
Shoemaker, Blackley	Horse found	2, Feb. 1822	S3
Shoemaker, Elias	Horse found	22, Dec. 1802	S3
Short, Ann Maria	Chancery case	7, Oct. 1824	E3
Short, Ann Maria	Chancery case	20, Jan. 1825	E3
Short, Betsey	Estate case	23, Dec. 1841	N2
Short, Charles	Chancery case	25, May 1830	N3
Short, Charles W.	Chancery case	7, Oct. 1824	E3
Short, Charles W.	Chancery case	20, Jan. 1825	E3
Short, J. Cleves	Horse lost	4, Oct. 1816	S3
Short, John	Run away apprentice	22, Oct. 1814	S3
Short, John C.	Horse found	9, June 1821	S3
Short, John C.	Chancery case	7, Oct. 1824	E3
Short, John C.	Chancery case	20, Jan. 1825	E3
Short, John Cleves	Estate case	23, Dec. 1841	N2
Short, Peyton	Petition filed	6, Apr. 1803	S3
Short, Peyton	Chancery case	7, Oct. 1824	E3
Short, Peyton	Chancery case	20, Jan. 1825	E3
Short, Thomas	Insolvent debtor	23, July 1830	N3
Shull, Burkhart & Rachel	Divorce/abandonment	21, Mar. 1817	S3
Shull, Peter	Horse found	25, July 1818	S3
Shullybarger, Jacob & Elizabeth	Divorce/abandonment	18, Mar. 1815	S3
Shuman, Jacob	Horse found	18, July 1812	S2

Name	Type of Notice	Date of Notice	Page
Shuman, Jacob	Horse found	31, July 1813	S3
Shutt, Peter	Court sentencing	4, Nov. 1836	N2
Silver, Enoch & Elizabeth	Divorce/abandonment	18, July 1826	N3
Silver, James	Notice store opened	22, Feb. 1794	C3
Silvers, Joseph	Horse lost	29, May 1802	S3
Simmerson, John	Deserter from army	30, Oct. 1813	S2
Simmons, Robert	Horse found	5, May 1815	S3
Simpson, Alexander & Rebecca	Divorce/abandonment	19, Sept 1804	S3
Simpson, James	Horse found	29, Jan. 1814	S3
Simpson, John & Nancy	Divorce/abandonment	15, Jan. 1814	S3
Simpson, Patrick	Petition	22, Aug. 1795	C3
Sinch, Philip	Cow lost	4, May 1809	H3
Sinks, Andrew	Horse lost	10, Aug. 1807	S3
Sisco, Henry	Horse found	21, Aug. 1819	S3
Sisson, Mary H.	Notice	19, Nov. 1814	S3
Skellman, Jacob	Horse lost	3, July 1805	S3
Skidmore, Jeremiah	Horse found	14, Feb. 1818	S1
Skilman, Samuel	Horse found	18, Mar. 1815	S3
Slayback, Abel	Court case	1, Mar. 1836	T2
Sloan, Elizabeth	Estate case	17, May 1816	S3
Sloan, James	Escaped prisoner	4, June 1796	C3
Sloan, James W.	Debtor	16, Jan. 1813	S3
Sloan, James W.	Attachment	19, July 1809	H1
Sloan, William	Estate case	17, May 1816	S3
Sloop, John	Horse lost	14, May 1814	S3
Sloop, Samuel	Run away apprentice	26, May 1815	S3
Slown, Margaret	Rape charge	25, Mar. 1796	C3
Sly, Jacob	Horse found	12, Nov. 1799	S3
Small, John	Horse found	8, Feb. 1808	S3
Smead, David H. & Jemima	Divorce/abandonment	11, Apr. 1823	N3
Smead, Ithiel & Diadamy	Divorce/abandonment	23, Mar. 1824	N3
Smead, Wesley	Chancery case	21, Mar. 1838	N2
Smiley, John	Horse found	4, July 1817	S3
Smith, Amos	Horse lost	5, Feb. 1800	S3
Smith, Benjamin	Insolvent debtor	27, Jan. 1829	N3
Smith, Charles	Hogs lost	7, Jan. 1800	S3
Smith, Charles	Horse lost	25, Feb. 1801	S3
Smith, Cyrus G. & Nancy	Divorce/abandonment	3, May 1850	P3
Smith, Daniel D.	Debt relief	2, Jan. 1818	S3
Smith, Edward	Deserter from army	15, June 1807	S3
Smith, Edwin B.	Debt relief	1, June 1820	S3
Smith, Elias	Insolvent debtor	23, July 1830	N3
Smith, Eliza Ann	Real estate case	9, Jan. 1838	N3
Smith, George	Chancery case	14, Dec. 1838	N2
Smith, George G.	Real estate case	9, Jan. 1838	N3
Smith, George G.	Court case witness	20, June 1850	P2
Smith, George W. & Cyntha	Divorce/abandonment	29, Jan. 1842	R3
Smith, Isaac	Horse found	19, Aug. 1825	N3
Smith, Jacob	Insolvent debtor	23, July 1830	N3
Smith, James	Horse lost	8, Aug. 1804	S3
Smith, James	Horse lost	19, June 1805	S3
Smith, James	Chancery case	19, Jan. 1811	S3
Smith, James (Capt)	Hamilton Co militia	28, Nov. 1801	S3
Smith, John	Horse lost	19, Dec. 1801	S3

Name	Type of Notice	Date of Notice	Page
Smith, John	Debt relief	11, May 1811	S3
Smith, John	Run away apprentice	25, Dec. 1813	S3
Smith, John	Horse found	11, June 1814	S3
Smith, John	Horse found	9, July 1796	F4
Smith, John	Chancery court case	17, June 1823	N4
Smith, John	Deserter from army	1, Sept 1836	N2
Smith, Joseph	Runaway apprentice	4, May 1820	S3
Smith, Joseph	Run away	20, Apr. 1820	D3
Smith, Justus	Horse lost	16, Jan. 1819	S3
Smith, Thomas	Guardian	8, Oct. 1830	N3
Smith, Willard M.	Debt relief	25, May 1820	S3
Smith, William	Horse lost	8, Aug. 1804	S3
Smith, William	Horse found	9, Nov. 1811	S3
Smith, William	Letter at P.O.	18, Oct. 1794	C3
Smith, William	Court sentencing	4, Nov. 1836	N2
Smith, William J. & Nancy	Divorce/abandonment	19, Mar. 1814	S1
Smith, William L. & Eveline	Divorce/abandonment	13, Dec. 1841	N3
Smith, Wright	Committee member	15, Nov. 1838	N2
Snell, Michael	Horse found	21, Mar. 1818	S2
Snider, Cornelius	Guardianship	20, Sept 1816	S1
Snider, David	Horse found	11, July 1818	S3
Snider, David	Chancery case	4, Mar. 1828	N3
Snodgrass, William	Horse found	11, July 1812	S3
Snodgrass, William	Fraud caution	23, July 1796	F4
Snowden, Peter	Run away notice	11, Nov. 1828	N1
Snowe, Isaac	Horse found	24, Sept 1808	S4
Snyder, John	Horse found	16, Nov. 1822	S3
Solomonson, Gottschalk	Birth notice	23, Jan. 1802	S3
Sorency, Jacob	Reward notice	11, Mar. 1797	F4
Southard, Abraham	Horse lost	2, July 1799	S2
Sparks, Kesiah	Guardian	17, June 1837	N2
Sparks, Martha	Guardian	17, June 1837	N2
Sparks, William	Land purchase	23, July 1814	S3
Spear, William	Horse lost	5, May 1815	S3
Speer, John	Horse found	19, June 1813	S3
Speer, John	Horse found	26, Dec. 1818	S3
Speer, William & Mary Ann	Divorce/abandonment	13, Sept 1816	S3
Spencer, Francis W.	Chancery case	11, Oct. 1847	K2
Spencer, H.E.	Committee member	15, Nov. 1838	N2
Spencer, Hannah	Real estate sale	17, June 1825	N3
Spencer, John	Deserter from army	1, Jan. 1814	S3
Spencer, Oliver	Horse lost	9, Sept 1801	S3
Spencer, Oliver	Run away apprentice	15, June 1803	S4
Spencer, Warner	Chancery case	11, Oct. 1847	K2
Spinning, Ichabod	Horse lost	24, June 1806	S3
Spinning, Isaac	Horse lost	26, Aug. 1806	S1
Spring, Nahum	Deserter from army	2, Feb. 1807	S3
Squire, Abraham	Horse found	23, Nov. 1811	S3
St.Clair, Ar.	Horse lost	12, Aug. 1801	S3
St.Clair, Ar., Jun.	Horse lost	28, May 1800	S3
St.Clair, Arthur, Jr.	Petition filed	6, Apr. 1803	S3
St.Clair, Esther	Estate case	4, July 1826	N3
St.Clair, Francis	Estate case	4, July 1826	N3
St.Clair, Jane	Estate case	4, July 1826	N3

Name	Type of Notice	Date of Notice	Page
St.Clair, Juliett	Estate case	4, July 1826	N3
St.Clair, Nancy	Estate case	4, July 1826	N3
St.Clair, Rebecca	Estate case	4, July 1826	N3
St.John, John	Horse lost	5, Feb. 1800	S3
Stackhouse, Thomas	Run away apprentice	12, Sept 1804	S3
Stafford, John & Mary	Divorce/abandonment	24, June 1836	N2
Staggs, Jonathan	Horse found	6, Aug. 1817	S3
Stailey, Samuel & Margaret	Divorce/abandonment	3, Sept 1834	T2
Staler, John L.	Debtor	17, Aug. 1822	S1
Staley, Susan	Run away	20, June 1812	S3
Stall, Edward	Guardianship	28, May 1830	N3
Stall, Edward H.	Debt relief	13, June 1817	S3
Stall, Frances	Guardianship	28, May 1830	N3
Stanley, Isaac	Run away	17, Oct. 1804	S3
Stanley, William (Lt)	Hamilton Co militia	28, Nov. 1801	S3
Stansbury, Thomas	Horse lost	24, Sept 1808	S4
Stanton, Latham	Horse lost	5, Nov. 1814	S3
Stanton, Richard	Letter at P.O.	18, Oct. 1794	C3
Stapp, A.	Run away notice	1, Apr. 1837	T2
Stapp, Hiram	Run away notice	1, Apr. 1837	T2
Starlin, Israel	Horse found	2, July 1814	S3
Starling, Samuel & Rebecca	Divorce/abandonment	6, Feb. 1824	N3
Starr, Rachel T.	Female Institution	19, Feb. 1830	N3
Starr, Sarah A.P.	Female Institution	19, Feb. 1830	N3
Stathagen, Jacob & Rachel	Divorce/abandonment	6, Nov. 1851	P2
Staunton, John	Deserter from army	15, May 1813	S3
Staunton, Joseph	Chancery case	31, Jan. 1835	N2
Staunton, Mary	Chancery case	31, Jan. 1835	N2
Stearns, Joseph	Deserter from army	10, Oct. 1812	S3
Steaurt, Matthew	Horse found	7, Nov. 1804	S3
Steel, John & Margaret	Divorce/abandonment	10, Apr. 1813	S3
Steele, Jesse	Deserter from army	1, Jan. 1814	S3
Steele, Richard	Horse lost	18, Nov. 1806	S3
Steer, Samuel	Partition petition	29, Mar. 1838	N2
Stemble, Henry	Letter at P.O.	18, Oct. 1794	C3
Stephens, James	Horse found	24, Sept 1808	S4
Stephens, Ruth	Horse found	16, Mar. 1811	S3
Stephenson, Jesse	Deserter from army	1, Jan. 1814	S3
Stevens, Ann	Guardian	21, Sept 1838	N3
Stevens, Benjamin	Horse found	24, Nov. 1815	S3
Stevens, Isaac	Inquiry	4, May 1822	S3
Stevens, John	Guardian	21, Sept 1838	N3
Stevens, Samuel	Inquiry	4, May 1822	S3
Steveson, Robert	Court case	21, Jan. 1801	S3
Steward, William	Deposition given	10, Sept 1842	Z3
Stewart, Arthur	Horse lost	13, Apr. 1807	S3
Stewart, F.R.	Deposition given	17, Sept 1842	Z4
Stewart, Gado	Horse found	13, Feb. 1819	S3
Stewart, Jacob	Notice of theft	2, Aug. 1794	C3
Stewart, John	Deserter from army	30, Nov. 1793	C3
Stewart, John M. & Hannah	Divorce/abandonment	21, Feb. 1851	P2
Stewart, Martin	Horse found	2, Jan. 1813	S3
Stewart, Palas P.	Chancery case	19, Jan. 1811	S3
Stewart, William	Escaped prisoner	7, Mar. 1795	C3

Name	Type of Notice	Date of Notice	Page
Stewart, William	Chancery case	29, Sept 1829	N3
Stickle, John N.	Deposition given	15, Sept 1842	Z4
Stilings, Joseph	Run away notice	15, May 1838	N2
Stinson, Alexander	Horse found	7, Aug. 1805	S3
Stites, Benjamin	Rape charge	25, Mar. 1796	C3
Stites, Benjamin	Chancery case	7, Oct. 1824	E3
Stites, Benjamin & Rachel	Divorce/abandonment	9, July 1796	F4
Stites, Hezekiah	Cows lost	5, Feb. 1800	S3
Stites, William & Elizabeth	Divorce/abandonment	7, Nov. 1823	N3
Stitt, Samuel	Horse lost	11, Feb. 1806	S3
Stockton, Aaron	Chancery case	10, Feb. 1824	N3
Stockton, John	Horse found	16, Jan. 1813	S3
Stockum, Joseph	Deposition given	17, Sept 1842	Z4
Stoddart, Thomas & Mary Ann	Divorce/abandonment	6, Jan. 1851	P3
Stokes, Benjamin	Run away apprentice	7, June 1795	C3
Stokes, Nathaniel	Horse found	2, May 1795	C3
Stokes, Nathaniel	Cow found	9, Apr. 1796	C2
Stone, E.	Horse lost	24, Oct. 1804	S3
Stone, Ethan	Horse found	24, Oct. 1828	N3
Stone, Ezra	Insolvent debtor	23, July 1830	N3
Stonemits, Casper	Horse found	2, Jan. 1813	S3
Stoner, Andrew R.	Horse found	26, Dec. 1818	S3
Stoner, Benedic	Horse found	8, Dec. 1810	S3
Stonesiffer, Ann	Horse found	20, Oct. 1815	S3
Stonmets, Casper	Horse found	20, June 1812	S3
Stonmoss, Casper	Horse found	8, Nov. 1809	H3
Storer, Bellamy & Euretta	Divorce/abandonemtn	28, Aug. 1838	T2
Storer, Charles & Jemima	Partition petition	23, Jan. 1837	N3
Stouder, Joseph	Horse found	1, June 1811	S3
Stout, Ephraim B.	Court case witness	20, June 1850	P2
Stout, Henry	Horse found	16, Apr. 1814	S3
Stout, Henry & Lydia	Divorce/abandonment	22, Apr. 1815	W3
Stouten, Joseph & Mary	Divorce/abandonment	30, Jan. 1813	S3
Stouten, William	Horse found	7, Nov. 1812	S3
Stratten, Cephas	Horse found	30, Jan. 1824	N3
Stratton, William	Attachment	19, July 1809	H1
Streets, John	Horse found	11, Aug. 1815	S3
Strickland, Henry	Horse found	9, Feb. 1811	S3
Strickler, John & Catharine	Divorce/abandonment	15, Sept 1851	P3
Strickler, John & Catharine	Divorce/abandonment	8, Nov. 1851	P2
Stuart, Pallas P.	Horse lost	5, Dec. 1804	S5
Studebaker, John	Land purchase	23, July 1814	S3
Sugrue, Charles & Mary	Divorce/abandonment	16, Dec. 1835	T3
Sullivan, George	Debt relief	11, Apr. 1817	S3
Sullivan, Henry	Horse found	11, July 1812	S3
Summers, William & Sarah	Divorce/abandonment	29, Sept 1815	S1
Summers, William & Sarah	Divorce/abandonment	4, Apr. 1817	S4
Supplee, Azael	Horse stolen	31, Aug. 1822	S3
Sutton, James	Horse lost	7, Jan. 1800	S3
Sutton, James	Cow lost	25, Mar. 1797	F4
Swain, Solomon	Horse found	25, May 1822	S3
Swearingen, Isaac	Letter at P.O.	18, Oct. 1794	C3
Sweney, William	Horse lost	28, May 1800	S3
Swin, William	Run away apprentice	14, Dec. 1836	N2

Name	Type of Notice	Date of Notice	Page
Symmes, Ann	Chancery case	20, Jan. 1825	E3
Symmes, Cilladon	Horse found	5, Sept 1817	S2
Symmes, Daniel	Cow found	17, Dec. 1799	S3
Symmes, Daniel	Petition	22, Aug. 1795	C3
Symmes, Daniel	Cow lost	22, Oct. 1796	F1
Symmes, Daniel (Capt)	Hamilton Co militia	28, Nov. 1801	S3
Symmes, John C.	Ox lost	7, Jan. 1800	S3
Symmes, John C., Jr.	Horse found	27, May 1801	S3
Symmes, P.S.	Committee member	15, Nov. 1838	N2
Tait, William	Notice	12, July 1794	C3
Talliford, Richard	Horse found	22, Aug. 1812	S3
Tanner, James	Horse found	23, Nov. 1811	S3
Tarrants, Samuel	Notice	5, Oct. 1803	S3
Tatman, Edward	Horse found	4, July 1817	S3
Taulman, Joseph	Deceased	8, Oct. 1830	N3
Tayler, Samuel & Nancy	Divorce/abandonment	20, Apr. 1835	T3
Taylor, Anna	Estate case	23, Dec. 1841	N2
Taylor, Cornelius	Horse found	18, July 1812	S4
Taylor, Harriet	Chancery case	31, Jan. 1835	N2
Taylor, Henry	Horse lost	15, Jan. 1806	S3
Taylor, Henry	Horse found	26, Oct. 1807	S1
Taylor, James	Horse found	30, Mar. 1811	S3
Taylor, James	Fraud caution	23, July 1796	F4
Taylor, James D.	Chancery case	31, Jan. 1835	N2
Taylor, Jonah	Horse found	7, Nov. 1818	S2
Taylor, Jonah	Insolvent debtor	27, Jan. 1829	N3
Taylor, Jonathan	Horse lost	15, Nov. 1794	C3
Taylor, William H.H.	Estate case	23, Dec. 1841	N2
Teed, Lemuel	Horse found	28, Aug. 1819	S3
Teirnan, Michael	Cow lost	6, Feb. 1802	S3
Temple, John & Sarah	Divorce/abandonment	5, Dec. 1795	C3
Terrel, Alexander	Deserter from army	2, May 1795	C3
Terril, Abner	Horse found	24, July 1813	S3
Terry, William	Horse lost	27, Oct. 1798	F4
Terwilliger, Nathaniel	Chancery case	4, Mar. 1828	N3
Test, John	Chancery court case	17, June 1823	N3
Tetrick, Joseph	Run away apprentice	13, Apr. 1809	H4
Tharp, (daughter of Boaz)	Daughter lost	11, Jan. 1812	S3
Thatcher, Thomas	Inquiry	8, Dec. 1821	S4
Thecker, John & Nancy	Divorce/abandonment	20, June 1818	S3
Theobald, Garret	Court sentencing	4, Nov. 1836	N2
Thomas, Edward	Insolvent debtor	11, Nov. 1828	N1
Thomas, George	Horse found	30, June 1815	S1
thomas, George	Horse found	13, June 1826	N3
Thomas, Jonathan	Horse found	31, Dec. 1814	S3
Thomas, Samuel	Escaped convict	3, Oct. 1818	S2
Thompson, Benjamin	Horse found	16, Jan. 1813	S3
Thompson, Charles	Horse stolen	18, July 1818	S3
Thompson, Charles	Horse lost	21, Aug. 1819	S3
Thompson, Charles	Cow found	29, Jan. 1820	S3
Thompson, David	Reward notice	24, Jan. 1810	H2
Thompson, J.G.	Deposition given	17, Sept 1842	Z4
Thompson, James	Horse found	10, Nov. 1815	S3

Name	Type of Notice	Date of Notice	Page
Thompson, John	Run away apprentice	6, Aug. 1799	S4
Thompson, John	Deserter from army	2, Feb. 1807	S3
Thompson, John	Horse found	13, Apr. 1809	H3
Thompson, Lewis	Debtor	23, Jan. 1813	S3
Thompson, Samuel	Horse found	16, May 1817	S3
Thompson, Samuel	Horse lost	22, Feb. 1794	C3
Thompson, Samuel	Horse lost	6, Dec. 1794	C3
Thompson, Samuel & Cath.	Divorce/abandonment	29, Aug. 1804	S4
Thompson, Smith & Sally	Divorce/abandonment	18, Dec. 1805	S3
Thompson, William	Deserter from army	24, Apr. 1813	S3
Thompson, William & Anne W.	Divorce/abandonment	22, Aug. 1817	S3
Thompson, Wilson	Horse found	12, Feb. 1820	S3
Thomson, Aaron	Horse found	10, Aug. 1811	S3
Thorn, Samuel	Horse found	12, Mar. 1814	S3
Thornton, John	Run away slave	26, Oct. 1836	T2
Thornton, John H.	Estate case	23, Dec. 1841	N2
Thornton, Mary T.	Estate case	23, Dec. 1841	N2
Thorp, Alex	Land partition	9, July 1835	N2
Thorp, Alvira	Land partition	9, July 1835	N2
Thorp, David	Land partition	9, July 1835	N2
Thorp, Elizabeth	Land partition	9, July 1835	N2
Thorp, George	Land partition	9, July 1835	N2
Thorp, James	Land partition	9, July 1835	N2
Thorp, John	Land partition	9, July 1835	N2
Thorp, Mary	Land partition	9, July 1835	N2
Thorp, Perry	Deposition given	17, Sept 1842	Z4
Thorp, Sarah	Land partition	9, July 1835	N2
Thorp, Sturges	Attachment	10, Oct. 1823	N3
Thorp, Truma	Land partition	9, July 1835	N2
Thorp, William	Land partition	9, July 1835	N2
Thorpe, William L. & Sarah	Divorce/abandonment	20, Jan. 1837	N3
Threasher, Charles	Horse found	29, Apr. 1820	S3
Throckmorton, Richard	Court case	21, Jan. 1801	S3
Thurston, William	Horse found	12, Sept 1812	S3
Thutsbey, Thomas	Notice	12, July 1794	C3
Tibbetts, Jeremiah	Debt relief	9, Oct. 1819	S3
Tice, John	Horse lost	24, Oct. 1804	S3
Timmons, Margaret	Run away notice	16, July 1824	N3
Tinbrook, Jacob	Horse lost	30, May 1823	N3
Titterton, Thomas	Inquiry	2, Jan. 1818	S3
Todd, Adeline	Chancery case	14, Oct. 1836	N2
Todd, Andrew A.	Chancery case	14, Oct. 1836	N2
Todd, Charlotte	Chancery case	14, Oct. 1836	N2
Todd, James	Chancery case	14, Oct. 1836	N2
Todd, Mary	Chancery case	14, Oct. 1836	N2
Tolbert, Davis B.	Escaped convict	3, Oct. 1818	S2
Tomlinson, John	Horse stolen	20, July 1820	S3
Tompson, John	Horse found	4, Dec. 1813	S3
Tomson, Samuel	Horse lost	11, Oct. 1794	C3
Toner, Edward	Lost item	6, Aug. 1796	F3
Toors, Paul	Inquiry	16, Nov. 1822	S3
Torrence, Samuel	Horse found	6, Oct. 1810	S3
Townsend, John B.	Horse lost	24, July 1802	S3
Traver, John	Insolvent debtor	11, Nov. 1828	N1

Name	Type of Notice	Date of Notice	Page
Traverse, Mercy	Caution on a note	9, July 1796	F1
Travis, William & Silas	Court case	21, Jan. 1801	S3
Treadway, John	Horse found	1, June 1820	S3
Trexler, Peter	Deserter from army	2, July 1800	S3
Trotter, Robert	Horse lost	22, Oct. 1814	S3
Trout, John	Horse found	28, Dec. 1807	S3
Trout, John	Horse found	15, Apr. 1818	S3
Troy, Daniel	Chancery case	9, Dec. 1824	E3
Trulock, Thomas	Cow found	22, Oct. 1796	F1
Tryon, Jeremiah	Debt relief	1, June 1820	S3
Tucker, Elias	Horse borrowed	18, Aug. 1815	S3
Tucker, Henry	Horse lost	3, Apr. 1807	S3
Tucker, James	Horse lost	24, Dec. 1800	S3
Tucker, William	Deserter from army	30, Nov. 1793	C3
Tull, Whetely	Horse found	13, Aug. 1830	N3
Tulley, John	Escaped prisoner	9, May 1795	C3
Turner, D.E. (Capt)	Letter at P.O.	18, Oct. 1794	C3
Turner, G.	Paintings lost	10, May 1794	C3
Turner, George	Court case	4, Feb. 1801	S3
Turner, George	Run away notice	2, May 1823	N3
Turner, James	Debt relief	5, Jan. 1822	S3
Turner, John B.	Court sentencing	4, Nov. 1836	N2
Turner, Will	Horse lost	15, Nov. 1794	C3
Tyzer, Augustin	Horse found	5, May 1815	S3
Underwood, John	Horse found	24, Dec. 1830	N3
Vail, Samuel	Horse lost	8, July 1806	S3
Vail, Samuel	Horse found	7, Mar. 1808	S3
Vanausdol, Garret	Chancery case	10, Oct. 1823	N3
VanBlaricum, Garret	Horse found	5, Feb. 1800	S4
Vandivert, Jonah	Horse found	7, Mar. 1808	S3
VanDyke, John	Run away apprentice	11, Feb. 1815	S3
Vandyke, Joseph L.	Insolvent debtor	23, July 1830	N3
VanGorder, Elijah	Horse found	17, Apr. 1829	N3
Vanhart, James	Horse found	21, Apr. 1826	N3
VanHorne, Elizabeth	Inquiry	16, Nov. 1822	S3
VanHorne, William & Hannah	Divorce/abandonment	5, Mar. 1814	S3
VanKamp, John	Escaped prisoner	4, July 1795	C3
VanKirk, John D. & Mary	Divorce/abandonment	27, Jan. 1824	N3
VanMatre, Isaac	Horse found	29, Jan. 1800	S3
VanMiddlesworth, Peter	Horse found	17, Jan. 1837	N2
VanNuys, Isaac	Cow lost	1, May 1802	S3
VanNuys, John	Run away apprentice	16, July 1799	S3
VanSickel, Gilbert	Horse found	30, May 1817	S3
VanSickle, Abraham	Horse lost	9, Jan. 1805	S2
Vantreese, Emanuel	Horse lost	16, Nov. 1807	S3
VanZandt, James	Deserter from army	30, Oct. 1813	S2
Vanzant, Higbee	Insolvent debtor	23, July 1830	N3
Vattier, Charles	Convicted	27, Apr. 1807	S3
Vattier, Charles	Chancery court case	17, June 1823	N4
Veal, Peter	Horse found	31, May 1816	S3
Vignon, Hipolite	Inquiry	6, July 1822	S1
Vinal, Barnabas	Horse found	22, June 1820	S3

Name	Type of Notice	Date of Notice	Page
Virgin, Brice	Horse found	9, Sept 1801	S3
Vitiar, Charles	Notice	9, May 1795	C3
Voorhees, Abraham	Horse found	23, Nov. 1811	S3
Voorhees, Balinda	Guardian	17, June 1837	N2
Voorhees, Jacob	Horse found	18, Mar. 1815	S3
Voorhees, William	Guardian	17, June 1837	N2
Vorhees, Jacob	Guardian	17, June 1847	N2
Wade, Horatio	Runaway apprentice	10, Oct. 1817	S2
Wagoner, Jacob	Horse found	11, Jan. 1808	S3
Wait, Reuben & Keturah	Divorce/abandonment	6, June 1823	N3
Wakefield, Daniel	Horse found	26, June 1827	N3
Wakefield, Thomas	Runaway apprentice	12, Feb. 1820	S1
Walden, Charles W.	Partition petition	25, Aug. 1837	N3
Walden, Elizabeth	Partition petition	25, Aug. 1837	N3
Walden, William C.	Partition petition	25, Aug. 1837	N3
Waldman, Peter & Magdalena	Divorce/abandonment	6, Jan. 1851	P3
Waldo, Frederick	Horse found	28, Sept 1811	S3
Waldo, Otis	Run away apprentice	15, Apr. 1815	S3
Waldrem, Joseph	Deserter from army	10, Oct. 1812	S3
Waldron, Francis	Deserter from army	24, May 1794	C3
Waldsmith, Christian	Cow lost	1, Jan. 1806	S4
Walker, Christopher	Horse found	10, Jan. 1823	N3
Walker, Edward	Horse found	2, Jan. 1824	N1
Walker, J.	Committee member	15, Nov. 1838	N2
Walker, John C.	Stabbing case	20, June 1850	P2
Walker, Joseph	Cow found	12, Mar. 1800	S3
Walker, Peter	Horse found	15, Apr. 1820	S1
Walker, Thomas	Court sentencing	4, Nov. 1836	N2
Wallace, Andrew (Sargeant)	Biography	11, Dec. 1834	T2
Wallace, John (Major)	Hamilton Co militia	28, Nov. 1801	S3
Wallace, William	Horse lost	7, Nov. 1804	S3
Wallace, William	Insolvent debtor	11, Nov. 1828	N1
Walsh, Peter & Peggy	Divorce/abandonment	26, Apr. 1828	R3
Ward, C.D. & Eleanor	Divorce/abandonment	4, Aug. 1832	R3
Ward, George	Cow lost	1, June 1822	S3
Ward, John	Horse found	12, Sept 1812	S1
Ward, John	Horse found	14, May 1814	S1
Ward, William	Horses stolen	1, Jan. 1806	S3
Ware, Andrew	Deserter from army	30, Nov. 1793	C3
Warmsley, William	Horse found	19, June 1813	S3
Warnam, John	Deserter from army	16, May 1812	S3
Warner, Jabez	Horse found	19, Oct. 1820	S3
Warrell, William & Elizabeth	Divorce/abandonment	1, June 1811	S3
Warren, Levi	Horse found	6, Apr. 1822	S3
Washburn, Alvan	Chancery case	28, May 1830	N3
Washburn, John	Court sentencing	4, Nov. 1836	N2
Washington, William	Run away apprentice	24, Dec. 1814	S3
Wason, Henry	Horse found	11, Sept 1802	S4
Waters, Jacob & Phebe	Divorce/abandonment	2, Nov. 1822	S3
Waters, Jacob & Phebe	Divorce/abandonment	31, Oct. 1822	J3
Waters, Wilks Wesley	Run away notice	19, Nov. 1824	N3
Watkins, Robert	Land purchase	9, Oct. 1805	S3
Watson, David & Agness	Divorce/abandonment	7, Mar. 1817	S3

Name	Type of Notice	Date of Notice	Page
Watson, James	Horse lost	16, Sept 1801	S3
Watt, David	Cow lost	11, Dec. 1819	S3
Watters, Catharine	Poor house inmate	14, Nov. 1851	P2
Watts, Benjamin	Land partition	29, Apr. 1828	N3
Watts, Nancy	Land partition	29, Apr. 1828	N3
Weaver, Henry	Chancery court case	20, June 1823	N3
Weaver, Henry	Chancery case	28, May 1830	N3
Webb, Jacob	Chancery case	9, Dec. 1824	E3
Webb, Joseph	Horse stolen	19, Feb. 1820	S3
Weber, David & Catharine	Divorce/abandonment	8, June 1820	S3
Webster, Benajah & Ruth	Divorce/abandonment	5, Sept 1851	P3
Webster, Isaac H. & Nancy	Divorce/abandonment	7, Apr. 1837	N2
Weidner, Jacob	Horse found	25, July 1812	S3
Weiman, George	Horse lost	9, Jan. 1818	S3
Weir, Alexander	Horse lost	26, Jan. 1803	S3
Welch, George W.	Deserter from army	13, Apr. 1809	H4
Welch, John	Escaped prisoner	9, Dec. 1806	S3
Welch, Samuel	Horse lost	29, Oct. 1800	S3
Welden, John R. & Rachel	Divorce/abandonment	20, Jan. 1825	E3
Weldon, John R.	Chancery case	7, Oct. 1824	E3
Weldon, John R. & Rachel	Divorce/abandonment	2, Jan. 1824	N3
Weldon, Rachael	Chancery case	7, Oct. 1824	E3
Weller, Lodowick	Horse found	6, June 1817	S3
Wellman, Robert	Horse found	16, Dec. 1825	N3
Wells, Aaron	Horse found	10, Aug. 1807	S3
Wells, William	Chancery case	19, Jan. 1811	S3
Welsh, John	Notice	24, Jan. 1817	S3
Wentworth, Amasa	Partition petition	22, Mar. 1837	N3
Wentworth, Luther	Horse found	26, July 1816	S3
Wentworth, Nathan	Partition petition	22, Mar. 1837	N3
Wentworth, Nelson	Partition petition	22, Mar. 1837	N3
Wert, Henry	Horse found	25, Aug. 1836	N2
Wescott, John	Runaway apprentice	27, Jan. 1821	S3
West, Enos	Horse found	22, June 1820	S3
Westbrook, Abraham P.	Escaped prisoner	13, Feb. 1813	S3
Western, George	Chancery case	6, Dec. 1838	N2
Western, Thomas	Chancery case	6, Dec. 1838	N2
Western, Wardell	Chancery case	6, Dec. 1838	N2
Western, William	Chancery case	6, Dec. 1838	N2
Westfall, Andrew & Susannah	Divorce/abandonment	28, May 1800	S3
Weston, Aaron	Horse found	19, Sept 1812	S3
Whalen, James	Horse found	21, Nov. 1817	S2
Whallon, Barnabas H.	Horse found	29, May 1829	N3
Wheelar, William	Run away apprentice	24, Aug. 1811	S3
Wheeler, Aquilla	Horse lost	15, Jan. 1806	S3
Wheeler, Jacob	Run away apprentice	7, Sept 1803	S4
Wheeler, Jacob	Run away apprentice	22, May 1805	S3
Wheeler, Jacob	Chancery court case	20, June 1823	N3
Wheeler, Robert	Horse found	15, Mar. 1816	S1
Wheeler, Stephen	Run away apprentice	27, Apr. 1803	S3
Wheelock, Daniel W.	Debt relief	30, Oct. 1819	S3
Wheler, Aquilla	Horse lost	13, Nov. 1805	S3
Whetstone, John	Horse found	21, Dec. 1803	S3
Whetstone, Rheuben	Notice	28, Mar. 1795	C3

Name	Type of Notice	Date of Notice	Page
Whitcomb, John	Horse found	24, Oct. 1818	S3
White, Alexander	Deserter from army	2, Oct. 1813	S3
White, Ann	Guardian	11, Dec. 1827	N3
White, Betsy	Guardian	11, Dec. 1827	N3
White, Betsy Ann	Guardianship	8, Oct. 1830	N3
White, Catharine	Guardianship	8, Oct. 1830	N3
White, Catharine	Guardian	11, Dec. 1827	N3
White, Catherine	Guardian	22, Dec. 1829	N3
White, Edward	Chancery case	2, Jan. 1829	N3
White, Edward	Chancery case	25, May 1830	N3
White, Elizabeth Ann	Guardian	22, Dec. 1829	N3
White, Francis	Horse lost	22, Jan. 1806	S3
White, Jacob	Horse lost	2, Sept 1801	S3
White, Jacob	Chancery case	25, May 1830	N3
White, Joseph	Run away apprentice	9, Apr. 1814	S3
White, Joseph	Land partition	29, Apr. 1828	N3
White, Lucy	Land partition	29, Apr. 1828	N3
White, Providence	Horse found	27, July 1811	S3
White, Thomas	Horse lost	27, May 1801	S3
White, Thomas	Horse found	3, June 1811	S3
Whitehead, John	Horse found	1, Dec. 1815	S3
Whitelock, James	Insolvent debtor	27, Jan. 1829	N3
Whiteman, Benjamin	Letter at P.O.	18, Oct. 1794	C3
Whitemore, William & Sarah	Divorce/abandonment	29, Jan. 1814	S3
Whitmore, William & Sarah	Divorce/abandonment	3, Jan. 1817	S3
Whitstone, John	Debt notice	18, July 1795	C3
Whittaker, Thomas & Nancy	Divorce/abandonment	15, Jan. 1814	S3
Whittington, Benjamin	Deserter from army	12, Sept 1795	C3
Wickliff, Charles	Runaway slave	9, July 1796	F4
Wiley, John	Horse found	24, July 1813	S3
Wiley, Thomas	Horse found	20, June 1826	N3
Wilkins, Peter	Horse found	22, Jan. 1830	N3
Wilkinson, Andrew	Horse lost	6, Feb. 1824	N3
Wilkinson, Joseph	Horse lost	13, Dec. 1816	S3
Wilkinson, William	Insolvent debtor	23, July 1830	N3
Willard, Samuel	Letter at P.O.	18, Oct. 1794	C3
Willcox, P.L.	Cow lost	1, Feb. 1794	C3
Willey, Burzilla	Horse found	13, Apr. 1809	H3
Willey, Harrison	Horse found	11, Apr. 1812	S3
Willey, James	Horse found	5, July 1816	S3
Willey, Judah	Horse found	20, Dec. 1816	S3
Williams, A.M.	Run away notice	18, May 1837	T2
Williams, Benajah & Ruth	Divorce/abandonment	6, Nov. 1851	P2
Williams, Caroline	Female school award	28, July 1835	N2
Williams, Catharine	Guardian	21, Sept 1838	N3
Williams, David	Horse found	18, June 1799	S3
Williams, Eleanor S.	Guardianship	14, Apr. 1829	N3
Williams, Eleazer	Debt relief	1, Dec. 1821	S3
Williams, Elisha	Horse found	8, Aug. 1818	S3
Williams, Elisha	Horse found	8, Dec. 1821	S3
Williams, Elmore	Horse found	6, Aug. 1799	S3
Williams, Elmore	Horse lost	5, Feb. 1800	S3
Williams, Elmore	Horse found	5, Mar. 1800	S3
Williams, Euretta	Guardian	21, Sept 1838	N3

Name	Type of Notice	Date of Notice	Page
Williams, F.B.	Guardian	21, Sept 1838	N3
Williams, Isaac	Escaped prisoner	7, Mar. 1795	C3
Williams, J.R.	Committee member	15, Nov. 1838	N2
Williams, Jacob	Horse lost	29, July 1801	S3
Williams, Jacob	Horse found	29, July 1806	S3
Williams, James	Deserter from army	23, Apr. 1814	S1
Williams, Joel	Petition	22, Aug. 1795	C3
Williams, Joel	Caution on a note	27, Oct. 1798	F4
Williams, Joel	Chancery case	25, May 1830	N3
Williams, John H.	Horse lost	3, Apr. 1802	S3
Williams, Joseph T. & Mary	Divorce/abandonment	13, Feb. 1838	T2
Williams, M.T.	Committee member	15, Nov. 1838	N2
Williams, Miles	Horse found	23, Nov. 1811	S3
Williams, Peter	Horse found	26, Feb. 1830	N3
Williams, Rachel	Missing child case	15, Aug. 1836	T2
Williams, Samuel	Horse found	27, Apr. 1822	S3
Williams, Samuel	Cow found	27, Aug. 1796	F3
Williams, Samuel	Cow found	10, Dec. 1796	F3
Williams, Thomas O.	Insolvent debtor	27, Jan. 1829	N3
Williams, William	Inquiry	9, Dec. 1824	E3
Williamson, Columbus	Guardian	19, Dec. 1826	N3
Williamson, David & Agnes J	Divorce/abandonment	20, Feb. 1851	P2
Williamson, George	Horse lost	1, Apr. 1806	S3
Williamson, George	Guardian	19, Dec. 1826	N3
Williamson, John	Horse lost	31, Oct. 1812	S3
Williamson, Richard	Run away notice	5, June 1829	N3
Williamson, Stephen D.	Horse found	30, May 1828	N3
Williard, Simon & Ann	Divorce/abandonment	8, Nov. 1851	P2
Willis, Isaac & Hannah	Divorce/abandonment	19, Oct. 1803	S3
Willis, William	Horse lost	7, Aug. 1802	S3
Willson, Peter	Horse lost	28, May 1800	S3
Wilmouth, Thomas	Land petition	25, June 1830	N3
Wilson, Abraham	Horse found	20, Oct. 1815	S3
Wilson, Charles	Inquiry	30, Nov. 1820	S3
Wilson, Cynthia	Runaway servant	2, Oct. 1819	S3
Wilson, Cynthia	Runaway	17, Oct. 1822	J1
Wilson, Elias	Horse found	12, June 1813	S3
Wilson, Francis	Departure notice	14, Jan. 1801	S3
Wilson, Francis	Debt notice	9, Aug. 1794	C3
Wilson, Isaac	Cow lost	30, Jan. 1805	S3
Wilson, James	Deserter from army	2, Oct. 1813	S3
Wilson, James	Horse found	1, Dec. 1815	S3
Wilson, James	Court sentencing	4, Nov. 1836	N2
Wilson, Joseph	Land purchase	23, July 1814	S3
Wilson, Lemuel & Caroline	Divorce/abandonment	4, Mar. 1836	T2
Wilson, Lemuel & Catharine	Divorce/abandonment	12, Feb. 1836	T3
Wilson, Samuel	Horse lost	20, July 1803	S3
Wilson, Sarah A.	Guardian	21, Sept 1838	N3
Wilson, William	Horse found	7, Dec. 1811	S3
Wilson, William	Horse found	27, Feb. 1813	S3
Wilson, William	Inquiry	30, Nov. 1820	S3
Wing, Isaiah	Committee member	15, Nov. 1838	N2
Wingate, Abraham	Horse found	11, Jan. 1812	S3
Wingate, Joseph	Horse found	29, July 1806	S1

Name	Type of Notice	Date of Notice	Page
Winslow, John	Insolvent debtor	23, July 1830	N3
Winter, Frederick	Inquiry	1, Mar. 1851	P2
Winters, Benjamin	Horse found	11, Oct. 1816	S3
Winters, John	Horse found	16, Jan. 1802	S3
Winton, Matthew	Horse lost	4, Jan. 1794	C3
Winton, Matthew	Notice of sale	17, Jan. 1795	C3
Winton, Matthew	Cow lost	6, Feb. 1796	C3
Winton, Matthew	Chancery case	28, May 1830	N3
Wise, John	Horse found	11, Aug. 1815	S3
Wise, John (Sargeant)	Letter at P.O.	18, Oct. 1794	C3
Wist, James	Horse found	9, Jan. 1813	S3
Witham, Gideon	Horse found	9, Feb. 1811	S3
Wolf, John G. & Nancy Jane	Divorce/abandonment	4, Jan. 1837	N3
Wolff, Leonard	Horse lost	6, July 1803	S2
Wolverton, John	Horse found	27, Dec. 1816	S3
Wolverton, Thomas	Horse found	9, Jan. 1813	S3
Wood, Eliza	Information wanted	2, Sept 1835	N2
Wood, Enoch & Sabra	Divorce/abandonment	4, June 1824	N3
Wood, Harriet	Guardian	17, June 1837	N2
Wood, Jesse	Horse lost	24, May 1816	S1
Wood, John & Polly	Divorce/abandonment	14, Aug. 1813	S3
Wood, John H.	Committee member	15, Nov. 1838	N2
Wood, Stephen	Petition filed	6, Apr. 1803	S3
Wood, Stephen	Horse found	28, May 1814	S3
Wood, William & Nancy	Divorce/abandonment	4, May 1850	P1
Woodbury, Jonathan	Horse found	5, July 1816	S3
Woodruff, John	Horse found	26, Jan. 1816	S1
Woodruff, Nathaniel	Horse found	13, June 1817	S3
Woodruff, Stephen & Betsey	Divorce/abandonment	8, Nov. 1809	H3
Woods, Alex	Chancery case	10, Oct. 1823	N3
Woodward, Horace	horse found	8, Dec. 1826	N3
Woodward, Levi	Run away apprentice	30, Sept 1801	S3
Woodward, Levi	Saddle bag found	30, Nov. 1793	C3
Woodward, Levi	Public notice	17, May 1794	C3
Woodworth, Benjamin & Ibby	Divorce/abandonment	20, Jan. 1825	E3
Woodworth, Daniel	Horse found	25, July 1812	S2
Workman, Richard	Escaped prisoner	26, Sept 1795	C3
Worley, Malcom	Horse lost	12, Oct. 1803	S3
Worman, Samuel	Chancery court case	20, June 1823	N3
Worman, Samuel	Chancery case	28, May 1830	N3
Worthington, Elizabeth R.	Gold medal	19, Feb. 1830	N3
Worthington, William	Horse found	19, July 1809	H3
Wray, James	Horse found	13, Apr. 1809	H3
Wright, N.	Committee member	15, Nov. 1838	N2
Wright, Nathaniel	Chancery court case	20, June 1823	N3
Wright, Simon	Insolvent debtor	27, Jan. 1829	N3
Wright, William C.	Insolvent debtor	11, Nov. 1828	N1
Wyatt, Joseph	Run away apprentice	11, Dec. 1813	S3
Wyley, Thomas	Horse found	26, Feb. 1830	N3
Wyncoop, Henry & Elizabeth	Divorce/abandonment	7, Mar. 1840	R3
Yancey, Charles W. & Mary A	Divorce/abandonment	31, May 1816	S3
Yapp, Joel & Sarah	Divorce/abandonment	15, Feb. 1836	N2
Yardly, William	Chancery court case	20, June 1823	N3

Name	Type of Notice	Date of Notice	Page
Yeatman, Griffin	Committee member	15, Nov. 1838	N2
Yost, J.W.	Committee member	15, Nov. 1838	N2
Young, Charles	Court case	4, Feb. 1801	S3
Young, Frances M.	Female Institution	19, Feb. 1830	N3
Young, Harry	Horse found	23, Apr. 1808	S3
Young, John	Chancery case	19, Jan. 1811	S3
Young, Jonathan	Horse found	10, Oct. 1817	S1
Young, Roger	Horse found	19, July 1809	H3
YoungHusband, (Lt)	Letter at P.O.	18, Oct. 1794	C3
Youtsey, Peter	Horse lost	17, June 1806	S3
Zeigler, David	Horse for sale	18, Mar. 1797	F3
Zeumer, Augustus	Debt relief	29, June 1820	S3